HANDBOOK OF RESEARCH METHODS AND APPLICATIONS IN EMPIRICAL FINANCE

HANDBOOKS OF RESEARCH METHODS AND APPLICATIONS

Series Editor: Mark Casson, *University of Reading, UK*

The objective of this series is to provide definitive over-views of research methods in important fields of social science, including economics, business, finance and policy studies. The aim is to produce prestigious high quality works of lasting significance. Each *Handbook* consists of original contributions by leading authorities, selected by an editor who is a recognised leader in the field. The emphasis is on the practical application of research methods to both quantitative and qualitative evidence. The *Handbooks* will assist practising researchers in generating robust research findings that policy-makers can use with confidence.

While the *Handbooks* will engage with general issues of research methodology, their primary focus will be on the practical issues concerned with identifying and using suitable sources of data or evidence, and interpreting source material using best-practice techniques. They will review the main theories that have been used in applied research, or could be used for such research. While reference may be made to conceptual issues and to abstract theories in the course of such reviews, the emphasis will be firmly on real-world applications.

Titles in this series include:

Handbook of Research Methods and Applications in Urban Economies
Edited by Peter Karl Kresl and Jaime Sobrino

Handbook of Research Methods and Applications in Empirical Finance
Edited by Adrian R. Bell, Chris Brooks and Marcel Prokopczuk

Handbook of Research Methods and Applications in Empirical Finance

Edited by

Adrian R. Bell

University of Reading, UK

Chris Brooks

University of Reading, UK

Marcel Prokopczuk

Zeppelin University, Germany

HANDBOOKS OF RESEARCH METHODS AND APPLICATIONS

Edward Elgar
Cheltenham, UK • Northampton, MA, USA

Published by
Edward Elgar Publishing Limited
The Lypiatts
15 Lansdown Road
Cheltenham
Glos GL50 2JA
UK

Edward Elgar Publishing, Inc.
William Pratt House
9 Dewey Court
Northampton
Massachusetts 01060
USA

A catalogue record for this book
is available from the British Library

Library of Congress Control Number: 2012946675

This book is available electronically in the ElgarOnline.com
Economics Subject Collection, E-ISBN 978 0 85793 609 7

MIX
Paper from
responsible sources
FSC
www.fsc.org   FSC® C018575

ISBN 978 0 85793 608 0 (cased)

Typeset by Servis Filmsetting Ltd, Stockport, Cheshire
Printed by MPG PRINTGROUP, UK

Contents

PART IV CORPORATE FINANCE

PART V RISK MODELLING

Contributors

Edward I. Altman, Stern School of Business, New York University, New York, USA; ealtman@stern.nyu.edu.

Manuel Ammann, Swiss Institute of Banking and Finance, University of St Gallen, Switzerland; manuel.ammann@unisg.ch.

Keith Anderson, The York Management School, University of York, UK; keith.anderson@york.ac.uk.

Adrian R. Bell, ICMA Centre, Henley Business School, University of Reading, UK; a.r.bell@icmacentre.ac.uk.

Chris Brooks, ICMA Centre, Henley Business School, University of Reading, UK; c.brooks@ icmacentre.ac.uk.

David A. Carter, Department of Finance, College of Business Administration, Oklahoma State University, USA; dcarter@okstate.edu.

Geraldo Cerqueiro, Universidade Católica Portuguesa Católica – Lisbon School of Business and Economics, Portugal; Geraldo.cerqueiro@ucp.pt.

Ke Chen, Manchester Business School, University of Manchester, UK; kechen1998@gmail.com.

Hans Degryse, Department of Accountancy, Finance and Insurance, KU Leuven, Belgium, CentER – Tilburg University, The Netherlands, CEPR, and CESifo; hans.degryse@kuleuven.be.

Deniz Erdemlioglu, University of Namur – FUNDP, Belgium; deniz.erdemlioglu@fundp.ac.be.

Andrey Golubov, Cass Business School, City University London, UK; andrey.golubov.1@city.ac.uk.

Massimo Guidolin, CAIR, Manchester Business School, University of Manchester, UK and IGIER, Bocconi University, Italy; massimo.guidolin@mbs.ac.uk.

Ólan T. Henry, University of Liverpool Management School, University of Liverpool, UK; Olan.Henry@liverpool.ac.uk.

Thomas Johann, University of Mannheim, Germany; johann@uni-mannheim.de.

Apostolos Katsaris, Albourne Partners Limited, London, UK; a.katsaris@albourne.com.

Sébastien Laurent, Department of Quantitative Economics, Maastricht University, The Netherlands; s.laurent@maastrichtuniversity.nl.

Yongwoong Lee, Research Centre, Deutsche Bundesbank, Germany; uomhero@gmail.com.

Woon Sau Leung, Cardiff Business School, Cardiff University, UK; leungws1@cardiff.ac.uk.

Hong Liu, Department of Accounting and Finance, University of Glasgow, UK; h.liu@accfin.gla.ac.uk.

Phil Molyneux, Bangor Business School, Bangor University, UK; p.molyneux@bangor.ac.uk.

Christopher J. Neely, Research Division, Federal Reserve Bank of St Louis, USA; neely@stls.frb.org.

David Oesch, Swiss Institute of Banking and Finance, University of St Gallen, Switzerland; david.oesch@unisg.ch.

Nilss Olekalns, Department of Economics, University of Melbourne, Australia; nilss@unimelb.edu.au.

Steven Ongena, CentER – Tilburg University and CEPR, Department of Finance, The Netherlands; steven.ongena@uvt.nl.

Dimitris Petmezas, Surrey Business School, Faculty of Business, Economics and Law, University of Surrey, UK; d.petmezas@surrey.ac.uk.

Ser-Huang Poon, Manchester Business School, University of Manchester, UK; Ser-huang.poon@manchester.ac.uk.

Marcel Prokopczuk, Zeppelin University, Germany; marcel.prokopczuk@zu.de.

Daniel A. Rogers, School of Business Administration, Portland State University, USA; danr@sba.pdx.edu.

Markus Schmid, Swiss Institute of Banking and Finance, University of St Gallen, Switzerland; markus.schmid@unisg.ch.

Kalvinder K. Shields, Department of Economics, University of Melbourne, Australia; k.shields@unimelb.edu.au.

Betty J. Simkins, Department of Finance, College of Business Administration, Oklahoma State University, USA; simkins@okstate.edu.

Silvia Stanescu, Kent Business School, University of Kent, UK; s.stanescu@kent.ac.uk.

Lars Stentoft, HEC Montréal, CIRANO, CIRPÉE and CREATES, Canada; lars.stentoft@hec.ca.

Nicholas Taylor, Cardiff Business School, Cardiff University, UK; taylorn@cardiff@ac.uk.

Erik Theissen, University of Mannheim, Germany; theissen@uni-mannheim.de.

Nickolaos G. Travlos, ALBA Graduate Business School at The American College of Greece, Greece; ntravlos@alba.edu.gr.

Stephen D. Treanor, Department of Finance and Marketing, College of Business, California State University, USA; streanor@csuchico.edu.

Radu Tunaru, Kent Business School, University of Kent, UK; R.Tunaru@kent.ac.uk.

John O.S. Wilson, School of Management, University of St Andrews, UK; jsw7@st-andrews.ac.uk.

Yingying Wu, ICMA Centre, Henley Business School, University of Reading, UK; y.wu@icmacentre.ac.uk.

William T. Ziemba, Sauder School of Business, University of British Columbia, Canada; wtzimi@mac.com.

Preface

Although the theoretical foundations of modern finance were laid almost half a century ago (and indeed, many would argue that surprisingly little theoretical progress has been made since then), the empirical side of finance has grown beyond all recognition both in terms of the volume of studies and their rigour. Several key developments coincided to facilitate this development in the subject. Firstly, considerable progress was made in statistical theory and an array of new econometric approaches was developed. Secondly, the availability of computers and computing power increased manyfold, which not only allowed the estimation of sophisticated models and the utilization of approaches involving processor-intensive techniques, but also enabled researchers to store and manipulate large financial databases. Thirdly, researchers are increasingly well trained in advanced quantitative techniques, and the availability of more powerful and yet at the same time more user-friendly statistical software packages have meant that models previously requiring weeks of code writing can now be estimated at the click of a mouse.

Of course, this computing power and ease of implementation have brought their own problems, perhaps not the least of which is the bewildering array of possible approaches from which a researcher could select to address a particular issue. Making this choice optimally and implementing the model validly requires considerable technical knowledge, and this constitutes the point of departure for the present collection. Our objective is to draw together in a single volume a set of chapters that will assist the reader in determining the appropriate method or model to solve a specific problem in finance, and to provide the reader with an example that demonstrates how to implement it. The book is divided into thematic parts in order to more closely group the chapters around five key subfields of research in empirical finance. Renowned experts within their field have produced each chapter.

The book is aimed primarily at doctoral researchers and academics who are engaged in conducting original empirical research in finance. It is written at the intermediate to advanced level using a 'cookbook' type approach and is highly practical in nature, with extensive use made of data and examples. Depending on the nature of the material covered, some chapters are organized more in the form of critical reviews of the literature with emphasis on the research designs of the studies, while others constitute worked illustrations of many of the key techniques that are commonly implemented in leading research in this area.

In addition, the book will be useful to researchers in the financial markets and also advanced Masters-level students who are writing dissertations. The objective has been to present the quantitative techniques together with real-world, state-of-the-art research examples. Our approach is to describe a question or issue in finance and then to demonstrate the methodologies that may be used to solve it. All of the techniques described are used to address real problems rather than being presented for their own sake, and the areas of application have been carefully selected so that a broad range of methodological approaches can be covered.

In Part I, we consider asset pricing and investments, the foundation and the subject of a broad range of research. The first chapter by Massimo Guidolin surveys the application of Markov switching models in financial economics, with a particular emphasis on tackling asset pricing questions. This is followed by a chapter from William T. Ziemba who reconsiders the classical portfolio optimization problem and discusses strategies for real-world implementations. Over the past few years, financial bubbles have been regularly discussed both in the academic literature and in the popular media. In Chapter 3, Keith Anderson, Chris Brooks and Apostolos Katsaris demonstrate, using a range of models, how researchers can test for the presence of bubbles in asset markets.

In Part II, we move to looking at research in the area of derivatives. Chapter 4 by Marcel Prokopczuk and Yingying Wu demonstrates how to estimate a commodity futures or interest rate term structure model using the Kalman filter. This is followed by Chapter 5 from Lars Stentoft, who explains how simulation methods can be used to price American options. In Chapter 6, Ke Chen and Ser-Huang Poon discuss how to numerically compute derivatives prices in affine model frameworks. Finally, in Chapter 7, Yongwoong Lee and Ser-Huang Poon describe how Markov Chain Monte Carlo estimation techniques can be used in the context of credit risk models.

Part III examines banking and microstructure. The former area was traditionally thought of as being predominantly discursive in nature, but more recently a wide range of relatively sophisticated approaches have been employed, while the latter field has witnessed some of the biggest advances in modelling techniques across the whole of finance, partly due to the increasing availability of very large databases in this area. Chapter 8 by Hong Liu, Phil Molyneux and John O.S. Wilson tackles a key issue by discussing and evaluating possible approaches for measuring competition in banking. Next, in Chapter 9, Geraldo Cerqueiro, Hans Degryse and Steven Ongena look at the choice to lend by banks and demonstrate how heteroscedastic regression models can be employed in this context. Liquidity is the subject of Chapter 10 by Thomas Johann and Erik Theissen. Whilst comparing and contrasting traditional methods of measuring liquidity, they also question these in light of recent developments in international equity markets. In Chapter 11, Woon Sau Leung and Nicholas Taylor present a contagion analysis of the US subprime crisis and investigate how financial markets in the rest of the world felt its spillover effects.

Part IV is devoted to the subfield of corporate finance. Chapter 12 by Andrey Golubov, Dimitris Petmezas and Nickolaos G. Travlos presents a review of empirical research into mergers and acquisitions of corporations and the impact these activities have. Manuel Ammann, David Oesch and Markus Schmid discuss the importance of constructing accurate corporate governance indices from an international perspective in Chapter 13. Finally, Chapter 14 by David A. Carter, Daniel A. Rogers, Betty J. Simkins and Stephen D. Treanor shows how the multivariate regression model methodology is employed and analyses the impact of the decision to hedge fuel prices for airlines in relation to unpredictable weather patterns in the United States (US).

In Part V we conclude the book by looking at risk modelling. Firstly, in Chapter 15, Silvia Stanescu and Radu Tunaru examine the accuracy of the popular value-at-risk (VaR) approach and explain how to compute confidence intervals for this risk measure. Next, Deniz Erdemlioglu, Sébastien Laurent and Christopher J. Neely look at problems in foreign exchange modelling, focusing on models for volatility and jumps. In Chapter

17, Edward I. Altman then reviews how techniques for analysing the financial distress of corporations have developed through to the present. The final chapter by Ólan T. Henry, Nilss Olekalns and Kalvinder K. Shields outlines new methods for detecting and quantifying dynamic responses to news on unobservable variables. They demonstrate the applicability of their method in the context of the international capital asset pricing model.

PART I

ASSET PRICING AND INVESTMENTS

1 Markov switching models in asset pricing research
Massimo Guidolin

1.1 INTRODUCTION

Recent years have marked an acceleration in the number and quality of asset pricing papers that have placed regime-switching and in particular Markov switching models (henceforth, MSMs) at the heart of their framework. In this chapter I survey applications of MS modeling to financial economics, with a particular emphasis on tackling asset pricing questions and problems. As a result, I shall keep separate the task of building (equilibrium) dynamic asset pricing models in which beliefs are informed by some MSM framework from the (simpler) goal of fitting MSMs on the data and loosely using MSM implications to test one or more hypotheses of interest. One equivalent way to understand this difference is that it stems from the fact that while in simple fitting exercises, a researcher only cares for modeling (at most, predicting) the physical (conditional) density under the physical measure, P, when MSMs are used to build dynamic asset pricing models (DAPMs), then she cares for the role of regime shifts both under P as well as under the risk neutral measure, Q.[1]

A brief overview of the structure of this survey may help a reader to ease into the material covered in this chapter. Section 1.2 provides a primer to MSMs and briefly deals with their specification and estimation (see Guidolin, 2012, or Hamilton, 1994, for additional details concerning testing and prediction). Section 1.3 deals with important contributions based on the intuition of MS in economic fundamentals to address a number of puzzles concerning the risk–return trade-off. Although this conclusion will be subject to many qualifications, we shall show that within macro-style DAPMs in which fundamentals follow a MSM, it is possible to estimate a positive relationship between risk premia and risk, as first principles normally postulate – a task that has proved elusive in extensive empirical tests.

Section 1.4 takes a different approach: instead of contrasting macro-based models that link asset returns to fundamentals with MS-driven models, I review the literature that has built rational pricing frameworks on and around MSMs for consumption, output or dividend growth. Section 1.5 extends this literature to a discussion of the early evidence on the cross-sectional implications of MS. Section 1.6 represents the core of this survey and goes into considerable detail in reviewing papers that – especially in the subfield of default risk-free term structure modeling – have developed a consistent and structural approach to the role of MS dynamics in the process of asset price formation. These papers directly incorporate MS dynamics in the key pricing measure, the stochastic discount factor (SDF). Section 1.7 performs a similar operation with reference to derivative pricing. Section 1.8 offers a few directions for future research.

Let me conclude with the usual caveats and disclaimers. This is just one survey of a (small, alas) portion of existing papers that have used MS methods in financial economics. There is no suggestion that my review may be complete in terms of discussing (or even just citing) all the relevant papers. It is also important to openly state that this chapter does not aim at becoming a reference on MSMs in financial economics. My more modest goal is to review a number of papers that can be taken as a sample of what MS tools may achieve when applied to asset pricing questions. Any reader interested in acquiring the basic tools to specify and estimate MSMs are invited to consult the excellent textbooks by Frühwirth-Schnatter (2006), Kim and Nelson (1999), Krolzig (1997) and McLachlan and Peel (2000). Moreover, my survey does not even attempt to scratch the surface of the important problem of the forecasting performance of MSMs. It has sometimes been reported that non-linear models provide a deeper understanding of the in-sample dynamics, but that they could also be much less useful for prediction purposes (see, e.g., Brooks, 1997). Yet, the literature abounds of cases in which MSMs outperform single-state benchmarks in prediction tests.[2] Finally, let me stress that – also in the light of the sheer size of the literature I have reviewed – I have made a conscious choice to limit my efforts to MSMs only, and thus left aside the equally important family of threshold models.

1.2   AN INTRODUCTION TO MARKOV SWITCHING MODELS

Suppose that the $N \times 1$ random vector $\mathbf{y}_t$ follows a K-regime Markov switching (MS) $VAR(p)$ (MSVAR) heteroskedastic process, compactly written $MSIAH(K, p)$ following Krolzig (1997):

$$\mathbf{y}_t = \boldsymbol{\mu}_{S_t} + \sum_{j=1}^{p} \mathbf{A}_{j,S_t}\mathbf{y}_{t-j} + \boldsymbol{\Sigma}_{S_t}\boldsymbol{\varepsilon}_t, \tag{1.1}$$

with $\boldsymbol{\varepsilon}_t \sim NID(\mathbf{0}, \mathbf{I}_N)$, where NID means normally and independently distributed. Even though the hypothesis of Gaussian shocks is not necessary, it will be maintained unless otherwise noted in what follows. $S_t = 1, 2, \ldots, K$ is a latent state variable driving all the matrices of parameters appearing in (1): $\boldsymbol{\mu}_{S_t}$ is a $N \times 1$ vector that collects N regime-dependent intercepts, while the $N \times N$ matrices $\mathbf{A}_{j,S_t}$ and $\boldsymbol{\Sigma}_{S_t}$ represent the state-dependent VAR matrices and Choleski factorization of the covariance matrix, $\boldsymbol{\Omega}_{S_t} = \boldsymbol{\Sigma}_{S_t}\boldsymbol{\Sigma}'_{S_t}$. In fact, conditionally on the unobservable state S_t, (1.1) defines a standard Gaussian reduced form VAR(p) model. When $K > 1$, alternative hidden states are possible and they will influence both the conditional mean and the volatility/correlation structures characterizing the process in (1.1). These unobservable states are generated by a discrete-state, homogeneous, irreducible and ergodic first-order Markov chain:[3]

$$\Pr(S_t = j | \{S_j\}_{j=1}^{t-1}, \{\mathbf{y}_j\}_{j=1}^{t-1}) = \Pr(S_t = j | S_{t-1} = i, \Im_t) = p_{ij,t}, \tag{1.2}$$

where $p_{ij,t}$ is the generic $[i,j]$ element of the $K \times K$ transition matrix $\mathbf{P}_t$. When $\mathbf{P}_t$ is constant over time, we shall speak of a homogeneous Markov chain.[4]

Multivariate MSMs may be estimated by maximum likelihood.[5] Parameter constraints (e.g., on transition probabilities) are imposed using the re-parameterizations illustrated in Kim and Nelson (1999, pp. 14–17), who also show how the standard errors need to be adjusted as a function of the transformations selected. In particular, estimation and inference are based on the EM (expectation-maximization) algorithm proposed by

Dempster et al. (1977) and Hamilton (1990), a filter that allows the iterative calculation of the one-step ahead forecast of the state vector $\xi_{t+1|t}$ given the information set $\mathfrak{I}_t$ and the consequent construction of the log-likelihood function of the data. Maximization of the log-likelihood function within the M-step is made faster by the fact that the first-order conditions defining the maximum likelihood estimation (MLE) may often be written in closed form (see, e.g., Hamilton, 1990). In particular, such first-order conditions can be shown to all depend on the smoothed probabilities $\hat{\xi}_{t|T} \equiv \Pr(\xi_t|\mathfrak{I}_T; \theta)$ (i.e., the state probabilities estimated on the basis of the full sample of data) and therefore they all present a high degree of non-linearity in the parameters, collected in the vector θ (and including the estimable elements of the transition matrix $\mathbf{P}$). As a result, these first-order conditions have to be solved numerically, although convenient iterative methods exist.

As for the properties of the resulting ML estimators, under standard regularity conditions (such as identifiability, stability and the fact that the true parameter vector does not fall on the boundaries), Hamilton (1994) and Leroux (1992) have proven consistency and asymptotic normality of the ML estimator $\tilde{\theta}$:

$$\sqrt{T}(\tilde{\theta} - \theta) \xrightarrow{D} N(0, \mathbf{I}_a(\theta)^{-1}) \tag{1.3}$$

where $\mathbf{I}_a(\gamma)$ is the asymptotic information matrix.[6]

A first, natural extension consists of including the autoregressive conditional heteroskedastic (ARCH) model in covariance matrices, when the associated parameters are themselves switching over time. In the simplest of the two-regime cases explored by Cai (1994), a univariate MS AR(1) ARCH process is:

$$r_t = \mu_0 + \mu_1 S_t + \phi(r_{t-1} - \mu_0 - \mu_1 S_{t-1}) + \varepsilon_t, \ \varepsilon_t = \sqrt{h_t} u_t, \ u_t \sim NID(0,1)$$

$$h_t = \omega_0 + \omega_1 S_t + \sum_{i=1}^{p} \alpha_i \varepsilon_{t-i}^2, \ \omega_0, \omega_1, \alpha_i \geq 0, \tag{1.4}$$

where $S_t = 0,1$ follows a first-order, homogeneous and irreducible two-state Markov chain. Hamilton and Susmel (1994) have proposed a switching-regime ARCH (SWARCH) model in which changes in regime are captured as changes in the scale of the ARCH process:

$$r_t = \mu + \sqrt{\delta_0 + \delta_1 S_t} \varepsilon_t, \ \varepsilon_t = \sqrt{h_t} u_t, \ u_t \sim NID(0,1)$$

$$h_t = \omega + \sum_{i=1}^{p} \alpha_i \varepsilon_{t-i}^2, \ \alpha_i \geq 0, \ S_t = 0,1,2. \tag{1.5}$$

In this case, the dynamic process of conditional variance is affected, although only through a scaling factor. Unfortunately, truly combining the MS model with generalized ARCH (GARCH) – i.e., making GARCH parameters follow regime switching patterns – induces tremendous complications in actual estimation. As a result of the particular lag structure of a GARCH model – by which all past lags of squared shocks affect conditional variance – the standard equations characterizing the EM algorithm for MS parameter estimation would depend on the entire history of the Markov states through the smoothed probabilities $\Pr(S_T, S_{T-1}, \ldots, S_1|\mathfrak{I}_t)$. Because each of the S_t's may take K values, this implies a total of K^T probabilities that need to be computed and stored. A first, important stab at this important problem came from Gray (1996), who has developed a two-state generalized MS GARCH(1,1) model:

$$r_t = (\mu_0 + \mu_1 S_t) + (\phi_0 + \phi_1 S_t)r_{t-1} + \sqrt{h_t(S_t)}\varepsilon_t \quad \varepsilon_t \sim NID(0,1)$$

$$h_t(S_t) = (\omega_0 + \omega_1 S_t) + (\alpha_0 + \alpha_1 S_t)\varepsilon_{t-1}^2 + (\beta_0 + \beta_1 S_t)h_{t-1}(S_{t-1}), \tag{1.6}$$

$(S_t = 0,1)$ which implies an infinite memory because $Var_{t-1}[r_t|S_t]$ can be now solved backwards to show that the conditional variance depends on the entire history of shocks to the short-term rate, $\varepsilon_0, \varepsilon_1, \ldots, \varepsilon_{t-1}$. Gray tackles the problem of path dependence in MS GARCH adopting an approach – in which $Var_{t-1}[r_t|S_t]$ is written as a difference of averages across regimes (with probabilities given by filtered probabilities) of the first and second moments – that preserves the essential nature of GARCH and yet allows tractable estimation.

Haas et al. (2004) have recently returned to the issue of the most efficient approximation to be used in the implementation of univariate MS GARCH models. They propose a way to write MS GARCH models that is different from Gray's (1996) and that better fits the standard intuition of volatility persistence in a GARCH framework. Similarly to previous papers, Haas et al. assume that $r_{t+1} = E_t[r_{t+1}] + \varepsilon_{t+1}$, where ε_{t+1} follows a K-component mixture of normals, $\varepsilon_{t+1} \sim NM(\pi_1, \pi_2, \ldots, \pi_K; \mu_1, \mu_2, \ldots, \mu_K; \sigma_{1t+1}^2, \sigma_{2t+1}^2, \ldots, \sigma_{Kt+1}^2)$, with zero unconditional mean and GARCH(1,1)-type variances that can be written in compact form as:

$$\boldsymbol{\sigma}_{t+1}^{(2)} = \boldsymbol{\omega} + \sum_{i=1}^{q}\boldsymbol{\alpha}_i\varepsilon_t^2 + \sum_{j=1}^{p}\mathbf{B}_j\boldsymbol{\sigma}_t^{(2)}, \tag{1.7}$$

where $\boldsymbol{\sigma}_{t+1}^{(2)} \equiv [\sigma_{1t+1}^2\sigma_{2t+1}^2\ldots\sigma_{Kt+1}^2]'$, $\boldsymbol{\omega}$ is a $K \times 1$ vector of constants, $\boldsymbol{\alpha}_i$ is a $K \times 1$ vector of coefficients that load the lagged shock ε_t^2 into the K regime-specific variances $\boldsymbol{\sigma}_{t+1}^{(2)}$, and $\mathbf{B}_j$ is a $K \times K$ matrix that loads past variances in each of the K regimes into the predicted K regime-specific variances $\boldsymbol{\sigma}_{t+1}^{(2)}$. This model is easily generalized to its persistent, Markov chain counterpart in which at each point in time one of the K components generates observation r_{t+1}, where the process that selects the actual component is a (first-order) hidden Markov chain with K-dimensional state space. Alexander and Lazar (2009) have extended this work to two-state mixture GARCH models with asymmetric effects, such as:

$$\boldsymbol{\sigma}_{t+1}^{(2)} = \boldsymbol{\omega} + \sum_{i=1}^{q}\boldsymbol{\alpha}_i\varepsilon_t^2 + \sum_{i=1}^{d}\boldsymbol{\delta}_i I_{\{\varepsilon_t < 0\}}\varepsilon_t^2 + \sum_{j=1}^{p}\mathbf{B}_j\boldsymbol{\sigma}_t^{(2)}. \tag{1.8}$$

Pelletier (2006) has recently proposed an extension of the now classical multivariate constant conditional correlation framework to incorporate MS dynamics in the conditional variance and covariance functions. Similarly to a standard DCC model, Pelletier's regime switching dynamic correlation (RSDC) model decomposes the covariances into standard deviations and correlations, but these correlations are allowed to change over time as they follow an MSM:

$$\mathbf{r}_t = \mathbf{H}_t^{1/2}\boldsymbol{\varepsilon}_t \quad \boldsymbol{\varepsilon}_t \; IID(\mathbf{0}, \mathbf{I}_N) \quad \mathbf{H}_t = \boldsymbol{\Psi}_t\boldsymbol{\Gamma}_{S_t}\boldsymbol{\Psi}_t, \tag{1.9}$$

where $\mathbf{\Psi}_t$ is a diagonal matrix composed of the standard deviations (Pelletier simply suggests that each of them may follow a standard univariate GARCH(1,1) process) of N return series and the regime-dependent matrix $\mathbf{\Gamma}_{S_t}$ contains the correlations that are assumed to be constant within a regime but different across regimes.

A different line of extension of the basic framework concerns the opportunity to model the Markov chain transition probabilities as depending on (endogenous or exogenous) state variables or factors. Moreover, as we shall see in section 1.7, in many asset pricing applications of MSMs, assuming that transition probabilities are time-varying is not only an empirical matter, but on the contrary this choice has first-order asset pricing implications. For instance, Gray (1996) assumes that the switching probabilities depend on the level of the short rate, to capture the phenomenon that a switch to the high-volatility regime may be more likely when interest rates are high, which fits the historical experience in the United States (US); formally:

$$\Pr(S_t = k | \Im_{t-1}) = \Phi(c_k + d_k i_{t-1}), \, k = 0,1, \tag{1.10}$$

where c_k and d_k are unknown parameters and $\Phi(\cdot)$ is the Normal CDF which ensures that $0 < \Pr(S_t = k | \Im_{t-1}) < 1$. Maheu and McCurdy (2000) have extended Gray's (1996) intuition on the importance of the non-linearities induced by time-varying regime durations to an empirical analysis of high-frequency stock returns and put their emphasis on the fact that MSMs with time-varying probabilities (TVTPs) may allow researchers to capture the existence of important non-linear dynamics in the conditional mean.

1.3   THE RISK–RETURN TRADE-OFF

Despite its key role in many applications, estimating and understanding the market risk premium has proven difficult. Recent empirical studies have documented two puzzling results. Firstly, there is evidence of a weak, or even negative, relationship between conditional expected returns and the conditional volatility of returns. In fact, a number of researchers have uncovered a negative relationship between volatility and average returns, the so-called 'volatility feedback' effect, which is the idea that an exogenous change in the level of market volatility initially generates additional return volatility as stock prices adjust in response to new information about future discounted expected returns.[7] Secondly, many papers have documented significant time variation in the relationship between volatility and excess (stock) returns. For instance, in a modified GARCH-in mean framework and using post- Second World War monthly data, Glosten et al. (1993) find that the estimated coefficient on volatility in a return–volatility regression is negative; using similar data, Whitelaw (1994) finds that the long-run correlation between fitted moments is also negative. Harrison and Zhang (1999) show that at intermediate horizons (i.e., 1–2 years) there is a significantly positive relationship.

However, the failure to find a positive relationship between excess returns and market volatility may result from not controlling for shifts in investment opportunities. This idea dates back at least to a seminal paper that had first traced a connection between MS as a time series technique and asset pricing theory, namely Turner et al. (1989, henceforth TSN). TSN introduce a model of the market portfolio in which market excess returns are generated from a mixture of two normal densities. The states are characterized as a high-variance and a low-variance state Markov process. TSN develop two models based on this framework. Each incorporates a different assumption about the agents' information sets. In the first model, economic agents know the realization of the Markov state process, even though the econometrician does not observe it. There are two sources of risk premia in this specification. The first is the difference between the mean of the distribution in the low-variance state and the riskless return: agents require compensation in excess of the riskless rate to hold an asset with a risky return. The second premium is a compensation of increased risk in the high-variance state:

$$E[r_t|S_t] = \begin{cases} \mu_0 & \text{if } S_t = 0 \\ \mu_1 & \text{if } S_t = 1 \end{cases} \tag{1.11}$$

The parameter estimates from this model suggest that whereas the first risk premium is positive, the second is negative, that is, $\hat{\mu}_0 > 0$ and $\hat{\mu}_1 < 0$. Monthly data on Standard & Poor's (S&P) 500 index returns for 1946–1987 reveal that the two regimes are persistent, with median durations of three months for the high-variance regime and of 43 months for the low-variance one. Estimates of this simple MSIH model, in which agents are assumed to know the state, do not support a risk premium that increases with risk, which is puzzling. The parameter estimates indicate that agents require an excess return of approximately 10 percent to hold the risky asset in *low*-variance periods, that is, $\hat{\mu}_1 < \hat{\mu}_0$. Further, not only is $\hat{\mu}_1$ significantly less than $\hat{\mu}_0$, it is also significantly negative. Therefore TSN reject the hypothesis of a risk premium increasing in the variance. Misspecification is a likely explanation for this finding: if agents are uncertain of the state, so that they are basing their decisions on their forecasts of the regime, estimates of risk premia that rely on the assumption that the state is known with certainty will be inconsistent.

Therefore in their second model, TSN assume that neither economic agents nor the econometrician observe the states. In each period, agents infer the probabilities of each possible state in the following period conditional on current and past excess returns from Bayes's rule, and use these probabilities in portfolio decisions. We are then interested in estimating the increase in return necessary to compensate the agents for a given increase in the probability of the high-variance state. Agents' portfolio choices are specified as a simple but ad hoc function of this probability, $\mu_t = \alpha + \theta \Pr(S_t = 1|\Im_{t-1})$, where the constant α represents agents' required excess returns for holding an asset in the low-variance state. In fact, TSN slightly generalize this model to:

$$\mu_t = (1 - S_t)\alpha_0 + S_t\alpha_1 + \theta \Pr(S_t = 1|\Im_{t-1}). \tag{1.12}$$

They are able to sign all the parameters using the fact that the stock price at time t should reflect all available information. This requires that the price at t should fall below its value at $t - 1$ if some unfavorable news, such as an increase in variance, arrives between $t - 1$ and t. This fall guarantees that the return from t to $t + 1$ is expected to be higher than usual to compensate stockholders for the additional risk. In this scenario, the return between $t - 1$ and t will be negative on average for periods in which adverse information is acquired, and positive on average when favorable information emerges. This implies that the coefficient θ attached to $\Pr(S_t = 1|\Im_{t-1})$ represents the effect when agents anticipate in $t - 1$ that the time t return will be drawn from the high-variance regime. According to standard mean-variance theory, advance knowledge of a high-variance regime should be compensated by a higher expected return. The expected variance in this model is:

$$E[\sigma_t^2|\mathfrak{I}_{t-1}] = [1 - \Pr(S_t = 1|\mathfrak{I}_{t-1})]\sigma_0^2 + \Pr(S_t = 1|\mathfrak{I}_{t-1})\sigma_1^2$$

$$+ [1 - \Pr(S_t = 1|\mathfrak{I}_{t-1})]\Pr(S_t = 1|\mathfrak{I}_{t-1})(\alpha_1 - \alpha_0)^2. \tag{1.13}$$

Thus when $\Pr(S_t = 1|\mathfrak{I}_{t-1}) \in (0, 1/2)$ is high, because:

$$\frac{\partial E[\sigma_t^2|\mathfrak{I}_{t-1}]}{\partial \Pr(S_t = 1|\mathfrak{I}_{t-1})} = (\sigma_1^2 - \sigma_0^2) + [1 - 2\Pr(S_t = 1|\mathfrak{I}_{t-1})](\alpha_1 - \alpha_0)^2 \tag{1.14}$$

is positive when $\Pr(S_t = 1|\mathfrak{I}_{t-1}) < 0.5$, the expected excess return should be positive so that the parameter θ is positive. On the other hand, it could be that today's high-variance state, $S_t = 1$, was not anticipated in the previous period. In this case, $\Pr(S_t = 1|\mathfrak{I}_{t-1})$ is small so that the average return between $t - 1$ and t is dominated by α_1. During a period in which agents are surprised by the high-volatility regime, the stock price must fall below what would have been seen had the low-volatility regime occurred instead. This will make the return between $t - 1$ and t lower and will yield a negative value for α_1. A related line of reasoning implies that if the variance unexpectedly decreases, the return between $t - 1$ and t will be higher than usual, suggesting that α_0 should be positive. TSN also sign a linear combination of the parameters that appears in the expression for the risk premium in t, the expected value of r_t conditional on the current information set:

$$\mu_t = [1 - \Pr(S_t = 1|\mathfrak{I}_{t-1})]\alpha_0 + (\alpha_1 + \theta)\Pr(S_t = 1|\mathfrak{I}_{t-1}). \tag{1.15}$$

If agents are risk-averse, this expression should always be positive and increase with the probability of a high-volatility state. The expectation will be positive if $\alpha_0 \geq 0$ and $\alpha_1 + \theta \geq 0$. Finally, if both these restrictions hold with inequality and $\alpha_1 + \theta > \alpha_0$, then:

$$\frac{\partial E[r_t|\mathfrak{I}_{t-1}]}{\partial \Pr(S_t = 1|\mathfrak{I}_{t-1})} = \alpha_1 + \theta - \alpha_0 > 0, \tag{1.16}$$

i.e., the risk premium is increasing with agents' probability of the high-variance regime.

When estimated using monthly S&P 500 data, this model yields parameter estimates that are largely consistent with asset pricing theory. The estimates ($\hat{\alpha}_0 = 0.70$ percent, $\hat{\alpha}_1 = -3.36$ percent, and $\hat{\theta} = 2.88$) support the hypothesis of a risk premium rising as the (anticipated) level of risk rises. If agents are certain that the next period's return will be drawn from the low-variance regime, they anticipate a monthly return of 5 percent; likewise, if agents are certain that the next period's return will be drawn from the high-variance regime, they require an annualized return of 180 percent. It seems that agents perceive stocks to be very risky during high-variance regimes. The unconditional probability of the high-variance state is only 0.0352, however. This suggests that the risk premium will average approximately 9 percent on an annual basis. Which is close to the average excess return observed in the data (7.5 percent).[8]

Mayfield (2004) has refined TSN's seminal intuition on the role played by a MS risk premium, the compensation for the additional risk caused by the presence of regimes in volatility, and developed a method for estimating the market risk premium based on the equilibrium relationship between volatility and expected returns under discrete shifts in investment opportunities, as governed by a two-state MSM for volatility, where $\sigma_H^2 \geq \sigma_L^2$, $\Pr(S_{t+1} = L|S_t = L) = 1 - \pi_L$, $\Pr(S_{t+1} = H|S_t = H) = 1 - \pi_H$, and the Markov state $S_t = L, H$ is observable. Mayfield solves the utility maximization problem of a representative investor in an infinite horizon, continuous-time model. Preferences are described by a power utility function with a constant relative risk aversion (CRRA) coefficient γ. There are only two investable assets: a risk-free bond yielding a certain rate of return equal to r_t^f and a risky stock yielding a rate of return equal to dS_t/S_t. The investor chooses an amount of consumption C_t and a fraction ω_t of her wealth W_t to invest in the stock:

$$\max_{C_t, \omega_t} E_v \int_v^{\infty} e^{-\rho s} \frac{C_t^{1-\gamma}}{1 - \gamma} dt \quad C_t > \overline{C}$$

$$\text{s.t. } dW_t = \omega_t W_t \frac{dS_t}{S_t} + (1 - \omega_t) r_t W_t dt - C_t dt$$

$$dS_t = \mu_t S_t dt + \sigma_t S_t dZ + J_t S_t dN(\pi_t), \tag{1.17}$$

where dZ is the increment of a standard Wiener process, $dN(l)$ is a Poisson process that equals either zero or one with intensity l, and the process followed by the drift, volatility and the state probabilities are $d\mu_t = 2(\overline{\mu} - \mu_t)dN(\pi_t)$, $d\sigma_t = 2(\overline{\sigma} - \sigma_t)dN(\pi_t)$, and $d\pi_t = 2(\overline{\pi} - \pi_t)dN(\pi_t)$. Barred variables are averages of the state-dependent variables, for instance $\overline{\pi} = 0.5\pi_L + 0.5\pi_H$. The process of the drift, μ_t, is determined in equilibrium. When $dN = 1$, this causes the drift, volatility and transition parameters to jump to the alternative state. The parameter, J_t, is the magnitude of the jump in the stock price that occurs when the economy switches state. The value of the jump parameter J_t takes two values, J_L and J_H, such that $dJ_t = 2(\overline{J} - J_t)dN(\pi_t)$. Using the principle of optimality, Mayfield proves that the optimal consumption–wealth ratio is given by:

$$\frac{\hat{C}_t}{W_t} = \frac{\rho + (\gamma - 1)\mu_t - 0.5\gamma(\gamma - 1)\sigma_t^2}{\gamma(1 - \lambda_t)} + \frac{\pi_t}{\gamma}\left[1 - \frac{(1 + J_t)^{\gamma}}{(1 + K_t)^{\gamma}}\right], \tag{1.18}$$

where K_t is the jump in consumption that is expected conditional on switching state while – assuming that $\pi_t J_t = \pi_t' \ln(1 + J_t)$, that is, that over the expected duration of each volatility state, the continuously compounded expected change in wealth is equal to the actual change in wealth associated with a change in state, the expression for the conditional equilibrium risk premium is:

$$E_t\left[\frac{dS_t}{S_t}\right] - r_t^f = E_t[r_{t+1}] - r_t^f = \gamma\sigma_t^2 + \hat{\pi}_t \ln(1 + J_t)[1 - (1 + K_t)^{-\gamma}], \tag{1.19}$$

where $\hat{\pi}_t$ is a discrete time estimate of the probability of a switch. This equation shows that the risk premium in each state can be decomposed into two state-dependent risk premia. The first term, $\gamma\sigma_t^2$, describes the intrastate risk premium that compensates diffusion risk within the current state. The second term, $\hat{\pi}_t \ln(1 + J_t)[1 - (1 + K_t)^{-\gamma}]$, describes the required interstate risk premium that compensates for potential jump risk arising from a change in volatility state. Notice that $E_t[r_{t+1}] - r_t^f < \gamma\sigma_t^2$ in the low-volatility state (i.e., $K_L < 0$) because investors expect a reduction in wealth when the economy enters the high-volatility state, because of a positive precautionary savings motive; similarly, when the economy is in the high-volatility state $E_t[r_{t+1}] - r_t^f > \gamma\sigma_t^2$ (i.e., $K_H > 0$) because when the economy re-enters the low-volatility state, consumption jumps up.

The expression for the equilibrium risk premium in Mayfield's model is a special case of Merton's (1973) intertemporal CAPM in which, because individuals anticipate future changes in volatility and corresponding changes in stock prices, *ex post* measured returns are not equal to *ex ante* expected returns. When individuals place a non-zero probability on the likelihood of a future change in the volatility regime, expected returns include the expected change in stock prices associated with a change in the state. While the economy is in the low-volatility regime, actual *ex post* returns are higher on average than expected returns. Conversely, while the economy is in the high-volatility regime, actual *ex post* returns will be lower than expected returns. Within each state, the difference between *ex post* returns and expected returns is similar to the peso-type problem discussed in Rietz (1988). Therefore Mayfield's model generates periods of low volatility and high *ex post* returns alternating with periods of high volatility and low *ex post* returns, thus explaining the finding that returns may be lower in periods of high volatility with the theoretical intuition that expected returns should be increasing with the level of market volatility.

Empirical estimation on value-weighted CRSP index data (in excess of one-month T-bills) of an MSM for volatility shows that market returns can be described as having been drawn from two distributions: an low-volatility, high-return distribution, from which about 88 percent of the returns are drawn, and a high-volatility, low-return distribution, from which about 12 percent of the returns are drawn. In the low-volatility state, the annual standard deviation of returns is 13.0 percent and the mean annualized excess return is 12.4 percent. In contrast, the annual standard deviation of returns in the high-volatility state is 38.2 percent and the mean annualized excess return is −17.9 percent. After having estimated the state-dependent moments and transition probabilities using standard methods, Mayfield uses (1.18) and the optimal consumption process to find the values of γ, J_t, and K_t that are consistent with the sample moments. Next, he uses the expression for the risk premium together with the estimated parameters to calculate the intrastate and interstate components of the risk premium in each volatility state. The estimate of the jump parameter, J_L, is 29.6 percent and is significantly different from zero; the corresponding value of J_H is 42.1 percent. The resulting estimates of the annualized state-dependent risk premia in the low- and high-volatility regimes are 5.2 percent and 32.5 percent, respectively. Therefore, based on the estimated preference parameters, about 50 percent of the unconditional risk premium is related to the risk of future changes in market volatility.

Kim et al. (2004; hereafter KMN) have tackled the volatility feedback puzzle of Mayfield (2004) and Turner et al. (1989) using Campbell and Shiller's (1988) log-linear present-value framework to derive an estimable model of stock returns under the assumption of MS volatility. The log-linear present-value framework is used to derive an analytical expression for the volatility feedback in terms of the parameters of the model:

$$r_t = E_{t-1}[r_t] - \underbrace{\left\{ E_t^*\left[\sum_{j=1}^{\infty}\kappa^j r_{t+j}\right] - E_{t-1}\left[\sum_{j=1}^{\infty}\kappa^j r_{t+j}\right] \right\}}_{\text{volatility feedback } (-f_t)} + \underbrace{\left\{ E_t^*\left[\sum_{j=1}^{\infty}\kappa^j \Delta d_{t+j}\right] - E_{t-1}\left[\sum_{j=1}^{\infty}\kappa^j \Delta d_{t+j}\right] \right\}}_{\text{news about dividend } (\varepsilon_t)} \quad (1.20)$$

or $r_t = E_{t-1}[r_t] - f_t + \varepsilon_t$, where d_{t+j} is the log dividend at time $t + j$, and $\kappa \leqslant 1$ is the average (steady-state) ratio of the stock price to the sum of the stock price and the dividend. Starred time t expectations, $E_t^*[\cdot]$, denote expectations conditional on all information at time t except the final realized return, r_t, which makes them different from the standard conditional operator $E_t[\cdot]$. Different from Campbell and Hentschel (1992), a time-homogeneous MSM for dividend news (ε_t) is found to be more plausible than GARCH specifications in the light of Hamilton and Susmel's (1994) result that most of the ARCH dynamics disappear at monthly frequencies, when switching variance is allowed. Implicitly, KMN use this evidence to support a conjecture that an alternative theory for the negative empirical relationships between realized stock returns, the 'leverage hypothesis', is inconsistent with the data. Under the leverage hypothesis, a large movement in stock prices alters the debt–equity ratio of firms, changing their risk profiles and therefore, the volatility of future returns. A log-linear present-value model implies that the expected return for a given period $t + j$ is a linear function of the market expectation on the volatility of news. Given this assumption and a MS specification for volatility, the expected return is assumed to be a linear function of the conditional probability of the high-volatility regime, $E_t[r_{t+j}] = \mu_0 + \mu_1 \Pr(S_{t+j} = 1|\mathfrak{I}_t)$, where μ_0 is the expected return in a perfectly anticipated low-variance state and μ_1 reflects the marginal effect on the expected return of an anticipated high-variance state. Because this implies that:

$$E_t[r_{t+j}] = \mu_0 + \mu_1 \Pr(S_t = 1) + \mu_1 [\Pr(S_t = 1|\mathfrak{I}_t)(p + q - 1)^j - \Pr(S_t = 1)] \quad (1.21)$$

and

$$E_t^*\left[\sum_{j=1}^{\infty}\kappa^j r_{t+j}\right] = \sum_{j=1}^{\infty}\kappa^j E_t^*[r_{t+j}] = \frac{\mu_0}{1 - \kappa} + \frac{\mu_1}{1 - \kappa}\Pr(S_t = 1)$$
$$+ \frac{\mu_1}{1 - \kappa(p + q - 1)}[\Pr(S_t = 1|\mathfrak{I}_t^*) - \Pr(S_t = 1)],$$

$$(1.22)$$

it is easy to show that:

$$-f_t = \sum_{j=1}^{\infty}\kappa^j E_1^*[r_{t+j}] - \sum_{j=1}^{\infty}\kappa^j E_{t-1}[r_{t+j}] = \frac{\mu_0}{1 - \kappa} + \frac{\mu_1}{1 - \kappa}\Pr(S_t = 1) +$$

$$+ \frac{\mu_1}{1 - \kappa(p + q - 1)}[\Pr(S_t = 1|\mathfrak{I}_t^*) - \Pr(S_t = 1)] - \frac{\mu_0}{1 - \kappa} - \frac{\mu_1}{1 - \kappa}\Pr(S_t = 1) +$$

$$-\frac{\mu_1}{1-\kappa(p+q-1)}[\Pr(S_t=1|\mathfrak{I}_{t-1})-\Pr(S_t=1)]=\varphi[\Pr(S_t=1|\mathfrak{I}_t^*)-\Pr(S_t=1|\mathfrak{I}_{t-1})]$$

(1.23)

so that:

$$r_t=\mu_0+\mu_1\Pr(S_t=1|\mathfrak{I}_{t-1})+\varphi[\Pr(S_t=1|\mathfrak{I}_t^*)-\Pr(S_t=1|\mathfrak{I}_{t-1})]+\varepsilon_t$$

(1.24)

where $\varepsilon_t\sim N(0,\sigma_{S_t}^2)$ and $\varphi\equiv\mu_1/[1-\kappa(p+q-1)]$. Under a volatility feedback effect, if market volatility is persistent ($p+q>1$) and positively related to the equity premium ($\mu_1>0$), then stock prices should immediately move in the opposite direction of the level of market volatility, that is, $\varphi<0$. Notice that a necessary and sufficient condition for a volatility feedback to occur is that $\mathfrak{I}_t^*\supseteq\mathfrak{I}_{t-1}$; when $\mathfrak{I}_t^*$ and $\mathfrak{I}_{t-1}^*$ are identical, $\Pr(S_t=1|\mathfrak{I}_t^*)=\Pr(S_t=1|\mathfrak{I}_{t-1})$ so that $r_t=\mu_0+\mu_1\Pr(S_t=1|\mathfrak{I}_{t-1})$ holds, as in Turner et al. (1989).[9]

Using monthly excess returns on the value-weighted NYSE equity portfolio for the sample periods 1926–51 and 1952–2000, KMN find that the evidence of time-varying risk premia is mixed. When agents are assumed to observe only past returns (i.e., $\mathfrak{I}_t^*$ and $\mathfrak{I}_{t-1}^*$ are identical but do not include S_t), a likelihood ratio test (LRT) for the null hypothesis of a constant mean has a p-value of 0.38 for the 1926–51 sample but of 0.02, for the 1952–2000 sample. When agents are assumed to observe the true volatility regime (i.e., $\mathfrak{I}_t^*$ and $\mathfrak{I}_{t-1}^*$ are identical and include S_t), there is strong evidence of a time-varying mean, with p-values of 0.03 and 0.01 for the two samples. However, in this case, the estimated trade-off between mean and variance is significantly negative, that is, the high-volatility regime is the one that implies a negative risk premium. When investors are assumed to learn the prevailing volatility regime only by the end of each month as in Mayfield (2004), that is, $\mathfrak{I}_t^*\supseteq\mathfrak{I}_{t-1}$, there is evidence of a positive relationship between volatility and the equity premium. The volatility feedback effect is significantly negative for both sample periods when the feedback parameter is unrestricted, $\hat{\varphi}<0$. The estimated partial effect, $\hat{\mu}_1$, is positive, though not significant, for the 1952–2000 sample. Since volatility regimes appear to be very persistent (i.e., $\hat{p}+\hat{q}\gg1$), these results are strongly in support of a positive relationship between market volatility and the equity premium. Similarly, when the restriction $\varphi=\mu_1/[1-\kappa(p+q-1)]$ is imposed, the estimated relationship is always positive, although this restriction can be rejected at the 10 percent level for the 1926–51 sample. KMN's work implies that taking volatility feedbacks into account is important to avoid confusing a negative relationship between volatility and realized returns with the underlying feedback relationship between volatility and the equity risk premium.

Bae et al. (2007; hereafter BKN) have used an MS GARCH framework to formally test the two key competing explanations for a negative relationship between average excess returns and their conditional volatility, that is: (1) Black's (1976) leverage story; and (2) volatility feedbacks; furthermore, they decompose the volatility feedback into intra- and inter-regime feedbacks. BKN argue that the test results in Turner et al. (1989), Kim et al. (2004) and Mayfield (2004) – who find evidence in support of volatility feedback effects – are unsatisfactory because they fail to disentangle leverage and feedback effects.[10] Moreover, the typical monthly estimates in the GARCH literature may be puzzling in light of the evidence (see, e.g., Hamilton and Susmel, 1994) that ARCH effects in equity returns die out within a month under switching volatility, so that the usefulness of ARCH is debatable. However, MSMs in which volatility is constant across states may also ignore a potential source of asymmetric volatility stemming from changing volatility within a regime. As a result, BKN propose a model of asymmetric volatility that identifies leverage and feedback effects by controlling for the actual change in the leverage ratio and that is based on MS GARCH, so nesting both MS ARCH and MSIH models. BKN take steps from an accounting identity by which the sum of equity and debt equals total assets: the return on total assets is therefore identical to a value-weighted sum of returns on equity and debt. An assumption of risk-free debt and some manipulations of the identity yields the following relationship between excess returns on total assets and excess returns on equity: $r_t \equiv l_t r_t^a$, where r_t is the return on equity in excess of the risk-free rate, r_t^a is the return on total assets in excess of the risk-free rate, and l_t is one plus the leverage ratio. Since the leverage effect matters only for equity, BKN formulate asymmetric volatility at the level of total assets and interpret the asymmetric volatility as a volatility feedback:

$$r_{t+1}^a = \mu_1 E_t[\sigma_{t+1}^2] + \mu_2 (E_t[\sigma_{t+1}^2] - E_t[\sigma_t^2]) + \varepsilon_{t+1} \quad \varepsilon_{t+1} \sim N(0, \sigma_{t+1}^2)$$

$$\sigma_{t+1}^2 = \omega_{S_{t+1}} + \alpha \varepsilon_t^2 + \delta I_{\{\varepsilon_t \leq 0\}} \varepsilon_t^2 + \beta \sigma_t^2 \quad S_{t+1} = 1, 2 \text{ and } \omega_1 > \omega_2 \tag{1.25}$$

If volatility is priced as implied by volatility feedback, market participants require compensation for the risk associated with volatility, which can be expressed as $\mu_1 E_t[\sigma_{t+1}^2]$. Evidence of a significant and positive μ_1 reflects that risk, measured by volatility, and returns are positively related, and support volatility feedback. Similar to Mayfield (2004), market participants face another risk: switches in the volatility regime, so that they require a compensation $\mu_2 (E_t[\sigma_{t+1}^2] - E_t[\sigma_t^2])$, where μ_2 is expected to be positive. In BKN's model, MS effects simply involve the GJR GARCH(1,1) constant, $\omega_{S_{t+1}}$, and therefore only affect the implied unconditional variance, $\omega_{S_{t+1}}/(1 - \alpha - \delta/2 - \beta)$. If $\omega_1 = \omega_2$, then the volatility process collapses to a typical asymmetric GARCH process with only one volatility regime; if $\alpha = \delta = \beta = 0$, the model reduces to the MSH variance model considered by Turner et al. (1989) and Kim et al. (2004). $\delta > 0$ suggests the existence of a negative correlation between returns and subsequent volatility. The negative correlation can be interpreted as volatility feedback if intra-regime conditional volatility is persistent and priced. BKN call this volatility feedback channel of asymmetric volatility an intra-regime feedback. While changes in conditional volatility within regimes may induce volatility feedback, shifts in the volatility regime provide an additional source which they call inter-regime feedback.[11] Finally, BKN combine the volatility feedback model formulated at the level of total assets with the financial leverage ratio to produce a model for equity returns, which represents interactions between leverage and volatility feedback effects:

$$r_{t+1} = l_t \mu_1 E_t[\sigma_{t+1}^2] + l_t \mu_2 (E_t[\sigma_{t+1}^2] - E_t[\sigma_t^2]) + u_{t+1} \quad u_{t+1} \sim N(0, l_t^2 \sigma_{t+1}^2), \tag{1.26}$$

where the expression for σ_{t+1}^2 is reported above. This model enables BKN to assess the relative contribution of each type of volatility to asymmetric feedbacks.

Using monthly 1952–99 returns on the value-weighted NYSE index in excess of one-month US T-bill yields and data on the leverage ratio constructed as in Schwert (1989), BKN assess the importance of each source of a negative relationship between expected returns and volatility, by first estimating the model under the restriction $\omega_1 = \omega_2$. The resulting model is an asymmetric GARCH model with no MS. The model allows for volatility feedback stemming from changing conditional volatility but no inter-regime volatility feedback. The point estimate of δ is 0.256 with a standard error of 0.126, suggesting that there is a significant negative correlation between returns and subsequent volatility. This negative correlation can be interpreted as a volatility feedback, if the volatility process is persistent and the price of risk is positive. The estimate of the price of risk parameter, μ_1, is significantly positive. With a 1987 crash dummy variable included, the volatility process is also reasonably persistent, $\hat{\alpha} + \hat{\beta} + \hat{\delta}/2 = 0.79$. Thus, in the absence of MS, the volatility feedback arising from changing conditional volatility plays an important role in explaining asymmetric volatility in returns, which is consistent with the single-regime results in Campbell and Hentschel (1992) and Bekaert and Wu (2000). To examine the implications of MS volatility, the full model with $\omega_1 \neq \omega_2$ is then estimated (using a Gray-type approximation in the MS GARCH case). The α estimate is zero as above, but MS volatility significantly affects the δ and β estimates: the point estimate of δ is 0.189 in the absence of MS but almost zero in the presence of MS; β is estimated to be 0.694 in its absence but almost zero in its presence. This has two important implications. Firstly, in the presence of MS, conditional volatility within regimes is neither persistent nor correlated with returns, suggesting that GARCH is not an important source of asymmetric volatility. Secondly, the potential of MS to act as a source of asymmetric volatility is not affected by the presence of varying volatility within regimes. While intra-regime feedback does not exist, BKN results support inter-regime volatility feedback; there is evidence of negative correlation between return innovations and the subsequent volatility regime, with negative shocks increasing the probability of switching from the low-volatility regime to the high-volatility regime. After controlling for the leverage effect, inter-regime volatility feedback weakens intra-regime volatility feedback, indicating that recurrent regime shifts are the main source of the negative correlation between returns and volatility.

Whitelaw (2000) has also investigated the issue of whether it may be sensible to find a negative relationship between market expected returns and conditional variance. He re-examines this question using a representative agent, Lucas-type exchange economy in which consumption growth is modeled as an MS autoregressive process with two regimes and in which the probability of a regime shift is a function of the level of consumption growth. When the parameters are estimated using monthly consumption data over the period 1959–96, the two-regime MSM identifies the expansionary and contractionary phases of the business cycle consistent with National Bureau of Economic Research (NBER) business cycle dates. Moreover, the model generates results that are consistent with commonly known empirical findings: expected returns and conditional volatility exhibit a complex, non-linear relationship; they are negatively (positively) related in the short (long) run and this relation varies widely over time. On the other hand, a single-regime consumption capital asset pricing model (CAPM) (CCAPM) calibrated to the same data generates a strong positive, and essentially linear, relation between returns and volatility. As a result, Whitelaw concludes that this evidence is consistent with reasonable parameterizations of a relatively simple MS version of the

CCAPM. The intuition is that under CRRA preferences, the equity premium is a function of the correlation between equity returns and the intertemporal marginal rate of substitution (IMRS):

$$E_t[r_{t+1} - r_t^f] = -r_t^f \sigma_t[r_{t+1}] \sqrt{Var_t[M_{t+1}]} Corr_t[r_{t+1}, M_{t+1}]$$

$$= -r_t^f \sigma_t[r_{t+1}] \sqrt{Var_t[M_{t+1}]} Corr_t \left[\frac{c_{t+1}}{c_t} \frac{\psi_{t+1} + 1}{\psi_t}, \left(\frac{c_{t+1}}{c_t} \right)^{-\gamma} \right], \qquad (1.27)$$

where ψ_{t+1} is the time-varying price–dividend ratio (PDR). The conditional moments of returns will be positively related (period by period) as long as the correlation between $M_{t+1} \equiv (c_{t+1}/c_t)^{-\gamma}$ and equity returns is negative. Holding the PDR constant (for the sake of argument), this condition holds (for $\gamma > 0$) since $Corr_t[c_{t+1}/c_t, (c_{t+1}/c_t)^{-\gamma}] < 0$. However, the marginal rate of substitution depends only on the next period's consumption growth, while the equity return depends on the infinite future via its dependence on the stock price next period (via ψ_{t+1}). The only way to duplicate these features of the data (i.e., weak or negative short-run and positive long-run relations between expected returns and volatility) is to formulate a model in which variation in the PDR partially offsets the variation in the dividend growth component of the equity return in some states. In other words, the PDR must either co-vary positively with the IMRS or co-vary weakly, but be volatile enough to reduce the overall correlation between the IMRS and the return on equity. In these states of the world, the magnitude of the correlation will be reduced, and high volatility will no longer correspond to high expected returns. Whitelaw observes that these requirements are difficult, if not impossible, to overcome if consumption growth follows a simple ARMA process. The correlation will be weakly time-varying because the PDR, which is an expectation of future consumption growth, will be less variable than consumption growth itself. Moreover, correlations will be stable because both the immediate and the distant future depend on a limited number of past values of consumption growth.[12] Whitelaw notices that one appealing way to overcome these problems is to consider an MSM with TVTPs. For regimes that are sufficiently far apart in terms of the time-series behavior of consumption growth, the transition probabilities will control the conditional volatility of returns. That is, regimes with a high probability of switching to a different regime will have high volatility. At the same time, however, increasing the probability of a switch may decrease the correlation between equity returns and the SDF, reducing the risk premium. This second effect will occur because the PDR, which depends on expected future consumption growth, will be related to the regime, not to short-run consumption growth. Put differently, regime shifts introduce large movements in the investment opportunity set, and therefore induce a desire among investors to hedge adverse changes. In some states of the world, the market claim provides such a hedge. Specifically, when a regime shift is likely, its value is high and its expected return is low as a consequence. These are also states of the world with high volatility, generating the required negative relation between volatility and expected returns. In other states of the world, regime shifts are less likely and the standard positive relation dominates.

Whitelaw (2000) and a handful of related papers have kept the MS specification simple on purpose, to preserve tractability. Consequently, the reduced form model, while providing insights on the relationship between risk and return, fails to match other features of equity data. For instance, the magnitude of the equity premium in Whitelaw (2000) is low. Calvet and Fisher (2007) develop a parsimonious CCAPM with shocks of heterogeneous durations to capture the fact that equity prices are driven by news with heterogeneous persistence, ranging from intra-day intervals (e.g., corporate and macroeconomic announcements) to several decades (e.g., demographics, technological innovation and regime shifts in consumption, dividends and macroeconomic uncertainty, as in Lettau et al., 2008; see section 1.5). Calvet and Fisher present an MS multifractal model, which is a stochastic volatility (SV) model characterized by a small number of parameters but an arbitrarily large number of frequencies, as in Calvet and Fisher (2001). In their model, volatility is hit by exogenous shocks with heterogeneous durations, which range from one day to more than a decade. That is, given a state vector $\mathbf{S}_{t+1}$ that contains K positive elements, $S_{j,t+1} = 1, 2,\ldots, K$, volatility follows the process:

$$\sigma^d_{S_{t+1}} = \bar{\sigma}^d \left(\prod_{j=1}^{K} S_{j,t+1} \right)^{1/2}, \tag{1.28}$$

where $\bar{\sigma}^d > 0$. This specification permits each component to evolve at a separate frequency. For example, the first component may have transitions measured in years or decades, matching low-frequency shocks to technology or demographics; medium-run components may represent business cycles; high-frequency components may capture liquidity and other transient effects. To maintain parsimony, Calvet and Fisher assume that the components of $\mathbf{S}_{t+1}$ evolve independently; further, the $S_{j,t+1}$ are first-order Markov, and for each component $S_{j,t+1}$, a single parameter controls the persistence of innovations. Multifrequency (MS) models are sufficiently flexible to account for market conditions that change considerably over a long time span and capture return outliers, volatility persistence and power variation of financial series (see e.g., Calvet and Fisher, 2001).

In Calvet and Fisher (2007), one Epstein–Zin consumer receives an exogenous consumption stream to price a flow of dividends under multifrequency MS. The agent receives an exogenous consumption stream, C_t, with the continuously compounded growth rate of consumption follows a random walk with constant drift and volatility (called μ^c and σ^c respectively), where the consumption growth shocks are IID Normal. The model separates stock returns from aggregate consumption growth and the SDF. This assumption is consistent with the imperfect correlation between real consumption growth and real dividend growth. The log-dividend follows a random walk with MS drift and volatility,

$$\ln D_{t+1} - \ln D_t = \mu^d_{S_{t+1}} - \frac{1}{2}(\sigma^d_{S_{t+1}})^2 + \sigma^d_{S_{t+1}} \varepsilon^d_{t+1} \quad \varepsilon^d_{t+1} \sim NID(0,1), \tag{1.29}$$

where ε^d_{t+1} is correlated with shocks to consumption growth (with coefficient $\rho_{c,d}$), and S_{t+1} is a first-order Markov state that may take K different values.[13] When the representative agent directly observes the true state of the economy, the SDF satisfies:

$$M_{t+1} = \beta \{ (E_t[C_{t+1}/C_t])^{1-\gamma} \}^{\frac{1}{\alpha-1}} \left(\frac{C_{t+1}}{C_t} \right)^{-\gamma}, \tag{1.30}$$

which is proportional to the SDF obtained under expected utility (when $\alpha \equiv (1 - \gamma)/(1 - 1/\psi) = 1$), suggesting that the elasticity of intertemporal substitution (EIS) affects the interest rate but not the price of risk. Given this SDF, the real interest rate $r_f = -\ln E_t[SDF_{t+1}]$ is constant and obeys the relationship:

$$r_f = -\ln\beta + (\alpha - 1)\ln E_t\left[\left(\frac{C_{t+1}}{C_t}\right)^{1-\gamma}\right] + \ln E_t\left[\left(\frac{C_{t+1}}{C_t}\right)^{-\gamma}\right]$$

$$= -\ln\beta + \frac{1}{\psi}\mu^c - \left(\gamma + \frac{\gamma - 1}{\psi}\right)\frac{(\sigma^c)^2}{2}. \tag{1.31}$$

Similar to Hung (1994), the equilibrium PDR is controlled by the Markov state, $P_t/D_t = \Psi_{S_t}$ so that the equilibrium price–dividend ratio therefore solves the fixed-point:

$$\Psi_{S_t} = E_t\left[(1 + \Psi_{S_{t+1}})\frac{D_{t+1}}{D_t}\right] = E_t[(1 + \Psi_{S_{t+1}})e^{-r_f + \mu^d_{S_{t+1}} - \gamma\rho_{c,d}\sigma^c\sigma^d_{S_{t+1}}}]. \tag{1.32}$$

and the equilibrium PDR can be computed numerically for every possible state.

Calvet and Fisher use US equity data over the period 1926–2003 to perform MLE estimation and report that using between six and eight volatility components provides significant improvements relative to lower-dimensional specifications. The model generates volatility feedback that, under sensible parameterizations, is substantially higher than in previous research. In particular, the strength of the feedback rises with the number of components, increasing to between 20 percent and 40 percent for the preferred specifications. As a result, the multifrequency equilibrium model generates an unconditional feedback that is 10 to 40 times larger than in previous literature.

1.4   GENERAL EQUILIBRIUM FOUNDATIONS OF MS IN ASSET RETURNS

A number of papers have shown that – under a variety of asset pricing frameworks and assumptions concerning preferences and market completeness – simple MSMs for the fundamentals (such as real dividends, real consumption, short-term interest rates, output, etc.) underlying asset prices may generate the ubiquitous finding that most asset classes appear to be characterized by MS dynamics. On the one hand, this literature seems removed from the main bulk of empirical finance papers that have implemented MS estimation: in the papers that I review in this section, the framework is extremely simple because their goal is to derive equilibrium asset prices and return processes from MS assumptions on fundamentals. Often the papers have performed only rough calibrations of the resulting models, in the form of estimation of simple MSMs for fundamentals and then simulation of the models to reproduce key stylized facts concerning asset returns. On the other hand, there is little doubt that even though these early papers proceeded in a mechanical way to assemble MS assumptions for the forcing variables to deliver models – often themselves containing MS dynamics – for the SDF, this is the literature that has provided the background to the development of the state-of-the-art knowledge of MS in SDFs to be reviewed in sections 1.6 and 1.7.

The context for a number of the papers to be discussed below is a quest to develop models for preferences and/or the dynamics of beliefs that can explain a number of pricing puzzles (below, I shall refer to them simply as 'the puzzles') that had been discussed in the literature starting in the 1980s. For instance, Mehra and Prescott (1985) had examined whether Lucas's 1978 model could account for the average rates of return on stocks and short-term T-bills in the US. They found that over the period 1889–1978 the average real rate of return was 6.98 percent per year on equities but only 0.80 percent per year on short-term bills. The 6.18 percent per year excess return on stocks relative to bills – the equity premium – is much larger than Mehra and Prescott could account for using a version of the Lucas model in which stocks are priced assuming that the aggregate stock market pays out consumption flows directly, instead of dividends (i.e., the CCAPM) under reasonable preferences. The failure of the CCAPM to account for the average risk premium has been dubbed the equity premium puzzle.[14]

Let me briefly introduce first, keeping details to a very minimum, a number of papers that since the late 1980s have ventured into an analysis of the effects of MS fundamentals for equilibrium asset returns. Abel (1994) has addressed the puzzles assuming that the conditional growth rates of consumption and dividends – assumed to be different – may depend on an underlying state of the world that evolves according to an MSM and derived closed-form solutions for the conditional and unconditional expected rates of return on stocks and short-term riskless bills.[15] However, Abel reports that the unconditional short-term interest rate is higher under MS than under conditional IID shocks, which further exacerbates the risk-free rate puzzle. In addition, under conditional lognormality, the added stochastic richness of MS fundamentals generally reduces the size of the equity premium predicted by his DAPM, and thus exacerbates rather than resolves the equity premium puzzle. More precisely, Abel shows that if the conditional expected growth rates of consumption and dividends are positively correlated with each other (as they must be in models that cannot distinguish between consumption and dividends), then introducing MS will reduce the unconditional equity premium under conditional lognormality and CRRA preferences.

Another early paper with negative results for the ability of MSMs to solve the puzzles is Bonomo and Garcia (1994). In the face of the apparent success of earlier papers such as Cecchetti et al. (1990; hereafter CLM) and Kandel and Stambaugh (1990) at calibrating simple DAPMs in which consumption equals dividends that follow a MS process to reproduce the predictability patterns in (aggregate) stock returns,[16] Bonomo and Garcia show that one needs to carefully avoid misspecifications in the MSM, lest the effects on the asset pricing implications may be disruptive. In particular, they emphasize that if instead of restricting our attention to one particular MSM, one specifies a larger class of MSMs and lets the data on the endowment decide on the best model according to standard testing procedures, the chosen specification turns out to be a two-state MSM with constant mean and regime-dependent variances. Therefore, they reject CLM's (1990) specification, an MS with regime-dependent means and constant variance, as well as Kandel and Stambaugh's (1990) specification with four regimes (two states for the mean and two states for the variance) for consumption growth. In a standard version of the CCAPM, Bonomo and Garcia report that their DAPM is unable to produce negative serial correlation in stock returns of the magnitude observed in the data, similarly to single-state models.

What are the mechanics of MS entering a standard macro-style DAPM? One key example is represented by Hung (1994) because it pursues goals and solution methods common to many of the papers reviewed in section 1.3, extending them to encompass a class of preferences richer than classical power utility, in particular, non-expected utility preferences à la Kreps and Porteus (1978).[17] In practice, the representative investor is assumed to care for the timing of the resolution of uncertainty over temporal lotteries and their preferences are represented recursively by $V_t = U(C_t, E_t[V_{t+1}])$, where $U(\cdot, \cdot)$ is an aggregator function, and C_t is consumption. As shown by Kreps and Porteus, agents prefer an early resolution of uncertainty over temporal lotteries if $U(\cdot, \cdot)$ is convex in its second argument. Let me now specialize to the parameterization:

$$[(1 - \beta)C_t^{1-\rho} + \beta E_t[V_{t+1}]^{\frac{1-\rho}{1-\gamma}}]^{\frac{1-\gamma}{1-\rho}}, \tag{1.33}$$

where β is the agent's subjective time discount factor, γ can still be interpreted as the Arrow–Pratt coefficient of relative risk aversion, and $1/\rho$ measures EIS. If the agent's CRRA coefficient γ exceeds the reciprocal of their EIS (ρ), then they prefer an early resolution of uncertainty; if $\gamma = \rho$, the agent's utility is an isoelastic von Neumann–Morgenstern utility function and they are indifferent to the timing of uncertainty resolution. In this case, the basic Euler condition for the wealth portfolio, the value-weighted portfolio of all assets, simplifies to

$$1 = \beta E_t\left\{\left(\frac{C_{t+1}}{C_t}\right)^{-\gamma} R_{t+1}^W\right\}, \tag{1.34}$$

where R_{t+1}^W is the gross return on the wealth portfolio, which is equivalent to

$$P_t^W u'(C_t) = \beta E_t[(P_{t+1}^W + C_{t+1})u'(C_{t+1})] \tag{1.35}$$

when $u(C_t)$ is a standard power utility function. Epstein and Zin (1989) have shown that when $\gamma \neq \rho$, because the SDF is given by:

$$\left[\beta\left(\frac{C_{t+1}}{C_t}\right)^{-\rho}\right]^{\frac{1-\gamma}{1-\rho}} (R_{t+1}^W)^{\frac{1-\gamma}{1-\rho}-1}, \tag{1.36}$$

the Euler condition that pins down the price of any asset or portfolio i is instead:

$$1 = E_t\left\{\left[\beta\left(\frac{C_{t+1}}{C_t}\right)^{-\rho}\right]^{\frac{1-\gamma}{1-\rho}} (R_{t+1}^W)^{\frac{1-\gamma}{1-\rho}-1} R_{t+1}^i\right\}. \tag{1.37}$$

At this point, one needs to solve the model using numerical methods. Although equivalent solution methods have been proposed (see, e.g., Abel, 1994), what follows represents a very common approach. To derive equilibrium asset prices and returns under Epstein and Zin's preferences, one needs to start off with the pricing function for the wealth portfolio, which is assumed to pay off C_t. Denote its price and return by P_t^W and R_t^W, respectively. As in Mehra and Prescott (1985) and Weil (1989), a stationary equilibrium is assumed such that $P_t^W = \psi_{S_t} C_t$, where S_t is the state prevailing at time t and ψ_{S_t} is an undetermined, regime-dependent PDR (defined over consumption) for the wealth portfolio. The one-period rate of return for the wealth portfolio if the current state is $S_t = i$ and the next period state is $S_{t+1} = j$ $(i, j = 0, 1)$, is $R^W(i, j) = [(\psi_j + 1)/\psi_i]g_j$, where g_j is the consumption growth rate in state $S_{t+1} = j$. Substituting this definition into (1.36) and using the log-normal moment generator, the following equation is obtained:

$$1 = \beta^{\frac{1-\gamma}{1-\rho}} \exp[0.5(1 - \gamma)^2 \sigma_c^2]\left\{ \Pr(S_{t+1} = 1|S_t = i)\exp[(1 - \gamma)g_1]\left[\left(\frac{1 + \psi_1}{\psi_i}\right)^{\frac{1-\gamma}{1-\rho}}\right] + \right.$$

$$\left. + \Pr(S_{t+1} = 0|S_t = i)\exp[(1 - \gamma)g_0]\left[\left(\frac{1 + \psi_0}{\psi_0}\right)^{\frac{1-\gamma}{1-\rho}}\right]\right\}. \tag{1.38}$$

These equations form a non-linear system in which the ψ_i s $(i = 0 \text{ and } 1)$ are positive solutions if the equilibrium exists. It is possible to solve ψ_i as a function of the estimated parameters in the bivariate MS process, and the preference parameters γ, β, and ρ. After obtaining the solutions for ψ_i, the expression for returns on the market portfolio follows easily. The stock market pays D_t in period t. Denote its price and return by P^M and R^M, respectively. In a stationary equilibrium, the price for the stock market can be expressed as $P_t^M(i) = \kappa_i D_t$, where D_t is the dividend level at t, i is the state of nature at t and κ_i is an undetermined PDR. Let $d_{t+1} = D_{t+1}/D_{t+1}$ be the dividend growth rate at t. Then the one-period rate of return for the stock market, if the current state is i and the next period state is j, can be written as $R^M(i, j) = [(\kappa_j + 1)/\kappa_i]d_j$. Substituting this expression into (1.37) and using the log-normal moment generator implies:

$$\kappa_i = \beta^{\frac{1-\gamma}{1-\rho}} \exp[0.5\,\gamma^2\sigma_c^2 + 0.5\,\sigma_d^2 - \gamma\sigma_{cd}]\left\{ \Pr(S_{t+1} = 1|S_t = i)\exp[-\gamma g_1 + d_1]\left[\left(\frac{1 + \psi_1}{\psi_i}\right)^{\frac{1-\gamma}{1-\rho} - 1}(1 + \kappa_1)\right] \right.$$

$$\left. + \Pr(S_{t+1} = 0|S_t = i)\exp[-\gamma g_0 + d_0]\left[\left(\frac{1 + \psi_0}{\psi_0}\right)^{\frac{1-\gamma}{1-\rho} - 1}(1 + \kappa_0)\right]\right\}. \tag{1.39}$$

These equations form a linear system. The κ_i are positive solutions to these equations if the equilibrium exists. If the current state is i, the regime-switching risk-free rate $R^f(i)$, can be calculated as follows:

$$1/R^f(i) = \beta^{\frac{1-\gamma}{1-\rho}} \exp[0.5\gamma^2\sigma_c^2]\left\{ \Pr(S_{t+1} = 1|S_t = i) \exp[-\gamma g_1]\left[\left(\frac{1 + \psi_1}{\psi_i}\right)^{\frac{1-\gamma}{1-\rho} - 1}\right] + \right.$$

$$\left. + \Pr(S_{t+1} = 0|S_t = i) \exp[-\gamma g_0]\left[\left(\frac{1 + \psi_0}{\psi_i}\right)^{\frac{1-\gamma}{1-\rho} - 1}\right]\right\}. \tag{1.40}$$

Through the estimation of a bivariate MS model on US annual (real) data for the period 1889–1985, Hung (1994) finds that the combination of non-expected utility preferences and of MS fundamentals over recessions and expansions can resolve the equity premium and risk-free rate puzzles. His ML estimates illustrate the presence of powerful asymmetries in the process of fundamentals: the probability that consumption and dividends will *both* be in a high-growth state in the next period, given that they are in a high-growth state in this period, is inferred to be 0.96. If dividends and consumption are depressed at time t, there is only a probability of 0.30 that *both* will still be depressed at time $t+1$. The resulting asymmetric transition matrix implies that the unconditional probabilities of both consumption and dividends being in either a boom state or a depression state are 0.94 and 0.06, respectively. Asymmetric market fundamentals are capable of matching the negative sample correlation between the risk premium and the risk-free rate. Although Hung's model is not capable of exactly matching all relevant first and second moments of the risk premium and the risk-free rate, the MS-driven model cannot be rejected using Cecchetti et al.'s (1993) generalized method of moments (GMM)-style tests. The importance of the findings in Hung (1994) and the role of MS in capturing the asymmetric dynamics of consumption and dividends over business cycles, as well as their time-varying correlations, is difficult to play down. CLM (1990) and Kocherlakota (1990) had already emphasized that consumption and dividend growth rates are less than perfectly correlated, so that the return on aggregate wealth and the return to the stock market portfolio are different. Consequently, instead of using a univariate degenerate process to govern consumption, they had adopted a bivariate, single-state VAR process for consumption and dividends. However, they all found that a DAPM governed by a bivariate linear process is not capable of resolving the puzzles. Moreover, CLM (1990) had also experimented with simple, bivariate MSVAR models with switching mean growth rates, when preferences are described by simple, time-separable power utility functions in which CRRA is the inverse of EIS. Similarly to Abel (1994), they had reported that although MSVAR processes are able to capture business cycle asymmetries, the solution to the equity premium puzzle could not be found. Hence the importance of Hung's results is that by putting together regime-switching consumption–dividends and Epstein–Zin preferences, an explanation to the puzzles could be found.

Cecchetti et al. (2000; CLM) have recently re-examined the issue of whether a MSM for fundamentals may be nested within a standard endowment-type CCAPM with isoelastic preferences to produce realistic implications. Their main conclusion is that the representative investor's beliefs need to be severely distorted in order for a calibrated model under MS to produce plausible implications for the mean equity premium and risk-free rate, volatility, persistence and long-horizon predictability of asset returns and its relationship to the business cycle. These belief distortions enter in two empirically plausible dimensions. Firstly, they introduce systematic deviations of the subjective probabilities of transitions between high- and low-growth state, that are motivated by showing how agents who use simple rules of thumb may form subjective probabilities that deviate from ML estimates derived from US per capita consumption data. Rule-of-thumb estimates that imply relatively pessimistic beliefs about the persistence of the expansion state and relatively optimistic beliefs about the persistence of the contraction state, and allow CLM to match the mean equity premium and risk-free rate found in the data. Unfortunately, such distortions alone are insufficient to rationalize the volatility of asset returns or the patterns of serial correlation and predictability commonly found in the data.

To go beyond an explanation of the first moments of asset returns, CLM introduce a second distortion in which beliefs about the transition probabilities fluctuate randomly around their subjective (distorted) means. However, fluctuations of a special kind are required to match the data, not randomization per se: it is random fluctuations in beliefs around the persistence of the low-endowment growth state that generate volatility and predictability in stock returns.[18] When the subjective discount rate is instead selected to match the risk-free rate and the representative agent is entirely rational with beliefs that match the ML estimates of their two-state MSMs, as expected from Abel (1994) and Bonomo and Garcia (1994), CLM's model fails badly: there is virtually no equity premium, the volatility of stock returns is far below their sample values, and excess returns have neither the persistence nor the predictability shown by the data. Unmistakably, CLM's use of MSMs to examine the asset pricing implications acquires a distinct behavioral flavor and it may be interpreted as a description not of a rational expectations equilibrium framework, but of the deviations that would be required of an MSM for it to appropriately price the aggregate US market.[19] Moreover, it may be questionable that CLM end up – through specific parametric choices for their behavioral perturbations – specifying a rich eight-state MSM, which appears to be unusual.

Another successful attempt at tackling complex asset pricing issues using an MSM for fundamentals has been made by Lettau et al. (2008; hereafter LLW). LLW's impetus comes from the fact that the relationship between stock prices and fundamentals gives the impression to have changed in the 1990s. A body of literature has studied the evidence of structurally higher PDRs in the 1990s, and explanations have ranged from declining costs of equity market participation and diversification, to irrational exuberance, to changes in technology and demography. LLW propose a CCAPM with Epstein–Zin preferences with an IES greater than one to study the influence of a decline in macroeconomic risk on aggregate stock prices. They estimate a four-state Markov switching in heteroskedasticity (MSIH) model with unobservable regimes for the volatility and mean of consumption growth and find indications of a shift to substantially lower consumption volatility at the beginning of the 1990s.[20] LLW's MSM is built on two different Markov states driving the mean and the variance of consumption growth (assumed to be equal to dividend growth), similarly to Kandel and Stambaugh (1990); the probability of changing mean states is independent of the probability of changing volatility states, and vice versa, so that $S_{t+1}^\mu = 1,2$ and S_{t+1}^σ may be equivalently summarized by a four-state Markov chain, $S_{t+1} \equiv S_{t+1}^\mu \times S_{t+1}^\sigma = 1, 2, 3, 4$, under restrictions on the transition matrix. The smoothed probabilities from the model show a sharp increase in the probability of being in a low-volatility state at the beginning of the 1990s. Over a period of approximately six years, the probability of being in a low-volatility regime goes from essentially zero, where it stayed for most of the post-Second World War period prior to 1991, to unity, where it remained for the rest of the decade. Thus, the series shows a marked decrease in volatility in the 1990s relative to previous periods.

In contrast to CLM (1990, 2000) and Bonomo and Garcia (1994, 1996), LLW assume that agents cannot observe the regime but must infer it from consumption data. The filtered probabilities summarize the information upon which conditional expectations are based; the PDR may be then computed by summing the discounted value of future expected dividends across regimes, weighted by the posterior probabilities of being in each regime. When historical quarterly filtered probabilities from the MSIH are used as inputs in the asset pricing model, LLW find that plausible parameterizations of the model can account for an important fraction of the run-up in PDRs observed in the late 1990s. Moreover, the increase in valuation ratios predicted by the model is not well described as a sudden jump upward, but instead occurs progressively over several years, as in the data.[21] Interestingly, LLW's predictions for the risk-free rate are also reasonable. However, it must be recognized that when LLW do not use their uncommon volatility regime persistence parameter of 0.9999 (or even of 1, an absorbing state) for both Markov states, but instead calibrate the consumption volatility Markov chain to the exact point estimates obtained in the paper, the model explains only about 20 percent of the total run-up in the price–dividend ratio, with the equilibrium PDR rising from 35 to 40 only. These results illustrate the importance of the perceived permanence of the volatility decline in determining the magnitude of the rise in the equilibrium PDR: only assuming that the volatility moderation has been perceived to be highly persistent – lasting many decades – can a large fraction of the run-up in stock prices be explained. If the volatility decline were expected to be transitory, less of the run-up could be understood through LLW's mechanism.[22]

Up to this point, MS has been exogenously assumed to characterize the process for the state variables, the fundamentals (e.g., dividends, consumption, output) that drive asset prices in simple endowment DAPMs. Branch and Evans (2010) is an interesting paper because they endogenously derive MS in equilibrium asset returns when the process of fundamentals is *not* assumed to contain MS. They develop a model of bounded rationality in which investors behave as econometricians, that is, in which agents estimate and select their models in real time. In particular, they study an asset pricing model in which the stock price depends on expected future returns and on an exogenous process for share supply that proxies for asset float and in which investors under-parameterize their forecasting models: agents perceive prices as depending on dividends or share supply, but not both; they only choose between models, or trading strategies, that lead to the highest (or nearly the highest) risk-adjusted trading profits. Within this class of under-parameterized models, the key condition restricting beliefs is that model parameters must satisfy a least-squares orthogonality condition that means that forecasting models are statistically optimal. This simple set-up is meant to parsimoniously describe a more complex framework in which traders face uncertainty about their model specification and choose simple trading strategies.[23] Branch and Evans entertain a simple linear static asset pricing model in which agents optimize with respect to the mean-variance efficient frontier, so that demands are bounded and linear. There is a single risky asset that yields a dividend stream $\{D_t\}$ and trades at price P_t, net of dividends. There is a risk-free asset that pays a rate of return $R = 1/\beta > 1$. Households, at time t, solve:

$$\max_{\omega_t} E_t^*[W_{t+1}] - \frac{\gamma}{2} Var_t^*[W_{t+1}] \tag{1.41}$$

subject to a standard budget constraint, where starred moments denote (possibly) non-RE beliefs, and ω_t is the amount of the risky asset demanded by households. Both dividends and the supply of shares are assumed to follow two stationary AR(1) processes. There are two types of agents, each omitting some relevant information from their prediction model when they solve portfolio problems. One type omits the role of supply in affecting price, while the other omits dividends. Each agent type solves a different mean-variance problem, but financial market equilibrium requires that the price adjusts to guarantee market clearing. Agents forecast by projecting a perceived law of motions (PLM) for the price; there are two sets of PLMs and plugging these into the market-clearing condition leads to an actual law of motion (ALM). At this point an RE equilibrium imposes restrictions that come from the fact that although agents in the model are assumed to have underparameterized forecasting models that make the PLMs deviate from the ALM, they require that they forecast in a statistically optimal manner, that is, the belief parameters in the PLMs satisfy least-squares orthogonality conditions.[24] Branch and Evans demonstrate that when there are multiple equilibria, traders will hold different perceptions of return and risk at each equilibrium. When they consider a real-time learning and dynamic predictor selection version of their model, they obtain that, with the model calibrated to US stock data as the model switches in real time between equilibria, simulated data match the MS dynamics in returns found, for example, in Guidolin and Timmermann (2006).

1.5 CROSS-SECTIONAL APPLICATIONS

Modern asset pricing theory insists that any good model ought to explain much more than the level and dynamics of the market risk premium, the (real) riskless rate, and possibly the dynamic second moments of these key quantities. On the contrary, a good model should also explain the cross-sectional variation (for instance, over industry, size and book-to-market sorted equity portfolios) of risk premia for all traded securities. Recently, applications of MS-based asset pricing models have recorded novel efforts at investigating cross-sectional implications. In this respect, the seminal paper is Ang and Chen (2002), who have investigated the conditional correlation properties of US equity portfolios using an MS framework. For US equity portfolios sorted on size, industry, past performance and book-to-market ratios, they find an asymmetric correlation structure where correlations increase more for downside moves than for upside moves. Ang and Chen also compute exceedance correlations, as in Longin and Solnik (2001), benchmarked to the bivariate normal and observe that simple MSMs may adequately fit this feature of the data while other models (e.g., multivariate GARCH) cannot.

Balyeat and Muthuswamy (2009) use a simple MSM to examine the correlation structure of US equity portfolios – ten size and ten book-to-market sorted portfolios – excess returns with market unexpected returns and derive the adjustments to the unconditional hedging strategy necessary to achieve the optimal hedge conditional on different market regimes.[25] In a first stage, they estimate a two-state MS for the market portfolio; in a second stage, they use the smoothed market state probabilities to estimate expected returns for equity portfolios via a reduced-form Fama and French (1993) three-factor regression (with constant coefficients) in which market regimes are allowed to affect slope coefficients through dummies; this choice forces the probability of being in either regime to be constant across the equity portfolios because the regime probabilities are solely determined by market data. Using weekly NYSE, NASDAQ and AMEX return series for a 1963–2005 sample, they find that, after adjusting correlations to reflect the presence of MS effects, the return data-generating process exhibits a natural hedging characteristic: when the market experiences a sharp drop, many of the portfolios decrease by less than expected; similarly, when the market experiences a sharp rise, many of the portfolios increase by more than expected. Thus, traditional hedging strategies based on unconditional correlations would overhedge during market declines and underhedge during market increases. Moreover, while there does not appear to be a large difference across states for the SMB betas, in all 20 of the portfolios, the HML beta is larger in the second crisis regime.

Of course, Balyeat and Muthuswamy's approach suffers from the awkward imposition of an identical market state process across 20 very different equity portfolios, which implies a severe loss of information versus the case in which the portfolios were allowed to contribute to the identification of the regime-switching dynamics. It is also unclear why the three-factor Fama–French regression is not implemented in a full MS mode, allowing the coefficient to be a function of the smoothed probabilities of the two Markov regimes for market data, which contradicts the evidence in Coggi and Manescu (2004).

Such loose ends appear to have been dealt with by Guidolin and Timmermann (2008), although their work follows a dynamic portfolio optimization logic. They propose a simple MSIH model of the joint distribution of returns on the market portfolio and the size (SMB) and book-to-market (HML) portfolios and find evidence of four regimes that capture important time-variations in mean returns, volatilities and return correlations. Two states capture periods of high volatility and large mean returns that accommodate skews and fat tails in stock returns. The other two states are associated with shifts in the distribution of size and value returns. Although they do not pursue the cross-sectional, asset pricing implications of the four regimes in the joint density of portfolio returns, Guidolin and Timmermann's economic value calculations (in pseudo out-of-sample recursive exercises) illustrate that the MS dynamic linkages between market portfolio returns and the US cross-section may strongly affect optimal portfolio choices because these command large hedging demands.

The leading attempt at using the properties of MS fundamentals to explain the cross-section of US stock returns has been made by Ozoguz (2009), who argues that when investors do not have perfect knowledge of the processes associated with macro-level variables (e.g., stock dividends) but instead learn them using Bayes's rule, the variance of their own beliefs (their 'Bayesian uncertainty') introduces a new source of time-variation in the investment opportunity set. Ozoguz employs this intuition to investigate whether and how the level of uncertainty is related to expected returns, and how uncertainty risk is priced in the cross-section of equity returns. Because Bayesian uncertainty is a notion that is hard to pin down, Ozoguz uses empirical proxies to measure investors' conditional beliefs and uncertainty about the aggregate state of the economy that are derived from simple two-state MSMs with TVTPs (for market returns or aggregate output). Motivated by these theoretical insights, Ozoguz studies a model with two new state variables, the conditional (filtered) probability $\pi_t \equiv \Pr(S_t = good|\Im_t)$ and investors' uncertainty, $UC_t \equiv \pi_t(1 - \pi_t)$. UC_t has a straightforward interpretation as an uncertainty index: when investors are uncertain about the future direction of the economy, suggesting that their beliefs linger around $\pi_t = 0.5$, UC_t approaches its maximum value of 0.25. This implies the following conditional multifactor representation of expected returns in the cross-section:

$$E_t[r_{t+1}^i - r_t^f] = \beta_{i,t}^m \lambda_{m,t} + \beta_{i,t}^\pi \lambda_{\pi,t} + \beta_{i,t}^{UC} \lambda_{UC,t}, \tag{1.42}$$

where $\beta_{i,t}^m$ is the loading on the excess market return, $\beta_{i,t}^\pi$ is the asset's sensitivity to changes in π, $\beta_{i,t}^{UC}$ is the asset's sensitivity to uncertainty risk (defined as the sensitivity of the return on asset i to an unanticipated change in uncertainty), $\lambda_{m,t}$ is the price of market risk, and $\lambda_{\pi,t}$, $\lambda_{UC,t}$ denote the risk premia associated with changing investor beliefs and uncertainty risk. Ozoguz finds that investors' uncertainty about the state of the economy has a negative impact on asset prices both at the aggregate level and at the individual portfolio level, with substantial variation across portfolios sorted by size, book-to-market and past returns. Following the typical spirit of the intertemporal CAPM, Ozoguz also tests whether there is a premium associated with uncertainty risk, measured as the covariance between stock returns and unexpected changes in investors' uncertainty. Ozoguz reports that there exists a positive, albeit non-linear, relationship between the level of uncertainty and expected returns. This drive towards linking the dynamics in beliefs to the cross-section of asset returns may hold the key to new and significant advances in modern asset pricing theory.

1.6   STRUCTURAL MODELS OF MS IN THE SDF

Recently, the asset pricing literature has proposed increasingly sophisticated models in which MS does not simply occur in the data under investigation – one can say, under the physical, objective measure P – but they also (or better, they emerge in P because they) occur under the risk-neutral pricing measure Q, also called the equivalent martingale measure. As we shall see, this is equivalent to modeling the SDF as containing MS effects. A few papers have not only assumed MS in the Q measure, but also that MS itself may represent a priced risk factor that is reflected in the SDF. This has a insightful meaning: if the state variables vary over time not only as a result of continuous (diffusive) shocks, but also because of discrete shifts in the parameters, it is natural to ask whether such shifts may represent a source of risk that is priced in equilibrium. Interestingly, these papers have at first appeared in a specific subfield of asset pricing research, that is, among papers that examine (default risk-free) yield curve models.[26]

Before reviewing the key lessons from the leading papers in this subfield, it is useful to stress that similar to the body of work surveyed in section 1.4, Markov switching term structure models (MSTSMs) find their underpinning in theoretical papers such as Veronesi and Yared (1999), who have presented a DAPM in which a representative investor prices nominal and real bonds when fundamentals (consumption and the inflation rate) contain MS components in their drift functions, and the investor cannot observe the current drift rates. It turns out that the no-arbitrage price of (real) bonds are just filtered probability-weighted sums of expected discounted values of one unit of (real) consumption good in the future. Veronesi and Yared (1999) report a number of interesting calibration results. For instance, a range of flexible and heterogeneous shapes – including humped and inverted hump yield curves – for both the nominal and real term structure may be generated using three regimes for the deflator process and two regimes for the real consumption one (independent of inflation), for a total of six. In addition, real rates can be high or low independently of whether nominal rates are high or low.

Bansal and Zhou (2002) represents the seminal contribution on MSTSMs. In the simplest, single-factor case, their model can be written as:

$$\Delta x_{t+1} = \kappa_{S_{t+1}}(\theta_{S_{t+1}} - x_t) + \sigma_{S_{t+1}}\sqrt{x_t}\varepsilon_{t+1}\ \varepsilon_{t+1} \sim NID(0,1),\tag{1.43}$$

where S_{t+1} follows a two-state, time homogeneous Markov chain, x_{t+1} is a continuous variable that describes the state of the economy, and $\kappa_{S_{t+1}}$, $\theta_{S_{t+1}}$ and $\sigma_{S_{t+1}}$ are the regime-dependent mean reversion, long-run mean and volatility parameters. All of these parameters are subject to discrete regime shifts. The agents observe the regimes, although the econometrician may possibly not observe them. The pricing kernel has a standard form, except for incorporating regime shifts:

$$M_{t+1} = \exp\left[-i_t - \left(\frac{\lambda_{S_{t+1}}}{\sigma_{S_{t+1}}}\right)^2 \frac{x_t}{2} - \frac{\lambda_{S_{t+1}}}{\sigma_{S_{t+1}}}\sqrt{x_t}\varepsilon_{t+1}\right].\tag{1.44}$$

The $\lambda_{S_{t+1}}$ parameter that affects the risk premium on bonds is also subject to regime shifts.[27] Bansal and Zhou develop a DAPM of a standard Lucas-type (with log-preferences and a Cox, Ingersoll and Ross, CIR-type, process for consumption growth) that leads to this pricing kernel. Importantly, this MSTSM does not entertain the possibility of separate risk compensation for regime shifts. In other words, the risk premium for a security that pays \$1 contingent on a regime shift at date $t + 1$ is zero. Under MS, Bansal and Zhou conjecture that the bond price with n periods to maturity at date t depends on the regime $S_t = 1, 2$ as well as x_t according to a simple linear affine function, $P_{S_t}(t, n) = \exp[-A_{S_t}(n) - B_{S_t}(n)x_t]$, so that the bond return is:

$$r_{t+1}(n) = \ln P_{S_{t+1}}(t+1, n-1) - \ln P_{S_t}(t, n)$$

$$= [A_{S_t}(n) - A_{S_{t+1}}(n-1) + B_{S_t}(n)x_t - B_{S_{t+1}}(n-1)\kappa_{S_{t+1}}\theta_{S_{t+1}}] + B_{S_{t+1}}(n-1)\sigma_{S_{t+1}}\sqrt{x_t}\varepsilon_{t+1}\tag{1.45}$$

and the volatility is $B_{S_{t+1}}(n-1)\sigma_{S_{t+1}}\sqrt{x_t}$. Under the standard boundary conditions $A_{S_t}(0) = B_{S_t}(0) = 0$ and the normalization $A_{S_t}(1) = 0$, $B_{S_t}(1) = 1$, for $S_t = 0,1$ (so that $P_{S_t}(t, 1) = \exp(-x_t)$, which means that the continuous state is just the short-term rate, $x_t = i_t$) and exploiting a log-linear approximation $(\exp(z) - 1 \cong z)$ of the key asset pricing condition $E[r_{t+1}(n)M_{t+1}|x_t, S_t] = 1$, it can be proven that the bond risk premium is:

$$E\left[\mu_{n,S_{t+1}} + \frac{\sigma^2_{n,S_{t+1}}}{2} - i_t\Big|x_t, S_t\right] \cong -x_t\sum_{k=1}^{K}\Pr(S_{t+1} = k|S_t)B_k(n-1)\lambda_k$$

$$= -x_t\sum_{k=1}^{K}p_{ik}\xi_{it}B_k(n-1)\lambda_k,\tag{1.46}$$

where p_{ik} is the probability of a transition from state i to state k $(k = 1,2)$. In the absence of MS, the risk premium would simply be $-x_tB(n-1)\lambda$. Hence incorporating regime shifts makes the beta of the asset (i.e., the coefficient on x_t) time-varying and dependent on the regime. Given (1.46), the solution for bond prices can be derived by recursively solving for the unknown coefficients $A_{S_t}(n)$ and $B_{S_t}(n)$ with initial conditions

$A_1(0) = A_2(0) = B_1(0) = B_2(0) = 0$. The bond yield $(y_{S_t}(t,n))$ of a K-regime MSTSM can be then simply derived as $y_{S_t}(t, n) \equiv -(1/n) \ln P_{S_t}(t, n) = A_{S_t}(n) + B_{S_t}(n)x_t$.

Using six-month and five-year US Treasury yield monthly data from 1964 to 1995, Bansal and Zhou estimate three types of models: one- and two-factor MSTSMs, one-, two- and three-factor CIR models, and three-factor linear affine models. They find that by a large amount the preferred model has two regimes and two factors. In both regimes, the first factor has far higher mean reversion than the second factor. Regime 1 volatility is larger for both factors. Additionally, the risk premium parameters for the factors are larger in regime 1, the more volatile regime. Both regimes are highly persistent, with $\hat{p}_{11} = 0.91$ and $\hat{p}_{22} = 0.94$. All the parameters are estimated rather accurately. The recovered first factor tracks the short yield well, while the second tracks the long yield. The model-implied regime changes usually lead or coincide with macroeconomic recessions: regimes with low yield spreads occur before or for the duration of business contractions. During NBER business cycle expansions, the yield spread is 86 basis points, while in recessions it is −8 basis points. The other important result is that the benchmark CIR and affine model specifications with up to three factors are sharply rejected with p-values of nearly zero. The only model specification that is not inconsistent with the data (with a p-value of 0.143) is the preferred two-factor MSTSM where the market price of risks depends on regime shifts. The two-state MSTSM can also duplicate in simulations the violations of the expectations hypothesis as recognized in Campbell and Shiller (1991) while the affine and CIR specifications are in trouble in matching these violations.[28]

Unfortunately, Bansal and Zhou (2002) assume that MS risk is not priced, which is the same as restricting MS not to be an aggregate risk, and therefore that regime-switching shocks do not affect the SDF. Because most empirical MSMs are motivated by business cycle fluctuations or monetary policy regimes, it is important to treat regime shifts as an aggregate risk. MS risk premia in the yield curve may appear because regime shifts have a direct impact on the SDF: if the regime-switching shocks generate movements in bond returns and the SDF in the same direction, the covariance is positive and the risk premium is negative as the bond offers investors a hedge against the risk of regime shifts. On the other hand, if regime shifts generate movements in the bond return and the SDF in opposite directions, the covariance is negative and the risk premium is positive. In this case, MS makes bonds riskier because they decrease the asset's return when investors' marginal utility is high. Dai and Singleton (2003) have generalized the intuitions in Bansal and Zhou (2002) with reference to MSTSMs. They write their general pricing model as a specification of the physical process for an $M \times 1$ vector of state variables $\mathbf{X}(t)$:

$$d\mathbf{X}(t) = \mu^P(\mathbf{X}, t)dt + \sigma_Y(z, t)d\mathbf{Z}(t), \tag{1.47}$$

and an SDF:

$$\frac{d\mathbf{M}(t)}{\mathbf{M}(t)} = -i(\mathbf{X}, t)dt - \lambda'(\mathbf{X}, t)d\mathbf{Z}(t), \tag{1.48}$$

where $i(\mathbf{X}, t)$ is the instantaneous riskless rate, $d\mathbf{Z}(t)$ is a vector of W independent Brownian motions, and $\lambda(\mathbf{X}, t)$ is the W-vector of market prices of risk. For simplicity, they take the risk factors driving M and $\mathbf{X}(t)$ to be the same, that is, they impose market completeness. For a fixed income security with a continuous coupon rate $h(\mathbf{X}, t)$ for $t < T$ and terminal payoff $g(\mathbf{X}(T))$ at date T, its price at date $t < T$ can be expressed in terms of the SDF as:

$$P(\mathbf{X}, t), t) = E_t\left[\int_t^T \frac{M(s)}{M(t)} h(\mathbf{X}(s), s) ds\right] + E_t\left[\frac{M(T)}{M(t)} g(\mathbf{X}(T))\right], \tag{1.49}$$

which can be alternatively written as a conditional expectation taken with respect to a risk-neutral measure Q, under which $\mathbf{X}(t)$ follows the process:

$$d\mathbf{X}(t) = [\boldsymbol{\mu}^P(t) - \boldsymbol{\sigma}_Y(\mathbf{X}, t)\boldsymbol{\lambda}(\mathbf{X}, t)]dt + \boldsymbol{\sigma}_Y(\mathbf{X}, t)d\mathbf{Z}^Q(t). \tag{1.50}$$

and $P(\mathbf{X}(t), t) = E_t^Q[\int_t^T \exp(-r(s)ds)h(\mathbf{X}(s), s)ds] + \exp(-r(T)T)E_t^Q[g(\mathbf{X}(T))]$.

Within this general framework, Dai and Singleton develop a general family of MSTSMs by assuming that the evolution of regimes is described by an $(S + 1)$-state continuous-time Markov chain with a state-dependent $(S + 1) \times (S + 1)$ rate matrix $\boldsymbol{\Lambda}^P$ in which all rows sum to zero. For simplicity, they assume that regimes are observable. Intuitively, $\boldsymbol{\Lambda}^P[i, j]dt$ represents the probability of moving from regime i to regime j over the next short interval of time. Under MS, the SDF becomes:

$$\frac{dM(t)}{M(t)} = -i(S_t; \mathbf{X}, t)dt - \boldsymbol{\lambda}'(S_t; \mathbf{X}, t)d\mathbf{Z}(t) - \sum_{j=0}^S \varsigma_t^j\left(dI_{\{S_t = j\}} - \sum_{i=0}^S I_{\{S_t = i\}}R^P[i, j]dt\right), \tag{1.51}$$

where $\boldsymbol{\lambda}(S_t; \mathbf{X}, t)$ is the vector of market prices of diffusion risk and $\varsigma^j(S_t; \mathbf{X}, t)$ the $S + 1$ market prices of a shift from the current regime S_t to regime j an instant later. MSTSMs in which regimes carry a specific risk price imply a highly flexible specification of bond risk premia that are time-varying both because they are a function of the underlying state variables as in standard affine models and also because the coefficients of the diffusion risk premia vary across regimes and regimes are themselves rewarded with a specific risk premium. The risk-neutral distribution of the short rate is governed by $i(S_t = i; \mathbf{X}, t) = \boldsymbol{\delta}_0^i + (\boldsymbol{\delta}_1^i)'\mathbf{X}(S_t; t)$, while the risk-neutral process for $\mathbf{X}(t)$ follows an affine diffusion with regime-dependent drifts and volatilities:[29]

$$d\mathbf{X}(t) = \left[\sum_{j=0}^S I_{\{S_t = j\}}K_j^Q(\theta_j^Q - \mathbf{X}(t))\right]dt + \left[\sum_{j=0}^S I_{\{S_t = j\}}diag(\alpha_j^k + (\boldsymbol{\beta}_j^k)'\mathbf{X}(t))\right]d\mathbf{Z}^Q(t). \tag{1.52}$$

Dai and Singleton prove that the regime-dependent prices of a T-maturity zero coupon bond, $P_{S_t}(t, T)$ $S_t = 0, 1, \ldots, S$, can be determined by solving a system of $S + 1$ partial differential equations under $S + 1$ terminal conditions $P_{S_t}(T, T) = 1$. These PDEs involve a rate matrix for the conditional Markov chain under the risk-neutral measure,

$$\boldsymbol{\Lambda}^Q[i, j; \mathbf{X}, t] = (1 - \varsigma^j(S_t = i; \mathbf{X}, t))\boldsymbol{\Lambda}^P[i, j] \text{ for } i \neq j \tag{1.53}$$

and $\boldsymbol{\Lambda}^Q[i, j; \mathbf{X}, t] = -\sum_{j \neq i}^Q \boldsymbol{\Lambda}[i, j; \mathbf{X}, t]$, which is in general not diagonal. Moreover, (1.53) implies that even when $\boldsymbol{\Lambda}^P[i, j]$ is constant over time – as assumed by Dai and

Singleton – provided the market prices of MS risk, $\varsigma^j(S_t; \mathbf{X}, t)$, are time-varying, then $\Lambda^Q[i,j; \mathbf{X}, t]$ becomes time-varying. Additionally, $1 - \Lambda^Q[i,j; \mathbf{X}, t]/\Lambda^P[i,j] = \varsigma^j(S_t = i; \mathbf{X}, t)$ which means that the (complement to one) of the ratio between the risk-neutral and the physical transition probabilities has a peculiar interpretation, being the market price of regime-switching risk in correspondence to the initial state i. However, the solution for bond prices will incorporate a regime-shifting nature even when $\varsigma^j(S_t; \mathbf{X}, t) = 0$ for $j = 0, 1, \ldots, S$ (as in Bansal and Zhou, 2002) as excess bond returns may still be time varying through the coefficients $\{\alpha_j^k, \boldsymbol{\beta}_j^k\}_{j=0}^S$.

Dai and Singleton show in their paper that allowing both the diffusion risk prices $\boldsymbol{\lambda}(S_t; \mathbf{X}, t)$ to follow a MS process and $\varsigma^j(S_t; \mathbf{X}, t) > 0$ is crucial not only for elegance, but also in empirical terms. This is obvious from the empirical work presented to match Campbell and Shiller's regression-style violations of the EH:[30] when MS risk is not priced and risk premia are restricted to be identical across regimes, the fact that regime-dependence of the bond risk premium is driven entirely by the state-dependence of volatility prevents MSTSMs capturing violations of the EH. When (as in Bansal and Zhou, 2002) the market price of risk is allowed to vary across regimes – even when regime shifts are not specifically priced – the model fits the evidence of bond return predictability very accurately.

A related paper is Dai et al. (2007; hereafter DSY) who have developed and empirically implemented an arbitrage-free MSTSM with priced regime-switching risks. Therefore they extend Bansal and Zhou's (2002) study of an (approximate) discrete-time CIR-style MSTSM to the case in which MS risk is priced but regimes are observable to investors. DSY's strategy is straightforward: they parameterize the risk-neutral distribution of the factors so as to ensure closed-form solutions for bond prices, and then overlay flexible specifications of the market prices of risk to describe the historical distribution of bond yields. The risk factors are assumed to follow a discrete-time Gaussian process, and regime shifts are governed by a discrete-time Markov process with TVTPs (under the measure P), according to a Gray-style logistic function that depends on the risk factors. Within each regime, the short rate is assumed to be a linear affine function of a vector $\mathbf{X}_t$ of three risk factors, $r_{t, S_t} = \delta_{0, S_t} + \boldsymbol{\delta}_1 \mathbf{X}_t$, where $\mathbf{X}_t$ follows a Gaussian VAR with constant conditional variances, and the market prices of factor risks depend on $\mathbf{X}_t$ as in Duffee (2002):

$$\mathbf{X}_{t+1} = \boldsymbol{\mu}_{t, S_t}^Q + \boldsymbol{\Sigma}_{S_t} \boldsymbol{\varepsilon}_{t+1} \quad \boldsymbol{\varepsilon}_{t+1} \sim NID(\mathbf{0}, \mathbf{I}_3), \tag{1.54}$$

where $\boldsymbol{\mu}_{t, s}^Q \equiv E[\mathbf{X}_{t+1} | S_t = s] = \mathbf{X}_t + \mathbf{K}^Q(\boldsymbol{\theta}_s^Q - \mathbf{X}_t)$ is the risk-neutralized drift function, $\boldsymbol{\theta}_s^Q$ follows a MS process, and $S_t = L, H$. There are two regimes characterized by low (L) and high (H) volatility. The transition probabilities are restricted to be constant under the risk-neutral measure Q. For simplicity, agents are assumed to know both the current state of the economy and the regime they are currently in. This leads to regime-dependent risk-neutral pricing of zero-coupon bond prices:

$$P_{t, n}^s = \exp\{-A_{n, s} - \boldsymbol{\varphi}_n' \mathbf{X}_t\}$$

$$A_{n+1, s} = \delta_{0, s} + (\mathbf{K}^Q \boldsymbol{\theta}_s^Q)' \boldsymbol{\varphi}_n - \frac{1}{2} \boldsymbol{\varphi}_n' \boldsymbol{\Sigma}_s \boldsymbol{\Sigma}_s' \boldsymbol{\varphi}_n - \ln\left(\sum_{j=1}^2 \Pr^Q(S_{t+1} = j | S_t = s) e^{-A_{n, j}}\right) \quad A_{0, s} = 0 \tag{1.55}$$

$$\boldsymbol{\varphi}_{n+1} = \boldsymbol{\delta}_1 + \boldsymbol{\varphi}_n - (\mathbf{K}^Q)' \boldsymbol{\varphi}_n \quad \boldsymbol{\varphi}_0 = 0,$$

and to a natural decomposition of bond risk premia into components corresponding to MS and linear affine, continuous factor risks. The conditional distributions of
$(\mathbf{X}_t, S_{t+1})$ under P and Q are linked by the Radon-Nikodym derivative $(dP/dQ)_{t,t+1}$,
$P(d\mathbf{X}_{t+1}, S_{t+1}|\mathfrak{T}_t) = (dP/dQ)_{t,t+1} Q(d\mathbf{X}_{t+1}, S_{t+1}|\mathfrak{T}_t)$ or equivalently, under the assumption of no arbitrage opportunities, by the SDF $\mathrm{M}_{t,t+1}$ underlying the time-t valuation of
payoffs at date $t + 1$:

$$\mathrm{M}_{t,t+1} = \exp\left\{ -r_t - \varsigma(\mathbf{X}_t, S_t; S_{t+1}) - \frac{1}{2}\boldsymbol{\Lambda}'(\mathbf{X}_t, S_t)\boldsymbol{\Lambda}(\mathbf{X}_t, S_t) - \boldsymbol{\Lambda}'(\mathbf{X}_t, S_t)\boldsymbol{\Sigma}^{-1}(S_t)[\mathbf{X}_{t+1} - \boldsymbol{\mu}^Q(S_t)] \right\},$$

(1.56)

where $\varsigma(\mathbf{X}_t, S_t; S_{t+1})$ is the market price of regime risk from S_t to S_{t+1}, and $\boldsymbol{\Lambda}(\mathbf{X}_t, S_t)$ is
the (vector of) market price(s) of factor risks. The SDF depends implicitly on the regimes
$(S_t; S_{t+1})$, because agents know both the regime S_{t+1} and the regime from which they have
transitioned, S_t. DSY also extend the essentially affine, Gaussian model of Duffee (2002)
to the case of multiple regimes by assuming that:[31]

$$\boldsymbol{\Lambda}(\mathbf{X}_t, S_t) = \boldsymbol{\Sigma}_{S_t}^{-1} (\boldsymbol{\lambda}_{0, S_t} + \boldsymbol{\lambda}_{1, S_t}\mathbf{X}_t).$$

(1.57)

Using monthly data on US Treasury zero-coupon bond yields for a sample 1972–2003
to estimate by ML a two-regime, three-factor MSTSM, DSY show that priced MS risk
plays a critical role in capturing time variations in risk premia, and document remarkable differences in the behavior of the factor risk component of risk premia across high-
and low-volatility states. The ML estimates of the parameters show that variances in the
H regime are all larger than in the L regime, so that omitting MS risk may lead single-
regime models to understate the fluctuations in excess returns in occasion of transitions
between regimes, and to overstate the volatility of factor risk premia and excess returns
during quiet times. An LRT of the null hypothesis that the transition matrix is constant
under P which is equivalent to a test of zero market prices for regime-switching risks,
because of DSY's result that the MS market price of regime-switching risk may be measured as the log-ratio of time-varying transition probabilities under P and of constant
transition probabilities under Q leads to a strong rejection. The state-dependence of the
TVTPs under P is shown to capture an interesting asymmetry in the cyclical behavior
of interest rates. If we view regime H as capturing periods of downturns and regime L
as periods of expansions, this result can be interpreted as a manifestation of an asymmetry in US business cycles: recoveries tend to last longer than recessions. The model
does a very good job at matching the first and second unconditional moments of the
data, as the sample curves fall well within the two standard deviation bands of simulated
yield curves. Finally DSY stress that, following the result in Duffee (2002) and Dai and
Singleton (2002) that only sufficiently persistent and variable factor risk premia in affine
models may shed light on the empirical failure of the EH, their MSTSM resolves the EH
puzzles summarized in Campbell and Shiller (1991).

A potential weakness of DSY's MSTSM is that the within-regime conditional variances of the factor process are constant. Even though DSY emphasize that their experi-

ence with estimating and forecasting single-regime affine DTSMs is that the conditional volatility in bond yields induced by conditional volatility in the factors tends to be very small relative to the volatility of excess returns, it may be important to further accommodate rich patterns of regime dependence of the vector of market prices of the risk factors, for instance of an MS ARCH type. Similarly, one problem with MSTSMs is a potential conflict between the transition probabilities between regimes and the market price of MS risk: a considerable fraction of DSY's asset pricing insights derive from the one-to-one mapping from the log-ratio of the TVTPs under P and of the constant transition probabilities under Q to the market price of MS, that rests on the maintained hypothesis that the transition probabilities are constant under Q. Therefore, at least in principle, one cannot rule that a rejection of the hypothesis of zero risk premia for regime shift risk may spuriously derive from the fact that transition probabilities are not constant under Q.

Ang et al. (2008; hereafter ABW) have overcome Dai et al.'s (2007) assumption that regimes are observable to investors. ABW develop a similar MSTSM framework but devote their efforts not only to the pricing of nominal bonds, but to investigating the dynamics of the real term structure of interest rates, decomposing changes in nominal interest rates into movements in real interest rates, expected inflation and the inflation risk premium. Relative to DSY, ABW use a more flexible MS structure with four regimes and link the regime-dependent parameters at time $t + 1$ not to S_t but to S_{t+1} which is unobservable, as typical in the empirical literature. As a result, the conditional variances of ABW factors embed a jump term reflecting the difference in conditional means across regimes which is absent in DSY.[32] In their paper, ABW infer the dynamics of real rates, expected inflation, and inflation risk premia, using a framework with three key features: (1) absence of arbitrage opportunities; (2) MS, with an emphasis on disentangling the real and nominal sources of the regimes; (3) flexible time-varying risk premia. As for the sources of MS, ABW introduce two different regime variables, $S_t^f \in \{1,2\}$ affecting the drift and variance of the latent factor process, and $S_t^\pi \in \{1,2\}$ affecting the drift and variance of the inflation process. The latter is therefore a nominal MS component – because S_t^π enters the conditional mean of inflation, this regime potentially affects expected inflation and can capture non-linear expected inflation components not directly related to past inflation realizations – while the former is a real MS component. To reduce the number of parameters in the resulting 4×4 transition probability matrix, ABW consider two restricted models of the correlation between S_t^f and S_t^π: in a first case, independence is imposed; in an alternative case they specify a restricted form of the transition probability matrix so that S_{t+1}^π depends on S_t^f as well as the previous inflation environment, but future f_{t+1} regimes depend only on S_t^f.[33]

Using 1-, 4-, 12- and 20-quarter zero-coupon risk-free rates and US CPI inflation for the period 1952–2004, ABW find that of all the models, only the four-state MSVAR(1) dynamics term structure model (DTSM) fits the mean, variance, and autocorrelogram of inflation. The prices of risk for the f_t factor are both significantly different from zero and significantly different across regimes. q_t can be interpreted as a level factor. The MS term structure factor f_t is highly correlated with the nominal spread, in absolute value, so f_t is a slope factor. In terms of ABW's four-state categorization, the first regime is a low real rate, high-inflation regime, where both real rates and inflation are not very volatile. The US economy spends most of the time in this normal state. The volatilities of real short rates, inflation compensation and nominal short rates are all lowest in regime 1. The regime with the second-largest ergodic probability is regime 3, which is also a low real rate regime. In this regime, the mean of inflation compensation is the highest. Regimes 2 and 4 are characterized by relatively high and volatile real short rates. The inflation compensation in these regimes is low. Regimes 2 and 4 are also associated with downward-sloping term structures of *real* yields. Finally, regime 4 has the highest volatility of real rates, inflation compensation and nominal rates. Unconditionally, the term structure of real rates assumes a somewhat flat shape around 1.3 percent, with a slight hump, peaking at a one-year maturity. However, there are some regimes in which the real rate curve is downward sloping. There is no significant real term spread. Finally, ABW's model is able to reproduce an unconditional upward-sloping nominal yield curve by generating an inflation risk premium that grows with maturity.

Bansal et al. (2004; hereafter BTZ) have stressed that the success of MSTSMs opens up the possibility that this class of models may be able to capture the dynamics of risk premia on bonds. Besides the common strategy of understanding bond risk premia in the form of deviations from the EH, mostly as negative slope coefficient in regressions of yield changes on yield spreads à la Campbell and Shiller (1991) – addressed in an MS framework by Bansal and Zhou (2002), and Dai and Singleton (2003) – another form of violation of the EH is that the forward rate can predict excess bond returns. In particular, Cochrane and Piazzesi (2005) have shown that using multiple forward rates to predict bond excess returns generates very high predictability statistics, with adjusted R^2s of around 30 percent, and coefficients of multiple forward rate regressors forming a now well-known tent-shaped pattern related to the maturity of the forward rate:

$$x_{t+12}^n \equiv \ln P_{t+12}^{n-1} - \ln P_t^n - y(t,1) = \delta_0^n + \delta_1^n y(t,1) + \sum_{i=2}^{5} \delta_i^n f(t,i) + \varepsilon_{t+12}^n \; n = 2,\ldots,5, \quad (1.58)$$

where x_{t+12}^n is the excess return of a *n*-year bond and $f(t,i) = \ln P_t^{n-1} - \ln P_t^n$ is the forward rate. BTZ set out to account for this predictability evidence from the perspective of latent factor term structure models, in the form of a simple, two-factor Bansal and Zhou (2002)-style MSTSM.[34] Using, six-month and five-year US Treasury yields for the 1964–2001 period, BTZ find that MSTSMs can fit the high predictability and the tent-shaped regression coefficients documented by Cochrane and Piazzesi (2005). Their two-factor MS CIR model produces an inverted and skewed tent shape, and an MS three-factor linear affine model produces a inverted tent shape. Both models achieve R^2s of around 10–20 percent at most. These results suggest that the prediction capability of forward rates for excess returns may be explained by two or three linear factors, whereas the tent pattern of regression coefficients appears to be due to the MS nature of the yield curve. This result is in no way trivial because while Duffee (2002) had shown that allowing for a more flexible (essentially affine) specification of the risk premium parameters, an affine conditional Gaussian factor model can dramatically improve its ability to match the predictability of excess returns, yet, when estimated on Bansal and Zhou's data, the best-performing model in Duffee's paper – with three Gaussian factors and eight market price-of-risk parameters – is severely rejected.

Monfort and Pegoraro (2007) have generalized these results on the importance of including MS risk prices within the SDF and developed a generalized DTSM which captures simultaneously a number of key features, such as MSVAR factor processes – possibly of a non-homogeneous kind, that is, with TVTPs – an exponential-affine specification of the SDF with time-varying and regime-dependent risk premia, and closed- (or quasi-closed) form solutions for zero-coupon bonds and interest rate derivative prices, when yields are restricted to be positive at each maturity. These ambitious objectives are reached by matching the historical distribution and the SDF in order to get a cumulative autoregressive (CAR) risk-neutral joint dynamics for the factors and the regimes, and by using the property of the CAR family of being able to incorporate lags and regimes. An N-dimensional process $\mathbf{x}_t$ follows a CAR(p) if the distribution of $\mathbf{x}_{t+1}$ given the past values $\mathbf{X}_t \equiv [\mathbf{x}_t, \mathbf{x}_{t-1}, \ldots]'$ admits a real Laplace transform:

$$E[\exp(\mathbf{u}'\mathbf{x}_{t+1})|\mathbf{X}_t] = \exp\left[\sum_{j=1}^{p} a_j(\mathbf{u})'\mathbf{x}_{t+1-j} + b(\mathbf{u})\right] \quad \forall \mathbf{u} \in R^N, \qquad (1.59)$$

where $\{a_j(\mathbf{u})\}_{j=1}^{p}$ and $b(\mathbf{u})$ are non-linear functions. The existence of the Laplace transform in a neighborhood of $\mathbf{u} = \mathbf{0}$, implies that all the conditional moments exist, and that the conditional expectations and covariance matrices (and all conditional cumulants) are affine functions of $\mathbf{x}_t$. In fact, one can immediately notice that a K-state homogeneous Markov chain, $S_{t+1} = 1, \ldots, K$, can be represented as a vector state ξ_{t+1} that is also a CAR(1) process. The log-Laplace transform – that is inherently controlling the conditional cumulants of $\mathbf{x}_{t+1}$ – will then be affine in $\mathbf{X}_t$ which implies that all the conditional cumulants and, in particular, the conditional mean and the conditional covariance matrix of $\mathbf{x}_{t+1}$ are affine in $\mathbf{X}_t$ (see Bertholon et al., 2008). To get closed-form pricing expressions, Monfort and Pegoraro proceed by imposing that the risk-neutral dynamics are also MS Gaussian (extended) CAR(p), which implies that the process for $[x_{t+1}\xi_{t+1}]'$ under Q has to satisfy a few additional restrictions (see Bertholon et al., 2008, for details); in particular, similar to what I have already noted above, one such condition is that a homogeneous, time-invariant underlying Markov chain, $Pr^Q(\xi_{t+1} = e_j|\xi_t = e_i; \mathbf{X}_t) = \pi^Q(e_j, e_i)$ exists to imply:

$$\exp[(\varsigma(\Xi_t, \mathbf{X}_t))'e_j] = \frac{\pi(e_j, e_i; \mathbf{X}_t)}{\pi^Q(e_j, e_i)} \Rightarrow \varsigma_j(\Xi_t, \mathbf{X}_t) = \frac{\pi(e_j, \xi_t; \mathbf{X}_t)}{\pi^Q(e_j, \xi_t)} j = 1, 2, \ldots, K, \quad (1.60)$$

that is, the state-dependent MS risk premia are simply ratios of historical (P) and risk-neutralized (Q) transition probabilities. Pegoraro and Monfort's MSVAR DTSM model nests Ang et al.'s (2008) Gaussian MSVAR(1) term structure model driven by a homogeneous Markov chain where MS is not priced, and Dai et al.'s (2007) trivariate Gaussian MSVAR(1) with time-varying probabilities under the risk-neutral measure. In qualitative terms, Monfort and Pegoraro show that the MSVAR(1) price at date t of a zero-coupon bond with residual maturity $n \geq 1$ is:

$$B_{t,n} = \exp\{\mathbf{C}_n'\mathbf{X}_t + \mathbf{D}_n'\Xi_t\}, \qquad (1.61)$$

where the vectors $\mathbf{C}_n$ and $\mathbf{D}_n$ satisfy some recursive equations that look complex but that can be easily computed starting from the initial conditions $\mathbf{C}_n = \mathbf{D}_n = \mathbf{0}$.

1.7   OPTION PRICING APPLICATIONS

It is useful to start with the case in which option pricing under MSM is easy to obtain. Consider the case in which a standard, K-state Gaussian MSM specifies K conditionally normal distributions for the underlying asset return at any point in time. Since the governing Markov state can switch randomly, the volatility of log exchange rate changes can also switch randomly. Therefore option valuation methods under MS must contend with the issue of SV. In the early models, such as Bollen et al. (2000), SV is driven by regime risk and it is standard to assume that regime risk is diversifiable. If such is the case, the price of regime risk in equilibrium is zero, and option valuation may be conducted in a risk-neutral framework. Under risk neutrality, the volatility dynamics are equivalent to the volatility dynamics in the real world. In addition, any K_m-regime model (for moment m, here either the mean or the variance) in which there is a difference between K_μ and K_σ (so that $K = K_\mu \times K_\sigma$), will then collapse – for the purposes of risk-neutral valuation pricing – to a K_σ-regime model in which the regimes differ only in volatility and persistence.[35]

Bollen et al. (2000; hereafter BGW) is probably the seminal paper on option pricing under MS that has exploited this simple intuition. BGW use a numerical valuation method based on a discrete-time approximation to the K_σ-regime risk-neutral process. Since each regime is characterized by a conditionally normal distribution, we can represent the two-regime model by a pair of binomial distributions.[36] The parameters implied by the option prices are estimated using non-linear least squares by minimizing the sum of squared deviations between model and observed option prices. Using weekly spot exchange rates for the British pound, the Japanese yen and the Deutsche mark versus the US dollar and daily (US) option prices, BGW find that the variance is significantly different across the two regimes whereas the mean parameters are approximately the same. The four-regime model performs much better than the single-regime and two-regime models, as it adds flexibility in allowing the mean and the variance regimes to switch independently. The two mean regimes correspond to periods of appreciation and depreciation of the dollar and the transition probabilities indicate persistence in the mean regimes. Although the parameters inferred from exchange rate data refer to the physical measure (P) whereas those inferred from the options refer to the risk-neutral process (Q), the volatility dynamics from the two processes are similar; moreover, the inferred Markov chain is more persistent under Q than under P. For two currencies series, joint tests fail to reject the null hypothesis that the true parameter values are the same under Q versus P.

Of course, nothing restricts option pricing applications from being based on relatively simple MSMs. For instance, Alexander and Lazar (2009) is a recent paper that emphasizes that while single-state GARCH models imply unrealistic shapes for the implied volatility skew surface – the relationship between Black and Scholes implied volatilities and option strikes – for stock indices, in contrast, asymmetric MS GARCH models provide a rich structure that can match all the observed features of volatility surfaces. This demonstrates their superiority over single-state GARCH models, which must resort to assuming that the volatility risk premia are time-varying, to explain the observed skew characteristics. Duan et al. (2002) is a related example in which a family of option pricing models when the underlying asset process is MSM with feedback from returns to volatility is obtained. Their volatility process is established in such a way to nest both MS, symmetric ARCH, asymmetric and non-linear GARCH models. If the transition matrix that characterizes the MS process is independent of the return innovations, then the model reduces to a plain MS in volatility; when the transition probabilities are influenced by the return innovations, this leads to a more complex, MS ARCH-type framework. Interestingly, Duan et al. demonstrate that it is possible to establish models with a relatively small number of volatility regimes that produce option prices indistinguishable from models with a continuum of volatility states, such as in the GARCH option pricing case (see, e.g., Duan, 1995). However, in Duan et al. (2002), regime risk is priced, similar to the most recent fixed-income literature. Duan et al. investigate the pricing and prediction of European S&P 500 index options using Monte Carlo pricing methods and find that incorporating asymmetric GARCH and volatility feedback effects in an MSM leads to a substantial removal of biases that exist when using a simpler MS for volatility; only for the long term, in the money options, does a simple MSM outperform more complex MS ARCH models, and in this case the improvement is marginal.

A number of technical issues and open questions remain. For instance, Aingworth et al. (2006) have proposed a computationally efficient Cox–Ross–Rubinstein (CRR) binomial tree algorithm to price US (hence, also European) options under MS that has a polynomially increasing run time, it can price options under SV, including MS, and converges rapidly. However, extending the CRR algorithm to the case of switching volatility means that the standard recombining feature may be lost: it is no longer true that an up-move followed by a down-move results in the same asset price as a down-move followed by an up-move; this is because the volatility multiplying through the value varies at each point in time. Aingworth et al. (2006) develop an algorithm that exploits the intuition that to the extent that volatility stays within the same state the binomial process is still recombining, while a certain extent of recombination occurs in an MS model, as a number of up and down moves in the same state will cancel each other out. The technical root of the algorithm proposed consists of showing that the recombination attained is sufficient, even in the worst case, to deliver a polynomial algorithm instead of an exponential one. Chen and Hung (2010) have extended these seminal ideas from plain MSMs to MS non-linear GARCH models (i.e., Duan's, 1995, version of GARCH). They develop a discrete Markov chain approximation for the dynamics of both asset returns and MS volatility that converges to the MS non-linear GARCH model. Based on a small-scale application to European currency options sampled on a weekly basis, Chen and Hung conclude that the prediction errors resulting from the GARCH model and the MS-GARCH model are lower than that of the BS model and a plain MSM.

1.8   DIRECTIONS FOR FUTURE RESEARCH

Our survey of applications of MSMs to asset pricing modeling has yielded a number of insights, some of them so powerful as to possibly change the ways asset pricing phenomena and puzzles are commonly perceived. For instance, section 1.3 has shown that in an MS world it may be perfectly normal to find that realized excess returns are high (low) when asset return variance is low (high) because MSMs create powerful volatility feedbacks that are hard to generate using continuous GARCH models. Section 1.4

emphasizes how MSMs may solve a number of important asset pricing puzzles. Section 1.6 and 1.7 have documented how fixed-income securities and derivatives could be priced when the SDF contains priced regimes itself.

Of course, our review has been incomplete at best and dozens of excellent papers have been left out. Similarly, a number of exciting applications have not been surveyed just because it would be hard to make these topics and papers fit within the structure of my chapter. For instance, recently some applications of MSMs have been directed at topics that lie at the intersection of asset pricing theory and corporate finance. Among many others, Ang et al. (2007) have used two- and three-state MSMs to examine peso problem explanations for IPO overpricing. They find that an MS-induced small sample bias is unlikely to account for the magnitude of initial public offering (IPO) underperformance.

Finally, it is pointless to list the myriad of unresolved issues that could or should be tackled using MS technologies within the field of asset pricing. Among many, let me briefly refer to the issue of developing a general, encompassing DAPM with Markov regimes that could map primitive assumptions on preferences, technology and frictions into MS dynamics in fundamentals, and from there into equilibrium price processes. Although we are currently far from this ambitious target, a few recent papers have marked progress in this direction. Examples are the papers by Elliott et al. (2007; hereafter EMY) and Baele et al. (2010; hereafter BBI). EMY propose a MS extension of a CIR representative agent DAPM of an economy with a single physical good in which there are a finite number of N risky assets and one riskless asset and in which there are two possible regimes. EMY find closed-form solutions for the equilibrium instantaneous interest rate, for the SDF, and determine a partial differential equation (PDE) satisfied by the price of any contingent claim written on a risky asset. Although their results are certainly promising, their work still seems to make a number of primitive assumptions on the MS dynamics of important objects (such as the value function) that I am hopeful could be soon grounded in deeper economic foundations. BBI have proposed a smart set of innovative tools to handle the problem of mapping fundamentals into MS: dynamic factor models (DFMs). They study the economic sources of US stock-bond return co-movements and their time variation. They develop a DFM that imposes structural restrictions inspired by recent New Keynesian models and that incorporates MS, to find that macroeconomic fundamentals contribute little to explaining stock and bond return correlations but that other factors, especially liquidity proxies, play an important role. Clearly, more work will be needed to deeply root the DFM structure into truly encompassing general equilibrium models.

NOTES

1. For a discussion of the differences between the two tasks and of the related difficulties, see for example Bertholon et al. (2008) and Dai et al. (2007).
2. See Guidolin (2012), Guidolin et al. (2009) or Clements and Hendry's (1998) book for a summary introduction to this debate.
3. The assumption of a first-order Markov process is not restrictive, since a higher-order Markov chain can always be reparameterized as a higher dimensional first-order Markov chain, that is, substitutability exists between the order of the Markov chain driving S_t and the number of regimes K.
4. Ergodicity implies the existence of a stationary vector of probabilities $\bar{\xi}$ satisfying $\bar{\xi} = P'\bar{\xi}$. Irreducibility implies that $\bar{\xi} > 0$, meaning that all unobservable states are possible. In practice, $\mathbf{P}$ is unknown and hence

$\bar{\xi}$ can be at most estimated given knowledge on **P** extracted from the information set $\Im_t = \{y_j\}_{j=1}^t$. For simplicity, I will also denote as $\bar{\xi}$ such an estimated vector of ergodic (unconditional) state probabilities.

5. However, Hahn et al. (2009) have recently re-examined a few issues related to the estimation of continuous-time MSMs and emphasized the considerable advantages of a Bayesian approach based on Markov chain Monte Carlo (MCMC) methods.

6. Although other choices exist – that is, either to use the conditional scores or a numerical evaluation of the second partial derivative of the log-likelihood function with respect to $\hat{\theta}$ – in applied work it has become typical to employ a White-style sandwich sample estimator of $\mathbf{I}_a(\theta)$.

7. See for example French et al. (1987) and Campbell and Hentschel (1992). While a positive relationship between volatility and the risk premium is a reasonable partial equilibrium hypothesis, it is not a necessary implication of modern DAPMs for asset prices; see for example Abel (1988) and Backus and Gregory (1993).

8. However, one problem remains: because $\hat{\alpha}_1 + \hat{\theta} - \hat{\alpha}_0 = -1.18 < 0$, the risk premium does not increase with the anticipated variance; the variance of the linear combination is large in relation to the point estimate, and the t-statistic is −0.21, so that the model provides no evidence for a risk premium changing with or against the variance.

9. $\Im_t^* \supseteq \Im_{t-1}$ means that investors observe past returns at the beginning of the trading period and obtain information through the process of trading about the volatility regime.

10. The only exception is Bekaert and Wu (2000), who are successful in disentangling leverage and volatility feedback effects simultaneously, but in a simpler, single-state GARCH framework.

11. In order to capture the negative relationship between returns and subsequent volatility regimes, BKN also make the transition probabilities governing the dynamics of S_{t+1} dependent upon past return innovations and assume that the TVTPs have a logistic functional form. Hence, shocks are negatively correlated with the subsequent volatility regime. This negative correlation represents a further volatility feedback channel.

12. Alternative specifications of preferences may deliver these empirical features even when consumption growth follows an autoregressive moving average (ARMA) process. For instance, habit persistence, as in Campbell and Cochrane (1999), and recursive utility as in Epstein and Zin (1989), have been shown to be able to match other features of stock return data, particularly the magnitude and volatility of the equity premium. Both approaches permit a separation between the IMRS and the inverse of the relative risk aversion coefficient, contrary to CRRA preferences. However, the principal effects of these generalizations are on the volatility of the SDF, not on the correlation between the SDF and equity returns.

13. The drift adjustment (Ito's term) $-0.5(\sigma_{S_{t+1}}^d)^2$ guarantees that expected dividend growth $E_t[D_{t+1}/D_t]$ is controlled only by $\mu_{S_{t+1}}^d$.

14. Subsequently, Weil (1989) had emphasized a risk-free rate puzzle, the fact that models that can produce a large equity premium produce a riskless rate that is much higher than the historically observed average riskless rate.

15. Differently from Mehra and Prescott (1985) (or earlier MS papers, such as Cecchetti et al., 1990) – where dividends on unlevered equity are identically equal to capital income, which is identically equal to total income, which is identically equal to consumption – Abel allows aggregate consumption and aggregate dividends to differ from each other. Obviously, aggregate consumption can deviate from aggregate dividends in a DAPM if there is labor income in addition to capital income.

16. For instance, the evidence of negative serial correlation at long horizons and the finding that ratios of variances of long- and short-horizon returns decline as the horizon grows.

17. Von Neumann–Morgenstern time additive expected utility functions imply that the reciprocal of the CRRA coefficient equals the elasticity of intertemporal substitution (EIS). Kreps and Porteus establish a nonexpected utility framework which is capable of distinguishing the CRRA coefficient from EIS. However, Kocherlakota (1990) and Weil (1989) demonstrate that relaxing the restriction linking the CRRA coefficient and EIS is by itself insufficient to resolve key asset pricing puzzles.

18. Of course, CLM need to assume that investors are incapable of learning that their distorted beliefs are distorted. With more than a century of quarterly data at their disposal, Bayesian learners would almost surely have learned how to be rational by now.

19. It bears emphasizing that CLM are permitting distortions only to subjective beliefs concerning the endowment, and not to the actual endowment which continues to evolve according to the estimated DGP. This is a subtle but important point that distinguishes their approach from that of Rietz (1988), in which the actual endowment evolves according to a distorted process.

20. This phenomenon has been often described as the Great Moderation. Stock and Watson (2003) conclude that a decline in volatility has occurred broadly across sectors: it has appeared in employment growth, consumption growth, inflation and sectoral output growth, as well as in gross domestic product (GDP) growth, in both US and international data. Reductions in standard deviations are on the order of 60–70 percent relative to the 1970s and 1980s, and the marked change seems to be better described as

a structural break, or regime shift, than a gradual, trending decline. However, casual evidence seems to show that such a break may have been overturned by the surge in volatility that has accompanied the financial crisis and deep recession of 2008–09.

21. This is a result of the learning built into the model by the assumption that agents cannot observe the underlying state, as in Veronesi (1999).

22. A related point had already been made by Mayfield (2004) with reference to the Great Depression: as a result of a structural shift in the likelihood of future high-volatility periods, the simple historical average of excess market returns may have substantially overstated the magnitude of the market risk premium for the period since the Great Depression, which is tantamount to stating that the PDR may have been artificially depressed for many decades in a row, as conjectured by LLW (2008). When Mayfield augments his MSM to account for time-variation in transition probabilities, in the form of a single structural shift in the transition probabilities governing the evolution of the two volatility states, he finds evidence of a decline in the expected duration of the high-volatility state after 1940 (from 19 to less than two months). Given the lower likelihood of entering the high-volatility state, the risk premium falls from about 20.1 percent before 1940 to 7.1 percent after 1940, so that *ex post* returns after 1940 might be a biased estimate of *ex ante* expected returns.

23. Importantly, Branch and Evans's model is derived imposing rational expectations (RE). In an RE framework, the self-referential feature of the model requires that both the forecasts generated from the model and the market outcomes be jointly determined. Therefore the parameters of the forecasting model, the perceived riskiness of stocks, and the distribution of agents across models, are jointly determined. The additional equilibrium feedback effect makes multiple equilibria possible, which is similar to Timmermann (1994).

24. Although a general existence result for the RE equilibrium is not available, Branch and Evans show that when dividends and supply share shocks are weakly correlated, and γ is sufficiently small, restricted perceptions RE equilibria (RPEs) will exist.

25. Empirical evidence has linked variations in the cross-section of stock returns to firm characteristics such as market capitalization (e.g., represented by a small minus big, SMB, portfolio long in small stocks and short in large stocks) and book-to-market values (e.g., represented by a high minus low, HML, portfolio long in high book-to-market stocks and short in low book-to-market stocks), as in Fama and French (1993). Cross-sectional return variations associated with these characteristics are non-trivial by conventional measures.

26. In a way, this is not surprising because the role of MSMs is to effectively capture the fact that the aggregate economy is subject to discrete changes in the business cycle. Business cycle fluctuations, together with the monetary policy responses to them, have a significant impact on the term structure of interest rates. As a result, there is now an extensive empirical literature on bond yields suggesting that MSMs may describe the historical interest rate data better than single-regime models do (see Guidolin, 2012); it is logical that fixed-income scholars were the ones who first felt a need to develop structural models of the effects of MS on equilibrium asset prices.

27. Naik and Lee (1997) had proposed a version of this family of MSTSMs in which l does not depend on the current regime, while $\kappa_{S_{t+1}}$, $\theta_{S_{t+1}}$, and $\sigma_{S_{t+1}}$ do. Bansal and Zhou (2002) compare their model against this simpler benchmark and find that the latter is largely outperformed.

28. Campbell and Shiller (1991, p. 505) reported that 'the slope of the term structure almost always gives a forecast in the wrong direction for the short-term change in the yield on the longer bond', that is, the coefficient θ_1 is normally well below its EH-restricted value of one (in fact, it tends to be significantly negative) in the regression $r_{t+m,n-m} - r_{t,n} = \theta_0 + \theta_1 \frac{m}{n-m}(r_{t,n} - r_{t,m}) + u_{t+m}$, where $r_{t+k,q}$ is the spot rate measured at time $t + k (k \geq 0)$ for a bond maturing at time $t + m (m \geq 1)$, with $m > k$.

29. If δ_1^i is regime-dependent, an analytical solution for the yield curve is unavailable. Bansal and Zhou (2002) assume that δ_1^i depends on regimes and obtain the term structure of interest rates using log-linear approximations.

30. A related paper is Bekaert et al. (2001; hereafter BHM), who tackle the failure of the expectations hypothesis (EH) of the term structure of (riskless) interest rates focusing on 'peso problem' issues, whenever the *ex post* frequencies of states within the sample differ substantially from their *ex ante* probabilities, so that sample moments calculated from the data may not coincide with population moments. BHM assume a three-state MSM with time-varying transition probabilities to capture that observed short rates move up and down gradually and it is implausible for them to jump among regimes. While the single-state version of this model is well known to be unable to generate population distributions for the term premia that resolve the EH puzzles, BHM confirm that their stylized asset pricing model with peso problems considerably weakens the evidence against the EH.

31. In standard affine models, the market price of (diffusion) risk is assumed to be proportional to the volatility of the state variables $\mathbf{X}_t$. Such a structure is intuitive: risk compensation goes to zero as risk goes to zero. However, since variances are non-negative, this specification limits the variation of the compens-

ations that investors anticipate to receive when bearing a risk: since the compensation is bounded below by zero, it cannot change sign over time. This restriction, however, is relaxed in the essentially affine models of Duffee (2002) by including λ_0, an extension that Dai and Singleton (2003) show to be crucial for empirical models to account for the failure of the EH.

32. The three-factor structure imposed by ABW is more tightly parameterized than in DSY: ABW employ a three-factor representation of yields in which one factor, π_t (inflation) is observed; the other two factors are unobservable; the second factor, f_t, represents a latent MS term structure factor; the third latent factor is q_t, a time-varying but regime-invariant price of risk factor. Moreover, while the conditional means and volatility of f_t and π_t follow an MS process, the conditional mean and volatility of q_t do not. Thanks to these restrictions, ABW's model produces closed-form solutions for bond prices.

33. Intuitively, this specification captures the fact that aggressively high real rates, for example according to an activist Taylor rule in the implementation of monetary policy as captured by a specific S_t^i regime, could stave off a regime of high inflation.

34. Notice that the existence of predictability from forward rates to excess bond returns is easily explained by any DTSM with time-varying risk premia. However, the interesting challenge consists of explaining the tent-shaped pattern of the slope coefficients when multiple forward rates are used as regressors.

35. Naik (1993) is the first paper presenting an analytical solution for the value of European-style options in an MSM. His approach uses the regime persistence parameters to compute the expected duration for each regime over the option's life, similar to Hull and White's (1987) use of expected average volatility in their SV framework. See also Alexander (2004).

36. In a lattice framework, this approximation translates into four branches stemming from each node. One pair of branches corresponds to one regime and the other pair of branches corresponds to the other regime. An extra branch is added to one of the regimes to allow for more efficient recombining in the lattice, resulting in the number of nodes growing linearly through time. This five-branch lattice uses a binomial distribution to represent one regime and a trinomial distribution to represent the other.

REFERENCES

Abel, A. (1988), 'Stock prices under time-varying dividend risk: an exact solution in an infinite-horizon general equilibrium model', *Journal of Monetary Economics*, **22**, 375–393.

Abel, A. (1994), 'Exact solutions for expected rates of return under Markov regime switching: implications for the equity premium', *Journal of Money, Credit, and Banking*, **26**, 345–361.

Aingworth, D., S. Das and R. Motwani (2006), 'A simple approach for pricing equity options with Markov switching state variables', *Quantitative Finance*, **6**, 95–105.

Alexander, C. (2004), 'Normal mixture diffusion with uncertain volatility: modeling short and long-term smile effects', *Journal of Banking and Finance*, **28**, 2957–2980.

Alexander, C. and E. Lazar (2009), 'Modelling regime-specific stock price volatility', *Oxford Bulletin of Economics and Statistics*, **71**, 761–797.

Ang, A., G. Bekaert and M. Wei (2008), 'Term structure of real rates and expected inflation', *Journal of Finance*, **63**, 797–849.

Ang, A. and J. Chen (2002), 'Asymmetric correlations of equity portfolios', *Journal of Financial Economics*, **63**, 443–494.

Ang, A., L. Gu and Y. Hochberg (2007), 'Is IPO underperformance a peso problem?', *Journal of Financial and Quantitative Analysis*, **42**, 565–594.

Backus, D. and A. Gregory (1993), 'Theoretical relations between risk premiums and conditional variances', *Journal of Business and Economic Statistics*, **11**, 177–185.

Bae, J., C.J. Kim and C. Nelson (2007), 'Why are stock returns and volatility negatively correlated?', *Journal of Empirical Finance*, **14**, 41–58.

Baele, L., G. Bekaert and K. Inghelbrecht (2010), 'The determinants of stock and bond return comovements', *Review of Financial Studies*, **23**, 2374–2428.

Balyeat, B. and J. Muthuswamy (2009), 'The correlation structure of unexpected returns in US equities', *Financial Review*, **44**, 263–290.

Bansal, R., G. Tauchen and H. Zhou (2004), 'Regime-shifts, risk premiums in the term structure, and the business cycle', *Journal of Business and Economic Statistics*, **22**, 396–409.

Bansal, R. and H. Zhou (2002), 'Term structure of interest rates with regime shifts', *Journal of Finance*, **57**, 1997–2043.

Bekaert, G., R. Hodrick and D. Marshall (2001), 'Peso problem explanations for term structure anomalies', *Journal of Monetary Economics*, **48**, 241–270.

Bekaert, G. and G. Wu (2000), 'Asymmetric volatility and risk in equity markets', *Review of Financial Studies*, **13**, 1–42.

Bertholon, H., A. Monfort and F. Pegoraro (2008), 'Econometric asset pricing modelling', *Journal of Financial Econometrics*, **6**, 407–458.

Black, F. (1976), 'Studies of stock price volatility changes', *Proceedings of the Meetings of the American Statistical Association*, Business and Economics Statistics Division, pp. 177–181.

Bollen, N., S. Gray and R. Whaley (2000), 'Regime switching in foreign exchange rates: evidence from currency option prices', *Journal of Econometrics*, **94**, 239–276.

Bonomo, M. and R. Garcia (1994), 'Can a well-fitted equilibrium asset pricing model produce mean reversion?', *Journal of Applied Econometrics*, **9**, 19–29.

Bonomo, M. and R. Garcia (1996), 'Consumption and equilibrium asset pricing: an empirical assessment', *Journal of Empirical Finance*, **3**, 239–265.

Branch, W. and C. Evans (2010), 'Asset return dynamics and learning', *Review of Financial Studies*, **23**, 1651–1680.

Brooks, C. (1997), 'Linear and non-linear (non-)forecastibility of high frequency exchange rates', *Journal of Forecasting*, **16**, 125–145.

Cai, J. (1994), 'A Markov model of switching-regime ARCH', *Journal of Business and Economic Statistics*, **12**, 309–316.

Calvet, L. and A. Fisher (2001), 'Forecasting multifractal volatility', *Journal of Econometrics*, **105**, 27–58.

Calvet, L. and A. Fisher (2007), 'Multifrequency news and stock returns', *Journal of Financial Economics*, **86**, 178–212.

Campbell, J. and J. Cochrane (1999), 'By force of habit: a consumption-based explanation of aggregate stock market behavior', *Journal of Political Economy*, **107**, 205–251.

Campbell, J. and L. Hentschel (1992), 'No news is good news', *Journal of Financial Economics*, **31**, 281–318.

Campbell, J. and R. Shiller (1988), 'The dividend-price ratio and expectations of future dividends and discount factors', *Review of Financial Studies*, **1**, 195–227.

Campbell, J. and R. Shiller (1991), 'Yield spreads and interest rate movements: a bird's eye view', *Review of Economic Studies*, **58**, 495–514.

Cecchetti, S., P. Lam and N. Mark (1990), 'Mean reversion in equilibrium asset prices', *American Economic Review*, **80**, 398–418.

Cecchetti, S., P. Lam and N. Mark (1993), 'The equity premium and the risk-free rate: matching the moments', *Journal of Monetary Economics*, **31**, 21–45.

Cecchetti, S., P. Lam and N. Mark (2000), 'Asset pricing with distorted beliefs: are equity returns too good to be true?', *American Economic Review*, **90**, 787–805.

Chen, C.-C. and M.-Y. Hung (2010), 'Option pricing under Markov-switching GARCH processes', *Journal of Futures Markets*, **30**, 444–464.

Clements, M. and D. Hendry (1998), *Forecasting Economic Time Series*, Cambridge: Cambridge University Press.

Cochrane, J. and M. Piazzesi (2005), 'Bond risk premia', *American Economic Review*, **95**, 138–160.

Coggi, P. and B. Manescu (2004), 'A multifactor model of stock returns with stochastic regime switching', working paper, Universitat St Gallen.

Dai, Q. and K. Singleton (2002), 'Expectations puzzles, time-varying risk premia, and Affine models of the term structure', *Journal of Financial Economics*, **63**, 415–441.

Dai, Q. and K. Singleton (2003), 'Term structure dynamics in theory and reality', *Review of Financial Studies*, **16**, 631–678.

Dai, Q., K. Singleton and W. Yang (2007), 'Are regime shifts priced in US Treasury markets?', *Review of Financial Studies*, **20**, 1669–1706.

Dempster, A.P., N.M. Laird and D.B. Rubin (1977), 'Maximum likelihood from incomplete data via the EM algorithm', *Journal of the Royal Statistical Society B*, **39** (1), 1–38.

Duan, J.-C. (1995), 'The GARCH option pricing model', *Mathematical Finance*, **5**, 13–32.

Duan, J.-C., I. Popova and P. Ritchken (2002), 'Option pricing under regime switching', *Quantitative Finance*, **2**, 116–132.

Duffee, G. (2002), 'Term premia and interest rate forecasts in affine models', *Journal of Finance*, **57**, 405–443.

Elliott, R.J., H. Miao and J. Yu (2007), 'General equilibrium asset pricing under regime switching', working paper, University of Calgary, Canada.

Epstein, L. and S. Zin (1989), 'Substitution risk aversion and the temporal behavior of consumption and asset returns: a theoretical framework', *Econometrica*, **57**, 937–968.

Fama, E. and K. French (1993), 'Common risk factors in the returns on stocks and bonds', *Journal of Financial Economics*, **33**, 3–36.

French, K., W. Schwert and R. Stambaugh (1987), 'Expected stock returns and volatility', *Journal of Financial Economics*, **19**, 3–29.

Frühwirth-Schnatter, S. (2006), *Finite Mixture and Markov Switching Models*, New York: Springer.

Glosten, L., R. Jagannathan and D. Runkle (1993), 'On the relation between the expected value and the volatility of the nominal excess return on stocks', *Journal of Finance*, **48**, 1779–1801.

Gray, S. (1996), 'Modeling the conditional distribution of interest rates as a regime-switching process', *Journal of Financial Economics*, **42**, 27–62.

Guidolin, M. (2012), 'Markov switching models in empirical finance', in D. Drukker (ed.), *Missing Data Methods: Time-series Methods and Applications, Advances in Econometrics*, Vol. 2 27B, Bingley: Emerald Group Publishing, pp. 1–86.

Guidolin, M., S. Hyde, D. McMillan and S. Ono (2009), 'Non-linear predictability in stock and bond returns: when and where is it exploitable?', *International Journal of Forecasting*, **25**, 373–399.

Guidolin, M. and A. Timmermann (2006), 'An econometric model of nonlinear dynamics in the joint distribution of stock and bond returns', *Journal of Applied Econometrics*, **21**, 1–22.

Guidolin, M. and A. Timmermann (2008), 'Size and value anomalies under regime shifts', *Journal of Financial Econometrics*, **6**, 1–48.

Haas, M., S. Mittnik and M. Paolella (2004), 'A new approach to Markov-switching GARCH models', *Journal of Financial Econometrics*, **2**, 493–530.

Hahn, M., S. Frühwirth-Schnatter and J. Sass (2009), 'Estimating continuous-time Markov processes based on merged time series', *ASTA Advances in Statistical Analysis*, **93**, 403–425.

Hamilton, J. (1990), 'Analysis of time series subject to changes in regime', *Journal of Econometrics*, **45**, 39–70.

Hamilton, J. (1994), *Time Series Analysis*, Princeton, NJ: Princeton University Press.

Hamilton J. and R. Susmel (1994), 'Autoregressive conditional heteroskedasticity and changes in regime', *Journal of Econometrics*, **64**, 307–333.

Harrison, P. and H. Zhang (1999), 'An investigation of the risk and return relation at long horizons', *Review of Economics and Statistics*, **81**, 1–10.

Hull, J. and A. White (1987), 'The pricing of options on assets with stochastic volatility', *Journal of Finance*, **42**, 281–300.

Hung, M.-W. (1994), 'The interaction between nonexpected utility and asymmetric market fundamentals', *Journal of Finance*, **49**, 325–343.

Kandel, S. and R. Stambaugh (1990), 'Expectations and volatility of consumption and asset returns', *Review of Financial Studies*, **3**, 207–232.

Kim, C.-J., J. Morley and C. Nelson (2004), 'Is there a positive relationship between stock market volatility and the equity premium?', *Journal of Money, Credit, and Banking*, **36**, 336–360.

Kim, C.J. and C. Nelson (1999), *State-Space Models with Regime Switching: Classical and Gibbs-Sampling Approaches with Applications*, Cambridge, MA: MIT Press.

Kocherlakota, N. (1990), 'Disentangling coefficient of relative risk aversion from elasticity of intertemporal substitution: an irrelevance result', *Journal of Finance*, **45**, 175–191.

Kreps, D. and K. Porteus (1978), 'Temporal resolution of uncertainty and dynamic choice theory', *Econometrica*, **46**, 185–200.

Krolzig, H.M. (1997), *Markov-Switching Vector Autoregressions: Modeling, Statistical Inference, and Application to Business Cycle Analysis*, Berlin: Springer-Verlag.

Leroux, B. (1992), 'Maximum likelihood estimation for hidden Markov models', *Stochastic Processes and their Applications*, **40**, 127–143.

Lettau, M., S. Ludvigson and J. Wachter (2008), 'The declining equity premium: what role does macroeconomic risk play?', *Review of Financial Studies*, **21**, 1653–1687.

Longin, E. and B. Solnik (2001), 'Correlation structure of international equity markets during extremely volatile periods', *Journal of Finance*, **56**, 649–676.

Maheu, J. and T. McCurdy (2000), 'Identifying bull and bear markets in stock returns', *Journal of Business and Economic Statistics*, **18**, 100–112.

Mayfield, S. (2004), 'Estimating the market risk premium', *Journal of Financial Economics*, **73**, 465–496.

McLachlan, G. and D. Peel (2000), *Finite Mixture Models*, New York: John Wiley & Sons.

Mehra, R. and E. Prescott (1985), 'The equity premium: a puzzle', *Journal of Monetary Economics*, **15**, 145–162.

Merton, R. (1973), 'An intertemporal asset pricing model', *Econometrica*, **41**, 867–888.

Monfort, A. and F. Pegoraro (2007), 'Switching VARMA term structure models', *Journal of Financial Econometrics*, **5**, 105–153.

Naik, V. (1993), 'Option valuation and hedging strategies with jumps in the volatility of asset returns', *Journal of Finance*, **48**, 1969–1984.

Naik, V. and M. Lee (1997), 'Yield curve dynamics with discrete shifts in economic regimes: theory and estimation', working paper, University of British Columbia.

Ozoguz, A. (2009), 'Good times or bad times? Investors' uncertainty and stock returns', *Review of Financial Studies*, **22**, 4377–4422.

Pelletier, D. (2006), 'Regime switching for dynamic correlations', *Journal of Econometrics*, **131**, 445–473.

Rietz, T. (1988), 'The equity premium: a solution', *Journal of Monetary Economics*, **22**, 117–131.

Schwert, G. (1989), 'Why does stock market volatility change over time?', *Journal of Finance*, **44**, 1115–1153.

Stock, J. and M. Watson (2003), 'Has the business cycle changed? Evidence and explanations', in M. Gertler and K. Rogoff (eds), *NBER Macroeconomics Annual: 2002*, Cambridge, MA: MIT Press, pp. 159–230.

Timmermann, A. (1994), 'Can agents learn to form rational expectations? Some results on convergence and stability of learning in the UK stock market', *Economic Journal*, **104**, 777–798.

Turner, C., R. Startz and C. Nelson (1989), 'A Markov model of heteroskedasticity, risk, and learning in the stock market', *Journal of Financial Economics*, **25**, 3–22.

Veronesi, P. (1999), 'Stock market overreaction to bad news in good times: a rational expectations equilibrium model', *Review of Financial Studies*, **12**, 975–1007.

Veronesi, P. and F. Yared (1999), 'Short and long horizon term and inflation risk premia in the US term structure: evidence from an integrated model for nominal and real bond prices under regime shifts', CRSP Working Paper No. 508.

Weil, P. (1989), 'The equity premium puzzle and the risk-free rate puzzle', *Journal of Monetary Economics*, **24**, 401–421.

Whitelaw, R. (1994), 'Time variations and covariations in the expectation and volatility of stock market returns', *Journal of Finance*, **49**, 515–541.

Whitelaw, R. (2000), 'Stock market risk and return: an equilibrium approach', *Review of Financial Studies*, **13**, 521–547.

2 Portfolio optimization: theory and practical implementation[1]

William T. Ziemba

2.1 INTRODUCTION

In this chapter, I review the classical portfolio optimization problem and examine various applications of portfolio theory. I begin with pure portfolio theory where it is assumed that the means, variances and other parameters are known and there is a static one-period horizon. The analysis uses Arrow–Pratt risk aversion theory. The advantage of accurate means in static portfolio problems and, indeed, in all models, is stressed as is its relationship to the investor's risk aversion. Then the stochastic programming approach to asset–liability management is discussed from a practitioner's perspective. There it is assumed that there are scenarios on the asset parameters in the assets-only case and asset and liability parameters in asset–liability situations in multiple periods. Kelly and fractional Kelly investment strategies which maximize long-run wealth are discussed. This leads to a winning system for place and show betting. This is followed by a discussion of some great investors who have behaved as if they were using Kelly betting strategies.

2.2 STATIC PORTFOLIO THEORY

In the static portfolio theory case, suppose there are n assets, $i = 1,\ldots, n$, with random returns $\xi_1,\ldots,\xi_n$. The return on asset i, namely ξ_i, is the capital appreciation plus dividends in the next investment period such as monthly, quarterly, yearly or some other time period. The n assets have the distribution $F(\xi_1,\ldots,\xi_n)$ with known mean vector $\overline{\xi} = (\overline{\xi}_1, \ldots, \overline{\xi}_n)$ and known $n \times n$ variance–covariance matrix Σ with typical covariance σ_{ij} for $i \neq j$ and variance σ_i^2 for $i = j$. A basic assumption is that the return distributions are independent of the asset weight choices.

A mean-variance frontier is:

$$\phi(\delta) = \text{Maximize } \overline{\xi}'x$$
$$st. \quad x'\sum x \leq \delta$$
$$e'x = w_0$$
$$x \in K$$

where e is a vector of ones, $x = (x_1,\ldots,x_n)'$ are the asset weights, K represents other constraints on the x and w_0 is the investor's initial wealth.

When the variance is parameterized with $\delta > 0$, it yields a concave curve, as in Figure 2.1a. This is the Markowitz (1952, 1987) mean-variance efficient frontier and

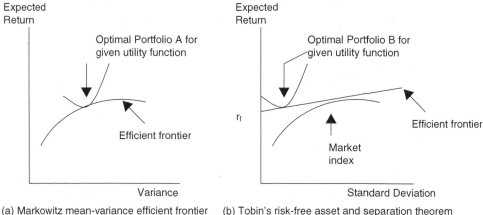

Figure 2.1   Two efficient frontiers

optimally trades off mean which is desirable with variance which is undesirable. Tobin (1958) extended the Markowitz model to include a risk-free asset with mean $\xi_0 = r_f$ and no variance. Then the efficient frontier concave curve becomes the straight line as shown in Figure 2.1b. The standard deviation here is plotted rather than the variance to make the line straight. An investor will pick an optimal portfolio in the Markowitz model using a utility function that trades off mean for variance or, equivalently, standard deviation as shown in Figure 2.1a to yield portfolio A. For the Tobin model, one does a simpler calculation to find the optimal portfolio which will be on the straight line in Figure 2.1b between the risk-free asset and the market index M. Here the investor picks portfolio B that is two-thirds cash (risk-free asset) and one-third market index. The market index may be proxied by the S&P 500 or Wilshire 5000 value weighted indices. Since all investors choose between cash and the market index, this separates the investor's problem into finding the market index independent of the investor's utility function and then where to be on the line for a given utility function, which is called Tobin's separation theorem. Ziemba et al. (1974) discuss this and show how to compute the market index and optimal weights of cash and the market index for various utility functions and constraints. They show how to calculate the straight line efficient frontier in Figure 2.1(b) with a simple n-variable deterministic linear complementary problem or a quadratic program. That calculation of Tobin's separation theorem means that for every concave, non-decreasing utility function, u the solution of the optimal ratio of risky assets, $i = 1, \ldots, n$ is the same. Hence $x_i^*/x_j^*, i, j = 1, \ldots, n, i \neq j$ is the same for all $u \in U_2 = [u|u' \geq 0, u'' \leq 0]$.

The portfolio problem is:

$$\max_{x \geq 0} E_\xi u(\xi' x)$$

$$e'x = 1 \qquad\qquad (2.1)$$

where $\hat{\xi} = (\xi_0, \xi_1, \ldots, \xi_n) = (\xi_0, \xi), \xi_0$ is the return on the risk-free asset, $\xi \sim N(\bar{\xi}, \Sigma)$ and initial wealth $w_0 = 1$.

In step 1, one solves the n-variable deterministic linear complementary problem (LCP):

$$w = Mz - \overline{\overline{\xi}}, \quad w'z = 0, \quad w \geq 0, \quad z \geq 0$$

where the optimal risky asset weights are:

$$x_i^* = \frac{z_i^*}{e^* z^*}, \quad i = 1,\ldots,n.$$

This LCP is derived as follows. The slope of the efficient frontier line in Figure 2.1(b) is found by maximizing:

$$\frac{\overline{\xi}'x - \xi_0}{(x' \sum x)^{1/2}} \quad \text{s.t.} \quad e'x = 1, x \in K,$$

which is equivalent to:

$$\text{Max} \, g(x) = \frac{\overline{\overline{\xi}}'x}{(x' \sum x)^{1/2}} \quad \text{s.t.} \quad e'x = 1, x \in K$$

where $\overline{\overline{\xi}}_i = \overline{\xi}_i - \xi_0$.

Since $g(x)$ is linear homogeneous and assuming $\lambda x \in K$, where $g(\lambda x) = g(x)$ for $\lambda \geq 0$, then the Kuhn–Tucker conditions can be written as the LCP problem above, where $w_i = -\overline{\overline{\xi}}_i + \Sigma_i z$ and Σ_i is the ith row of Σ. From the theory of the LCP, see, for example, Murty (1972), there is a unique solution since Σ is positive definite.

This gives the market index $\mathbf{M} = \Sigma_{i=1}^{n} \overline{\xi}_i' x_i^*$ independent of u. Then in step 2, one determines the optimal ratio of M and the risk-free asset. So for a given $u \in U_2$ from the single variable $\alpha \in (-\infty, 1]$, in Figure 2.1(b), $\alpha = 1$ is $\mathbf{M}$, $\alpha = 1/2$ if half $\mathbf{M}$ and half the risk-free asset and $\alpha = -3$ means that 4 of the risk-free asset is borrowed to invest in $\mathbf{M}$. Then optimal allocation in the risk-free asset is α^* and the optimal allocation in risky asset i, $i = 1,\ldots,n$, is $(1 - \alpha^*)x_i^*$, which is obtained by solving:

$$\max_{-\infty \leq \alpha \leq 1} E_M u(\alpha \xi_0 + (1 - \alpha) M) \tag{2.2}$$

where $M = \xi' x^* \sim N (\overline{\xi}' x^*, x^{*'} \Sigma x^*)$ and $\xi = (\xi_1, \ldots, \xi_n)$.

One may solve (2.2) using a search algorithm such as golden sections or a bisecting search; see Zangwill (1969). Examples with data and specific utility functions appear in Ziemba et al. (1974). Ziemba (1974) generalized all this to certain classes of infinite variance stable distributions. That analysis, though more complex, follows the normal distribution case. In place of variances, dispersions are used. Under some assumptions, one has the convexity of the risk measure property that is analogous to Figure 2.1. That paper, as well as many other classic papers, discussions and extensive problems are reprinted in Ziemba and Vickson (1975 [2013]).

Figure 2.1(b) illustrates the Sharpe (1964), Lintner (1965), Mossin (1966) capital asset pricing model which has $E(R_i) = \alpha_i + \beta_i E(R_M)$, where $E(R_i)$ and $E(R_M)$ are the mean return of the asset and the market, respectively, α_i is the excess return from this asset and β_i measures the asset's correlation with the market, M.

Referring to Figure 2.1(a), the point A is determined through a trade-off of expected return and variance. This trade-off is determined through risk aversion. The standard way to measure absolute risk aversion is via the Arrow (1965), Pratt (1964) absolute risk aversion index:

$$R_A(w) = \frac{-u''(w)}{u'(w)}.$$

Risk tolerance as used in industry is:

$$R_T(w) = \frac{100}{\frac{1}{2}R_A(w)}.$$

$R_A = 4$, represents the standard pension fund strategy 60:40 stock bond mix corresponds to $R_T = 50$ (independent of wealth).

$R_A(w)$ represents all the essential information about the investor's utility function $u(w)$, which is only defined up to a linear transformation, while eliminating everything arbitrary about u, since:

$$u(w) \sim \int e^{\int R_A(w)}.$$

The major theoretical reason for the use of R_A is that:

$$R_A^1(w) \geq R_A^2(w) \Leftrightarrow \pi_1(w,z) \geq \pi_2(w,z) \quad \text{for all } w, z$$

$$\Leftrightarrow p_1(w,h) \geq p_2(w,h) \quad \text{for all } w, h$$

$$\underbrace{}_{\text{formula replicates behavior}} \quad \underbrace{}_{\text{Behavior}}$$

where the risk premium $\pi(w, z)$ is defined so that the decision maker is indifferent to receiving the random amount z and the non-random amount $\bar{z} - \pi = -\pi$, where $\bar{z} = 0$ and $u[w - \pi] = E_z u(w + z)$ (this defines π). When u is concave, $\pi \geq 0$.

For σ_z^2 small, a Taylor series approximation yields $\pi(w,z) = \frac{1}{2}\sigma_z^2 R_A(w) +$ small errors. For the special case:

$$z = \begin{cases} +h & pr = \frac{1}{2} \\ -h & pr = \frac{1}{2} \end{cases}$$

where $p(w, h) =$ probability premium $= P(z = h) - P(z + h)$, the decision maker is indifferent between status quo and the risk z:

$$u(w) = E_z u(w + z) = \frac{1}{2}[1 + p(w, h)]u(w + h) + \frac{1}{2}[1 - p(w,h)]u(x - h). \quad (2.3)$$

This equation defines p. Again, by a Taylor series approximation we get $p(w,h) = \frac{1}{2}h R_A(w)$ + small errors. So risk premiums and probability premiums rise when risk aversion rises and vice versa.

Good utility functions include those in the general class of decreasing risk aversion functions $u'(w) = (w^a + b)^{-c}, a > 0, c > 0$, which contain log, power, negative power, arctan, and so on. Decreasing absolute risk aversion utility functions are preferred because they are the class where a decision maker attaches a positive risk premium to any risk ($\pi(w, z) > 0$), but a smaller premium to any given risk the larger his wealth:

$$\left(\frac{\partial \pi(w, z)}{\partial w} \leq 0 \right).$$

A key result is:

$$\underbrace{\frac{\partial R_A(w)}{\partial w} \leq 0}_{\text{replicates behavior}} \Leftrightarrow \underbrace{\frac{\partial \pi(w, z)}{\partial w} \leq 0 \Leftrightarrow \frac{\partial p(w, h)}{\partial w} \leq 0}_{\text{behavior}} \quad \text{for all } w, z, h > 0.$$

So decreasing absolute risk aversion utility functions replicate those where the risk premium and probability premium are decreasing in wealth.

An individual's utility function and risk aversion index can be estimated using the double exponential utility function:

$$u(w) = -e^{-aw} - be^{-cw}$$

where a, b and c are constants. An example using the certainty-equivalent and gain-and-loss equivalent methods is defined in Figure 2.2 for Donald Hausch (my co-author of

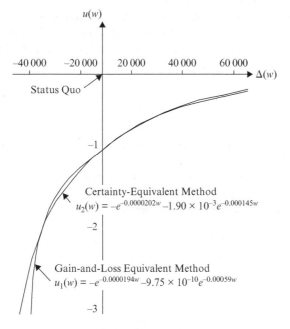

Figure 2.2   Utility of wealth function for Donald Hausch

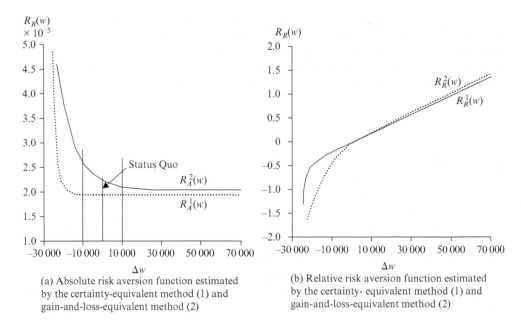

(a) Absolute risk aversion function estimated
by the certainty-equivalent method (1) and
gain-and-loss-equivalent method (2)

(b) Relative risk aversion function estimated
by the certainty- equivalent method (1) and
gain-and-loss-equivalent method (2)

Figure 2.3   Risk aversion functions for Donald Hausch

various horse racing books and articles) when he was a student – see the Appendix which describes these estimation methods. This function is strictly concave, strictly increasing and has decreasing absolute risk aversion.

Donald Hausch's utility function was fitted by least squares and both methods provide similar curves. His absolute risk aversion is decreasing – see Figure 2.3(a) and 2.3(b) – and nearly constant in his investment range where initial wealth w_0 changes by $\pm 10\,000$, corresponding to a value of R_A between 2.0 and 2.5:

$$-w\left[\frac{u''(w)}{u'(w)}\right]$$

His relative risk aversion is increasing and linear in his investment range.

The Arrow–Pratt risk aversion index is the standard way to measure risk aversion but the less-used known Rubinstein risk aversion measure is actually optimal. Indeed, Kallberg and Ziemba (1983) show that given utility functions u_1 and u_2, initial wealth w_1 and w_2, and assets $(\xi_1, \ldots, \xi_n) \sim N(\bar{\xi}, \Sigma)$ then if:

$$\frac{E_\xi u_1''(w_1\xi'x^*)}{E_\xi u_1'(w_1\xi'x^*)} = \frac{E_\xi u_2''(w_2\xi'x^*)}{E_\xi u_2'(w_2\xi'x^*)}$$

where x^* solves:

$$\max_{\text{s.t. } x \in K, e'x = w} E_\xi u_1(w_1\xi'x)$$

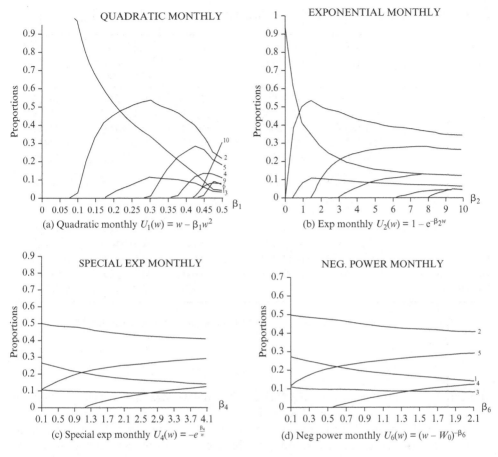

Source: Kallberg and Ziemba (1983).

Figure 2.4 Functional forms asset weights

then x^* solves:

$$\max_{\text{s.t. } x \in K, e'x=1} E_\xi u_2(w_2\xi'x).$$

Hence if two investors have the same Rubinstein risk aversion measure, they will have the same optimal portfolio weights. As shown in Figure 2.4(a) to 2.4(d) special exponential and negative power utility functions with the same average risk aversion have very similar mean, variance, expected utility and portfolio weights and these are very different compared to quadratic or exponential utility. When two utility functions have the same average risk aversion, then they have very similar optimal portfolio weights. Here $u_4(w) = e^{-\beta_4/w}$ and $u_6(w) = (w - w_0)^{-\beta_6}$ are different utility functions but their average risk aversions have similar ranges and these are very different than the quadratic

Table 2.1   Optimal portfolio weights for alternative utility functions and $R_A = 4$

Security/ Statistic	Exponential (4.0)	Quadratic (0.351447)	Log (−0.832954)	Special Exponential (2.884400)	Negative Power (1.443557)
1	0.088239	0.082991	0.046975	0.021224	0.047611
2	0.169455	0.165982	0.116220	0.185274	0.112794
3	0.106894	0.106663	0.080160	0.104064	0.079600
4	0.194026	0.198830	0.161247	0.048522	0.154474
5	0.441385	0.445533	0.343318	0.441182	0.328958
6					
7					
8					
9					
10			0.252077	0.199733	0.258232
Mean	1.186170	1.185175	1.151634	1.158397	1.149527
Variance	0.037743	0.037247	0.024382	0.027802	0.023756
Expected utility	0.988236	0.988236	0.987863	0.987589	0.987821
Percent error	−	0	0.703000	0.709900	0.782700

Note: Parameter values are in parentheses. Zeros and blanks indicate values less than 10^{-4}.

Source: Kallberg and Ziemba (1983).

and exponential utilities in Figure 2.4(a) and 2.4(b). The size of the errors is shown in Table 2.1 for fixed risk aversion of $R_A = 4$.

The basic theory of Markowitz, Sharpe and Tobin assumes that the parameters are known. The real world, of course, does not have constant (or known) parameters. So let us look first at what are the errors associated with parameter estimation and later at models (stochastic programming) where the probability distribution of asset returns is explicitly considered.

2.3   THE IMPORTANCE OF MEANS

Means are by far the most important part of any return distribution for actual portfolio results. If you are to have good results in any portfolio problem, you must have good mean estimates for future returns.

If asset X has cumulative distribution $F(\cdot)$, asset Y has $G(\cdot)$ and these cumulative distribution functions cross only once, then asset X dominates asset Y for all increasing concave utility functions, that is has higher expected utility, if and only if the mean of X exceeds the mean of Y.

This useful result of Hanoch and Levy (1969) means that the variance and other moments are unimportant for single crossing distributions. Only the means count. With normal distributions, X and Y cross just once if and only if the standard deviation of asset X is less than the standard deviation of asset Y. This is the basic equivalence of

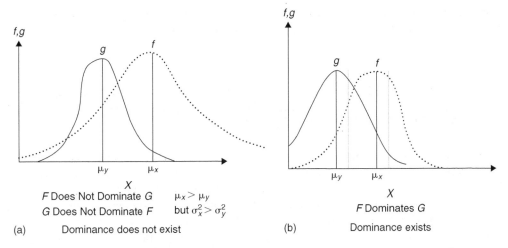

Figure 2.5 Mean variance and second-order stochastic dominance

mean-variance analysis and expected utility analysis via second-order (concave, non-decreasing) stochastic dominance. Figure 2.5 displays this where the second-degree and mean-variance dominance is on the right. There is no dominance on the left because the distributions cross twice. This F has a higher mean but also higher variance than G. The densities f and g are plotted here for convenience and give the same results as if the cumulative distribution functions F and G were plotted.

Errors in parameter inputs can lead to significant losses and larger turnover. Additional calculations appear in Kallberg and Ziemba (1981, 1984) and Chopra and Ziemba (1993).

The size of the error depends on the risk tolerance, the reciprocal of the Arrow–Pratt risk aversion $(R_T = \frac{100}{\frac{1}{2}R_A})$. However, errors in means, variances and covariances are roughly 20:2:1 times as important, respectively (Table 2.2). But with low risk aversion, such as that embodied by a logarithmic utility function, the ratios can be 100:2:1. So good mean estimates are by far the most crucial aspect for successful application of a mean-variance analysis and we will see that in all other stochastic modelling

Table 2.2 Average ratio of CEL for errors in means, variances and covariances

Risk tolerance	Errors in means vs covariances	Errors in means vs variances	Errors in variances vs covariances
25	5.38	3.22	1.67
50	22.50	10.98	2.05
75	56.84	21.42	2.68
	↓	↓	↓
	20	10	2
	Error mean	Error var	Error covar
	20	2	1

approaches. The sensitivity of the mean carries over into multiperiod models. There the effect is strongest in period one and less in future periods; see Geyer and Ziemba (2008).

2.4   APPLYING PORTFOLIO THEORY IN PRACTICE: THE STOCHASTIC PROGRAMMING APPROACH TO ASSET–LIABILITY MANAGEMENT

I now discuss an approach using scenarios and optimization to model asset–liability decisions for pension funds, insurance companies, individuals, retirement, bank trading departments, hedge funds, and so on. It includes the essential problem elements: uncertainties, constraints, risks, transactions costs, liquidity, and preferences over time, to provide good results in normal times and avoid or limit disaster when extreme scenarios occur. The stochastic programming (SP) approach, while complex, is a practical way to include key problem elements that other approaches are not able to model.

Other approaches (static mean-variance, fixed-mix, stochastic control, capital growth, continuous time finance etc.) are useful for the micro-analysis of decisions and the SP approach is useful for the aggregated macro (overall) analysis of relevant decisions and activities. They yield good results most of the time but are frequently a recipe for disaster: overbetting and not being truly diversified at a time when an extreme scenario occurs. It pays to make a complex stochastic programming model when a lot is at stake and the essential problem has many complications.

The accuracy of the actual scenarios chosen and their probabilities contributes greatly to model success. However, the scenario approach generally leads to superior investment performance even if there are errors in the estimations of both the actual scenario outcomes and their probabilities. It is not possible to include all scenarios or even some that may actually occur. The modeling effort attempts to cover well the range of possible future evolution of the economic environment. The predominant view is that such models do not exist, are impossible to successfully implement or are prohibitively expensive. I argue that given modern computer power, better large-scale stochastic linear programming codes and better modeling skills, such models can be widely used in many applications and are very cost effective. We know that professionals adjust means (mean-reversion, James–Stein, etc.) and constrain output weights. They do not change asset positions unless the advantage of the change is significant. Also, they do not use mean-variance analysis with liabilities and other major market imperfections except as a first test analysis. Mean-variance models can be modified and applied in various ways to analyze many problems – see Markowitz (1987) and Grinold and Khan (1999), for example. But mean-variance models define risk as a terminal wealth surprise regardless of direction and make no allowance for skewness preference. Moreover, they treat assets with option features inappropriately. In my models I use a relative of variance, namely the convex risk measure weighted downside target violations and that will avoid such objections. Possible approaches to model asset and liability management (ALM) situations include: simulation, mean-variance, expected log, stochastic control, stochastic programming and control and stochastic programming.

The stochastic programming approach is ideally suited to analyze such problems with the following features:

- Multiple time periods; end effects – steady state after decision horizon adds one more decision period to the model.
- Consistency with economic and financial theory for interest rates, bond prices, and so on.
- Discrete scenarios for random elements – returns, liability costs, currency movements.
- Utilize various forecasting models, handle fat tails.
- Institutional, legal and policy constraints.
- Model derivatives, illiquid assets and transactions costs.
- Expressions of risk in terms understandable to decision makers; the more you lose, the greater the penalty for losing.
- Maximize long-run expected profits net of expected discounted convex penalty costs for shortfalls; pay more, and more penalty for shortfalls as they increase.
- Model as constraints or penalty costs in the objective to maintain adequate reserves and cash levels and meet regularity requirements.
- We can now solve very realistic multiperiod problems on personal computers (PCs).
- If the current situation has never occurred before, then use one that is similar to add scenarios. For a crisis in Brazil, use Russian crisis data, for example. The results of the SP will give you good advice when times are normal and keep you out of severe trouble when times are bad.
- Those using SP models may lose 5–10–15 percent but they will not lose 50–70–95 percent like some investors and hedge funds. If the scenarios are more or less accurate and the problem elements reasonably modeled, the SP will give good advice. You may slightly underperform in normal markets but you will greatly overperform in bad markets when other approaches may blow up.

Table 2.3 illustrates the models my colleagues and I built at Frank Russell in the 1990s.

In Cariño and Ziemba (1998) we showed that stochastic programming models usually beat fixed-mix models. The latter are basically volatility pumping models (buy low, sell high); see Luenberger (1998). Figure 2.6 illustrates how the optimal weights change depending on the previous periods' results. Despite good results, fixed-mix and buy-and-hold strategies do not utilize new information from return occurrences in their construction. By making the strategy scenario dependent using a multi-period stochastic programming model, a better outcome is possible.

I compare two strategies:

1. the dynamic stochastic programming strategy, which is the full optimization of the multiperiod model; and
2. the fixed-mix strategy in which the portfolios from the mean-variance frontier have allocations rebalanced back to that mix at each stage; buy when low and sell when high. This is like covered calls, which is the opposite of portfolio insurance.

Table 2.3   Russell business engineering models

Model	Type of application	Year delivered	Number of scenarios	Computer hardware
Russell-Yasuda (Tokyo)	Property and Casualty Insurance	1991	256	IBM RISC 6000
Mitsubishi Trust (Tokyo)	Pension Consulting	1994	2000	IBM RISC 6000 with Parallel Processors
Swiss Bank Corp (Basle)	Pension Consulting	1996	8000	IBM UNIX 2
Daido Life Insurance Company (Tokyo)	Life Insurance	1997	25 600	IBM PC
Banca Fideuram (Rome)	Assets Only Personal	1997	10 000	IBM UNIX 2 and PC
Consulting Clients	Assets Only Insurance	1998	Various	IBM UNIX 2 and PC

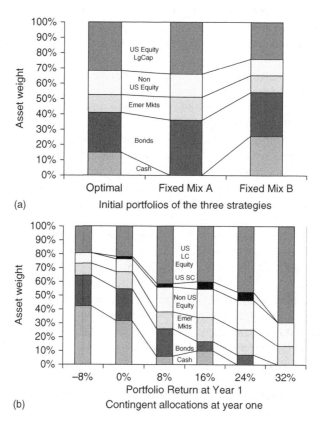

Figure 2.6   Example portfolios

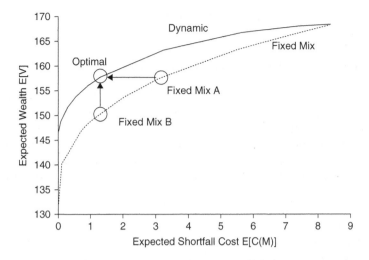

Figure 2.7   The optimal stochastic strategy dominates fixed-mix

Consider fixed-mix strategies A (64:36 stock bond mix) and B (46:54 stock bond mix). The optimal stochastic programming strategy dominates, as shown in Figure 2.7.

A further study of the performance of stochastic dynamic and fixed-mix portfolio models was made by Fleten et al. (2002). They compared two alternative versions of a portfolio model for the Norwegian life insurance company Gjensidige NOR, namely multistage stochastic linear programming and the fixed-mix constant rebalancing strategy. They found that the multiperiod stochastic programming model dominated the fixed-mix approach but the degree of dominance is much smaller out-of-sample than in-sample. This is because out-of-sample the random input data is structurally different from in-sample, so the stochastic programming model loses its advantage in optimally adapting to the information available in the scenario tree. Also, the performance of the fixed-mix approach improves because the asset mix is updated at each stage.

The Russell–Yasuda Kasai project was the first large-scale multiperiod stochastic programming model implemented for a major financial institution. As a consultant to the Frank Russell Company during 1989–91, I designed the model. Experience has shown that we should not be concerned with getting all the scenarios exactly right when using stochastic programming models. You cannot do this, and it does not matter much anyway. Rather, you should worry that you have the problem periods laid out reasonably, and the scenarios basically cover the means, the tails and the chance of what could happen.

Back in 1990–91, computations were a major focus of concern. Originally we had ten periods and 2048 scenarios. It was too big to solve at that time and became an intellectual challenge for the stochastic programming community. We quickly realized that ten periods made the model far too difficult to solve and also too cumbersome to collect the data and interpret the results, and the 2048 scenarios were at that time a large number to deal with. The liability structure of the property and casualty insurance business had become very complex, and the insurance industry had various restrictions in terms of asset management. It was concluded that existing models, such as Markowitz mean-variance, would not function well and that we needed to develop a new asset–liability management model.

2.4.1   The Yasuda Fire and Marine Insurance Company

The Yasuda Fire & Marine Insurance Company called Yasuda Kasai is based in Tokyo. In 1988, Yasuda Kasai and Russell signed an agreement to deliver a dynamic stochastic asset allocation model by April 1, 1991. The goal was to implement a model of Yasuda Kasai's financial planning process to improve their investment and liability payment decisions and their overall risk management. In 1989, I proposed a stochastic programming model which we then built at Russell in Tacoma. The business goals were to:

1. maximize long-run expected wealth;
2. pay enough on the insurance policies to be competitive in current yield;
3. maintain adequate current and future reserves and cash levels, and
4. meet regulatory requirements especially with the increasing number of saving-oriented policies being sold that were generating new types of liabilities.

The following is a summary of the Russell Yasuda model and its results. See also the original papers Cariño et al. (1998), Cariño and Ziemba (1998) and the survey in Zenios and Ziemba (2007):

- The model needed to have more realistic definitions of operational risks and business constraints than the return variance used in previous mean-variance models employed at Yasuda Kasai.
- The implemented model determines an optimal multiperiod investment strategy that enables decision makers to define risks in tangible operational terms such as cash shortfalls.
- The risk measure used is convex and penalizes target violations, more and more as the violations of various kinds and in various periods increase.
- The objective is to maximize the discounted expected wealth at the horizon net of expected discounted penalty costs incurred during the five periods of the model.
- This objective is similar to a mean-variance model except that it is over five periods and only counts downside risk through target violations.
- I greatly prefer this approach to value-at-risk (VaR) or conditional VaR (CVaR) and its variants for ALM applications because for most people and organizations, the non-attainment of goals is more and more damaging and not linear in the non-attainment (as in CVaR) or not considering the size of the non-attainment at all (as in VaR).
- A reference on VaR and CVaR as risk measures is Artzner et al. (1999). They argue that good risk measures should be coherent and satisfy a set of axioms.

The convex risk measure I use is coherent. Rockafellar and Ziemba (2000) define a set of axioms that justify these convex risk measures:

- The model formulates and meets the complex set of regulations imposed by Japanese insurance laws and practices.
- The most important of the intermediate horizon commitments is the need to produce a sufficiently high income to pay the required annual interest in the savings-type insurance policies without sacrificing the goal of maximizing long-run expected wealth.
- During the first two years of use, 1991 and 1992, the investment strategy recommended by the model yielded a superior income return of 42 basis points (US$79 million) over what a mean-variance model would have produced. Simulation tests also showed the superiority of the stochastic programming scenario-based model over a mean-variance approach.
- In addition to the revenue gains, there have been considerable organizational and informational benefits.
- The model had 256 scenarios over four periods plus a fifth end effects period.
- The model was flexible regarding the time horizon and length of decision periods, which are multiples of quarters.
- A typical application had initialization; plus period 1 to the end of the first quarter; period 2 the remainder of fiscal year 1; period 3 the entire fiscal year 2; period 4 fiscal years 3, 4 and 5; and period 5, the end effects years 6 and forever.

Figure 2.8 shows the multistage stochastic linear programming structure of the Russell–Yasuda Kasai model.

The objective of the model is to allocate discounted fund value among asset classes to maximize the expected wealth at the end of the planning horizon T less expected penalized shortfalls accumulated throughout the planning horizon:

$$Maximize \ E\left[W_T - \sum_{t=1}^{T} c_i(w_t) \right]$$

subject to budget constraints:

$$\sum_{n} X_{nt} - V_t = 0,$$

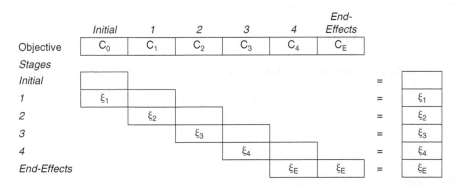

Figure 2.8   Layout of the Russell–Yasuda Kasai model

Table 2.4   The dimensions of a typical implemented problem

heightPer	BrPar	Scen	Assets	Alloc Var	Rows	Cols	Coeff	GLP: Rows	Cols	Coeff
INI	1	1	7	59	22	60	257	22	60	257
Q01	8	8	7	59	48	85	573	384	680	4 584
Y01	4	32	7	59	54	96	706	1 728	3 072	22 592
Y02	4	128	7	29	52	66	557	6 656	8 448	71 296
Y05	2	256	7	29	52	66	407	13 312	16 896	104 192
YFF	1	256	5	21	35	58	450	8 960	14 848	11 5200

asset accumulation relations:

$$V_{t+1} - \sum_n (1 + RP_{nt+1} + RI_{nt+1}X_{nt}) = F_{t+1} - Pt+1 - I_{t+1},$$

income shortfall constraints:

$$\sum_n RI_{nt+1}X_{nt} + w_{t+1} + - v_{t+1} = g_t + L_t$$

and non-negativity constraints:

$$X_{nt} \geq 0, \quad v_{t+1} \geq 0, \quad w_{t+1} \geq 0,$$

for $t = 0,1, 2,\ldots, T - 1$. Liability balances and cash flows are computed to satisfy the liability accumulation relations:

$$L_{t+1} = (1 + g_{t+1})L_t + F_{t+1} - P_{t+1} - I_{t+1}, t = 0,\ldots, T - 1.$$

Publicly available codes to solve such models are discussed in Wallace and Ziemba (2005); see also Gondzio and Kouwenberg (2001). The Russell–Yasuda model is small by current standards but in 1991 it was a challenge. The dimensions of a typical implemented problem are shown in Table 2.4. Figure 2.9 shows Yasuda Kasai's asset–liability decision-making process.

Yasuda Fire and Marine faced the following situation:

- An increasing number of savings-oriented policies were being sold which had new types of liabilities.
- The Japanese Ministry of Finance imposed many restrictions through insurance law leading to complex constraints.
- The firm's goals included both current yield and long-run total return and that led to multidimensional risks and objectives.

The insurance policies were complex, with a part being actual insurance, and another part an investment with a fixed guaranteed amount plus a bonus dependent on general

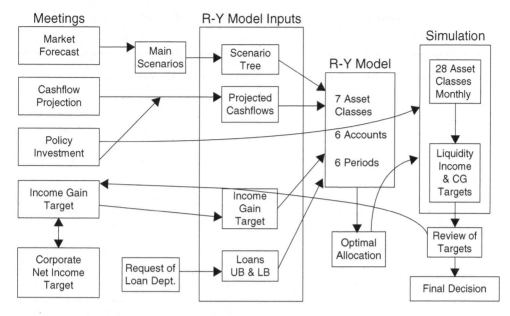

Figure 2.9   Yasuda Kasais asset and liability decision process

business conditions in the industry. The insurance contracts are of varying length; maturing, being renewed or starting in various time periods; and subject to random returns on assets managed, insurance claims paid and bonus payments made. There are many regulations on assets including restrictions on equity, loans, real estate, foreign investment by account, foreign subsidiaries and *tokkin* (pooled accounts). The asset classes were as shown in Table 2.5.

Dividing the universe of available investments into a manageable number of asset classes involves a trade-off between detail and complexity. A large number of asset classes would increase detail at the cost of increasing size. Therefore, the model allows

Table 2.5   Asset classes and their associated indices

Asset	Associated Index
Cash bonds	Nomura bond performance index
Convertible bonds	Nikko research convertible bond index
Domestic equities	TOPIX
Hedged foreign bonds	Salomon Brothers world bond index (or hedged equivalent)
Hedged foreign equities	Morgan Stanley world equity index (or hedged equivalent)
Unhedged foreign bonds	Salomon Brothers world bond index
Unhedged foreign equities	Morgan Stanley world equity index
Loans	Average lending rates (trust/long-term credit (or long-term prime rates))
Money trusts, etc.	Call rates (overnight with collateral)
Life insurance company general accounts	

Table 2.6   Expected allocations for initialization period: INI (100 million yen: % by account)

Total		%
Cash	2053	9
Loans-fl	5598	26
Loans-fx	5674	26
Bonds	2898	13
Equity	1426	7
Foreign bonds	3277	15
Foreign equity	875	4
Total	21800	100

Note: Total book value 1: 22510; total book value 2: 34875.

Table 2.7   Expected allocations in the end effects period

	General	Savings	Spec Savings 1	Spec Savings 2	Exogenous	Total	%
Cash	0	44	0	36	0	80	0.1
Bonds	5945	17	14846	1311	0	22119	40.1
Equity	0	0	4	0	18588	18592	33.7
For bonds	2837	1094	0	0	0	3931	7.1
For equity	0	4650	6022	562	0	11234	20.4
Total	8782	5804	20072	1908	18588	55154	

Note: Total book value 1: 28566; total book value 2: 50547.

the number and definition of asset classes to be specified by the user. There can be different asset classes in different periods. For example, asset classes in earlier periods can be collapsed into aggregate classes in later periods.

A major part of the information from the model is provided in terms of reports consisting of tables and figures of model output. Actual asset allocation results from the model are confidential. But we have the following expected allocations in the initialization (Table 2.6) and end effects periods (Table 2.7). These are averages across scenarios in 100 million yen units and percentages by account.

In summary:

1. The 1991 Russsell–Yasuda Kasai model was then the largest application of stochastic programming in financial services.
2. There was a significant ongoing contribution to Yasuda Kasai's financial performance: US$79 million and US$9 million in income and total return, respectively, over FY91–92, and it has been in use since then.
3. The basic structure is portable to other applications because of flexible model gen-

eration. Indeed, the other models in Table 2.3 are modified versions of the Russell–Yasuda Kasai model.

4. A substantial potential impact in performance of financial services companies.
5. The top 200 insurers worldwide have in excess of $10 trillion in assets.
6. Worldwide pension assets are also about $7.5 trillion, with a $2.5 trillion deficit.
7. The industry is also moving towards more complex products and liabilities and risk based capital requirements.

2.5   DYNAMIC PORTFOLIO THEORY AND PRACTICE

2.5.1   The Kelly Capital Growth Approach

The first category of multiperiod models are those reducable to static models. Part IV of Ziemba and Vickson (1975 [2006]) reprints key papers and discusses important results. It is well known in stochastic programming that n-period concave stochastic programs are theoretically equivalent to concave static problems; see Dantzig (1955). In the theory of optimal investment over time, it is not quadratic utility (the utility function behind the Sharpe ratio) but log utility that yields the most long-term growth. The elegant results based on the Kelly (1956) criterion, as it is known in the gambling literature, and on the capital growth theory, as it is known in the investments literature,[2] that were proved rigorously by Breiman (1961) and generalized by Algoet and Cover (1988), are long-run asymptotic results. However, the Arrow–Pratt absolute risk aversion of the log utility criterion, namely $1/\omega$, is essentially zero. Hence, in the short run, a log utility function can be exceedingly risky with wide swings in wealth values and fractional Kelly strategies are not much safer as their risk aversion indices are $1/\gamma\omega$ where the negative power utility function αW^{α}, $\alpha < 0$. The formula:

$$\gamma = \frac{1}{1 - \alpha}$$

is exact for log-normal assets and approximately correct otherwise; see MacLean et al. (2005).

The myopic property of log utility (optimality is secured with today's data and you do not need to consider the past or future) is derived as follows in the simplest Bernoulli trials (p = probability you win, $q = 1 - p$ = probability you lose a fixed amount). Final wealth after N trials is:

$$X_N = (1 + f)^M (1 - f)^{N-M} X_0$$

where f = fraction bet, X_0 = initial wealth and you win M of N trials. The exponential rate of growth is:

$$G = \lim_{N \to \infty} \log\left(\frac{X_N}{X_0}\right)^{1/N}$$

$$G = \lim_{N \to \infty} \left[\frac{M}{N} \log(1+f) + \frac{N-M}{N} \log(1-f) \right]$$

$$= p\log(1 + f) + q\log(1-f) \text{ by the strong law of large numbers}$$

$$= \text{Elog W}.$$

Thus the criterion of maximizing the long-run exponential rate of asset growth is equivalent to maximizing the one period expected logarithm of wealth. So an optimal policy is myopic. See Hakansson (1971) for generalizations of this myopic policy:

$$\text{Max} \, G(f) = p\log(1+f) + q\log(1-f) \to f^* = p - q.$$

The optimal fraction to bet is the edge $p - q$. The bets can be large: $-\frac{u''}{u'} = \frac{1}{w} \approx 0$:

p	.5	.51	.6	.99
q	.5	.49	.4	.01
f^*	.0	.02	.2	.98

$$f^* = \frac{\text{edge}}{\text{odds}} = \frac{\text{edge}}{10} \text{ with 10-1 situation.}$$

The key to the size of the bet is not the edge, it is the risk. An example was the bet to place and show on Slew O'Gold in the inaugural Breeders' Cup Classic in 1984. $f^* = 64$ percent for place or show suggests fractional Kelly (that is, a lower bet where you blend the Kelly full expected log bet with cash). See the discussion of the Thorp–Ziemba bets on that day in Ziemba and Hausch (1986). In continuous time:

$$f^* = \frac{\mu - r}{\sigma^2} - \frac{\text{edge}}{\text{risk (odds)}}$$

$$g^* = \frac{1}{2} \left(\frac{(\mu - r)^2}{\sigma^2} \right) + r$$

$$= \frac{1}{2}(\text{Sharpe Ratio})^2 + \text{risk free asset.}$$

The classic Breiman (1961) results are: in each period $t = 1, 2, \ldots$, there are K investment opportunities with returns per unit invested $X_{N_1}, \ldots, X_{N_k}$, intertemporally independent with finitely many distinct values:

$$X_N = \sum_{i=1}^{K} \lambda_i X_{N_i}$$

$$\text{Max E log } X_N$$

Property 1: maximizing $E \log X_N$ asymptotically maximizes the rate of asset growth. If, in each time period, two portfolio managers have the same family of investment opportunities and one uses a Λ^* maximizing:

Table 2.8   Simulation results for the Kelly and half-Kelly criteria

Strategy	Final wealth				Number of times the final wealth out of 1000 trials was:				
	Min	Max	Mean	Median	>500	>1000	>10000	>50000	>100000
Kelly	18	483883	48135	17269	916	870	598	302	166
Half Kelly	145	111770	13069	8043	990	954	480	30	1

$$\text{E} \log X_N = \sum_{i=1}^{K} \lambda_i X_{N_i}$$

whereas the other uses an essentially different strategy, for example:

$$\text{Max E} \log X_N(\Lambda^*) - \text{E} \log X_N(\Lambda) \rightarrow \infty$$

then:

$$\lim_{N \rightarrow \infty} \log \frac{X_N(\Lambda^*)}{X_N(\Lambda)} \rightarrow \infty$$

where essentially different means they differ infinitely often. So the actual amount of the fortune exceeds that of any other strategy by more and more as the horizon becomes more distant.

Property 2: the expected time to reach a pre-assigned goal is, asymptotically as X increases, least with a strategy that maximizes E log X_N.

We can learn a lot from the following Kelly and half-Kelly medium time simulations from Ziemba and Hausch (1986). This simulation had 700 independent investments all with a 14 percent advantage, with 1000 simulated runs and w_0 = $1000 (Table 2.8).

The power of the Kelly criterion is shown when 16.6 percent of the time final wealth is 100 times the initial wealth with full Kelly but only once with half Kelly. Thirty percent of the time, final wealth exceeds 50 times initial wealth. But the probability of being ahead is higher with half Kelly 87 percent versus 95.4 percent. So Kelly is much riskier than half Kelly since the minimum wealth is 18 and it is only 145 with half Kelly. With 700 bets all independent with a 14 percent edge, the result is that you can still lose over 98 percent of your fortune with bad scenarios, and half Kelly is not much better with a minimum of 145 or a 85.5 percent loss. Here financial engineering is important to avoid such bad outcomes.

2.5.2   Some Great Investors

The portfolio optimization survey in Figure 2.10 includes the wealth plots of a number of great investors who have successfully used Kelly and fractional Kelly strategies. These include John Maynard Keynes at King's College, University of Cambridge; Warren Buffett of Berkshire Hathaway Hedge Fund (in Figure 2.11); Bill Benter the top race-track bettor in Hong Kong; Ed Thorp, Princeton Newport Hedge Fund; and Jim Simons of Renaissance Medallion.

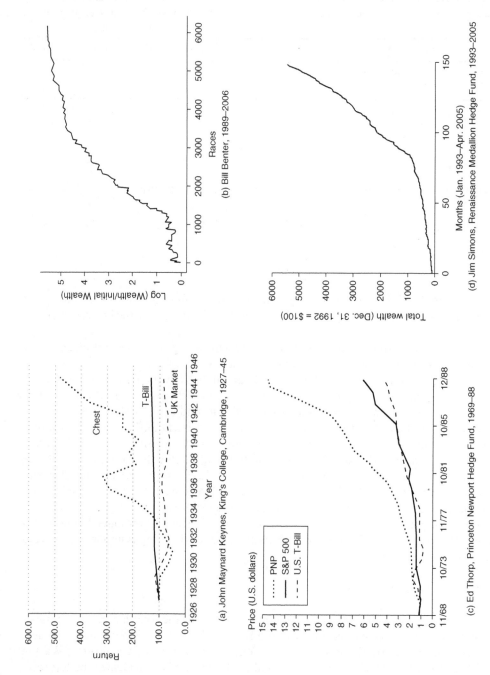

Figure 2.10 Four great investors

Table 2.9   *Comparison of ordinary and symmetric downside Sharpe yearly performance measures, monthly data and arithmetic means*

	Ordinary	Downside
Ford Foundation	0.970	0.920
Tiger Fund	0.879	0.865
S&P 500	0.797	0.696
Berkshire Hathaway	0.773	0.917
Quantum	0.622	0.458
Windsor	0.543	0.495

Source: Ziemba (2005).

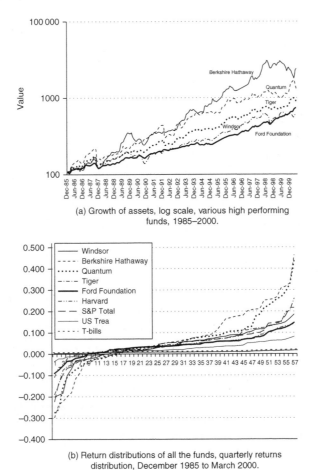

(a) Growth of assets, log scale, various high performing
funds, 1985–2000.

(b) Return distributions of all the funds, quarterly returns
distribution, December 1985 to March 2000.

Sources: Ziemba (2003, 2005).

Figure 2.11   *The wealth paths and return distributions of Berkshire Hathaway, Quantum, Tiger, Windsor, the Ford Foundation and the S&P 500, 1985–2000*

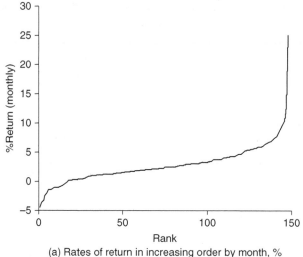

(a) Rates of return in increasing order by month, %

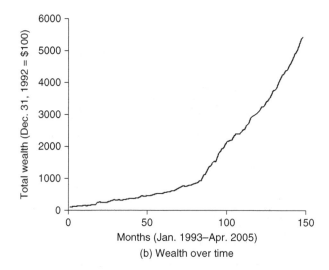

(b) Wealth over time

Source: Ziemba and Ziemba (2007).

Figure 2.12   Medallion Fund, January 1993 to April 2005

Ziemba (2005) argues that a modification of the Sharpe ratio is needed to properly evaluate the great investors as the ordinary Sharpe ratio:

$$S = \frac{\overline{R}_P - R_F}{\sigma_P}$$

penalizes gains. See also the updated paper by Gergaud and Ziemba (2012). The modified measures uses only losses in the calculation of σ_P, namely:

$$\sigma_p = \frac{\sum_{i=1}^{n} (r_i - \bar{r})^2}{n - 1},$$

Where $\bar{r} = 0$ and ( ) – means that only the losses are counted. Using this measure, only Buffett improves upon his Sharpe ratio as shown in Table 2.9. But Buffett is still below the Ford Foundation and the Harvard endowment with downside symmetric Sharpe ratios (DSSRs) near 1.00. The reason for that can be seen in Figure 2.11(b) where Berkshire has the highest monthly gains but also the largest monthly losses of the funds studies. It is clear that Warren Buffett is a long-term Kelly-type investor who is not concerned with monthly losses, just with having a high final wealth. The great hedge fund investors, Thorp at DSSR = 13.8 and Simons at 26.4, dominate the others dramatically. In their cases, the ordinary Sharpe ratio does not show their brilliance. For Simons, the Sharpe was only 1.68.

Simons's wealth graph is one of the best I have seen – see Figure 2.12(b) and Figure 2.12(a) for the distribution of gains and losses; Renaissance Medallion has had a remarkable record and its net of 5 percent management fees and 44 percent incentive fees so the gross returns are about double these net returns. Thorp's returns (Figure 2.10c) are a model for successful hedge fund performance with no yearly or quarterly losses and only three monthly losses in 20 years. See Gergaud and Ziemba (2012) for some funds with even higher DSSRs and one whose results are too good to be true with an infinite DSSR. That one turned out to be a fraud.

NOTES

1. This chapter updates some of my previous work in this area which is cited in the text.
2. See the surveys by Hakansson and Ziemba (1995), MacLean and Ziemba (2006) and Thorp (2006).

REFERENCES

Algoet, P.H. and T. Cover (1988), 'Asymptotic optimality and asymptotic equipartition properties of log-optimum investment', *Annals of Probability*, **16** (2), 876–898.
Arrow, K.J. (1965), 'Aspects of the theory of risk bearing. Technical report', Yrjö Jahnsson Foundation, Helsinki.
Artzner, P., F. Delbaen, J.-M. Eber and D. Heath (1999), 'Coherent measures of risk', *Mathematical Finance*, **9**, 203–228.
Breiman, L. (1961), 'Optimal gambling system for favorable games', *Proceedings of the 4th Berkeley Symposium on Mathematical Statistics and Probability*, **1**, pp. 63–68.
Cariño, D., D. Myers and W.T. Ziemba (1998), 'Concepts, technical issues and uses of the Russell–Yasuda Kasai financial planning model', *Operations Research*, **46** (4), 450–462.
Cariño, D. and W.T. Ziemba (1994), 'The Russell–Yasuda Kasai model: an asset/liability model for a Japanese insurance company using multistage stochastic programming', *Interfaces*, January–February, **24** (1), 29–49.
Cariño, D. and W.T. Ziemba (1998), 'Formulation of the Russell–Yasuda Kasai financial planning model', *Operations Research*, **46** (4), 433–449.
Chopra, V.K. and W.T. Ziemba (1993), 'The effect of errors in mean, variance and co-variance estimates on optimal portfolio choice', *Journal of Portfolio Management*, **19**, 6–11.
Dantzig, G. (1955), 'Linear programming under uncertainty', *Management Science*, **1**, 197–206.
Fleten, S.-E., K. Høyland and S. Wallace (2002), 'The performance of stochastic dynamic and fixed mix portfolio models', *European Journal of Operational Research*, **140** (1), 37–49.
Gergaud, O. and W.T. Ziemba (2012), 'Great investors: their methods, results and evaluation', *Journal of Portfolio Management*, **38** (4), 128–147.

Geyer, A. and W.T. Ziemba (2008), 'The Innovest Austrian pension fund planning model InnoALM', *Operations Research*, **56** (4), 797–810.
Gondzio, J. and R. Kouwenberg (2001), 'High performance computing for asset liability management', *Operations Research*, **49**, 879–891.
Grinold, R.C. and R.N. Khan (1999), *Active Portfolio Management: Quantitative Theory and Applications*, New York: McGraw-Hill.
Hakansson, N.H. (1971), 'On optimal myopic portfolio policies with and without serial correlation', *Journal of Business*, **44**, 324–334.
Hakansson, N.H. and W.T. Ziemba (1995), 'Capital growth theory', in R.A. Jarrow, V. Maksimovic and W.T. Ziemba (eds), *Finance Handbook*, Amsterdam: North-Holland, pp. 123–144.
Hanoch, G. and H. Levy (1969), 'The efficiency analysis of choices involving risk', *Review of Economic Studies*, **36**, 335–346.
Kallberg, J.G. and W.T. Ziemba (1981), 'Remarks on optimal portfolio selection', in G. Bamberg and O. Opitz (eds), *Methods of Operations Research*, Vol. 44, Oelgeschlager: Gunn & Hain, pp. 507–520.
Kallberg, J.G. and W.T. Ziemba (1983), 'Comparison of alternative utility functions in portfolio selection problems', *Management Science*, **29** (11), 1257–1276.
Kallberg, J.G. and W.T. Ziemba (1984), 'Mis-specifications in portfolio selection problems', in G. Bamberg and K. Spremann (eds), *Risk and Capital*, New York: Springer Verlag, pp. 74–87.
Kelly, J. L., Jr (1956), 'A new interpretation of information rate', *Bell System Technical Journal*, **35**, 917–926.
Lintner, J. (1965), 'The valuation of risk assets and the selection of risky investment in stock portfolios and capital budgets', *Review of Economics and Statistics*, **47**, 13–37.
Luenberger, D.G. (1998), *Investment Science*, New York: Oxford University Press.
MacLean, L.C. and W.T. Ziemba (2006), 'Capital growth theory and practice', in S.A. Zenios and W.T. Ziemba (eds), *Handbook of Asset and Liability Management, Volume 1*, Handbooks in Finance, Amsterdam: North-Holland, pp. 139–197.
MacLean, L., W.T. Ziemba and Y. Li (2005), 'Time to wealth goals in capital accumulation and the optimal trade-off of growth versus securities', *Quantitative Finance*, **5** (4), 343–357.
Markowitz, H.M. (1952), 'Portfolio selection', *Journal of Finance*, **7** (1), 77–91.
Markowitz, H.M. (1987), *Mean-Variance Analysis in Portfolio Choice and Capital Markets*, Cambridge, MA: Basil Blackwell.
Mossin, J. (1966), 'Equilibrium in a capital asset market', *Econometrica*, **34**, 768–783.
Murty, K.G. (1972), 'On the number of solutions to the complementarity problem and spanning properties of complementarity cones', *Linear Algebra*, **5**, 65–108.
Pratt, J.W. (1964), 'Risk aversion in the small and in the large', *Econometrica*, **32**, 122–136.
Rockafellar, T. and W.T. Ziemba (2000), 'Modified risk measures and acceptance sets', mimeo, University of Washington, July.
Sharpe, W.F. (1964), 'Capital asset prices: a theory of market equilibrium under conditions of risk', *Journal of Finance*, **19**, 425–442.
Thorp, E.O. (2006), 'The Kelly criterion in blackjack, sports betting and the stock market', in S.A. Zenios and W.T. Ziemba (eds), *Handbook of Asset and Liability Management*, Handbooks in Finance, Amsterdam: North-Holland, pp. 385–428.
Tobin, J. (1958), 'Liquidity preference as behavior towards risk', *Review of Economic Studies*, **25** (2), 65–86.
Wallace, S.W. and W.T. Ziemba (2005), *Applications of Stochastic Programming*, Philadelphia, PA: Society for Industrial and Applied Mathematics.
Zangwill, W.I. (1969), 'Nonlinear programming: a unified approach', Englewood Cliffs, NJ: Prentice Hall.
Zenios, S.A. and W.T. Ziemba (2007), *Handbook of Asset and Liability Management, Volume 2: Applications and Case Studies*, Handbooks in Finance, Amsterdam: North-Holland.
Ziemba, R.E.S. and W.T. Ziemba (2007), *Scenarios for Risk Management and Global Investment Strategies*, Chichester: John Wiley.
Ziemba, W.T. (1974), 'Calculating investment portfolios when the returns have stable distributions', in P.L. Hammer and G. Zoutendijk (eds), *Mathematical Programming in Theory and Practice*, Amsterdam: North-Holland, pp. 443–482.
Ziemba, W.T. (2003), *The Stochastic Programming Approach to Asset Liability and Wealth Management*, Charlottesville, VA: AIMR.
Ziemba, W.T. (2005), 'The symmetric downside risk sharpe ratio and the evaluation of great investors and speculators', *Journal of Portfolio Management*, Fall, 108–122.
Ziemba, W.T. and D.B. Hausch (1986), 'Betting at the racetrack', San Luis Obispo, CA: Dr Z Investments Inc.
Ziemba, W.T., C. Parkan and F.J. Brooks-Hill (1974), 'Calculation of investment portfolios with risk free borrowing and lending', *Management Science*, **21**, 209–222.
Ziemba, W.T. and R.G. Vickson (eds) (1975), *Stochastic Optimization Models in Finance*, New York: Academic Press, reprinted (2013) with a new preface, Singapore: World Scientific.

APPENDIX: ESTIMATING UTILITY FUNCTIONS AND RISK AVERSION

Certainty Equivalent Method

Set $u(w_L) = 0$, $u(w_U) = 1$
Find $w_{0.5}$:

$$u(w_{0.5}) = \tfrac{1}{2}u(w_L) + \tfrac{1}{2}u(w_U)$$

Find $w_{0.25}$, $w_{0.75}$:

$$u(w_{0.25}) = \tfrac{1}{2}u(w_{0.5}) + \tfrac{1}{2}u(w_L)$$

$$u(w_{0.75}) = \tfrac{1}{2}u(w_U) + \tfrac{1}{2}u(w_{0.5})$$

The five points generate u:

$$u(w_{0.25}) = .25$$
$$u(w_{0.5}) = .5$$
$$u(w_{0.75}) = .75$$

Split each range one more to generate nine points.
For Donald Hausch, see Figure 2.2. These values were:

w	−30,000	−26,000	−20,000	−14,000	−5,000	+5,000	20,000	28,000	70,000
$u_2(w)$	0.000	0.125	0.250	0.375	0.500	0.625	0.750	0.875	1.000
	↑								↑
	$u(w_L)$								$u(w_U)$

Gain and Loss Equivalent Method

1. Consider the gambles:

$$A \begin{cases} \text{lose } \tfrac{1}{2} \text{ wealth} & \text{pr} = \tfrac{1}{2} \\ \text{gain x} & \text{pr} = \tfrac{1}{2} \end{cases}$$

or:

$$B \begin{cases} \text{gain } \$5000 & \text{pr} = 1 \end{cases}$$

x_0 is the gain that would make the subject indifferent to a choice between A and B (gain equivalence):

$$u(5000 + w_0) = \frac{1}{2}u(w_0 + x_0) + \frac{1}{2}u\left(\frac{w_0}{2}\right).$$

Set $u(\frac{w_0}{2}) = a, u(w_0 + 5000) = b$.
Hence this yields $u(w^0 + x_0)$.

2. Repeat with probability of winning = 0.2, 0.3, 0.4, 0.6, and 0.8.
3. Consider the gambles:

$$A \begin{cases} \text{lose fraction } y \text{ of wealth} & \text{pr} = \frac{1}{2} \\ \text{gain } x^1 & \text{pr} = \frac{1}{2} \end{cases}$$

or:

$$B \begin{cases} \text{gain } \$5000 & \text{pr} = 1 \end{cases}$$

$\rightarrow y_0$ (loss equivalence)

$$u(5000 + w^2) = \tfrac{1}{2}u(w_0 + x_0) + \tfrac{1}{2}u(w^0(1 - y^0)).$$

Set $u\left(\dfrac{w_0}{2}\right) = a$, and $u(w_0 + 5000) = b$.

4. Repeat with probability of winning = 0.2, 0.3, 0.4, 0.6 and 0.8.
   For Donald Hausch, these values were:

w	− 35,000	− 25,000	− 15,000	− 7,500	+ 2,500	10,000	14,000	18,000	20,000	39,000	70,000
$u1(w)$	− 15.0	− 5.00	− 3.00	− 1.67	0.00	1.00	1.25	1.67	2.00	2.50	5.00

$\uparrow$ $\uparrow$

$u(.5\,w_0)$ $u(w_0 + 5000)$

Points determined by 1,2 are above the loss-equivalent ($w_0 + 5000$) and by 3, 4 are below; see Figure 2.2.

The Kallberg and Ziemba (1983) Method

Kallberg and Ziemba showed that the average Arrow–Pratt risk aversion approximates closely the optimal Rubinstein measure under the normality assumptions. So a consequence is that one can devise risk attitude questions to determine if a particular investor is a $R_A = 4$ (pension fund investor 60:40 mix type) or a risk taker $R_A = 2$ or a conservative investor $R_A = 6$. Kallberg and Ziemba show that the accuracy of such questions is most crucial when R_A is low. The Chopra and Ziemba (1993) results discussed above are consistent with this.

3 Testing for speculative bubbles in asset prices

Keith Anderson, Chris Brooks and Apostolos Katsaris

3.1 INTRODUCTION

Like the prices of assets themselves, interest in speculative bubbles as a research topic moves in cycles. At the time of writing (early 2012), it is a hot topic. Currently, much popular discussion is made of the possibility of bubbles in Chinese real estate prices and precious metal commodities; but, it is argued, bubbles in Western stock and real estate markets have already collapsed, leading to heavy financial losses for some and precipitating deep recessions around the world. Bubbles are certainly not new phenomena, and have been argued to have existed for centuries; examples of very early bubbles include 'tulipmania' (see Garber, 1989, 2000) and the South Sea Bubble (Garber, 2000; Dale et al., 2005, 2007).

Some early approaches to testing for bubbles were implicitly based on the premise that such behaviour in price series can only be caused by investor irrationality. During the growth phase of the bubble, it is argued that investors become 'irrationally exuberant', caught up in their own overenthusiasm such that they become willing to pay too much for assets. Eventually, something (probably a minor outside event) triggers a change in sentiment that causes a rapid reduction in prices and the bubble collapses.

However, while behavioural finance has itself grown in popularity and gained acceptability as a re-emerged subject for research in the past decade, many would still feel uncomfortable at the idea that bubbles can only be generated by irrational behaviour. If that were the case, why would rational investors not be able to see a bubble emerging and start to sell, forcing prices quickly back down before the bubble really took off? And why would the irrational investors who pay too much for assets during periods of bubble growth not be eradicated from the markets when the crash eventually comes (because they lose either their wealth or their jobs)? Of course, there are behavioural answers to these questions but an alternative and perhaps more palatable theory is based on the concept of rational speculative bubbles.

The key argument behind the existence of rational speculative bubbles is that, as the algebra in section 3.2 below will show, at every point during the cycle of a bubble, investors are earning the market-required rate of return, and therefore it will always be rational collectively for the markets to remain invested in the bubble asset. When we look at the rise in prices during the formation and growth of a speculative bubble, it becomes apparent that they tend to rise fairly slowly during the early stages of the bubble's development, but they then grow more and more quickly as the bubble becomes larger and a collapse in prices looks more likely. Thus, as the riskiness of being invested in the asset increases, so do the returns right until the point when the bubble bursts. Those who are holding the bubble asset at this point will inevitably sustain heavy losses, but key to the formation of a bubble is that investors cannot predict precisely when it will collapse. All they can do, perhaps, is to estimate the likelihood of collapse at any given point in time.

If investors were able to forecast when the bubble would collapse, the bubble would unravel back to its inception and could therefore never exist.

An important initial consideration here is the question of exactly what is a bubble. Unfortunately, no universally accepted definition exists, but the best working definition that we have found is from Santoni (1987), which is that bubbles are persistent, systematic and increasing deviations of actual prices from their fundamental values. This is a useful statement of what constitutes a bubble because it compares the actual, traded price of an asset to its underlying or intrinsic value, which is based on the stream of cashflows that will accrue to the holder. For applications to stock markets, fundamentals are usually measured using dividends, and this will be discussed more extensively in section 3.3.

Speculative bubbles are generated when investors include the expectation of a future price in their information set. In essence, they are self-fulfilling prophecies, and Keynes (1936) notes that 'an equity market is an environment in which speculators anticipate what average opinion expects average opinion to be' and thus bubbles can be created when investors include the expectation of the future price in their information set. In a universe comprising a finite number of securities and finite investment horizons, this will lead demand for the security and therefore its price to be a function of expected future prices. As we demonstrate below, when a speculative bubble is present in the price of an asset, bubble returns will lead to increased demand and thus actual prices will increasingly diverge from their fundamental values until such point as the bubble collapses.

The purpose of this chapter is to explain how to test for speculative bubbles in stock prices using a variety of techniques which we then apply to a standard and widely available stock index series (the S&P 500). It draws heavily on material from Brooks and Katsaris (2003) and Brooks and Katsaris (2005a, 2005b), but provides a unifying, integrated approach to testing for bubbles and interpreting the results. The remainder of the chapter is organized as follows. Section 3.2 outlines the core theory and definitions that lie behind the development of tests for the presence of speculative bubbles. Then section 3.3 presents the data that we employ for illustration of the techniques and discusses how a measure of fundamentals can be formed. Section 3.4 proceeds to describe the first of the tests for bubbles that we employ, namely the variance bounds approach, which is then applied and the results discussed. The bubble specification test is considered in section 3.5, followed by the cointegration approach in section 3.6. Section 3.7 presents the regime switching regression model for periodic, partially collapsing speculative bubbles; and finally section 3.8 offers some brief concluding comments.

3.2 DEVELOPING BUBBLE MODELS AND TESTS

We start with some notation and definitions. According to the discounted dividend model, the fundamental value of a stock is the present value of all of its future dividends:

$$p_t^f = \sum_{g=1}^{\infty} \frac{1}{(1 + i)^g} E_t(d_{t+g}) \tag{3.1}$$

where p_t^f is the fundamental price at time t, d_t is the dividend in period t, i is the market discount rate (the required rate of return, which is assumed constant), and $E_t(.)$ is the expectations operator conditioning on information available at time t. If the actual price of the stock, p_t^a, contains a bubble, we can write the following equation for the path of its movements:

$$p_t^a = p_t^f + b_t + u_t \qquad (3.2)$$

where b_t is the bubble component, and u_t is a zero mean, random disturbance term. For a rational speculative bubble to exist, the bubble component of equation (3.2) must grow by the required rate of return (i). In order to ensure no arbitrage opportunities, the bubble in period $t + 1$ must be expected to grow by i relative to its size in the previous period:

$$E_t(b_{t+1}) = (1 + i)b_t \qquad (3.3)$$

It would also be possible to write this equation for the bubble component at time t as:

$$b_t = \frac{E_t(b_{t+1})}{(1 + i)} \qquad (3.4)$$

However, if we are modelling an actual bubble process rather than its expectation, we would write:

$$b_{t+1} = (1 + i)b_t + e_{t+1} \qquad (3.5)$$

where e_{t+1} is the deviation of the bubble at $t + 1$ from its expected value and so it is the 'surprise' in the asset's bubble, which is a zero mean white noise process:

$$e_{t+1} = b_{t+1} - E_t(b_{t+1}) \qquad (3.6)$$

It can already be seen from equation (3.3) that the bubble process is explosive for $i > 0$; however, it is not realistic since it would continue to grow infinitely, only being buffeted up or down by the random shocks, e_t. Therefore, Blanchard (1979) and Blanchard and Watson (1982) propose modifying this set-up by allowing for the bubble to crash to zero with some probability. In mathematical terms, Blanchard suggests that if the bubble survives (the 'surviving regime', S), then the expected bubble in period $t+1$ is:

$$E_t(b_{t+1}) = \frac{1}{q}(1 + i)b_t \qquad (3.7)$$

where q is the probability that the bubble will continue to exist in period $t + 1$, ($0 < q < 1$).

On the other hand, the bubble might burst in period $t + 1$ with probability $1 - q$ (the 'collapsing regime', C) and in that case:

$$E_t(b_{t+1}) = 0 \qquad (3.8)$$

If the bubble does not burst, then the investor will receive the bubble return given by the equation:

$$r_b = \frac{E_t(b_{t+1}) - b_t}{b_t} \tag{3.9}$$

Setting the error term to its expected value of zero, if we substitute (3.7) into (3.9), we will see that for $0 < q < 1$, the return of the bubble component when it survives is bigger than i, which is the required rate of return, and is equal to:

$$r_b = \frac{(1 + i - q)}{q} \tag{3.10}$$

Equation (3.10) expresses the explosive nature of bubble returns because as the probability of the bubble continuing to exist, q, reduces, the return of the bubble component increases disproportionately. Equation (3.10) is thus in accordance with the assumption that risk-averse investors require higher returns as risk increases. Of course, whether the additional return from holding an asset containing a large bubble is sufficient to compensate a specific investor will depend on how risk-averse they are. Needless to say, very risk-averse investors will never knowingly hold bubbly assets.

3.3   DESCRIPTION OF THE DATA USED AND THE CONSTRUCTION OF FUNDAMENTALS

The data that we employ in this chapter comprise the total return index and dividend yield for the S&P 500 Composite Index from January 1965 to October 2011, a total of 562 monthly observations, obtained from Thomson Datastream. However, since total returns are only available from January 1988, for the observations prior to this date we generate a set of total percentage returns by adding the monthly 'cash' dividend to the corresponding price index and dividing by the previous price index. In order to construct the 'cash' dividend series, d_t, we multiply the price index by the dividend yield.[1] The bubble models require the use of real returns, and we therefore deflate the nominal returns using the all items consumer price index (CPI), again obtained from Thomson Datastream.

Some summary statistics for the price and dividend series are presented in Table 3.1. The 'cash' dividend series and stock index series are clearly non-stationary, since the augmented Dickey–Fuller test does not reject the null hypothesis of a unit root even at the 10 per cent level. On the other hand, the first differenced series are both comfortably stationary, although they are skewed and leptokurtic.

There are numerous possible approaches to constructing an appropriate measure of the fundamental price for stocks. The majority are based on dividends, and this makes sense since they represent the actual cashflow that investors receive from holding stocks, although it would also be possible to construct the measure based on earnings (or a combination of earnings and dividends). There also exist several different quantitative approaches to actually constructing the fundamental series from the raw dividend yield

Table 3.1   Summary statistics for S&P and dividend index and change series, January 1965–October 2011

	S&P Price Index	'Cash' dividend series	Monthly change in S&P Index (%)	Monthly change in cash dividend
Mean	512.6153	0.9337	0.5744	0.4552
Median	284.1550	0.8112	1.0512	0.3981
Maximum	1552.500	2.4481	19.6822	16.7873
Minimum	65.20000	0.2155	−23.8836	−9.4113
Standard Dev.	477.7608	0.6156	4.4578	2.5077
Skewness	0.7416	0.6605	−0.4132	0.6451
Kurtosis	1.9420	2.4248	5.6045	9.335
ADF	−0.3780	0.3131	−24.2232	−5.5665
	(0.9101)	(0.9789)	(0.0000)	(0.0000)

Note: The lag length for the augmented Dickey–Fuller (ADF) test is selected using SBIC. The figures in parentheses for the ADF test are *p*-values. The 10% critical value is −2.5695.

data. For instance, the Campbell and Shiller (1987) methodology can allow for predictable time-variation in the growth rate of dividends, although the approach assumes that both the actual spread and the dividend growth rate are stationary. However, if the actual spread is not stationary, this may lead to spurious regression problems and inefficient forecasts of the theoretical spread for those sectors.

We therefore adopt for illustrative purposes two methods for constructing the fundamental series based on dividends. Firstly, we employ the Gordon growth model for the variance bounds, bubble specification and cointegration tests. We then employ the dividend multiple fundamental measure in connection with the regime switching approach. It would be possible to use either approach with any of the tests, and we only employ both to demonstrate that different techniques are possible.

3.3.1   The Gordon Growth Model

The approach involves using a constant discount rate i and a constant growth rate of dividends, g, calculated using only data available up to that point in time. The Gordon growth fundamental value estimate for time t is then:

$$p_t^f = \frac{(1 + g)}{(g \quad i)} d_{t-1} \tag{3.11}$$

3.3.2   The Dividend Multiple Fundamental Measure

The dividend multiple measure of fundamentals is employed by van Norden and Schaller (1999). Assuming that dividends follow a geometric random walk, that is, that log dividends follow a random walk with a drift, it can be shown that the fundamental price of a stock will be equal to a multiple of current dividends:

$$p_t^f = \rho d_t \qquad (3.12)$$

Where $\rho = \dfrac{1 + r}{e^{(a+\frac{\sigma^2}{2})} - 1}$.

Our measure of ρ is an approximation based on the sample mean of the long-term price–dividend ratio, that is, the inverse of the long-term dividend yield. To ensure that there is no look-ahead bias in the calculation of this measure, the long-term average is calculated using only data available up to that month. The dividend-based fundamental price is then the current annual dividend being paid multiplied by ρ as per equation (3.12).

Hence the relative bubble size as a proportion of the actual value is given by:

$$B_t = \frac{b_t}{p_t^a} = \frac{p_t^a - p_t^f}{p_t^a} = 1 - \frac{\rho d_t}{p_t^a} \qquad (3.13)$$

3.4   VARIANCE BOUNDS TESTS

In general, if a speculative bubble is present, the variance of the stock price will be greater than the variance of the fundamental price and hence tests for the presence of excess volatility are based on a comparison of the variance of actual prices with the variance of fundamental prices. In most cases, the fundamental prices are constructed using *ex post* analysis, but several researchers have tried to model and forecast the dividend series in order to construct fundamental prices that are similar to the prices perceived by investors.

Mankiw et al. (1985) developed a 'second-generation' variance bounds test. They augment the simple variance bound with a naive forecast of fundamental values that is formed based on a naive information set:[2]

$$p_t^n = E_t \sum_{g=0}^{\infty} i^g (d_{t+g}|I_t) \qquad (3.14)$$

where p_t^n is a naive forecast of fundamental values estimated under the assumption that the last dividend payment will be the level of dividends for all future dates: $(E_t^n(d_{t+g}) = d_{t-1}, \forall g = 1,2,\ldots,\infty)$ and I_t is a naive information set. Mankiw et al. then argue that the following identity must hold:

$$(p_t^f - p_t^n) \equiv (p_t^f - p_t^a) + (p_t^a - p_t^n) \qquad (3.15)$$

Note that the first term in parentheses on the right-hand side is equal to the error term of the first variance bounds test. If this error term is rational then it will be uncorrelated with the naive information set and thus the two terms on the right-hand side will be uncorrelated:

$$E[(p_t^f - p_t^a)(p_t^a - p_t^n)|I_t] = 0 \qquad (3.16)$$

If equation (3.16) holds, then we can take the square of equation (3.15):

$$E[(p_t^f - p_t^n)^2 | I_t] = E[(p_t^f - p_t^a)^2 | I_t] + E[(p_t^a - p_t^n)^2 | I_t] + 2E[((p_t^f - p_t^a)(p_t^a - p_t^n))^2 | I_t]$$
(3.17)

$$E[(p_t^f - p_t^n)^2 | I_t] = E[(p_t^f - p_t^a)^2 | I_t] + E[(p_t^a - p_t^n)^2 | I_t]$$
(3.18)

If we assume rational expectations, then we can solve equation (3.18) for any past information set and thus rewrite the equation as:

$$E[(p_t^f - p_t^n)^2 | I_{t-g}] = E[(p_t^f - p_t^a)^2 | I_{t-g}] + E[(p_t^a - p_t^n)^2 | I_{t-g}] \ \forall g \geq 0$$
(3.19)

Equation (3.16) implies two testable implications:

$$E[(p_t^f - p_t^n)^2 | I_0] \geq E[(p_t^f - p_t^a)^2 | I_0]$$
(3.20)

$$E[(p_t^f - p_t^n)^2 | I_0] \geq E[(p_t^a - p_t^n)^2 | I_0]$$
(3.21)

Equation (3.20) states that the *ex post* rational fundamental process (p_t^f) is better forecasted by the *ex ante* rational process (p_t^a) than by the naive process (p_t^n). Equation (3.21) states that the *ex post* rational fundamental process must fluctuate more around the naive forecast of fundamentals than the *ex ante* rational fundamental process.

Mankiw et al. show that in order to derive these inequalities, there is no need to assume stationarity of the fundamentals and that these inequalities avoid the bias of the original variance bounds test caused by the *ex ante* assumption of a limited information set. They apply this variance bounds test to annual S&P 500 data for the period 1872–1983, and find that it still rejects the joint null hypothesis of market efficiency and of no bubbles for all reasonable values of the discount factor. Other variance bounds tests that take into account the non-stationarity of the fundamental processes are due to Meese and Singleton (1983), West (1986, 1988), Campbell and Shiller (1988), Shiller (1989) and LeRoy and Parke (1992).

Early versions of the variance bounds tests assume that the discount rate is exogenous and constant. In an effort to deal with changing investor risk aversion, Grossman and Shiller (1981) try to insert a variable discount rate that is generated from a variable risk aversion utility function. Their results show that although these *ex post* fundamental prices have larger variance than constant discount rate, *ex post* fundamentals, the no-bubble hypothesis is again rejected, as actual prices are still more volatile. A similar variance bounds test, with fundamental values that allow for varying expected returns, is presented in Campbell and Shiller (1988). Their results on annual data of the S&P 500 for the same period show that the variation of actual prices is not warranted by the fundamental model.

A different critique of variance bounds tests for the presence of speculative bubbles is presented in Kleidon (1986). Kleidon notes that we should not compare time series variances of actual prices and fundamental values. On the contrary, the inequalities stated above should in fact restrict the variance of prices with the cross-sectional variance of expected fundamental values at any point in time. Kleidon shows through simulation that even constructed *ex post*, fundamental prices with no bubbles reject the simple variance bounds. This is because actual prices are the present value of all the possible future economies and thus we should compare the variance of actual prices with the variance of the distribution of expected future economies.

From the above, we conclude that the violation of condition (3.21) should not be taken as a rejection of the no-bubble hypothesis, since a violation of the variance bound(s) can be caused by several other factors that cannot be statistically quantified and included in the fundamental model. Overall, variance bounds tests are unreliable since they have very low statistical power and are biased towards rejection of the no-bubble hypothesis. Most models of fundamentals are mis-specified as they are not formed based on an information set similar to the one investors use, and thus they exclude relevant variables. Furthermore, some of these tests use dividend and price series that are non-stationary. This leads to biased variance estimates and so the test results are unreliable. Moreover, the variance bounds approach can only test for bubbles that are uncorrelated with fundamentals. If the bubble process is correlated with the fundamental process then it might have the same variance and will thus be undetected. Finally, variance bounds tests are not just examining the presence of bubbles but are joint tests of the validity of the fundamental model and of no bubbles. Although we cannot draw any certain conclusion for the existence of bubbles from these tests, a violation of the variance bound is a necessary but not sufficient condition, and thus merely constitutes a hint of the existence of speculative bubbles.

Not withstanding the problems that exist with variance bounds tests, we still consider this approach a logical starting point for testing the presence of speculative bubbles. Because dividends and prices are not stationary in their levels, as seen in Table 3.1, we cannot use the original variance bounds tests and we therefore initially examine the improved version of Mankiw et al. (1985).

As the variances of both fundamental and actual values are taken around the naive forecast, there is no problem of non-stationarity in this test. We examine whether equations (3.20) and (3.21) are violated by the data. Since the naive forecast assumes that dividends are constant over time, our measure of naive fundamental values is now given from the following equation:

$$p_t^n = \frac{d_{t-1}}{i} \tag{3.22}$$

In equation (3.22), we use the average monthly real total return of the entire sample as the discount rate. Note that the naive fundamental value is not required to be well specified. Furthermore, Mankiw et al. only examine the *ex post* warranted fundamental values, whereas we apply this test to the Gordon growth fundamentals described above. All regressions and calculations are performed in Matlab 7.12.0 except for the computation of summary statistics and the cointegration test, which is conducted using EViews 6.

The results of both variance bounds for the S&P 500 for the period January 1965 to October 2011 are found in Table 3.2. The figures in the table show the mean squared error of the spreads described in equations (3.20) and (3.21). In order to adjust for heteroscedasticity, since the S&P 500 grows through time and thus the errors may grow accordingly, we follow Mankiw et al. and divide each error by the corresponding actual value of the S&P 500. Equations (3.20) and (3.21) are thus calculated using percentage errors.

Table 3.2   S&P 500 Mankiw, Romer and Shapiro (1985) variance bounds test results, January 1965–October 2011

Variance inequality (20)	$E[(p_t^f - p_t^n)^2\|I_0]$	$E[(p_t^f - p_t^a)^2\|I_0]$
	0.0173	0.1060
Variance inequality (21)	$E[(p_t^f - p_t^n)^2\|I_0]$	$E[(p_t^a - p_t^n)^2\|I_0]$
	0.0173	0.0464

Note: Fundamental values are calculated using the Gordon growth model. The naive forecast of fundamentals is calculated using equation (3.22).

From the results, we can see that both inequalities are violated for the constructed fundamental values. The first part of Table 3.2 examines the hypothesis that the actual price is a more accurate forecast of the rational fundamental value than the naive forecast of the fundamentals. This variance bound is rejected, implying that the naive estimate is a better forecast of the fundamental process than the actual price. This could be attributed to the presence of a speculative bubble in the S&P 500. The second part of the table examines the hypothesis that the fundamental value is more volatile around the naive forecast than the actual price. This hypothesis is also rejected, thus suggesting that prices are too volatile to be explained by fundamental values.

3.5   BUBBLE SPECIFICATION TEST

In this section we apply the Dezhbakhsh and Demirguc-Kunt (1990) specification test to the monthly series of S&P 500 for the period 1965–2011, as described below. We first identify the dividend process and examine its structural stability. Dezhbakhsh and Demirguc-Kunt apply the test to the levels of the series. However, the price and dividend series are non-stationary in the levels throughout our entire sample. For this reason, we must model dividends in first differences. Therefore, we run regressions of the form (using standard notation):

$$\Delta(d_t) = \phi_o + \phi_1\Delta(d_{t-1}) + \ldots + \phi_p\Delta(d_{t-p}) + \theta_1 u_{t-1} + \ldots + \theta_q u_{t-q} + u_t \quad (3.23)$$

In order to select the lag length of the dividend process, we use the Breusch–Godfrey serial correlation LM test for model misspecification and find that the 'best' model for dividend changes is one where the current change in dividends is modelled on the one lagged and seven lagged dividend changes as well as an MA(2) process:

$$\Delta(d_t) = \phi_o + \phi_1\Delta(d_{t-1}) + \phi_2\Delta(d_{t-7}) + \theta_1\Delta(u_{t-1}) + \theta_2\Delta(u_{t-2}) + u_t \quad (3.24)$$

The results of regression (3.24) are presented in Table 3.3. As shown in the second part of the table, there is no residual autocorrelation in the model and it appears to be structurally stable, since the test rejects the hypothesis that the series contains a breakpoint

Table 3.3   S&P 500 results for dividend process specification equation January 1965–
October 2011

Coefficient	Coefficient value	Test statistic
φ_0	0.0011	0.5577
φ_1	0.9810	18.3271***
φ_2	−0.0614	−2.2022**
θ_1	−1.4241	−24.6625***
θ_2	0.5168	13.0526***
Serial Correlation χ^2_p Test (12 Lags)		1.1535
χ^2_1 Breakpoint Test 1989:01		1.1393
Ramsey RESET F-Test		1.4561

Note: The results are for equation (3.24). The serial correlation test is the Breusch–Godfrey test performed on 12 lags. The breakpoint test is the Chow Test for a breakpoint in 1989:01. The Ramsey RESET test is performed using one fitted value of the dependent variable.

in January 1989. We employ this date somewhat arbitrarily since it is approximately the middle of our sample. Finally, as an additional check, we perform a Ramsey RESET test with one fitted value to see if the model is correctly specified. This test does not reject the hypothesis of correct model specification. We can therefore continue with this process of testing for bubbles as the model is sufficient to estimate future dividend changes.

We can now proceed to examine the validity of the two-period present-value model described in equation (3.25) below. In order to estimate the equation, we follow West (1987) and Dezhbakhsh and Demirguc-Kunt (1990) and examine the present value relationship in a single period setting:[3]

$$p_t^a = \theta(p_{t+1}^a + d_{t+1}) + z_t \qquad (3.25)$$

where $\theta = 1/(1 + i)$ is the real discount factor $(0 < \theta < 1)$.

In equation (3.25), the residuals must be serially uncorrelated if expectations are formed rationally since $z_t = \theta(E[p_{t+1}^a + d_{t+1}|H_t] - (p_{t+1}^a + d_{t+1}))$ where H_t is the information set used to form expectations and contains variables such as current and past dividends and prices. However, the residuals are heteroscedastic and correlated with the regressors. For this reason, we follow West (1987) and estimate equation (3.25) using a two-stage instrumental variables method. The instruments used are the first and seventh lagged dividend differences identified in equation (3.24) since Hansen and Sargent (1981) state that only the autoregressive terms should be taken into account.

The first step is a standard two-stage least squares estimation, while the second stage uses the Newey and West (1987) method to adjust for arbitrary heteroscedasticity and thus provides a consistent and efficient coefficient estimate for equation (3.25). The results from estimating this equation are presented in Table 3.4. We can see that the estimate of the real discount factor is 0.9961, implying a discount rate of approximately 0.39

*Table 3.4   Results for S&P 500 single period present value relationship January 1965–
October 2011*

Coefficient	Coefficient Value	p-value
θ	0.996124	0.0000
Serial Correlation χ^2_p Test (12 Lags)	18.0686	0.1136
χ^2_1 Breakpoint Test 1989:01	0.0458	0.8306
Ramsey RESET	0.2077	0.6487

Note: See the notes of Table 3.3. The results are for equation (3.25) estimated using two-step, two-stage
least squares with the instruments being the significant dividend lags identified for equation (3.24).

per cent on a monthly basis, which is close to the average total return for the S&P 500 in
our sample (0.48 per cent on a monthly basis).

In the third row of Table 3.4, we find, as in West (1987) and Dezhbakhsh and
Demirguc-Kunt (1990), that the residuals are serially uncorrelated up to 12 lags. This is
a prerequisite if expectations are to be rational over the entire sample. Furthermore, we
test the series for the presence of a breakpoint in January 1989. This is useful in order
to identify whether the assumption of a constant discount rate over the entire sample is
correct, since if there is a breakpoint in the series, it would imply that the discount rate is
different across time. As can be seen, there is no breakpoint in the data halfway through
the sample, implying that the assumption of a constant discount rate is adequate, at least
with respect to this potential break date.

Furthermore, we examine the specification of the present value relationship using a
RESET Test. The result of this test are presented in the final row of Table 3.4 and we can
see that the present-value relationship is valid and well specified for the entire sample,
and therefore we can use equations (3.24) and (3.25) to test the presence of a bubble.
This test is performed by omitting the bubble term from the following equation and then
examining:

$$p_t^a = \gamma_o + \gamma_1 \Delta d_{t-1} + \gamma_2 \Delta d_{t-7} + u_t \tag{3.26}$$

If prices are only a function of dividends, then omitting a possible bubble term b_t should
not affect the specification of equation (3.26). However, if a bubble that is correlated
with the fundamentals is present, then the omission of the bubble term will render the
coefficient estimates of (3.26) inconsistent. We run equation (3.26) without the bubble
term, and use Newey and West's (1987) method to adjust for heteroscedasticity; the
results are presented in Table 3.5.

The findings indicate that equation (3.26) is correctly specified for the entire sample
(despite the fact that none of the parameters in the first panel of Table 3.5 are statistically
significant) and hence no bubble premium can be detected in this period. However, when
we examine sub-periods (see Table 3.6), we see that the model is not correctly specified
for the period January 1984 to December 1999, implying that there was a bubble of this
form in that period.

Table 3.5   Results for the S&P 500 index bubble specification test January 1888–January 2001, transformed data

Coefficient	Coefficient Value	p-value
γ_0	1.0996	0.5382
γ_1	−81.5210	0.0522
γ_2	−65.3622	0.1244
Serial Correlation χ_p^2 Test	17.9666	0.1167
χ_{q+1}^2 Breakpoint Test 1989:01	2.9164	0.4047
Ramsey RESET F-Test	0.3606	0.8495

Note: See the notes of Table 3.3. The results are for equation (3.26) estimated with OLS and by omitting the unobservable bubble term.

Table 3.6   Results for the S&P 500 Index bubble specification test subsample RESET test results

Subsamples	Test value	p-value
1965:01–1983:12	0.0300	0.8627
1984:01–1999:12	4.1545**	0.0429
2000:01–2009:03	0.0321	0.8581
2009:04–2011:10	0.0029	0.9573

Note: See the notes of Table 3.3.

3.6   COINTEGRATION TESTS

Diba and Grossman (1988a, 1988b) employ a cointegration approach to test for the presence of speculative bubbles. If prices and dividends are unit root processes in their levels, which is indeed the case according to the Dickey–Fuller test results in Table 3.1, then if the two series are not cointegrated this is usually taken as evidence for speculative bubbles. We could adopt either the Engle–Granger or Johansen procedures here, and we opt for the latter with an intercept but no trend in both the cointegrating equation and the vector autoregression (VAR), together with an arbitrary four lags in the latter. The trace statistic value for the null hypothesis of no cointegrating vectors is 5.2955 with critical value 15.4947 and p-value 0.7767; the maximum test statistic has a value 5.0929 with critical value 14.2646 and p-value 0.7300. The conclusion is therefore that the price index and 'cash' dividend index are not cointegrated, and this is consistent with the existence of speculative bubbles in the S&P 500. This finding therefore contradicts that of the whole sample results in section 3.5, but it appears to be in the nature of bubble tests that different approaches sometimes yield different conclusions.

3.7   THE REGIME SWITCHING APPROACH

While the key advantage of the early approaches to modelling bubbles without presuming investor irrationality described in section 3.2 is their simplicity, there are several crucial disadvantages. Firstly under this specification, in order for a bubble to exist at any point in time, it must have been present since the asset's first trading day. Secondly when a bubble collapses, it does so completely to zero and can then never subsequently regenerate. Finally, this framework cannot entertain the possibility of negative bubbles, where actual prices are below fundamentals, and yet empirical observation suggests that there have been periods throughout history where this phenomenon has occurred.

These limitations led Evans (1991) to propose a slightly more general formulation where partial collapses are possible. However, the model relies upon an arbitrary threshold for determining when the process is in the surviving and collapsing regimes and was never empirically implemented. Subsequently, in a series of important papers, van Norden and Shaller (1993, 1997, 1999; hereafter vNS) develop a regime switching approach that can allow for periodically, partially collapsing bubbles. They consider the following bubble process:

$$
E_t(b_{t+1}) \;=\;
\begin{cases}
\dfrac{(1+r)b_t}{q(B_t)} - \dfrac{1 - q(B_t)}{q(B_t)} u(B_t)p_t^a & \text{with probability } q(B_t) \\[4mm]
u(B_t)p_t^a & \text{with probability } 1 - q(B_t)
\end{cases}
\tag{3.27}
$$

where B_t is the size of the bubble relative to the actual price p_t^a, $(B_t = b_t/p_t^a)$, $u(B_t)$ is a continuous and everywhere differentiable function such that: $u(0) = 0$, and $0 \le \partial u(B)/\partial B_t < 1$. $q(B_t)$ is the probability of the bubble continuing to exist, and is a negative function of the absolute size of the bubble relative to the stock's fundamental value.

To ensure that the estimates of the probability of survival are bounded between zero and one, vNS employ a probit specification:

$$
q(B_t) = \Omega(\beta_{q,0} + \beta_{q,b}|B_t|)
\tag{3.28}
$$

where Ω is the standard normal cumulative density function, $\Omega(\beta_{q,0})$ is the constant probability of being in the surviving regime when the size of the bubble is equal to zero, and $\beta_{q,b}$ is the sensitivity of the probability of survival to the absolute size of the bubble as a proportion of the price. vNS also allow for partial bubble collapses by letting the expected bubble size in the collapsing state be a function of the relative bubble size.

The vNS model can be used in order to specify asset returns as state dependent, where the state is unobservable. This implies that the security's gross returns are given, under certain assumptions about the dividend process, by the following non-linear switching model:[4]

$$
E_t(r_{t+1}|W_{t+1} = S) = \left[M(1 - B_t) + \frac{MB_t}{q(B_t)} - \frac{1 - q(B_t)}{q(B_t)}u(B_t) \right] \text{ with probability } q(B_t)
\tag{3.29}
$$

$$E_t(r_{t+1}|W_{t+1} = C) = [M(1 - B_t) + u(B_t)] \text{ with probability } 1 - q(B_t) \quad (3.30)$$

where $(r_{t+1}|W_{t+1} = S)$ denotes the gross return of period $t + 1$ conditioning on the fact that the state at time $t + 1$ is the survival state (S) and on all other available information at time t, W_{t+1} is an unobserved indicator that determines the state in which the process is at time $t + 1$, C denotes the collapsing state and M is the gross fundamental return on the security.

In order to estimate the model, vNS linearize equations (3.29) and (3.30) to derive a linear regime switching model for gross stock market returns where $q(B_t)$ is the probability of being in regime S:

$$r_{t+1}^S = \beta_{S,0} + \beta_{S,b}B_t + u_{S,t+1} \quad (3.31a)$$

$$r_{t+1}^C = \beta_{C,0} + \beta_{C,b}B_t + u_{C,t+1} \quad (3.31b)$$

$$q(B_t) = \Omega(\beta_{q,0} + \beta_{q,b}|B_t|) \quad (3.31c)$$

In (3.31), $u_{S,t+1}$ and $u_{C,t+1}$ are the unexpected gross returns of period $t + 1$ in the surviving and collapsing regimes respectively, and are assumed zero mean and constant variance normal random variables.

Several further extensions of the model have been developed, including the addition of trading volume as an explanatory variable in (3.31a) and (3.31c) (see Brooks and Katsaris, 2005b), and a three-regime model, where the additional regime allows for the bubble to remain dormant for a period and grow only at the required rate of return (see Brooks and Katsaris, 2005a). A multivariate extension that allows the joint modelling of the bubbles in several related assets was proposed by Anderson et al. (2010).

Under the assumption that the disturbances follow a normal distribution, the model given by (3.31a) to (3.31c) can be estimated using maximum likelihood via the following log-likelihood function:

$$\ell(r_{t+1}|\xi) = \sum_{t=1}^{T} \ln\left[P(r_{t+1}|W_{t+1} = S)\frac{\omega\left(\frac{r_{r+1} - \beta_{S,0} - \beta_{S,b}B_t}{\sigma_S}\right)}{\sigma_S} \right.$$
$$\left. + P(r_{t+1}|W_{t+1} = C)\frac{\omega\left(\frac{r_{t+1} - \beta_{C,0} - \beta_{C,b}B_t}{\sigma_C}\right)}{\sigma_C} \right] \quad (3.32)$$

where ξ is the set of parameters over which we maximize the likelihood function including $\beta_{S,0}, \beta_{S,b}, \beta_{S,V}, \beta_{C,b}, \beta_{C,0}, \beta_{q,0}, \beta_{q,B}, \gamma_{q,V}, \sigma_S, \sigma_C$. ω is the standard normal probability density function (pdf), σ_S (σ_C) is the standard deviation of the disturbances in the surviving (collapsing) regime, and $P(r_{t+1}|W_{t+1} = C) = 1 - P(r_{t+1}|W_{t+1} = S)$. Note that the maximization of this log-likelihood function produces consistent and efficient estimates of the parameters in ξ as it does not require any assumptions about which regime generated a given observation.

The regime switching approach to testing for bubbles essentially involves estimating the model given by equations (3.31a) to (3.31c) above using maximum likelihood with the function given by equation (3.32) and examining the plausibility of the coefficients obtained. Then, from the first-order Taylor series expansion, we can derive certain conditions that must hold if the periodically collapsing speculative bubble model has explanatory power for stock market returns. If the above model can explain the variation in future returns, then this would be evidence in favour of the presence of in the periodically collapsing speculative bubbles data. These restrictions are:

$$\beta_{S,0} \neq \beta_{C,0} \tag{a}$$

$$\beta_{C,b} < 0 \tag{b}$$

$$\beta_{S,b} > \beta_{C,b} \tag{c}$$

$$\beta_{q,b} < 0 \tag{d}$$

Restriction (a) implies that the mean return across the two regimes is different, so that there exist two distinct regimes, although we cannot say anything about the relative size of these coefficients. Restriction (b) implies that the expected return should be negative if the collapsing regime is observed. This means that the bubble must be smaller in the following period if the bubble collapses. Note that the opposite holds for negative bubbles: the larger the negative bubble, the more positive the returns in the collapsing regime. Restriction (c) ensures that the bubble yields higher (lower) returns if a positive (negative) bubble is observed in the surviving regime than in the collapsing regime. Restriction (d) must hold since the probability of the bubble continuing to exist is expected to decrease as the size of the bubble increases.

We examine the power of the model to capture bubble effects in the returns of the S&P 500 by testing it against three simpler specifications that capture stylized features of stock market returns using a likelihood ratio test. Firstly, we examine whether the effects captured by the switching model can be explained by a more parsimonious model of changing volatility. In order to test this alternative, we follow vNS and jointly impose the following restrictions:

$$\beta_{C,0} = \beta_{S,0} \tag{3.33a}$$

$$\beta_{S,b} = \beta_{C,b} = \beta_{q,b} = 0 \tag{3.33b}$$

$$\sigma_S \neq \sigma_C \tag{3.33c}$$

Restriction (3.33a) implies that the mean return across the two regimes is the same, and restriction (3.33b) states the bubble deviation has no explanatory power for next-period returns or for the probability of being in the surviving regime. The later point suggests that there is a constant probability of being in the surviving regime as stated in restriction (3.33c).

In order to separate restrictions (3.33a) and (3.33b), we examine whether returns can be characterized by a simple mixture of normal distributions model, which only allows mean returns and variances to differ across the two regimes. This mixture of normal distributions model implies the following restrictions:

$$\beta_{S,b} = \beta_{C,b} = \beta_{q,b} = 0 \tag{3.34}$$

Another possible alternative is that of mean reversion in prices as described by Cutler et al. (1991). Under the fads model, returns are linearly predictable although mean returns do not differ across regimes. Furthermore, the deviation of actual prices from the fundamentals has no predictive ability for the probability of being in the surviving regime. The returns in the two regimes are characterized by different variances of residuals but are the same linear functions of bubble deviations. The fads model is thus:

$$r_{t+1}^S = \beta_0 + \beta_b B_t + u_{S,t+1}$$

$$r_{t+1}^C = \beta_0 + \beta_b B_t + u_{C,t+1} \tag{3.35}$$

$$q_t = \Omega(\beta_{q,0})$$

In the above equations, $u_{t+1} \sim N(0, \sigma_S^2)$ with probability q_t, and $u_{t+1} \sim N(0, \sigma_C^2)$ with probability $1-q_t$.

3.7.1   Results from the Regime Switching Model

The first panel of Table 3.7 presents the results from the van Norden and Shaller model. Although several of the key parameters are not statistically significantly different from zero, all have correct signs and are of plausible magnitudes. The intercept parameter in the surviving regime, $\beta_{S,0}$, is 1.0075, which corresponds to an expected return conditional upon a zero bubble size of 0.75 per cent per month (or around 9.4 per cent on an annualized basis with a p–value of less than 0.001). On the other hand, the intercept parameter in the collapsing regime, $\beta_{C,0}$, is 0.9930, which corresponds to an expected return conditional upon a zero bubble size of −0.70 per cent per month (or around −8.7 per cent on an annualized basis with a p–value of <0.001). The coefficients in the surviving and collapsing regimes on the bubble terms, $\beta_{S,b}$ and $\beta_{C,b}$ respectively, have positive and negative signs as expected, implying that returns are a positive function of the size of the bubble in the surviving regime and a negative function of it in the collapsing regime, although neither is statistically significant. The probability of being in the surviving regime in the next period is a negative and significant (p-value 0.0412) function of the size of the bubble. Finally, the standard deviation of the error terms in the surviving regime (0.0358) is around half its value in the collapsing regime (0.0736), indicating as expected that returns in the collapsing regime will typically be considerably more volatile.

In the next panel of Table 3.7, we present the results from the restriction tests for whether the regime switching speculative bubble model parameters are appropriate. There are four tests, and for the model to be deemed well specified, we would want to reject the null hypothesis of equality in all cases. However, only for the final restriction, that the probability of bubble survival is a negative function of the size of the bubble, is the null rejected (and even then, only at the 10 per cent level of significance). For the

Table 3.7   Parameter estimates from the van Norden and Shaller model

Coefficient	Estimate	Std. error	p-value
$\beta_{S,0}$	1.0075	0.0030	0.0000
$\beta_{S,b}$	0.0022	0.0075	0.3815
$\beta_{C,0}$	0.9930	0.0124	0.0000
$\beta_{C,b}$	−0.0216	0.0295	0.2316
$\beta_{q,0}$	1.4727	0.6170	0.0087
$\beta_{q,b}$	−1.5363	0.8827	0.0412
σ^S	0.0358	0.0033	0.0000
σ^C	0.0736	0.0150	0.0000

Speculative bubble model restrictions LR tests

Restriction	LR test statistic	p-value
$\beta_{S,0} \neq \beta_{C,0}$	1.1344	0.2868
$\beta_{C,b} < 0$	0.6859	0.4076
$\beta_{S,b} > \beta_{C,b}$	0.6125	0.4338
$\beta_{q,b} < 0$	3.4851	0.0619

Robustness of speculative bubble models against stylized alternatives LR tests

Restriction	LR test statistic	p-value
Volatility Regimes	2.3144	0.6781
Mixture of Normals	4.3618	0.2249
Fads	6.6595	0.0836

Notes: The model is given by equations (3.31a) to (3.31c) and the coefficients are estimated using maximum likelihood via equation (3.32). The *p*-values are calculated using standard errors estimated from the inverse of the Hessian matrix at the optimum. The volatility regimes test imposes the restrictions: $\beta_{S,0} = \beta_{C,0}$ and $\beta_{S,b} = \beta_{C,b} = \beta_{q,b} = 0$. The mixture of normals test imposes the restrictions $\beta_{S,b} = \beta_{C,b} = \beta_{q,b} = \beta_{S,V} = \gamma_{q,b} = 0$. The fads test imposes the restrictions $\beta_{S,0} = \beta_{C,0}$, $\beta_{S,b} = \beta_{C,b}$ and $\beta_{q,b} = 0$.

other three tests – that the intercepts in the two regimes are equal, that the return is a negative function of the size of the bubble in the collapsing regime, and that the parameter on the lagged bubble size is larger in the surviving regime – than the collapsing regime, the null is not rejected.

Together, the evidence in the three panels of Table 3.7 provides only very limited support for the notion that a periodic, partially collapsing speculative bubble model is a good description of the S&P 500 Composite Index over our sample period. However, a key issue that can provide further evidence on the appropriateness of the model is whether it is able to predict market collapses; in other words, does the probability of collapse rise before the S&P 500 index falls? In another context, this argument is often used by defenders of the capital asset pricing model: the assumptions might stretch credibility, but the acid test is whether its predictions are useful in the real world. In anticipation of our findings, the answer to this question is yes, but only to some extent. To this end, Figure 3.1 plots the S&P 500 Return Index and its fundamental value (on the left-hand scale) against the probability of collapse estimated from the vNS model (on the right-hand scale).

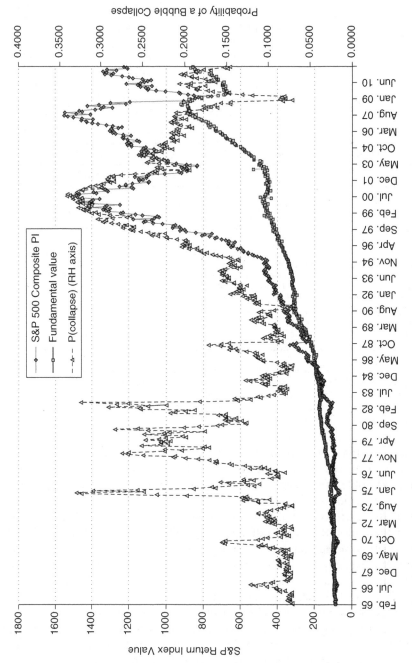

Figure 3.1   A plot of the S&P 500 return index, its fundamental value and the probability of collapse estimated from the vNS model

If we examine the major market 'corrections' over our sample period, the first occurs from February 1973 when the index fell for seven consecutive months by a total of around 13 per cent. Although there were some modest rises thereafter, the market was highly volatile by its own previous standards and the general drift downwards in prices continued until September 1974. By that time, the S&P 500 was around 45 per cent below its previous peak. While the probability of collapse, as shown in Figure 3.1, had risen slightly, it was only at around 10 per cent in February 1973, slightly above its long-term average up to that point of 9 per cent.

The next prolonged fall occurred during the famous market crash of 1987. At that time, prices fell from September 1987 right through to December, by which time the index had dropped 27 per cent. Over this period, the model performed better at delivering an early warning sign, as the probability of a collapse had risen to around 16 per cent by July 1987, up from less than 10 per cent in early 1986. The value of this probability remained high until the crash actually took place, but by November 1987 it had fallen back to around 9 per cent.

The bursting of the 'tech bubble' was the next large and prolonged stock price adjustment, most notably from March 2001, when prices fell by over 11 per cent in a single month. The model had suggested that the market was becoming overvalued right from the mid-1990s, and by around 2000 the probability of a bubble collapse had reached historically unprecedented levels of over 30 per cent. Thereafter, the probability gradually drifted downwards, to reach only 8 per cent by the end of 2009. As a result, the model completely missed the stock price falls that occurred in 2009 as a result of the subprime banking crisis.

There are several reasons why the model may have performed poorly over this latter part of the sample period. A first possibility is that the measure of fundamentals did not work well. It is certainly true that the propensity of firms to pay dividends varied over the sample period, with investors being increasingly rewarded via share repurchases; thus, arguably, dividends no longer represent the key distribution to shareholders in some cases. Secondly, it may be that using a different approach to construct the fundamental measure, still based on dividends (e.g. using the Campbell and Shiller model or the Gordon growth model), may lead to a better-fitting regime switching model. A final possibility is that the behaviour of the stock markets has been different during the recent market turbulence starting in 2007 from what it was previously. As Figure 3.1 shows, unlike the bubble collapses of 1987 and 2000, prices as a multiple of dividends were not at historically unprecedented levels – during the mid-2000s, dividend payments were increasing at a considerable rate. Therefore, perhaps it is not surprising that the model performed poorly in predicting a collapse that was in character unlike all of those that occurred before and from which it was calibrated.

3.8   CONCLUSIONS

This chapter has illustrated how several models for speculative bubbles in asset pricing series can be applied. Approaches based on variance bounds, bubble specification tests, cointegration and regime switching have all been employed to test for speculative bubbles in the S&P 500 using dividend-based measures of fundamentals. It is clear that the results are mixed: the first three tests all demonstrated evidence consistent with the presence of bubbles, while most of the parameters in the regime switching model were insignificant and the coefficient restrictions not in favour of bubble presence.

It is clear that the poor fit of the regime switching model over parts of our sample period 1965–2011 is not only perhaps surprising, but also goes against findings in previous studies that have examined a longer and earlier run of data. It is the case that the behaviour of prices and fundamentals is different at the end of our sample period (2007–2011) from what it had been in the past, with considerable market falls in the absence of strong overvaluation and consequently no bubble; this may have caused problems for the test. Further work on the development of more refined tests for speculative bubbles in asset markets is still warranted.

NOTES

1.   We then divide this by 1200 to turn it from an annualized percentage to a monthly proportion.
2.   Note that the information set I_t is part of the full information set available, Φ_t, since it includes only 'naive' information on dividends.
3.   ·Note that we assume that the dividend payment occurs at the end of the month, and therefore technically, we use the dividend of period t in our analysis, keeping this notation for simplicity. ·
4.   For a derivation of the equations, the reader is referred to the working paper version, van Norden and Schaller (1997), available at the Bank of Canada website: http://www.bankofcanada.ca/en/res/wp97-2.htm.

REFERENCES

Anderson, K., C. Brooks and A. Katsaris (2010), 'Speculative bubbles in the S&P 500: was the tech bubble confined to the tech sector?', *Journal of Empirical Finance*, **17**, 345–361.
Blanchard, O.J. (1979), 'Speculative bubbles, crashes and rational expectations', *Economics Letters*, **3** (4), 387–389.
Blanchard, O.J. and M.W. Watson (1982), 'Bubbles, rational expectations and financial markets', NBER Working Paper no. 945, Cambridge, MA: National Bureau of Economic Research.
Brooks, C. and A. Katsaris (2003), 'Rational speculative bubbles: an investigation of the London Stock Exchange', *Bulletin of Economic Research*, **55** (4), 319–346.
Brooks, C. and A. Katsaris (2005a), 'A three-regime model of speculative behavior: modelling the evolution of bubbles in the S&P 500 Composite Index', *Economic Journal*, **115** (505), 767–797.
Brooks, C. and A. Katsaris (2005b), 'Trading rules from forecasting the collapse of speculative bubbles for the S&P 500 composite index', *Journal of Business*, **78** (5), 2003–2036.
Campbell, J.Y. and R.J. Shiller (1987), 'Cointegration and tests of present value models', *Journal of Political Economy*, **95**, 1062–1088.
Campbell, J.Y. and R.J. Shiller (1988), 'Stock prices, earnings and expected dividends', *Journal of Finance*, **43** (3), 661–676.
Cutler, D., J. Poterba and L. Summers (1991), 'Speculative dynamics', *Review of Economic Studies*, **58**, 529–546.
Dale, R.S., J.E.V. Johnson and L. Tang (2005), 'Financial markets can go mad: evidence of irrational behaviour during the South Sea Bubble', *Economic History Review*, **58** (2), 233–271.
Dale, R., J.E.V Johnson and L. Tang (2007), 'Pitfalls in the quest for South Sea rationality', *Economic History Review*, **60** (4), 766–772.
Dezhbakhsh, H. and A. Demirguc-Kunt (1990), 'On the presence of speculative bubbles in stock prices', *Journal of Financial and Quantitative Analysis*, **25** (1), 101–112.
Diba, B.T. and H. Grossman (1988a), 'The theory of rational bubbles in stock prices', *Economic Journal*, **98**, 746–754.
Diba, B.T. and H. Grossman (1988b), 'Explosive rational bubbles in stock prices?', *American Economic Review*, **78**, 520–530.

Evans, G.W. (1991), 'Pitfalls in testing for explosive bubbles in asset prices', *American Economic Review*, **81**, 922–930.

Garber, P.M. (1989), 'Tulipmania', *Journal of Political Economy*, **97** (3), 535–560.

Garber, P.M. (2000), *Famous First Bubbles*, Cambridge, MA: MIT Press.

Grossman, S.J. and R.J. Shiller (1981), 'The determinants of the variability of stock market prices', *American Economic Review Papers and Proceedings*, **71** (2), 222–227.

Hansen, L.P. and T.J. Sargent (1981), 'Formulating and estimating dynamic linear rational expectations models', in R.E. Lucas and T.J. Sargent (eds), *Rational Expectations and Econometric Practise*, Minneapolis MN: University of Minnesota Press, pp. 91–126.

Keynes, J.M. (1936), *The General Theory of Employment, Interest and Money*, London: Palgrave Macmillan.

Kleidon, A.W. (1986), 'Bias in small sample tests of stock price rationality', *Journal of Business*, **59** (2), 237–261.

LeRoy, S.F. and W.R. Parke (1992), 'Stock price volatility: tests based on the geometric random walk', *American Economic Review*, **82** (4), 981–992.

Mankiw, G., D. Romer and M. Shapiro (1985), 'An unbiased re-examination of stock market volatility', *Journal of Finance*, **40** (3), 677–687.

Meese, R.A. and K.J. Singleton (1983), 'Rational expectations and the volatility of floating exchange rates', *International Economic Review*, **24** (3), 721–734.

Newey, W.K. and K.D. West (1987), 'A simple, positive semi-definite, heteroskedasticity and autocorrelation consistent covariance matrix', *Econometrica*, **55** (3), 703–708.

Santoni, G.J. (1987), 'The great bull markets of 1924–29 and 1982–87: speculative bubbles or economic fundamentals?', Working paper, Federal Reserve Bank of St. Louis.

Shiller, R.J. (1989), *Market Volatility*, 5th edn, Cambridge, MA: MIT Press.

van Norden, S. and H. Schaller (1993), 'The predictability of stock market regimes: evidence from the Toronto Stock Exchange', *Review of Economics and Statistics*, **75**, 505–510.

van Norden, S. and H. Schaller (1997), 'Fads or bubbles?', Bank of Canada Working Paper 97–2.

van Norden, S. and H. Schaller (1999), 'Speculative behavior, regime-switching, and stock market crashes', in P. Rothman (ed.), *Nonlinear Time Series Analysis of Economic and Financial Data*, Boston, MA: Kluwer, pp. 321–356.

West, K.D. (1986), 'Empirical assessment of present value relations: comment', *Econometric Reviews*, **5** (2), 273–278.

West, K.D. (1987), 'A specification test for speculative bubbles', *Quarterly Journal of Economics*, **102** (3), 553–580.

West, K.D. (1988), 'Dividend innovations and stock price volatility', *Econometrica*, **56** (1), 37–61.

PART II

DERIVATIVES

4 Estimating term structure models with the Kalman filter

Marcel Prokopczuk and Yingying Wu

4.1 INTRODUCTION

Models for the term structure of interest rates and for the term structure of commodity futures prices are of central interest for academics and practitioners alike. Consequently, an enormous literature on these topics exists. The estimation of term structure models is complicated by the fact that the relevant data have two dimensions. The first is calendar time, that is, the underlying variables evolve over time. The second is time-to-maturity, that is, at each point in time several bonds or futures with different maturity dates are available. Theoretical models link these two dimensions, usually by assuming no-arbitrage. On the empirical front, the Kalman filter allows the researcher to exploit the two dimensions, calendar time and time-to-maturity, simultaneously and thus enables the use of all available data in a consistent way. The aim of this chapter is to explain how term structure models can be efficiently estimated using the Kalman filter. We first describe the general idea of the Kalman filter and then demonstrate its implementation for a joint three-factor model of commodity futures and interest rates.

The remainder of this chapter is organized as follows. Section 4.2 introduces the Kalman filter and describes how it can be used for parameter estimation. In section 4.3, we first introduce the three-factor model under study. We then outline two possible estimation approaches, both based on Kalman filtering. We compare these two approaches in a simulation study and finally apply the superior method to real crude oil futures and Treasury security data. Section 4.4 briefly outlines two extensions of the general Kalman filter. Section 4.5 concludes by describing other applications of the Kalman filter in the finance and economics literature.

4.2 THE KALMAN FILTER

4.2.1 The General Idea

The Kalman filter was not developed for finance or economics applications. Its origin was in the field of engineering. The name is derived from its developer R.E. Kalman (Kalman, 1960; Kalman and Bucy, 1961). The Kalman filter was first designed to extract a state estimation from noisy observations in a situation where the nature of the mechanism and parameters of the state variables are known. However, Schweppe (1965) showed how, with the help of a state space specification in terms of prediction error decomposition, the Kalman filter can be used for parameter inference based on the maximum likelihood principle.[1] Dynamic models in state space form provide a wide range of applications to economic problems. Work by Chow (1975), Pagan (1975), Engle (1979) and Engle and Watson (1981) on dynamic factor analysis introduced the techniques to the empirical finance and economics literature. For example, Engle and Watson (1981) employ this methodology to formulate and estimate unobserved wage rates.

The basic Kalman filter is a recursive method to estimate the state of a system, and this is what it is used for in engineering. However, as noted above, it can also be used to estimate any unknown parameters of a model via the method of maximum likelihood. We first describe the basic idea in a simple example:[2] consider the situation in which one wants to track a satellite in space using two measurement devices with potentially different precisions. Each device provides different measurement results. How can we determine a point estimate of the satellite's location? One way would be to ignore the less precise estimate. However, although less precise, it still provides some information.

Let us denote the unknown position of the satellite by p (of course this would be a three-dimensional problem in reality but we want to keep it simple here). Now assume that we have measured this position with the two different devices and that they have normally distributed measurement errors with mean zero and variances σ_1^2 and σ_2^2. We denote these two measurements by m_1 and m_2. To combine the two measurements, we take the weighted average, that is:

$$\hat{p} = wm_1 + (1 - w)m_2 \tag{4.1}$$

But how should we chose w? As we have Gaussian errors, it makes sense to minimize the error variance of the total measurement, that is, minimize:

$$\hat{\sigma}_p^2 = w^2\sigma_1^2 + (1 - w)^2\sigma_2^2 \tag{4.2}$$

The solution to this problem is:

$$\omega^* = \frac{\sigma_2^2}{\sigma_1^2 + \sigma_2^2} \tag{4.3}$$

Defining $K = \frac{\sigma_1^2}{\sigma_1^2 + \sigma_2^2}$ we can rewrite the above equations as:

$$\hat{p} = m_1 + K(m_2 - m_1) \tag{4.4}$$

$$\hat{\sigma}^2 = (1 - K)\sigma_1^2 \tag{4.5}$$

Now assume that the measurements do not take place at the same time, but sequentially. We first observe the measurement m_1 with error variance σ_1^2 and then the second measurement m_2 with error variance σ_2^2. At time 1, m_1 is the only information we have so we would only use this, that is, $\hat{p}_{t=1} = x_1$ and $\hat{\sigma}_{p,t=1}^2 = \sigma_1^2$. At time 2, more information, that is, m_2 with error variance σ_2^2, becomes available which we want to use together with the previous one. Thus, we combine the information as described above. We obtain:

$$\hat{p}_{t=2} = \hat{p}_{t=1} + K(m_2 - \hat{p}_{t=1}) \tag{4.6}$$

$$\hat{\sigma}^2_{p,t=2} = (1 - K)\hat{\sigma}^2_{p,t=1} \tag{4.7}$$

This shows how new information can be sequentially used to improve the measurement. The quantity K determines how much weight the second measurement receives relative to the first one, and it is therefore called the *update gain*. The more precise one of the measurement technologies is compared to the other, the more weight is put on its measurement.

4.2.2   State Space Form

'The state space form is an enormously powerful tool which opens the way to handling a wide range of time series models' (Harvey, 1989).

Let y_1, y_2,...y_T be an n-dimensional multivariate time series of observable quantities, for example, yields of bonds with different maturities or commodity futures prices with different maturities. These observables depend on a vector of unobservable (latent) quantities of size m, z_t, which is often referred to as the state of nature or the state vector. For example, this might be the instantaneous interest rate or the spot price of a commodity. The model relates y_t to z_t through the so-called *measurement equation*:

$$y_t = F_t z_t + d_t + \varepsilon_t \tag{4.8}$$

where F_t is an $n \times m$ matrix and d_t is an $n \times 1$ vector. The term ε_t is called the observation error and is assumed to be serially uncorrelated and normally distributed with mean zero and covariance matrix H_t, that is, $\varepsilon_t \sim N(0, H_t)$. The state vector evolves through time according to the so-called *transition equation*:

$$z_t = G_t z_{t-1} + c_t + \omega_t \tag{4.9}$$

where G_t is an $m \times m$ matrix, c_t is an $m \times 1$ vector and ω_t is a vector of serially uncorrelated and normally distributed random variables with mean zero and variance W_t, that is, $\omega_t \sim N(0, W_t)$.

In the context of the above engineering application, equation (4.8) would describe the measurement technology, and equation (4.9) the physical laws determining the satellite's movements. As such, all parameters would be known and the task would be to determine z_t only. In the context of financial modeling, we start with an assumption on the dynamics of the state variables, that is, equation (4.9), and then derive equation (4.8) from it. The system's quantities G_t, c_t, F_t, d_t, H_t and W_t depend on the model's parameters, θ, which are usually not known and need to be estimated.

4.2.3   Estimating State Variables and Parameters

The basic Kalman filter is a recursive procedure for inference about the state vector z_t, based on information available at time t. For a linear and Gaussian system, the Kalman filter is optimal in the mean square sense. Given initial values $z_0 = E[z_0]$ and $V_0 = Var[z_0]$, it consists of the following steps.

Firstly, prediction. First one obtains the simple estimates of the state vector and its variance. Denoting by $z_{t|t-1}$ and $V_{t|t-1}$ the optimal forecast of z_t and V_t respectively at time $t-1$ we get:

$$z_{t|t-1} = G_t z_{t-1} + c_t \tag{4.10}$$

$$V_{t|t-1} = G_t V_{t-1} G_t' + W_t \tag{4.11}$$

Secondly, update. Once y_t has been observed, one can compute the forecast error v_t and the forecast error variance C_t:

$$v_t = y_t - (F_t z_{t|t-1} + d_t) \tag{4.12}$$

$$C_t = F_t V_{t|t-1} F_t' + H_t \tag{4.13}$$

Now one obtains a new estimate of the state vector and its variance:

$$z_t = z_{t|t-1} + V_{t|t-1} F_t' C_t^{-1} v_t \tag{4.14}$$

$$V_t = V_{t|t-1} - V_{t|t-1} F_t' C_t^{-1} F_t V_{t|t-1} \tag{4.15}$$

Essentially, the Kalman filter procedure combines past information and new measurements of the state vector in an optimal (least squares) way. The derivation mainly relies on the fact that a linear combination of multivariate normal random variables is again multivariate normal.[3]

Thirdly, parameter estimation. The last part of the procedure, which is not part of the initial aim of obtaining the state vector, is to estimate the system's parameters. In the previous step, we have assumed that we know the parameters and have obtained an optimal estimate for the state vector given these values. Collecting all model parameters in θ, the log-likelihood function of the state vector is given by:

$$\mathcal{L}(z_t; \theta) = -\frac{nT}{2} \ln 2\pi - \frac{1}{2} \sum_{t=1}^{T} (\ln|C_t| + v_t' C_t^{-1} v_t) \tag{4.16}$$

One now (numerically) maximizes the likelihood function with respect to θ. For each new θ the Kalman filter produces a new estimate of the state vector which is then an input to the likelihood function. Standard errors for the estimate $\hat{\theta}$ are computed from the covariance matrix after taking the inverse of the information matrix.[4] The information matrix is defined as the negative of the expected value of the Hessian matrix of the log-likelihood function. The standard errors are the square roots of the diagonal entries in this matrix.[5]

A few things are worth mentioning. Firstly, as noted above, the algorithm requires starting values for the state vector and its variance. Moreover, one needs to supply initial values for the model's parameters. Depending on the complexity and number of parameters and state variables, these might have a significant impact on the numerical optimization. Sometimes, economic theory or existing research can provide some guidance on reasonable choices. It is important to try a range of different values in order to ensure the stability and robustness of the results.

Secondly, we denote the parameter matrices and vectors in the measurement and transition equations with a time index. This is not to reflect time-varying parameters but the possibility of changing sizes of the vectors and matrices. For example, the number of observations might change over time, perhaps because of missing values in the data set. This flexibility is a great advantage of the Kalman filter.

Thirdly, the measurement errors covariance matrix needs to be specified. If one has specific information on the precision of measurements one might just set them at certain values. In the situation considered here, this is very unlikely. Therefore, it is common to treat these as unknown parameters and therefore include them in θ. Usually it is assumed that the errors are uncorrelated, which means that H_t is a diagonal matrix. If the system is large, it is sometimes also assumed that the errors' variances are equal for each measurement so that only one parameter must be estimated for H_t.

4.3 APPLICATION TO COMMODITY AND INTEREST RATE MODELING

We want to demonstrate the use of Kalman filtering in the context of estimating the parameters (and state variables) of dynamic commodity price and interest rate models. To do this, we have chosen to describe and analyze the estimation of the three-factor model developed in Schwartz (1997). This model captures the joint dynamics of commodity prices and interest rates. It can be seen as a combination of the two-factor Gibson and Schwartz (1990) commodity pricing model and the one-factor interest rate model proposed by Vasicek (1977). We first introduce the model and then we discuss two possible ways of estimating it by means of Kalman filtering. We analyze these two competing approaches in a simulation experiment and, afterwards, implement the superior one using real data from the crude oil and Treasury security markets.

Applications of the Kalman filtering method to interest rate term structure models can be found in, among many others, Pennacchi (1991), Lund (1997), Duan and Simonato (1999), Babbs and Nowman (1999), de Jong (2000) and Chen and Scott (2003).

In the context of commodity futures pricing models, the Kalman filter has been applied by, again among many others, Schwartz (1997), Schwartz and Smith (2000), Sorensen (2002), Cortazar and Naranjo (2003), Geman and Nguyen (2005), Korn (2005), Paschke and Prokopczuk (2009, 2010).

4.3.1 The Schwartz Three-Factor Model

The commodity pricing model developed by Schwartz (1997) contains three stochastic factors: the commodity spot price (S), the instantaneous convenience yield (δ) and the instantaneous interest rate (r). The joint model dynamics are given as follows:

$$dS_t = (\mu - \delta_t)S_t dt + \sigma_1 S_t dz_t^1 \tag{4.17}$$

$$d\delta_t = \kappa(\alpha - \delta_t)dt + \sigma_2 dz_t^2 \tag{4.18}$$

$$dr_t = a(m - r_t)dt + \sigma_3 dz_t^3 \tag{4.19}$$

with:

$$dz_t^1 dz_t^2 = \rho_1 dt, \quad dz_t^2 dz_t^3 = \rho_2 dt, \quad dz_t^1 dz_t^3 = \rho_3 dt \tag{4.20}$$

where z_t^1, z_t^2 and z_t^3 are three standard Brownian motions with correlations ρ_1, ρ_2 and ρ_3, respectively. σ_1, σ_2 and σ_3 describe the volatilities of the three processes. The parameter μ governs the spot price drift. The convenience yield and interest rate are mean-reverting with speed κ and a to the long-run equilibrium levels α and m, respectively.[6] As mentioned above, the dynamics for the commodity spot price and the convenience yield are the same as in the model of Gibson and Schwartz (1990) that treats interest rates as constant. The interest rate process is identical to the well-known Vasicek (1977) model.

In order to derive expressions for commodity futures and bond prices, one needs to consider the risk-neutral version of the model. Assuming a constant market price of risk, the joint stochastic process for the three state factors under the risk-neutral measure is given as:

$$dS_t = (r_t - \delta_t) S_t dt + \sigma_1 S_t dz_1^* \tag{4.21}$$

$$d\delta_t = \kappa(\alpha^* - \delta_t) dt + \sigma_2 dz_2^* \tag{4.22}$$

$$dr_t = a(m^* - r_t) dt + \sigma_3 dz_3^* \tag{4.23}$$

$$dz_1^* dz_2^* = \rho_1 dt, \quad dz_2^* dz_3^* = \rho_2 dt, \quad dz_1^* dz_3^* = \rho_3 dt \tag{4.24}$$

where in (4.22), $\alpha^* = \alpha - \frac{\lambda}{\kappa}$ and λ is the constant market price of convenience yield risk. m^* denotes the risk-adjusted mean short rate.[7]

Schwartz (1997) shows that, assuming no-arbitrage, a commodity futures price f in this model must satisfy the partial differential equation (PDE):

$$\frac{1}{2}\sigma_1^2 S^2 f_{SS} + \frac{1}{2}\sigma_2^2 f_{\delta\delta} + \frac{1}{2}\sigma_3^2 f_{rr} + \sigma_1\sigma_2\rho_1 Sf_{S\delta} + \sigma_2\sigma_3\rho_2 f_{\delta r} + \sigma_1\sigma_3\rho_3 Sf_{sr}$$

$$+ (r - \delta) Sf_s + \kappa(\alpha^* - \delta)f_\delta + a(m^* - r)f_r - f_T = 0 \tag{4.25}$$

subject to the boundary condition $f(S, \delta, r, 0) = S$. The solution of this PDE is:

$$f(S,\delta,r,T) = S \exp\left[\frac{-\delta(1 - e^{-\kappa T})}{\kappa} + \frac{r(1 - e^{-aT})}{a} + A(T) \right] \tag{4.26}$$

$$A(T) = \frac{(\kappa a^* + \sigma_1\sigma_2\rho_1)((1 - e^{-\kappa T}) - \kappa T)}{\kappa^2}$$

$$- \frac{\sigma_2^2(4(1 - e^{-\kappa T}) - (1 - e^{-2\kappa T}) - 2\kappa T)}{4\kappa^3}$$

$$- \frac{(am^* + \sigma_1\sigma_3\rho_3)((1 - e^{-aT}) - aT)}{a^2}$$

$$-\frac{\sigma_3^2\big(4(1 - e^{-aT}) - (1 - e^{-2aT}) - 2aT\big)}{4a^3}$$

$$+ \sigma_2\sigma_3\rho_2\left(\frac{(1 - e^{-\kappa T}) + (1 - e^{-aT}) - (1 - e^{-(\kappa+a)T})}{\kappa a(\kappa + a)}\right.$$

$$+ \left.\frac{\kappa^2(1 - e^{-aT}) + a^2(1 - e^{-\kappa T}) - \kappa a^2 T - a\kappa^2 T}{\kappa^2 a^2(\kappa + a)}\right) \tag{4.27}$$

The yield to maturity (R) of a zero coupon bond with price (D) and maturity (T) is given by $R = -\frac{1}{T}\ln(D)$. Solving the model for R, one obtains the following expression (see, e.g., Duan and Simonato, 1999; Babbs and Nowman, 1999):

$$R = r\frac{1 - e^{-aT}}{aT} + B(T) \tag{4.28}$$

$$B(T) = -\frac{1}{T}\left[\left(m^* - \frac{\sigma_3^2}{2a^2}\right)\left(\frac{1}{a}(1 - e^{-aT}) - T\right) - \frac{\sigma_3^2(1 - e^{-aT})^2}{4a^3}\right] \tag{4.29}$$

4.3.2   Estimation Approaches

The three state variables of the model are not observable. In Schwartz (1997), this three-factor model is estimated in two steps. Firstly, the interest rate process is estimated separately by assuming that the instantaneous interest rate can be approximated by the three-month Treasury bill yield. The volatility of the interest rate process, σ_3, is then simply estimated by the standard deviation of this time series. The speed of mean reversion, a, is simply assumed to be 0.2. The risk-adjusted drift rate, m^*, is chosen such that the long-term yield resembles 0.07. In the second step, Schwartz (1997) uses the Kalman filter to estimate the remaining parameters of the model. Although these approximations and assumptions are reasonable, there is no need to do this.[8]

We therefore propose two different alternative methods. The first one (*method 1* hereafter) is, as the one described above, a two-step procedure. However, we apply the Kalman filter not only in the second, but also in the first step to estimating the parameters of the interest rate processes. On the one hand, this approach essentially follows the argument of Schwartz (1997) that it is reasonable to assume that the interest rate parameters are not determined or affected by the commodity futures prices. On the other hand, we treat the instantaneous short rate as unobservable state variable (which it is) and employ the filtering approach to determine it and the parameters, avoiding the assumption that it can be approximated by the three month yield. Moreover, the Kalman filter approach allows us to employ information from the entire yield curve, not only one particular maturity. Once we have obtained the parameters and state vector, that is, σ_3, a, m^* and r_t, we can use them in the second step to estimate the remaining model parameters.

Besides assuming no effect of the commodity futures prices on the interest rate model parameter, this approach has another disadvantage. It neglects the estimation error of the first step in the second step. Clearly, it might be advantageous to estimate the model at once – as also pointed out by Schwartz: 'Ideally, the commodity spot price process, the convenience yield process, and the interest rate process should be estimated simulta-neously from a time series and cross-section of futures prices and discount bond prices.' This is exactly what we do in *method 2*.[9]

We now describe the Kalman filter estimation of *method 1* and *method 2* in detail, that is, we explicitly provide the transition and measurement equations. We generally work with time series of $N_1 + N_2 = N$ observed variables. Here, N_1 denotes the number of observed commodity futures prices (with different maturities) and N_2 the number of Treasury debt discount yields (with different maturities). The time interval between the observation dates is denoted Δt.

Method 1:   firstly, we use the N_2 time series of Treasury debt discount yields for esti-mating the one-factor interest rate model. The measurement equation (4.8) is given as:

$$
\underbrace{\begin{bmatrix} R(T_1) \\ \vdots \\ R(T_{N_2}) \end{bmatrix}}_{N_2 \times 1} = \underbrace{\begin{bmatrix} \frac{1 - e^{-aT_1}}{aT_1} \\ \vdots \\ \frac{1 - e^{-aT_{N_2}}}{aT_{N_2}} \end{bmatrix}}_{N_2 \times 1} r_t + \underbrace{\begin{bmatrix} B(T_1) \\ \vdots \\ B(T_{N+2}) \end{bmatrix}}_{N_2 \times 1} + \varepsilon_t
\tag{4.30}
$$

and the transition equation (4.9) can be obtained by taking the discrete-time distribution of the state variables and has the following specification:

$$
r_t = am\Delta t + (1 - a\Delta t)r_{t-1} + \omega_t
\tag{4.31}
$$

where ω_t are serially uncorrelated and normally distributed random variables with mean zero, $E(\omega t) = 0$ and variance $W = \sigma_3^2 \Delta t$. Having obtained the parameters a, m^*, σ_3 and state variable r_t by applying the Kalman filter and maximum likelihood methodology, they are regarded as known in the remaining estimation part. The second part aims at the commodity spot price and convenience yield processes. Denote $X_t = \ln S_t$. The measure-ment equation for the N_1 observed commodity futures series is:

$$
\underbrace{\begin{bmatrix} \ln f(T_1) \\ \vdots \\ \ln f(T_{N_1}) \end{bmatrix}}_{N_1 \times 1} = \underbrace{\begin{bmatrix} 1 & -\frac{1 - e^{-\kappa T_1}}{\kappa} \\ \vdots & \vdots \\ 1 & -\frac{1 - e^{-\kappa T_{x_1}}}{\kappa} \end{bmatrix}}_{N_1 \times 2} \underbrace{\begin{bmatrix} X_t \\ \delta_t \end{bmatrix}}_{2 \times 1} + \underbrace{\begin{bmatrix} A(T_1) + r_t\frac{1 - e^{-aT_1}}{a} \\ \vdots \\ A(T_{N_1}) + r_t\frac{1 - e^{-aT_{N_1}}}{a} \end{bmatrix}}_{N_1 \times 1} + \varepsilon_t
\tag{4.32}
$$

The transition equation (4.9) is given as:

$$
\begin{bmatrix} X_t \\ \delta_t \end{bmatrix} = \begin{bmatrix} (\mu - \frac{1}{2}\sigma_1^2)\Delta t \\ \kappa\alpha\Delta t \end{bmatrix} + \begin{bmatrix} 1 & -\Delta t \\ 0 & 1 - \kappa\Delta t \end{bmatrix} \begin{bmatrix} X_{t-1} \\ \delta_{t-1} \end{bmatrix} + \omega_t
\tag{4.33}
$$

Method 2:   here we estimate the entire model simultaneously. The quantities y_t, F_t, d_t and ε_t of the general measurement equation (4.8) are given as follows:

$$
\begin{bmatrix} \ln f(T_1) \\ \vdots \\ \ln f(T_{N_1}) \\ R(T_{N_1+1}) \\ \vdots \\ R(T_N) \end{bmatrix} = \begin{bmatrix} 1 & -\dfrac{1-e^{-\kappa T_1}}{\kappa} & \dfrac{1-e^{-aT_1}}{a} \\ \vdots & \vdots & \vdots \\ 1 & \dfrac{1-e^{-\kappa T_{N_1}}}{\kappa} & \dfrac{1-e^{-aT_{N_1}}}{a} \\ 0 & 0 & \dfrac{1-e^{-aT_{N_1+1}}}{aT_{N_1+1}} \\ \vdots & \vdots & \vdots \\ 0 & 0 & \dfrac{1-e^{aT_N}}{aT_N} \end{bmatrix} \underbrace{\begin{bmatrix} X_t \\ \delta_t \\ r_t \end{bmatrix}}_{3\times 1} = \begin{bmatrix} A(T_1) \\ \vdots \\ A(T_{N_1}) \\ B(T_{N_1+1}) \\ \vdots \\ B(T_N) \end{bmatrix} + \varepsilon_t
$$

$$
\underbrace{}_{N\times 1} \qquad \underbrace{}_{N\times 3} \qquad\qquad \underbrace{}_{N\times 1} \qquad\qquad (4.34)
$$

where ε_t is serially uncorrelated noise with $E(\varepsilon_t) = 0$ and $Var(\varepsilon_t) = H_t$. The transition equation is given as:

$$
\begin{bmatrix} X_t \\ \delta_t \\ r_t \end{bmatrix} = \begin{bmatrix} (\mu - \tfrac{1}{2}\sigma_1^2)\Delta t \\ \kappa\alpha\Delta t \\ am\Delta t \end{bmatrix} + \begin{bmatrix} 1 & -\Delta t & 0 \\ 0 & 1-\kappa\Delta t & 0 \\ 0 & 0 & 1-a\Delta t \end{bmatrix} \begin{bmatrix} X_{t-1} \\ \delta_{t-1} \\ r_{t-1} \end{bmatrix} + \omega_t \qquad (4.35)
$$

where ω_t are serially uncorrelated and normally distributed random variables with:

$$
E(\omega_t) = 0, Var[\omega_t] = W = \begin{bmatrix} \sigma_1^2\Delta t & \sigma_1\sigma_2\rho_1\Delta t & \sigma_1\sigma_3\rho_3\Delta t \\ \sigma_1\sigma_2\rho_1\Delta t & \sigma_2^2\Delta t & \sigma_2\sigma_3\rho_2\Delta t \\ \sigma_1\sigma_3\rho_3\Delta t & \sigma_2\sigma_3\rho_2\Delta t & \sigma_3^2\Delta t \end{bmatrix}
$$

Having written the model in its state space form for both estimation methods, one can proceed to estimate the parameters of this three-factor model by maximizing the log-likelihood function (4.16) of the state vector. For the numerical optimization, we use the function *fmincon* in Matlab and impose parameter constraints determined by the model specification or economic reasoning: a, $\kappa > 0.001$ (to ensure that the latent factors are mean reverting), σ_1, σ_2 and $\sigma_3 > 0.001$ and $-1 \le \rho_1$, ρ_2 and $\rho_3 \le 1$.

4.3.3   Simulation Results

When implementing Kalman filter-based estimation techniques (or any other estimation method), it is usually a good idea to test the procedure using simulated data first. This mainly serves two purposes. Firstly, one can check whether it works properly; and, secondly, one gets an idea what one can expect in terms of accuracy. In the simulation experiment, we set all model parameters to some fixed values. We then simulate data assuming that it follows the model's processes, add some random observation noise and then apply our estimation technique to it. The random noise is assumed to be serially and cross-sectionally uncorrelated Gaussian with the true values of their standard deviation chosen at similar levels as in the estimation results of Schwartz (1997) and Babbs and Nowman (1999).[10]

More precisely, we simulate time series of length 1000 for the three state variables using

Table 4.1   Estimation results for 100 simulations

Parameter	True value	Method 2		Method 1		Initial range
		Mean	SD	Mean	SD	
μ	0.30	0.2991	0.0888	0.2988	0.0927	[0.10, 0.60]
κ	1.30	1.3000	0.0033	1.2990	0.0054	[0.60, 2.00]
α	0.25	0.2521	0.0717	0.2517	0.0776	[0.04, 0.50]
σ_1	0.34	0.3400	0.0046	0.3396	0.0058	[0.01, 0.60]
σ_2	0.37	0.3699	0.0043	0.3705	0.0064	[0.01, 0.60]
ρ_1	0.90	0.9009	0.0054	0.8997	0.0060	[0.20, 1.00]
λ	0.35	0.3528	0.0934	0.3510	0.1001	[0.10, 0.60]
X_0	3.20	3.1999	0.0023	3.1977	0.0225	[2.00, 4.00]
δ_0	0.30	0.2996	0.0057	0.2967	0.0302	[0.10, 0.60]
r_0	0.06	0.0600	0.0007	0.0601	0.0009	[0.01, 0.12]
σ_3	0.008	0.0080	0.0003	0.0080	0.0003	[0.001, 0.01]
a	0.20	0.1988	0.0143	0.1999	0.0162	[0.01, 0.40]
m^*	0.07	0.0700	0.0006	0.0700	0.0006	[0.01, 0.12]
ρ_2	−0.30	−0.2998	0.0345	−0.0087	0.9045	[−0.50, 0.50]
ρ_3	−0.20	−0.2003	0.0369	−0.0969	0.8822	[−0.50, 0.50]
ξ_1	0.002	0.0019	0.0002	0.0019	0.0003	−
ξ_2	0.00003	0.0002	0.0002	0.0002	0.0003	−
ξ_3	0.0025	0.0025	0.0001	0.0025	0.0001	−
ξ_4	0.004	0.0040	0.0001	0.0040	0.0001	−
ξ_5	0.005	0.0050	0.0001	0.0054	0.0036	−
ξ_6	0.001	0.0010	0.0000	0.0010	0.0000	−
ξ_7	0.002	0.0020	0.0001	0.0020	0.0001	−
ξ_8	0.009	0.0090	0.0002	0.0090	0.0002	−

Notes: This table displays mean and standard deviation for each model parameter estimates from 100 simulations. For each estimation, time series of length 1000 observations are simulated using the parameters values listed in the second column ('True values'). The initial guess for each parameter and each simulation is drawn from a uniform distribution with range as provided in the last column ('Initial range').

the transition equations. We then construct eight observable quantities per time step using the measurement equations – specifically five futures prices and three Treasury security yields per date. Futures prices are set to have maturities of 0.05, 0.4, 0.7, 1.05 and 1.4 years. The Treasury security maturities are three months, one year and ten years. The parameter values used to simulate the state vector are chosen from a range where we would usually expect them to be (reflecting the empirical literature on interest rate and commodity futures modeling). The exact values are shown in Table 4.1. We then employ *method 1* and *method 2* to estimate the parameters, that is, we assume them to be unknown. Comparing the two methods in terms of computational time first, we find that *method 2* takes about twice as long as *method 1*. On a standard office computer, method 1 needs about 30 minutes for one simulated dataset, whereas *method 2* needs about one hour.

As discussed above, the Kalman filter procedure requires initial guesses for all parameters. In a first step, one might choose the values employed in the simulation step. This means that one essentially starts the optimization at the optimal solution. This is an ideal setting, so the result should be close to the initial guess and can confirm that the algorithm contains no major errors. To make the simulation experiment more realistic (in reality we do not know the optimal solution before we conduct the estimation), we draw the initial guess for each parameter from a uniform distribution spanning a reasonable range of possible values. Of course, 'reasonable' is subjective and chosen by us. The ranges used for each parameter are provided in the last column of Table 4.1. We repeat the simulation and estimation procedures 100 times for each method.[11]

Table 4.1 presents the mean values of the estimated parameters and their standard deviations for *method 1* and *method 2*. In order to have a good estimation methodology we would want the mean to be close to the input parameter used and the standard deviation to be small.

Considering *method 1* first, we can observe that the mean values of most of the parameters are close to the input values. Some parameters, for example κ, are estimated with very high precision, whereas other parameters, for example μ and λ, exhibit larger standard deviations but might be considered reasonable. However, the two model parameters that relate the interest rate process to the commodity price and convenience yield processes, ρ_2 and ρ_3, show severely biased estimates. Not only that, but the standard deviations of these estimates are enormous, indicating that the two-step procedure of *method 1* does not work well for estimating these two parameters.

In contrast, looking at the results for *method 2*, we can observe that both correlation parameters, ρ_2 and ρ_3, are estimated quite well. The mean estimates are almost identical to the true values and the standard deviations are of moderate size. All other model parameters are also estimated well. Moreover, we can observe that the estimation standard deviations are smaller for all parameters using *method 2* compared to *method 1*. Therefore, our simulation experiment provides clear evidence in favor of a simultaneous estimation of the entire model, that is, *method 2*.

4.3.4 Empirical Results

In this section, we apply the superior *method 2* to real market data. We consider the market for crude oil, which is one of the most heavily traded commodities and also studied in numerous research papers, including Schwartz (1997). The commodity futures data are collected from the Commodity Research Bureau (CRB). We consider weekly observations over the period from 2 January 1990 to 15 December 2011 for the first nearby contract (NBF01), fifth nearby contract (NBF05), ninth nearby contract (NBF09), thirteenth nearby contract (NBF13) and seventeenth nearby contract (NBF17). These nearby time series are created by rolling over at the last trading day of a given maturity to the contract maturing one month later. Therefore, the exact maturity of the observed futures is not constant as in the simulation study. This is not a problem, as time-to-maturity is considered explicitly in the measurement equation. The corresponding Treasury securities yields for the same observation dates are obtained from Thomson Reuters. The yields used correspond to discount bonds with maturities of three months, one year and ten years.

An estimation output that one might be interested in is the evolution of the state vector. Figure 4.1 displays the estimated log spot price, the convenience yield and the risk-free rate over the sample period. In context, the convenience yield is probably of most interest as it is the most difficult to obtain from observed market variables. We can

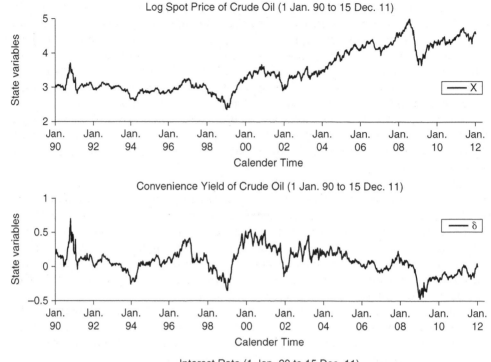

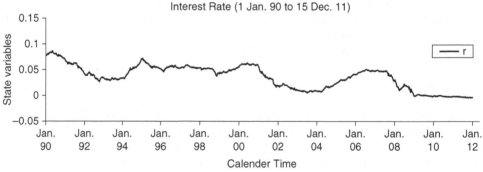

Notes: This figure displays the estimated state variables (log spot price, (*X*), convenience yield, (δ), and instantaneous interest rate, (*r*)) from the crude oil futures and Treasury securities data over the period from 1 January 1990 to 15 December 2011.

Figure 4.1   Estimated state variables

see meaningful variations of the convenience yield over time, indicating that it is a useful and necessary component in the pricing model. A model without convenience yield would not be able to match the data well (Gibson and Schwartz, 1990; Schwartz, 1997).

Table 4.2 presents the results of all parameters together with their standard errors. To make our results comparable to those estimated by Schwartz (1997), we repeat the estimation for the time period covered in his work, that is, 2 January 1990 to 17 February 1995, and we also present his estimates.

Table 4.2 Estimation results from crude oil data

	Our results		Our results		Schwartz (1997)	
period	1/2/90 to 12/15/11		1/2/90 to 2/17/95		1/2/90 to 2/17/95	
# weeks	1102		259		259	
parameter	estimate	SE	estimate	SE	estimate	SE
μ	0.2433	0.0446	0.0991	0.1353	0.315	0.125
κ	0.8920	0.0127	1.2407	0.0346	1.314	0.027
α	0.1030	0.0366	0.0789	0.1101	0.249	0.093
σ_1	0.3454	0.0066	0.3194	0.0134	0.334	0.009
σ_2	0.2727	0.0064	0.3219	0.0143	0.372	0.014
ρ_1	0.8076	0.0093	0.9012	0.0137	0.915	0.007
λ	0.1076	0.0327	0.0101	0.1454	0.353	0.123
X_0	3.0688	0.0514	3.1199	0.0520	–	–
δ_0	0.1922	0.0713	0.2815	0.0800	–	–
r_0	0.0777	0.0016	0.0778	0.0017	–	–
σ_3	0.0088	0.0002	0.0083	0.0004	0.0081	–
a	0.1077	0.0039	0.1727	0.0082	0.2000	–
m^*	0.0846	0.0014	0.0969	0.0014	0.0692	–
ρ_2	0.1085	0.0280	0.0266	0.0612	−0.0039	–
ρ_3	0.0947	0.0282	−0.0242	0.0581	−0.0293	–
ξ_1	0.0470	0.0010	0.0446	0.0025	0.045	0.002
ξ_2	0.0095	0.0002	0.0076	0.0009	0.007	0.001
ξ_3	0.0000	0.0004	0.0027	0.0003	0.003	0.000
ξ_4	0.0000	0.0002	0.0000	0.0003	0.000	–
ξ_5	0.0045	0.0001	0.0036	0.0002	0.004	0.000
ξ_6	0.0031	0.0001	0.0000	0.0002	–	–
ξ_7	0.0000	0.0004	0.0035	0.0001	–	–
ξ_8	0.0080	0.0002	0.0042	0.0002	–	–

Notes: This table displays parameter estimates and standard errors (SE) when applying the simultaneous estimation approach to crude oil futures and T-Bill data. We also report the results obtained by Schwartz (1997) for comparison.

Firstly, we can observe that the assumptions on the interest rate parameters *a*, *m** and σ_3 made by Schwartz were quite reasonable, although there are some differences. The results of the subperiod using our estimation methods show that two of the three long-term average levels of the three factors are at lower levels. The correlation between the convenience yield and interest rate, ρ_2, has the opposite sign but is still close to zero. The market price of convenience yield risk, λ, changes substantially and is now close to zero, although with a relatively high standard error. The standard deviations of measurement errors of the observed futures prices (ξ_1 to ξ_5) are close to the ones found in Schwartz (1997). Among these five estimates, the first nearby futures contract (NBF01), which is also the most heavily traded in the market, implies the highest level of embedded noise. The values for the Treasury yields' measurement errors are at similar level as the ones from the futures prices.

Comparing our results for the full sample period until December 2011 and the shorter subperiod, we can observe some differences. The standard errors of most estimates decrease by a substantial amount, which is of course not a surprising result of increasing the sample size. However, one might argue that especially for μ and λ, the decreased standard errors make the estimation results more meaningful than for the shorter period where they are statistically indistinguishable from zero. The speed of mean reversion of the convenience yield process, κ, decreases by about 30 percent. The spot price volatility, σ_1, increases whereas the convenience yield volatility, σ_2, decreases. The market price of convenience yield risk, λ, is now significantly positive. Moreover, correlations between the interest rate process and the other two state variables, ρ_2 and ρ_3, increase by a fair amount.

4.4   EXTENSIONS

4.4.1   Extended Kalman Filter

For more complex models, it might be the case that either the transition equation or the measurement equation (or both) are non-linear, that is, they take the following form:

$$y_t = g(z_t) + \varepsilon_t \qquad (4.36)$$

and:

$$z_t = h(z_{t-1}) + \omega_t \qquad (4.37)$$

where g and h are some non-linear functions. For example, if one wanted to estimate an interest rate or commodity pricing model as the one discussed in this chapter using option prices, the measurement equation (i.e., the option pricing formula) would be non-linear. In this situation, the standard Kalman filter cannot be applied any more. However, a modified version, the so-called 'extended Kalman filter', might be used. The idea is to 'linearize' the model by applying a first-order Taylor series expansion. Given that g and h are sufficiently smooth, this approximation can perform very well. More details can be found in Harvey (1989). Lund (1997) demonstrates how to use the extended Kalman filter for interest rate models when applied to coupon bonds. Duffee and Stanton (2004) study the properties of several econometric techniques for estimating term structure models. These include the technique of inverting the pricing equation and employing maximum likelihood as suggested by Chen and Scott (1993), a simulation-based maximum likelihood approach developed by Pedersen (1995) and Santa-Clara (1995), the method of efficient moments suggested by Gallant and Tauchen (1996) and a variant of the (extended) Kalman filter. They conclude that the Kalman filter is superior to all other methods. For a recent example of the extended Kalman filter in the context of commodity derivatives pricing, see Trolle and Schwartz (2009).

4.4.2   Unscented Kalman Filter

If g and h are highly non-linear one might consider another extension, the so-called 'unscented Kalman filter' developed by Julier and Uhlmann (1997). This technique avoids linearizing the model but employs the so-called 'unscented transformation' to directly account for the non-linear relationship in the model.

Christoffersen et al. (2008) conduct extensive simulation experiments and conclude that the unscented Kalman filter produces smaller estimation errors than the extended Kalman filter when dealing with non-linearities in the context of term structure modeling. An application to currency options can be found in Carr and Wu (2007).

4.5 CONCLUSION

This chapter has described how the Kalman filter can be used to estimate dynamic interest rate and commodity futures models. We applied the methodology to the Schwartz (1997) three-factor model and analyzed two possible estimation approaches in a simulation study. Estimating the entire model simultaneously was found to be superior to a stepwise procedure. We then applied this method to a real data set of crude oil commodity futures and Treasury security yields.

Although the application of the Kalman filter (or one of its extensions) to term structure model estimation is one of the most popular in finance, there are many other areas where it can be employed. For example, Kim et al. (1994) and Prokopczuk (2011) utilize the Kalman filter to estimate multivariate jump diffusion models of stock prices. Similarly, volatility of financial assets is a crucial component for the valuation of derivatives securities. However, the unobservable nature of volatility makes estimation nontrivial. Among many others, Ruiz (1994), Barndorff-Nielsen (2002) and Forbes et al. (2007) employ the Kalman filter for this inference problem.

The Kalman filter has also been applied in the context of estimating time-varying betas; see, for example, Bos and Newbold (1984) and Ohlson and Rosenberg (1982). Another stream of literature concerns hedging strategies under partial observation. The optimal hedge ratio is generally not observable and the Kalman filter can be utilized to estimate time-varying hedge ratios. Hatemi-J and Roca (2006) demonstrate the superiority of a filtered hedging strategy by using the Kalman filter, and Fischer et al. (1999) discuss the situation where some of the underlying price observations are missing. Moreover, the Kalman filter can be used to investigate the tracking and investment methods of hedge funds; see, for example, Roncalli and Weisang (2011) and Racicot and Théoret (2007).

Other interesting applications include situations where measurement errors are substantial and unavoidable. This is often the case in survey-based studies. For example, Beck (1989) employs the Kalman filter for analyzing the impact of economic conditions on presidential popularity in this context. Of course, the literature listed above is by no means comprehensive and many other applications exist.

NOTES

1. See also Mehra (1974), who discusses the similarity of model identification across the stochastic control and econometric literatures.
2. This example can be found in De Schuter et al. (1999).
3. See, for example, Harvey (1989, Chapter 3). See also Meinhold and Singpurwalla (1983) for a derivation from a Bayesian point of view.

4.   A detailed derivation can be found in Harvey (1989, subsections 3.4.5 and 3.4.6).
5.   The Hessian matrix is often provided as an output of numerical optimization routines, such as the function *fmincon* in Matlab which we use for the estimations in this chapter.
6.   This type of stochastic process is known as Ornstein–Uhlenbeck process.
7.   An extended model allowing for a dynamic market price of risk can be found in, for example, Casassus and Collin-Dufresne (2005).
8.   Considering computational speed, this might have been different at the time when the original paper had been written.
9.   Schwartz (1997, p. 933). Note that we will employ time series of discount bond yields and not prices. This is for convenience only as both contain the same information.
10. See Dempster and Tang (2011) for an analysis of the case of correlated measurement errors.
11. Note that we use the same simulation data for both methods, that is, for each of the 100 simulations, we use the same dataset for *method 1* and *method 2*. Therefore there is no error introduced by random differences in the simulated data.

REFERENCES

Babbs, S. and K. Nowman (1999), 'Kalman filtering of gernalized Vasicek term structure models', *Journal of Financial and Quantitative Analysis*, **34**, 115–130.
Barndorff-Nielsen, O. (2002), 'Econometric analysis of realized volatility and its use in estimating stochastic volatility models', *Journal of the Royal Statistical Society: Series B*, **64**, 253–280.
Beck, N. (1989), 'Estimating dynamic models using Kalman filtering', *Political Analysis*, **1**, 121–156.
Bos, T. and P. Newbold (1984), 'An empirical investigation of the possibility of stochastic systematic risk in the market model', *Journal of Business*, **57**, 35–41.
Carr, P. and L. Wu (2007), 'Stochastic skew in currency options', *Journal of Financial Economics*, **86**, 213–247.
Casassus, J. and P. Collin-Dufresne (2005), 'Stochastic convenience yield implied from commodity futures and interest rates', *Journal of Finance*, **60**, 2283–2331.
Chen, R. and L. Scott (1993), 'Maximum likelihood estimation for a multifactor equilibrium model of the term structure of interest rates', *Journal of Fixed Income*, **3**, 14–31.
Chen, R. and L. Scott (2003), 'Multi-factor Cox-Ingersoll-Ross models of the term structure: estimates and tests from a Kalman filter model', *Journal of Real Estate Finance and Economics*, **27**, 143–172.
Chow, G. (1975), *Analysis and Control of Dynamic Economic Systems*, New York: Wiley.
Christoffersen, P., K. Jacobs, L. Karoui and K. Mimouni (2008), 'Nonlinear filtering in affine term structure models: evidence from the term structure of swap rates', Working Paper, McGill University.
Cortazar, G. and L. Naranjo (2003), 'A multi-factor stochastic model and estimation procedure for the valuation and hedging of commodity contingent claims', Working Paper, Pontificia Universidad Catolica de Chile.
de Jong, F. (2000), 'Time series and cross-section information in affine term-structure models', *Journal of Business and Economic Statistics*, **18**, 300–314.
De Schuter, J., J. De Geeter, T. Lefebvre and H. Bruyninckx (1999), 'Kalman filters: a tutorial', Working Paper, Katholieke Universiteit Leuven.
Dempster, M. and K. Tang (2011), 'Estimating exponential affine models with correlated measurement errors: application to fixed income and commodities', *Journal of Banking and Finance*, **35**, 639–652.
Duan, J.-C. and J.-G. Simonato (1999), 'Estimating and testing exponential-affine term structure models by Kalman filter', *Review of Quantitative Finance and Accounting*, **13**, 111–135.
Duffee, G. and R. Stanton (2004), 'Estimation of dynamic term structure models', Working Paper, University of California at Berkeley.
Engle, R. (1979), 'Estimating structural models of seasonality', in A. Zellner (ed.), *Seasonal Analysis of Economic Time Series*, Washington, DC: NBER, pp. 281–308.
Engle, R. and M. Watson (1981), 'A one-factor multivariate time series model of metropolitan wage rates', *Journal of the American Statistical Association*, **76**, 774–781.
Fischer, P., E. Platen and W. Runggaldier (1999), 'Risk minimizing hedging strategies under partial observation', *Progress in Probability*, New York: Springer-Verlag, pp. 175–188.
Forbes, C., G. Martin and J. Wright (2007), 'Inference for a class of stochastic volatility models using option and spot prices: application of a bivariate Kalman filter', *Econometric Reviews*, **26**, 387–418.
Gallant, A. and G. Tauchen (1996), 'Which moments to match?', *Econometric Theory*, **12**, 657–681.
Geman, H. and V.-N. Nguyen (2005), 'Soybean inventory and forward curve dynamics', *Management Science*, **51**, 1076–1091.

Gibson, R. and E. Schwartz (1990), 'Stochastic convenience yield and the pricing of oil contingent claims', *Journal of Finance*, **45**, 959–976.

Harvey, A. (1989). *Forecasting, Structural Time Series Models and the Kalman Filter*, Cambridge: Cambridge University Press.

Hatemi-J, A. and E. Roca (2006), 'Calculating the optimal hedge ratio: constant, time varying and the Kalman filter approach', *Applied Economics Letters*, **13**, 293–299.

Julier, S. and J. Uhlmann (1997), 'A new extension of the Kalman filter to nonlinear systems', Proceedings of AeroSense: The 11th International Symposium on Aerospace/Defence Sensing, Simulation and Controls.

Kalman, R. (1960), 'A new approach to linear filtering and prediction problems', *Journal of Basic Engineering*, **82**, 35–45.

Kalman, R. and R. Bucy (1961), 'New results in linear filtering and prediction theory', *Journal of Basic Engineering*, **83**, 95–107.

Kim, M.-J., Y.-H. Oh and R. Brooks (1994), 'Are jumps in stock returns diversifiable? evidence and implications for options pricing', *Journal of Financial and Quantitative Analysis*, **29**, 609–631.

Korn, O. (2005), 'Drift matters: an analysis of commodity derivatives', *Journal of Futures Markets*, **25**, 211–241.

Lund, J. (1997), 'Non-linear Kalman filtering techniques for term structure models', Working Paper, Aarhus.

Mehra, R. (1974), 'Topics in stochastic control theory identification in control and econometrics: similarities and differences', in S.U. Berg (ed.), *Annals of Economic and Social Measurement*, Washington, DC: NBER, pp. 21–48.

Meinhold, R. and N. Singpurwalla (1983), 'Understanding the Kalman filter', *American Statistician*, **37**, 123–127.

Ohlson, J. and B. Rosenberg (1982), 'Systematic risk of the CRSP equal-weighted common stock index: a history estimated by stochastic-parameter regression', *Journal of Business*, **55**, 121–145.

Pagan, A. (1975), 'A note on the extraction of components from time series', *Econometrica*, **43**, 163–168.

Paschke, R. and M. Prokopczuk (2009), 'Integrating multiple commodities in a model of stochastic price dynamics', *Journal of Energy Markets*, **2**, 47–82.

Paschke, R. and M. Prokopczuk (2010), 'Commodity derivatives valuation with autoregressive and moving average components in the price dynamics', *Journal of Banking and Finance*, **34**, 2742–2752.

Pedersen, A. (1995), 'A new approach to maximum-likelihood estimation of stochastic differential equations based on discrete observations', *Scandinavian Journal of Statistics*, **2**, 55–71.

Pennacchi, G. (1991), 'Identifying the dynamics of real interest rates and inflation: evidence using survey data', *Review of Financial Studies*, **4**, 53–86.

Prokopczuk, M. (2011), 'Optimal portfolio choice in the presence of domestic systemic risk: empirical evidence from stock markets', *Decisions in Economics and Finance*, **34**, 141–168.

Racicot, F. and R. Théoret (2007), 'A study of dynamic market strategies of hedge funds using the Kalman filter', *Journal of Wealth Management*, **10**, 94–106.

Roncalli, T. and G. Weisang (2011), 'Tracking problems, hedge fund replication, and alternative beta', *Journal of Financial Transformation*, **31**, 19–29.

Ruiz, E. (1994), 'Quasi-maximum likelihood estimation of stochastic volatility models', *Journal of Econometrics*, **63**, 289–306.

Santa-Clara, P. (1995), 'Simulated likelihood estimation of diffusions with an application to the short term interest rate', PhD dissertation, INSEAD.

Schwartz, E. (1997), 'The stochastic behavior of commodity prices: implications for valuation and hedging', *Journal of Finance*, **52**, 923–973.

Schwartz, E. and J. Smith (2000), 'Short-term variations and long-term dynamics in commodity prices', *Management Science*, **46**, 893–911.

Schweppe, F. (1965), 'Evaluation of likelihood functions for Gaussian signals', *Information Theory, IEEE Transactions on Information Theory*, **11**, 61–70.

Sorensen, C. (2002), 'Modeling seasonality in agricultural commodity futures', *Journal of Futures Markets*, **22**, 393–426.

Trolle, A. and E. Schwartz (2009), 'Unspanned stochastic volatility and the pricing of commodity derivatives', *Review of Financial Studies*, **22**, 4423–4461.

Vasicek, O. (1977), 'An equilibrium characterization of the term structure', *Journal of Financial Economics*, **5**, 177–188.

5 American option pricing using simulation with an application to the GARCH model
Lars Stentoft

5.1 INTRODUCTION

To date, pricing options in general and options with early exercise in particular remains a challenge and an area of interest in empirical finance. There are several reasons for this. In reality, many exchange traded options do have the possibility of early exercise and hence this feature needs to be considered when pricing these claims. This is the case for most if not all options written on individual stocks and if neglected their values could be severely underestimated. However, potentially much more important is the fact that many decisions made in real life, not only of the financial kind, can be regarded as problems of deciding on the optimal stopping time and hence correspond to the American option pricing situation. A classical example is that of real options – for instance, the option to develop an area for mining. The decision of when to develop the mine is essentially one of deciding on the optimal stopping time, and the value of the mine should be calculated taking this into consideration.

As a result of the wide applicability of the American option pricing problem it is of immediate interest to develop a flexible pricing framework. For example, theoretically it is well known that the price of an equity option on a financial asset depends on multiple factors including the strike price and the maturity of the option, the interest rate, the value of the underlying asset, the volatility of this asset and the value of dividends paid on it. While some of these factors, for example the strike price and the time to maturity, are fixed or vary only deterministically, the other factors are potentially stochastic and if so should be modeled accordingly. More generally, any real option will likely depend on several stochastic factors. Therefore a valuation framework should be able to accommodate multiple factors in a realistic way.

Historically, the American option pricing problem has been solved using numerical procedures such as the binomial model, see for example Cox et al. (1979), or the finite difference method, see, for example Brennan and Schwartz (1977). However, though it is possible to incorporate the early exercise feature in these models, it is not computationally feasible to include more than a couple of stochastic factors. For example, the finite difference method simply cannot be extended to more than two or three stochastic factors and although it is possible to extend the binomial model – see for example Boyle (1988), Boyle et al. (1989) and Amin (1991) – the problem is that the computational complexity increases exponentially with the number of stochastic factors. Whereas in one dimension a recombining binomial model with k steps has $k + 1$ final nodes in two dimensions, the number of final nodes is $(k + 1)^2$. In the literature this problem is known as the 'curse of dimensionality', and in principle it is thus computationally difficult to accommodate all of the potential stochastic factors and instead alternative solutions are called for. One alternative is to use simulation techniques.

Simulation methods are very flexible and can easily accommodate multiple stochastic factors.[1] Indeed, simulation methods can immediately be used to price European options. In fact this approach was introduced to finance at least as early as in Boyle (1977) and even before the binomial model was suggested. Simulation methods generally do not suffer from the curse of dimensionality as the computational complexity only grows linearly with the number of stochastic factors. However, for a long period it remained a challenge to solve the optimal stopping time problem using this technique. This chapter contains an introduction to how simulation methods can be used to price American options with an application to the generalized autoregressive conditional heteroskedastic (GARCH) option pricing model.

Section 5.2 presents the option pricing framework and explains how the price of an American option can be calculated using dynamic programming. Section 5.3 introduces how simulation techniques can be used to solve this problem and discusses various existing methods for how to accommodate the early exercise feature of the American option. Section 5.4 explains how the flexibility of simulation techniques can be used to model more realistically the dynamics of financial assets using the GARCH framework and in section 5.5 this framework is used to examine the effect on estimated option prices of the specification of the price of risk. Finally, section 5.6 provides some concluding remarks.

5.2   THE OPTION PRICING FRAMEWORK

The theoretical framework I use closely follows that of Stentoft (2013). In particular, assume that the time to expiration of an option can be divided into K periods, $t_0 = 0 < t_1 \leq t_2 \leq \ldots \leq t_K = T$. Thus, I am essentially approximating the American option price with the so-called Bermudan option price.[2] As the number of periods increase this approximation becomes better and better. Next, assume a complete probability space $(\Omega, \mathcal{F}, P)$ equipped with a discrete filtration $\mathcal{F}((t_k))_{k=0}^{K}$ and assume that the underlying model is Markovian with state variables $(X(t_k))_{k=0}^{K}$ adapted to $(\mathcal{F}(t_k))_{k=0}^{K}$. Further denote by $(Z(t_k))_{k=0}^{K}$ an adapted payoff process for the derivative, satisfying $Z(t_k) = h(X(t_k), t_k)$ for a suitable function $h(\cdot, \cdot)$. As an example, consider the American put option for which the only state variable of interest is the stock price, $X(t_k) = S(t_k)$. We have that $Z(t_k) = \max(\bar{S} - S(t_k), 0)$, where $\bar{S}$ denotes the strike price. Finally, assume that $X(0) = x$ is known and hence $Z(0)$ is deterministic and let $\tau(t_k)$ denote the set of all stopping times with values in $\{t_k, \ldots, t_K\}$.

Following, for example, Karatzas (1988) and Duffie (1996), in the absence of arbitrage we can specify the object of interest, the American option price, as the solution to the following problem:

$$P(0) = \max_{\tau(t_1) \in \tau(t_1)} E[Z(\tau)]. \tag{5.1}$$

The problem of determining the American option price in (5.1) is referred to as a discrete time optimal stopping time problem and one of the preferred ways to solve this problem is to use the dynamic programming principle. Intuitively, this procedure can be motivated by considering the choice faced by the option holder at time t_k: that is, to exercise the option immediately or to continue to hold the option until the next period. The optimal choice is to exercise immediately if the value of this is positive and larger than the expected payoff from continuing to hold the option. In this section I explain in detail how this is done.

5.2.1   Exact Algorithms

Let $V(t_k)$ denote the value function of the option at a time t_k prior to expiration.[3] If the option holder keeps the option until the next period and acts optimally from this time onwards the expected payoff will be $E[Z(\tau(t_{k+1}))|X(t_k)]$. On the other hand, if the option is exercised immediately the payoff is $Z(t_k)$. Thus, the value of the option at time t_k may be written as:

$$V(t_k) = \max(Z(t_k), E[Z(\tau(t_{k+1}))|X(t_k)]). \tag{5.2}$$

Furthermore, since it is always optimal to exercise at expiration, the optimal stopping time $\tau(t_k)$ can be generated iteratively according to the following algorithm:

$$\begin{cases} \tau(t_K) = T \\ \tau(t_k) = t_k 1_{\{Z(t_k) \geq E[Z(\tau(t_{k+1}))|X(t_k)]\}} + \tau(t_{k+1}) 1_{\{Z(t_k) < E[Z(\tau(t_{k+1}))|X(t_k)]\}}, \ 1 < k \leq K - 1. \end{cases} \tag{5.3}$$

From the algorithm in (5.3), the value of the option in (5.1) can be calculated as:

$$P(0) = E[Z(\tau(t_1))|X(0)]. \tag{5.4}$$

By definition, this price corresponds to the true option price in (5.1).

Alternatively, one can formulate the dynamic programming problem directly in terms of the value function $V(t_k)$. To see this, note that if the option holder keeps the option until the next period and acts optimally from this time onwards, the expected payoff will be $E[V(t_{k+1})|X(t_k)]$. Thus, the value of the option at time t_k may equivalently be written as:

$$V(t_k) = \max(Z(t_k), E[V(t_{k+1})|X(t_k)]). \tag{5.5}$$

Furthermore, since the value at expiration equals the intrinsic value, the value functions can be generated iteratively according to the following algorithm:

$$\begin{cases} V(t_K) = Z(t_K) \\ V(t_k) = \max(Z(t_k), E[V(t_{k+1})|X(t_k)]), \ 1 < k \leq K - 1. \end{cases} \tag{5.6}$$

From the algorithm in (5.6), the value of the option in (5.1) can be calculated as:

$$P(0) = E[V(t_1)|X(0)]. \tag{5.7}$$

The backward induction theorem of Chow et al. (1971) provides the theoretical foundation for the algorithm in (5.6) and establishes the optimality of the price in (5.7).

Although it might not be clear that these two algorithms lead to the same optimal stopping time and hence the same price this is in fact the case. To show this, note that it can be optimal to exercise the option at time t_k if and only if the value of the option equals the immediate exercise value, that is, if and only if $V(t_k) = Z(t_k)$. Hence, the optimal stopping time identified at any time t_k, $\tau(t_k)$, can be written as:

$$\tau(t_k) = \sum_{n=k}^{K} t_n \mathbf{1}_{\{Z(t_n) < V(t_n),\, k \leq h < n \text{ and } V(t_n) = Z(t_n)\}}$$

$$= t_k \mathbf{1}_{\{Z(t_k) = V(t_k)\}} + \left[\sum_{n=k+1}^{K} t_n \mathbf{1}_{\{Z(t_n) < V(t_n),\, k+1 \leq h < n \text{ and } V(t_n) = Z(t_n)\}} \right] \mathbf{1}_{\{Z(t_k) < V(t_k)\}}$$

$$= t_k \mathbf{1}_{\{Z(t_k) = V(t_k)\}} + \tau(t_{k+1}) \mathbf{1}_{\{Z(t_k) < V(t_k)\}}$$

$$= t_k \mathbf{1}_{\{Z(t_k) \geq E[V(t_{k+1})|X(t_k)]\}} + \tau(t_{k+1}) \mathbf{1}_{\{Z(t_k) < E[V(t_{k+1})|X(t_k)]\}}, \tag{5.8}$$

where the last equality follows from (5.5). Finally, by definition it follows that:

$$E[Z(\tau(t_{k+1}))|X(t_k)] = E[V(t_{k+1})|X(t_k)], \tag{5.9}$$

and substituting this into (5.8) one obtains the algorithm in (5.3).

5.2.2 Approximate Algorithms

First consider how to implement an approximate method in the case of the stopping time algorithm in (5.3). Define the function $F(\omega, t_k) \equiv E[Z(\omega, \tau(\omega, t_{k+1}))|X(\omega, t_k)]$, where ω represents a sample path, and let $F_M(\omega, t_k)$ denote an approximation to $F(\omega, t_k)$ based on M 'parameters', where 'parameters' is used in a broad sense. Assume that these parameters can be estimated based on N observations and denote the estimated approximation by $\hat{F}_M^N(\omega, t_k)$. The estimated approximate stopping time can then be derived from the following algorithm:

$$\begin{cases} \hat{\tau}_M^N(\omega, t_K) = T \\ \hat{\tau}_M^N(\omega, t_k) = t_k \, \mathbf{1}_{\{Z(\omega, t_k) \geq \hat{F}_M^N(\omega, t_k)\}} + \hat{\tau}_M^N(\omega, t_{k+1}) \mathbf{1}_{\{Z(\omega, t_k) < \hat{F}_M^N(\omega, t_k)\}}, \quad 1 < k \leq K - 1. \end{cases} \tag{5.10}$$

From the algorithm in (5.10), a natural estimate of the option value in (5.4) can be calculated as:

$$\hat{P}_M^N(0) = \frac{1}{N} \sum_{n=1}^{N} Z(\omega_n, \hat{\tau}_M^N(\omega_n, 1)). \tag{5.11}$$

For the value function algorithm in (5.6), a similar approach can be taken. Now define the function $H(\omega, t_k) \equiv E[V(\omega, t_{k+1})|X(\omega, t_k)]$, let $H_M(\omega, t_k)$ denote an approximation to $H(\omega, t_k)$ based on M parameters, assume that these parameters can be estimated based on N observations, and denote the estimated approximation $\tilde{H}_M^N(\omega, t_k)$. The estimated approximate value functions can then be derived from the following algorithm:

$$\begin{cases} \tilde{V}_M^N(\omega, t_K) = Z(\omega, t_K) \\ \tilde{V}_M^N(\omega, t_k) = \max(Z(\omega, t_k), \tilde{H}_M^N(\omega, t_k)), \ 1 < k \le K - 1. \end{cases} \tag{5.12}$$

From the algorithm in (5.12), a natural estimate of the option value in (5.7) can be calculated as:

$$\tilde{P}_M^N(0) = \frac{1}{N} \sum_{n=1}^{N} \tilde{V}_M^N(\omega_n, t_1). \tag{5.13}$$

In the case of the exact algorithms, it was straightforward to show that the price in (5.4) and (5.7) coincide, and one might think that this is also the case for the approximate price obtained with (5.11) and (5.13). Unfortunately, this is not the case and instead it can be shown that the two methods lead to approximations with bias of opposite sign. In particular, the approximate stopping time algorithm leads to downwardly biased estimates since by definition any approximate stopping time is suboptimal. The approximate value function algorithm, on the other hand, leads to upwardly biased estimates because of the 'max' operator in (5.12).[4] Since the biases are of different sign a direct comparison of the two methods is somewhat difficult. However, it is in fact possible to quantify the magnitude of the bias and based on this argue that the absolute size of the bias will be negligible for the approximate stopping time algorithm. The approximate value function algorithm, on the other hand, will generally have a non-negligible positive bias, see Stentoft (2008a).

Finally, it may be argued that there should be less accumulation of errors for the approximate stopping time algorithm than for the approximate value function algorithm. Consider, as an example, the case above with an approximate value function which is biased upward compared to the true value function. In this situation the resulting price estimate from the approximate value function method is affected by two sources of error. Firstly, the bias means that exercise is chosen relatively late compared to the optimal time due to the higher value attributed to continuation. Secondly, the future value attributed to a path, for which the choice is to continue to hold the option, is too high because of the biased estimation. For the approximate stopping time algorithm, on the other hand, only the error due to choosing to exercise relatively late occurs. Hence we can expect there to be less accumulation of errors with this method; see Stentoft (2008a).

5.3   OPTION PRICING USING SIMULATION

It should be clear from the previous section that pricing American-style options is a complicated task. Indeed, it remains a challenge to develop flexible methods that can be used in a multidimensional setting. As discussed in the introduction, many of the methods that have been used, such as the binomial model and the finite difference method, cannot be extended to accommodate more than a couple of stochastic factors. Therefore, alternative methods are needed and this is where simulation techniques are interesting.

In this section I explain how simulation can be used to price both European and American-style options. I first consider the case of the European option which is a 'special case' of the framework above where $\tau(t_1) = T$. Although this type of option is not the main focus of this chapter, considering this case first allows me to discuss some important properties of the simulation approach. Next I discuss how American-style options can be priced using simulation. I review several existing methods and discuss their advantages and potential problems.

5.3.1   European Options

Using the fact that for the European option it is optimal to exercise at time T, that is, $\tau(t_1) = T$ by definition, and substituting this into (5.1), one obtains the following formula:

$$p(0) = E[Z(T)], \tag{5.14}$$

where lower case letters are used to denote that this is the European price and where $Z(t_k) = h(X(t_k), t_k)$ is the payoff from exercising the option at time t_k. From (5.14), it is clear that all that is needed to price the option are the values of the state variables, $X(t_k)$, on the day the option expires. Thus, an obvious estimate of the true price in (5.14) can be calculated using N simulated paths as:

$$\hat{p}^N(0) = \frac{1}{N}\sum_{n=1}^{N} h(X(\omega_n, T), T), \tag{5.15}$$

where $X(\omega_n, T)$ is the value of the state variables at the time of expiration T along path number n.

    Equation (5.15) does not necessarily rely on the discretized framework since all that is needed is the values of the state variables at maturity. For example, if one considers options in the constant volatility log-normal model of Black and Scholes (1973) and Merton (1973), or BSM, these values can be generated directly. However, there are several situations where this is not the case. Firstly, the framework may be discrete by definition as is the case in the GARCH framework I use in sections 5.4 and 5.5. Next, when simulating from many models with stochastic volatility and jumps, discretization methods are needed. Finally, as I discuss below, in some situations the payoff of the option is in fact path dependent which also requires a discrete time framework as the one used here. Clearly, as the number of periods K tends to infinity one would expect that the estimates converge to those obtained with a truly continuous time formulation in the latter two cases.

Extensions

One of the most important advantages of the simulation method is its flexibility, and one might argue that 'if we can simulate it, we can price it'.[5] For example, simulation methods can be used to price European options whose payoffs depend on a function of the path of the underlying asset and not just the terminal value. A classic example is the so-called Asian option or average value option, where the option payoff is determined by the average underlying price over some pre-set period of time. This type of option is of particular interest in thinly traded markets since price manipulation is difficult. One of the first methods proposed to price this type of product was simulation, see Kemna and Vorst (1990). Other types of path-dependent options are look-back options and barrier options. Note that some path-dependent options depend on the entire path of the underlying asset. In this case, simulation methods only provide an approximation to the true price, the precision of which depends on the precision of the discretization used for simulation.

Simulation methods are also well suited to pricing European-style options when the simple BSM model is generalized. For example, one could consider treating the volatility as an additional stochastic factor. This allows for a large degree of flexibility and in the literature many such models have been suggested. Some early examples which use simulation methods for pricing are Hull and White (1987) and Scott (1987). Simulation methods have also been used to price options in discrete-time models with time-varying volatility such as the GARCH option pricing model of Duan (1995). Although the binomial model can be extended to accommodate stochastic volatility and jumps, see for example Amin (1993), and GARCH features, see for example Ritchken and Trevor (1999), these extensions lack the flexibility available with the simulation method.

Finally, the simulation approach is easily extended to more complex types of European options such as options on multiple stocks, see, for example, Margrabe (1978), Stulz (1982) and Johnson (1987) for multivariate extensions of the constant volatility Gaussian model; Da Fonseca et al. (2007) and Gourieroux and Sufana (2010) for multivariate stochastic volatility models; and Rombouts and Stentoft (2011) for a multivariate discrete-time model with time-varying volatility and correlations. Classical examples of options on multiple stocks are basket options, for which the payoff is based on the average of a basket of securities; spread options, where the payoff is based on the difference between the prices of two or more assets; and options which pay the best or worst of N assets. Note also that the most traded type of options, index options, are in principle options on an average of multiple assets. Simulation methods can easily accommodate all these types of extensions as the computational complexity increases only linearly in the number of underlying assets.

Properties

Simulation methods are not only very flexible but they also have very nice asymptotic properties. For example, another advantage of the simulation method is that it is well known that the price estimate in (5.15) will be unbiased and asymptotically normal under very mild assumptions. In fact, the only restriction is that the payoff function should be square integrable, which is a relatively mild assumption. The reason is that after all the European price is just an expected value and estimating this by an average of independent simulation values is (very) sensible.

The fact that a central limit holds for the option price estimate in (5.15) immediately tells us that the standard error of this estimate tends to zero with $1/\sqrt{N}$. Therefore, in order to obtain an estimate with half the variance, one needs to double the number of simulated paths. Although this is very 'reasonable' in statistics, compared to many other numerical methods this approach would be considered slow. For this reason, a lot of research has been conducted to reduce the variance of the estimated price. Among the simplest and most widely used methods are antithetic simulation, see, for example, Boyle (1977); control variables, see, for example, Boyle (1977) and Kemna and Vorst (1990); and moment matching methods, see, for example, Barraquand (1995), who termed this 'quadratic re-sampling', and Duan and Simonato (1998), who call it 'empirical martingale simulation'. Other more specialized methods are importance sampling and methods that use stratified sampling or samples from low-discrepancy sequences. For an early discussion of how these methods may be applied to security pricing in general and option pricing in particular, see the review of Boyle et al. (1997), and for a detailed introduction to these methods see Glasserman (2004).

Finally, it should be noted that one potential additional challenge in using simulation for pricing is that sometimes future values of the state variables cannot be simulated directly, or only simulated at great cost. In particular, whereas simulation is straightforward in the simple constant volatility log-normal Black, Scholes and Merton (BSM) model, this is not the case with many of the stochastic volatility and jump models which generalize this framework. Whenever this is the case, discretization methods are needed and these will affect the properties of the estimates obtained. For a general introduction to this, see Kloeden et al. (1994) and for applications of particular relevance in finance, see Glasserman (2004). This issue is also of particular importance if the derivative is path dependent as discussed above. However, note that for other applications, for example to the GARCH framework which is discrete in nature and therefore simple to simulate from, this is not a problem.

5.3.2 American Options

Though simulation techniques are simple to use for pricing European options, even those with path dependence, this is by no means the case for American-style options. Essentially, the problem at hand is that pricing American options is backward looking; that is, one starts at maturity and then solves the problem in (5.1) by going backwards. In contrast, simulations are forward-looking; that is, tomorrow's stock price is generated from today's value. Thus, for a long time it was believed that it would be difficult if not impossible to price this type of option using simulation. For example, earlier editions of standard textbooks such as Hull (2000) remark that simulation methods 'cannot easily handle situations where there are early exercise opportunities'.[6]

In order to illustrate the problem, consider the simplest possible two-period framework and assume that the simulated paths are as illustrated in Figure 5.1. Further assume that we wish to price a put option with a strike price of $\bar{S}$. While the payoff is known at time T, at time t_1 it has to be decided if early exercise would be optimal along each path. Using next period's payoff along the path would lead to biased results as this implies perfect foresight on behalf of the option holder. To be specific, the problem is that in order to determine the optimal stopping time one needs to know the conditional expectation of the future payoff.

Overview of existing methods
In the literature, several methods have been proposed to approximate this conditional expectation using simulation techniques. Examples include the bundling or state space partitioning methods of Tilley (1993) and Barraquand and Martineau (1995); the regression-based methods of, for example, Carriere (1996), Tsitsiklis and Van Roy (2001) and Longstaff and Schwartz (2001); and the stochastic mesh method of Broadie and Glasserman (2004). In the following I provide an overview of these methods.[7] I also consider the parameterized stopping time method of Garcia (2003) and Ibanez and Zapatero (2004), although this method does not approximate the continuation value directly.

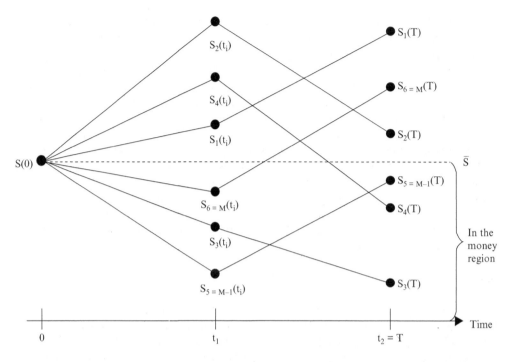

*Figure 5.1   The American option pricing problem when using simulation in the simple
two-period case*

Parameterized stopping strategy   A first idea of how to solve the American option
pricing problem is to parameterize the early exercise decision. For example, if this decision can be determined by a low dimensional set of parameters, θ, then solving the
optimal stopping time problem amounts to optimizing over this set. To be specific,
consider the put option with only one possible early exercise time in Figure 5.1. Here, θ
could simply be the threshold price of the underlying asset at which it becomes optimal to
exercise the option. This type of method was suggested by Garcia (2003) and Ibanez and
Zapatero (2004). More generally, one could estimate a separate threshold price for each
early exercise date or alternatively one could approximate the threshold value across the
early exercise dates by a low order function.

Though at first sight this method appears straightforward, in real applications the
problem is that the optimization is generally not simple and often the problem fails to
be well behaved. For example, even in the simplest possible case the simulated option
price is in general not continuous in the parameter over which the optimization is conducted. As a result, it may be impossible for standard optimization algorithms to find
the optimum. This is illustrated in Figure 5.1 where the function is flat between the three
paths that are in the money and jumps discretely at each point. Though this becomes less
of an issue as the number of paths increases, with a large number of paths the numerical
maximization becomes computationally very demanding.

Another potential problem with the parametric method is the curse of dimensionality
of the optimization problem, both in terms of the number of exercise steps and in the

number of stochastic factors. For example, extending the simple two-period problem to, for example, one with 50 early exercise points would result in a 50-dimensional optimization problem. This is very difficult to solve and typically more than 50 times as difficult as solving the one-dimensional problem. Although this type of issue could be circumvented by approximating the 50 points by a low-order function, this would introduce an approximation bias unless the functional form is sufficiently flexible. Moreover, although this type of approximation could decrease the computational burden in the one-dimensional case, this may not be the case when the number of stochastic factors increase. To illustrate this, consider again the case with only one possible early exercise time but let the option be multidimensional on the average of several underlying assets. In one dimension the threshold is a point, in two dimensions it is a line, and in three dimensions it is a plane.[8]

Bundling methods and state space partitioning The real problem in using simulation to price American options is that as one moves backwards through time one simply cannot use the future path to determine the optimal stopping time as this would imply perfect foresight on behalf of the option holder. One way to avoid this is to bundle several paths together and use the average future values within a bundle as an estimate of the expected future value. This approach was one of the first suggestions made for the American option pricing problem and dates back to Tilley (1993). To be specific, let M be the number of equally sized bundles and let $b(\omega_n, t)$ denote which bundle path number ω_n belongs to at time t. Then the algorithm of Tilley (1993) calculates the value along path ω_n at time t as:

$$\hat{V}(\omega_n, t) = \max\left[Z(\omega_n, t), \frac{1}{N/M} \sum_{\{j : b(\omega_j, t) = b(\omega_n, t)\}} \hat{V}(\omega_j, t + 1) \right]. \tag{5.16}$$

That is, the continuation value is a simple average of future payoffs.[9] Because of this averaging, the issue of perfect foresight is mitigated.

More generally, the underlying idea of this type of algorithm is that when simulated paths are bundled together one can calculate the probability of transitioning to a future bundle conditional on today's bundle. Moreover, average future values within a bundle can be used as estimates of actual future values without assuming perfect foresight. With these probabilities and the future values, the conditional expected future values can be approximated. Let M be the number of (now not necessarily equally sized) bundles and let $b(\omega_n, t)$ denote which bundle path number ω_n belongs to at time t. Furthermore, let $p(i, j, t)$ be the probability of moving from bundle i to bundle j from time t to $t + 1$, calculated by simply counting the number of transitions. Then the bundling algorithm estimates the value along path ω_n at time t as:

$$\hat{V}(\omega_n, t) = \max\left[Z(\omega_n, t), \sum_{j=1}^{M} p(b(\omega_n, t), j, t) \times \overline{V}(j, t + 1) \right], \tag{5.17}$$

where $\overline{V}(j, t + 1)$ denotes the average option value of all paths in bundle j at time $t + 1$. Note that in the limit, when the number of bundles equals the number of paths, we obtain the perfect foresight solution.

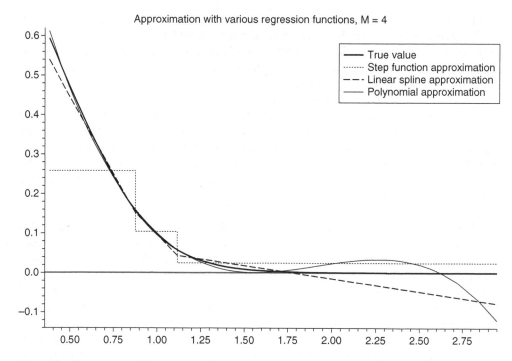

Note: Results are reported for approximations based on step functions, linear splines, and simple polynomials. The true value corresponds in this case to the BSM price of an option with one period to maturity.

Figure 5.2   The approximation obtained with various regression functions

The main problem with the bundling algorithm is that the partition has to be chosen before the simulation and choosing the partition is particularly tricky in high-dimensional problems. For example, for a given number of partitions along each underlying asset value, the total number of partitions grows exponentially in the dimension of the problem. To circumvent this problem, Barraquand and Martineau (1995) suggest that instead of partitioning the state space along the simulated paths, one should use the payoff for stratification. In particular, instead of partitioning the (high-dimensional) state space of the underlying asset, partitions are chosen based on the (one-dimensional) payoff. The algorithm is termed stratified state aggregation along the payoff, or SSAP, and it ensures that the partition is feasible even in high dimensions.[10]

Regression-based methods   In the bundling algorithms, the conditional expectation term, the second term in (5.17), is constant for all paths in a given bundle. Hence this method essentially approximates the conditional expectation function by a step function. While this may be a reasonable method for approximating some functions, it most likely is not so for functions such as the conditional expectation. For example, in the two-period case in a BSM world, we know that at time t_1 this expectation is given by the one-period European option value. Thus, unless the number of bundles is very large, the approximation is poor and so is the estimate of the option price. In Figure 5.2 I illustrate this using four partitions with a dotted line. Thus, in actual applications of the bundling method, a large number of bundles, say 100, is required.

The step functions needed in the bundling algorithm can actually be estimated in one go by using simple dummy variables for the bins of the state variables as regressors in a simple linear regression using the cross-section of simulated paths. This is in fact how I generated the approximation in Figure 5.2 in which the regression used four partitions: that is, a constant term and three 'steps'. However, as an obvious alternative to the step functions, one could then use other more refined regression functions. For example, one could use (linear) spline functions as suggested by Carriere (1996) or a given polynomial family as suggested by Longstaff and Schwartz (2001), and these methods are now collectively referred to as regression-based methods. They have been analyzed in quite some detail, see, for example, Moreno and Navas (2003), Stentoft (2004a) and Areal et al. (2008). To be specific, let $\{\phi_m(\cdot)\}_{m=1}^M$ denote a 'family' of functions, also called basis or approximation architecture, to be used for the approximation. Then a regression-based method would estimate the value along path ω_n at time t by:

$$\hat{V}(\omega_n, t) = \max\left[Z(\omega_n, t), \sum_{m=1}^M \phi_m(X(\omega, t_k))\hat{b}_m(t_k)\right],$$
(5.18)

where $\hat{b}_m(t_k)$ is found from a regression of future values on the regression functions $\{\phi_m(\cdot)\}_{m=1}^M$. Though the regression-based methods do not involve choosing a partition as in the bundling algorithm, they do involve a choice of regression functions. However, in the existing literature there is a significant amount of evidence that the actual choice of regressors is in fact of minor importance in actual applications; see, for example, Moreno and Navas (2003) and Stentoft (2004a).

Regression-based methods differ first in terms of how the approximation is carried out. In Figure 5.2 I also plot the approximation obtained using three regressors plus a constant term with linear splines, the dashed line, and polynomials, the thin solid line, respectively. From this figure it can be seen that both approximate the true value quite well in the centre, whereas the approximation in the tails is much worse. When compared to the step function approximation though, it is evident that the spline and polynomial approximation methods have clear advantages. Secondly, the methods differ in terms of the interval over which the approximation is conducted. For example, Longstaff and Schwartz (2001) suggest that only the in-the-money (ITM) paths should be used. In Figure 5.3 I compare the approximation when using only the ITM paths and when using all the paths. This figure clearly shows how much better the fit is for a given number of parameters, M, when using only the ITM paths and lends support to the suggestion of Longstaff and Schwartz (2001).[11]

Stochastic mesh methods   In the bundling and state space partitioning method the transition densities are approximated for the bundles. However, if these were known one could simply estimate the value along path ω_n at time t by:

$$\hat{V}(\omega_n, t) = \max\left[Z(\omega_n, t), \sum_{j=1}^N p(\omega_n, j, t) \times \hat{V}(\omega_j, t + 1)\right].$$
(5.19)

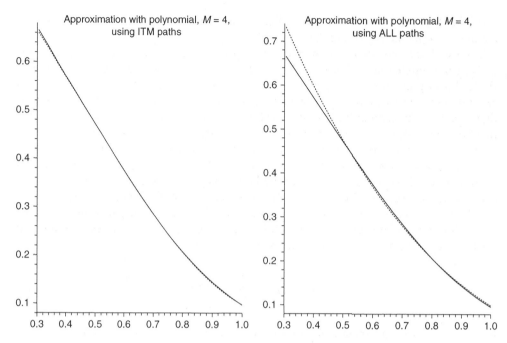

Note: The left-hand plot shows the results when only ITM paths are used and the right-hand plot when all paths are used.

Figure 5.3   The approximations obtained with a polynomial of order M = 4

Unlike the bundling algorithm in (5.17), here all the N paths are used. This method is known as the stochastic mesh method; see for example Broadie and Glasserman (2004). The reason for the name is that at any time step all current knots are 'connected' to all future knots, which creates a mesh-like structure.

A major drawback of the stochastic mesh method is that often computationally complex operations are required to obtain the transition densities. Moreover, in many cases the transition densities are not known analytically and will have to be approximated. This further adds to the computational complexity of the method. Broadie et al. (2000) suggest two methods which can be used to determine the transition densities when these are either unknown or fail to exist. Both methods rely on constraining the weights to correctly replicate certain basic theoretical quantities, such as moments of the state variables. Since there will generally be many more weights than constraints this problem is underdetermined, requires the imposition of an optimization criterion and is non-trivial to solve.

Nevertheless, the stochastic mesh method is not only closely connected to the stratified state partitioning method, it is in fact also related to the regression-based methods. To see this, note that one can rewrite the predicted value given by $\sum_{m=1}^{M}\phi_m(X(\omega,t_k))\hat{b}_m(t_k)$ in (5.18) as:

$$\frac{1}{N}\sum_{j=1}^{N}\Phi(X(\omega,t_k))\,(\Phi(X(\omega,t_k))'\Phi(X(\omega,t_k)))^{-1}\Phi(X(\omega_j,t_k))'\hat{V}(\omega_j,t+1),$$

where $\Phi(X(\omega, t_k))$ is the $N \times M + 1$ matrix of regressors used and $\Phi(X(\omega_n, t_k))$ is the $M + 1$ row vector of the regressors evaluated for path ω_n. Thus, the regression-based methods correspond to a particular choice of weights in the stochastic mesh method.

Discussion

Of the methods discussed above, the regression-based methods in general and the least squares Monte Carlo (LSM) method of Longstaff and Schwartz (2001) in particular are some of the most popular methods for pricing American options using simulation. For example, a web search performed in early 2012 using http://scholar.google.com resulted in 41 citations of Garcia (2003) and 116 citations of Ibanez and Zapatero (2004) for the parameterized stopping strategy method; 305 citations of Tilley (1993) and 306 citations of Barraquand and Martineau (1995) for the state space partitioning method; 239 citations of Carriere (1996), 272 citations of Tsitsiklis and Van Roy (2001) and a massive 1519 citations of Longstaff and Schwartz (2001) for the regression-based methods; and 126 citations of Broadie and Glasserman (2004) for the stochastic mesh method.[12]

Moreover, regression-based methods are not only the most cited methods for pricing American options using simulation; they are also very likely the most flexible methods. After all, regression-based methods use nothing but the simulated paths together with linear regression to determine the option price. The flexibility is illustrated by the many applications of the method to price: among other things, life insurance contracts (e.g. in Bacinello et al., 2010), real-estate derivatives (e.g. in Longstaff, 2005) and real options (e.g. in Gamba, 2002), which has several applications such as gas storage, mine expansion decisions, timber harvest contracts and executive stock options (e.g. in León and Vaello-Sebastià, 2009). In addition to being very flexible it can be argued that regression-based methods have advantages both in terms of computational efficiency and in terms of their asymptotic properties.

Computational efficiency   One of the main advantages of regression-based methods is that they are computationally efficient. In fact, as shown in Stentoft (2004a), in multiple dimensions the LSM method is actually more efficient than the binomial model which is notoriously difficult to outperform. When comparing the methods it should be clear that computationally the challenge is to determine the parameters; that is, the transition probabilities in the bundling algorithm, the coefficients in the regression-based algorithm, and the transition densities in the stochastic mesh method. The reason that regression-based methods are computationally efficient is that they rely on nothing but simple linear regression to calculate the coefficients needed for the approximation of the conditional expectation function. I now examine the computational time of the different methods using the example of an American put option in a BSM model. The option matures in one year and has a strike price of 40, the interest rate is 6 percent, and the underlying asset's price is 40, it pays no dividend and has a volatility of 40 percent.

In Figure 5.4 I report the computational time for the regression-based method. Since this method relies on linear regressions to determine the M parameters, it is expected to be of order $K \times N \times M^2$.[13] The left-hand plot shows computational time against the number of time steps, K, for different number of paths and confirms that computational time is linear in the number of time steps. The right-hand plot shows computational time against the number of regressors, M, and shows that this indeed grows faster than

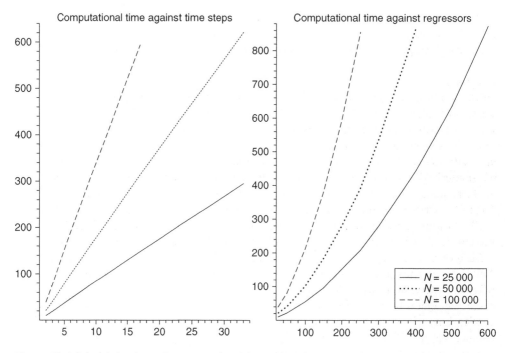

Figure 5.4   *The computational time for the regression algorithm for different values of*
N, *the number of simulated paths*

linearly. However, this is to be expected as the regression is of order $N \times M^2$. Finally, when comparing computational time for a given number of time periods or regressors while increasing the number of paths, N, Figure 5.4 shows that there is a linear relationship. Put differently, computing a price with 50 000 paths takes roughly twice as much time as with 25 000 paths, and half the time as with 100 000 paths.

In Figure 5.5 I report the corresponding results for the bundling algorithm. The left-hand plot shows that for this method computational time is linear in the number of time steps, K, as it was the case with the regression-based method. The right-hand plot shows that computational time is also linear in the number of partitions, M. This is in contrast to the regression-based method for which computational time grew faster. Finally, note that Figure 5.5 confirms that computational time increases linearly in the number of paths, N, with the bundling method as it was the case with the regression-based method. Essentially these results show that the bundling algorithm is of order $K \times N \times M$.

Finally, consider the stochastic mesh method. Compared to the state space partitioning method, each valuation of (5.19) in the stochastic mesh is of order $N \times N$, and therefore the method is at least of order $K \times N^2$ even if the transition densities are known. The computational complexity is further increased when the transition densities are either unknown or fail to exist and have to be estimated using, for example, the method of Broadie et al. (2000). In particular, using the simplest method the weights are determined using linear

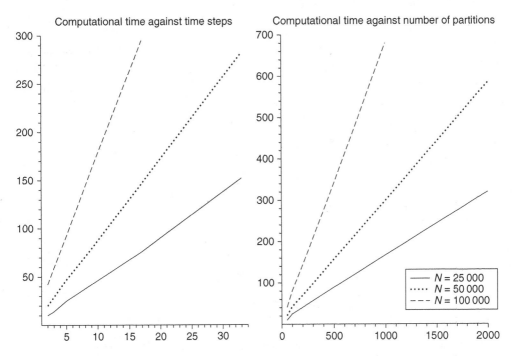

Note: The left-hand plot shows the computational time against the number of time steps, K, and the right-hand plot against the number of partitions, M.

Figure 5.5   The computational time for the bundling algorithm for different values of N, the number of simulated paths

regression and therefore it is of order $N \times B^2$, where B is the number of constraints imposed to obtain the weights. However, this problem has to be solved for all N paths and at each time step. Therefore the overall complexity of the method is in fact of order $K \times N^2 \times B^2$. Thus, even if the number of constraints is low and the method is implemented with few paths, the computational cost is large with this method due to the factor N^2.

Based on the results above it may appear that the bundling algorithm is in fact the most efficient since the computational time only grows linearly in the number of partitions. However, this is true only if the same number of regressors and partitions are needed. In real applications, this is rarely the case since it is possible to obtain a much better approximation using, for example a polynomial function than a step function as Figure 5.2 shows. Moreover, when comparing the actual performance of the methods, the price estimates and not only computational time needs to be compared. In Figure 5.6 I plot the root mean square error, $RMSE$, of a particular estimate, $\hat{P}_M^N(0)$, which I define as:

$$RMSE(\hat{P}_M^N(0)) = \sqrt{E[(\hat{P}_M^N(0) - P(0))^2]}, \qquad (5.20)$$

against computational time. I estimate the expected value by the sample mean from 1000 independent simulations, and compare the estimate from the parametric method, the bundling algorithm, the SSAP method and the regression-based method.

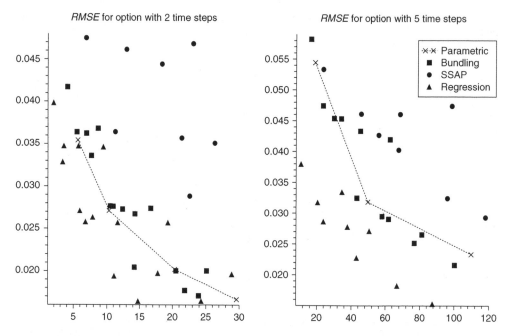

Note: The left-hand plot shows results for an option with two time steps and the right-hand plot for an option with five time steps. Results are reported for the parametric stopping time, the bundling method, the SSAP method, and the regression based method. The best models are close to the origin.

Figure 5.6   The RMSE of the different estimators against computational time

The left-hand plot of Figure 5.6 shows the results for an option with two time periods. From this plot it is seen that the best approach is the regression-based method as this is closest to the origin and offers the best trade-off between computational time and precision. The next best is the bundling method, although the parametric method has similar performance when computational speed is important. The SSAP method is always dominated by the other methods, even the parametric method, in this example. The results for the option with five time periods in the right-hand plot of Figure 5.6 are very similar and the ranking of the methods is the same. However, when comparing the two plots it is seen that the relative performance of the regression-based method compared to, for example, the bundling method improves with the number of time steps. For example, estimates with an *RMSE* ≈ 0.02 can be obtained roughly 22 percent faster with regression-based methods in the first case and 57 percent faster in the second case.[14]

Asymptotic properties   Another advantage of regression-based methods is that they have nice asymptotic properties. In particular, it can be shown that the estimated price converges to the true price as the number of paths and regressors tend to infinity under some regularity assumptions. Stentoft (2004b) proves this for the LSM algorithm in a general multi-period and multidimensional setting and shows that to achieve convergence the number of regressors, M, should not be increased too fast and has to satisfy $M < C \times N^{1/3}$. Glasserman and Yu (2004) study the case where all the paths are used in the regression and prove convergence in the normal and log-normal cases provided that $M < C \times \ln(N)$ and $M < C \times \sqrt{\ln(N)}$, respectively. Thus, this shows that the speed with which M can be increased is much slower when all the paths are used than when only the ITM paths are used. See Gerhold (2011) and references therein for generalizations of these results to other processes. Although it is difficult if not impossible to derive the actual convergence rates for the price estimate, the numerical evidence provided in Stentoft (2012) shows that in many cases this happens as quickly as with the European price estimate.

For the bundling method, on the other hand, significantly less research has been conducted in terms of convergence results. In particular, though it is argued in Tilley (1993) that for a fixed bundling parameter α, where $0 < \alpha < 1$, if the number of bundles, M, is picked as $M = N^{\alpha}$ the algorithm converges as N tends to infinity, no formal proof is provided. This type of result can likely be generalized to the multidimensional situation, although here the standard bundling method suffers from the curse of dimensionality. Moreover, as shown in Boyle et al. (1997), an important disadvantage of the SSAP method is its potential lack of convergence. The reason for this is that the payoff is not a sufficient statistic for determining the optimal exercise strategy. This limits the potential use of these methods in particular for multidimensional problems.[15]

The asymptotic properties of the parameterized stopping strategy method are examined in Garcia (2003), who shows that if the stopping time can actually be parameterized by θ then the simulation method converges. Likewise, in Broadie and Glasserman (2004), the stochastic mesh estimator is shown to converge to the true price when the mesh weights, $p(\omega_n, j, t)$, are known. Thus, the existing results are for the 'idealized' algorithms and therefore of little use for practical purposes. In fact, this is similar in spirit to assuming that the exact conditional expectation in, for example, $F(\omega, t_k)$ is given by some finite element function $F_M(\omega, t_k)$ with known form. In this case, it is simple to show that $\hat{F}_M^N(\omega, t_k)$ converges to $F_M(\omega, t_k)$ as N tends to infinity and therefore the regression-based method converges. To obtain convergence of the two methods in the general case one would need results when the stopping time is approximated or when the weights of the mesh are estimated, respectively, and these are, to my knowledge, not available.

5.4   THE GARCH OPTION PRICING MODEL

In the previous section I illustrated how American options can be priced using simulation. In particular, I argued that a framework relying on cross-sectional regressions to determine the conditional expectations is computationally efficient and very flexible. It should therefore be an obvious candidate to be used to price options in very realistic models.

In this section I illustrate this using the generalized autoregressive conditional heteroskedastic (GARCH) model originally suggested by Engle (1982) and Bollerslev (1986). I first introduce the GARCH framework and I explain how the risk neutral dynamics needed for option pricing can be obtained. Next, I provide a detailed algorithm for American option pricing in this model. I also discuss some alternative methods and review some of the existing results.

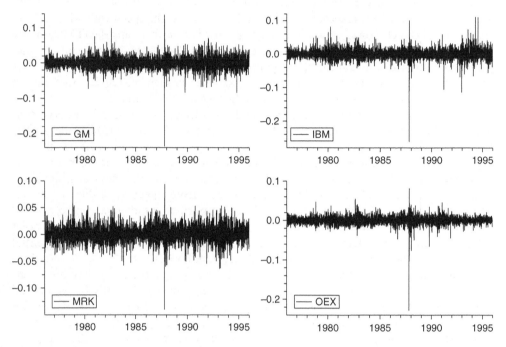

Note: The sample period is January 2, 1976, to December 29, 1995, for a total of 5055 observations.

Figure 5.7   Time series plots of the annualized continuously compounded returns for the four assets considered

5.4.1   The GARCH Framework

As elegant as it is, the BSM model with constant volatility and log-normal returns is unsatisfying as a model for financial data. There exists an extensive empirical literature which has documented that the return variance of many assets is time varying. For illustrative purposes I plot in Figure 5.7 the return through time for four assets. The assets considered are General Motors (GM), International Business Machines (IBM), Merck and Company Inc. (MRK) and the Standard & Poor's 100 index (OEX). The sample period is January 2, 1976, to December 29, 1995, for a total of 5055 observations. The figure clearly shows that periods of high volatility are clustered, that is, periods of high return variance are followed by periods of low return variance, and hence the variance is time varying.

In the empirical literature the GARCH framework has been used extensively to model financial time series with similar properties as the ones considered in Figure 5.7; see, for example, the surveys by Bollerslev et al. (1992) and Poon and Granger (2003). To illustrate this framework, consider a discrete time economy with the price of an asset denoted S_t and the dividends of that asset denoted δ_t. Then assume that the continuously compounded return process, $R_t = \ln((S_t + \delta_t)/S_{t-1})$, can be modelled using the GARCH framework. In the most general form one can specify the dynamics as:

$$R_t = m_t(\,\cdot\,;\theta_m) + \sqrt{h_t}\varepsilon_t \qquad (5.21)$$

$$h_t = g(h_s,\varepsilon_s;-\infty < s \le t - 1,\theta_h) \qquad (5.22)$$

$$\varepsilon_t = Z_t, \qquad (5.23)$$

where Z_t, conditional on the information set F_{t-1} containing all information up to and including time $t - 1$, is a standard normal variable.

In (5.21) the term $m_t(\,\cdot\,;\theta_m)$ denotes the conditional mean which is allowed to be governed by a set of parameters θ_m as long as the process is measurable with respect to the information set F_{t-1}. This means that besides the various exogenous variables one might consider using in the mean equation, the mean term may include lagged values of, for example, the variance as is the case for the GARCH-in-mean specifications. Likewise, in (5.22) the parameter θ_h governs the variance process which is allowed to depend on lagged values of innovations to the return process and lagged values of the volatility itself. Two classical specifications are the GARCH process of Bollerslev (1986) given by:

$$h_t = \omega + \alpha h_{t-1}\varepsilon_{t-1}^2 + \beta h_{t-1}, \qquad (5.24)$$

and the non-linear asymmetric GARCH process, or NGARCH, of Engle and Ng (1993) given by:

$$h_t = \omega + \alpha h_{t-1}(\varepsilon_{t-1} + \gamma\sqrt{h_{t-1}})^2 + \beta h_{t-1}. \qquad (5.25)$$

The NGARCH specification can potentially accommodate asymmetric responses to negative and positive return innovations and thus allows for the so-called leverage effect. Moreover, note that the GARCH specification is obtained when the asymmetry parameter, γ, is zero.[16]

A major advantage with the discrete-time GARCH model in (5.21)–(5.23) is that data are readily available for estimation. Moreover, estimation is computationally simple and can be performed using maximum likelihood techniques, for example. In particular, conditional on starting values the log likelihood function for a sample of T_{obs} observations is, up to a constant, given by:

$$L_{T_{obs}}(\theta) = \frac{1}{T_{obs}}\sum_{t=1}^{T_{obs}} -\frac{1}{2}(\log(h_t) + \varepsilon_t^2/h_t), \qquad (5.26)$$

where θ denotes the set of parameters in θ_m and in θ_h. This is very different from the continuous time framework in which volatility is modelled as a separate stochastic process. Although this framework allows for a large degree of flexibility in the specification and sometimes leads to elegant solutions for the price of European options, in real applications a problem with continuous-time models is that volatility is unobservable. Hence estimation of these models is rather complicated. Moreover, when pricing claims for which numerical procedures are required, as it is the case with, for example, American options, future values of the unobservable volatility are needed. This variable is latent and hence potentially complicated to predict.[17]

The risk-neutral dynamics
Although there are clear advantages of the discrete-time GARCH framework in terms of estimation, when deriving a theoretical option pricing model discreteness poses a potential problem as the asset market models easily become incomplete. This is indeed the case for the GARCH-type models. Heuristically, the reason is that, unlike in the binomial model where the stock can take only two different values next period conditional on the price today, in a GARCH model the number of future possible values is infinite. Thus, in order to obtain the appropriate risk-neutral dynamics, further assumptions about preferences, apart from non-satiation, or about the risk premium, have to be made in order to obtain a risk-neutral valuation relationship.

The approach used in Duan (1995), where an extension of the risk-neutralization principle of Brennan (1979) referred to as the locally risk-neutral valuation relationship (LRNVR) is used, falls in the first category. The LRNVR can be shown to hold under some familiar assumptions on preferences and under the assumed conditional normality in (5.23). Using the LRNVR it can be shown that the appropriate risk-neutralized dynamics are given by:

$$R_t = m_t(\cdot\,;\theta_m) + \sqrt{h_t}\varepsilon_t \tag{5.27}$$

$$h_t = g(h_s,\varepsilon_s; -\infty < s \le t-1, \theta_h) \tag{5.28}$$

$$\varepsilon_t = Z_t - \lambda_t, \tag{5.29}$$

where Z_t, conditional on F_{t-1}, is a standard normal variable under the risk-neutral measure Q.[18] Furthermore, in (5.29) above, λ_t is the solution to:

$$\lambda_t = \frac{m_t(\cdot\,;\theta_m) - r_t + \frac{1}{2}h_t}{\sqrt{h_t}}. \tag{5.30}$$

Thus, it is immediately observed that the risk-neutral dynamics depend only on parameters that can be estimated using historical returns. Note also that in this set-up risk-neutralization happens through a change of the mean of the risk-neutral innovations.

Accommodating the time-varying volatility via the GARCH framework has one drawback: in general no closed-form solutions can be found for the future distribution of stock prices and hence the pricing of even European options is difficult. However, it is immediately clear that using the system in (5.27)–(5.30) a large number of paths of the risk-neutralized asset prices can be generated and hence the simulation-based methods discussed previously can be used. In particular, this is the method used originally by Duan (1995), who recognized that the asset price S_t and the conditional volatility h_{t+1} together serve as sufficient statistics to simulate from the risk-neutral dynamics.

Extensions and alternatives
There are several interesting extensions to the GARCH framework above. For example, an interesting generalization is to consider situations where the conditional distribution is non-Gaussian. This situation was considered theoretically by Duan (1999), who shows how to derive the risk-neutral dynamics in this case. However, although non-Gaussian

distributions have been shown to be important, the problem remains that this complicates pricing. For example, it is generally not possible to find a closed-form expression for λ_t like that in (5.30) for the Gaussian case, and therefore it is difficult if not impossible to directly examine the effect of different mean specifications on option prices. Moreover, when using the method of Duan (1999) with non-Gaussian innovations, the risk-neutral innovations in (5.29) are generally not available explicitly and instead one needs to generate these using a numerical procedure; see, for example, Stentoft (2008a). This complicates pricing and adds to the computational complexity.

The Gaussian GARCH option pricing model of Duan (1995) and the generalization in Duan (1999) are not the only methods for obtaining the risk-neutral dynamics to be used for option pricing. More recently, Christoffersen et al. (2010b) have demonstrated that option pricing is possible in a non-Gaussian framework with time-varying volatility using only the no-arbitrage principle. In particular, they show that under certain assumptions, the resulting risk-neutral return dynamics are from the same family of distributions as the physical return dynamics in the non-Gaussian case as well. Thus, the paper shows that similar results can be provided under a more general pricing framework which does not rely on particular assumptions regarding the preferences of the representative agent. Note that in the log-normal case this method and that of Duan (1999) coincide and lead to equivalent risk-neutral dynamics. In the more general non-Gaussian case, however, the methods differ since in the approach of Christoffersen et al. (2010b), risk-neutralization happens directly through a change of the parameters of the risk-neutral distribution instead of by transforming the risk-neutral innovations.[19]

Finally, it should be noted that multivariate extensions of the GARCH framework exist. For example, these models have been used extensively in recent years to model the behavior of financial data. The resulting dynamics are generally more realistic as they take into account the interaction and correlation between assets. In Rombouts and Stentoft (2011) the dynamics needed for option pricing are derived for a general multivariate discrete-time model with time-varying volatility and correlations. This framework generalizes the method of Christoffersen et al. (2010b), which is obtained as a special case when only one asset is considered.

5.4.2 American Option Pricing with the GARCH Framework

In the following I will use the American put option as an example, and for simplicity I will assume that the option can be exercised only at the end of each trading day. Furthermore, I assume that the one-period continuously compounded dividend yield, δ_t, and the one-period interest rate, r_t, are both constant and I denote them simply by δ and r, respectively.

The algorithm
To fix the notation, let the present time be denoted by $t = 0$ and assume that the option expires in K trading days at time T. For notational convenience I denote the K trading days simply as $t_k = k$. The pricing algorithm consists of the following four steps: a parameter identification step, a simulation step and two pricing steps.

Step 1: identification and initialization of the relevant parameters. The relevant parameters in the GARCH framework are obtained. This can be done by estimating the parameters in (5.21)–(5.23) using maximum likelihood techniques. The parameter values are stored together with the necessary historical values for S_s, h_s, ε_s, and $m_s(\cdot\,;\theta_m)$, for $s \le 0$ as specified in the particular choice of variance equation in (5.22).

Step 2: simulation of the risk-neutral asset price. Given the historical values for S_s, h_s, ε_s, and $m_s(\cdot\,;\theta_m)$, for $s \le 0$, one can immediately calculate the conditional volatility through period one, h_1. From (5.28) this is simply $h_1 = g(h_s, \varepsilon_s, S_s; s \le 0)$, and with this a realization of the next period stock price S_1 can be calculated from the starting level S_0 as:

$$S_1 = S_0 \exp\{m_1(\cdot\,;\theta_m) - \delta + \sqrt{h_1}\varepsilon_1\}, \tag{5.31}$$

where $\varepsilon_1 = Z_1 - \lambda_1$ with $Z_1 \sim N(0,1)$. Likewise, the conditional volatility through the next period should now be calculated as:

$$h_2 = g(h_s, \varepsilon_s, S_s; s \le 1). \tag{5.32}$$

Iterating on (5.31) and (5.32) a further $K - 1$ times until the time of expiration is reached yields a single realization of a stock path. The simulation consists of N such stock paths, each of which is labeled $S(n)$, $n = 1, \ldots, N$, generated using different random Gaussian variates or using different seeds in the random number generator.[20]

Step 3: calculation of the payoff along each path. Let Z be an $N \times K$ payoff matrix, with typical element $z_t(n)$. At time T the payoff along each path is the maximum of zero and the value of exercising the option. Hence, the elements of the last column in the matrix Z may be calculated as:

$$z_K(n) = \max(0, X - S_K(n)), \quad 1 \le n \le N. \tag{5.33}$$

Next, at any time t, $0 < t < K$, ordinary least squares (OLS) is used to estimate the conditional expectation of the payoff if the option is kept alive, along the paths for which the option is in the money and thus immediate exercise should be considered. As the dependent variable, use the discounted pathwise future payoff:

$$y_t(n) = \sum_{\tilde{\imath} = t+1}^{K} e^{-(\tilde{\imath} - t)r} z_{\tilde{\imath}}(n), \tag{5.34}$$

where r is the risk-free interest rate. As regressors use powers and cross-products of the two state variables which in this case are the stock price S_t and the level of the volatility h_{t+1}. Denote the state variables by $x_t(n)$ and let $\Xi(x_t(n))$ be the transformation with powers and cross products. Then the conditional expectation $F(x_t(n)) \equiv E[y_t(n) | x_t(n)]$ from section 5.2.2 is approximated by:

$$\hat{F}(x) = \Xi(x_t(n))\hat{\beta}_t, \tag{5.35}$$

where $\hat{\beta}_t$ is a vector of coefficients determined by OLS. The fitted values correspond to the estimated conditional expectation of the payoff from the option assuming that it is kept alive. Now use the following rule to determine whether or not to exercise at time t for all the in the money paths, n:

$$z_t(n) = \begin{cases} S_t(n) - X \text{ and } z_{\tilde{t}}(n) = 0, t < \tilde{t} \le K \text{ if } S_t(n) - X > \hat{F}(x) \\ 0 \qquad\qquad\qquad\qquad\qquad\qquad \text{otherwise} \end{cases} \quad (5.36)$$

Step 4: calculating the value of the option. At $t = 0$ the value of the option is calculated from the payoff matrix by discounting the payoffs to period zero using the risk-free rate of interest and averaging across the simulated paths. Since there is at most one non-zero element along each path in Z this yields:

$$\hat{P}^N(0) = \frac{1}{N} \sum_{n=1}^{N} \sum_{t=1}^{K} e^{-tr} z_t(n). \quad (5.37)$$

This ends the pricing algorithm.

In relation to the algorithm a couple of remarks are in order. Firstly, the European price estimate is obtained by discounting the values in (5.33) back to time zero and averaging as:

$$\hat{p}^N(0) = \frac{1}{N} \sum_{n=1}^{N} e^{-Kr} z_K(n). \quad (5.38)$$

Again, it is well established that (5.38) is an unbiased and asymptotically normally distributed estimate of (5.14) if the paths are independent. Secondly, in terms of the conditional expectation approximation, a choice has to be made as to which transformation to use. I choose to use monomials and cross-products of the state variables as regressors. From Stentoft (2004b) we know that as the number of regressors, M, and the number of paths, N, tend to infinity, the price estimate in (5.37) converges to the American option price in (5.1) where exercise is allowed once at the end of each trading day.

Discussion and review of some existing results

In addition to the simulation-based algorithm outlined above, alternative methods have been developed for pricing American options in the GARCH framework. For example, Ritchken and Trevor (1999) develop a lattice algorithm which approximates the NGARCH processes with conditional normality. Their algorithm can be seen as a generalization of the well-known binomial tree which is used as an approximation to, for example, the constant volatility BSM model. Duan et al. (2003) provide an alternative way to price options using a binomial tree approach that allows reducing the dimensionality of the tree from two to one. Another alternative is proposed in Duan and Simonato (2001) in which a Markov chain approximation to the underlying asset price process for an NGARCH specification is developed and used for option pricing purposes. See also Ben-Ameur et al. (2009) who develop a dynamic programming approach combined with interpolation that has the method of Duan and Simonato (2001) as a special case.

The methods proposed by Ritchken and Trevor (1999) and Duan and Simonato (2001) are compared to the simulation method above in Stentoft (2005) who finds that the LSM algorithm provides estimates which are very close to those reported for American option prices in these two papers. However, compared to these other numerical methods, the simulation method has clear advantages. In particular, the simulation-based method is more flexible than the others and is therefore indeed a useful alternative. For example, it is not immediately obvious how to extend the algorithms developed in Ritchken and Trevor (1999) and Duan and Simonato (2001) to other GARCH specifications.

Moreover, although the dynamic programming approach of Ben-Ameur et al. (2009) can be used with a large class of GARCH models, it is developed under the assumption of Gaussian innovations. The simulation approach, on the other hand, does not suffer from this shortcoming and can be applied to virtually any GARCH specification as well as to models with non-Gaussian innovations.

The widespread use of simulation methods in the empirical applications of the GARCH model is a testament to its flexibility. For example, simulation methods have been used to price options on the Standard & Poor's 500 Index using various GARCH specifications together with Gaussian innovations in, among others, Bollerslev and Mikkelsen (1996, 1999), Christoffersen and Jacobs (2004) and Hsieh and Ritchken (2005); and with non-Gaussian innovations in Christoffersen et al. (2010a) and Rombouts and Stentoft (2010). Moreover, simulation techniques have been used together with the regression-based method to price American-style options with success in Stentoft (2005, 2008a, 2011b). In fact, the only empirical paper that prices American-style options in a GARCH framework and does not use simulation is Weber and Prokopczuk (2011). In this paper a binomial method is used and the GARCH models are calibrated directly to the option prices.

The empirical literature mentioned above generally finds support not only for GARCH effects, particular with asymmetries, but also for non-Gaussian innovations and this so for both European and American-style options. For example, when considering options on the Standard & Poor's 500 Index, the above papers all find that the GARCH models diminish the mispricings found when using the constant-volatility BSM model. Moreover, Stentoft (2011b) provides what is likely the largest analysis ever conducted of individual stock options using 30 stocks from the Dow Jones Industrial Average (DJIA), and prices a total of 139 879 option contracts over the 11-year period from 1996 to 2006. The results of the paper provide clear support for using an asymmetric volatility specification together with a non-Gaussian distribution, particularly of the normal inverse Gaussian type, and statistical tests show that this model is most frequently among the set of best-performing models.

5.5   THE PRICE OF RISK AND THE EFFECT ON OPTION PRICES

As the discussion above shows, several GARCH specifications and underlying distributions have been used for empirical option pricing in the GARCH framework. However, comparatively little work has examined the importance of the price of risk. This may appear somewhat puzzling as this parameter is what drives a wedge between the historical and the risk-neutral dynamics.

In this section I consider this question in detail as an illustration of the flexibility of the GARCH framework and of the simulation-based approach. To keep the analysis tractable I consider only models with Gaussian innovations since this allows for a closed form solution for λ_t given $m_t(\cdot\,;\theta_m)$. I first explain how alternative specifications of the risk premium can be accommodated in the above framework, and then provide pricing results for the different specifications.

5.5.1   Specifications of the Price of Risk

The original GARCH option pricing paper by Duan (1995) specifies the mean as:

$$R_t = r + \lambda\sqrt{h_t} - \frac{1}{2}h_t + \sqrt{h_t}\varepsilon_t, \tag{5.39}$$

where ε_t is standard normally distributed and r is the risk-free interest rate. The particular specification corresponds to one where the mean part, $m_t(\,\cdot\,;\theta_m)$, of (5.21) is given by:

$$m_t(\,\cdot\,;\theta_m) = r + \lambda\sqrt{h_t} - \frac{1}{2}h_t. \tag{5.40}$$

Substituting this into (5.30) yields a very simple expression for λ_t which is given by:

$$\lambda_t = \frac{r + \lambda\sqrt{h_t} - \frac{1}{2}h_t - r_t + \frac{1}{2}h_t}{\sqrt{h_t}} = \lambda. \tag{5.41}$$

Hence, for this model the unit risk premium is constant and λ is often interpreted as the price of risk.

Although the specification in Duan (1995) may be considered quite realistic in terms of the way the volatility influences the mean, other functional forms could equally well be considered. In particular, it is equally reasonable to specify the mean as:

$$m_t(\,\cdot\,;\theta_m) = r + \lambda h_t - \frac{1}{2}h_t. \tag{5.42}$$

This corresponds to the specification used in Heston and Nandi (2000), which in terms of the risk-neutral dynamics, would lead to the following equation for λ_t:

$$\lambda_t = \frac{r + \lambda h_t - \frac{1}{2}h_t - r_t + \frac{1}{2}h_t}{\sqrt{h_t}} = \lambda\sqrt{h_t}. \tag{5.43}$$

Thus, with this specification, the unit risk premium is increasing in the level of volatility. Likewise, one might consider specifying the mean as:

$$m_t(\,\cdot\,;\theta_m) = r + \lambda - \frac{1}{2}h_t, \tag{5.44}$$

which would lead to the following specification for λ_t:

$$\lambda_t = \frac{r + \lambda - \frac{1}{2}h_t - r_t + \frac{1}{2}h_t}{\sqrt{h_t}} = \lambda/\sqrt{h_t}. \tag{5.45}$$

In this situation the unit risk premium is decreasing in the level of the volatility.

The mean specifications in (5.40), (5.42) and (5.44) are closely related. For example, if we specify the functional form of the risk premium as λh_t^β we are essentially considering

Table 5.1   Estimation results for the risk parameter λ

Panel A: GARCH model

	GM		IBM		MRK		OEX	
	λ	*SE* (λ)	λ	*SE* (λ)	λ	*SE* (λ)	λ	*SE* (λ)
Model 2	0.0412	(0.0205)	0.0352	(0.0212)	0.0693	(0.0189)	0.0393	(0.0122)
Model 3	0.0322	(0.0140)	0.0316	(0.0171)	0.0512	(0.0139)	0.0529	(0.0150)
Model 4	0.0206	(0.0077)	0.0216	(0.0102)	0.0346	(0.0095)	0.0513	(0.0126)

Panel B: NGARCH model

	GM		IBM		MRK		OEX	
	λ	*SE* (λ)	λ	*SE* (λ)	λ	*SE* (λ)	λ	*SE* (λ)
Model 2	0.0187	(0.0101)	0.0095	(0.0185)	0.0550	(0.0191)	0.0271	(0.0120)
Model 3	0.0191	(0.0102)	0.0100	(0.0140)	0.0407	(0.0141)	0.0380	(0.0142)
Model 4	0.0198	(0.0103)	0.0039	(0.0087)	0.0276	(0.0097)	0.0328	(0.0122)

Notes: This table reports the estimation results for the risk parameter. Panel A reports results for the GARCH models and Panel B results for the NGARCH models. In each panel I report the estimate as well as the standard error for each of the four assets, GM, IBM, MRK and OEX. Each row reports the results for the three models specified in the text where the risk premium is specified as λh_t^β for β equal to 0, ½, and 1, respectively model 2, model 3, model 4.

the cases of $\beta = 1$ and $\beta = 0$ as alternatives to setting $\beta = ½$ as was done in Duan (1995). Whether either one of these is a more plausible specification from a theoretical point of view will not be discussed here. Instead I examine the empirical performance of the GARCH option pricing model with these alternative specifications. In Table 5.1 I report estimation results for λ with the three specifications considered for the four assets plotted in Figure 5.7. Each row reports the results for the three models with β equal to 0, ½ and 1; respectively model 2, model 3 and model 4.[21] Model 1 is used to denote a specification without any risk premium, that is when $\lambda = 0$, and therefore no results are reported for this model.

Panel A in Table 5.1 reports the results for the GARCH specification and shows that in general the risk parameter is estimated to be significantly positive. In fact, the parameter is insignificant only for IBM and this so only for models 2 and 3. The panel also shows that the estimates are similar in size. The specification with the largest likelihood value, not reported here, is model 4 for three out of the four stocks. Panel B in Table 5.1 reports the results for the NGARCH specification and shows that once asymmetries are accommodated in the variance specification, the size of the estimated risk parameter decreases. In fact, once asymmetries are considered the estimate is insignificant for half of the specifications, that is, for all the models for GM and IBM. When comparing the likelihoods, model 3 now has the largest value for three out of the four stocks. Thus, overall the estimation results show that λ is statistically significant for most of the specifications considered.

Table 5.2   Pricing errors in dollar terms for individual stock options

Panel A: BIAS

	All (obs = 8424)		Put (obs = 3009)		Call (obs = 5415)	
	GARCH	NGARCH	GARCH	NGARCH	GARCH	NGARCH
Model 1	−0.1212	−0.1417	−0.0839	−0.0642	−0.1420	−0.1848
Model 2	−0.1212	−0.1429	−0.0819	−0.0654	−0.1431	−0.1859
Model 3	−0.1189	−0.1423	−0.0789	−0.0646	−0.1411	−0.1855
Model 4	−0.1184	−0.1424	−0.0778	−0.0646	−0.1410	−0.1857

Panel B: RMSE

	All (obs = 8424)		Put (osb = 3009)		Call (obs = 5415)	
	GARCH	NGARCH	GARCH	NGARCH	GARCH	NGARCH
Model 1	0.4438	0.4511	0.4275	0.4321	0.4526	0.4613
Model 2	0.4430	0.4509	0.4267	0.4314	0.4518	0.4613
Model 3	0.4439	0.4513	0.4282	0.4320	0.4525	0.4616
Model 4	0.4449	0.4530	0.4298	0.4339	0.4530	0.4632

Notes: This table reports the pricing errors in dollar terms for individual stock options. Panel A reports the BIAS and Panel B the RMSE. In each panel I report the errors for the four models specified in the text, a model with no price of risk, model 1, and 3 models where the risk premium is specified as λh_t^β for β equal to 0, ½, and 1, respectively model 2, model 3, model 4. I report results for both the GARCH and the NGARCH specification and for all options as well as put and call options separately.

5.5.2   Pricing Results

I now examine the effect of the alternative specifications of the price of risk in terms of the estimated option prices. For more details on the sample of options, see Stentoft (2005). As a natural benchmark, I consider a model without any price of risk, that is, a model with $\lambda = 0$. In Tables 5.2 and 5.3 pricing errors are reported for the individual stock options and the index options, respectively.[22] I report results across models as well as for put and call options individually. I consider two metrics for option pricing comparison using the dollar errors. Specifically, letting P_k and $\tilde{P}_k$ denote the kth observed price and the kth estimated price respectively I use the bias, $BIAS = K^{-1}\Sigma_{k=1}^{K}(P_k - \tilde{P}_k)$, and the root mean square error, $RMSE = \sqrt{K^{-1}\Sigma_{k=1}^{K}(P_k - \tilde{P}_k)^2}$.

The first thing to note from the table is that the overall pricing errors are generally of a similar order of magnitude and close to those reported previously in the literature. In particular, for model 3, which corresponds to the specification proposed in Duan (1995) and used empirically in Stentoft (2005) for the same assets considered here, the reported results are very close to those found in Stentoft (2005, Tables 8 and 9) for the *BIAS*. Moreover, when compared to what is obtained with the constant volatility model, the results show that allowing for GARCH-type volatility specifications can explain a large fraction of the mispricing often found for models with constant volatility, and this so irrespective of the specification of the price of risk.

Table 5.3   Pricing errors in dollar terms for index options

Panel A: BIAS

	All (obs = 8291)		Put (obs = 4804)		Call (obs = 3487)	
	GARCH	NGARCH	GARCH	NGARCH	GARCH	NGARCH
Model 1	−0.0893	−0.0453	−0.3909	−0.2761	0.3261	0.2726
Model 2	−0.0787	−0.0427	−0.3732	−0.2737	0.3271	0.2756
Model 3	−0.0858	−0.0465	−0.3792	−0.2776	0.3184	0.2719
Model 4	−0.0848	−0.0349	−0.3795	−0.2679	0.3213	0.2860

Panel B: RMSE

	All (obs = 8291)		Put (obs = 4804)		Call (obs = 3487)	
	GARCH	NGARCH	GARCH	NGARCH	GARCH	NGARCH
Model 1	0.9299	0.8699	0.9200	0.8521	0.9435	0.8937
Model 2	0.9242	0.8719	0.9112	0.8534	0.9417	0.8967
Model 3	0.9210	0.8702	0.9105	0.8529	0.9352	0.8935
Model 4	0.9228	0.8756	0.9119	0.8548	0.9376	0.9034

Notes: This table reports the pricing errors in dollar terms for index options. Panel A reports the BIAS and Panel B the RMSE. In each panel I report the errors for the four models specified in the text, a model with no price of risk, model 1, and 3 models where the risk premium is specified as λh_t^β for β equal to 0, ½, and 1, respectively model 2, model 3, model 4. I report results for both the GARCH and the NGARCH specifications and for all options as well as put and call options separately.

However, although the results are similar there are differences. For example, for the individual stock options, Table 5.2 shows that allowing for a risk premium generally decreases the overall *BIAS* of the GARCH models. In particular, the pricing errors of model 3 and model 4 are 1.9 percent and 2.3 percent lower than for model 1, respectively. For the NGARCH model the differences are, on the other hand, quite small and this is also the case when considering the *RMSE* metric. When considering the put and call options separately the table shows that the differences in performance are largest for the put options where the BIAS is 2.3 percent, 5.9 percent and 7.3 percent, smaller with models 2, 3 and 4, respectively, than with model 1 when using a GARCH specification.

For the index options the differences are more pronounced than for the individual stock options and occur for both the GARCH and NGARCH specifications. For example, Table 5.3 shows that compared to the model with no risk premium, the pricing errors are 11.9 percent smaller with model 2 for the GARCH specification and 22.9 percent smaller with model 4 for the NGARCH specification. When considering the GARCH model, the table also shows that the reason for model 2's superior fit is that it performs well for the put options. For the call options the difference between models 1 and 2 is, on the other hand, only minor. Note though that models 3 and 4 outperform model 1 for both put and call options by between 1.5 percent and 3.0 percent. For the NGARCH model things are less clear. For example, whereas model 4 outperforms model 1 for put options, the opposite is the case for the call options. In fact, once asymmetries in the volatility specification are allowed for, neither of the specifications with a risk premium outperforms the model with no premium for both puts and calls. Finally, the table shows that when considering the *RMSE* metric, the differences in pricing errors for the index options are generally very small and in most cases less than 1 percent.

5.6   CONCLUSION

This chapter contains an introduction to how simulation methods can be used to price American options and a discussion of various existing methods. In particular, I provide a review of four methods: the parameterized stopping time method of Garcia (2003) and Ibanez and Zapatero (2004), the bundling or state space partitioning methods of Tilley (1993) and Barraquand and Martineau (1995), the regression-based methods of, for example, Carriere (1996), Tsitsiklis and Van Roy (2001) and Longstaff and Schwartz (2001), and the stochastic mesh method of Broadie and Glasserman (2004). I compare the methods in terms of their computational efficiency and asymptotic properties and argue that the regression-based methods have clear advantages.

To illustrate the flexibility of the regression-based method, an application to the GARCH option pricing model is provided. In particular, I present a detailed algorithm for how to price options in the GARCH framework using simulation and the regression-based method. A discussion of the benefits of the proposed algorithm compared to other existing methods is provided. In an empirical application, I examine the effect on the estimated option prices of using different specifications for the price of risk. I find that the specification of the price of risk has a non-negligible effect on the pricing performance. In particular, the best model has pricing errors that are up to 2.3 percent lower than the benchmark for the individual stock options and up to 22.9 percent lower than the benchmark for the index options.

NOTES

1. For an excellent introduction to the use of Monte Carlo simulation methods, not just for option pricing but for many other problems in finance, see Glasserman (2004).
2. The reason for this name is that this type of option is somewhere in between a European and an American option, just as Bermuda geographically is located between Europe and North America.
3. Though $V(0) = P(0)$, at all other times $V(t_k)$ is a function of the option parameters and the state variables.
4. This was first pointed out by Carriere (1996) in a regression setting and follows from Jensen's inequality which implies that:

$$E[\tilde{V}_M^N(t_{K-1})|X(t_{K-1})] = E[\max(Z(t_{K-1}),\tilde{H}_M^N(t_{K-1}))|X(t_{K-1})]$$

$$\geq \max(Z(t_{K-1}),E[\tilde{H}_M^N(t_{K-1})|X(t_{K-1})])$$

$$= \max(Z(t_{K-1}),H(t_{K-1}))$$

$$= V(t_{K-1}).$$

5. In the movie *The Cowboy Way* Woody Harrelson's character Pepper says: 'If it's got hair, I can ride it. If it's got a beat, I can dance to it'. The situation is similar here.
6. In later versions of Hull's book, some of the methods I review below are included.
7. The random tree method of Broadie and Glasserman (1997) also uses simulation to price American options. However, this method is closer in spirit to the binomial model and requires additional sub-sampling at each time step. Hence it is not a true simulation method and it suffers from the curse of dimensionality.
8. For other option payoffs, say the maximum of several stocks, there are early exercise regions which cannot be easily approximated by simple functions, see, for example, Ibanez and Zapatero (2004). In this case the method of Garcia (2003), which parameterizes directly the early exercise region, also requires the use of approximations.
9. In Tilley (1993), a refined version of the algorithm called the 'sharp boundary' algorithm is also considered.
10. Barraquand and Martineau (1995) also suggest an alternative formulation of the payoff calculations, or backward integration, in which only the average values are used. Backward induction is then performed as:

$$\overline{V}(i, t) = \max\left[\overline{Z}(i, t), \sum_{j=1}^{M} p(i, j, t) \times \overline{V}(j, t + 1)\right],$$

    where $\overline{V}(i, t)$ and $\overline{Z}(i, t)$ denotes the averages across bundle i at time t.
11. However, note that with this method only the stopping time method can be used.
12. Even when correcting for the year of publication, the LSM method is, with 138 citations per year, cited almost ten times as often as the average of the other methods.
13. In fact, it may be slightly faster depending on the regressors and the regression method chosen.
14. The computational times for the regression method are 11.1 and 43, and for the bundling method, they are 14.2 and 100.2, respectively.
15. In Raymar and Zwecher (1997) a generalization of the SSAP method to stratification along two dimensions is used. Although this method is shown to perform better in finite samples, asymptotically it has the same drawback as the original SSAP method.
16. The specification, however, is much more general and can accommodate most, if not all, conceivable specifications used in the extant GARCH literature.
17. Nevertheless, it is somewhat surprising that very few papers compare the option pricing performance of these two strands of the literature, though see Stentoft (2011a) for an exception.
18. In fact, the system above is somewhat more general than that used in Duan (1995). Nevertheless, this more general specification can be obtained, for example, by considering the restriction to the log-normal model of the generalized LRNVR of Duan (1999).
19. Yet another approach, which would provide a similar set of conditions, is to specify a candidate stochastic discount factor directly as is done in, for example Gourieroux and Monfort (2007).
20. Most modern computer programs allow for generating all paths at once using simple matrix operations.
21. I only report estimation results for the parameter of interest, λ. The remainder of the parameters are for all specifications close to those reported in Stentoft (2005).
22. I have chosen to report only results for the combined sample of individual stock options. The results for each stock are available on request.

REFERENCES

Amin, K.I. (1991), 'On the computation of continuous time option prices using discrete approximations', *Journal of Financial and Quantitative Analysis*, **26**, 477–495.
Amin, K.I. (1993), 'Jump diffusion option valuation in discrete time', *Journal of Finance*, **48**, 1833–1863.
Areal, N., A. Rodriques and M.R. Armada (2008), 'Improvements to the least squares Monte Carlo option valuation method', *Review of Derivatives Research*, **11**, 119–151.
Bacinello, A.R., E. Biffis and P. Millossovich (2010), 'Regression-based algorithms for life insurance contracts with surrender guarantees', *Quantitative Finance*, **10** (9), 1077–1090.
Barraquand, J. (1995), 'Numerical valuation of high dimensional multivariate european securities', *Management Science*, **41** (12), 1882–1891.
Barraquand, J. and D. Martineau (1995), 'Numerical valuation of high dimensional multivariate American securities', *Journal of Financial and Quantitative Analysis*, **30**, 383–405.
Ben-Ameur, H., M. Breton and J.-M. Martinez (2009), 'Dynamic programming approach for valuing options in the GARCH model', *Management Science*, **55** (2), 252–266.

Black, F. and M. Scholes (1973), 'The pricing of options and corporate liabilities', *Journal of Political Economy*, **81**, 637–654.

Bollerslev, T. (1986), 'Generalized autoregressive conditional heteroskedasticity', *Journal of Econometrics*, **31**, 307–327.

Bollerslev, T., R.Y. Chou and K.F. Kroner (1992), 'ARCH modelling in finance', *Journal of Econometrics*, **52**, 5–59.

Bollerslev, T. and H.O. Mikkelsen (1996), 'Modelling and pricing long memory in stock market volatility', *Journal of Econometrics*, **73**, 151–184.

Bollerslev, T. and H.O. Mikkelsen (1999), 'Long-term equity anticipation securities and stock market volatility dynamics', *Journal of Econometrics*, **92**, 75–99.

Boyle, P.P. (1977), 'Options: a Monte Carlo approach', *Journal of Financial Economics*, **4**, 323–338.

Boyle, P.P. (1988), 'A lattice framework for option pricing with two state variables', *Journal of Financial and Quantitative Analysis*, **23**, 1–12.

Boyle, P.P., M. Broadie and P. Glasserman (1997), 'Monte Carlo methods for security pricing', *Journal of Economic Dynamics and Control*, **21**, 1267–1321.

Boyle, P.P., J. Evnine and S. Gibbs (1989), 'Numerical evaluation of multivariate contingent claims', *Review of Financial Studies*, **2**, 241–250.

Brennan, M.J. (1979), 'The pricing of contingent claims in discrete time models', *Journal of Finance*, **24** (1), 53–68.

Brennan, M.J. and E.S. Schwartz (1977), 'The valuation of American put options', *Journal of Finance*, **32** (2), 449–462.

Broadie, M. and P. Glasserman (1997), 'Pricing American-style securities using simulation', *Journal of Economic Dynamics and Control*, **21**, 1323–1352.

Broadie, M. and P. Glasserman (2004), 'A stochastic mesh method for pricing high-dimensional American options', *Journal of Computational Finance*, **7** (4), 35–72.

Broadie, M., P. Glasserman and Z. Ha (2000), 'Pricing American options by simulation using a stochastic mesh with optimized weights', in S.P. Uryasev (ed.), *Probabilistic Constrained Optimization: Methodology and Applications*, Dordrecht: Kluwer Academic Publishers, pp. 32–50.

Carriere, J.F. (1996), 'Valuation of the early-exercise price for options using simulations and nonparametric regression', *Insurance: Mathematics and Economics*, **19**, 19–30.

Chow, Y.S., H. Robbins and D. Siegmund (1971), *Great Expectations: The Theory of Optimal Stopping*, New York: Houghton Mifflin.

Christoffersen, P., C. Dorion, K. Jacobs and Y. Wang (2010a), 'Volatility components, affine restrictions, and nonnormal innovations', *Journal of Business and Economic Statistics*, **28** (4), 483–502.

Christoffersen, P., R. Elkamhi, B. Feunou and K. Jacobs (2010b), 'Option valuation with conditional heteroskedasticity and non-normality', *Review of Financial Studies*, **23**, 2139–2183.

Christoffersen, P. and K. Jacobs (2004), 'Which GARCH model for option valuation?', *Management Science*, **50** (9), 1204–1221.

Cox, J., S. Ross and M. Rubinstein (1979), 'Option pricing: a simplified approach', *Journal of Financial Economics*, **7**, 229–264.

Da Fonseca, J., M. Grasselli and C. Tebaldi (2007), 'Option pricing when correlations are stochastic: an analytical framework', *Review of Derivatives Research*, **10**, 151–180.

Duan, J.-C. (1995), 'The GARCH option pricing model', *Mathematical Finance*, **5** (1), 13–32.

Duan, J.-C. (1999), 'Conditionally fat-tailed distributions and the volatility smile in options', working paper, Hong Kong University of Science and Technology.

Duan, J.-C., G. Gauthier, C. Sasseville and J.-G. Simonato (2003), 'Approximating American option prices in the GARCH framework', *Journal of Futures Markets*, **23** (10), 915–929.

Duan, J.-C. and J.-G. Simonato (1998), 'Empirical martingale simulation for asset prices', *Management Science*, **44** (9), 1218–1233.

Duan, J.-C. and J.-G. Simonato (2001), 'American option pricing under GARCH by a Markov chain approximation', *Journal of Economic Dynamics and Control*, **25**, 1689–1718.

Duffie, D. (1996), *Dynamic Asset Pricing Theory*, Princeton, NJ: Princeton University Press.

Engle, R.F. (1982), 'Autoregressive conditional heteroscedasticity with estimates of the variance of United Kingdom inflation', *Econometrica*, **50** (4), 987–1007.

Engle, R.F. and V.K. Ng (1993), 'Measuring and testing the impact of news on volatility', *Journal of Finance*, **48** (5), 1749–1778.

Gamba, A. (2002), 'Real options valuation: a Monte Carlo approach', working paper, University of Verona, Italy.

Garcia, D. (2003), 'Convergence and biases of Monte Carlo estimates of American option prices using a parametric exercise rule', *Journal of Economic Dynamics and Control*, **27**, 1855–1879.

Gerhold, S. (2011), 'The Longstaff-Schwartz algorithm for Lévy models: results on fast and slow convergence', *Annals of Applied Probability*, **21** (2), 589–608.

Glasserman, P. (2004), *Monte Carlo Methods in Financial Engineering*, New York: Springer-Verlag.

Glasserman, P. and B. Yu (2004), 'Number of paths versus number of basis function in American option pricing', *Annals of Applied Probability*, **14** (4), 2090–2119.

Gourieroux, C. and A. Monfort (2007), 'Econometric specification of stochastic discount factor models', *Journal of Econometrics*, **136**, 509–530.

Gourieroux, C. and R. Sufana (2010), 'Derivative pricing with Wishart multivariate stochastic volatility', *Journal of Business and Economic Statistics*, **28** (3), 438–451.

Heston, S.L. and S. Nandi (2000), 'A closed-form GARCH option valuation model', *Review of Financial Studies*, **13** (3), 585–625.

Hsieh, K.C. and P. Ritchken (2005), 'An empirical comparison of GARCH option pricing models', *Review of Derivatives Research*, **8**, 129–150.

Hull, J.C. (2000), *Options, Futures, and Other Derivatives*, Upper Saddle River, NJ: Prentice-Hall.

Hull, J. and A. White (1987), 'The pricing of options on assets with stochastic volatilities', *Journal of Finance*, **42** (2), 281–300.

Ibanez, A. and F. Zapatero (2004), 'Monte Carlo valuation of American options through computation of the optimal exercise frontier', *Journal of Financial and Quantitative Analysis*, **39** (2), 253–275.

Johnson, H. (1987), 'Options on the maximum or the minimum of several assets', *Journal of Financial and Quantitative Analysis*, **22**, 277–283.

Karatzas, I. (1988), 'On the pricing of American options', *Applied Mathematics and Optimization*, **17**, 37–60.

Kemna, A.G.Z. and A.C.F. Vorst (1990), 'A pricing method for options based on average asset values', *Journal of Banking and Finance*, **14**, 113–129.

Kloeden, P.E., E. Platen and H. Schurz (1994), *Numerical Solutions of SDE Through Computer Experiments*, Berlin: Springer-Verlag.

Léon, A. and A. Vaello-Sebastià (2009), 'American GARCH employee stock option valuation', *Journal of Banking and Finance*, **33**, 1129–1143.

Longstaff, F.A. (2005), 'Borrower credit and the valuation of mortgage-backed securities', *Real Estate Economics*, **33**, 619–661.

Longstaff, F.A. and E.S. Schwartz (2001), 'Valuing American options by simulation: a simple least-squares approach', *Review of Financial Studies*, **14**, 113–147.

Margrabe, W. (1978), 'The value of an option to exchange one asset for another', *Journal of Finance*, **33**, 177–186.

Merton, R.C. (1973), 'Theory of rational option pricing', *Bell Journal of Economics and Management Science*, **4**, 141–183.

Moreno, M. and J.F. Navas (2003), 'On the robustness of least-squares Monte Carlo (LSM) for pricing American options', *Review of Derivatives Research*, **6**, 107–128.

Poon, S.-H. and C.W.J. Granger (2003), 'Forecasting volatility in financial markets: a review', *Journal of Economic Literature*, **41**, 478–539.

Raymar, S.B. and M.J. Zwecher (1997), 'Monte Carlo estimation of American call options on the maximum of several stocks', *Journal of Derivatives*, **5** (1), 7–23.

Ritchken, P. and R. Trevor (1999), 'Pricing options under generalized GARCH and stochastic volatility processes', *Journal of Finance*, **59** (1), 377–402.

Rombouts, J. and L. Stentoft (2010), 'Option pricing with asymmetric heteroskedastic normal mixture models', CIRANO – Scientific Publications No. 2010s–38.

Rombouts, J.V. and L. Stentoft (2011), 'Multivariate option pricing with time varying volatility and correlations', *Journal of Banking and Finance*, **35**, 2267–2281.

Scott, L.O. (1987), 'Option pricing when the variance changes randomly: theory, estimation, and an application', *Journal of Financial and Quantitative Analysis*, **22** (4), 419–438.

Stentoft, L. (2004a), 'Assessing the least squares Monte-Carlo approach to American option valuation', *Review of Derivatives Research*, **7** (3), 129–168.

Stentoft, L. (2004b), 'Convergence of the least squares Monte Carlo approach to American option valuation', *Management Science*, **50** (9), 1193–1203.

Stentoft, L. (2005), 'Pricing American options when the underlying asset follows GARCH processes', *Journal of Empirical Finance*, **12** (4), 576–611.

Stentoft, L. (2008a), 'American option pricing using GARCH models and the normal inverse Gaussian distribution', *Journal of Financial Econometrics*, **6** (4), 540–582.

Stentoft, L. (2011a), 'American option pricing with discrete and continuous time models: an empirical comparison', *Journal of Empirical Finance*, **18** (5), 880–902.

Stentoft, L. (2011b), 'What we can learn from pricing 139 879 individual stock options', available at SSRN: http://ssrn.com/abstract=1975779.

Stentoft, L. (2012), 'American option pricing using simulation and regression: numerical convergence results', *Topics in Numerical Methods for Finance*, **19**, 57–94.

Stentoft, L. (2013), 'Value function approximation or stopping time approximation: a comparison of two recent numerical methods for American option pricing using simulation and regression', *Journal of Computational Finance*, forthcoming.

Stulz, R. (1982), 'Options on the minimum or maximum of two risky assets: analysis and applications', *Journal of Financial Economics*, **10**, 161–185.

Tilley, J.A. (1993), 'Valuing American options in a path simulation model', *Transactions, Society of Actuaries, Schaumburg*, **45**, 499–520.

Tsitsiklis, J.N. and B. Van Roy (2001), 'Regression methods for pricing complex American-style options', *IEEE Transactions on Neural Networks*, **12** (4), 694–703.

Weber, M. and M. Prokopczuk (2011), 'American option valuation: implied calibration of GARCH pricing models', *Journal of Futures Markets*, **31** (10), 971–994.

6 Derivatives pricing with affine models and numerical implementation
Ke Chen and Ser-Huang Poon[1]

6.1 INTRODUCTION

Affine models are popular in finance, especially since the publication of Duffie et al. (2000). They represent a compromise between tractibility and empirical complexity. The characteristic function of the underlying dynamics in affine models is an exponential affine function of the state variables. As a result, the price and characteristic function of a contingent claim can be expressed as an integral and evaluated numerically. In this chapter we present the most popular theory of derivatives pricing with affine models and explain their numerical implementation.

The remainder of this chapter is outlined as follows. In section 6.2, we present some stochastic differential equations (SDE) that underly well-known affine models in finance. Section 6.3 links the SDE of the underlying dynamics to the partial differential equation (PDE) of the characteristic function. Some pricing examples are presented in section 6.4. Section 6.5 summarizes the reasons why affine models are so attractive in option pricing, and finally, section 6.6 introduces two different ways for calculating the option price numerically.

6.2 CANDIDATE SDE

Not all SDEs lead to an affine model. We will present a more general specification of the affine model from Duffie et al. (2000) in the next section. In this section, we introduce a few well-known affine models and their associated SDEs. The most famous affine model is, perhaps, the Heston (1993) stochastic volatility (SV) model as shown below:

$$d\ln S_t = \left(r - \frac{v_t}{2}\right)dt + \sqrt{v_t}dW_t^1$$

$$dv_t = \kappa(\theta - v_t)dt + \sigma\sqrt{v_t}dW_t^2$$

$$[dW_t^1, dW_t^2] = \rho dt$$

The popularity of the Heston model is largely due to the resulting semi-closed form solution for European option prices as a direct consequence of the affine formulation.

In the Heston model above, there are two state variables, S_t and v_t, but generally affine models can have many state variables. For example, in Duffie et al. (2000), the long-run mean of stochastic variance is driven by a second square root process:

$$d\ln S_t = \left(r - \frac{v_t}{2}\right)dt + \sqrt{v_t}dW_t^1$$

$$dv_t = \kappa(\theta_t - v_t)dt + \sigma\sqrt{v_t}dW_t^2$$

$$d\theta_t = \kappa_\theta(\theta_\theta - \theta_t)dt + \sigma_\theta\sqrt{\theta_t}dW_t^3$$

$$[dW_t^1, dW_t^2] = \rho dt$$

Here, only dW_t^1 and dW_t^2 are correlated; dW_t^3 is not correlated with dW_t^1 and dW_t^2. In the two-speed mean reversion SV model below, there are two independent Brownian motions for volatility, each of which is correlated with the Brownian motion that drives the stock price. All the other correlations between dW_t^i are zero:

$$d\ln S_t = \left(r - \frac{v_{1,t} + v_{2,t}}{2}\right)dt + \sqrt{v_{1,t}}dW_t^1 + \sqrt{v_{2,t}}dW_t^2$$

$$dv_{1,t} = \kappa_1(\theta_1 - v_{1,t})dt + \sigma_1\sqrt{v_{1,t}}dW_t^3$$

$$dv_{2,t} = \kappa_2(\theta_2 - v_{2,t})dt + \sigma_2\sqrt{v_{2,t}}dW_t^4$$

$$[dW_t^1, dW_t^3] = \rho_1 dt$$

$$[dW_t^2, dW_t^4] = \rho_2 dt$$

As in Bates (1996), we can further extend the affine model to include a discrete jump process as shown below:

$$d\ln S_t = \left(r - \frac{v_t}{2}\right)dt + \sqrt{v_t}dW_t^1 + J_x dN(t)$$

$$dv_t = \kappa(\theta - v_t)dt + \sigma\sqrt{v_t}dW_t^2$$

$$[dW_t^1, dW_t^2] = \rho dt$$

where J_x is the jump in log returns with a constant jump intensity. Since jumps are normally modelled as a discrete process, it is common practice to assume that it is not correlated with the continuous Brownian motions. The model remains affine whether J_x follows a normal distribution or a double exponential distribution. Furthermore, the model remains affine with a closed form characteristic function even if we introduce another jump process, J_v, into the SV process (see Duffie et al. 2000) as long as J_v is linear in the state variables.

The constraint imposed by a constant jump intensity can be further relaxed. For example, Fang and Oosterlee (2008) introduce the stochastic jump intensity model:

$$d\ln S_t = \left(r - \frac{v_t}{2}\right)dt + \sqrt{v_t}dW_t^1 + J_x dN(t)$$

$$dv_t = \kappa(\theta - v_t)dt + \sigma\sqrt{v_t}dW_t^2$$

$$d\lambda_t = \kappa_\lambda(\theta_\lambda - \lambda_t)dt + \sigma_\lambda\sqrt{\lambda_t}dW_t^3$$

$$[dW_t^1, dW_t^2] = \rho dt$$

It should be noted that dW_t^3 has no correlation with dW_t^1 and dW_t^2, otherwise, the model is no longer affine. The key issue with this correlation restriction is the need to maintain linearity after applying Ito's lemma. This means that all the variance–covariance terms must be linear in the state variables.

6.3   FROM SDE TO PDE

Duffie et al. (2000) present a general affine framework with n state variables as:

$$dX_t = u(X_t, t)dt + \sigma(X_t, t)dW_t + \int_{\mathbb{R}^n} h(J)\mu(dJ, dt) \tag{6.1}$$

where X and J are n-dimensional vectors; $h(J)$ is a function of the jump size, $\mu(dJ, dt)$ is the random measure of the Poisson jump, and W_t represents an n-dimensional independent Brownian motion.

6.3.1   Kolmogorov Backward Equation

Many finance problems involve estimating the probability distribution of future values of the state variable given the current values. Such a problem is called the 'forward' problem. The Kolmogorov backward equation, on the other hand, is more useful when one is interested in the (hitting) probability that the state variable will reach a target region B at some future point in time. As we will soon see, the Kolmogorov backward equation is very useful for derivative pricing because the price of the derivatives is the expectation of the future payoff, which is a function of future values of the state variables.

For the diffusion case without jumps, the Kolmogorov backward equation is:

$$-\frac{\partial}{\partial t}p(X_t, t) = \frac{\partial}{\partial X}p(X_t, t) \cdot u(X_t, t) + \frac{1}{2}\mathrm{tr}\left(\Sigma(X_t, t)\frac{\partial^2}{\partial X^2}p(X_t, t)\right) \tag{6.2}$$

where $\Sigma(X_t, t) = \sigma(X_t, t)\sigma(X_t, t)^T$ is the covariance matrix of the diffusion part, tr is the sum of the diagonal of the matrix, $p(X_t, t)$ is the hitting probability with terminal condition:

$$p(X_T, T) = 1_{X(T) \in B} \tag{6.3}$$

and B is a predefined set. As an example, one could have a digital option that pays £1 if S_T is within the set B.

We can extend the backward equation in (6.2) to include jumps. Assuming that the jump time is independent of the jump size, that is, $\mu(dJ, dt) = \mu(dt)\mu(dJ)$, equation (6.2) becomes:

$$-\frac{\partial}{\partial t}p(X_t,t) = u(X_t,t)\frac{\partial}{\partial X}p(X_t,t) + \frac{1}{2}\text{tr}\left(\Sigma(X_t,t)\frac{\partial^2}{\partial X^2}p(X_t,t)\right)$$

$$+ \lambda_t\int_{\mathbb{R}^n}(p(X_t+h(J))-p(X_t))\mu(dJ) \tag{6.4}$$

where λ_t, as one of the state variables, is the jump intensity such that $\lambda_t dt = v(dt)$, which is the compensator of the random measure $\mu(dt)$.

To simplify the equation, we can introduce the differential operator:

$$\mathcal{L}(\cdot) = \frac{\partial}{\partial t}(\cdot) + u(X_t,t)\frac{\partial}{\partial X}(\cdot) + \frac{1}{2}\text{tr}\left(\Sigma(X_t,t)\frac{\partial^2}{\partial X^2}\right)(\cdot) + \lambda_t\int_{\mathbb{R}^n}\Delta(\cdot)\mu(dJ)$$

and now the backward equation in (6.4) can be written as:

$$\mathcal{L}p(X_t,t) = 0. \tag{6.5}$$

6.3.2   Green's Function

Green's function is an integral kernel that can be used to solve a differential equation that is itself inhomogeneous or one with inhomogeneous boundary conditions. In the latter case, the solution involves changing the boundary condition in (6.3) into the delta function below:

$$p(X_T,T) = \delta(X_T - x) \tag{6.6}$$

where x is a particular realisation of X_T. That is, x is the only element in the set B in equation (6.3). Moreover:

$$p(X_T = x|X_t,t) = \mathbb{E}[p(X_T,T) \times 1_{X_{T=x}}|X_t,t] = \mathbb{E}[\delta(X_T - x)|X_t,t].$$

Using the Black–Scholes model as an example, we have in place of equation (6.1):

$$dS_t = rS_t dt + \sigma S_t dW_t \tag{6.7}$$

Here, S_t is the only state variable in the vector X_t. Let f denote the option whose payoff, $g(S)$, depends on S, and:

$$\mathcal{L}f = \frac{\partial f}{\partial t} + rS\frac{\partial f}{\partial S} + \frac{1}{2}\sigma^2 S^2\frac{\partial^2 f}{\partial S^2} \tag{6.8}$$

The value of the derivative at time T can now be expressed in terms of equation (6.6) as follows:

$$f_T = \int\delta(S_T - s)g(s)ds$$

The current option price is the discounted expectation of the future payoff:

$$f_T = e^{-r(T-t)}E\left[\int \delta(S_T - s)g(s)\,ds\right] = e^{-r(T-t)}\int p(S_T = s|S_T,t)g(s)\,ds$$

and by applying the differential operator:

$$\mathcal{L}f = re^{-r(T-t)}\int p(S_T = s|S_T,t)g(s)\,ds + \mathcal{L}\int p(S_T = s|S_T,t)g(s)\,ds$$

$$= rf + \int \mathcal{L}p(S_T = s|S_T,t)g(s)\,ds$$

$$= rf \tag{6.9}$$

where the second equality is due to the fact that $\mathcal{L}$ is a linear operator. Since we know $\mathcal{L}p(S_T = s|S_T,t) = 0$ in the Kolmogorov backward equation (6.5), the last term $\int \mathcal{L}p(S_T = s|S_T,t)g(s)\,ds = 0$. Then the PDE for the current price of a contingent claim on the future payoff function $g(S)$ is, by combining (6.8) and (6.9):

$$\frac{\partial f}{\partial t} + rS\frac{\partial f}{\partial S} + \frac{1}{2}\sigma^2 S^2 \frac{\partial^2 f}{\partial S^2} = rf$$

which is exactly the same as the Black–Scholes fundamental PDE derived by hedging arguments.

6.3.3   The Feynman–Kac Formula

The Feynman–Kac formula provides a relationship between a solution of a PDE and the expectation of a stochastic process. For a one-dimensional diffusion process:

$$dX_t = \mu(X_t,t)\,dt + \sigma(X_t,t)\,dW,$$

the Feynman–Kac formula states that any function $f(X_t, t)$ defined as:

$$f(X_t,t) = \mathbb{E}[f(X_T,T)|X(t)]$$

is the solution to the following PDE:

$$\frac{\partial f}{\partial t} + \mu(X_t,t)\frac{\partial f}{\partial x} + \frac{1}{2}\sigma^2(X_t,t)\frac{\partial^2 f}{\partial x^2} = 0. \tag{6.10}$$

This result is closely connected with the results in the previous sections. Note that equation (6.10) can be applied to any function $f(X_t,t)$, which is not necessary to be a derivative pricing formula. For example, we can define $f(X_T,T) = e^{\omega X_T}$; then $f(X_t,t)$ is the characteristic function conditional on $\mathcal{F}_t$. One condition for $f(X_t,t)$ is that it must be twice differentiable.

Let us define $f(X_T, T) = \delta(X_T - x)$ and let us assume that the SDE has exactly the same form as (6.7). Then, from equation (6.6):

$$f(X_T, T) = p(X_T, T)$$

$$f(X_t, T) = \mathbb{E}[p(X_T = x | X_t, t)]$$

and we get the Kolmogorov backward equation in (6.5).

One of the most important results derived from the Feynman–Kac formula is related to the characteristic function. Let:

$$f(X_T, T) = \phi(\omega, X_T, T) = e^{i\omega X_T}$$

$$f(X_t, t) = \phi(\omega, X_t, T) = \mathbb{E}[e^{i\omega X_T} | X_t]$$

Then the Feynman–Kac formula implies:

$$\mathcal{L}\phi(\omega, X_t, T) = 0 \tag{6.11}$$

Here, $\phi(\omega, X_t, T)$ is the characteristic function of X_T and is the key to many option pricing solutions as explained in the following sections. It should be noted that the characteristic function can also be derived from the Kolmogorov forward equation. Here, we have decided to use the Kolmogorov backward equation as it is more straightforward to apply.

6.4   CHARACTERISTIC FUNCTION EXAMPLES

In this section, we show three examples of how the PDE can be solved through the use of characteristic functions.

6.4.1   The Jump Diffusion Model

The first example has only one state variable, and we have a jump diffusion process for a stock price with SDE below:

$$dx_t = \left(r - \frac{1}{2}\sigma^2 - \lambda m \right) dt + \sigma dw_t + J dN_t \tag{6.12}$$

where x equals the log price, $\ln S_t$, N_t is a Poisson process with constant jump intensity, $\lambda, m = \mathbb{E}[e^J - 1]$ is the mean value of jump size J, and the jump size J has a distribution π_J.

Based on the convolution property of characteristic functions, the $\mathcal{F}_t$-conditional characteristic function of X_T is:

$$\phi(\omega, x_t, \sigma^2, \lambda, t, T)$$

$$= \phi_{Diffusion} \times \phi_{Jump}$$

$$= e^{x_t i\omega + r(T-t)i\omega - \lambda m i\omega(T-t) - \frac{1}{2}(i\omega + \omega^2)(T-t)\sigma^2} e^{(\phi_{Jump}(\omega) - 1)(T-t)\lambda} \tag{6.13}$$

where ϕ_{Jump} is the characteristic function of jump size distribution π_J. The first equality holds because of the independence of the diffusion and jump parts. In this simple example, the characteristic function can be easily derived in closed form by evaluating the mean of the diffusion part and the jump part in (6.12) separately. Note that the characteristic function in (6.13) is an exponent of the affine function of σ^2, λ and the state variable x_t.

As we have a jump component in the stock price, the PDE includes an integral term for the jump as shown below:

$$\frac{\partial f}{\partial t} + \mu(X_t, t)\frac{\partial f}{\partial x} + \frac{1}{2}\sigma^2(X_t, t)\frac{\partial^2 f}{\partial x^2} + \lambda_t \int (f(X_t + h(J)) - f(X_t))\mu(dJ) = 0$$

Such a PDE is called a PIDE (partial integral differential equation). Invoking the Feynman–Kac formula in characteristic functional form in (6.11) and using the fact that the moment generating function (MGF) is $G(\omega) = \phi(-i\omega)$, we have:

$$G_t + \left(r - \frac{1}{2}\sigma^2 - \lambda m\right)G_x + \frac{1}{2}\sigma^2 G_{xx}$$

$$+ \lambda \int_R (G(x + J) - G(x))f_J dJ$$

$$= 0 \tag{6.14}$$

with boundary condition $G_T = e^{x_T \omega}$. From the PIDE and the boundary condition, one may guess the solution to be of the form:

$$G(\omega, x_t, v_t, \lambda_t, t, T) = e^{\omega x_t + r(T-t)\omega + A(\omega,t,T) + B(\omega,t,T)\sigma^2 + C(\omega,t,T)\lambda} \tag{6.15}$$

and for the jump component:

$$G(x + J) - G(x) = G(x)(e^{J\omega} - 1). \tag{6.16}$$

Substituting the solution forms (6.15) and (6.16) into equation (6.14), we have:

$$\left(r - \frac{1}{2}\sigma^2 - \lambda m\right)\omega G + \frac{1}{2}\sigma^2 \omega^2 G$$

$$+ \lambda G \int_R (e^{J\omega} - 1)dJ$$

$$= \left(r\omega - \frac{\partial A(\omega,t,T)}{\partial t} - \frac{\partial B(\omega,t,T)}{\partial t}\sigma^2 - \frac{\partial C(\omega,t,T)}{\partial t}\lambda\right)G$$

Canceling G on both sides, we get:

$$-\frac{1}{2}\sigma^2\omega + \frac{1}{2}\sigma^2\omega^2$$

$$+ \lambda \int_R (e^{J\omega} - 1)dJ - \lambda m\omega$$

$$= -\frac{\partial A(\omega,t,T)}{\partial t} - \frac{\partial B(\omega,t,T)}{\partial t}\sigma^2 - \frac{\partial C(\omega,t,T)}{\partial t}\lambda$$

Regrouping the equation with respect to the parameters yields:

$$\left(-\frac{1}{2}\omega + \frac{1}{2}\omega^2 + \frac{\partial B(\omega,t,T)}{\partial t}\right)\sigma^2$$

$$+ \left(\int_R (e^{J\omega} - 1)dJ - m\omega + \frac{\partial C(\omega,t,T)}{\partial t}\right)\lambda$$

$$+ \frac{\partial A(\omega,t,T)}{\partial t}$$

$$= 0$$

which means that the following system of ODEs must have a solution:

$$\frac{\partial A(\omega,t,T)}{\partial t} = 0$$

$$\frac{\partial B(\omega,t,T)}{\partial t} = \frac{1}{2}(\omega - \omega^2)$$

$$\frac{\partial C(\omega,t,T)}{\partial t} = -\int_R (e^{J\omega} - 1)\pi_J dJ + m\omega$$

given the boundary condition, $G(\omega,x_T,V_T,T,T) = e^{x_T\omega}A(\omega,T,T) = 0$, $B(\omega,T,T) = 0$, and $C(\omega,T,T) = 0$. Therefore we have the solutions:

$$A = 0$$

$$B = -\frac{1}{2}(\omega - \omega^2)(T - t)$$

$$C = \left(\int_R (e^{J\omega} - 1)\pi_J dJ - m\omega\right)(T - t)$$

where $\int_R e^{J\omega}f_J dJ = \phi_{Jump}(\omega)$ is the MGF of the jump size distribution. For normal distribution, $J \sim N(\varepsilon, \delta^2)$:

$$\int_R (e^{J\omega} - 1)dJ = e^{\varepsilon\omega + \delta^2\omega^2/2}.$$

Substituting A, B and C into equation (6.15), we have $G(\omega) = \phi(-i\omega)$, which is exactly the relationship between the MGF and the characteristic function that was defined above.

6.4.2   The Heston Model

The Heston SDE has two state variables as follows:

$$d\ln S_t = \left(r - \frac{v_t}{2}\right)dt + \sqrt{v_t}dW_t^1$$

$$dv_t = \kappa(\theta - v_t)dt + \sigma\sqrt{v_t}dW_t^2$$

$$[dW_t^1, dW_t^2] = \rho dt$$

The characteristic function is given as:

$$\phi(\omega, x_t, v_t, t, T) = \mathbb{E}[e^{i\omega x_T}|x_t, v_t]$$

where $x_t = \ln S_t$. As in the previous subsection, we invoke the Feynman–Kac formula in the characteristic functional form and use the moment generating function (MGF) of $\ln S_T$, $G(\omega) = \phi(-i\omega)$:

$$G_t + \left(r - \frac{1}{2}v_t\right)G_x + \frac{1}{2}v_t G_{xx} + \kappa(\theta - v_t)G_v$$

$$+ \frac{1}{2}\sigma^2 v_t G_{vv} + \rho\sigma v_t G_{xv}$$

$$= 0$$

$$G_T = e^{x_T\omega}. \tag{6.17}$$

From the PDE and the boundary condition, one may guess that the solution of (6.17) is an exponential affine function of the state variables, x_t and v_t, and thus a possible solution is:

$$G(\omega, x_t, v_t, \lambda_t, t, T) = e^{\omega x_t + r(T-t)\omega + A(\omega, t, T) + B(\omega, t, T)v_t} \tag{6.18}$$

Substituting the solution into equation (6.17), we have:

$$-\frac{1}{2}v_t\omega + \frac{1}{2}v_t\omega^2 + \kappa(\theta - v_t)B(\omega, t, T)$$

$$+ \frac{1}{2}\sigma^2 v_t B(\omega, t, T)^2 + \rho\sigma v_t\omega B$$

$$= -\frac{\partial A(\omega, t, T)}{\partial t} - \frac{\partial B(\omega, t, T)}{\partial t}v_t.$$

Regrouping the equation with respect to the state variables v_t:

$$\left(-\frac{1}{2}\omega + \frac{1}{2}\omega^2 - \kappa B(\omega, t, T) + \frac{1}{2}\sigma^2 B(\omega, t, T)^2 + \rho\sigma\omega B + \frac{\partial B(\omega, t, T)}{\partial t}\right)v_t$$

$$+ \kappa\theta B(\omega, t, T) + \frac{\partial A(\omega, t, T)}{\partial t}$$

$$= 0$$

Since v_t is a time varying process, in order to get zero on the right-hand side, we have:

$$\frac{\partial A(\omega, t, T)}{\partial t} = -\kappa\theta B(\omega, t, T) \tag{6.19}$$

$$\frac{\partial B(\omega, t, T)}{\partial t} = \frac{(\omega - \omega^2)}{2} + (\kappa - \rho\sigma\omega)B(\omega, t, T) - \frac{\sigma^2 B(\omega, t, T)^2}{2} \tag{6.20}$$

Therefore, the PDE is now decomposed as a set of ODEs. The second non-linear ODE is known as the Riccati differential equation, whose analytical solution can be obtained by applying a change of variable. The solutions of (6.19) and (6.20) are:

$$A(\omega, t, T) = -\frac{\kappa\theta}{\sigma^2}\left(\psi_- + (T - t) + 2\ln\frac{\psi_- + \psi_+ e^{-\zeta(T-t)}}{2\zeta}\right)$$

$$B(\omega, t, T) = -(\omega - \omega^2)\frac{1 - e^{-\zeta(T-t)}}{\psi_- + \psi_+ e^{-\zeta(T-t)}}$$

$$\zeta = \sqrt{(\kappa - \rho\sigma\omega)^2 + \sigma^2(\omega - \omega^2)}$$

$$\psi_\pm = \zeta \mp (\kappa - \rho\sigma\omega)$$

Finally, we verify that given the terminal boundary condition $G(\omega, x_T, V_T, T, T) = e^{x_T\omega}$, $A(\omega, T, T) = 0$ and $B(\omega, T, T) = 0$.

6.4.3   Multiple Factors Affine Models

Here, we add stochastic jump intensity to Heston's stochastic volatility model:

$$d\ln S_t = \left(r - \frac{v_t}{2}\right)dt + \sqrt{v_t}dW_t^1 + J_x dN(t)$$

$$dv_t = \kappa(\theta - v_t)dt + \sigma\sqrt{v_t}dW_t^2$$

$$d\lambda_t = \kappa_\lambda(\theta_\lambda - \lambda_t)dt + \sigma_\lambda\sqrt{\lambda_t}dW_t^3$$

$$[dW_t^1, dW_t^2] = \rho dt$$

Following the same procedure as in the previous section, we derive the PIDE for the moment-generating function of $\ln S_T$:

$$G_t + \left(r - \frac{1}{2}v_t - \lambda m\right)G_x + \frac{1}{2}v_t G_{xx}$$

$$+ \kappa(\theta - v_t)G_v + \frac{1}{2}\sigma^2 v_t G_{vv} + \rho\sigma v_t G_{xv}$$

$$+ \kappa_\lambda(\theta_\lambda - \lambda_t)G_v + \frac{1}{2}\sigma_\lambda^2\lambda_t G_{\lambda\lambda}$$

$$+ \lambda_t\int_R (G(x + J) - G(J))f_J dJ$$

$$= 0$$

$$G_T = e^{x_T\omega} \tag{6.21}$$

We propose the solution of equation (6.21) as an exponential affine function of the state variables x_t, v_t and λ_t as follows

$$G(\omega, x_t, v_t, \lambda_t, t, T) = e^{\omega x_t + r(T-t)\omega + A(\omega,t,T) + B(\omega,t,T)v_t + C(\omega,t,T)\lambda_t} \tag{6.22}$$

and when substituted into equation (6.21), we have:

$$-\frac{1}{2}v_t\omega + \frac{1}{2}v_t\omega^2$$

$$+ \kappa(\theta - v_t)B(\omega,t,T) + \frac{1}{2}\sigma^2 v_t B(\omega,t,T)^2 + \rho\sigma v_t\omega B$$

$$+ \kappa_\lambda(\theta_\lambda - \lambda_t)C(\omega,t,T) + \frac{1}{2}\sigma_\lambda^2\lambda_t C(\omega,t,T)^2$$

$$= -\frac{\partial A(\omega,t,T)}{\partial t} - \frac{\partial B(\omega,t,T)}{\partial t}v_t - \frac{\partial C(\omega,t,T)}{\partial t}\lambda_t$$

Regrouping the equation with respect to the state variables v_t and λ_t:

$$\left(-\frac{1}{2}\omega + \omega^2 - \kappa B(\omega,t,T) + \frac{1}{2}\sigma^2 B(\omega,t,T)^2 + \rho\sigma\omega B + \frac{\partial B(\omega,t,T)}{\partial t}\right)v_t$$

$$+ \left(-\kappa_\lambda C(\omega,t,T) + \frac{1}{2}\sigma_\lambda^2 C(\omega,t,T)^2 + \frac{\partial C(\omega,t,T)}{\partial t}\right)\lambda_t$$

$$+ \kappa\theta B(\omega,t,T) + \kappa_\lambda\theta_\lambda C(\omega,t,T) + \frac{\partial A(\omega,t,T)}{\partial t}$$

$$= 0$$

The corresponding set of ODEs is:

$$\frac{\partial A(\omega,t,T)}{\partial t} = -\kappa\theta B(\omega,t,T) \tag{6.23}$$

$$\frac{\partial B(\omega,t,T)}{\partial t} = \frac{(\omega - \omega^2)}{2} + (\kappa - \rho\sigma\omega)B(\omega,t,T) - \frac{\sigma^2 B(\omega,t,T)^2}{2} \tag{6.24}$$

$$\frac{\partial C(\omega,t,T)}{\partial t} = \kappa_\lambda C(\omega,t,T) - \frac{1}{2}\sigma_\lambda^2 C(\omega,t,T)^2 \tag{6.25}$$

and the solution, as shown in Sepp (2003), is:

$$A(\omega,t,T) = -\frac{\kappa\theta}{\sigma^2}\left(\psi_- + (T-t) + 2\ln\frac{\psi_- + \psi_+ e^{-\zeta(T-t)}}{2\zeta}\right)$$

$$- \frac{\kappa_\lambda\theta_\lambda}{\sigma_\lambda^2}\left(\chi_- + (T-t) + 2\ln\frac{\chi_- + \chi_+ e^{-\xi(T-t)}}{2\xi}\right)$$

$$B(\omega,t,T) = -(\omega - \omega^2)\frac{1 - e^{-\zeta(T-t)}}{\psi_- + \psi_+ e^{-\zeta(T-t)}}$$

$$C(\omega,t,T) = 2\Lambda\frac{1 - e^{-\xi(T-t)}}{\chi_- + \chi_+ e^{-\xi(T-t)}}$$

$$\Lambda = \int_R e^{J\omega}f_J dJ - 1 - \omega\left(\int_R e^J f_J dJ - 1\right)$$

$$\zeta = \sqrt{(\kappa - \rho\sigma\omega)^2 + \sigma^2(\omega - \omega^2)}$$

$$\psi_\pm = \zeta \mp (\kappa - \rho\sigma\omega)$$

$$\xi = \sqrt{\kappa_\lambda^2 - 2\sigma_\lambda^2\Lambda}$$

$$\chi_\pm = \xi \mp \kappa\lambda$$

6.5   WHY AFFINE?

As shown in the three examples in the previous section, if the SDE is affine, the characteristic function is an exponential affine function of the state variables, $X_t = [X_1,...,X_n]'$ for example $\phi(\omega, X_t, T) = e^{g(X_t)}$ and $g(X_t) = A_0 + A_1 X_1 + \cdots + A_n X_n$. Then we can solve the PDE (6.11) in terms of the characteristic function as follows:

$$\mathcal{L}\phi = \frac{\partial\phi}{\partial t} + u(X_t,t)\frac{\partial\phi}{\partial X} + \frac{1}{2}\text{tr}\left(\Sigma(X_t,t)\frac{\partial^2\phi}{\partial X^2}\right) + \lambda_t\int_{\mathbb{R}^n}\Delta\phi(\mu(dJ))$$

$$= [\dot{A}_1,...,\dot{A}_t][X_1,...,X_n]'e^{g(X_t)} + u(X_t,t)[A_1,...,A_n]'e^{g(X_t)}$$

$$+ \frac{1}{2} [A_1, \ldots, A_n] \Sigma (X_t, t) [A_1, \ldots, A_n]' e^{g(X_t)}$$

$$+ e^{g(X_t)} \lambda_t \int_{\mathbb{R}^n} (e^{h(J)} - 1) \mu(dJ)$$

$$= 0$$

where $\dot{A}$ represents the derivative of A with respect to time t. We first eliminate the term $e^{g(X_t)}$ to get:

$$\dot{A}_0 + [\dot{A}_1, \ldots, \dot{A}_t][X_1, \ldots, X_n]' + u(X_t, t)[A_1, \ldots, A_n]'$$

$$+ \frac{1}{2} [A_1, \ldots, A_n] \Sigma (X_t, t) [A_1, \ldots, A_n]'$$

$$+ \lambda_t \int_{\mathbb{R}^n} (e^{h(J)} - 1) \mu(dJ)$$

$$= 0 \qquad (6.26)$$

Recall that jump intensities are part of the state variables. We let the first m states be from the diffusion part and the remaining $n - m$ states be from the jump part, for example $X_q = \lambda_{q-m}$ for $q = m + 1, \ldots, n$. Using the features of affine models that:

$$u(X, t)[A_1, \ldots, A_n]' = \alpha_0 + \alpha_1 X_1 + \cdots + \alpha_n X_n$$

$$[A_1, \ldots, A_n] \Sigma (X(t), t)[A_1, \ldots, A_n]' = \beta_0 + \beta_1 X_1 + \cdots + \beta_m X_m$$

$$\lambda_t \int_{\mathbb{R}^n} (e^{h(J)} - 1) \mu(dJ) = \beta_{m+1} \lambda_{1,t} + \cdots + \beta_n \lambda_{n-m,t}$$

Now, the PDE (6.26) can be regrouped as:

$$\begin{bmatrix} \dot{A}_0 + \alpha_0 + \beta_0 \\ \dot{A}_1 + \alpha_1 + \beta_1 \\ \vdots \\ \dot{A}_n + \alpha_n + \beta_n \end{bmatrix}' \begin{bmatrix} 1 \\ X_1 \\ \vdots \\ X_n \end{bmatrix} = 0$$

Since $X_{t,i}$ represents the individual dynamics of the underlying state variable, the coefficient must be zero to make the above equation hold all the time. Therefore, we have the decomposed ODE set as follows:

$$\begin{bmatrix} \dot{A}_0 + \alpha_0 + \beta_0 \\ \dot{A}_1 + \alpha_1 + \beta_1 \\ \vdots \\ \dot{A}_n + \alpha_n + \beta_n \end{bmatrix} = 0$$

Compared with the original PDE, the ODE set is much easier to solve, either in closed form or numerically.

6.6   NUMERICAL INTEGRATION

In the previous section, we show that it is relatively easy to solve the characteristic function if the SDE is affine. In this section, we are going to introduce several ways of using the characteristic function to price options.

6.6.1   The Fourier Transform

For any contingent claim, the current price is the discounted expectation of future payoff under the risk-neutral measure:

$$f(X_t, t)_T = e^{-r(T-t)}\mathbb{E}^{\mathbb{Q}}[f(X_T, T)|X_t]$$

$$= e^{-r(T-t)}\int_{\mathbb{R}^n} f(X_T, T)p(X_T|X_t)dX_T. \tag{6.27}$$

Let us denote $\phi(-\omega, X_t, T)$ the characteristic function of the transition distribution $p(X_T|X_t)$, and $\hat{f}(\omega)$ the Fourier transform of the payoff function $f(X_T, T)$, or alternatively $f(X_T, T)$ as the inverse Fourier transform of $\hat{f}(\omega)$. Then:

$$\phi(-\omega, X_t, T) = \int_{\mathbb{R}^n} e^{-i\omega X_T}p(X_T|X_t)dX_T$$

$$\hat{f}(\omega) = \int_{\mathbb{R}} f(x, T)e^{i\omega x}dx$$

$$f(X_T, T) = \frac{1}{2\pi}\int_{-\infty}^{\infty} \hat{f}(\omega)e^{-i\omega X_T}d\omega$$

Take the European call option for example:

$$\hat{f}(\omega) = \int_{\mathbb{R}} f(x, T)e^{i\omega x}dx$$

$$= \int_{\ln K}^{\infty} (e^x - K)e^{i\omega x}dx \tag{6.28}$$

$$= \int_{\ln K}^{\infty} e^{(1+i\omega)x}dx - \int_{\ln K}^{\infty} e^{\ln K + i\omega x}dx \tag{6.29}$$

$$= \frac{e^{(1+i\omega)x}}{1+i\omega}\Big|_{\ln K}^{\infty} - \frac{Ke^{i\omega x}}{i\omega}\Big|_{\ln K}^{\infty} \tag{6.30}$$

where $x = \ln S_T$. Given that $(\frac{e^{(1+i\omega)x}}{1+i\omega})$ or $(\frac{Ke^{i\omega x}}{i\omega})$ does not necessary exist as $x \to \infty$, we have to put some constrains to ensure their existence. To make $e^{(1+i\omega)x} \to 0$ and $e^{i\omega x} \to 0$

when $x \to 0$, we need $\Im(\omega) > 1$, where $\Im(\cdot)$ denotes the imaginary part. The necessary constraint varies and depends on the option payoffs. For example, for put option, the constraint is $\Im(\omega) < 0$.

The integral can further be evaluated as:

$$\hat{f}(\omega) = -\frac{Ke^{i\omega\ln K}}{1 + i\omega} + \frac{Ke^{i\omega\ln K}}{i\omega}$$

$$= \frac{e^{k(i\omega + 1)}}{i\omega - \omega^2}$$

where $k = \ln K$.

Substituting the definition of the inverse Fourier transform of $f(X_T, T)$ into (6.27), we have:

$$f(X_t, t)_T = \frac{e^{-r(T-t)}}{2\pi} \int_{\mathbb{R}^n} \int_{-\infty}^{\infty} \hat{f}(\omega) e^{-i\omega X_T} d\omega p(X_T | X_t) dX_T$$

$$= \frac{e^{-r(T-t)}}{2\pi} \int_{-\infty}^{\infty} \hat{f}(\omega) \int_{\mathbb{R}^n} e^{-i\omega X_T} p(X_T | X_t) dX_T d\omega \qquad (6.31)$$

$$= \frac{e^{-r(T-t)}}{2\pi} \int_{-\infty}^{\infty} \hat{f}(\omega) \phi(-\omega, X_t, T) d\omega \qquad (6.32)$$

Here, we rearranged the order of integration in equation (6.31) and applied the definition of the characteristic function in (6.32).

It is not critical to have a closed form solution in order to calculate the option price. As long as the value inside the integral in (6.32) at each point of ω can be calculated, the integration can be evaluated numerically.

6.6.2   The Fast Fourier Transform

Carr and Madan (1999) applied the method of FFT (fast Fourier transform) to speed up the calculation of the integral. However, equation (6.32) is not in the form of a Fourier transform, whereas the FFT can only be used on an integral of a Fourier transform. To take advantage of the FFT technique, the trick is to transform the target integral to a Fourier transform.

Firstly, according to Carr and Madan (1999), it is important that the condition in Plancherel's theorem is satisfied, which requires the price function to be square integrable in order to apply the (inverse) Fourier transform.[2] Using the European call option as example, we can see that $C(k) \to S$ as $k \to -\infty$, which is not square integrable. Carr and Madan (1999) suggest transforming the call price as follows:

$$c_T(k) \equiv e^{\alpha k} C_T(k)$$

for some suitable α, which makes $c_T(k)$ square integrable. Now we can apply the Fourier transform on $c_T(k)$:

$$\psi_T(\omega) = \int_{-\infty}^{\infty} e^{i\omega} c_T(k)\, dk.$$

Substituting the inverse Fourier transform in equation (6.32) and the payoff function in (6.28), we have:

$$\psi_T(\omega) = \int_{-\infty}^{\infty} e^{i\omega} e^{\alpha k} C_T(k)\, dk$$

$$= e^{-r(T-t)} \int_{-\infty}^{\infty} e^{i\omega k} \int_{k}^{\infty} e^{\alpha k} (e^x - e^k) p(x_T | x_t)\, dx\, dk$$

$$= e^{-r(T-t)} \int_{-\infty}^{\infty} p(x_T | x_t) \int_{-\infty}^{x} e^{(i\omega + \alpha)k} (e^x - e^k)\, dk\, dx$$

$$= e^{-r(T-t)} \int_{-\infty}^{\infty} \left(-\frac{e^{(i\omega + 1 + \alpha)x}}{\alpha + 1 + i\omega} + \frac{e^{(i\omega + 1 + \alpha)x}}{\alpha + i\omega} \right) p(x_T | x_t)\, dx$$

$$= e^{-r(T-t)} \frac{\phi(\omega - (\alpha + 1)i, S_t, T)}{\alpha^2 + \alpha + i(2\alpha + 1)\omega - \omega^2} \tag{6.33}$$

The last equality is obtained through the application of a Fourier transform of the pdf $p(x_T | x_t)$ with the variable change $v = -i(i\omega + 1 + \alpha) = \omega - (\alpha + 1)i$.

Now we can back out the original option price $C_T(k)$ through an inverse Fourier transform:

$$C_T(k) = e^{-\alpha k} c_T(k)$$

$$= \frac{e^{-\alpha k}}{2\pi} \int_{-\infty}^{\infty} \psi_T(\omega) e^{-i\omega k}\, d\omega$$

$$\approx \frac{e^{-\alpha k}}{\pi} \sum_{j=0}^{N} \psi_T(j\Delta\omega) e^{-ij\Delta\omega k}\, d\omega \tag{6.34}$$

with $\Delta\omega = \frac{u}{N+1}$ and u is the upper bound for the truncation of the characteristic function $\psi_T(\omega)$. We refer the reader to Carr and Madan (1999) for further discussions of the choice of u.

As mentioned before, we should choose α to make $c_T(k)$ square integrable. Since $C(k) \to S_T$ as $k \to -\infty$, the call option price is not square integrable. One necessary condition is $\alpha > 0$. Another condition we need, as pointed out by Carr and Madan (1999), is $\psi(0)$ being finite, which is to ensure that $\frac{\phi(-(\alpha+1)i)}{\alpha^2 + \alpha}$ is finite. Using the definition of the characteristic function, this condition is equivalent to:

$$\mathbb{E}[S_T^{\alpha+1}] < \infty$$

A popular choice for α is $\frac{1}{2}$. Then the integral (6.34) can be calculated efficiently by the FFT method.

The calculation of the FFT requires $N\log_2 N$ operations which makes it much more efficient than the direct numerical integration in section 6.6.1, which requires at least N^2 operations.

6.6.3 The Fourier Cosine Transform

Recently, Fang and Oosterlee (2008) proposed the use of the Fourier cosine transform (FCT) to calculate the integral in equation (6.32). The FCT method is normally more efficient than the FFT method, but it is not without other pitfalls. For any contingent claim with final payoff $f(x_T)$, the current value $f(x_t)$ is the discounted value of the expectation of the final payoff under the risk-neutral measure:

$$f(x_t) = e^{-r(T-t)}\mathbb{E}^Q[f(x_T|\Im_t)]$$

$$= e^{-r(T-t)}\int_R f(x_T)p(x_T|x_t)dx_T \tag{6.35}$$

The idea of the FCT is to express the pdf, $p(x_T|x_t)$, as a series of cosine functions. As long as the pdf is smooth enough, the number of terms required for the integral approximation is much smaller than that for the FFT method to achieve the same level of accuracy. An additional requirement for the FCT method to work effectively is that the function to be decomposed must have finite support so that the tail of the distribution can be truncated as follows:

$$p(x_T|x_t) = \sum_{j=0}^{\infty} a_j(x_t)\cos\left(j\pi\frac{x_T - l}{u - l}\right)$$

$$\approx \sum_{j=0}^{M} a_j(x_t)\cos\left(j\pi\frac{x_T - l}{u - l}\right)$$

with:

$$a_j(x_t) = \frac{2}{u - l}\int_l^u p(x_T|x_t)\cos\left(j\pi\frac{x_T - l}{u - l}\right)dx_T$$

where $[l, u]$ are the lower and upper boundaries for the truncated pdf $p(x_T|x_t)$.

The option price in equation (6.35) now becomes:

$$f(x_t) = e^{-r(T-t)}\int_R f(x_T)p(x_T|x_t)dx_T$$

$$\approx e^{-r(T-t)}\int_l^u f(x_T)\sum_{j=0}^{M} a_j(x_t)\cos\left(j\pi\frac{x_T - l}{u - l}\right)dx_T$$

$$= e^{-r(T-t)}\sum_{j=0}^{M} a_j(x_t)\int_l^u f(x_T)\cos\left(j\pi\frac{x_T - l}{u - l}\right)dx_T$$

$$= e^{-r(T-t)} \sum_{j=0}^{M} a_j(x_t) V_i \tag{6.36}$$

where V_i is the coefficient for the cosine transform of payoff function. Using European call and put options as examples, Fang and Oosterlee (2008) show that:

$$V_j^{Call} = \frac{2}{u-1} K(\chi_j(0,u) - \psi_j(0,u))$$

$$V_j^{Put} = \frac{2}{u-1} K(-\chi_j(l,0) + \psi_j(l,0))$$

with:

$$\chi_j(a,b) = \frac{1}{1 + (\frac{j\pi}{u-1})^2} \left[\cos\left(j\pi\frac{b-l}{u-l}\right) e^b - \cos\left(j\pi\frac{a-l}{u-l}\right) e^a \right.$$

$$+ \frac{j\pi}{u-1} \sin\left(j\pi\frac{b-l}{u-1}\right) e^b - \frac{j\pi}{u-1} \sin\left(j\pi\frac{a-l}{u-1}\right) e^a \right]$$

$$\psi_j(a,b) = \begin{cases} \left[\sin\left(j\pi\frac{b-l}{u-1}\right) - \sin\left(j\pi\frac{a-l}{u-1}\right) \frac{u-l}{j\pi} \right] & j \neq 0 \\ b - a & j = 0 \end{cases}$$

Now, we need to revisit the coefficients of the cosine transform of the transition distribution $p(x_T|x_t)$. Noting that:[3]

$$e^{i\omega x} = \cos(\omega x) + i \sin(\omega x)$$

where $a_i(x_t)$ is just the real part of the Fourier transform of $p(x_T|x_t)$,

$$a_j(x_t) = \frac{2}{u-1} \int_l^u p(x_T|x_t) \cos\left(j\pi\frac{x_T-l}{u-l}\right) dx_T$$

$$\approx \Re\left(\frac{2}{u-1} \int_{\mathbb{R}} p(x_T|x_t) e^{ij\pi\frac{x_T-l}{u-l}} dx_T\right)$$

$$= \frac{2}{u-1} \Re\left(\phi\left(\frac{j\pi}{u-l}, X(t), T\right) \times e^{-i\frac{j\pi l}{u-l}}\right)$$

and the option price is given by equation (6.36).

6.6.4 Fast Fourier Transform versus Fourier Cosine Transform

Both the FFT and FCT methods require the truncation of the target distribution; FFT in the ω domain and FCT in the x domain. Furthermore, the FFT works by separating the integration interval into buckets. It is very inefficient for long intervals and it introduces discretization errors. The FCT works in a similar way to a Taylor series expansion by

Table 6.1   Model parameters

	Jump diffusion	Heston	Multiple factors
r	3%	3%	3%
σ^2	0.1		
κ		2	2
θ		0.05	0.05
ρ		−0.6	−0.6
σ		0.6	0.6
V_0		0.05	0.05
κ_λ			8
θ_λ			1
σ_λ			2
λ_0	3		3
μ	−5%		−5%
δ	10%		10%

Note: The distribution of jump sizes is $N(\mu,\delta)$.

Table 6.2   Performance comparison, FFT ($N = 4096$)/FCT ($M = 128$)

$T = 1$	K	Call	Put	Error
Jump diffusion	20	80.5912/80.5912	0.0001/0.0001	4.2988e-013/−4.9984e-006
	100	15.8844/15.8797	12.9290/12.9243	5.2580e-013/5.6843e-014
	200	0.6418/0.6389	94.7309/94.7280	1.2506e-012/6.4801e-012
Heston	20	80.5920 /80.5902	0.0009/0.0009	3.8725e-013/−0.0019
	100	9.6921/9.6838	6.7367/6.7283	4.5475e-013/4.1243e-005
	200	0.0020/0.0019	94.0911/94.0891	1.3074e-012/0.0019
Multiple factors	20	80.5923/80.5922	0.0012/0.0012	3.8725e-013/−2.2915e-006
	100	11.0256/11.0185	8.0701/8.0630	4.6896e-013/2.3078e-006
	200	0.0076/0.0075	94.0967/94.0965	1.3074e-012/1.1117e-004

ignoring the higher-order terms of the cosine expansion of the target distribution. If the distribution function is smooth, the FCT is much more efficient, as shown in Fang and Oosterlee (2008), because the FCT uses far fewer terms in the cosine expansion in (6.36) than the number of points needed to calculate the FFT integral in (6.34), that is, $M \ll N$.

For illustration, we implemented the three examples used in section 6.4 in Matlab. The parameter values used in each case are reported in Table 6.1. Since the FFT algorithm is optimized in Matlab, we will not compare the computation speed of the two algorithms. Instead, we focus on the pricing accuracy when valuing ATM (at-the-money), deep ITM (in-the-money) and deep OTM (out-of-the-money) European call and put options, given the current stock price $S = 100$ and two times to maturity, namely one year and one month. The pricing error is measured by put–call parity, $Error = C - P - S + e^{-r(T-t)}K$. The results for one-year to maturity options are reported in Table 6.2. The first number

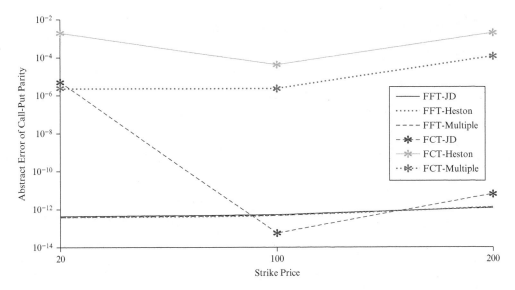

Figure 6.1   Pricing errors for options with one year to maturity, FFT vs. FCT

Table 6.3   Performance comparison, FFT (N = 4096)/FCT (M = 128)

T = 1/12	K	Call	Put	Error
Jump diffusion	20	80.0499/11.6896	0.0000/0.0000	4.6185e-013/−68.3603
	100	4.2725/4.2548	4.0228/4.0051	3.9790e-013/4.3815e-008
	200	0.0000/0.0000	99.5006/99.4705	1.3642e-012/0.0301
Heston	20	80.0499/0.0002	0.0000/5.4632	−3.7097e-011/−85.5130
	100	2.6758/2.6470	2.4262/2.3973	1.0601e-011/2.9512e-008
	200	0.0000/0.0000	99.5006/87.7105	3.2031e-011/11.7902
Multiple factors	20	80.0499/1.0551	0.0000/0.2905	−9.4254e-010/−79.2853
	100	3.2053/3.1803	2.9556/2.9307	−3.8989e-010/2.4047e-006
	200	0.0000/0.0000	99.5006/98.4884	−4.5102e-010/1.0122

reported is from the FFT and the second number from the FCT. Here we have specifically chosen $M = 128$, which is much smaller than $N = 4096$. The same set of results is
presented in Figure 6.1. Both Table 6.2 and Figure 6.1 show that the pricing errors produced by the FCT is of the same order as those produced by FFT, despite the small M.
The speed of FCT becomes more relevant in empirical studies that require, for example,
daily calibration (or optimization) of the option pricing model using a large amount of
market data each day.

   As shown in Table 6.3, at short maturities such as one month, the option pricing starts
to go wrong for the FCT when the payoff strongly depends on the tail of the distribution (for deep OTM options). Figure 6.2 illustrates the results in Table 6.3. This problem
can be easily fixed by readjusting the truncated domain, $[u,l]$, to include the full set with

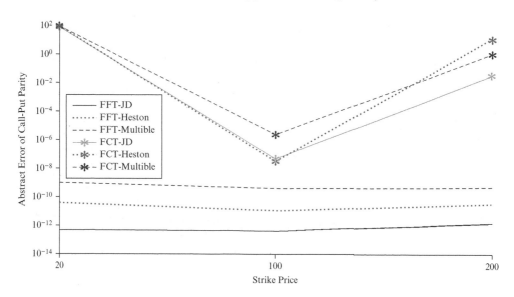

Figure 6.2   Pricing errors for options with one month to maturity, FFT vs. FCT

positive payoff. But this example serves to remind us of the potential problem of using the FCT. On the other hand, given a large N, the FFT result is much more stable, regardless of the payoff functions and how they relate to the underlying distribution.

NOTES

1. We would like to thank Boda Kang, Eberhard Mayerhofer and Heikki Seppälä for many helpful comments.
2. Note that actually $\mathcal{L}^1$ is sufficient for the Fourier transform and inverse Fourier transform. The discussion here follows Carr and Madan (1999) and uses $\mathcal{L}^2$, the Plancherel condition.
3. It should be noted that in Fang and Oosterlee (2008), $x = \ln(S/K)$.

REFERENCES

Bates, D.S. (1996), 'Jumps and stochastic volatility: exchange rate processes implicit in Deutschmark options', *Review of Financial Studies*, **9**, 69–107.
Carr, P. and D.B. Madan (1999), 'Option valuation using the fast Fourier transform', *Journal of Computational Finance*, **2** (4), 61–73.
Duffie, D., J. Pan and K. Singleton (2000), 'Transform analysis and asset pricing for affine jump-diffusions', *Econometrica*, **68**, 1343–1376.
Fang, F. and C.W. Oosterlee (2008), 'A novel pricing method for European options based on Fourier-cosine series expansions', *SIAM Journal on Scientific Computing*, **31**, 826–848.
Heston, S.L. (1993), 'A closed-form solution for options with stochastic volatility with applications to bond and currency options', *Review of Financial Studies*, **6**, 327–343.
Sepp, A. (2003), 'Fourier transform for option pricing under affine jump-diffusions: an overview', working paper, SSRN eLibrary.

7 Markov Chain Monte Carlo with particle filtering

Yongwoong Lee and Ser-Huang Poon

7.1 INTRODUCTION

Markov Chain Monte Carlo (MCMC) is a method of making Bayesian inference from the posterior distribution of model parameters based on their prior distribution and the likelihood of the observed data. It is especially powerful when dealing with complicated and un-normalized posterior distributions of parameters in a multidimensional or non-linear model. However, if the likelihood evaluation involves a latent or unobservable process, as in the case of state space models, then the latent process needs to be estimated through a pure Bayesian method or filtering methods such as a Kalman filter or a particle filter. In this chapter, we present the MCMC method for sampling from the posterior distribution where particle filtering is nested in the likelihood evaluation. Firstly, we introduce the general concepts and procedures for Bayesian inference. Next, we establish the general MCMC framework with a few useful algorithms. Finally, we introduce particle filtering and combine it with MCMC for drawing random samples from the posterior distribution. Throughout this chapter, examples based on the Basel II single-factor portfolio credit risk model are used to illustrate the concepts and procedures.

7.2 BAYESIAN INFERENCE

In this section, MCMC is not used because we assume the posterior distribution has a closed form. Let us suppose that the task at hand is to estimate the parameter θ given a subjective prior distribution for θ and the observed data set y. Bayesian inference for the posterior distribution of θ can be conducted through the prior distribution of θ and the likelihood of observing y. First, we write the joint probability of θ and y as the product of $p(\theta)$, the prior density, and $p(y|\theta)$, the likelihood (or the sampling distribution) of y, as follows:

$$\underbrace{p(\theta, y)}_{\text{joint}} = \underbrace{p(\theta)}_{\text{prior}} \cdot \underbrace{p(y|\theta)}_{\text{likelihood}} \tag{7.1}$$

Then, by Bayes's rule, the posterior density of θ conditional on the observed data y can be written as:

$$p(\theta|y) = \frac{p(\theta, y)}{\int p(\theta)p(y|\theta)d\theta} = \frac{p(\theta)p(y|\theta)}{p(y)} \tag{7.2}$$

where $p(y)$ is called the normalizing constant, which can be omitted since its value does not depend on θ by being integrated out. Hence the posterior distribution can be simplified into the unnormalized form:

$$\underbrace{p(\theta|y)}_{\text{posterior}} \propto p(\theta)p(y|\theta) \qquad (7.3)$$

Given the prior density, the posterior density above is determined by the likelihood function $p(y|\theta)$. Therefore, Bayesian inference follows the likelihood principle that, given the prior, the likelihood estimation will always lead to the same posterior distribution. While classical modelling normally involves setting up the likelihood function $p(y|\theta)$, Bayesian statistical inference is based on the posterior distribution $p(y|\theta)$ by modelling the joint distribution $p(\theta, y)$. For example, the expectation of some arbitrary function of θ, $g(\theta)$, can be obtained by:

$$\mathbb{E}(g(\theta)|y) = \int g(\theta)p(\theta|y)\,d\theta. \qquad (7.4)$$

The expectation in (7.4) can easily be calculated by Monte Carlo methods, if the posterior density $p(\theta|y)$ is from a standard distribution, for example the normal, binomial or beta distribution. We provide an example in the next section for this simple case. However, if the posterior density has many parameters or has no closed form, then it will not be possible to directly draw samples from it. In this case, MCMC methods can be employed; this is explained in section 7.3.

7.2.1   An Example: Bayesian Inference for the Vasicek Model

As the simplest example of Bayesian inference with Monte Carlo but without the Markov Chain, we consider the Vasicek single-factor model for a loan portfolio loss distribution. Vasicek (1987, 1991) derives the loss distribution for a homogeneous portfolio of N loans of equal amount, with identical default probabilities and equi-correlation. The log-return of the asset value, A, of firm i is represented by:

$$A_i = \sqrt{\rho_i}X + \sqrt{1 - \rho_i}\varepsilon_i,$$

for $i = 1, 2, \ldots, N$, where $X \sim N(0, 1)$ is a systematic common factor and $\varepsilon_i \sim N(0, 1)$ is firm i's idiosyncratic factor which is independent of X. Note that X is usually a latent factor. In this simple example, we assume that X is exogeneous and observable. As in Merton (1974), firm i defaults when asset value A_i drops below a default threshold h_i. Then, conditional on $X = x$, the default probability of firm i is given by:

$$p_i(x) = \mathbb{P}[A_i \leq h_i | X = x]$$

$$= \mathbb{P}[\sqrt{\rho_i}x + \sqrt{1 - \rho_i}\varepsilon_i \leq h_i]$$

$$= \mathbb{P}\left[\varepsilon_i \leq \frac{h_i - \sqrt{\rho_i}x}{\sqrt{1 - \rho_i}}\right]$$

$$= \Phi\left(\frac{h_i - \sqrt{\rho_i}x}{\sqrt{1 - \rho_i}}\right). \tag{7.5}$$

Let the loss rate of the portfolio be:

$$Y_N = \frac{1}{N}\sum_{i=1}^{N}I_{\{A_i \le h_i\}},$$

where $I_{\{A_i \le h_i\}}$ is the default indicator which has the value 1 if $A_i \le h_i$, and 0 otherwise. As $N \to \infty$, Y_N converges to the conditional default probability, $p(x)$, by the law of large numbers, that is:

$$Y \doteq \lim_{N \to \infty} Y_N \to p(x). \tag{7.6}$$

Let y_t denote the realization of Y at time t. As $N \to \infty$, y_t is equal to the conditional default probability $p(x_t)$. So from (7.5) and omitting the subscript i for convenience and due to the homogeneity of the loans, we obtain:

$$y_t = p(x_t) = \Phi\left(\frac{h - \sqrt{\rho}x_t}{\sqrt{1 - \rho}}\right). \tag{7.7}$$

Rearranging terms yields the inverse of the loss ratio as:

$$\tilde{y}_t = \Phi^{-1}(y_t) = \frac{h}{\sqrt{1 - \rho}} - \frac{\sqrt{\rho}}{\sqrt{1 - \rho}}x_t \tag{7.8}$$

for $t = 1, 2, \ldots, T$. Additionally, we assume that the systematic factor X_t follows an $AR(1)$ process:

$$X_t = \varphi X_{t-1} + \sqrt{1 - \varphi^2}\eta_t, \tag{7.9}$$

where $-1 < \varphi < 1$ and $\eta_t \sim N(0, 1)$. By inserting equation (7.9) into equation (7.8), the probit of the loss ratio can be written as:

$$\tilde{y}_t = \frac{h}{\sqrt{1 - \rho}} - \frac{\sqrt{\rho}}{\sqrt{1 - \rho}}\varphi x_{t-1} + \frac{\sqrt{\rho}}{\sqrt{1 - \rho}}\sqrt{1 - \varphi^2}\eta_t, \tag{7.10}$$

which is essentially a non-linear regression model with parameters $\{h, \rho, \varphi\}$. Due to the non-linearity in equation (7.10), it is difficult to find the posterior distribution of the parameters. We will illustrate how to estimate such a non-linear model in the next section. Here, we take a simple approach by transforming the non-linear regression model in (7.10) into a linear one by reparameterization such that:

$$\tilde{y}_t = \beta_0 + \beta_1 x_{t-1} + v_t, \tag{7.11}$$

where $\beta_0 = \frac{h}{\sqrt{1-\rho}}$, $\beta_1 = -\frac{\sqrt{\rho}}{\sqrt{1-\rho}}\varphi$, $v_t \sim N(0, \sigma^2)$ and $\sigma^2 = \frac{\rho(1-\varphi^2)}{1-\rho}$. Now, equation (7.11) is a simple linear regression and allows a straightforward Bayesian inference. First, we make Bayesian inferences on β_0, β_1 and σ^2, and then estimate h, ρ and φ by solving the system of linear equations.

We assume a non-informative prior distribution given by $p(\beta, \sigma^2) \propto \frac{1}{\sigma^2}$, where $\beta = (\beta_0, \beta_1)'$. Since $\tilde{y}_t \sim N(\beta_0 + \beta_1 x_{t-1}, \sigma^2)$, under the regression model in (7.11), the posterior distribution is:

$$p(\beta, \sigma^2|\tilde{y}, \tilde{X}) \propto \underbrace{\sigma^{-2} \cdot \left(\frac{1}{\sigma^2}\right)^{\frac{T}{2}}}_{\text{prior}} \underbrace{\exp\left\{-\frac{1}{2\sigma^2}(\tilde{y}-\tilde{X}\beta)'(\tilde{y}-\tilde{X}\beta)\right\}}_{\text{likelihood}} \qquad (7.12)$$

where $\tilde{y}$ is the $T \times 1$ vector of $\Phi^{-1}(y_t)$, $\tilde{X}$ is a $T \times 2$ matrix of ones and the time series of the systematic risk factor, that is:

$$\tilde{X} = \begin{pmatrix} 1 & x_0 \\ \vdots & \vdots \\ 1 & x_{T-1} \end{pmatrix}.$$

We define $\hat{\beta} = (\tilde{X}'\tilde{X})^{-1}\tilde{X}'\tilde{y}$ as the ordinary least square estimate of β and

$$s^2 = \frac{(\tilde{y}-\tilde{X}\hat{\beta})'(\tilde{y}-\tilde{X}\hat{\beta})}{T-2}$$

as the estimate of σ^2 based on $\hat{\beta}$. Since:

$$(\tilde{y}-\tilde{X}\beta)'(\tilde{y}-\tilde{X}\beta) = (\tilde{y}-\tilde{X}\hat{\beta})'(\tilde{y}-\tilde{X}\hat{\beta}) + (\beta-\hat{\beta})'(\tilde{X}'\tilde{X})(\beta-\hat{\beta}),$$

the posterior distributions can be written as:

$$p(\beta, \sigma^2|\tilde{y}, \tilde{X}) \propto p(\sigma^2|\tilde{y}, \tilde{X}) \cdot p(\beta|\sigma^2, \tilde{y}, \tilde{X}), \qquad (7.13)$$

where:

$$p(\sigma^2|\tilde{y}, \tilde{X}) \propto (\sigma^2)^{-\frac{T}{2}} \exp\left\{-\frac{(T-2)s^2}{2\sigma^2}\right\} \qquad (7.14)$$

and:

$$p(\beta|\sigma^2, \tilde{y}, \tilde{X}) \propto (\sigma^{-2})\exp\left\{-\frac{1}{2\sigma^2}(\beta-\hat{\beta})'(\tilde{X}'\tilde{X})(\beta-\hat{\beta})\right\}. \qquad (7.15)$$

Therefore, the posterior of σ^2 conditional on $\tilde{y}$ in (7.14) is an inverse-gamma distribution, that is $\sigma^2|\tilde{y}, \tilde{X} \sim IG(\frac{T-2}{2}, \frac{(T-2)s^2}{2})$, and the posterior of β conditional on $\tilde{y}$ and σ^2 in (7.15) is a normal distribution, that is $\beta|\sigma^2, \tilde{y}, \tilde{X} \sim N(\hat{\beta}, \sigma^2(\tilde{X}'\tilde{X})^{-1})$.

To demonstrate the estimation procedures, we simulate an artificial data set based on the regression model in (7.11) with $h = -1.5$, $\rho = 0.3$, $\varphi = 0.8$ and $T = 100$. Figure 7.1 presents the simulated systematic risk factor x_t and default probability y_t. To start the estimation process, we first obtain the ordinary least square estimates β and s^2 using the simulated x_t and y_t. Next, we draw samples of σ^2 from $IG(\frac{T-2}{2}, \frac{(T-2)s^2}{2})$ and the corresponding β from $N(\hat{\beta}, \sigma^2(\tilde{X}'\tilde{X})^{-1})$. For each set of β and σ^2 sampled, we calculate the parameters h, ρ and φ. Figure 7.2 plots a histogram of the samples from the posterior distributions of β_0, β_1 and σ^2, and Figure 7.3 plots the histogram for the corresponding samples, h, ρ and φ. Table 7.1 presents the OLS estimates, mean, median and 95 per cent posterior confidence interval based on 10 000 samples from the posterior distributions and the values of the true parameters. The results reported in Table 7.1 demonstrate that the procedure is indeed able to recover the true value of h, ρ and φ.

7.3   MARKOV CHAIN MONTE CARLO

It is hard to evaluate the (unnormalized) porterior distribution, $p(\theta|y)$, if $p(\theta)p(y|\theta)$ has an irregular and ill-behaved shape or the dimension of the parameter space is large. For complicated models, it is very rare that we have standard posterior densities from which samples can be drawn. Markov Chain simulation allows us to draw samples from a complicated multidimensional posterior density. The key idea of MCMC is to construct a Markov process for θ which moves around the parameter space of θ and eventually converges to a stationary (unnormalized) distribution of $p(\theta|y)$. The most popular and general MCMC method is the Metropolis–Hastings algorithm.

7.3.1   The Metropolis–Hastings Algorithm

The Metropolis–Hastings method was initially proposed by Metropolis et al. (1953) and generalized by Hastings (1970). Each sequence of the Markov Chain is considered as a sample vector from the posterior distribution $p(\theta|y)$. With a sufficiently long chain, convergence leads to a stationary posterior distribution. The general Metropolis–Hastings algorithm works as follows:

1. Draw an initial sample θ^0 from some proposed distribution. A good proposal must have the property that $p(\theta^0|y) > 0$.
2. For the i-th iteration of the Markov Chain (starting from $i = 1$), draw a candidate sample $\theta*$ with jump probability $J(\theta*|\theta^{i-1})$ that governs the relationship between consecutive draws of the same parameter.
3. Calculate the importance ratio:

$$r = \frac{p(\theta*|y)/J(\theta*|\theta^{i-1})}{p(\theta^{i-1}|y)/J(\theta^{i-1}|\theta*)}.$$

4. Generate a uniform random number $u \sim U(0, 1)$.
5. Set:

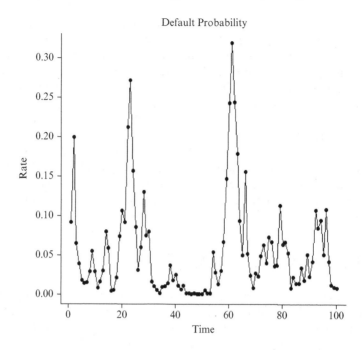

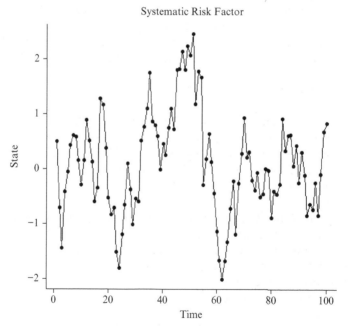

Figure 7.1   Simulated default probability and systematic risk factor

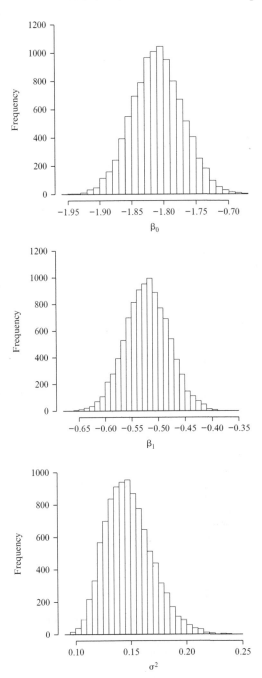

Figure 7.2   Histograms of β_0, β_1 and σ^2 from the posterior distributions with 10 000 simulations

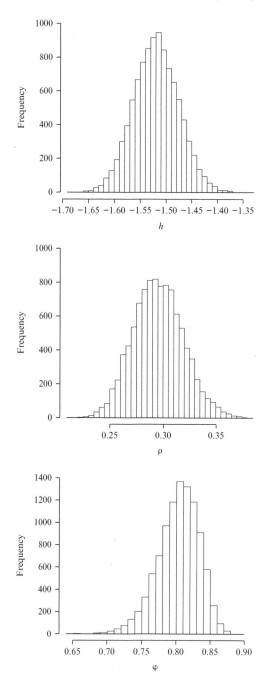

Figure 7.3   *Histograms of* h, ρ *and* φ *with 10 000 simulations*

Table 7.1   Summary of the posterior distributions

	β_0	β_1	σ^2	h	ρ	φ
True	−1.7928	−0.5237	0.1543	−1.5000	0.3000	0.8000
OLS	−1.8106	−0.5202	0.1458	−1.5214	0.2940	0.8061
Mean	−1.8101	−0.5206	0.1485	−1.5190	0.2956	0.8028
2.5%	−1.8738	−0.5890	0.1172	−1.5897	0.2581	0.7490
Median	−1.8100	−0.5204	0.1467	−1.5195	0.2949	0.8056
97.5%	−1.7451	−0.4540	0.1861	−1.4466	0.3358	0.8471

$$\theta^i = \begin{cases} \theta^* & \text{if } u \leq \min(r,1) \\ \theta^{i-1} & \text{otherwise.} \end{cases}$$

6.   Iterate from step 2 to step 4.
7.   To check the efficiency of the jump rules, calculate an acceptance rate:

$$R = \frac{\sum_{i=1}^{N} I_{\{\theta^i \neq \theta^{i-1}\}}}{N},$$

where N is the total length of the Markov Chain.

Jump distribution
The jump distribution in step 2 could be symmetric with $J(\theta^*|\theta^{i-1}) = J(\theta^{i-1}|\theta^*)$ or asymmetric with $J(\theta^*|\theta^{i-1}) \neq J(\theta^{i-1}|\theta^*)$. If the jump distribution is symmetric, then the importance ratio becomes:

$$r = \frac{p(\theta^*|y)}{p(\theta^{i-1}|y)},$$

since $J(\theta^*|\theta^{i-1}) = J(\theta^{i-1}|\theta^*)$. A Metropolis–Hastings algorithm with symmetric jump distribution is sometimes refered to as the Metropolis algorithm. As an example, the random walk chain Metropolis–Hastings algorithm, where the jump rule has a random walk structure $\theta^* = \theta^{i-1} + \varepsilon_i$, $\varepsilon_i \sim N(0, \sigma)$, has a symmetric jump distribution.
   If θ^* is independent of θ^{i-1}, then $J(\theta^*|\theta^{i-1}) = J(\theta^*)$ and the importance ratio becomes:

$$r = \frac{p(\theta^*|y)/J(\theta^*)}{p(\theta^{i-1}|y)/J(\theta^{i-1})}. \tag{7.16}$$

Such a Metropolis–Hastings algorithm is called independence chain Metropolis–Hastings.
   The jump distribution critically influences the efficiency of the Metropolis–Hastings algorithm and the speed by which the Markov Chain converges to the posterior distribution. For the simulation to be efficient, it must be easy to draw samples from the jump

distribution $J(\theta^*|\theta^{i-1})$. The jump distribution should be tuned to achieve an acceptance rate of around 30–40 per cent. We will provide an example to illustrate this below. The principle of Markov Chain convergence in the Metropolis–Hastings algorithm is well presented in Gelman et al. (1995).

Gibbs sampler

For a multidimensional parameter set $\theta = (\theta_1, \theta_2, \ldots, \theta_d)'$, samples of $\theta_1, \theta_2, \ldots, \theta_d$ can be drawn sequentially. The Gibbs sampler constructs a Markov Chain whose j-th parameter θ_j is sampled from the conditional posterior distribution given all the other parameters. As the chain gets longer, a Gibbs-sampled Markov Chain converges to the joint posterior distribution of the parameter vector θ. Suppose that θ_j can be sampled from its conditional posterior distribution:

$$p(\theta_j|\theta_{-j}, y), \tag{7.17}$$

where $\theta_{-j} = (\theta_1, \theta_2, \ldots, \theta_{j-1}, \theta_{j+1}, \ldots, \theta_d)'$. The Gibbs sampling method considers the conditional posterior distribution in (7.17) as the jump distribution. For θ_j and the i-th iteration, the jump distribution is given by:

$$J_j(\theta^*|\theta^{i-1}) = p(\theta_j^*|\theta_{-j}^{i-1}, y),$$

where $\theta_{-j}^{i-1} = (\theta_1^i, \theta_2^i, \ldots, \theta_{j-1}^i, \theta_{j+1}^{i-1}, \ldots, \theta_d^{i-1})'$. With this jump distribution, the importance ratio for θ_j at the i-th iteration is:

$$r_j = \frac{p(\theta^*|y)/p(\theta_j^*|\theta_{-j}^{i-1}, y)}{p(\theta_{i-1}|y)/p(\theta_j^{i-1}|\theta_{-j}^{i-1}, y)} = 1,$$

which means that every candidate θ^* is accepted with probability 1. The j-th updated parameter vector at the i-th iteration is:

$$(\theta_1^i, \theta_2^i, \ldots, \theta_{j-1}^i, \theta_j^*, \theta_{j+1}^{i-1}, \ldots, \theta_d^{i-1})'.$$

Therefore, the Gibbs sampling method can be thought of as a special case of the Metropolis–Hastings algorithm with unit importance ratio.

7.3.2   Convergence of the Chain

Checking that the chain converges to the posterior distribution is an important part of MCMC. The convergence of the chain is affected by the starting values, the within-chain correlations and the length of the chain. Firstly, the arbitrary starting point selection 'contaminates' the front part of the chain. For this reason, the early part of the simulated chain is 'burned in', that is, discarded, and only the latter part of the chain is used for making inferences. Secondly, the convergence speed of the chain depends on the within-chain correlations; the higher the within-chain correlations, the lower the convergence speed. Given a fixed chain length, the distribution of a correlated chain is less precise than an independent and identical chain. This means that with a highly correlated chain, more samples are needed to achieve the same accuracy of inference as in the case of an independently and identically distributed chain. One way to reduce the within-chain correlation is to keep only every second, third, fifth or tenth samples, a practice known as 'thinning'. Thirdly, the simulated chain must be long enough to cover the real domain of the posterior distribution.

Geweke's χ^2-test and the Raftery–Lewis diagnostics are often used to check whether the chain converges to the stationary posterior distribution. Geweke's χ^2-test determines whether the first 20 per cent of the chain has the same distribution as the last 50 per cent. The Raftery–Lewis diagnostics list the thinning ratio, burning ratio, and the total number of samples needed to achieve the prescribed accuracy of the posterior statistics. Le Sage (1999) implements both Geweke's χ^2-test and the Raftery–Lewis diagnostics in the Matlab function 'coda'.[1] We provide an example of how these diagnostics are used in the next subsection.

7.3.3   An Example: MCMC for the Vasicek Model with Known Systematic Factor

In the simple example of subsection 7.2.1, the Vasicek non-linear regression model in (7.10) was transformed into a linear regression by reparameterization. Here, we will estimate the non-linear regression directly by drawing samples for h, ρ and φ based on the MCMC methods presented in the previous subsection. In terms of h, ρ and φ, the posterior distribution defined in (7.12) is equivalent to:

$$p(h,\rho,\varphi|\tilde{y},x) \propto \sigma^{-(T+2)} \exp\left\{ -\frac{1}{2}\sigma^{-2}\sum_{t=1}^{T}\left(\tilde{y}_t - \frac{h - \sqrt{\rho}\varphi x_{t-1}}{\sqrt{1-\rho}}\right)^2\right\} \tag{7.18}$$

where $\sigma^2 = \frac{1-\rho}{\rho(1-\varphi^2)}$. This posterior distribution is not a standard probability distribution. Moreover, since it is hard to find the conditional posterior distributions, $p(h|\rho,\varphi,\tilde{y},x)$, $p(\rho|h,\varphi,\tilde{y},x)$ and $p(\varphi|h,\rho,\tilde{y},x)$, the Gibbs sampler is not applicable in this case. Hence, we will use the independence chain Metropolis–Hastings algorithm to draw samples for h, ρ and φ from the posterior distribution in (7.18). Specifically, let $\theta_1 = h$, $\theta_2 = \rho$ and $\theta_3 = \varphi$:

1.   Draw starting values from jump distributions $\theta_1^0 \sim N(\mu_{\theta_1},\sigma_{\theta_1}^2)$, $\theta_2^0 \sim N(\mu_{\theta_2},\sigma_{\theta_2}^2)$ and $\theta_3^0 \sim N(\mu_{\theta_3},\sigma_{\theta_3}^2)$.
2.   For the i-th iteration of the Markov Chain and for the j-th parameter:
     (a)   Draw a candidate sample θ_j^* from jump distribution $N(\mu_{\theta_j},\sigma_{\theta_j}^2)$.
     (b)   Calculate the importance ratio:

$$r = \frac{p(\theta_j^*,\boldsymbol{\theta}_{-j}^{i-1}|\tilde{y},x)/J_j(\theta_j^*)}{p(\theta_j^{i-1},\boldsymbol{\theta}_{-j}^{i-1}|\tilde{y},x)/J_j(\theta_j^{i-1})},$$

where $J_j(\cdot)$ denotes the jump probability of θ_j, which in this case is simply the Gaussian density from $N(\mu_{\theta_j},\sigma_{\theta_j}^2)$.
     (c)   Generate a uniform random number $u \sim U(0, 1)$.
     (d)   Set:

$$\theta_j^i = \begin{cases} \theta^* & \text{if } u \leq \min(r,1) \\ \theta_j^{i-1} & \text{otherwise.} \end{cases}$$

(e)   Iterate from steps (a) to (d) for all j.

3.   Iterate step 2 up to $i = N$, where N is the total length of the Markov Chain.
4.   To check the efficiency of the jump rules, calculate the acceptance rate for each parameter:

$$R_j = \frac{\sum_{i=1}^{N} I_{\{\theta_j^i \neq \theta_j^{i-1}\}}}{N}.$$

As mentioned before, the jump distribution is the most important factor affecting the efficiency of the Metropolis–Hastings algorithm. To enhance its efficiency, we first assume a normal distribution for the jump rule. Secondly, we take advantage of the OLS estimates provided in subsection 7.2.1 for the starting values of chain and the means of the jump distributions, μ_{θ_j}. Thirdly, we adjust the variances of the jump distributions, $\sigma_{\theta_j}^2$, to achieve a 30–40 per cent acceptance rate R_j. As a result, the jump distributions of h, ρ and φ are selected as $N(-1.52, 0.09^2)$, $N(0.29, 0.05^2)$ and $N(0.81, 0.08^2)$, respectively.

Initially, based on the independence chain Metropolis–Hastings algorithm, we draw a million samples for each parameter, burn in the first 40 per cent of each chain and keep every tenth sample afterwards so that we have a total of 60000 samples for each parameter. Table 7.2 presents the acceptance ratio R of each parameter, within-chain correlation, Raftery–Lewis diagnostics, and p-values for the Geweke χ^2-test. Within-chain correlations are almost equal to zero across all parameters so that Raftery–Lewis's 'Thin' becomes 1.[2] Since we have already discarded the first 40 per cent of each chain, Raftery–Lewis's 'Burn' shows that only the first two or three samples from each chain needed to be 'burned in'. The Raftery–Lewis 'Total' is the total number of samples needed to achieve the same level of efficiency as 'Nmin' number of draws for i.i.d.

Table 7.2   Diagnostics of simulated chains

	h	ρ	φ
Acceptance ratio (R)	0.4151	0.3923	0.4206
Within-chain correlation			
Lag 1	0.104	0.115	0.034
Lag 5	0.004	0.003	0.004
Lag 10	0.004	0.003	0.000
Lag 50	0.006	−0.002	−0.001
Raftery–Lewis Diagnostics			
Thin	1	1	1
Burn	2	3	2
Total	977	1008	963
Nmin	937	937	937
I-stat	1.043	1.076	1.028
Geweke's χ^2–test	0.4410	0.7607	0.8604

samples. The Raftery–Lewis 'I-stat' is the ratio of Total to Nmin; a value close to one means that the chain has a weak within-chain correlation, and thus there is less need for a very long chain. Finally, a *p*-value of Geweke's χ^2-test larger than 0.05 means that the chain has converged to a stationary distribution based on the comparison of the first 20 per cent and last 50 per cent of the chain.

Figure 7.4 shows, for each parameter, the histogram of the draws and the mean tracking plot which traces the mean value of the parameter at the *i*-th iteration. Based on Table 7.2 and Figure 7.4, our Markov Chain simulated by the independence chain Metropolis–Hastings algorithm has converged to its posterior distribution. Table 7.3 reports the summary statistics of the posterior distributions which are very similar to the results reported in Table 7.1.

7.4 MCMC NESTING PARTICLE FILTERING

Until this point, we have been assuming that the state variable, x_t, is observable. In this section, we relax this assumption and treat x_t as a latent, unobservable factor. Firstly, we define a state space model with state equation

$$x_t = f(x_{t-1}, \eta_t; \theta_f) \tag{7.19}$$

where x_t is the state at time t, f is a known function with related parameters θ_f, and η_t is an i.i.d. white noise process with known density φ_η. The observation equation is:

$$y_t = h(x_t, \xi_t; \theta_h) \tag{7.20}$$

where y_t is the observation at time t, h is a known function with distribution parameters θ_h, ξ_t is an i.i.d. measurement noise with known density ϕ_ξ. The functions f and h can be linear or non-linear and η and ξ can have any distributions.

If f and h are both linear, and η and ξ are both Gaussian, then the Kalman filter is the optimal solution for tracking the evolution of state variable x_t. The Kalman filter cannot be used, however, if the state space model is non-linear or one of η_t or ξ_t is non-Gaussian. The particle filter is the more appropriate choice in this case. There are several existing particle filtering algorithms for non-linear or non-Gaussian state space models. Here, we focus on the sampling importance resampling (SIR) filter which is one of the more popular particle filters.

7.4.1 A Bayesian Solution to Filtering

Suppose that we are looking for the filtered estimates of x_t based on all information from the measurements up to time t, that is, $y_{1:t} = (y_1, y_2, \ldots, y_t)'$. This is related to obtaining the posterior distribution $p(x_t|y_{1:t})$, which can be obtained by the recursive procedure of prediction and update.

In the prediction step, x_t is predicted conditional on $y_{1:t-1}$ and its density is given by:

$$p(x_t|y_{1:t-1}) = \int p(x_t|x_{t-1}, y_{1:t-1}) p(x_{t-1}|y_{1:t-1}) dx_{t-1}$$

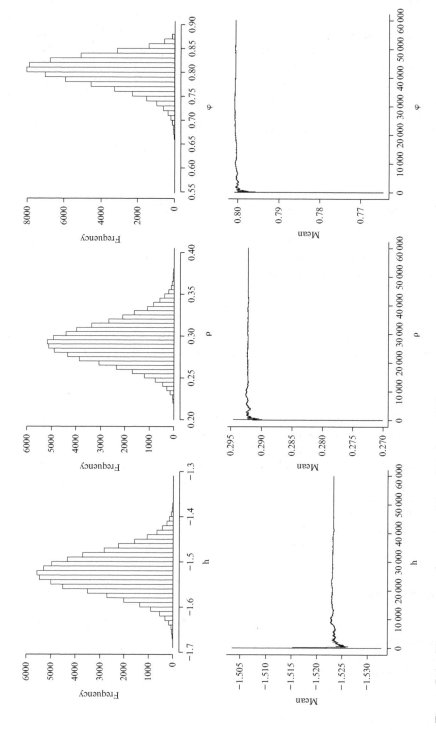

Figure 7.4   Histograms and mean tracking plots for model parameters

Table 7.3 Summary statistics of the simulated sample from independence Metropolis–Hastings

	True	Mean	2.5%	Median	97.5%
h	−1.5000	−1.5233	−1.5929	−1.5241	−1.4517
ρ	0.3000	0.2923	0.2550	0.2916	0.3317
φ	0.8000	0.8005	0.7440	0.8037	0.8462

$$= \int p(x_t|x_{t-1})p(x_{t-1}|y_{1:t-1})dx_{t-1} \tag{7.21}$$

where, by assumption, the posterior distribution $p(x_{t-1}|y_{1:t-1})$ is available from the previous update.

In the updating step, the prediction density in (7.21) is updated via Bayes's rule by including the most recent observation y_t as follows:

$$p(x_t|y_{1:t}) = p(x_t|y_t, y_{1:t-1})$$

$$= \frac{p(y_t|x_t, y_{1:t-1})p(x_t|y_{1:t-1})}{\int p(y_t|x_t, y_{1:t-1})p(x_t|y_{1:t-1})dx_t}$$

$$= \frac{p(y_t|x_t)p(x_t|y_{1:t-1})}{\int p(y_t|x_t)p(x_t|y_{1:t-1})dx_t} \tag{7.22}$$

Thus, the posterior distribution in (7.22) depends on the likelihood via $p(y_t|x_t)$. and the prediction density via $p(x_t|y_{1:t-1})$.

With linear functions f and h and Gaussian noises η and ξ, the posterior distribution $p(x_t|y_{1:t})$ is a normal, whose two moments, mean and variance, can be computed using the Kalman filter. With non-linear functions and non-Gaussian noises, the optimal filter is generally not available so that we are forced to use a particle filter, based on an approximation of the posterior distribution $p(x_t|y_{1:t-1})$ by Monte Carlo methods. Particle filtering is sometimes refered to as sequential Monte Carlo method, bootstrap filter or the condensation algorithm.

7.4.2 Posterior with Particle Filtered Likelihood

The particle filter uses randomly sampled particles with associated weights to approximate the posterior distribution $p(x_t|y_{1:t})$ for the state variable by performing Monte Carlo simulations via sequential importance sampling. According to the choice of the importance sampling density and resampling method, there are different versions of particle filtering such as the sampling importance resampling (SIR) filter, auxiliary sampling importance resampling (ASIR) filter, particle filters with improved sample diversity, local linearization particle filters, multiple-model particle filters, and so on. Details of these variants are available in Ristic et al. (2004). Here, we use the SIR filter because it is easy to implement and the assumptions are less restrictive. The SIR filter is applicable as long as we can sample the noise, η_t, of the state equation in (7.19) and evaluate the likelihood from the measurement equation in (7.20). We implement the SIR particle filter as follows. Suppose that M denotes the total number of particles. For $t = 0, \{x_{0|0}^m\}$ can be generated from the unconditional distribution of x. For $t = 1, 2, \ldots, T$:

1. Prediction: For $m = 1, 2, \ldots, M$:
   (a) Draw the predicted particles $\{x_{t|t-1}^m\}$ from state equation (7.19).
   (b) Calculate $\tilde{\omega}_t^m = \phi_\xi(\xi_t^m; \theta_h)$, where ξ_t^m is the measurement error calculated from y_t and $\{x_{t|t-1}^m\}$, and ϕ_ξ is the density of ξ.
2. For $m = 1, 2, \ldots, M$, calculate the normalized resampling weights:

$$\omega_t^m = \frac{\tilde{\omega}_t^m}{\sum_{m=1}^M \tilde{\omega}_t^m}.$$

3. Update: for $m = 1, 2, \ldots, M$, $\{x_{t|t}^m\}$ is resampled with replacement from the simulated $\{x_{t|t-1}^m\}$ in step 1 using the resampling weight ω_t^m in step 2. After the resampling, $\{x_{t|t}^m\}$ will have equal weights $\frac{1}{M}$.
4. Iterate steps 1, 2 and 3 up to $t = T$.

Through the SIR filter, the posterior distribution $p(x_t|y_{1:t})$ presented in (7.22) is approximated by the filtered particles $\{x_{t|t}^m\}$ for $t = 1, 2, \ldots, T$ and the accuracy of the approximation is increasing as $M \to \infty$.

The likelihood of the measurement equation in (7.20) can be produced by the SIR particle filter as follows. Suppose that $x_{t|t}^m$ denotes the m-th filtered particle at time t.

In the prediction step, the predicted particles $\{x_{t|t-1}^m\}$ are obtained using the state equation in (7.19) and fed into the measurement equation in (7.20) to calculate the measurement error ξ_t^m. Then the likelihood at time t can be approximated as:

$$\hat{p}(\xi_t|\theta) = \frac{1}{M}\sum_{m=1}^M \phi_\xi(\xi_t^m|x_{t|t-1}^m; \theta),$$

where $\phi_\xi(\cdot)$ is the probability density of measurement noise ξ and $\theta = (\theta_f, \theta_h)'$.

In the updating step, the updated particles $\{x_{t|t}^m\}$ are resampled from $\{x_{t|t-1}^m\}$ with associated sampling weights given by:

$$\omega_t^m = \frac{\phi_\xi(\xi_t^m|x_{t|t-1}^m, \theta)}{\sum_{m=1}^M \phi_\xi(\xi_t^m|x_{t|t-1}^m, \theta)} \tag{7.23}$$

based on equation (7.22). Thus, the distribution of the updated particles $\{x_{t|t}^m\}$ is represented by the posterior distribution in (7.22).

Then the likelihood can be obtained as:

$$\hat{p}(y_{1:T}|\theta) = \prod_{t=1}^T \hat{p}(\xi_t|\theta) \tag{7.24}$$

and the mean of the filtered process of x_t can be obtained as:

$$\hat{x}_{t|t} = \frac{1}{M}\sum_{m=1}^{M} x_{t|t}^m.$$

The posterior distribution of parameters presented in the state space model in (7.19) and (7.20) can be constructed as:

$$p(\theta|y_{1:T}) \propto p(\theta)\hat{p}(y_{1:T}|\theta)$$

by substituting the likelihood by the simulated likelihood from particle filtering in (7.24). In order to make inferences on the posterior distribution, we can perform MCMC simulations as presented in the previous sections.

7.4.3   An Example: MCMC Nesting Particle Filter for Vasicek Model

In the previous sections, the systematic risk factor is assumed to be known. However, in practice, the systematic risk factor is an unobservable latent process. Thus, in this section, we define a non-linear state space model for modelling the loss ratio with the observation equation as:

$$\tilde{y}_t = \Phi^{-1}(y_t) = \frac{h}{\sqrt{1-\rho}} - \frac{\sqrt{\rho}}{\sqrt{1-\rho}}x_t + \delta\xi_t \qquad (7.25)$$

where $\xi_t \sim N(0, 1)$ denotes Gaussian white noise and δ^2 is the variance of the measurement noise. The state equation is defined with the state variable following an AR(1) process as before:

$$x_t = \varphi x_{t-1} + \sqrt{1 - \varphi^2}\eta_t. \qquad (7.26)$$

To demonstrate the estimation procedure, we simulate the state space model in (7.25) and (7.26) with $h = -1.5$, $\rho = 0.3$, $\varphi = 0.8$ and $\delta = 0.3$. Figure 7.5 plots the simulated default ratio y_t and the systematic risk factor x_t.

With the estimated likelihood from particle filtering, the posterior distribution is represented as:

$$p(h,\rho,\varphi,\delta|\tilde{y}) \propto \left(\frac{1-\rho}{\rho(1-\varphi^2)}\right)^{-\frac{T+2}{2}} \prod_{t=1}^{T}\hat{p}(\xi_t|h,\rho,\varphi,\delta)$$

$$= \left(\frac{1-\rho}{\rho(1-\varphi^2)}\right)^{-\frac{T+2}{2}} \prod_{t=1}^{T}\frac{1}{M}\sum_{m=1}^{M}\phi_\xi(\xi_t^m|x_{t|t-1}^m;0,\delta),$$

where $\phi_\xi(\xi_t^m|x_{t|t-1}^m;0,\delta)$ is the normal density with mean 0 and standard deviation δ. In order to draw the posterior samples of h, ρ, φ and δ, the independence chain Metropolis–Hasting algorithm is employed by letting $\theta_1 = h$, $\theta_2 = \rho$, $\theta_3 = \varphi$ and $\theta_4 = \delta$:

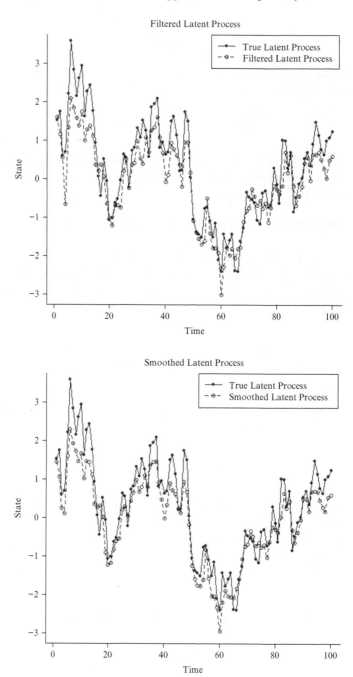

Figure 7.5   Simulated default probability

1. Draw starting values from jump distributions, $\theta_1^0 \sim N(\mu_{\theta_1}, \sigma_{\theta_1}^2)$, $\theta_2^0 \sim N(\mu_{\theta_2}, \sigma_{\theta_2}^2)$, $\theta_3^0 \sim N(\mu_{\theta_3}, \sigma_{\theta_3}^2)$ and $\theta_4^0 \sim N(\mu_{\theta_4}, \sigma_{\theta_4}^2)$.

2. For the i-th iteration of the Markov Chain and for the j-th parameter:

    (a) Draw a candidate sample θ_j^* from jump distribution $N(\mu_{\theta_j}, \sigma_{\theta_j}^2)$.

    (b) Set up the candidate parameter vector from $\boldsymbol{\theta}_{-j}^{i-1}$ and θ_j^*. For example, for $j = 3$, the candidate parameter vector is $(\theta_1^i, \theta_2^i, \theta_3^*, \theta_4^{i-1})'$ and the old parameter vector is $(\theta_1^i, \theta_2^i, \theta_3^{i-1}, \theta_4^{i-1})'$. Both sets of parameter values are needed in the computation below.

    (c) Calculate the likelihood via the particle filter for both the old and candidate parameter vector for time $t \le T$.

    i. Prediction: generate M numbers of $\eta_t^m \sim N(0, 1)$ to produce M numbers of predicted particles $\{x_{t|t-1}^m\}$ based on:

    $$\{x_{t|t-1}^m\} = \varphi\{x_{t-1|t-1}^m\} + \sqrt{1 - \varphi^2}\eta_t^m.$$

    For $t = 1$, $x_{0|0}^m$ is drawn from the unconditional distribution of x.

    ii. Likelihood: calculate the likelihood at time t as:

    $$\hat{p}(\xi_t | h, \rho, \varphi, \delta) = \frac{1}{M}\sum_{m=1}^{M}\phi_\xi(\xi_t^m | x_{t|t}^m; 0, \delta)$$

    where:

    $$\xi_t^m = \tilde{y}_t - \frac{h}{\sqrt{1-\rho}} + \frac{\sqrt{\rho}}{\sqrt{1-\rho}}\{x_{t|t-1}^m\}.$$

    iii. Update: updated particles $\{x_{t|t}^m\}$ are resampled from $\{x_{t|t-1}^m\}$ with associated sampling weights defined in (7.23).

    For the m-th particle:
    – Draw a uniform random number $u \sim U(0, 1)$.
    – Sort ω_t^m according to the values of $x_{t|t-1}^m$.
    – Calculate the smallest K such that $\sum_{k=1}^{K}\omega_t^k \ge u$.
    – Save $\{x_{t|t-1}^K\}$ as the m-th updated particle $\{x_{t|t}^m\}$.

    iv. Repeat (i) to (iii) for time $t = 1, \ldots, T$.

    (d) At time $t = T$, calculate the likelihoods $p(\theta_j^*, \boldsymbol{\theta}_{-j}^{i-1} | y)$ and $p(\theta_j^{i-1}, \boldsymbol{\theta}_{-j}^{i-1} | y)$ from:

    $$\prod_{t=1}^{T}\frac{1}{M}\sum_{m=1}^{M}\phi_\xi(\xi_t^m | x_{t|t}^m; 0, \delta).$$

    (e) Calculate the importance ratio:

    $$r = \frac{p(\theta_j^*, \boldsymbol{\theta}_{-j}^{i-1} | y)/J_j(\theta_j^*)}{p(\theta_j^{i-1}, \boldsymbol{\theta}_{-j}^{i-1} | y)/J_j(\theta_j^{i-1})}.$$

    where $J_j(\theta_j)$ denotes the probability density of θ_j, that is, $N(\mu_{\theta_j}, \sigma_{\theta_j}^2)$.

    (f) Generate a uniform random number $u \sim U(0, 1)$.

    (g) Set:

Table 7.4   Diagnostics of simulated chains

	h	ρ	φ	δ
Acceptance ratio (R)	0.4053	0.4309	0.4119	0.3908
Within-chain correlation				
Lag 1	0.005	0.030	0.009	0.099
Lag 5	0.003	0.007	-0.003	0.003
Lag 10	0.004	0.005	-0.004	-0.001
Lag 50	0.007	-0.003	0.001	0.001
Raftery–Lewis Diagnostics				
Thin	1	1	1	1
Burn	2	1	2	2
Total	950	940	942	940
Nmin	937	937	937	937
I-stat	1.014	1.003	1.005	1.003
Geweke's χ^2-test	0.5669	0.9362	0.8117	0.8541

$$\theta_j^i = \begin{cases} \theta^* & \text{if } u \le \min(r,1) \\ \theta_j^{i-1} & \text{otherwise}. \end{cases}$$

(h)   Iterate (a) to (g) for all j.

3.   Iterate step 2 up to $i = N$, where N is the total length of the Markov Chain.

4.   For checking the efficiency of the jump rules, calculate the acceptance rate for each parameter:

$$R_j = \frac{\sum_{i=1}^{N} I_{\{\theta_j^i \ne \theta_j^{i-1}\}}}{N}.$$

As shown in the example of the Vasicek model with known systematic risk factor, we need information on the parameters to propose jump distributions for the independence chain Metropolis–Hasting algorithm. Otherwise, the general Metropolis–Hastings algorithm should be applied to draw samples from the posterior distributions. In this example, we construct a four dimensional coarse grid on the parameter space and calculate the density of the posterior distribution on the grid. Based on the information from the grid method, we propose the jump distribution of h, ρ, φ and δ as $N(-1.5, 0.5^2)$, $N(0.3, 0.14^2)$, $N(0.8, 0.18^2)$ and $N(0.3, 0.04)$ to produce an acceptance rate R between 30 and 40 per cent.

We initially draw a million samples for each parameter, burn-in the first 40 per cent of each chain and keep every tenth sample. This leaves 60000 samples for each parameter. Table 7.4 presents the acceptance ratios R_j for each parameter and the respective diagnostics. Based on the results reported in Table 7.4, we conclude that the Markov Chain converges to the posterior distribution (see Table 7.2 and the previous section for a detailed interpretation of the diagnostic statistics).

Figure 7.6 displays a histogram of the samples and a tracking plot for the mean

Table 7.5   Summary of the simulated sample from Metropolis–Hastings

	True	Mean	2.5%	Median	97.5%
h	-1.5000	-1.6551	-2.1509	-1.6585	-1.1469
ρ	0.3000	0.3442	0.2338	0.3423	0.4611
φ	0.8000	0.8061	0.6252	0.8210	0.9367
δ	0.3000	0.3313	0.2686	0.3308	0.3958

value of each parameter and Table 7.5 presents the summary statistics of the converged chain. It is natural that the confidence interval of each parameter is wider than those reported in Table 7.2 since the information from the latent process is not available in this case.

Smoothing

While filtering concerns the estimation of the posterior distribution of x_t based on the information available up to time t, $p(x_t|y_{1:t})$, smoothing describes the estimation of the posterior distribution conditional on all information at time $t = 1, \cdots, T$ to give $p(x_t|y_{1:T})$. The trajectory of estimated states tends to be smoother than those by filtering. Among the few existing algorithms for smoothing, we introduce the forward–backward recursion method. The procedure starts from the last observation at $t = T$.

At time $t = T$, the filtered and the smoothed distribution of x_t are the same, that is, $p(x_T|y_{1:T})$. At time $t = T - 1$:

$$p(x_{T-1}|y_{1:T}) = p(x_{T-1}|x_T, y_{1:T}) = p(x_{T-1}|x_T, y_{1:T-1})$$

The information set needed from y is reduced because x_T contains the related information in y_T.

By Bayes's rule:

$$p(x_{T-1}|y_{1:T}) = p(x_{T-1}|y_{1:T-1}) \frac{f(x_T|x_{T-1})}{p(x_{T-1}|y_{1:T-1})}$$

The ratio, that is, the second component on the right-hand side (RHS), can be integrated out with respect to x_T as follows since the distribution $p(x_T|y_{1:T})$ is known:

$$p(x_{T-1}|y_{1:T}) = p(x_{T-1}|y_{1:T-1}) \int \frac{f(x_T|x_{T-1})}{p(x_{T-1}|y_{1:T-1})} p(x_T|y_{1:T}) dx_T.$$

The procedure is repeated for $t = T - 1, T - 2, \ldots, 1$.

Following the implementation procedures in the previous section, suppose that $\{x_{t|t}^m, \omega_t^m\}$ is the pair of the filtered particles and its associated weight at time t. Then the particle approximation of $p(x_t|y_{1:T})$ can be represented as $x_{t|t}^m$ with smoothed weight $\omega_{t|T}^m$ which can be obtained by:

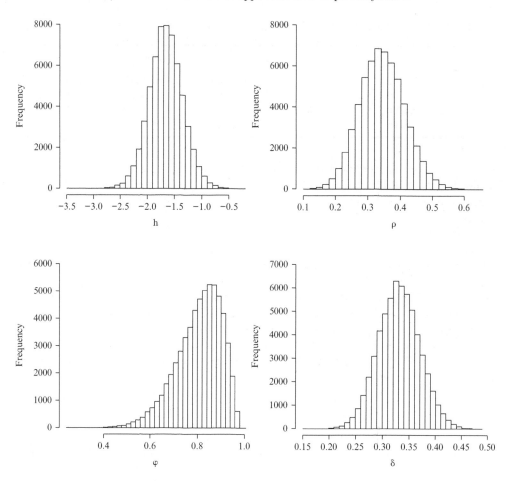

Figure 7.6   Histograms and mean tracking plots

$$\omega_{t|T}^{m} = \omega_{t}^{m} \left[\sum_{j=1}^{M} \omega_{t+1|T}^{j} \frac{f(x_{t+1}^{j}|x_{t}^{m})}{\sum_{i=1}^{M} \omega_{t}^{i} f(x_{t+1}^{j}|x_{t}^{i})} \right]$$ (7.27)

For the SIR filter, the weight of the resampled particle $x_{t|t}^{m}$ is given by $\frac{1}{M}$ for all m and t. Therefore, from the forward–backward smoothing formula in (7.27), the smoothed weight $\omega_{t|T}^{m}$ for the SIR filter is simplified as:

$$\omega_{t|T}^{m} = \frac{1}{M} \left[\sum_{j=1}^{M} \omega_{t+1|T}^{j} \frac{f(x_{t+1}^{j}|x_{t}^{m})}{\sum_{i=1}^{M} \frac{1}{M} f(x_{t+1}^{j}|x_{t}^{i})} \right]$$

and the expected smoothed state is estimated as:

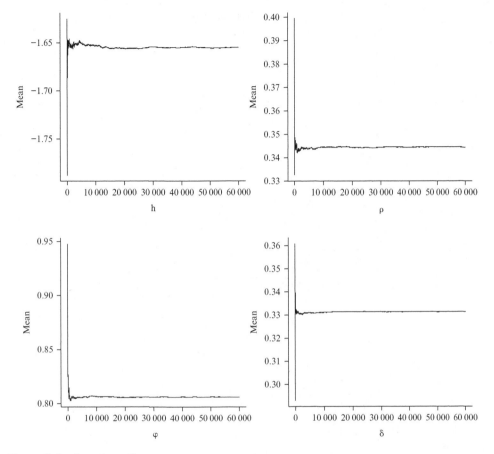

Figure 7.6 (continued)

$$\hat{x}_{t|T} = \sum_{m=1}^{M} x_{t|t}^{m} \omega_{t|T}^{m}.$$

Figure 7.7 displays the expected filtered and smoothed systematic risk factor.

7.5 LIMITATION

Throughout this chapter, we use a model that has only one set of observed variables and one set of unobserved variables. The MCMC and particle filtering procedures for the multivariate case are much more complex and are beyond the scope of this chapter.

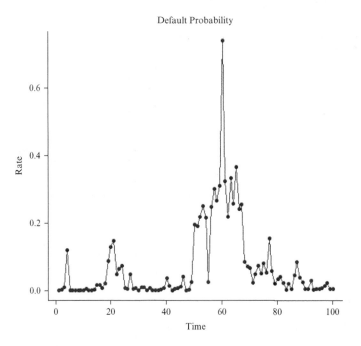

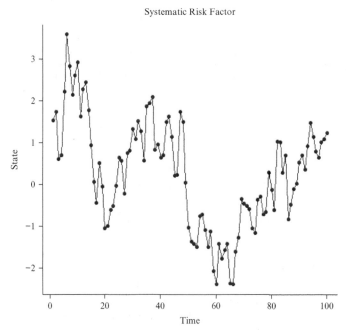

Figure 7.7   Simulated default probability

NOTES

1. The 'coda' Matlab function can be downloaded from http://www. spatial-econometrics. com.
2. This means we can accept every value simulated without thinning, or throwing away any samples.

REFERENCES

Gelman, A., J.B. Carlin, H.S. Stern and D.B. Rubin (1995), *Bayesian Data Analysis*, London: Chapman & Hall.

Hastings, W.K. (1970), 'Monte Carlo sampling methods using Markov Chains and their applications', *Biometrika*, **57**, 97–109.

LeSage, J.P. (1999), 'Applied econometrics using MATLAB', available at http://www.spatial-econometrics. com/html/mbook.pdf.

Merton, R.C. (1974), 'On the pricing of corporate debt: the risk structure of interest rates', *Journal of Finance*, **7**, 141–183.

Metropolis, N., A.W. Rosenbluth, M.N. Roshnbluth, A.H. Teller and E. Teller (1953), 'Equation of state calculations by fast computing machines', *Journal of Chemical Physics*, **21**, 1087–1092.

Ristic, B., S. Arulampalam and N. Gordon (2004), *Beyond the Kalman Filter: Particle Filters for Tracking Applications*, Boston, MA: Artech House.

Vasicek, O. (1987), 'Probability of loss on loan portfolio', working paper, KMV Corporation.

Vasicek, O. (1991), 'Limiting loan loss probability distribution', working paper, KMV Corporation.

PART III

BANKING AND MICROSTRUCTURE

8 Competition in banking: measurement and interpretation

Hong Liu, Phil Molyneux and John O.S. Wilson

8.1 INTRODUCTION

Competition in banking is important because it encourages efficiency in the production and allocation of financial services. In banking, the level of competition has implications for access to finance, the allocation of capital funds, the competitiveness and development of manufacturing and service sectors, the level of economic growth and the extent of financial stability (Petersen and Rajan, 1995; Cetorelli, 2004; Bonaccorsi Di Patta and Dell'Aricca, 2004; Beck et al., 2004). Competition can make markets more competitive by encouraging innovation, lower prices and higher-quality products to enhance consumer choice and welfare.

Given the importance of bank competition, it is crucial that researchers find precise ways of assessing not only the level of competition at a given moment in time, but also changes in competition over a sustained period. The more accurate the measure, the more precise any predictions of econometric models utilized are likely to be. Any policy measures following from such predictions can be misleading if the extent of competition measured is inaccurate.

The assessment of competition in the banking industry has a long empirical tradition. Early research focused on market structure–performance linkages starting from the structure–conduct–performance (SCP) paradigm and the Chicago Revisionist School. The former contested that a small number of banks may be able to collude either implicitly or explicitly, or use independent market power, to charge higher prices (lower rates paid on deposits, higher rates charged on loans) so as to earn abnormal profits. The latter contested that finding evidence of a positive-concentration–profitability relationship does not necessarily infer collusive behaviour as it may simply reflect the relationship between size and efficiency (larger banks gain from scale and other efficiency advantages, so more concentrated markets are inherently more profitable). The extent to which banks are able to earn high profits through collusion or the exercise of market power, or as a consequence of superior efficiency, has never been satisfactorily resolved (Goddard et al., 2001, 2007; Dick and Hannan, 2010).

Later research drew on contestable markets theory and its new empirical industrial organization (NEIO) counterpart to emphasize the influence of potential as well as actual competition, and consequently focus on competitive conduct of firms in response to changes in demand and supply conditions. Empirical banking research in this tradition has found differences in competitive conditions across banking sectors from the 1980s until the present day (Molyneux et al., 1994; Claessens and Laeven, 2004; Goddard and Wilson, 2009).

More recently, research (which in many ways is sympathetic to the Austrian and

Schumperterian notions of competition) has examined the dynamics of bank performance in an attempt to assess the extent to which entry, exit and governance mechanisms are efficient enough to drive banks' profit rates to converge towards the same long-run average value. The alternative hypothesis is that incumbent banks possess the capability to prevent imitation, or retard or block entry. If so, abnormal profit tends to persist from year to year, and differences in bank-level long-run average profit rates may be sustained indefinitely. Evidence suggests that barriers to competition and information constraints influence the degree of persistence of profitability (Berger et al., 2000; Goddard et al., 2004a, 2004b; Goddard et al., 2011).

It is against this background that this chapter outlines a number of ways in which researchers can use information on individual banks to compute various measures of competition. Using real-world data, we show that the extent of competition differs across countries. This has implications not only for the methods used to assess the extent of competition, but also for public policy approaches to competition. The rest of this chapter is structured as follows. Section 8.2 provides a basic introduction to competition in banking via an overview of the structure–conduct–performance (SCP) paradigm which utilizes measures of industry structure, and links these to measures of bank performance in order to say something about the extent of competition prevailing in an industry over a short period of time. Section 8.3 introduces the new empirical industrial organization (NEIO) approaches to measure bank conduct with an overview of the Panzar–Rosse H-statistic. Section 8.4 introduces other competition measures including the Lerner index, Boone indicator and persistence of profits (POP). Section 8.5 presents estimates of the aforementioned indicators for a sample of nine European Union (EU) banking systems from 2000 to 2009, highlighting similarities of various measures. Section 8.6 discusses recent literature that explores the relationship between competition and risk in banking. Section 8.7 concludes.

8.2   STRUCTURE–CONDUCT–PERFORMANCE (SCP) PARADIGM

8.2.1   Overview of SCP

Mason (1939, 1949) and Bain (1951, 1956, 1959) were the originators of what has become known as the structure–conduct–performance (SCP) paradigm. The SCP paradigm seeks to explain aspects of the conduct and performance of firms in terms of the structural characteristics of the industries or markets in which they operate. The structural features include the number of firms and their absolute and relative sizes, the extent of product differentiation and the nature of entry conditions.

According to the SCP approach, market structure is expected to influence the conduct of the firms that comprise the industry. Conduct variables include price setting, collusion and other forms of strategic behaviour, expenditure on advertising, research and development and innovation. Conduct, dictated or influenced by structure, in turn determines performance. Firm performance can be measured by a number of indicators, including: profit, growth, market share, technological progress and efficiency. The main insight from the SCP paradigm is that the smaller the number of firms in an industry,

Figure 8.1   The structure conduct performance paradigm

the easier it is for these firms to exploit their market power (and operate in an uncompetitive manner) in order to charge prices above marginal costs, and so the greater will be the profitability (market power) of incumbent firms. This is shown in Figure 8.1 where the bold arrows indicate the direction of the SCP relationship.

Early empirical work based on the SCP paradigm focused on the relationship between concentration and performance measured by profitability. A positive relationship between concentration and profit was typically interpreted as evidence that firms act collusively in order to achieve high profits. Bain (1951), for instance, tests the concentration hypothesis using data on United States (US) manufacturing firms between 1936–40, and finds that in industries with eight-firm concentration ratios (CR_8) above 70 per cent, profits were significantly higher than in those with CR_8 below 70 per cent. These results have been interpreted as supporting the hypothesis that concentration facilitates collusion and limits rivalry. Bain's findings were confirmed by numerous other studies, which at the time were interpreted as providing empirical justification for government intervention aimed at increasing competition. Gilbert (1984) reviews a large number of early concentration–profits studies, most of which report a significant positive relationship between these two variables.

Proponents of the SCP paradigm tend to view most existing markets as imperfect in terms of their competitive structure, and in need of some form of regulation in order to check the abuse of market power. The Chicago School, however, represented by academics including Stigler (1968) and Demsetz (1973), argue that government interference tends to lead to less competition rather than more. A positive link between concentration and profits does not necessarily imply collusive behaviour on the part of firms. It may simply reflect the fact that the larger firms tend to operate more efficiently, and tend to make higher profits as a result.

Demsetz argues that market structure affects profitability not through concentration, but by the association between market share and profitability. Because by definition concentrated industries contain firms with high market shares, the average level of profit also tends to be higher than in less intensively concentrated industries. A positive relationship between market share and profitability at the firm level therefore suggests a relationship between profit and concentration, even if concentration has no effect on conduct. If the positive relationship between market concentration and profitability reflects the exercise of market power, then it should affect all firms equally. If large firms in concentrated industries have higher profits than small firms, however, the correlation between profit and concentration is the result of the underlying relationship between profit and efficiency which has allowed these firms to become large. If some firms have an efficiency advantage, these firms tend to attain large market shares, and consequently the industry becomes concentrated. If all firms operate at similar levels of efficiency, concentration and average profitability tend to remain low. This implies that regulation or intervention aimed at achieving de-concentration is not an appropriate policy prescription, since it penalizes the largest and most efficient firms.

8.2.2   Measuring Industry Structure: Concentration Measures

Much of the empirical research into the relationship between market structure and the behaviour and performance of firms tends to rely heavily on a number of alternative measures of the first of these characteristics: the number and size distribution of firms. No doubt the emphasis on this aspect of structure is strongly influenced by the relative ease with which firm size distributions can be observed and quantified, in comparison with some of the other structural features.

Another important factor is to always bear in mind how we define the market from which the concentration measure is calculated. Usually, for ease, studies calculate national concentration measures where the size of the market is defined by the size of total banking sector assets or deposits in the country. This is relatively simple to calculate but rather crude as it provides only one simple concentration indicator for the banking system under study. In reality we know that the structure of different banking business areas – consumer loans, mortgage loans, credit cards, company lending and so on – vary enormously. In the United Kingdom (UK), for instance, mortgage lending is substantially less concentrated than small-firm lending. However, this type of information on specific market segments over time is problematic to obtain for many banking systems and that is why most studies resort to national market structure indicators and broad bank performance indicators to undertake SCP analysis.

Hannah and Kay (1977) argue that if a measure is to capture the structure of an industry adequately, it must satisfy a number of key criteria, including the following: (1) a concentration measure should rank Industry A as more concentrated than Industry B if the cumulative share of output when the firms in Industry A are ranked in descending order is everywhere greater than the cumulative share of the firms in Industry B; (2) a transfer of sales from a smaller to a larger firm should always increase concentration; (3) the entry of firms below a certain size threshold should always reduce concentration, while the exit of firms below the threshold should increase concentration; (4) a merger between two existing firms should always increase concentration.

As will be seen, not all of the measures of concentration defined below satisfy all of these criteria, and there is no perfect measure. Nevertheless, while all measures are subject to their own idiosyncracies and limitations, they do usually tend to correlate highly with one another (Lipczynski et al., 2009).

The n-firm concentration ratio measures the market share of the top n firms in the industry:

$$CR_n = \sum_{i=1}^{n} S_i$$

where S_i = market share of the i'th firm, when firms are ranked in descending order of market share.

Typically, market share in banking is measured in terms of deposits or assets and commonly used values of n include 3, 5 or 10. Unsurprisingly, researchers have found that there is a high correlation between concentration ratios defined using alternative values of n. The n-firm concentration ratio has the advantage of being easily measurable; one needs to know only the total size of the industry and the individual sizes of the top n firms. By focusing only on the share of the top n firms, however, it takes no account of the size distribution of remaining firms. It therefore fails to satisfy several of Hannah and Kay's (1977) criteria (see above): for example, a merger between two firms outside the top n does not affect CR_n.

In contrast, the much more data-intensive Herfindahl–Hirschman (H-H) index (Hirschman, 1945; Herfindahl, 1950) uses information about all points on the firm size distribution. It is simply defined as the sum of the squares of the market shares of all firms:

$$H - H = \sum_{i=1}^{N} S_i^2$$

where S_i is market share of firm i as before, and N is the total number of firms in the industry. In the calculation of H-H, the larger firms receive a weighting heavier than their smaller counterparts, reflecting their relative importance. The numbers equivalent of the H-H index is also sometimes used, $\frac{1}{H - H}$, that represents the number of equal-sized firms that the industry could sustain. Typically the simple n-firm concentration ratio and H-H index are most widely used in the empirical banking literature.[1]

8.2.3 Estimation of the SCP Relationship

As noted earlier, bank conduct is difficult to observe so tests of the SCP relationship typically link structure to performance from which they infer conduct. We have already explained that banking system structure is usually measured using a three- or five-firm deposits or assets concentration ratio (or a deposits or assets-based H-H index). It is generally assumed that different types of depository institutions (commercial banks, savings banks, co-operative banks, etc.) are competing against each other in the same market, while investment bank and insurance companies are competing with different product markets and are not included in calculating the concentration ratio. Studies exclude foreign banks if these are not viewed as direct competitors to their domestic counterparts.

Once the measure of market structure is chosen then one also has to choose a bank performance indicator. Usually, profit measures such as return on equity (ROE) or return on assets (ROA) are chosen. However, if a specific banking market is being analysed (e.g. car loans), it may be possible to obtain product prices such as the interest rates charged on car loans in different markets.[2] Unfortunately, it is often difficult to get product prices in different banking markets so researchers stick to bank profitability as the main performance indicator. The bulk of the literature uses simple OLS (although more recently various panel estimators have been used) to estimate the following type of regression:

$$ROE_{ij} \text{ or } ROA_{ij} = a + b\, CONC_j + c\, \Sigma\, BS_{ij} + d\Sigma\, MKT_j + u_{ij}$$

where:

ROE_{ij} = return on equity of bank i in market j

ROA_{ij} = return on assets of bank i in market j

$CONC_j$ = concentration measure (H-H index or 3-firm or 5-firm assets or deposits concentration measure) in market j

BS_{ij} = bank-specific variables (such as loan/asset ratio, liquid assets/total assets, capital/assets, bank size or market share, risk measures, bank ownership features and so on) for bank i in market j

MKT_j = market-specific variables (such as market-growth indicators, inflation, interest rates and so on) in market j

u_{ij} = error term.

In order to test for the SCP relationship, the model seeks to explain variation in bank performance (ROA or ROE) with a variety of bank-specific and market (or country) -specific variables. The finding of a positive and statistically significant b coefficient on $CONC_j$ confirms the positive link between profits and concentration confirming evidence of the traditional SCP paradigm. However, the findings of a positive relationship between concentration and profitability cannot be interpreted unambiguously as the result of collusion and the exercise of monopoly power. According to the efficiency hypothesis, it may simply reflect the fact that bigger banks are more efficient than their smaller counterparts. In other words, it is questionable whether the high profits enjoyed by large banks are a consequence of concentrated market structures and collusive price-setting behaviour, or of superior production and management techniques that allow larger banks to keep costs low, make high returns and grow larger. More concentrated banking sectors containing a high proportion of large banks will tend to have higher profitability on average, because the large banks are more efficient than their smaller counterparts operating in more competitive sectors. The existence of the competing collusion and efficiency interpretations of the concentration–profitability relationship has spawned a body of research which seeks to resolve the issue using empirical criteria.

As in the earlier SCP literature, concentration indicators are still used as the main structural indicators (mainly because this is easier to measure than other dimensions of structure, such as entry barriers and product differentiation). Furthermore, empirical research based on the SCP paradigm often finds the anticipated direction between structure, conduct and performance, although such relationships are usually weak in terms of their statistical significance. Overall, the aforementioned controversy has never been satisfactorily resolved (Berger et al., 2004; Wilson et al., 2010).

8.3   MEASURES OF BANK CONDUCT: THE PANZAR–ROSSE H-STATISTIC

Weaknesses in the SCP approach and more specifically in measures of concentration have led to a number of attempts to collect empirical evidence on the nature of competition by observing conduct directly. This approach has become known as the NEIO. One of the major strengths of NEIO is that it is grounded firmly in microeconomic (oligopoly) theory. SCP measures structure–performance relationships across a number of industries, and then draws inferences about what these relationships might mean for conduct. In contrast, NEIO makes direct observations of conduct in specific industries, and then draws inferences about what these observed patterns of conduct might mean for structure.

Empirical research in the NEIO stream attempts to estimate the behavioural equations that specify how firms set their prices and quantities. One of the main methodological challenges for NEIO research is to find ways of transforming behavioural relationships that are unobservable in their original theoretical form into relationships involving variables that can be observed, so that tests are available that can be implemented in practice.

Rosse and Panzar (1977) and Panzar and Rosse (1982, 1987) develop a test that examines whether firm conduct is in accordance with the models of perfect competition, imperfect or monopolistic competition, or monopoly. The Rosse–Panzar test is also known as the revenue test. This test is based on empirical observation of the impact on firm-level revenues of variations in the prices of the factors of production that are used as inputs in the production processes of a group of competing firms. Built into the test is an explicit assumption of profit-maximizing behaviour on the part of the firms.

Rosse and Panzar's test generates what is referred to as the H-statistic, defined simply as the sum of how the elasticities of a firm's total revenue with respect to each of its factor input prices, differs under perfectly competitive, imperfectly competitive and monopolistic market conditions. The intuition is straightforward in the polar cases of perfect competition and monopoly, but more complex in the intermediate case of imperfect or monopolistic competition. The following discussion focuses on the two polar cases. In each of these, we consider the impact of a simultaneous equiproportionate increase in all of the firm's factor input prices. This implies an equiproportionate increase in the total cost of producing any given level of output, and an upward shift in the positions of the long-run average cost (LRAC) and long-run marginal cost (LRMC) functions.

Under perfect competition as each firm's LRAC and LRMC functions shift upwards, the market price must increase in exactly the same proportion, so that each firm continues to earn only a normal profit when long-run equilibrium is restored. The increase in market price implies a reduction in the level of demand. The required adjustment in the total quantity of output is achieved by a reduction in the number of firms. However, for those firms that survive, total revenue increases in the same proportion as total cost; and in the same proportion as the original increase in factor prices. Therefore in perfect competition, the H-statistic is one.

Under monopoly (assuming horizontal LRAC and LRMC functions) as long-run average and marginal costs shift upwards, the monopolist's profit-maximizing price and output adjust. A monopolist with non-zero costs always operates on the price-elastic portion of the market demand function. This must be so, because for profit maximization, marginal revenue (MR) equals marginal cost, so if LRMC > 0, we must have MR > 0. And if MR > 0, price elasticity of demand (PED) > 1. This implies that the shift from an increase in costs causes a reduction in the monopolist's total revenue (if PED > 1, an increase in price causes total revenue to fall). In this case, the increase in factor prices causes total revenue to decline. Therefore in monopoly, the H-statistic is negative. Intermediate values between zero and one denote conduct consistent with imperfect competition. This approach has found particularly widespread application in the banking literature due to its modest data requirements and single-equation linear estimation (Shaffer, 2004a, 2004b).

The Panzar–Rosse revenue test is usually implemented through fixed effects (FE) estimation of the following regression, using bank-level panel data:

$$\log TR_{i,t} = \alpha + \sum_{j=1}^{J} \beta_i \log w_{j,i,t} + \theta' X_{i,t} + \eta_{i,t}$$

where $TR_{i,t}$ = total revenue of bank i in year t; $w_{j,i,t}$ = price of factor input j; $X_{i,t}$ is a vector of exogenous control variables; and $\eta_{i,t}$ is a random disturbance term. The factor input prices are usually imputed from bank account data. The Panzar–Rosse H-statistic is then defined as $H = \sum_{j=1}^{J} \beta_j$.

The dependent variable is defined as the natural logarithm of total revenue. Empirically, it is the natural logarithm of either interest income (II) or total income (TI), where the latter includes both the interest income and non-interest income arising from fee-based products and off-balance sheet activities. It is assumed that there are J = 3 factor inputs: deposits; labour; and fixed capital and equipment. In the vector $w_{j,i,t}$, the definitions of the factor input prices are interest expenses/total deposits and money market funding, personnel costs/total assets, and other non-interest expenses/total assets,[3] respectively.[4] The control variables comprise balance sheet ratios that reflect bank behaviour and risk profile. These normally include equity to total assets ratio, net loans to total assets ratio, diversification (the proportion of non-interest income among total operating income), and a full set of individual year dummy variables. The literature also suggests controlling for bank size (the logarithm of total bank assets) since larger banks tend to earn more revenue, *ceteris paribus*, in ways unrelated to variations in input prices. Alternatively, one can use log (P) = log (TR/TA) instead of log (TR) as the dependent variable, where TA is total assets (the so called price equation). Bikker et al. (2012), however, provide both theoretical and empirical evidence that the price and revenue equations may generate identical H-statistics when in long-run competitive equilibrium, but critically different H-statistics when in monopoly or oligopoly. The price equation and scaled revenue function should then be discarded. Bikker et al. further show that the appropriate H-statistic calculated from an unscaled revenue equation requires additional information about costs, market equilibrium and possibly market demand elasticity to infer the degree of competition, all of which are difficult to obtain.

Typically, equations are estimated using fixed effects (FE) estimators to deal with any unobserved bank-specific factors, although earlier literature used ordinary least squares (OLS) (as do various cross-sectional studies). Goddard and Wilson (2009), however, argue that the micro-theory underlying the Panzar–Rosse test is based on a static equilibrium framework, while in practice the speed of adjustment towards equilibrium might well be less than instantaneous, and markets might be out of equilibrium either occasionally, or frequently, or always. They consequently suggest using a generalized method of moments (GMM) dynamic panel estimation method instead. In practice, it is common to estimate a first-order autoregressive (AR(1)) specification:

$$\log TR_{i,t} = \alpha + \lambda \log TR_{i,t-1} + \sum_{j=1}^{J} \beta_i \log w_{j,i,t} + \theta' X_{i,t} + \eta_{i,t}$$

The Panzar–Rosse H-statistic is then defined as $H = \sum_{j=1}^{J}\beta_j/(1-\lambda)$. Applying the GMM method to estimate the H-statistic has stricter data requirements and requires that the number of banks be much larger than the number of years (Arellano and Bover, 1995; Blundell and Bond, 1998; Roodman, 2009).

8.4 OTHER COMPETITION MEASURES

8.4.1 Lerner Index

In perfect competition, price equals (short-run or long-run) marginal cost. This suggests that the degree to which price exceeds marginal cost provides a useful indicator or measure of market power. Accordingly, Lerner (1934) proposes the following measure of market power, known as the Lerner index:

$$L = \frac{P - MC}{P}$$

The Lerner index is subject to a minimum value of zero, and a maximum value of one. In perfect competition, $P = MC$ so $L = 0$. In monopoly $P > MC$, and if $MC > 0$, $0 < L < 1$. After some simple manipulation, the Lerner index can also be expressed in terms of the price elasticity of demand (PED):

$$MR = P\left(1 - \frac{1}{|PED|}\right) = P - \frac{P}{|PED|} \Rightarrow P - MR = \frac{P}{|PED|} \Rightarrow \frac{P - MR}{P} = \frac{1}{|PED|}$$

For a profit-maximizing firm, $MR = MC$. Therefore:

$$\frac{P - MC}{P} = \frac{1}{|PED|}, \text{ or } L = \frac{1}{|PED|}$$

The Lerner index is the reciprocal of the firm's price elasticity of demand. In perfect competition, $|PED| = \infty$ for each firm, so $L = 0$ (as above). In monopoly, if $MC > 0$ then $MR > 0$ and $|PED| > 1$, so $0 < L < 1$ (as above).

The Lerner index provides a convenient measure of a firm's market power based on the relationship between its price and marginal cost. It is a 'level' indicator of the proportion by which price exceeds marginal costs, and is calculated as $(P - MC)/P$ where P is the price of total assets computed as the ratio of total (interest and non-interest) revenue–total assets; and MC is the marginal cost of total assets computed from a standard translog function with a single output (total assets) and three input prices (deposits, labour and physical capital). The translog function is generally as follows:

$$\ln Cost_{i,t} = \beta_0 + \beta_1 \ln Q_{i,t} + \frac{\beta_2}{2}\ln^2 Q_{i,t} + \sum_{k=1}^{3}\gamma_{k,t}\ln W_{k,i,t} + \sum_{k=1}^{3}\varphi_k \ln Q_{i,t}\ln W_{k,i,t} +$$

$$\sum_{k=1}^{3}\sum_{j=1}^{3}\ln W_{k,i,t}\ln W_{j,i,t} + \delta_1 Trend + \delta_2 Trend^2 + \delta_3 Trend \times \ln Q_{i,t} + \sum_{k=1}^{3}\lambda_k Trend \times \ln W_{k,i,t} + \varepsilon_{i,t}$$

where *Cost* represents total bank cost, calculated as total expenses over total assets; Q represents a proxy for bank output or total assets. W_k represent three input prices of funding and fixed capital, and are calculated as the ratios of interest expenses to total deposits, other operating and administrative expenses to total assets and personnel expenses to total assets, respectively.[5] *Trend* represents yearly fixed effects to capture technical changes in the cost function over time.

8.4.2   Boone Indicator

A recent development has been the use of the Boone (2008) indicator, a new measure of competition based on the efficiency hypothesis proposed by Demsetz (1973), which stresses that industry performance is an endogenous function of the growth of efficient firms. Put simply, the indicator gauges the strength of the relationship between efficiency (measured in terms of average cost) and performance (measured in terms of profitability). In general, this indicator is based on the efficient structure hypothesis that associates performance with differences in efficiency. Under this hypothesis, more efficient banks (i.e. banks with lower marginal costs), achieve superior performance in the sense of higher profits at the expense of their less efficient counterparts and also attract greater market shares. This effect is monotonically increasing in the degree of competition when firms interact more aggressively and when entry barriers decline. The Boone indicator theoretically underpins the empirical findings by Stiroh and Strahan (2003) who state that increased competition allows banking markets to transfer considerable portions of assets from low-profit to high-profit banks.

As shown theoretically in Boone (2008), the reallocation effect is a general feature of intensifying competition, so that the indicator can be seen as a robust measure of competition. While different forces can cause increases in competition – for example increases in the number of suppliers of banking services via lower entry cost – more aggressive interaction between banks, or banks' relative inefficiencies, as long as the reallocation conditions holds, the indicator remains valid. As the industry becomes more competitive, given a certain level of efficiency of each individual bank, the profits of the more efficient banks increase relative to those of less efficient bank counterparts.

Schaeck and Cihák (2010) note that the Boone indicator has a number of appealing qualities compared with other competition indicators such as the Panzar and Rosse (1987) H-statistic (which imposes restrictive assumptions about the banking market being in long-run equilibrium), and the Lerner index (which often fails to appropriately capture the degree of product substitutability; see Vives, 2008). The Boone model does not require such restrictive assumptions. What is important for the Boone indicator is how aggressively the more efficient banks exploit their cost advantage to reallocate profits away from the least efficient banks. Various recent studies, including van Leuvensteijn et al. (2007) and Schaeck and Cihák (2010), have applied the Boone indicator to banking markets, although there remains some scepticism as to the efficacy of this new competition measure (Schiersch and Schmidt-Ehmcke, 2010).

The Boone indicator can be estimated from the following simple profitability equation:

$$\ln \pi_i = \alpha + \beta \ln mc_i + \varepsilon_i$$

Where π_i is the profit of each bank i, mc_i is marginal cost of bank i, and β is the Boone indicator of market power. This is based on the idea that the more efficient a company becomes (lower marginal cost), the greater the profit should be, *ceteris paribus*. Hence, the estimated β should be negative. As competition intensifies, the slope of the regression should become even more steeply negative, since inefficient banks are punished more harshly by fiercer competition.

Researchers (van Leuvensteijn et al., 2013) also use bank market shares of profits as the dependent variable, defined as the profits of bank i divided by the total profits of the whole market in the same year. The estimated beta coefficient should be the same as if the dependent variable is profit, since the logarithm of the profits of the whole market goes to the constant term.

Since profits are expressed in logarithms, they need to be positive. All observations of banks with losses should consequently be deleted. In doing so, the estimation of the Boone indicator introduces a bias in the sample towards profitable banks. However, banks with negative profits are common in the real world, particularly in the recent financial crisis of 2007/08.

Empirically, there are two ways to estimate the marginal cost. The first is to simply use average (variable) costs, defined as the total (variable) costs divided by total assets, as a crude proxy. This method has the advantage of being less complex but it is less accurate. The second method is to use a linear cost function, which could be the same function as the cost function described in the previous section.

8.4.3 Persistence of Profits

Another strand of empirical research that seeks to evaluate the competitive stance of markets is the persistence of profit (POP) literature that focuses on the dynamics of profitability recognizing the possibility that markets are out of equilibrium at the moment they are observed. The persistence of profit hypothesis developed by Mueller (1977, 1986) is that entry and exit are sufficiently free to eliminate any abnormal profit quickly, and that all firms' profit rates tend to converge towards the same long-run average value. The alternative is that some incumbent firms possess the capability to prevent imitation, or retard or block entry (inhibiting competition). If so, abnormal profit tends to persist from year to year, and differences in firm-level long-run average profit rates may be sustained indefinitely. The degree of first-order serial correlation in firm- or industry-level time-series profit data indicates the speed at which competition causes above- or below-average profit in one year to dissipate subsequently to converge to long-run values.

Berger et al. (2000) analyse profit persistence in the US banking industry. This study employs a non-parametric methodology in order to examine exogenous propagation mechanisms of persistence. Propagation mechanisms are identified as: local market power, informational opacity, and regional macroeconomic shocks. Results indicate that both local market power and informational opacity are correlated with profit persistence. Furthermore, bank performance is affected by macroeconomic shocks.

Tregenna (2009) provides an empirical analysis of the structure and profitability of the US banking system prior to the recent financial crisis. Using data for US banks covering the period 1994 to 2005, she finds a robust relationship between market concentration and profitability.

Cross-country studies also find evidence of profits persistence in banking.[6] A recent example is Goddard et al. (2011), who report that the persistence of profit is weaker for banks in developing countries than for those in developed countries. In particular, they note that banks located in North America and Western Europe display a relatively high degree of persistence relative to their counterparts located in East Asia. Furthermore, persistence is stronger when entry barriers are high and competition is low.

In order to eliminate the effect of cyclical fluctuations which impact similarly on the profit rates of all of the banks within each country, $\pi_{i,t}$ is expressed as a deviation from the cross-sectional mean profit rate in year t for each country. Therefore $\pi_{i,t}$ is the normalized profit rate of bank i in year t for each country. In the theoretical model, the change in the normalized profit rate of bank i between year $t-1$ and year t, denoted $\Delta\pi_{i,t}$, is assumed to be a function of bank i's lagged normalized profit rate; the component of current and past entry which impacts directly on bank i's profitability, denoted $E_{i,t-k}$ for $k = 0 \ldots \infty$; and an idiosyncratic component, denoted $u_{i,t}$:

$$\Delta\pi_{i,t} = \theta_i + \sum_{k=0}^{\infty} \beta_{j,k} E_{i,t-k} + u_{i,t}$$

where the coefficients $\beta_{j,k}$, which measure the impact of $E_{i,t-k}$ on $\Delta\pi_{i,t}$, are assumed to be the same for all banks that are located in country j. Entry is assumed to be a function of past realizations of bank i's normalized profit rate:

$$E_{i,t} = \phi + \sum_{k=1}^{\infty} \alpha_{j,k} \pi_{i,t-k} + e_{i,t}$$

Substituting this into the previous equation and re-parameterizing yields an autoregressive model for bank i's normalized profit rate:

$$\pi_{i,t} = \tilde{\pi}_i + \sum_{k=1}^{\infty} \lambda_{j,k} \pi_{i,t-k} + v_{i,t}$$

When employing panel data with a short time-dimension, it is convenient to estimate a AR(1) specification for $\pi_{i,t}$, with the higher-order lagged profit rates suppressed:

$$\pi_{i,t} = \tilde{\pi}_i + \lambda_j \pi_{i,t-1} + v_{i,t}$$

In the above, $\tilde{\pi}_i$ denotes bank i's long-run mean normalized profit rate, and λ_j replaces $\lambda_{j,1}$ in the previous equation. The adjustment of normalized bank profit rates described here is interpreted as a consequence of the interaction between profitability and the entry threat, as postulated in the contestable markets literature (Baumol et al., 1982; Bratland, 2004). Estimation of the persistence of profit coefficients (or short-run profit persistence parameter), λ_j, can be implemented using Arellano and Bover's (1995) system GMM estimator.

Table 8.1   Competition measures for the EU countries (2000–2009)

Country code	No. of Obs.	C3	HHI	H(II)	H(TI)	Lerner	Boone	POP
AT	1 529	0.66	4 595	0.58	0.50	9.17	−0.87	0.38
BE	352	0.85	2 851	0.52	0.56	20.21	−0.89	0.54
DE	11 227	0.69	1 067	0.39	0.37	7.30	−0.78	0.34
DK	606	0.78	3 000	−0.24	−0.13	15.14	−0.39	0.30
ES	643	0.76	1 024	0.02	0.10	25.81	−0.80	0.65
FR	1 652	0.56	710	−0.46	−0.15	22.71	−0.95	0.46
GB	682	0.57	2 251	−0.06	0.01	23.98	0.02	0.53
IT	2 702	0.49	592	0.55	0.49	10.92	−0.15	−0.03*
LU	583	0.26	739	−0.47	−0.03	32.98	−0.22	0.52
Mean	2 220	0.62	1 870	0.09	0.19	18.69	−0.56	0.41

Notes:
'C3' represents the three-bank assets concentration ratio; 'HHI' represents the Herfindahl–Hirschman index
(calculated using asset market shares); 'H(II)' represents the H-statistic by using the unscaled revenue equation
with interest income as the dependent variable; 'H(TI)' represents the H-statistic by using the unscaled revenue
equation with total income as the dependent variable; 'Lerner' represents the Lerner index, 'Boone' represents the
Boone indicator; and 'POP' represents the short-run profit persistence parameter using ROA as the profit ratio.
The measures are calculated using the raw data format from Bankscope over the period from 2000 to 2009.
* Not significant at the 10% significance level.

8.5   EMPIRICAL APPLICATION: MEASURES OF COMPETITION

Table 8.1 presents the competition measures outlined above for nine EU banking
markets. 'C3' represents the three-bank assets concentration ratio, 'HHI' represents
the Herfindahl–Hirschman index, 'H(II)' represents the Rosse–Panzar H-statistic using
the unscaled revenue equation with interest income as the dependent variable, 'H(TI)'
represents the H-statistic using the unscaled revenue equation with total income as the
dependent variable, 'Lerner' represents the Lerner index, 'Boone' represents the Boone
indicator, and 'POP' represents the short-run profit persistence parameter using ROA as
the profit ratio. The competition measures are calculated using 'raw' data obtained from
Bankscope over the period from 2000 to 2009.

We discuss these competition measures as follows. The three-bank concentration ratio
(C3) is from the World Bank Financial Development and Structure Database (updated
2010) collected by Beck et al. (2000). Belgium exhibits a concentrated market feature
where the three largest banks collectively own 85 per cent of the assets of the whole
banking system. In contrast, Luxembourg has the lowest concentration ratio given the
substantial presence of international banks (29 per cent). H-H shows a different competition pattern from the concentration ratio, with Austria being the most concentrated
banking market. One of the weaknesses of calculating H-H is that the information for
all the banks in the market is required. Data from Bankscope is self-reported and the
missing data for many small banks can sometimes be extensive. The calculated H-H
statistic may consequently be biased, even though it tends to provide more information
about the concentration condition than simple n-firm concentration ratios.

Table 8.2   Correlation matrix for the competition measures

	C3	HHI	H(II)	H(TI)	Lerner	Boone	POP
C3	1.00						
HHI	0.48	1.00					
H(II)	0.42	0.38	1.00				
H(TI)	0.28	0.30	0.96*	1.00			
Lerner	−0.41	−0.36	−0.7194*	−0.59	1.00		
Boone	−0.55	−0.20	−0.21	−0.25	0.23	1.00	
POP	0.17	0.09	−0.40	−0.34	0.67*	−0.32	1.00

Note: * Denotes significance at the 5% level.

Following Bikker et al. (2012), we use unscaled revenue equations to estimate the Rosse–Panzar H-statistic. The dependent variables are either interest income (II) or total income (TI). The estimated H-statistics for both methods are broadly consistent. The correlation coefficient between them is 96 per cent and significant at 5 per cent significance levels (see Table 8.2). The H-statistic suggests that banks in Denmark, France and Luxembourg earn revenues as if under monopoly conditions, while banks in other countries generate revenue under monopolistic competition. The H-statistic for the UK shows negative (−0.06) and positive (0.01) values, both of which are relatively small. This suggests that UK banks are relatively uncompetitive, earning revenues somewhere between monopoly and monopolistic competition.

The Lerner index is highly significantly correlated with the H-statistic (II) and the short-run profit persistence parameter (POP). Luxembourg has the highest Lerner index, which reflects the low level of competition. At the other extreme, Austria has the lowest Lerner index, indicating the highest level of competition. These results are broadly consistent those results suggested by H-statistics.

Boone indicators do not show any significant correlation with other competition measures, although the signs of the correlation are consistent with theory. France seems to have the fiercest bank competition (−0.95) while Austria, Belgium, Denmark and Spain all remain relatively competitive. These results tend to be contradictory with what we find for the Lerner index and H-statistic. On the other hand, Luxembourg has a relatively low level of competition (−0.22), which is consistent with the results suggested by the Lerner index and H-statistic. Again, the UK banking system shows some features of monopoly since its Boone indicator is positive, even though it is only marginally above zero.

Profit persistence shows significant correlation with the Lerner index but not with the other competition measures. In this case, Italy shows the highest competition level since the banks cannot keep any of their profit from previous years,[7] while the Spanish, Belgian and UK banks appear relatively less competitive since more than half of the bank's profits can be sustained from the previous year.

As we can observe, apart from the H-statistic, the Lerner index and possibly the profit persistence coefficient, most other competition measures do not provide consistent evidence of the competitive conditions in our sample of EU countries. Concentration measures (either the n-bank concentration ratio or H-H) are obviously not good competition indicators both from theoretical and empirical evidence. The effectiveness of the Boone indicator remains suspect since it is not significantly correlated with any of the other competition measures, although it is theoretically appealing and requires less information to estimate. The H-statistic and Lerner index are highly correlated and provide consistent results for competition conditions, which may justify their popularity in applied empirical research in banking. The profit persistence coefficient is highly significantly correlated with the Lerner index, but not with other measures. This may reflect the competition process in the banking market, although other factors like the regulatory environment, economic growth, and so on, may also impact upon the ability of banks to keep their profits from previous year.

8.6 RECENT DEVELOPMENTS: COMPETITION AND RISK IN BANKING[8]

So far we have outlined the various approaches to evaluating competition in banking. An important strand of the recent empirical banking literature seeks to investigate whether competition is linked to banking sector stability. Until the 1980s, there appeared to be a general view that competition worsened banking sector stability (Carletti, 2010), the main argument being that competition led to excessive risk-taking on the assets (loans) side of banks' balance sheets, and this led to a higher likelihood of individual bank failure.

More recently, studies have shown that competition may be beneficial to a bank's portfolio risk. The traditional theoretical set-up assumes that the allocation of bank assets is determined by solving a portfolio problem emphasizing the liability side of the balance sheet. Upon confronting increased competition on the deposit side, banks tend to increase their offered rate to attract depositors. When paying higher deposit rates, neglecting the effects of competition in the loans market, bank earnings decline. In order to cover lost profits, banks will tend to accept more risky investments. In contrast, when competition is restrained, banks exercise market power by paying lower deposit rates and can therefore increase their profits. As a result, banks in relatively uncompetitive markets are less willing to invest in low-probability, high-return projects. So the probability of failure is lower.

Another strand of the theoretical literature assumes that banks solve an optimal contracting problem. Here the modelling framework attempts to measure the impact of competition on both sides of the bank's balance sheet. In less competitive deposits markets, banks can earn greater rents (as noted above). However, banks can also charge higher rates in the lending market as well. The less competitive the market, the higher the interest rates borrowers pay. Facing higher rates, borrowers tend to invest in more risky projects and therefore their probability of bankruptcy increases. This risk mechanism is further exacerbated by moral hazard on the bank borrower's side. As a result, banks become more risky in a less competitive market (Boyd and De Nicolo, 2005). More recently, Martinez-Miera and Repullo (2009) suggest a non-linear relationship between bank competition and stability. They argue that the competition–stability view advocated by Boyd and De Nicolo (2005) does not necessarily hold when loan defaults are imperfectly correlated. More competition may reduce borrowers' probabilities of default, but it may also reduce the interest payments from performing loans, which serve as a buffer to cover loan losses. They find evidence of a U-shaped relationship between competition (measured by the number of banks) and bank stability.

In light of the 2007/08 banking crisis, it has become apparent that large banks are often deemed to be too big; too interconnected or too complex to fail. In these cases, they obtain implicit (or explicit) subsidies via government safety nets that may further increase moral hazard and encourage large banks to take on excessive risks (Herring and Carmassi, 2010; Demirguc-Kunt and Huizinga, 2010).

Empirical work that examines the relationship between bank competition and risk appears somewhat inconclusive. Studies by Keeley (1990) and Dick (2006) tend to find that banks with greater market power have lower risks – suggesting that competition leads to fragility. In contrast, the competition–stability view is confirmed by Jayaratne and Strahan (1998), De Nicolo et al. (2004) and Boyd et al. (2006).

This mixed picture is also confirmed in the most recent empirical literature. Jiménez et al. (2010), for instance, find that risks decrease with an increase in bank market power, whereas Turk-Ariss (2010), who looks at how market power influences bank efficiency and stability in 60 developing banking systems over 1999 and 2005, finds that competition leads to instability. Berger et al. (2009) analyse market power and risk issues using a sample of over 8000 banks across 23 developed countries between 1999 and 2005 and, using a standard Lerner index measure of competition, find that banks with a greater degree of market power also have less overall risk exposure. The results provide limited support for both the competition–fragility and competition–stability views in that market power increases credit risk, but banks with greater market power face lower risks.

8.7   CONCLUSIONS

This chapter highlights both theoretical and methodological issues associated with measuring competition in banking. Firstly, we examine market structure features and outline the traditional SCP paradigm and the alternative efficiency hypothesis approach. Different measures of market structure are provided, noting that simple asset or deposit concentration ratios (in addition to the H-H index) are the most widely used structural indicators. We note that while these may be appropriate structural indicators, they may not be too useful to gauge competitive conditions. As such, the empirical literature typically now focuses more on non-structural or NEIO competition measures that gauge bank conduct – indicators including the Lerner index, Panzar–Rosse H-statistic, POP and the Boone indicator. Using a sample of banks from nine EU countries, we compare these measures and illustrate how they can yield different competition outcomes. Finally, the chapter highlights recent work focusing on linking competition to banking sector risk.

From the analysis presented in the chapter, it is important for researchers in banking sector competition to realize that different measures can yield different outcomes, so any discussion on banking sector competition should be supported with a variety of estimates and, if they are to be policy-relevant, should present the same competition interpretation. Increasingly, empirical banking researchers are seeking to link measures of competition to a host of other factors including risk, efficiency, economic development and so on. Again, researchers should be aware of the limitations of their analysis if multiple measures of competition are not considered. Similarly, one should also be aware of policy announcements based on a view of limited competition in banking markets unless supported by credible empirical evidence.

NOTES

1. Other measures of industry structure that focus on inequality of firm size include the gini coefficient, the variance of the logarithms of market shares and the entropy coefficient (although these are rarely used in empirical banking studies).
2. Some of the earlier SCP studies looked at loan and deposit pricing in different markets to see whether the prices of bank products varied according to the degree of concentration.
3. In many of the banking databases, for example Bankscope, the data for non-interest expenses are quite often missing. Researchers may opt to use overheads instead.
4. The definition of the input factor may vary. For instance, Bikker et al. (2012) use the ratio of other non-interest expenses to fixed assets instead of total assets as proxy for the price of physical capital.
5. Some researchers (Turk-Ariss, 2010; Liu and Wilson, forthcoming) also scale cost and input prices by the price of labour to correct for heteroscedasticity and scale biases.
6. Other examples using datasets comprising banks located in various European countries include Goddard et al. (2004a, 2004b) and Athanasoglou et al. (2008).
7. The estimated profit persistence coefficient for Italy is actually −0.03 but is not significant at even the 10 per cent level.
8. An empirical analysis of the relationship between competition and risk is outside the scope of this chapter. Useful recent analyses and discussions can be found in Berger et al. (2009) and Liu and Wilson (forthcoming).

REFERENCES

Arellano, M. and O. Bover (1995), 'Another look at the instrumental variable estimation of error-components models', *Journal of Econometrics*, **68**, 29–51.

Athanasoglou, P.P., S.N. Brissimis and M.D. Delis (2008), 'Bank-specific, industry-specific and macro-economic determinants of bank profitability', *Journal of International Financial Markets, Institutions and Money*, **18**, 121–136.

Bain, J.S (1951), 'Relation of profit rate to industry concentration: American manufacturing', *Quarterly Journal of Economics*, **65**, 293–324.

Bain, J.S. (1956), *Barriers to New Competition*, Cambridge, MA: Harvard University Press.

Bain, J.S. (1959), *Industrial Organization*, New York: John Wiley & Sons.

Baumol, W.J., J.C. Panzar and R.D. Willig (1982), *Contestable Markets and the Theory of Industry Structure*, San Diego, CA: Harcourt Brace Jovanovich.

Beck, T., A. Demirguc-Kunt and R. Levine (2000), 'A new database on the structure and development of the financial sector', *World Bank Economic Review*, **14**, 597–605.

Beck, T., A. Demirguc-Kunt and V. Maksimovic (2004), 'Bank competition and access to finance', *Journal of Money Credit and Banking*, **36**, 627–648.

Berger, A.N., S.D. Bonime, D.M. Covitz and D. Hancock (2000) 'Why are bank profits so persistent? The roles of product market competition, information opacity and regional macroeconomic shocks', *Journal of Banking and Finance*, **24**, 1203–1235.

Berger, A.N., A. Demerguc-Kunt, R. Levine and J.C. Haubrich (2004), 'Bank concentration and competition', *Journal of Money Credit and Banking*, **36**, 433–451.

Berger, A.N., L.F. Klapper and R. Turk-Ariss (2009), 'Bank competition and financial stability', *Journal of Financial Services Research*, **35**, 99–118.

Bikker, J.A., S. Shaffer and L. Spierdijk (2012), 'Assessing competition with the Panzar–Rosse model: the role of scale, costs, and equilibrium', *Review of Economics and Statistics*, **94**, 1025–1044.

Blundell, R.W. and S.R. Bond (1998), 'Initial conditions and moment restrictions in dynamic panel data models', *Journal of Econometrics*, **87**, 115–143.

Bonaccorsi Di Patta, E. and Dell'Aricca, G. (2004), 'Bank competition and firm creation,' *Journal of Money Credit and Banking*, **36**, 225–252.

Boone, J. (2008), 'A new way to measure competition', *Economic Journal*, **118**, 1245–1261.

Boyd, J.H. and G. De Nicolo (2005), 'The theory of bank risk taking and competition revisited', *Journal of Finance*, **60**, 1329–1343.

Boyd, J.H., G. De Nicolo and A.M. Jalal (2006), 'Bank risk-taking and competition revisited: new theory and new evidence', IMF Working Paper WP/06/297.

Bratland, J. (2004), 'Contestable market theory as a regulatory framework: an Austrian postmortem', *Quarterly Journal of Austrian Economics*, **7**, 3–28.

Carletti, E. (2010), 'Competition, concentration and stability in the banking sector', Istituto Luigi Einaudi per gli Studi Bancari Finanziari e Assicurativi (IstEin), Working Paper 2010, Number 8.

Cetorelli, N. (2004), 'Real effects of bank competition', *Journal of Money, Credit and Banking*, **36**, 543–558.

Claessens, S. and L. Laeven (2004), 'What drives bank competition? Some international evidence', *Journal of Money, Credit, and Banking*, **36**, 563–583.

De Nicolo, G., P. Bartholomew, J. Zaman and M. Zephirin (2004), 'Bank consolidation, internationalization and conglomeration: trends and implications for financial risk', *Financial Markets, Institutions and Instruments*, **13**, 173–217.

Demirguc-Kunt, A. and H. Huizinga (2010), 'Are banks too-big-too fail or too big to save? International evidence from equity prices and CDS spreads', World Bank Policy Research Paper No. 5360.

Demsetz, H. (1973), 'Industry structure, market rivalry and public policy', *Journal of Law and Economics*, **16**, 1–9.

Dick, A.A. (2006), 'Nationwide branching and its impact on market structure, quality and bank performance', *Journal of Business*, **79**, 567–592.

Dick, A.A. and T.H. Hannan (2010), 'Competition and antitrust in banking', in A.N. Berger, P. Molyneux and J.O.S. Wilson (eds), *Oxford Handbook of Banking*, Oxford: Oxford University Press, pp. 405–429.

Gilbert, R.A. (1984), 'Bank market structure and competition – a survey', *Journal of Money, Credit and Banking*, **16**, 617–645.

Goddard, J., P. Molyneux, H. Liu and J.O.S. Wilson (2011), 'The persistence of bank profit', *Journal of Banking and Finance*, **35**, 2881–2890.

Goddard, J., P. Molyneux and J.O.S. Wilson (2001), *European Banking: Efficiency, Technology and Growth*, Chichester: John Wiley & Sons.

Goddard, J., P. Molyneux and J.O.S. Wilson (2004a), 'The profitability of European banks: a cross-sectional and dynamic panel analysis', *Manchester School*, **72**, 363–381.

Goddard, J., P. Molyneux and J.O.S. Wilson (2004b). 'Dynamics of growth and profitability in banking', *Journal of Money, Credit and Banking*, **36**, 1069–1090.

Goddard, J., P. Molyneux, J.O.S. Wilson and M. Tavakoli (2007), 'European banking: an overview', *Journal of Banking and Finance*, **31**, 1911–1935.

Goddard, J.A. and J.O.S. Wilson (2009), 'Competition in banking: a dis-equilibrium approach', *Journal of Banking and Finance*, **33**, 2282–2292.

Hannah. L. and J.A. Kay (1977), *Concentration in Modern Industry*, London: Macmillan.

Herfindahl, O.C (1950), 'Concentration in the US steel industry', unpublished PhD thesis, New York: Columbia University.

Herring, R.J. and J. Carmassi (2010), 'The corporate structure of international financial conglomerates: complexity and its implications for safety and soundness', in A.N. Berger, P. Molyneux and J.O.S. Wilson (eds), *Oxford Handbook of Banking*, Oxford: Oxford University Press, pp.195–232.

Hirschman, A.O (1945), *National Power and the Structure of Foreign Trade*, Berkeley, CA: University of California Bureau of Business and Economic Research.

Jayaratne, J. and P.E. Strahan (1998), 'Entry restrictions, industry evolution, and dynamic efficiency: evidence from commercial banking', *Journal of Law and Economics*, **41**, 239–273.

Jiménez, G., J. Lopez and J. Saurina (2010), 'How does competition impact on bank risk taking?', Banco De Espana Working Paper 1005.

Keeley, M.C. (1990), 'Deposit insurance, risk and market power in banking', *American Economic Review*, **80**, 1183–1200.

Lerner, A.P. (1934), 'The concept of monopoly and the measurement of monopoly power', *Review of Economic Studies*, **1**, 157–175.

Lipczynski, J., J.O.S. Wilson and J. Goddard (2009), *Industrial Organization: Competition, Strategy and Policy*, 3rd edn, Harlow: Financial Times, Prentice Hall.

Liu, H. and J.O.S. Wilson (forthcoming), 'Competition and risk in Japanese banking', *European Journal of Finance*.

Martinez-Miera, D. and R. Repullo (2009), 'Does competition reduce the risk of bank failure?', Centre for Economic Policy Research Working Paper DP6669, London: CEPR.

Mason, E.S (1939), 'Price and production policies of large scale enterprise', *American Economic Review*, **29**, 61–74.

Mason, E.S (1949), 'The current state of the monopoly problem in the United States', *Harvard Law Review*, **62**, 1265–1285.

Molyneux, P., M. Lloyd-Williams and J. Thornton (1994). 'Competitive conditions in European banking', *Journal of Banking and Finance*, **18**, 445–459.

Mueller, D.C. (1977), 'The persistence of profits above the norm', *Economica*, **44**, 369–380.

Mueller, D.C. (1986), *Profits in the Long Run*, Cambridge: Cambridge University Press.

Panzar, J.C. and J.N. Rosse (1982), 'Structure, conduct and comparative statistics', Bell Laboratories Economics Discussion Paper.

Panzar, J.C. and J.N. Rosse (1987), 'Testing for "monopoly" equilibrium', *Journal of Industrial Economics*, **35**, 443–456.

Petersen, M. and R.G. Rajan (1995), 'The effect of credit market competition on lending relationships', *Quarterly Journal of Economics*, **110**, 407–443.

Roodman, D. (2009), 'A note on the theme of too many instruments', *Oxford Bulletin of Economics and Statistics*, **71**, 135–158.

Rosse, J.N and J.C. Panzar (1977), 'Chamberlin vs Robinson: an empirical study for monopoly rents', Bell Laboratories Economic Discussion Paper.

Schaeck, K. and M. Cihák (2010), 'Competition, efficiency, and soundness in banking: an industrial organization perspective', European Banking Center Discussion Paper No. 2010-20S.

Schiersch, A and J. Schmidt-Ehmcke (2010), 'Empiricism meets theory: is the Boone-indicator applicable?', DIW Berlin Discussion Paper No. 1030.

Shaffer, S. (2004a), 'Patterns of competition in banking', *Journal of Economics and Business*, **56**, 287–313.

Shaffer, S. (2004b), 'Comment on "What drives bank competition? Some international evidence" by S.Claessens and L. Laeven', *Journal of Money, Credit and Banking*, **36**, 585–592.

Stigler, G.J. (1968), *The Organization of Industry*, Chicago, IL: Irwin.

Stiroh, K. and P.E. Strahan (2003), 'Competitive dynamics of deregulation: evidence for US banking', *Journal of Money, Credit and Banking*, **35**, 801–828.

Tregenna, F. (2009),'The fat years: the structure and profitability of the US banking sector in the pre-crisis period', *Cambridge Journal of Economics*, **33**, 4, 609–632.

Turk-Ariss, R. (2010), 'On the implications of market power in banking: evidence from developing countries', *Journal of Banking and Finance*, **34**, 765–775.

van Leuvensteijn, M., J.A. Bikker, A. Van Rixtel and C. Kok Sorensen (2007), 'A new approach to measuring competition in the loan markets of the Euro area', European Central Bank Working Paper, No. 768 June, Frankfurt: ECB.

van Leuvensteijn, M., C.K. Sorensen, J.A Bikker and A. Van Rixtel (2013), 'Impact of bank competition on the interest rate pass-through in the euro area', *Applied Economics*, **45**, 1359–1380.

Vives, X. (2008), 'Innovation and competitive pressure', *Journal of Industrial Economics*, **56**, 419–469.

Wilson, J.O.S., B. Casu, C. Girardone and P. Molyneux (2010), 'Emerging themes in banking: recent literature and directions for future research', *British Accounting Review*, **42**, 153–169.

9 Using heteroskedastic models to analyze the use of rules versus discretion in lending decisions
Geraldo Cerqueiro, Hans Degryse and Steven Ongena

9.1 INTRODUCTION

Little is known about the procedures and processes through which banks decide to grant loans and to price credit. For example, even after one takes into account the differences in borrowers, lenders and markets, loan rates still often exhibit substantial dispersion. This dispersion suggests that frictions in the credit market enable banks (i.e., through their loan officers) to price loans in a discretionary manner. The banks' use of 'discretion' should affect aggregate welfare as well as its distribution across different market participants. Consequently, understanding the nature of discretion is crucial for any analysis of the credit market.

This chapter demonstrates how to investigate the use of discretion by banks in the loan rate setting process with a heteroskedastic regression model. With such a model one can investigate what factors determine the dispersion in banks' loan rates to small and medium-sized enterprises, for example. One can then attribute this dispersion to the bank and loan officers' exploitation of market imperfections and assess the relevance of firm, loan officer and bank characteristics, as suggested by the theoretical literature, in explaining discretion.

An example illustrates what this investigation is aimed at (see also Cerqueiro et al., 2011). Imagine twins who apply for a bank loan and consider the setting of the loan rate. If the twins are fully identical in all respects (same sex, profession, street address, etc.) and the applications are made online through the same automated system, the twins are expected to receive the same loan rate, as both the inputs to the credit application and the model processing these inputs are identical. Even if the twins differed in a few characteristics, the potential gap between the offered rates would be fully explained by the objective differences between them.

If instead the identical twins conduct their loan applications in person at a particular bank but with different loan officers, they may not get the same loan rate, given that there is an extra input in the pricing decision, that is, the loan officer's judgment. This judgment may reflect a number of factors: experience, bargaining ability, uncertainty regarding the customer's prospects, and soft information. To a large extent, the loan officer's judgment could also be clouded by such eccentricities as the colour of the applicant's jacket or the loan officer's mood (which may not only depend on the weather conditions, for example, but also on many other personal and social environmental factors). In any case, all the aforementioned factors share a common denominator that outlines our definition of discretion – they have an idiosyncratic nature and hence are not verifiable by third parties.

This chapter discusses a methodology that allows the researcher to assess the extent to which these judgmental factors, or discretion, may matter in the final loan pricing decision. Hence, the methodology measures the factors that determine the dispersion in the loan rates offered to many different sets of twins. The methodology consists of empirically examining the determinants of the unexplained variance of a benchmark linear loan pricing model. The higher predictive power of the model can be interpreted as evidence of the greater importance of 'rules' in the loan rate setting process. A larger unexplained variance, on the other hand, is then associated with the prevalence of discretion. The determinants of the unexplained variance are then factors that drive loan officer discretion.

The motivation for such an analysis may go beyond the empirical regularity that contracted loan rates are typically difficult to predict (see e.g. Petersen and Rajan, 1994; Berger and Udell, 1995). What is even more interesting is that the fit of the loan pricing models seems to depend on the type of loans and borrowers in the sample that is being investigated. Degryse and Ongena (2005), for example, estimate the same loan pricing model for two independent subsamples: one with small loans (below $5000) and another with larger loans (above $50000). The fit of their regressions is strikingly different: the R-squares are 1 percent for small loans and 67 percent for large loans.

The story about the twins and the different fits of the same loan pricing models illustrate the adequacy of the heteroskedastic regression model. Rules and discretion can be seen as the extremes of a continuum along which any loan pricing model can be classified according to its level of standardization and the nature of its inputs. At one extreme, rules correspond to a standardized pricing model (for instance, using a computer) that generates loan rates that can be predicted by verifiable characteristics of the applicant. At the other extreme, discretion refers to an arbitrary pricing technology, where loan rates exclusively reflect the loan officer's judgment. Consequently, discretion decreases the researcher's ability to predict observed loan rates for two interrelated reasons. Firstly, loan rates are set on the basis of inputs that are only observed and understood by the loan officer (for instance, 'these are serious people', or 'that green hat is ridiculous'). Secondly, each pricing model – the relative weight of each input in the final loan rate – itself becomes arbitrary.

In a frictionless world there should be no room for discretion and loan rates should only vary with verifiable information. In contrast, economic theory predicts that the dispersion of loan rates, and hence discretion, characterizes the equilibrium of credit markets under asymmetric and imperfect information. The extent to which loan rates reflect the prevalence of rules or discretion should depend on the severity of information asymmetries in the credit market. Moreover, discretion can also result from information search costs, switching costs, imperfectly competitive credit market structures, and regulatory constraints. These market imperfections determine the bargaining power that banks and their loan officers have vis-à-vis firms, and set the boundaries within which banks can engage in discretionary loan pricing practices.

The heteroskedastic regression model is particularly useful when discretion cannot be directly observed. We want to acknowledge some recent work where discretion can be inferred more directly in the data, for example at the loan acceptance/rejection stage or regarding decisions on loan size. Puri et al. (2011) study discretion in the accept/reject decisions of small consumer loans in Germany. In particular, discretion in their setting is interpreted as deviations from a commonly implemented credit scoring model across savings banks in accept/reject decisions. They find that soft information drives discretion mainly for customers without credit history, whereas hard information drives it for consumers with a credit history. Accepted loans based on discretion do not perform differently than loans accepted on the basis of the scoring model. Degryse et al. (2011) observe loan officer discretion in setting the loan size granted to small and medium-sized enterprises (SMEs). Discretion is defined as the deviation from the model limit resulting from a credit scoring model. The maximum exposure allowed to firms may deviate from the model limit as a result of the loan officer's discretion. They show that this type of discretion is important, and that there is both positive and negative discretion. They find that soft information partially explains the use of discretion and that discretion is more used for collateralized loans. Loans based upon loan officer discretion do not perform differently than loans based on the credit scoring model only.

The remainder of this chapter is organized as follows. Section 9.2 discusses in detail linear regression models with heteroskedasticity and section 9.3 provides a simple example to illustrate the models' inner workings. Section 9.4 addresses some empirical concerns. Section 9.5 discusses alternative interpretations of discretion. Section 9.6 reviews some alternative applications of heteroskedastic models and section 9.7 concludes.

9.2   MODELS OF HETEROSKEDASTICITY

Suppose that one wants to investigate the determinants of the degree of discretion used by a bank (loan officer) in setting loan conditions. Such an investigation could reveal the drivers of the choice that the bank makes between offering relationship versus transactional-oriented banking.

In order to identify the determinants of the dispersion of loan rates, for example, one can employ the regression model with multiplicative heteroskedasticity introduced by Harvey (1976). The heteroskedastic version extends the linear regression model by also parametrizing the unexplained variance as function of exogenous covariates.

It is as if the heteroskedastic regression model comprises two equations: one to model the mean of the dependent variable, and one for the residual variance. In the example that is maintained throughout this chapter, the mean equation captures the loan pricing model while the variance equation (and its variables) determines the precision of the loan pricing model. Hence, in the example, a higher precision implies the stricter adherence to rules, possibly as a result of a focus on transactional banking, while a lower precision could indicate the presence of extensive discretion granted to loan officers under a relationship banking strategy.

Given a cross-section of N observations (i.e., interest rates of loan contracts) indexed by $i = 1,\ldots,N$, the regression model with multiplicative heteroskedasticity is formalized with the following two equations:

$$y_i = x_i'\beta + u_i, \qquad (9.1)$$

and:

$$\sigma_i^2 = \sigma^2 e^{z_i'\gamma}, \tag{9.2}$$

with the identifying assumptions:

$$E[u_i|x_i] = 0, \tag{9.3}$$

and:

$$Var[u_i|z_i] = \sigma_i^2 = \sigma^2 e^{z_i'\gamma}. \tag{9.4}$$

y_i is the dependent variable, x_i is a vector of explanatory variables in the mean equation that includes a constant, and u_i is a disturbance term. The variance of the error term is an exponential function of a vector of individual-specific attributes denoted by z_i. Although other functional forms of heteroskedasticity can be used, the exponential form is particularly convenient because it ensures a positive variance.

The interpretation of γ is crucial for the intended analysis here. Pick one variable from the vector z, say, z^k, and the respective parameter, γ^k. A positive γ^k indicates that the precision of the loan pricing model decreases in z^k. One can interpret such a result as evidence of a positive correlation between the variable z^k and the weight of discretion in the loan rate setting process. When $\gamma^k = 0$ the error term is homoskedastic and its variance equals σ^2.

In this setting, our interest lies only in the first two moments of the conditional distribution of y. It is therefore plausible to assume that the error term follows a normal distribution. Under this assumption, the conditional distribution of y is given by:

$$y_i|x_i, z_i \xrightarrow{d} N(x_i'\beta, \sigma^2 e^{z_i'\gamma}). \tag{9.5}$$

It is straightforward to obtain maximum-likelihood estimates in the heteroskedastic regression model by maximizing the following log-likelihood function with respect to the vector of parameters β and γ:

$$\log L(\beta, \gamma | X, Z) = \frac{N}{2}\log(2\pi\sigma^2) - \frac{1}{2}\sum_{i=1}^{N} z_i'\gamma - \frac{1}{2}\sum_{i=1}^{N} e^{z_i'\gamma}\left(\frac{y_i - x_i'\beta}{\sigma}\right)^2. \tag{9.6}$$

From a theoretical perspective, the maximum likelihood estimators for the parameters in the mean and variance equations are, in expectation, uncorrelated (see Harvey, 1976). To see this, consider the case in which a single covariate x that affects both the mean and variance of y. The estimator for β that arises from maximizing the log-likelihood function is:

$$\hat{\beta} = \frac{\sum_{i=1}^{N}\left(\dfrac{x_i y_i}{\hat{\sigma}_i^2}\right)}{\sum_{i=1}^{N}\left(\dfrac{x_i^2}{\hat{\sigma}_i^2}\right)}. \tag{9.7}$$

which is the well-known weighted-least squares (WLS) estimator. In this estimation method, the contribution of each observation in the sum of squares is weighted by the inverse of its estimated variance (i.e., its precision):

$$\frac{1}{\hat{\sigma}_i^2} = \frac{1}{\hat{\sigma}^2 e^{\hat{\gamma}x_i}}. \qquad (9.8)$$

In practice, estimation via WLS requires that one specifies the pattern of heteroskedasticity and estimates the individual variances. Virtually, all empirical applications assume the multiplicative heteroskedasticity model. When heteroskedasticity is present in the data, the WLS estimator for β will in general differ from the OLS estimator, because WLS shifts weight from high-variance to low-variance observations. As a result, the difference between OLS and WLS estimators is a direct consequence of heteroskedasticity. However, the parameters in the variance equation, γ, are simply factor loadings capturing variation in the residual variance that would otherwise be averaged out in $\hat{\sigma}^2$. Therefore, γ does not systematically affect β.

An alternative procedure to estimate the heteroskedastic regression model is to estimate the parameters in the mean equation by OLS and to use the squared errors as raw estimates of the individual variances. Then one obtains estimates of the parameters in the variance equation by regressing the log of squared errors on the set of covariates in the vector z. Despite being computationally simpler, there is a dramatic loss of efficiency in this two-step procedure (Harvey, 1976). For that reason, the estimates are usually obtained via maximum likelihood. In an example in the next section, we will demonstrate the two-step procedure. This two-step procedure can also be applied iteratively, where the mean equation is re-estimated by WLS using as weights the inverse of the estimated variances. Through this iterative process the estimates obtained in both equations converge to the maximum likelihood estimates.

9.3   EXAMPLE

We now present a simple example that allows us to further explain the basic characteristics of a heteroskedastic model. Table 9.1 provides the 20 observations that we will use in our analysis (although these values are invented, they are also not entirely unrealistic). We want to investigate the impact of the loan amount on the dispersion of the loan rate. For expositional reasons, we assume that the loan amount is predetermined and the result of both firm need and the common practice of granting rounded loan amounts, while once the loan amount is fixed the loan rate is determined by bargaining. The loans we have in our sample vary between €10 000 and €500 000.

Table 9.2 already provides a first glance at the basic intuition. For each loan amount we calculate the mean and (sample) standard deviation of the loan rate (having multiple loans with the same loan amount in this respect facilitates the exposition). The mean loan rate for the six €10 000 loans equals 9.67 percent, while the mean loan rate charged on the three €250 000 loans equals 3.50 percent. The loan rate on the single loan of 500 000 euro equals (only) 1.5 percent. Hence the mean loan rate is decreasing in loan amount.

Table 9.1   Example of loan contracts, loan rates and loan amounts

Observation loan contract	y loan rate (%)	X loan size (euros)
1	12	10 000
2	10	10 000
3	4	10 000
4	14	10 000
5	5	10 000
6	13	10 000
7	7	25 000
8	9	25 000
9	8	25 000
10	7	25 000
11	9	25 000
12	6	50 000
13	7	50 000
14	4	50 000
15	5	50 000
16	5	100 000
17	5.75	100 000
18	4	250 000
19	3	250 000
20	1.5	500 000
Mean	6.96	79 250
standard deviation	3.37	122 069

Table 9.2   Loan rate, by loan size

Loan size	Number of loan contracts	Loan rate	
		Mean	Standard deviation
>0	20	6.96	3.37
= 10 000	6	9.67	4.23
= 25 000	5	8.00	1.00
= 50 000	4	5.50	1.29
= 100 000	2	5.38	0.53
= 250 000	2	3.50	0.71
= 500 000	1	1.50	–

At the same time that the loan rate is decreasing in the loan amount, the sample standard deviation is also decreasing in the loan amount. The standard deviation equals 4.23 percent for €10 000 loans, 1.00 percent for 25 000 euro loans, and 0.53 percent for the €100 000 loans. At first sight, one could suspect that the lower number of observations in each bin (i.e., for the different loan amounts) is partly responsible for the decrease in standard deviation (the extreme case being the single €500 000 loan for which no

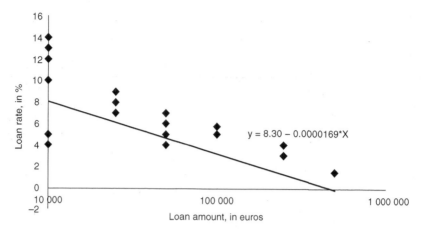

Figure 9.1   Loan rate versus loan amount

standard deviation can be calculated). This is not so. Remember that the standard deviation (s) is calculated as:

$$\sigma = \sqrt{\frac{1}{N-1} \sum_{i=1}^{N} (y_i - \bar{y})^2} \qquad (9.9)$$

with y_i being the loan rate on loan i within a bin, $\bar{y} = \sum_{i=1}^{N} \frac{y_i}{N}$, the mean loan rate, and N the number of loan contracts in each bin (to keep notation simple we do not index by bin). Hence the number of observations is accounted for (so to speak) when calculating the standard deviation.

To implement the (simple two-step) heteroskedastic model we now first estimate the parameters in the mean equation by OLS and use the squared errors as raw estimates of the individual variances. Then, we obtain estimates of the parameters in the variance equation by regressing the log of squared errors on the set of covariates in the variance equation. To keep things simple, we use the same covariate, that is, the loan amount, in the mean and variance equations. In general, there are no constraints or requirements (beyond those suggested by economic theory) with respect to the choice of covariates for either equation.

Figure 9.1 displays the values of the loan rate and the loan amount for the 20 observations and also the estimated coefficients: *Loan Rate* = 8.30 − 0.0000169 * *Loan Amount*. Given these estimated coefficients we calculate the projected loan rates and the logarithm of the squared residuals in Table 9.3. Table 9.4 then calculates the mean of the latter series for the various loan amounts. The mean of the logarithm of the squared residuals decreases from 1.14 percent for €10 000 loans, to 0.37 percent for €50 000 loans, to −1.09 percent for €250 000 loans. Figure 9.2 displays the logarithm of the squared residuals versus the loan amounts and the estimated coefficients: *Logarithm of the Squared Residuals* = 4.20 − 0.00000213 *Loan Amount*.

Hence, not only does the loan rate itself decrease in the loan amount, but also the

Table 9.3   Projected loan rates and log of the residuals squared

Observation Loan contract	y Loan rate (%)	X Loan size in euros	ŷ Projected loan rate (%)	$\log(y - \hat{y})^2$ Log residual squared (%)
1	12	10 000	8.13	1.18
2	10	10 000	8.13	0.54
3	4	10 000	8.13	1.23
4	14	10 000	8.13	1.54
5	5	10 000	8.13	0.99
6	13	10 000	8.13	1.37
7	7	25 000	7.88	−0.11
8	9	25 000	7.88	0.10
9	8	25 000	7.88	−1.82
10	7	25 000	7.88	−0.11
11	9	25 000	7.88	0.10
12	6	50 000	7.46	0.33
13	7	50 000	7.46	−0.68
14	4	50 000	7.46	1.08
15	5	50 000	7.46	0.78
16	5	100 000	6.61	0.41
17	5.75	100 000	6.61	−0.13
18	4	250 000	4.08	−2.25
19	3	250 000	4.08	0.06
20	1.5	500 000	−0.15	0.43

Table 9.4   Log loan rate residual squared, by loan size

Loan size	Number of loan contracts	Log loan rate residual squared	
		Mean	Standard deviation
>0	20	0.25	0.98
= 10 000	6	1.14	0.35
= 25 000	5	−0.37	0.82
= 50 000	4	0.37	0.77
= 100 000	2	0.14	0.39
= 250 000	2	−1.09	1.64
= 500 000	1	0.43	−

dispersion in the loan rate decreases. We could interpret the latter decrease as indicative of reduced discretion on the part of the loan officer to decide on loan rates. Indeed, typically for larger loans the decision about loan rates is taken at a higher level within the bank and this decision will be more in line with the output of pricing models and market conditions, the importance of search and switching costs, and hence much less discretionary. Our example provides an illustration in the case of one covariate in both the mean and variance equations. The same principles are at work when several covariates are included in both equations.

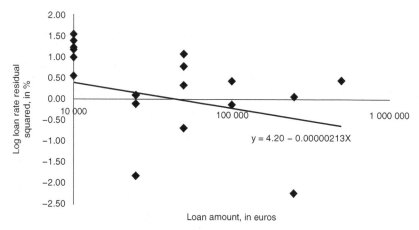

Figure 9.2   Logarithm of the squared residuals versus the loan amount

9.4   OMITTED VARIABLES IN THE MEAN EQUATION AND OTHER CONCERNS

Similar to the consistency of the coefficients being unaffected in a linear regression model by heteroskedasticity in the error term, the parameters in the mean (β) and the variance (γ) equations are uncorrelated. Put differently, what happens in the mean equation ultimately may not matter a great deal for the variance equation and its parameter estimates (as if what happens in the cellar of a house does not determine life of the household on the first floor). Nevertheless, as with any empirical model, this conclusion rests on the implicit assumption that the regression model is well specified.

To get some intuition on the lack of correlation between the parameters in the mean and the variance equations, consider the example in the previous section again. Suppose that we estimate the mean equation with only a constant, that is, without the loan amount included. The mean loan rate equals almost 7 percent. So in Figure 9.1 draw a (hypothetical) horizontal line through this value on the horizontal axis. Notice that at least up to the value of €100 000, the squared residuals (i.e., the difference between this 7 percent line and the actual loan rates) again decrease in the loan amount – that is, the estimate of the coefficient in the variance equation is unaffected by the set of variables in the mean equation. But beyond €100 000, the example unfortunately starts to break down somewhat (which is the hallmark of all good examples, we would claim) and the squared residuals start increasing again.

To allay any lingering concerns with respect to the specification of the mean equation, many possibilities exist to alter it. If the focus is on the estimation and interpretation of the parameters in the variance equation, their inclusion should be fully motivated by theory. But the 'work' in the mean equation will be to some extent secondary. The objective there should be to maximize and alter the space spanned by the mean equation to the fullest.

To tackle the concern that omitted variables in the mean equation determine the estimates in the variance equation, the researcher can throw all variables that are available into the mean equation. The objective of this exercise is to predict the dependent variable as accurately as possible, disregarding any collinearity problems that may occur. Robustness can then further be checked by a systematic series of exercises of exclusion and inclusion of variables. The mean equation can further be saturated with fixed effects to the extent that these can be generated, for instance on the basis of the identity of agents partaking in the transaction that is being studied.

To address the concern that the functional form in the mean equation is not correctly specified, squared and cubed terms of all (or a set of) variables can be introduced. Also, linearly predicted loan rates squared and cubed can be inserted (à la a Ramsey regression equation specification error test), terms which will stand in for an extensive polynomial form. All continuous variables can also be split into a set of splines (each spline represented by a dummy variable that equals one if the continuous variable takes a value between the minimum and maximum value of the spline, and equals zero otherwise).

9.5   INSIDE THE DISCRETION BOX

We have seen how the heteroskedastic regression model can be used to identify the presence of discretion in lending decisions. Below we discuss the precise interpretation of 'discretion' in the context of the heteroskedastic model.

As mentioned before, the difference between rules and discretion lies in the level of standardization of the pricing model. At one extreme, rules refers to maximum standardization, in which case all lenders have the same information set and employ the same pricing model. At the other extreme, under full discretion each loan is priced independently and according to a unique model, implying that each loan rate is idiosyncratic. Discretion can therefore explain why individuals who are identical *ex ante* could face different loan rates, or why the same individual could also face different loan rates when facing either different loan officers or the same loan officer under different circumstances.

The definitions of rules and discretion we provide above can be summarized, respectively, as standardized versus non-standardized loan pricing models. In order to clarify the precise meaning of these concepts, let us go back to the example presented in section 9.3. The results of the simulated data indicate that both expected loan rates and the amount of discretion that observed loan rates incorporate decrease with loan size. The interpretation of the reduction in discretion is clear in Figure 9.1. While the regression model can predict the loan rates of large loans quite tightly, it does a poor job at predicting loan rates of small loans. This reasoning implicitly assumes that there is a single model to price all these loans. Under this hypothesis, discretion results from unobserved inputs, such as private information and bargaining between the borrower and lender, that are added to the rules-based model in order to produce the observed loan rate.

There is, however, an alternative interpretation for discretion based on heterogeneity of the model itself, rather than of the private information embedded in the residuals. Suppose that the only information relevant to price loans is public and is contained in the vector x. Assume, however, that loan officers have access to a set of alternative pricing models among which they can choose. Each model combines the individual factors contained in x in a unique way. The following model formalizes this view:

$$y_i = x_i'\beta_i, \tag{9.10}$$

where β_i is i.i.d and independent of x_i, $E[\beta_i] = \beta$ and $Var[\beta_i] = \Gamma$. In this model, which is often referred to as the random coefficients model, the parameters in the pricing model vary arbitrarily across individuals. For this reason, again in this model two individuals with identical characteristics can face different loan rates.

The mean equation of the heteroskedastic model in (9.1) assumes that all individuals with given characteristics face the same standard rule. In contrast, the model in equation (9.10) specifies that rules are themselves idiosyncratic. Allowing ourselves to abuse semantics, we argue that such a diverse set of idiosyncratic rules represents de facto discretion, because each borrower faces a non-standard pricing model. This alternative interpretation demonstrates that the difference between rules and discretion transcends the nature of information used in any lending decision. Ultimately, the difference lies in the processes through which information is embedded in the observed loan rates.

We note, however, that the two alternative interpretations share similar methodological foundations. To see the relationship between the random coefficients model and the heteroskedastic model presented in section 9.2, note that equation (9.10) can be rewritten as:

$$y_i = x_i'\beta_i + \varepsilon_i. \tag{9.11}$$

where $\varepsilon_i = x_i'(\beta_i - \beta)$. Consequently:

$$E[\varepsilon_i|x_i] = 0, \tag{9.12}$$

and:

$$Var[\varepsilon_i|x_i] = x_i'\Gamma x_i \equiv \sigma^2(1 + z_i'\gamma). \tag{9.13}$$

The variance equation has levels and all cross-products of the components of the regression vector x, and hence it is heteroskedastic. From an econometric viewpoint, this model is similar to the one we presented in section 9.2, except for the functional form of the variance equation. There we argued that the exponential form is computationally more convenient because it ensures a positive variance.

The parameters of the random coefficients model have an interpretation consistent with discretion reflecting model heterogeneity. The key parameter in this model is the variance of the regression coefficients, Γ, which measures the degree of model heterogeneity. It turns out that Γ is also the parameter of interest in the variance equation (reparametrized as γ). A small γ means that the models used to price loans are quite standardized, which is consistent with rules-based pricing. As γ increases, so does the diversity of pricing models used, signaling the heavier use of discretion.

Figure 9.3 summarizes the full intuition of the heteroskedastic model. Panel A plots the individual observations, the loan rate, on the vertical axis, as a function of the loan amount, on the horizontal axis. Panel B plots the estimated mean equation, possibly capturing the model or the rules that prevail at the bank. Panel C indicates the residuals

Panel A

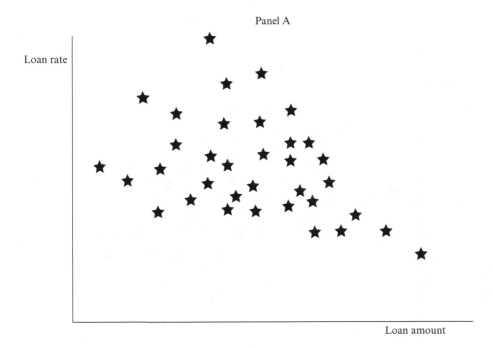

Panel B

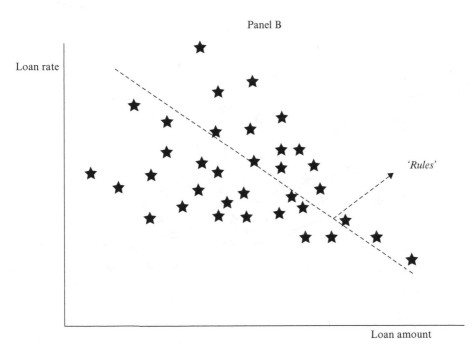

Figure 9.3   Loan rate versus loan amount illustrating rules and discretion

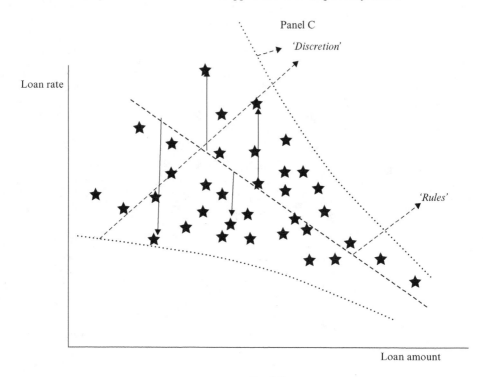

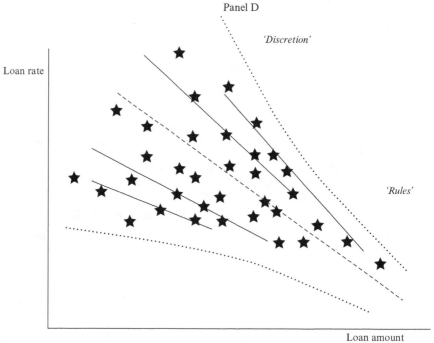

Figure 9.3   (continued)

Panel E

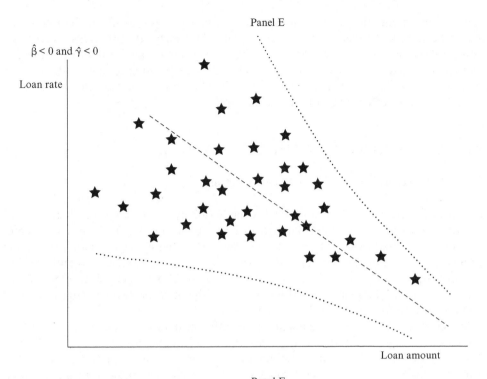

Panel F

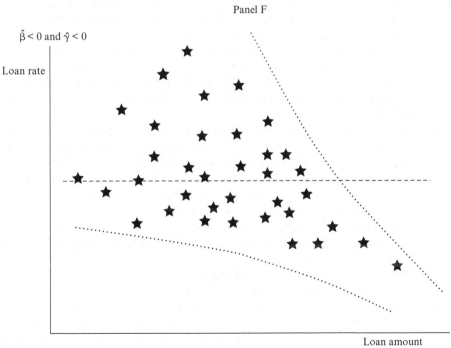

Figure 9.3 (continued)

from the mean equation with various arrows, which may represent the discretion that loan officers actually exercise at this bank. Panel D displays the alternative interpretation for discretion, which is based on model heterogeneity. Panel E points out that the estimated parameters in the mean ($\hat{\beta}$) and the variance ($\hat{\gamma}$) equation are both negative. Finally, Panel F illustrates that even when the loan amount is omitted, that is, making $\hat{\beta}$ equal to zero, the estimate of $\hat{\gamma}$ remains negative.

9.6   APPLICATIONS IN THE LITERATURE

9.6.1   Rules versus Discretion in Loan Rate Setting

In Cerqueiro et al. (2011) we apply this methodology to banking and focus on the impact of a set of variables on loan rate dispersion. In sum, we find that larger loans, incorporated firms, firms without tax problems, firms with longer relationships, and younger firms, exhibit a lower variance. These findings are economically significant. For example, an increase in loan amount from $25 000 (the 25th percentile) to $550 000 (the 75th percentile) implies a nearly sixfold increase in the fit of the mean equation, showing that residual variance becomes less important.

In Cerqueiro et al. (2011) we employ four different datasets in our analysis. But the primary dataset we study first is the 1993 Survey of Small Business Finances (SSBF). Table 9.5 describes the main variables that are present in the 1993 Survey, while Table 9.6 presents the estimated parameters of the benchmark mean and variance equations. While the estimates in the mean equation are directly interpretable in terms of their economic relevance, the estimates in the variance equation require some more work (beyond the scope of this chapter). To illustrate the usefulness of such potential calculations, however, Table 9.7 provides an example of two loans with different characteristics, their predicted loan rates that are derived from the mean equation, and the predicted standard errors and confidence intervals (on these predicted loan rates) that are based on the estimates of the variance equation.

We further supplement the 1993 Survey with the 1998 and 2003 SSBFs in order to identify potential changes over time in the use of discretion. Our findings suggest a decreasing role for discretion in small credits to opaque businesses over the period 1990–2005. This result could be explained by the proliferation in the US banking industry of automated decision making in small-business lending at most banks (for instance, Small Business Credit Scoring). We also investigate whether our results are driven by the pooling of heterogeneous lending technologies that may populate our sample. To this end, we investigate a subsample of lines of credit extended by commercial banks only. Consistent with the view that lines of credit are relationship-driven (Berger and Udell, 1995), we find no temporal change in discretion for this subsample.

To show the robustness of our results, we also study a dataset provided by an important Belgian bank. This dataset enables us to mitigate the concern that our results could be driven by the omission of relevant variables, since it contains all the information that was recorded and stored by the bank about each particular client. Moreover, the Belgian dataset allows us to include branch fixed-effects to control for potential heterogeneity across branches in lending technologies. Therefore we ensure that discretion will relate to

Table 9.5 Descriptive statistics, 1993 SSBF

Variable	Description	Mean	Med	SD	Min	Max
Interest rate variables						
Prime Rate	Prime rate (%)	6.50	6.00	0.71	6.00	10.00
Loan characteristics						
Loan rate	Loan rate (%) [Dependent Variable]	8.77	8.45	2.34	0.00	32.00
Loan amount	Loan size ($million)	0.32	0.04	2.05	0.0003	100.00
Loan maturity	Loan maturity (years)	3.50	1.00	4.80	0.08	30.00
Collateral	=1 if loan is collateralized	0.70	1.00	0.46	0.00	1.00
Floating	=1 if floating loan rate	0.50	1.00	0.50	0.00	1.00
Firm/owner characteristics						
Proprietorship	=1 if firm is a proprietorship	0.31	0.00	0.46	0.00	1.00
Partnership	=1 if firm is a partnership	0.08	0.00	0.28	0.00	1.00
S-corporation	=1 if firm is a S-corporation	0.26	0.00	0.44	0.00	1.00
Regular corporation	=1 if firm is a regular corporation	0.35	0.00	0.48	0.00	1.00
Owner's age	Age of firm's primary owner	48.00	47.00	10.00	25.00	89.00
Minority	=1 if firm is owned by minority race	0.05	0.00	0.21	0.00	1.00
Accounting information						
Assets	Total assets ($million)	1.01	0.18	4.10	0.00	240.00
Sales	= sales/assets	4.50	2.70	7.00	0.00	92.00
Profits	= profits/assets	0.54	0.14	2.50	-31.00	43.00
Inventories	= inventories/assets	0.19	0.06	0.26	0.00	1.00
Accounts receivable	= accounts receivable/assets	0.18	0.10	0.22	0.00	1.10
Accounts Payable	= accounts payable/assets	0.13	0.05	0.19	0.00	3.50
Total Loans	= total loans/assets	0.52	0.37	0.88	0.00	20.00
Leverage	= total liabilities/assets	0.70	0.56	0.94	0.00	21.00
Trade Credit Use	% of purchases on trade credit	56.00	75.00	41.00	0.00	100.00

Table 9.5 (continued)

Variable	Description	Mean	Med	SD	Min	Max
Credit history						
Bankrupt	=1 if firm declared bankruptcy in past 7 years	0.01	0.00	0.11	0.00	1.00
Owner delinquent	=1 if owner has been 60 or more days delinquent on personal obligations within past 3 years	0.07	0.00	0.26	0.00	1.00
Firm delinquent	=1 if firm has been 60 or more days delinquent on business obligations within past 3 years	0.17	0.00	0.37	0.00	1.00
Judgments	=1 if any judgments have been rendered against the principal owner within the past 3 years	0.03	0.00	0.17	0.00	1.00
Clean record	=1 if owner has clean record (the four previous variables equal zero)	0.78	1.00	0.41	0.00	1.00
IRS Problem	=1 if firm had IRS problems or penalties in the past year	0.33	0.00	0.47	0.00	1.00
Relationship characteristics						
Duration	Duration of relationship with the lender (years)	7.80	5.00	7.70	0.00	53.00
Main bank	=1 if loan granted by primary bank	0.72	1.00	0.45	0.00	1.00
Personal	=1 if firm mainly conducts business with lender in person	0.74	1.00	0.44	0.00	1.00
Competition/location						
Concentrated	=1 if HHI > 1800 (firm's headquarters office)	0.54	1.00	0.50	0.00	1.00
MSA	=1 if firm located in MSA	0.73	1.00	0.44	0.00	1.00
Distance	Distance to lender (miles)	42.00	3.00	197.00	0.00	2608.00

Notes: All variables are obtained from the 1993 Survey of Small Business Finance, except the Prime Rate which we obtain from the Federal Reserve Economic Database. The table defines the variables employed in the empirical specifications and provides some sample statistics: mean, median (Med), standard deviation (SD), minimum (Min) and maximum (Max). The statistics take into account the 1993 SSBF sample weights. The number of observations is 1625. Other variables used in our regressions (dummies): type of loan (5), one-digit SIC codes (9), year (4), census regions (8) and type of lender (8). We do not present descriptive statistics for these variables to conserve space.

Table 9.6   Results of heteroskedastic regression with 1993 SSBF

Variable	(I) Mean equation		(II) Variance equation	
	β	SE	γ	SE
Constant	842.2***	4.2	10.10***	0.04
Interest rate variables				
Prime Rate	50.8***	7.0		
Loan characteristics				
Ln (Loan Amount)	−10.1***	3.4	−0.27***	0.02
Ln (Loan Maturity)	0.2	4.4		
Collateral	31.4***	9.2	−0.18**	0.08
Floating Rate	−33.6***	8.8		
Firm/owner characteristics				
Corporation			−0.24***	0.09
Ln (Owner's Age)	8.6	9.6	0.39***	0.13
Minority	32.6*	17.1	0.34***	0.13
Accounting information				
Ln(Assets)	−14.2***	3.7		
Sales	−1.3*	0.8		
Profits	2.0	2.1		
Inventories	−25.6	19.0		
Accounts Receivable	−13.3	19.5		
Accounts Payable	15.3	29.2		
Total Loans	−4.6	17.4		
Total Debt	16.3	16.2		
Trade Credit Use (%)	−0.1	0.1		
Credit history				
Bankrupt	−2.6	30.7		
Owner Delinquent	77.2***	20.3		
Firm Delinquent	15.1	11.6		
Judgments	24.4	23.0		
Clean Record			−0.25***	0.09
IRS Problem	7.7	7.8	0.16**	0.07
Relationship characteristics				
Ln (Duration)	−2.4	5.2	−0.12**	0.05
Main Bank	15.7	10.1		
Personal	5.5	8.5		
Competition/location				
Concentrated	5.9	7.8	0.10	0.08
MSA	4.7	9.6	0.18**	0.09
Ln (Distance)	3.2	2.8	0.10***	0.02
Other controls				
Loan Type (5)	Yes**			
Firm Organization Type (3)	Yes**			
SIC (9)	Yes			
Year Dummies (4)	Yes**			
Regions (8)	Yes**			
Lender Type (8)	Yes***			

Table 9.6 (continued)

Variable	(I) Mean equation		(II) Variance equation	
	β	SE	γ	SE
Number of observations		1625		
Number of parameters		74		
χ^2-Statistic		980.4		
Pseudo-R^2 (%)		4.46		
VWLS R^2 (%)		28.26		

Note: The table lists the coefficients and standard errors (SE) for the mean equation (column I) and variance equation (column II) from a heteroskedastic regression with *Loan Rate* (in basis points) as the dependent variable. The explanatory variables in both the mean and variance equation, which we define in Table 9.5, are demeaned. We obtain the estimates by maximum likelihood. The symbols *, ** and *** denote significance at the 10, 5 and 1% level, respectively. Some measures of fit are provided. χ^2 (k) is the statistic for the joint test that all coefficients except the intercept are zero, for k degrees of freedom. Pseudo-R^2 is defined as 1-Likelihood (just a constant)/Likelihood (full model). The VWLS (variance-weighted least squares) R^2 is obtained by using the inverse of the estimated variances in the heteroskedastic model as weights in the corresponding linear regression model.

Table 9.7 *Economic relevancy of heteroskedastic regression with 1993 SSBF*

Variable	Loan A	Loan B
Loan Size ($)	$25 000	$550 000
Loan is Collateralized (0/1)	No	Yes
Firm is a Corporation (0/1)	No	Yes
Firm Has Clean Legal Record (0/1)	No	Yes
Duration of Relationship (years)	3	13
Predicted Loan Rate (%)	9.3	8.1
Predicted Standard Error	2.1	0.9
Confidence Interval (95%)	[5.1–13.5]	[6.3–9.9]
Predicted R^2 of Mean Equation	0.01	0.81

Notes: The table lists the different characteristics of two loans (of otherwise mean characteristics) and their predicted loan rates (derived from the mean equation), and the predicted standard errors and confidence intervals on the predicted loan rates (derived from the variance equation).

the information observed only by the loan officer and to the arbitrariness in their pricing decisions.

The estimates from all our heteroskedastic regression models generate four new robust findings. Firstly, the opaqueness and observable risk of borrowers are associated with a larger unexplained dispersion of loan rates. This result is actually in line with the so-called mixed strategy loan pricing equilibrium in von Thadden (2004), where discretion is increasing in the severity of information asymmetries in the credit market. Moreover, this result also suggests that discretion is positively related to the switching costs firms face. Secondly, banks price larger loans according to more objective criteria or rules. This finding illustrates that a firm's incentive to increase its search intensity constrains a bank's ability to price discriminate. Thirdly, we find that discretion is most important for large and highly concentrated banking markets. Fourthly, discretion increases with borrower–lender distance.

These findings are robust to the arbitrary manipulations in our benchmark linear pricing model (as discussed in section 9.4), and they are not driven by the endogeneity of other loan contract terms, or by sample selection. Furthermore, we show that the information set we use to explain loan rates quite accurately predicts the outcome of the banks' loan granting decisions. In particular, our results suggest that, while being heavily used in loan pricing, discretion is far less present in the loan granting decision.

While loan rate dispersion has itself been widely documented before, no study so far (to the best of our knowledge) had identified the actual sources of this dispersion. In fact, empirical research on price dispersion is limited to the product market (see Dahlby and West, 1986, for instance). Price dispersion in the product market is motivated by costly consumer search, that is, frictions on the demand side. In contrast to the product market, frictions in the credit market are present on both the demand side (firm uncertainty about the competitiveness of the loan offer) and the supply side (bank uncertainty about firm quality). Consequently, the credit market provides a richer environment to investigate how market imperfections translate into price dispersion.

9.6.2   Market Discipline

Baele et al. (2011) and Iannotta (2011) employ heteroskedastic models to assess the monitoring role of bank stockholders and bank bondholders, respectively. Baele et al. (2011) investigate the propensity of bank managers to manipulate key strategic variables following alarming signals that arrive in the form of risk or negative valuation. They interpret unexplained dispersion of total risk and performance as pressure from stock market investors, and assess how this dispersion is associated with the business model, managerial discretion, and bank opaqueness. Baele et al. (2011) provide evidence that stock markets penalize discretionary bank behavior. Moreover, banks actively react to negative signals by increasing their capital buffer, reducing dividends and their exposure to liquidity risk, and increasing their cost-efficiency.

Iannotta (2011) uses a heteroskedastic model to study the dispersion in bank bond credit spreads unexplained by easy-to-observe characteristics, such as rating, maturity and seniority. He argues that higher dispersion in credit spreads could reflect both bond opaqueness and investors' incorporation of proprietary information in bond prices. The study finds dispersion in bond spreads to be more prevalent when bonds have lower rating and a longer maturity, and when bonds are subordinated. Moreover, spread dispersion is also higher in open-priced offers and when the syndicate contains fewer banks. These results are affected by neither the inclusion of issuer fixed-effects nor the inclusion of non-linear terms in the spread equation.

9.6.3   Other Applications

Navone and Iannotta (2008) use a heteroskedastic model to study mutual fund fee dispersion, which they interpret in light of search cost theories. They find that fee dispersion is lower for highly visible funds and for funds that invest heavily in incentives for brokers and advisers to create and distribute information. Navone and Iannotta (2008) argue that these results could reflect limited competition in the United States (US) mutual fund market.

Stebunovs and Gaul (2009) investigate the determinants of the dispersion in interest rate spreads on corporate loans. Specifically, they test Leland and Pyle's (1977) theory that lenders can mitigate information asymmetries in the corporate loan market through loan ownership. To this end, Stebunovs and Gaul (2009) test whether the production of private information by lenders, which they measure as the unexplained variation in spreads, is positively associated with loan ownership. Their findings indicate that information problems seem to exist in the corporate loan market, and that loan ownership reduces – but does not eliminate – such problems.

9.7   CONCLUSIONS

It has frequently been shown that applications by similar borrowers yield differential lending outcomes. Indeed, lending decisions quite often exhibit the discretion exerted by banks and their loan officers. In some environments, discretion is directly observed and theoretically motivated factors can be employed to understand discretionary behaviour of managers, banks or loan officers.

Mostly, however, the environment does not allow us to observe discretion directly. This chapter demonstrates how to investigate the use of discretion in the loan rate setting process with a heteroskedastic regression model. This model allows us to investigate which factors determine the dispersion in banks' loan rates to similar borrowers. The heteroskedastic regression model allows us to introduce determinants that drive the dispersion around the mean. In particular, one can attribute this dispersion to the bank and loan officers' exploitation of market imperfections and can assess the relevance of firm, loan officer and bank characteristics, as suggested by the theoretical literature, in explaining discretion.

REFERENCES

Baele, L., V. De Bruyckere, O. De Jonghe and R. Vander Vennet (2011), 'Do stock markets discipline US bank holding companies: just monitoring, or also influencing?', CentER, Tilburg.

Berger, A.N. and G.F. Udell (1995), 'Relationship lending and lines of credit in small firm finance', *Journal of Business*, **68**, 351–381.

Cerqueiro, G., H. Degryse and S. Ongena (2011), 'Rules versus discretion in loan rate setting', *Journal of Financial Intermediation*, **20**, 503–529.

Dahlby, B. and D.S. West (1986), 'Price dispersion in an automobile insurance market', *Journal of Political Economy*, **94**, 418–438.

Degryse, H., J.M. Liberti, T. Mosk and S. Ongena (2011), 'Is loan officer discretion advised when viewing soft information?', CentER, Tilburg.

Degryse, H. and S. Ongena (2005), 'Distance, lending relationships, and competition', *Journal of Finance*, **60**, 231–266.

Harvey, A.C. (1976), 'Estimating regression models with multiplicative heteroscedasticity', *Econometrica*, **44**, 461–465.

Iannotta, G. (2011), 'Market discipline in the banking industry: evidence from spread dispersion', *European Journal of Finance*, **17**, 111–131.

Leland, H.E. and D.H. Pyle (1977), 'Informational asymmetries, financial structure, and financial intermediation', *Journal of Finance*, **32**, 371–387.

Navone, M. and G. Iannotta (2008), 'Search costs and mutual fund fee dispersion', CAREFIN, Milano.

Petersen, M.A. and R.G. Rajan (1994), 'The benefits of lending relationships: evidence from small business data', *Journal of Finance*, **49**, 3–37.

Puri, M., J. Rocholl and S. Steffen (2011), 'Rules versus discretion in bank lending decisions', ESMT, Berlin.

Stebunovs, V. and L. Gaul (2009), 'Ownership and asymmetric information problems in the corporate loan market: evidence from a heteroskedastic regression', Board of Governors of the Federal Reserve System, Washington DC.

von Thadden, E.-L. (2004), 'Asymmetric information, bank lending, and implicit contracts: the winner's curse', *Finance Reaserch Letters*, **1**, 11–23.

10 Liquidity measures
Thomas Johann and Erik Theissen

10.1 INTRODUCTION

The liquidity of a financial market is universally recognized as one of the most important, if not *the* most important, determinant of market quality. Liquidity affects the cost of trading in financial markets and is, therefore, an important determinant of the performance of asset portfolios. Liquidity is also a decisive factor in the competition between trading venues for investor order flow because it affects the decision of traders concerning where to trade. But its importance extends far beyond the realm of market microstructure. The liquidity of an asset has implications for its expected rate of return and, in turn, for the cost of capital (see e.g. Amihud and Mendelson, 1986; Pastor and Stambough, 2003; Acharya and Pedersen, 2005). Recent academic research has uncovered several channels through which liquidity and corporate financing decisions are interrelated.[1] Also, market liquidity varies systematically with the business cycle (Naes et al., 2011).

Given the importance of the concept, a large number of academic studies have tried to explain liquidity (i.e., liquidity is the dependent variable in these models) while an even larger number of studies have included liquidity as an explanatory variable. In both cases the researcher obviously needs a valid and reliable measure of liquidity. In the past decades a plethora of liquidity measures have been proposed. They differ with respect to their underlying assumptions, the dimension of liquidity they try to capture, and their data requirements. In this chapter we survey the most widely used measures, discuss their relative advantages and disadvantages, and derive conclusions on their suitability for various types of empirical applications. We briefly discuss recent developments in international equity markets (such as fragmentation, hidden liquidity and high-frequency trading) and their implications for the validity and reliability of traditional liquidity measures.

The chapter is structured as follows. Section 10.2 defines liquidity and describes the dimensions and determinants of liquidity. Section 10.3 discusses measures of liquidity that are based on the bid–ask spread. These measures require the availability of data on bid and ask quotes. Section 10.4 describes several procedures that try to estimate the bid–ask spread from low-frequency (e.g. daily) data. Section 10.5 presents approaches which aim to measure liquidity by the price impact of trades. Section 10.6 offers concluding remarks.

10.2 LIQUIDITY: DIMENSIONS AND DETERMINANTS

There is no universally accepted definition of liquidity. At a very general level, an asset's liquidity can be defined as 'the ease with which it is traded' (Brunnermeier and Pedersen,

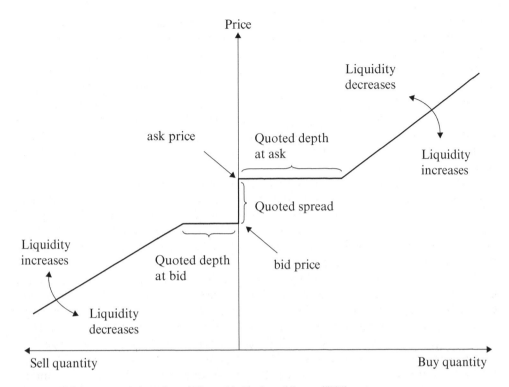

Source: This is an extended version of Figure 1 in Engle and Lange (2001).

Figure 10.1 The market reaction schedule

2009, p. 2201). Liquidity, broadly defined, is a multidimensional concept. There are three dimensions: price, quantity and time:

- The price dimension captures the deviation between the true value of an asset and the price at which it can actually be bought or sold.
- The quantity dimension captures the volume that can be transacted at a given price.
- The time dimension captures the time it takes to complete a trade of given size at a given price. A related, though not identical, concept is that of resiliency. Resiliency is the time it takes for the market to recover after a liquidity shock.[2]

These dimensions are, of course, not independent of each other. This is most obvious in an open limit order book[3] where, at any given point in time, larger volumes can be traded at worse prices. This price–quantity trade-off is captured by the slope of the limit order book (see Figure 10.1 for an illustration).

Obviously, a one-dimensional measure cannot capture all three dimensions of liquidity. Most of the measures that are surveyed in this chapter aim to capture the price dimension while others target the quantity dimension. Only few authors have attempted to explicitly measure resiliency.[4]

In order to put the various liquidity measures into perspective, it is useful to briefly discuss the economic reasons for the existence of execution costs in financial markets. The theory on which the discussion is based assumes that liquidity is supplied by designated market makers. The intuition, however, carries over to limit order markets in which limit order traders supply liquidity.[5] We will not discuss brokerage fees.

The market maker's gross revenue is the difference between the prices at which they buy assets (the bid price) and the prices at which they sell assets (the ask price). The difference between the best (lowest) ask price and the best (highest) bid price available in a market at a point in time is the (quoted) bid–ask spread. It is a source of transaction costs for investors.

Market makers face several types of costs. Most obviously, they incur the costs of doing business. These comprise fixed and variable costs (such as rental charges, information technology costs, etc.) as well as the opportunity cost of time. The bid–ask spread must incorporate a compensation for the costs of doing business (and potentially also a profit margin). This component of the spread is known as the order processing cost. It is unrelated to the value of the asset.

Market makers stand ready to buy and sell assets to satisfy their customers' trading needs. Their inventory of risky assets thus depends on their customers' decisions. Consequently, market makers will often hold portfolios that deviate from their target portfolios and expose them to additional risk. A risk-averse market maker will require compensation for bearing this risk. This compensation is known as the inventory holding cost component of the spread. Theoretical models of the inventory holding cost component[6] predict a specific dynamic pattern in the time series of bid, ask and transaction prices. Market makers who acquired a large position will be eager to sell but will be hesitant to buy additional assets. Therefore, they will lower their ask price and lower their bid price. We thus expect that the bid and ask quotes will decrease after a transaction at the bid price and, by an analogous argument, increase after a transaction at the ask price.

Finally, market makers face the risk of trading with counter-parties having superior information on the value of the asset (insiders) and will lose money on those transactions. Because market makers will typically not be able to identify traders with superior information, they are unable to avoid these transactions. They will thus increase the bid–ask spread to the point where gains from trades with uninformed traders compensate the losses to informed traders.[7] This component of the bid–ask spread is referred to as the adverse selection component. Given the existence of traders with superior information, the occurrence of a transaction provides information on the value of the asset. A transaction at the ask price (a buyer-initiated transaction) should therefore trigger an upward-revision of the market maker's beliefs. Thus, the existence of the adverse selection component also introduces a dynamic pattern in the time series of bid, ask and transaction prices.[8]

10.3   SPREAD-BASED MEASURES

The most obvious measure of liquidity, and the one that is most directly related to the theory briefly summarized above, is the bid–ask spread. Because the spread is defined as the difference between the best ask price and the best bid price, it is obvious that it can be estimated from data on bid and ask prices. However, as will be demonstrated below, the simple difference between the best bid and the best ask price may yield a biased measure of the true execution cost. Therefore, alternative measures have been developed. These approaches are reviewed in section 10.3.1. For many markets, data on bid and ask prices are not available. Roll (1984) has pioneered approaches that attempt to estimate the spread from transaction price data only. His approach is presented in section 10.3.2.

10.3.1   Estimating the Spread from Quote Data

As mentioned above, the quoted bid–ask spread is simply the difference between the lowest ask price and the highest bid price:

$$s_t^q = A_t - B_t. \tag{10.1}$$

The relative quoted spread:

$$s_t^{qr} = \frac{A_t - B_t}{M_t}; M_t = \frac{A_t + B_t}{2} \tag{10.2}$$

expresses the spread as a fraction of the quote midpoint. The advantage of a relative measure is that it makes shares with different price levels comparable.

The quoted spread is a valid forward-looking measure of execution cost under the assumptions that:

1.   The size of the transaction does not exceed the volume available at the best ask price (the quoted depth at the ask) or at the best bid price (the quoted depth at the bid), respectively.
2.   The transaction price will indeed be the ask price for a buy order and the bid price for a sell order.

A market order with a volume exceeding the depth at the respective quote (i.e., an order which violates assumption 1) will walk up or down the limit order book, thus triggering several transactions at different prices. The relevant price is then a volume-weighted average of the prices of the individual limit orders that are hit. If we denote these weighted average prices as $A_t(V)$ and $B_t(V)$ we can construct a forward-looking measure of the execution cost for orders of size V:[9]

$$CRT(V) = A_t(V) - B_t(V); CRT^r(V) = \frac{A_t(V) - B_t(V)}{M_t}. \tag{10.3}$$

In some markets, transactions may occur at prices which are more favourable than the best bid and ask prices displayed on the trading screens. We refer to this phenomenon as price improvement. Price improvement implies a violation of assumption 2 above. It can occur for various reasons:

- The specialists on the New York Stock Exchange (and similar intermediaries on other floor-based exchanges) may execute incoming market orders at prices inside the quoted spread.[10]
- Large market participants may have market power vis-à-vis market makers and use it to negotiate prices inside the quoted spread.[11]
- Nowadays many markets allow the submission of (partially or fully) hidden limit orders. A limit order is partially hidden if only a fraction of the true order size is displayed on the trading screens. If such an order exists, the actual volume that can be traded at a price equal to the limit price is larger than the volume displayed on the screen. A limit order is fully hidden if it is completely invisible. If a completely hidden limit order exists with a price limit that is within the visible spread, the transaction price will lie within the spread. It is thus generally true that a market order that executes against a hidden limit order will achieve a price that is more favourable than the price that could be forecasted using the information visible on the trading screen.

In all these cases the quoted spread and the CRT measure will overestimate the true execution cost. The effective bid–ask spread is calculated based on actual transaction prices. It therefore accounts for possible price improvement. The effective spread is defined as:

$$s_t^e = 2Q_t(P_t - M_t); \quad s_t^{er} = \frac{2Q_t(P_t - M_t)}{M_t} \tag{10.4}$$

where Q_t is a trade indicator variable that is 1 if the trade was initiated by a buyer and -1 if it was initiated by a seller. M_t is the quote midpoint immediately prior to the transaction.

A more common definition of the effective spread is:

$$s_t^{e*} = 2|P_t - M_t|; \quad s_t^{e*r} = \frac{2|P_t - M_t|}{M_t}. \tag{10.5}$$

The two versions of the effective spread are identical when buyer-initiated trades are always executed at prices which are equal to or above the quote midpoint, and vice versa for seller-initiated transactions. In some markets this condition is always satisfied by design. For example, in an electronic limit order book with no hidden liquidity inside the best bid and ask quote, a trade can only occur when a market buy order hits the best ask or when a market sell order hits the best bid. Buyer-initiated trades thus always execute at the ask price which is above the quote midpoint, and vice versa for seller-initiated trades. In many markets, however, the condition stated above may be, and often is, violated. Table 2 of Odders-White (2000) reveals that violations occur for slightly more than 9 per cent of the transactions in her sample from the New York Stock Exchange. 'Violation' here means that a trade is buyer-initiated but is executed at a price below the quote midpoint, and vice versa for seller-initiated trades. Ellis et al. (1999) report even higher figures for Nasdaq. In these cases the second version of the effective spread measure, s^{e*}, yields an upwardly biased estimate of the execution costs.

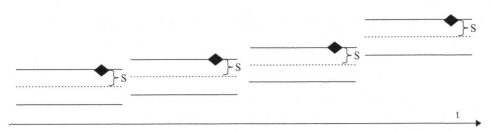

Figure 10.2   Splitting up a large buy order

Unfortunately it will often be impossible to quantify the bias because this would require data on trade initiation which are frequently unavailable. A typical data set contains bid prices, ask prices and transaction prices. Researchers then usually infer trade direction using algorithms such as the one proposed by Lee and Ready (1991). These algorithms assume that trades occurring at prices above (below) the quote midpoint are buyer-initiated (seller-initiated). If this assumption is wrong (and the empirical results alluded to above suggest that it often is wrong), the inferred trade direction will also be wrong.

Average effective spreads are typically smaller than average quoted spreads. This is not surprising in markets in which transactions can occur at prices inside the quoted spread. However, the same relationship is observed in markets in which transactions can only occur at the bid or the ask prices. In these markets the effective spread is equal to the quoted spread in effect immediately prior to the transaction. The average effective spread is then equal to the average quoted spread, conditional upon observing a trade. If trades are more likely to occur when quoted spreads are low, this conditional average will be smaller than the unconditional average quoted spread.

The effective spread is a backward-looking measure because it is calculated based on past transaction prices. It also implicitly assumes that an order is filled at once. If a large order is broken up into several small trades, a situation as in Figure 10.2 may arise. The average effective spread of the individual trades will clearly underestimate the true execution costs. A valid estimate of the execution cost is obtained by relating the weighted average price of all transactions to the quote midpoint prior to the first transaction.[12]

10.3.2   Estimating the Spread from Transaction Data

As mentioned above, data on bid and ask prices are often unavailable. Roll (1984) has proposed a simple procedure to estimate the spread from transaction data. It is based on the following assumptions:

1.   The quote midpoint (which is assumed to be the best available estimate of the asset value) follows a random walk:

$$M_t = M_{t-1} + \varepsilon_t \tag{10.6}$$

where ε_t is i.i.d. noise.
2.   The bid–ask spread, S, is constant.

3. Transactions occur at the bid price or at the ask price with equal probability. The price of transaction t is:

$$P_t = M_t + \frac{S}{2}Q_t + v_t. \tag{10.7}$$

Q_t is a trade indicator variable as defined in section 10.3.1. The error term, v_t, is assumed to be i.i.d.. It captures noise such as rounding errors (due to the existence of a minimum tick size).[13]

4. The trade indicator variable is serially uncorrelated and is independent of future changes in the quote midpoint.

First-differencing the price equation and inserting $\Delta M_t = \varepsilon_t$ yields the model:

$$\Delta P_t = \frac{S}{2}\Delta Q_t + \varepsilon_t^*; \varepsilon_t^* = \varepsilon_t + v_t - v_{t-1}. \tag{10.8}$$

From this, it follows that the covariance of successive price changes is:

$$Cov(\Delta p_t, \Delta p_{t-1}) = \frac{S^2}{4}Cov(\Delta Q_t, \Delta Q_{t-1}). \tag{10.9}$$

As Q_t is $+1$ or -1 with equal probabilities and is not serially correlated, we have $Cov(\Delta Q_t, \Delta Q_{t-1}) = -1$. Inserting this into (10.9) and solving for S yields the Roll (1984) spread estimator:

$$S = 2\sqrt{-Cov(\Delta p_t, \Delta p_{t-1})}. \tag{10.10}$$

As discussed in section 10.2, the existence of inventory holding costs and adverse selection costs implies that bid and ask quotes are adjusted after a transaction. This, in turn, implies that the trade indicator variable is correlated with future midquote changes. Assumption 4 above is thus much less innocent than it might seem at first sight. It is tantamount to assuming that order processing costs are the only reason for the existence of a positive bid–ask spread. This is an obvious shortcoming of the Roll (1984) spread estimator.

Empirically, it is often the case that the serial covariance of successive price changes is positive. This is particularly true for stocks with low spreads.[14] In these cases the Roll measure is not defined. A procedure commonly applied is to set the spread estimate to zero in these cases.

Notwithstanding its drawbacks, the Roll measure is widely used.[15] The most likely reason is that it is easy to compute and has low data requirements – the researcher only needs a time series of transaction prices.

10.4　ESTIMATING THE SPREAD FROM LOW-FREQUENCY DATA

Direct estimation of the spread requires intraday data on bid and ask prices and transaction prices. These data are often unavailable. Even if the data are available, direct estimation of the spread may be burdensome. This is because trading activity (and thus the amount of data to be processed) has increased tremendously. In the late 1990s, the average daily number of transactions for the 30 Dow Jones stocks hovered between 1000 and 2000. By 2009 that number had exceeded 130000. At the same time the ratio of order cancellations to executions (and thus the number of changes in the quoted spread and/or the CRT(V) measure) has more than tripled (Angel et al., 2011).

Therefore, researchers have developed methods to estimate the spread from low-frequency (usually daily) data. In this section we describe several of these methods.

10.4.1   The Roll Estimator Again

As discussed above, the Roll (1984) spread estimator is derived from the serial covariance of successive price changes. However, the logic of the estimator carries over to daily data. Thus, provided that the assumptions underlying the Roll estimator are met, the serial covariance of successive changes in daily closing prices can serve as an estimator of the spread. Recently, Hasbrouck (2009) has proposed to use a Bayesian approach. His estimates are constructed using a Gibbs sampling procedure.[16]

10.4.2   Zero-Return-Based Estimators

Lesmond et al. (1999) develop an estimator of total transaction costs denoted LOT. Total transaction costs include brokerage commissions and exchange fees besides the spread. Consequently, the LOT estimator should be larger than estimates of the bid–ask spread.

The intuition is simple: imagine that a trader receives private information on the value of stock i. Absent transaction costs, he will trade on his information up to the point where the marginal price is equal to his estimate of the asset value. The price then reflects his private information. If, however, the total transaction cost exceeds the expected gain, he will refrain from trading. His information will then not be impounded into prices. If transaction costs even for the trader with the highest expected gain from trading exceed those expected gains, a zero return will be recorded.

By this logic, a zero return observation is indicative of high transaction costs. Therefore, Lesmond et al. (1999) propose to use the fraction of zero return observations in a period (a month or a year) as a first and very simple proxy for transaction costs:

$$\text{Zero} = \frac{\text{\# of zero return days in period}}{\text{\# of days in a period}} \qquad (10.11)$$

Higher values of Zero indicate larger total transaction costs.

The Zero measure only makes use of the information provided by zero return days. Lesmond et al. (1999) develop an extended model that also uses the information provided by non-zero returns. Assume that the unobservable 'true' returns, $r_{i,t}^*$, are generated by a market model:

$$r_{i,t}^* = \beta_i r_{m,t} + \varepsilon_{i,t}. \qquad (10.12)$$

If transaction costs were zero, observable returns would also be generated by a market model. With non-zero transaction costs, however, observed returns will be different from those in a frictionless world. Denote by $\alpha_{1,i} < 0; \alpha_{2,i} > 0$ the transaction costs for a sale and a purchase, respectively. Then the observed return $r_{i,t}$ is:

$$r_{i,t} = r_{i,t}^* - \alpha_{1,i} \ \ if \ r_{i,t}^* < \alpha_{1,i}$$

$$r_{i,t} = 0 \ \ if \ \alpha_{1,i} < r_{i,t}^* < \alpha_{2,i}$$

$$r_{i,t} = r_{i,t}^* - \alpha_{2,i} \ \ if \ r_{i,t}^* > \alpha_{2,i} \tag{10.13}$$

The intuition is as above. The marginal trader (the trader with the highest expected benefit from trading) will only trade if the true expected return exceeds the transaction costs. Otherwise, there will be no trade and a zero return is observed. The rationale for allowing different transaction costs for buying and selling is that the marginal seller might be a short seller, and short sales cause higher transaction costs than regular trades.

Lesmond et al. (1999) provide the likelihood function which can be used to obtain maximum likelihood estimates of the parameters $\alpha_{1,i}$ and $\alpha_{2,i}$. The measure of the proportional roundtrip transaction costs is then:

$$LOT = \alpha_{2,i} - \alpha_{1,i}. \tag{10.14}$$

Fong et al. (2011) simplify the LOT measure. Firstly, they assume that transaction costs for buying and selling are identical $(-\alpha_{1,i} = \alpha_{2,i})$. Secondly, they replace the market model assumption by the assumption that true returns follow a normal distribution. Based on these assumptions they derive the transaction cost estimator:

$$FHT = 2\sigma\Phi^{-1}\left(\frac{1 + Zero}{2}\right). \tag{10.15}$$

Φ denotes the cumulative density of the standard normal distribution, σ is the standard deviation of daily returns, and Zero is the proportion of zero return days as defined above. The Fong, Holden, Trzcinka (FHT) estimator is easy to apply because it does not require maximum likelihood estimation.

10.4.3   The Effective Tick Estimator

The minimum tick size set by the exchange determines the set of admissible prices. If the minimum tick size is 1 cent, all prices ending in full cents are admissible while prices ending in a fraction of a cent (sub-penny prices) are not. Observed prices are not uniformly distributed over the full set of admissible prices. Rather, traders have a preference for particular (e.g. round) numbers. This phenomenon is referred to as price clustering (see Harris, 1991).

The observed price clustering can be used to draw inferences on the spread (Goyenko et al., 2009; Holden, 2009). Assume that the minimum tick size is 1 cent and the spread is 5 cents. It is assumed that a 5 cent spread is implemented on a 5 cent price grid.[17] That is, even though the minimum tick size is 1 cent, traders behave as if it were 5 cents. By that assumption, we will not observe bid and ask prices of 40.41 and 40.46, respectively. Rather, we would observe 40.40 and 40.45.

Now assume that we observe a transaction price of 40.41. This price will only be observed when the spread (and thus the price grid that traders use) is 1 cent. Thus, we can attach a 100 per cent probability to a 1 cent price grid. Assume next that we observe a price of 40.45. This price can result from a 1 cent grid or a 5 cent grid. The probability of observing a price ending in x5 cent when a 1 cent grid is used is 10 per cent (ten prices out of a total of 100). The probability of observing a price ending in x5 cents when a 5 cent grid is used is 50 per cent (ten prices out of a total of 20 because it is assumed that a 5 cent spread is implemented on a price grid that only comprises prices ending in x0 and x5). Thus, the price of 40.45 comes from a 1 cent grid with probability 0.167 (= 0.1/0.6) and from a 5 cent grid with probability 0.833 (= 0.5/0.6). Combining these numbers results in an expected spread equal to 4.33 cent (= 0.167*0.01 + 0.833*0.05).

By this logic each price implies a distribution of price grids from which it is drawn. We can then calculate the expected spread that is implied by the observed price. Averaging this over a sample of closing prices yields an estimate of the effective bid–ask spread (Goyenko et al., 2009; Holden, 2009).[18]

The critical assumption of the effective tick estimator is that traders agree on a price grid which is coarser than that implied by the minimum tick size, possibly in order to economize on negotiation costs (see Harris, 1991). Whether this assumption is justified in the era of computerized high-frequency traders is an open issue.

10.4.4   The High–Low Spread Estimator

The high–low spread estimator was proposed by Corwin and Schultz (2012). It is based on a simple intuition. The highest price observed on a trading day will typically originate from a buyer-initiated transaction (i.e., a transaction at the ask price) while the lowest price will typically originate from a transaction at the bid price. The difference between the daily high and low price thus contains one component which is related to the spread and one component which is related to the volatility of asset returns. The problem is to disentangle these components. Corwin and Schultz (2012) propose a procedure which is based on the assumptions that: (1) true asset prices follow a diffusion process; and (2) the spread is constant over a two-day period. Assumption (1) implies that the variance of changes in the true asset value increases proportional with time. The component related to the spread, on the other hand, is constant over time. Under these assumptions, then, the difference between the daily high and low price contains once the component related to the variance of price changes and once the component related to the spread. The difference between the highest and lowest prices measured over a two-day interval contains twice the component related to the variance of price changes but still only once the component related to the spread.[19] We thus essentially have two equations in two unknowns and can solve for the spread estimator:

$$CS = \frac{2(e^{\alpha} - 1)}{1 + e^{\alpha}}$$

$$\alpha = \frac{\sqrt{2\beta} - \sqrt{\beta}}{3 - 2\sqrt{2}} - \sqrt{\frac{\gamma}{3 - 2\sqrt{2}}}; \beta = \left[\ln\left(\frac{H_t}{L_t}\right)\right]^2 + \left[\ln\left(\frac{H_{t+1}}{L_{t+1}}\right)\right]^2; \gamma = \left[\ln\left(\frac{H_{t,t+1}}{L_{t,t+1}}\right)\right]^2$$

(10.16)

H and L denote the observed high and low prices. The parameter β contains the sum of the high–low price ratio for two individual days t and $(t + 1)$ while the parameter γ contains the high–low price ratio calculated from the high and low prices observed over the two-day interval from day t to day $(t + 1)$.

One advantage of the CS estimator is that it does not require a long time series. Observations from any two trading days are sufficient to derive a spread estimate. Corwin and Schultz (2009) even propose a method that yields a spread estimate for an individual day. They propose to estimate the spread over days $t - 1$ and t and over days t and $t + 1$. The CS estimate for day t is then the average of these two estimates:

$$CS_t = \frac{1}{2}(CS_{t-1,t} + CS_{t,t+1}) \tag{10.17}$$

This procedure can be applied to analyse the change in liquidity around corporate events such as merger announcements. However, applying it to the day immediately preceding or following the announcement would be inappropriate because we would mix pre-event and post-event observations. Corwin and Schultz (2009) thus propose to use the spread estimated from days $t - 2$ and $t - 1$ (days $t + 1$ and $t + 2$) for the day before (after) the announcement.

The CS estimator can become negative. As with the Roll estimator, this is more likely to happen when the spread is small. One remedy is to set negative spread estimates to zero.

10.4.5   Comparing the Approaches

The existence of several low-frequency data spread estimators immediately raises the question of how they compare against each other. Typically, authors who propose a new estimator compare its performance to that of existing measures. Usually, high-frequency data are used for the evaluation. The high-frequency data are used: to (1) directly estimate the effective spread from the bid and ask quotes; and (2) to construct the various estimators from data of lower frequency. The (cross-sectional and/or time series) correlation between the effective spread and the low-frequency estimators is then used as the metric to assess the performance of the estimators. These horse races yield ambiguous results. In almost all cases the measure which is proposed in a paper wins the horse race that is reported in that paper (see Goyenko et al., 2009; Holden, 2009; Corwin and Schultz, 2012; Fong et al., 2011).

Johann and Theissen (2013) is the only paper we are aware of that is independent in that it does not include a measure that is advocated by the authors of the paper. It is also the most comprehensive study in that it estimates both cross-sectional and time-series correlations, employs different weighting schemes (equal versus value-weighted), calculates average correlations between stock-wise correlations as well as correlations between averages of stock-wise liquidity measures, and uses data from different markets (NYSE, Nasdaq and the German stock market). The correlations between the effective spread and the low-frequency estimators reported in Johann and Theissen (2013) are lower than those reported in previous papers. The authors also report that the ranking of the estimators depends strongly on the methodology (e.g. the weighting scheme) used. In sum, the results are not very favourable for the low-frequency estimators.

A further issue deserves attention. Researchers typically use closing prices when apply-ing the low-frequency estimators. In many markets closing prices are determined in a call auction.[20] In a call auction no explicit bid–ask spread exists. It is thus not obvious how low-frequency spread estimates obtained from call auction prices should be interpreted. We are not aware of academic research into this issue.

10.5 PRICE IMPACT MEASURES

Trades move prices. This price change can be transitory or permanent (as is the case in Kyle's 1985 model in which trade size reveals private information on the asset value). Based on this intuition, several authors have proposed to use the sensitivity of prices to trading activity as a measure of liquidity. In this section we discuss several measures which are based on this intuition.

10.5.1 Trade Indicator Models

Trade indicator models can be interpreted as extensions of the Roll (1984) estimator. To see this, go back to equation (10.8):

$$\Delta P_t = \frac{S}{2}\Delta Q_t + \varepsilon_t^*; \varepsilon_t^* = \varepsilon_t + v_t - v_{t-1} \tag{10.8}$$

In a regression of price changes on the first differences of the trade indicator variable, the slope is (one half of) the Roll measure. However, as noted in section 10.3.2, the Roll measure does not take into account that trades move prices permanently because trades are informative. Trade indicator models extend the Roll model to allow for a perma-nent price impact. We present the Huang and Stoll (1997) trade indicator model here. It assumes that after a transaction the quote midpoint changes by an amount θ in the direction of the trade:

$$M_t = M_{t-1} + \theta Q_{t-1} + \varepsilon_t. \tag{10.18}$$

This specification results in the augmented model:

$$\Delta P_t = \frac{S}{2}\Delta Q_t + \theta Q_{t-1} + \varepsilon_t^*, \tag{10.19}$$

which can be estimated by ordinary least squares (OLS) with HAC standard errors (because of the obvious serial correlation in the error term). Equation (10.19) yields an estimate of the bid–ask spread S and an estimate of the adverse selection cost θ. This model can be further extended. The spread can be modelled as the sum of a transitory component ϕ and the adverse selection component θ. Both components can then be modelled as functions of trade size (Glosten and Harris, 1988). Similarly, predictability in the order flow can be accounted for (Foster and Viswanathan, 1993; Brennan and Subrahmanyam, 1996; Madhavan et al., 1997). The intuition of these approaches is that only unpredicted volume should move prices. Thus, if order flow is predictable, only the unpredicted component should be included in the model.

Estimation of the trade indicator models requires knowledge of the trade indicator variable, Q_t. Thus, to the extent that the trade indicator variable is observed with error, the models will yield biased results.[21]

10.5.2   A Direct Estimate of the Price Impact

The trade indicator models discussed in the previous section essentially decompose the spread into a transitory component and a permanent component. The transitory component ϕ is due to the existence of order processing costs. Transaction prices 'bounce' between the bid and the ask price. The permanent component θ captures the information content of a trade. This is the amount by which suppliers of liquidity revise their expectation of the asset value after observing the trade. Intuitively, then, we can also decompose the spread directly by applying the following procedure:

1. Consider transaction t and record: (a) the effective spread; and (b) whether the transaction is buyer-initiated (in which case $Q_t = +1$) or seller-initiated ($Q_t = -1$).
2. Record the change in the quote midpoint, $\Delta M_{t+\Delta t}$, over the interval Δt after the transaction. The interval should be long enough that the quote midpoint at time $t + \Delta t$ is not affected by the transitory price impact of the transaction.[22]
3. The price impact of the trade is then estimated to be $Q_t \cdot \Delta M_{t+\Delta t}$. It is an estimate of the adverse selection component of the spread.
4. The difference between the effective spread at time t and the price impact is the realized spread for transaction t. It is an estimate of the gross revenue earned by the suppliers of liquidity.

10.5.3   The Amihud (2002) Illiquidity Ratio

In a liquid market the price change in response to a given trading volume will be small; in an illiquid market it will be large. This intuition suggests relating price changes to trading activity. Amihud (2002) has proposed the illiquidity ratio:[23]

$$Illiq_{i,t} = \frac{1}{D_{i,t}} \sum_{t=1}^{D_{i,t}} \frac{|r_{i,t}|}{V_{i,t}}. \tag{10.20}$$

$r_{i,t}$ and $V_{i,t}$ are the return and the dollar trading volume of stock i on day t, respectively, and $D_{i,t}$ is the number of days in the evaluation period (often a month or a year). Only days with non-zero volume are included.

The illiquidity ratio has several advantages. It has low data requirements, it is easy to calculate, and it has a theoretical foundation based on Kyle (1985). Therefore it has become very popular and is widely used. However, the measure also has its drawbacks.[24] Most importantly, it is unable to differentiate between price changes that are related to new information and those that are not. Every event that causes a large price change (such as a merger announcement) is taken as evidence of illiquidity. Goyenko et al. (2009) and Johann and Theissen (2013) run horse races of different liquidity proxies and include the illiquidity ratio in their analysis. They conclude that the measure captures the price impact of trades reasonably well but is 'not appropriate' (Goyenko et al., 2009, p. 179) to use as proxy for effective or realized spreads.

Acharya and Pedersen (2005) contend that the illiquidity ratio is not stationary. Its unit of measurement is percentage return per dollar of trading volume. Thus, the measure ignores inflation. This is an important issue in asset pricing studies which typically cover very long sample periods. Acharya and Pedersen (2005, p. 386) propose to solve this problem by scaling the illiquidity ratio. Brennan et al. (2011) analyse the asset pricing implications of the illiquidity ratio in detail. They find that it is reliably priced, but that the pricing is caused by those components of the illiquidity ratio that are related to negative return days.

10.5.4 The Pastor and Stambough (2003) Measure

Pastor and Stambough (2003) propose to run the following regression:

$$(r_{i,t+1} - r_{m,t+1}) = \alpha_i + \beta_i r_{i,t} + \gamma_i Sign(r_{i,t} - r_{m,t}) V_{i,t} + \varepsilon_{i,t} \qquad (10.21)$$

where $r_{i,t}$ is the return of stock i on day t, $r_{m,t}$ is the return on a stock index on day t and $V_{i,t}$ is the dollar trading volume of stock i on day t. The coefficient γ_i measures the sensitivity of a stock's excess return over the index with respect to lagged signed volume. The intuition is as follows. Volume moves prices. However, some of the price change is transitory and will be reversed on the next trading day.[25] The coefficient γ_i measures this reversal and is thus expected to be negative. The less liquid a stock, the higher the temporary price change and the reversal should be. Thus, less liquid stocks should have higher absolute γ_i.

10.6 DISCUSSION

In this chapter we have reviewed the concept of liquidity as well as various approaches to measuring market liquidity. Measures based on intra-daily data on bid and ask quotes and transaction prices (such as the effective spread) provide the most reliable estimates. Results on the low-frequency measures and on the price impact measures discussed in sections 10.4 and 10.5 are ambiguous. Studies aimed at evaluating these measures do not produce a clear ranking. Therefore, researchers may be well advised to use more than one proxy in order to establish the robustness of their results.

Some final words of caution are appropriate. Recent developments in international equity markets may generally impair the validity and reliability of traditional liquidity measures. Trading today is highly-fragmented across different trading venues, and is dominated by high-frequency trading. Many trading systems allow for hidden liquidity, and many markets have adopted 'make/take' fee schedules. We now briefly discuss the potential implications.

If trading is fragmented, liquidity measures based on data from one market do not necessarily capture the overall liquidity of an asset. This is true for traditional measures such as the quoted spread (the market under investigation may not be offering the lowest spread), but it is also true for other measures. Consider the illiquidity ratio as an example and assume it is calculated from NYSE data. The market share of the NYSE in trading NYSE-listed stocks has declined from approximately 80 per cent ten years ago to about 25 per cent in 2010 (Angel et al., 2011). Therefore, the NYSE volume in the denominator of the illiquidity ratio captures 80 per cent of the total volume in 2002, but only 25 per cent ten years later. This may obviously affect the reliability of the measure.

Fragmentation may also lead to the duplication of liquidity. Traders (and high-frequency traders in particular) may submit limit orders to several markets but intend to only trade once. As soon as one of the limit orders is executed the others will be cancelled. Therefore, simply adding up the liquidity across markets is likely to overstate the true liquidity (see van Kervel, 2012). High-frequency traders submit very large numbers of limit orders. Most of these orders are cancelled after a very short time (see Hasbrouck and Saar, 2009). When high-frequency traders collectively withdraw their limit orders, the liquidity in a market may deteriorate within seconds. Liquidity may thus be futile – a fact that became evident during the 2010 'flash crash'.

As noted previously, many exchanges allow for hidden liquidity. When the researcher uses a data set that does not include the hidden liquidity, measures such as the quoted spread or the CRT(V) measure will understate the true liquidity. This does not apply to the effective spread as its calculation is based on actual transaction prices.

Some exchanges use a split fee schedule where market order traders (liquidity 'takers') pay a large fee while limit order traders (liquidity 'makers') pay a negative fee (i.e., they receive a rebate).[26] In equilibrium, the quoted spread will reflect the rebate and will thus be lower than in markets without a split fee structure (see Foucault et al., 2013; Colliard and Foucault, 2011; Malinova and Parks, 2011). Consequently, the quoted spread in a market with a make/take fee structure understates the true execution costs of a market order trader. Similarly, estimates of the realized spread earned by the suppliers of liquidity will fail to capture the rebate they receive.

NOTES

1. See the survey by Amihud and Mendelson (2008).
2. Traditionally, resiliency was defined as the time prices take to recover (i.e., to return to their equilibrium levels) after a shock (e.g. Black, 1971; Harris, 1990b). More recently, Foucault et al. (2005) have defined resiliency to be the time it takes until liquidity reverts to its equilibrium level.
3. In an auction market traders can submit limit orders. These orders are stored in the order book. The order book thus represents the demand for, and the supply of, the asset at a point in time.
4. Kempf et al. (2008) model liquidity as a mean-reverting process and use the mean reversion parameter as a measure of resiliency. Gomber et al. (2012) use an intraday event study approach to analyse how quickly liquidity reverts to 'normal' levels after a shock.
5. In many electronic limit order markets, high-frequency traders act as liquidity suppliers. They essentially behave like traditional market makers. See Menkveld (2012).
6. Such models have been developed by (among others) Stoll (1978) and Ho and Stoll (1981). Hansch et al. (1998) test the predictions of these models empirically.
7. See Bagehot (1971). Copeland and Galai (1983) and Glosten and Milgrom (1985), among others, developed formal models of the adverse selection component.
8. The dynamic patterns introduced by the inventory holding and adverse selection components are similar. It is therefore difficult to empirically disentangle the inventory holding and adverse selection components; see Stoll (1989) and Huang and Stoll (1997).

9. This measure has been proposed by Irvine et al. (2000). They called it the 'cost of round trip trade' (CRT).
10. Benveniste et al. (1992) provide an explanation for this behaviour. They argue that the specialist offers better terms of trade to brokers deemed uninformed. Theissen (2003), using data from the Frankfurt Stock Exchange, finds empirical support for this hypothesis.
11. Bernhardt et al. (2005) develop a model which explains the relationship between trade size and the price concessions market makers are willing to make.
12. This measure of the execution cost is one component of the implementation shortfall proposed by Perold (1988). The second component is an estimate of the opportunity cost that may arise when a large order is not fully executed.
13. The minimum tick size is the smallest admissible price increment in a market. Also see section 10.4.3.
14. For a detailed discussion of the statistical properties of the Roll estimator, see Harris (1990a).
15. Recent applications include Bao et al. (2011) and Naes et al. (2011).
16. The data set and program code are available from Joel Hasbrouck's homepage, see http://people.stern. nyu.edu/jhasbrou/Research/GibbsCurrent/gibbsCurrentIndex.html.
17. Holden (2009) explicitly assumes that traders agree on a price grid (e.g. pennies, nickels, dimes or quarters) and that the effective spread on a particular day is the increment of that price grid.
18. Holden (2009) also constructs combined estimators which are a linear combination of the effective tick and the Roll estimators.
19. This idea is reminiscent of the market efficiency coefficient (MEC) proposed by Hasbrouck and Schwartz (1988). The MEC is simply the ratio of a stock's return variance measured over a long interval divided by T times the return variance over a short interval. T is the length of the long interval divided by the length of the short interval. The MEC is expected to be smaller than one, and to decrease in the illiquidity of a stock.
20. In a call auction, buy and sell orders are collected over a period of time. They are then aggregated to a demand and a supply schedule. The intersection of these schedules determines the market clearing price. The call auction procedure thus results in a multilateral transaction (rather than a series of bilateral transactions as in a continuous trading mechanism).
21. See the brief discussion above in section 10.3.1.
22. A common choice is five minutes. The results are typically not very sensitive to the choice of the interval length; see Huang and Stoll (1996) for an example.
23. Similar measures have been proposed earlier. For example, Cooper et al. (1985) used the Amivest ratio which is defined as the sum of daily volume divided by the sum of absolute returns.
24. Grossman and Miller (1988) discuss the suitability of the Amivest ratio. Their arguments also apply to the illiquidity ratio.
25. Pastor and Stambough (2003) implicitly assume that aggregate order flow has a transitory price impact that shows up in daily returns and is reversed the next day. The trade indicator models discussed in section 10.5.1 and the price impact measure presented in section 10.5.2 consider the price impact at the level of individual transactions and implicitly assume that the transitory price impact is very short-lived.
26. Angel et al. (2011) discuss some regulatory implications of make/take fee structures.

REFERENCES

Acharya, V. and L.H. Pedersen (2005), 'Asset pricing with liquidity risk', *Journal of Financial Economics*, **77**, 375–410.
Amihud, Y. (2002), 'Illiquidity and stock returns: cross-section and time-series effects', *Journal of Financial Markets*, **5**, 31–56.
Amihud, Y. and H. Mendelson (1986), 'Asset pricing and the bid–ask spread', *Journal of Financial Economics*, **17**, 223–249.
Amihud, Y. and H. Mendelson (2008), 'Liquidity, the value of the firm, and corporate finance', *Journal of Applied Corporate Finance*, **20**, 32–45.
Angel, J., L. Harris and C. Spatt (2011), 'Equity trading in the 21st century', *Quarterly Journal of Finance*, **1**, 1–53.
Bagehot, W. (1971), 'The only game in town', *Financial Analysts Journal*, **27**, 12–14 and 22.
Bao, J., J. Pan and J. Wang (2011), 'The illiquidity of corporate bonds', *Journal of Finance*, **66**, 911–946.
Benveniste, L., A. Marcus and W. Wilhelm (1992), 'What's special about the specialist?', *Journal of Financial Economics*, **32**, 61–86.
Bernhardt, D., V. Dvoracek, E. Hughson and I. Werner (2005), 'Why do larger orders receive discounts on the London Stock Exchange?', *Review of Financial Studies*, **18**, 1343–1368.

Black, F. (1971), 'Toward a fully automated stock exchange', *Financial Analysts Journal*, **27**, 28–44.

Brennan, M., S.-W. Huh and A. Subrahmanyam (2011), 'An analysis of the Amihud liquidity premium', working paper, June.

Brennan, M. and A. Subrahmanyam (1996), 'Market microstructure and asset pricing: on the compensation for illiquidity in stock returns', *Journal of Financial Economics*, **41**, 441–464.

Brunnermeier, M. and L.H. Pedersen (2009), 'Market liquidity and funding liquidity', *Review of Financial Studies*, **22**, 2201–2238.

Colliard, J.-E. and T. Foucault (2011), 'Trading fees and efficiency in limit order markets', CEPR Discussion Paper, No. 8395, May.

Cooper, K., J. Groth and W. Avera (1985), 'Liquidity, exchange listing, and common stock performance', *Journal of Economics and Business*, **37**, 19–33.

Copeland, T. and D. Galai (1983), 'Information effects on the bid–ask spread', *Journal of Finance*, **38**, 1457–1469.

Corwin, S. and P. Schultz (2009), 'An application of the high-low spread estimator to daily event studies: stock splits from 1926–1982', working paper, February.

Corwin, S. and P. Schultz (2012), 'A simple way to estimate bid–ask spreads from daily high and low prices', *Journal of Finance*, **67**, 719–760.

Ellis, K., R. Michaely and M. O'Hara (1999), 'The accuracy of trade classification rules: evidence from NASDAQ', *Journal of Financial and Quantitative Analysis*, **35**, 529–551.

Engle, R. and J. Lange (2001), 'Predicting VNET: a model of the dynamics of market depth', *Journal of Financial Markets*, **4**, 113–142.

Fong, K., C. Holden and C. Trzcinka (2011), 'What are the best liquidity proxies for global research?', working paper, July.

Foster, D. and S. Viswanathan (1993), 'Variations in trading volume, return volatility, and trading costs: evidence on recent price formation models', *Journal of Finance*, **48**, 187–211.

Foucault, T., O. Kadan and E. Kandel (2005), 'Limit order book as a market for liquidity', *Review of Financial Studies*, **18**, 1171–1217.

Foucault, T., O. Kadan and E. Kandel (2013), 'Liquidity cycles and make/take fees in electronic markets', *Journal of Finance*, **68**, 299–341.

Glosten, L. and L. Harris (1988), 'Estimating the components of the bid-ask spread', *Journal of Financial Economics*, **21**, 123–142.

Glosten, L. and P. Milgrom (1985), 'Bid, ask and transaction prices in a specialist market with heterogeneously informed traders', *Journal of Financial Economics*, **14**, 71–100.

Gomber, P., U. Schweickert and E. Theissen (2012), 'Liquidity dynamics in an electronic open limit order book: an event study approach', working paper.

Goyenko, R., C. Holden and C. Trzcinka (2009), 'Do liquidity measures measure liquidity?', *Journal of Financial Economics*, **92**, 153–181.

Grossman, S. and M. Miller (1988), 'Liquidity and market structure', *Journal of Finance*, **43**, 617–627.

Hansch, O., N. Naik and S. Viswanathan (1998), 'Do inventories matter in dealership markets? Evidence from the London Stock Exchange', *Journal of Finance*, **53**, 1623–1656.

Harris, L. (1990a), 'Statistical properties of the Roll serial covariance bid-ask spread estimator', *Journal of Finance*, **45**, 579–590.

Harris, L. (1990b), 'Liquidity, trading rules, and electronic trading systems', NYU Salomon Center Monograph Series in Finance and Economics, 1990–4.

Harris, L. (1991), 'Stock price clustering and discreteness', *Review of Financial Studies*, **4**, 389–415.

Hasbrouck, J. (2009), 'Trading costs and returns for US equities: estimating effective costs from daily data', *Journal of Finance*, **64**, 1445–1477.

Hasbrouck, J. and G. Saar (2009), 'Technology and liquidity provision: the blurring of traditional definitions', *Journal of Financial Markets*, **12**, 143–172.

Hasbrouck, J. and R. Schwartz (1988), 'Liquidity and execution costs in equity markets', *Journal of Portfolio Management*, Spring, 10–16.

Ho, T. and H. Stoll (1981), 'Optimal dealer pricing under transactions and return uncertainty', *Journal of Financial Economics*, **9**, 47–73.

Holden, C. (2009), 'New low-frequency spread measures', *Journal of Financial Markets*, **12**, 778–813.

Huang, R. and H. Stoll (1996), 'Dealer versus auction markets: a paired comparison of execution costs on NASDAQ and the NYSE', *Journal of Financial Economics*, **41**, 313–357.

Huang, R. and H. Stoll (1997), 'The components of the bid-ask spread: a general approach', *Review of Financial Studies*, **10**, 995–1034.

Irvine, P., G. Benston and E. Kandel (2000), 'Liquidity beyond the inside spread: measuring and using information in the order book', working paper, July.

Johann, T. and E. Theissen (2013), 'A comprehensive evaluation of alternative low-frequency bid–ask spread estimators', working paper, March.

Kempf, A., D. Mayston and P. Yadav (2008), 'Resiliency in limit order book markets', working paper.

Kyle, A. (1985), 'Continuous auctions and insider trading', *Econometrica*, **53**, 1315–1336.

Lee, Ch. and M. Ready (1991), 'Inferring trade direction from intraday data', *Journal of Finance*, **46**, 733–746.

Lesmond, D., J. Ogden and C. Trzcinka (1999), 'A new estimate of transaction costs', *Review of Financial Studies*, **12**, 1113–1141.

Madhavan, A., M. Richardson and M. Roomans (1997), 'Why do securities prices change? A transaction-level analysis of NYSE stocks', *Review of Financial Studies*, **10**, 1035–1064.

Malinova, K. and A. Parks (2011), 'Subsidizing liquidity: the impact of make/take fees on market quality', working paper, April.

Menkveld, A. (2012), 'High frequency trading and the new-market makers', working paper, February.

Naes, R., J. Skjeltorp and B.A. Odegaard (2011), 'Stock market liquidity and the business cycle', *Journal of Finance*, **66**, 139–176.

Odders-White, E. (2000), 'On the occurrence and consequences of inaccurate trade classification', *Journal of Financial Markets*, **3**, 259–286.

Pastor, L. and R. Stambough (2003), 'Liquidity risk and expected stock returns', *Journal of Political Economy*, **111**, 642–685.

Perold, A. (1988), 'The implementation shortfall: paper versus reality', *Journal of Portfolio Management*, **14** (Spring), 4–9.

Roll, R. (1984), 'A simple implicit measure of the bid/ask spread in an efficient market', *Journal of Finance*, **39**, 1127–1139.

Stoll, H. (1978), 'The supply of dealer services in securities markets', *Journal of Finance*, **33**, 1133–1151.

Stoll, H. (1989), 'Inferring the components of the bid-ask spread: theory and empirical tests', *Journal of Finance*, **44**, 115–134.

Theissen, E. (2003), 'Trader anonymity, price formation and liquidity', *European Finance Review*, **7**, 1–26.

van Kervel, V. (2012), 'Liquidity: what you see is what you get?', working paper, March.

11 Testing for contagion: the impact of US structured markets on international financial markets

Woon Sau Leung and Nicholas Taylor

11.1 INTRODUCTION

The United States (US) subprime crisis, driven by the decline in US house prices and the subsequent threats of mortgage defaults, has had a significant (negative) impact on financial markets. From 2006 onwards, threats of US mortgage loan defaults heightened and prices of collateralized asset-backed securities (ABS) containing subprime mortgages and collateralized debt obligations (CDO) tumbled, all of which resulted in an almost complete halt in trading and disruption in the normal price discovery process. Furthermore, financial markets suffered from significant recessionary expectations as both market and funding liquidity shrunk within the financial system. Caruana and Kodres (2008) point out that the average maturity of US short-term asset-backed commercial paper (ABCP) shortened by six days with outstanding ABCP declines amounting to approximately $300 billion from August 2007 onwards. As the liquidity of both money markets and structured credit markets withered, the ability of banking institutions to raise external funds was severely impaired. Meanwhile, the level of interbank lending also declined as evidenced by the widening of LIBOR overnight index swap spreads. These national effects evolved into a global (and catastrophic) context, and was followed by a series of collapses and bailouts of renowned financial institutions, most notably, Lehman Brothers, Merrill Lynch, Washington Mutual, AIG, Fannie Mae and Freddie Mac. All of these effects led to a prolonged period of global economic recession characterized by frequent injections of liquidity and rescue actions by central banks and government authorities.

Longstaff's (2010) work is among the first papers to study the subprime crisis. He finds evidence of significant increases in cross-market linkages between the less liquid US subprime CDO market and a number of US financial markets. However, his paper is limited to examining spillover effects within the US domestic financial system, and does not consider cross-country contagious effects. There are a number of reasons that support the contention of cross-country contagion during the subprime crisis from the US structured markets to international financial markets. Firstly, financial institutions with their subprime portfolios written down are of significant size and are characterized by extensive cross-market functionality. The absorption of distressed subprime ABS portfolios into their balance sheets raised widespread concern on the insolvency of these institutions resulting in possible systematic changes in risk premia across economies. Investors, anticipating shock spillovers, might divert their investments from distressed sectors to Treasury markets giving rise to cross-market asset co-movement. Secondly, extreme market illiquidity in the US structured market reinforces lenders' desire to tighten their credit giving rise to severe funding illiquidity in a number of economies. Market makers and institutional investors, who faced higher funding costs, were unable to provide sufficient liquidity to the market leading to surging market illiquidity risks in a number of financial markets (Brunnermeier and Pedersen, 2009). Thirdly, hedge funds and professional investors with levered positions might be forced to liquidate assets in unaffected markets to meet margin calls and contingent liabilities while their ABS portfolio collateral values tumbled.[1] All these exert enormous downward pressures and signal pessimistic economic sentiments to various international markets suggesting possible spillover effects from the US structured market, and motivate this chapter.

This chapter is an empirical investigation into spillover effects from the US structured market to equity and bond markets in the G5 countries during the US subprime crisis. The US structured market in our chapter refers specifically to the US subprime residential CDO market and is regarded as the origin of contagion during the crisis. The G5 countries comprise the US, United Kingdom (UK), France, Germany and Japan, and represent a subset of global developed economies. Similar to the methodologies adopted by Longstaff (2010), we employ a vector autoregressive (VAR) framework and use lagged returns of the ABX indices as exogenous variables to test for any predictive power (Granger causality) over the returns of the international equity and bond markets. In other words, we test whether lagged returns of the ABX index can jointly explain the returns in these financial markets after accounting for possible interdependence between our sample countries during normal market conditions. We also evaluate the validity of contagion transmission mechanisms using liquidity, credit risk and implied correlation variables.

To anticipate some of the results, we identify significant spillover effects in a number of international financial markets that include the US equity and government bond markets, UK equity markets, French equity and government bond markets, German government bond markets, and Japanese equity markets during the US subprime crisis. This is evidenced by significant increases in the predictive power of the ABX returns over the subsequent weekly returns of our international markets during the crisis subperiod. In other words, the cross-market linkages increased substantially suggesting the possible existence of contagious effects during the crisis. We also find that ABX shocks have led to subsequent declines in equity market returns and increases in government bond market returns consistent with a possible flight-to-quality from stocks to bonds. The second part of our analysis shows that ABX index returns have significant predictive power over liquidity ratios in the US and Germany, interest rate swap spreads (IRSS) in the US, UK and Germany, and implied correlations (between domestic financial equity and government bond markets) in the US, UK and Germany. In particular, the widening of interest rate swap spreads during the crisis period, which reflects increases in the levels of credit and market illiquidity risks, can be significantly predicted by the ABX returns. In addition, higher trading intensity in the financial sectors relative to the broader markets are found to be associated with ABX returns. Besides, the negative time-varying implied correlation estimated using the MGARCH diagonal VECH specification model supports the existence of flights between financial stocks and government bonds in our sample countries. However, our findings reveal that a negative shock to the US subprime CDO market led to higher co-movement between financial stock and government bond returns in the US and UK, but lower co-movement in Germany. In other words, our findings suggest that the shock from the US structured market during the crisis might have lessened the extent of flight-to-quality between financial stocks and government bonds in the US and UK, but encouraged flights in the German market.

Our chapter makes a number of contributions to the body of knowledge. Firstly, we offer a detailed literature review on the major contagion transmission channels and distinguish between funding and market liquidity. Secondly, we contribute to the contagion literature by providing empirical evidence of cross-country contagion from the US structured market to five developed markets during the US subprime crisis. Thirdly, we test for the validity of the contagion transmission channel and, in particular, we lend support to the risk premia channel and the funding liquidity channel. Finally, we also contribute to the flight-to-quality literature and shed light on the dynamics of flights between financial equity and government bond markets during the subprime crisis.

The remainder of this chapter is organized as follows: section 11.2 reviews the contagion literature and develops our hypotheses; section 11.3 offers a brief overview of the causes of the US subprime mortgage crisis as well as its financial impacts on our sample of countries; section 11.4 introduces the US subprime CDO (ABX) indices; section 11.5 explicates our methodological framework; section 11.6 describes and explains our data; section 11.7 presents and discusses the empirical findings; section 11.8 examines the contagion transmission channels; and section 11.9 concludes.

11.2   WHAT IS CONTAGION?

In the literature, there is widespread disagreement about the definition of contagion. In a review by Pericoli and Sbracia (2003), at least five working definitions of contagion are summarized. These working definitions correspond with particular sets of methodologies that address specific sets of research questions. Some researchers define contagion as a significant increase in the probability of a crisis conditional on a crisis occurring in another country (Eichengreen et al., 1996), while some study the co-movement of assets prices (e.g. Dornbusch et al., 2000; Forbes and Rigobon, 2002) or returns volatilities (e.g. Park and Song, 1999; Edwards, 1998) between markets. Forbes and Rigobon (2002) point out the importance of distinguishing between normal market interdependence and contagion, and establish a more stringent definition of contagion.[2] Kaminsky et al. (2003) contend that contagious effects are 'fast and furious' and that gradual effects of shock propagation are not contagion but spillover effects.[3]

This chapter aims to detect any significant increases in cross-market linkages between the US structured market and our sample international markets during the subprime crisis, and hence, should relate and contribute to the market co-movement contagion literature. Similar to Forbes and Rigobon (2002), we define contagion as a significant increase in market co-movement conditional on a crisis event in another market. However, instead of measuring the correlations between the market returns directly, we examine the dependencies between lagged returns of the ABX index (which tracks the performance of the US subprime CDO market) and equity and government bond indices in the G5 countries to identify any significant increases in cross-market linkages. We control for interdependence between markets during normal market conditions by splitting the sample period into pre-crisis and crisis periods. Our definition relaxes the restriction by Kaminsky et al. (2003), who contend that contagious effects have to be 'fast and furious', and allows any possible contagious effects to transmit within weeks.[4]

11.2.1 Hypotheses

The first part of our analysis seeks to identify any increases in cross-market linkages via examining the dependencies between the US subprime CDO market and other financial markets before, during, and after the crisis period. Our first hypothesis can be written as:

H_0^1: There are significant increases in the predictive power of the US subprime CDO market returns (tracked by the ABX indices) over the equity and government bond returns in our sample of countries during the subprime crisis.

Prior to the crisis period, the explanatory power of the ABX index returns reflects the level of interdependence between the US structured market and the international markets in normal pre-crisis times. This pre-crisis window allows us to distinguish spillover effects from interdependence as a result of market integration. If shocks spill over from the US subprime CDO market to these markets during the crisis, then we shall expect to find substantial increases in the predictive power of the ABX index returns in the crisis subperiod only. We also include the after-crisis subperiod in our analysis and test whether the continual market declines from 2008 onwards are associated with the shocks from the US structured market or not.

On the theoretical side, there are a number of studies that explain how contagion may transmit from one market to another. These studies are of fundamental importance to understanding the dynamics of shock spillovers. A review of a few well-documented transmission mechanisms along with our hypotheses are provided below.

11.2.2 The Information Transmission Channel

The information transmission channel refers to the mechanism by which a shocked market may signal new market information that affects the prices in other markets. Kaminsky et al. (2003) contend that shocks transmit through the arrival of negative economic news that immediately affects the collateral values in other markets. King and Wadhwani (1990) present a rational expectation price equilibrium model that explains contagion as the result of market agents' attempts to infer equity values based on imperfect information about certain events. Their model implies that idiosyncratic changes in one market may affect other markets as a result of information asymmetries and result in subsequent co-movement of market volatilities. This information transmission mechanism relates closely to the efficient market hypothesis (EMH), which asserts that prices in efficient markets absorb new market information rapidly. In this sense, shocks transmitted via the information transmission should be 'fast and furious' (Kaminsky et al., 2003) with instantaneous adverse market co-movement.

This chapter examines the dependencies between returns of the US structured market and international markets using weekly data and hence does not directly test for the validity of the information transmission channel. Under our current research settings, we aim to identify cross-market contagious effects that took place and culminated over weeks.

In the cases in which we have identified contagious effects over a weekly frequency, we do not rule out the possibility that there was simultaneous information-transmitted contagion that evolved over a matter of hours and minutes (or 'fast and furious').

11.2.3   The Liquidity Transmission Channel

This liquidity transmission channel refers to the mechanism by which a shock in one market leads to a subsequent shrinkage of liquidity in other markets. In the literature, liquidity can be further defined as funding liquidity, which is the ability to fund any solvent agent to fulfil their immediate demand for money, and market liquidity, which refers to the ease by which an asset position can be sold in financial markets. Recent works have considered market illiquidity as a systematic risk factor within an asset pricing context (e.g. Amihud, 2002; Acharya and Pedersen, 2005) and have found significant relationships between market illiquidity and stock expected returns. It is therefore reasonable to review the market liquidity channel within the context of risk premia transmission.

The contagion transmission mechanism with regard to funding liquidity refers to the situation where institutional investors or mutual funds liquidate their assets to raise additional funds to account for future fund redemptions or contingent liabilities during adverse market conditions. Levered hedge funds may be obliged to liquidate assets in unaffected markets to meet margin calls, which in turn transmit shocks to other financial markets (Calvo, 2000; Kodres and Pritsker, 2002). Allen and Gale (2000) present a model that focuses on the role of banking systems in contagion transmission. The authors contend that financial shocks cause banks to liquidate cross-holding deposits across regions causing severe cross-market funding illiquidity and asset co-movement. Similarly, Kaminsky and Reinhart (2000) also point out that in tranquil markets banks may tighten credit lines for prudence motives and rebalance their overall risk exposure in anticipation of shocks. The main implication of these studies is that funding illiquidity may induce substantial increases in the amount of liquidations and short positions of assets as shown by higher trading volumes during the crisis. Our chapter tests whether lagged US subprime CDO market returns might predict the level of trading intensity in the equity markets in the G5 countries. Our second hypothesis is formulated as follows:

H_0^2:   There are significant increases in the predictive power of the US subprime CDO market returns for the level of trading intensity in domestic equity markets (measured by the liquidity ratios: the aggregate trading volume in market value of a financial equity index to the aggregate trading volume in market value of a broader equity index) during the crisis period.

The studies reviewed reflect the important role of funding liquidity in cross-market financial stability and lend theoretical justification to the injection of funding liquidity by authorities to contain the crises.

11.2.4   The Risk Premia Transmission Channel

The risk premia transmission channel refers to the co-movements of asset prices that occur as a result of changes in risk premia after a shock hits a market. For instance, an idiosyncratic shock to one market leads to subsequent increases in the risk premia expected by investors in other markets.

Recent papers by Amihud (2002) and Acharya and Pedersen (2005) have documented the significant roles of aggregate and idiosyncratic illiquidity in asset pricing. Their findings suggest time variation in market illiquidity risk premia and evidence of a flight-to-liquidity. Longstaff (2004) finds significant liquidity premia in the yield spreads between the more liquid US Treasury bonds over the Refcorp bonds, suggesting some market liquidity components in the Treasury bonds. Liu et al. (2006) also find significant time-varying liquidity premia in US Treasury bonds over the period from 1988 to 2002. These empirical studies have shown that investors have certain liquidity preferences and that the flight-to-quality phenomenon might be driven by liquidity apart from credit risk considerations. This channel suggests that shocks are transmitted via changes in market illiquidity risk premia that lead to subsequent flights to liquid assets and changes in trading patterns. Besides, funding and market illiquidity might be closely related. Brunnermeier and Pedersen (2009) present a model that studies the relationship between funding and market illiquidity. The authors contend that traders' funding illiquidity leads to higher transaction costs and thus higher market. Such an increase in perceived risks in financing trades then leads to higher volatility and results in cross-market asset co-movement and volatility spillovers.

Another well-documented set of risk premia are those for credit risk that compensate for default and counterparty risks. Vassalou and Xing (2004) find that equity credit risk premia are systematic and could significantly explain expected stock returns. Eichengreen et al. (2009) examine the common factors that drive the credit default swap spreads of major banks and find increasing importance for these factors during the subprime crisis. In particular, these factors are found to be associated with heightening credit risks within the US banking industry. These studies suggest possible time variation in the credit risk premia in equity markets, especially in the financial equity sectors. Moreover, the credit risk premia might have increased significantly during extreme market conditions. These higher credit risk premia may then lead to portfolio rebalancing and encourage risk-averse investors to move to less risky assets. Our study shall examine the validity of this risk premia transmission channel via testing of the following hypothesis:

H_0^3:   The level of credit and market illiquidity risks can be predicted by the US subprime CDO market returns during the subprime crisis period.

Significant increases in the predictive power of ABX index returns over the level of credit and market illiquidity risks (measured by IRSS) suggest evidence of shock spillovers via the risk premia transmission channel.

11.2.5   The Flight-to-Quality Phenomenon

A number of empirical studies examine the 'flight-to-quality' phenomenon in which investors switch from equity to bond markets during crises in order to reduce their risk exposures (e.g. De Goeij and Marquering, 2004; Baur and Lucey, 2009). Despite the fact that both directions of flights between stocks and bonds have been identified empirically, the 'flight-to-quality' phenomenon is consistent with the risk premia transmission channel in that an increase in the equilibrium risk premia in stock markets (for instance, as a result of market illiquidity or shifts in expectations) may induce risk-averse investors to pursue safer fixed-income investments. Our study investigates how the US subprime CDO market returns may predict the level of co-movement between financial equity sectors and government bond markets. Our hypothesis can be described as:

H_0^4:   The implied correlations (between the returns of domestic financial stocks and government bonds) are predicted by the US subprime CDO market returns during the subprime crisis period.

In the next section, we shall review briefly the causes of the US subprime crisis and examine its financial impact on our sample of countries.

11.3   BRIEF OVERVIEW OF THE US SUBPRIME MORTGAGE CRISIS

During the 1990s, a number of regulations and policies (e.g. the Financial Institutions Reform, Recovery and Enforcement Act, FIRREA; the Federal Deposit Insurance Corporation Improvement Act, FDICIA; and the Community Reinvestment Act) were enacted in an attempt to boost the declining mortgage loan and housing markets (see discussions in Lindsey, 2007; Udell, 2009). Since then, the US housing demand increased substantially and supported the consistent growth in housing prices. Loan granting institutions, which were largely under-regulated, accepted lower yields and gradually loosened their lending standards. These loans with poorer credit quality refer to those Alt-A and subprime mortgages and were marketed as new 'innovations' with features resembling prime mortgages (Weaver, 2008). Driven by rising housing markets and ever-easier credit, many new entrants came to the subprime loan markets. During the four years between 2001 and 2005, the number of subprime mortgage loans issued increased by about 450 per cent from approximately 624 000 to 3 440 000. Average subprime loan values increased by 72 per cent from $151 000 in 2001 to $259 000 in 2006. Moreover, the total value of subprime loans outstanding has risen by more than 700 per cent from $94 billion in 2001 to $685 billion in 2006 (Swan, 2009). The overcapacity of these subprime loans led to irrational competition and further deterioration in credit standards. In addition, the issuance of subprime mortgage loans in recent years tended to concentrate on a product called an adjustable-rate mortgage (ARM) (Deutsche Bank, cited in Weaver, 2008), which carries a fixed rate for some years and then resets to prevailing market rates thereafter. These mortgage loans were initiated at attractive fixed rates when the interest rates were flat and low, but were putting borrowers in a position exposed to interest rate risks. Borrowers may face payment shocks and possibly default on their mortgages at the time mortgage rates are reset. In short, the subprime mortgage markets were essentially fragile to any housing demand shocks as weak borrowers were barely able to repay their loans and relied heavily on house sales for loan financing.

One major complication of the current subprime mortgage crisis concerns the process of securitization. To securitize means packaging cash flows from fixed income securities as collateral and selling these cash flows to underwriter companies for the issuance of new securities. The process allows mortgage issuers to acquire immediate liquidity and make profits while transferring (almost all) the loan risk exposure to other parties. Facing strong demand and high profitability, issuers are incentivized to generate as much loan volume as possible regardless of the borrowers' credit quality. Underwriter companies then pool these loans and sell them to trusts, which then issue mortgage-backed securities (MBS) in various tranches and eventually market them to investors. From the underwriters' perspective, the financial risks of the mortgage loans are eliminated shortly after the MBS are sold (Udell, 2009). Therefore, underwriters are prone to issue large volumes of MBS regardless of the underlying collateral credit quality. Consequently, the MBS markets expanded rapidly with an increasing proportion of securitization and ever-deteriorating credit quality.[5] In addition, one important aspect of the subprime loans securitization with regard to the crisis refers to the extensive use of subprime subordinated MBS as collateral in CDO issuance, driven by the attractive ratings (Weaver, 2008). Under incorrect actuarial assumptions, rating agencies largely overlooked the high correlation between various subordinated MBS and allowed those mezzanine bonds of low credit quality to be pooled into new AAA-rated CDO bonds, which were then sold to investors as low-risk fixed-income products. A number of international financial institutions, assured that the AAA rating provided sufficient protection, held a large amount of such subprime CDO portfolios. Any failure in the US subprime mortgage markets would affect not only the US mortgage markets, but also a number of international markets.

The rise in US house prices appreciation began to slow down from 2006, with prices falling from mid-2007 onwards (Federal Housing Finance Agency, 2008). Lenders tightened lending standards, foreseeing a higher probability of mortgage defaults while home appraisers' assessments also became more restrictive. The subsequent increases in mortgage rates, as a result of the housing downward spiral, led to payment shocks that threatened a number of ARM borrowers. The buy-side of MBS markets almost disappeared in an instant and the subprime MBS prices declined sharply. The valuation of subprime CDOs was extremely difficult due to the high uncertainty with regard to the value of their collateral (i.e., the subordinated subprime MBS). While most of these subprime portfolios were held in off-balance sheet structured investment vehicles (SIVs), financial institutions were under pressure to rescue their investments by providing liquidity and absorbing these structured conduits onto their balance sheets. Therefore, a number of financial institutions with exposure to these toxic assets suffered from huge losses and substantial write-offs. Meanwhile, facing heightened insolvency risks, banking institutions further restricted their credit and interbank lending, resulting in a global shortage of funding liquidity. In the third quarter of 2008, suffering from the continuing losses from the subprime mortgage related business, Lehman Brothers, one of the largest investment banks in the world, filed for chapter 11 bankruptcy and was the largest bankruptcy filing in history. A number of institutions, such as AIG, Washington Mutual Inc., Wachovia Corp., Merril Lynch, Fannie Mae and Freddie Mac were bailed out or taken over.

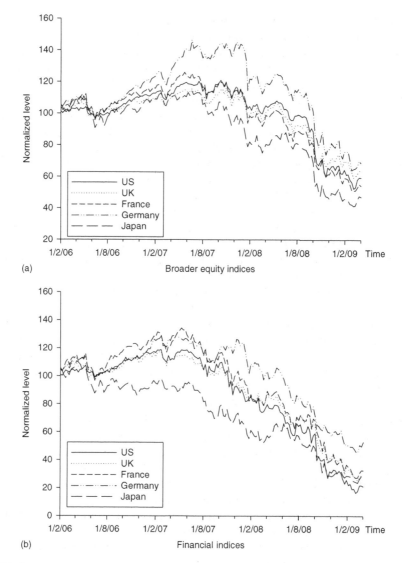

Note: This figure provides time series plots of broader equity indices, financial indices, government bond indices, and ABX indices for the G5 countries.

Source: Reuters and Datastream; normalized at initial level of 100 – authors' calculations.

Figure 11.1   Financial market performance

11.3.1   The Impacts on the Financial Markets of the G5 Countries

The financial consequences of the subprime crisis were devastating and prolonged and these shocks seemed to spill over to a number of international financial markets. Normalized at an initial level of 100, Figures 11.1(a) and 11.1(b) plot the broader equity

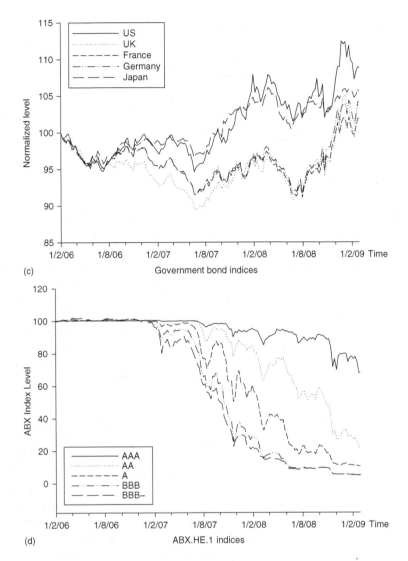

Figure 11.1   (continued)

and financial equity indices respectively, of our sample countries, the US, UK, France, Germany and Japan. The patterns of movement in the broader equity markets were largely identical. Although the German equity market outperformed the others over most of the sample period, all equity markets started to decline in late 2007 and fell dramatically from the third quarter of 2008 onwards. After Lehman Brothers' bankruptcy filing, all equity markets continued the downward trend and entered a period of distress that lasted about six months. Looking at the financial indices, we observe qualitatively similar patterns of price movements but with a higher magnitude of declines.

Figure 11.1(c) plots the government bond clean price indices for our sample countries. Year 2006 represents largely a period of stability for the government bond markets characterized by low volatility. The indices started to decline in the first half of 2007 and were then followed by steady growth from the third quarter of 2007 onwards. We find two distinctive patterns of movements in the government bond markets characterized by the US and Japanese markets as one group, and the rest of the countries as another group. The US and Japanese government bond markets outperformed the rest of the countries for most of our sample period. Our observation of the upward rising government bond markets in the second half of 2007 provides support for possible flight-to-quality between equities and government bond markets during the crisis.

11.4   THE ABX INDICES

Similar to Longstaff (2010), we use returns of the ABX indices to track the performance of the US subprime structured market. The ABX indices are equally weighted, static portfolios that reference 20 subprime home equity CDO transactions. Every six months, the ABX series are reconstituted with new on-the-run index vintages referencing 20 new subprime CDO transactions issued during the six months prior to the index initiation. There are five subindices of various ratings within the ABX family corresponding to AAA, AA, A, BBB and BBB- credit ratings of the underlying CDO deals. The AAA. HE.1 index is the first vintage and was followed by the ABX.HE.2 index formed in July 2006, while the ABX.HE.3 and ABX.HE.4 indices were issued in January 2007 and July 2007, respectively. Subprime home equity CDO issuance declined dramatically during the crisis and no more ABX indices were formed. The ABX.HE.4 index remained the on-the-run ABX index until the end of our sample period.[6]

This study uses the weekly lagged returns (based on quotes on Wednesdays) of the ABX.HE.1 index (the first vintage of the ABX index) as exogenous variables in our VAR system as it spans the longest period among the available ABX vintages and largely covers the entire subprime crisis. Figure 11.1(d) plots the ABX.HE.1 series from February 2006 to March 2009. All five subindices were in general close to their par value of $100 in 2006 and started to decline in 2007. In particular, the three lowest-rated subindices fell dramatically starting from the second quarter in 2007 and reached their troughs in 2009. The figure shows that the subprime crisis had more devastating effects on lower-rated CDO than the higher-rated ones. Table 11.1 summarizes the descriptive statistics for the log first difference of the ABX.HE.1 series. In the pre-crisis subperiod, the mean returns of the ABX indices were all positive and became negative in the crisis and post-crisis subperiods. The negative mean returns were largest for the BBB and BBB- subindices during the crisis subperiod. In addition, the standard deviations of all indices were significantly higher during and after the crisis. Throughout the entire sample period, the correlation between the returns of the AAA and AA indices was high while the returns of the A, BBB and BBB- indices were also highly correlated.

There are a few precautionary notes to make with regard to using lagged returns of the ABX.HE.1 index as exogenous variables in our analysis. First of all, each of the four vintages of ABX indices (the ABX HE.1, ABX HE.2, ABX HE.3 and ABX HE.4) are in fact only small subsets of the universe of subprime CDO products and hence are limited in market coverage. In addition, for each MBS deal tracked, only part of the capital structure is referenced by the five tranches of the ABX indices (Fender and Scheicher,

Table 11.1   Data description: the ABX indices

Year	Rating	Mean	Std. Dev.	Min.	Max.	Correlation				
						AAA	AA	A	BBB	BBB-
2006	AAA	0.003	0.02	−0.03	0.09	1.00				
	AA	0.012	0.04	−0.11	0.13	0.30	1.00			
	A	0.005	0.07	−0.23	0.15	0.41	0.66	1.00		
	BBB	0.009	0.20	−0.41	0.46	0.42	0.52	0.71	1.00	
	BBB-	0.011	0.31	−0.68	0.59	0.35	0.58	0.70	0.84	1.00
2007	AAA	−0.14	1.10	−5.28	3.78	1.00				
	AA	−0.33	2.41	−10.23	6.89	0.86	1.00			
	A	−0.95	6.21	−22.20	21.69	0.57	0.80	1.00		
	BBB	−2.10	8.38	−39.97	19.37	0.72	0.72	0.88	1.00	
	BBB-	−2.38	7.12	−31.65	15.07	0.68	0.69	0.74	0.93	1.00
2008–09	AAA	−0.51	3.72	−16.17	11.52	1.00				
	AA	−2.17	7.28	−30.58	10.95	0.86	1.00			
	A	−2.85	8.71	−21.27	19.17	0.54	0.73	1.00		
	BBB	−3.10	7.68	−25.73	8.32	0.49	0.59	0.74	1.00	
	BBB-	−2.89	7.04	−26.89	5.42	0.48	0.57	0.66	0.90	1.00

Notes: This table contains a descriptive summary of the weekly returns (based on Wednesday quotes) of the five ABX subindices. The summary is presented according to the three sample subperiods: Year 2006 (48 observations, from 1 February 2006 to 27 December 2006) refers to the tranquil pre-crisis subperiod; Year 2007 (51 observations, from 3 January 2007 to 26 December 2007) refers to the subprime crisis subperiod; and Year 2008–09 (62 observations) refers to the last subperiod that covers the period from 2 January 2008 to 4 March 2009. The table also presents the matrix of unconditional correlation between returns of the ABX subindices.

2008, p. 70). In particular, the ABX AAA index does not reference the most senior tranche of the MBS deals such that the ABX prices reflect higher durations than those remaining AAA-rated subprime MBS (Fender and Hördahl, 2007). Nonetheless, Fender and Hördahl also point out that the bias with regard to the insufficient market coverage may not be significant as the MBS deals referenced by the ABX indices are likely to be similar to the remaining subprime MBS in collateral and loan-to-value ratios.

11.5   METHODOLOGIES

Our chapter adopts a vector autoregressive (VAR) framework with exogenous variables to investigate spillover effects from the US structured market (measured by the ABX returns) during the subprime crisis. Having returns of the domestic equity and government bond markets modelled in a system of equations for each country, we account for any potential endogeneity between the markets and test for any predictive power of the ABX index for the returns of our international markets. Any significant predictive power (Granger-causality) of the ABX lagged returns for the international market returns suggests that shocks had spilled over from the US structured market to the international markets with some weeks' lag. To capture the dynamic effects of spillovers, we include four lags (without the contemporaneous ABX index returns) for our VAR models corresponding to one month and regress the endogenous variables against the lagged returns of the ABX indices. As the US subprime CDO market was largely driven by the US housing markets and subprime credit markets, lagged returns of the ABX indices are assumed exogenous to the VAR system (i.e. the ABX lagged returns appear on each VAR OLS equation). Our VAR(4) models can be expressed in the following reduced form with n endogenous variables:

$$\mathbf{y}_t = \alpha_0 + \sum_{i=1}^{4} \beta_i \mathbf{y}_{t-i} + \sum_{i=1}^{4} \phi_i x_{t-i} + \varepsilon_t, \tag{11.1}$$

where $\mathbf{y}_t$ is an $n \times 1$ vector of endogenous dependent variables (market returns), x_{t-i} is the lagged value of the ABX index assumed exogenous to the VAR system, β_i is an $n \times n$ matrix of coefficients estimated in the systems of equations, ϕ_i is an $n \times 1$ vector of coefficients of the ABX lagged returns, and ε_t is an $n \times 1$ vector of innovations that are uncorrelated with their own lagged values and all right-hand side variables.

All five ABX subindices are included in our analysis as exogenous variables to the VAR systems, and hence five VAR models are estimated and reported for each subperiod, amounting to 15 VAR models for three subperiods in each country. Within each VAR model, we include weekly returns of the broader equity, financial equity and government bond indices of the subject country as endogenous dependent variables. We also include a latent variable in our VAR models that captures the variation in the remaining four broader equity market returns under a principal component analysis (PCA).

11.6   DATA

All our sample data are collected from Datastream and comprise weekly returns of the broader equity, financial equity and government bond indices from our G5 countries. The G5 countries in our study are the US, UK, France, Germany and Japan, which represent the five largest global economies. Our sample covers the period from 1 February 2006 to 4 March 2009, which covers the entire subprime crisis and the six-month distress period after Lehman Brothers' collapse. Consistent with the contagion literature, we control for interdependence by splitting the sample period into three subperiods with the year 2006 (48 obs) as the tranquil pre-crisis period characterized by no significant cross-market shock spillover. Similar to Longstaff (2010), we regard the year 2007 (51 obs) as the subprime crisis subperiod and the last period (from 2 January 2008 to 4 March 2009, 62 obs) as the post-crisis subperiod.

11.6.1   Endogenous Dependent Variables

Table 11.2 summarizes and describes the data set for this study. Our data points are based on weekly Wednesday-to-Wednesday returns to avoid any potential calendar day bias and abnormal trading patterns. To measure changes in the domestic government bond markets, we use weekly returns of the FTSE Global Government 10+ year bond clean price indices for each country. For the equity markets, we use weekly returns of domestic

Table 11.2   Data description and transformation

Data Description	Time series	Country	Data Type	Transformation
Broader equity index:	S&P 500 composite index	US	Weekly	Log first difference
	FTSE 100 index	UK	Weekly	Log first difference
	France CAC 40 index	France	Weekly	Log first difference
	Germany DAX 30 index	Germany	Weekly	Log first difference
	Nikkei 225 index	Japan	Weekly	Log first difference
Financial equity index:	US Datastream financial index	US	Weekly	Log first difference
	UK Datastream financial index	UK	Weekly	Log first difference
	France Datastream financial index	France	Weekly	Log first difference
	Germany Datastream financial index	Germany	Weekly	Log first difference
	Japan Datastream financial index	Japan	Weekly	Log first difference
Government bond index:	FTSE global government US 10+ Y clean price index	US	Weekly	Log first difference
	FTSE global government UK 10+ Y clean price index	UK	Weekly	Log first difference
	FTSE global government France 10+ Y clean price index	France	Weekly	Log first difference
	FTSE global government Germany 10+ Y clean price index	Germany	Weekly	Log first difference
	FTSE global government Japan 10+ Y clean price index	Japan	Weekly	Log first difference
Interest rate swap spread: (Interest rate differential)	US (USD) interest rate swap 10 year (ICAP/TR) middle rate minus US Treasury 10 year bond yield	US	Weekly	Level
	UK (GBP) interest rate swap 10 year (ICAP/TR) – middle rate minus UK bond yield government 10 year (econ) middle rate	UK	Weekly	Level
	France (FRF) interest rate swap 10 year (ICAP/TR) middle rate minus France OAT constant maturity – tec 10 year red. yield	France	Weekly	Level
	Germany (DEM) interest rate swap 10 year (ICAP/TR) middle rate minus Germany government bond 10 year red. yield	Germany	Weekly	Level
	Japan (JPY) interest rate swap 10 year (ICAP/TR) middle rate minus Japan bond yield government 10 year (econ) middle rate	Japan	Weekly	Level

Note: This table contains a summary of the data description, the full title of the time series used, the country, the data type and the data transformation applied (whether the data are first-difference or log first-difference).

Source: Datastream.

269

Table 11.3   Principal component analysis of the broader equity market returns

Country	No. of components	Input series (Broader equity market returns)	Eigenvalue of the 1st component	% of variances accounted for
US	1	UK, France, Germany, Japan	3.485	87.12
UK	1	US, France, Germany, Japan	3.344	83.60
France	1	US, UK, Germany, Japan	3.288	82.20
Germany	1	US, UK, France, Japan	3.343	83.59
Japan	1	US, UK, France, Germany	3.586	89.65

Notes: This table contains a summary of the principal component analysis (PCA) for our sample of countries. For each subject country, the remaining four countries' broader equity market returns are used as inputs for the PCA to obtain the principal components and the corresponding factor scores. The Kaiser's significance rule is used to determine the number of significant principal components, i.e. any components with eigenvalues greater than one are retained. The number of components, the input countries, the eigenvalues of the first component, and the percentage of variances explained are reported here.

composite indices to track the performance of the broader equity markets and Datastream-calculated financial price indices for the performance of the financial equity sectors.

11.6.2   Latent Variables under Principal Component Analysis

From an international market perspective, we are aware that the transmission of contagion might not be unidirectional (i.e. not necessarily from the US subprime CDO market to other markets) and that the occurrence of shock spillovers might be sequential, that is, first from the US subprime CDO market to the US financial markets then to the international markets. In order to focus on the spillover effects from the US subprime CDO market, we account for cross-market dependencies and possible simultaneous spillover effects between broader equity markets in our sample of countries. To this end, we use PCA to extract the latent principal components that underlie the changes in the broader equity markets of our sample of countries. The factor scores obtained are then used as endogenous variables within our VAR models.

For each country, we use the remaining four countries' broader equity market returns as inputs for PCA to obtain the principal components and corresponding factor scores. For instance, the principal component for the US VAR models is computed by using the broader equity returns of the UK, France, Germany and Japan as inputs for the PCA. The Kaiser's significance rule is used to determine the number of significant principal components such that any components with eigenvalues greater than one are deemed statistically significant and retained. Table 11.3 presents the eigenvalues of the PCA and the percentages of variances explained by the first principal component for each country. Only one principal component has been identified and retained for each country, suggesting that all our broader equity markets are largely driven by the same latent factor and are quite correlated. Each of the first principal components in our sample countries explain more than 80 per cent of the variances of the input series of equity market returns.

The series of factor scores are then used in our VAR models as endogenous variables to control for any dependencies between our subject financial markets and the international equity markets.

11.7   EMPIRICAL FINDINGS

This section provides the empirical test results of our VAR models for each country. We report the sums of coefficients of the ABX index lagged returns, R^2 for each equation and the 1 per cent, 5 per cent and 10 per cent significance levels of standard F-tests denoted by ***, ** and * respectively. The F-test places restrictions on the lagged exogenous variables and tests the null hypothesis that $\phi_1 = \phi_2 = \phi_3 = \phi_4 = 0$. A significant F-statistic implies that the ABX lagged returns had significant predictive power (Granger causality) for returns of other markets, and in other words, there were spillover effects from the US subprime CDO market. Table 11.4 reports the findings from our VAR models for each country.

11.7.1   The Pre-Crisis Subperiod

As discussed in the previous sections, the year 2006 was largely free of any significant shocks and volatilities. The international equity markets had showed signs of stability and even growth during this subperiod. Findings based on this one-year window reveal the levels of dependencies between the US structured market and other markets at normal, tranquil market conditions.

Our findings for all countries are, in general, identical in that we find little predictive power of the lagged ABX returns for returns of the international equity and government bond markets. In other words, the cross-market linkages between the US subprime CDO market and the other markets were largely weak during normal market conditions. The results are sensible based on the fact that the US subprime residential mortgage market represents only a niche market accounting for approximately 12 per cent of the total national residential mortgage loan outstanding (Census Bureau, eMBS, Loan Performance, Deutsche Bank; cited in Weaver, 2008). Besides, subprime CDO products were relatively new, complex and opaque such that it may have been difficult to estimate the scope and severity of the financial consequences if these products became insolvent. These might be possible reasons why the dependencies between the US subprime CDO market and our sample of international markets were rather low prior to the crisis. Our findings are consistent with Longstaff (2010) in that interdependence was documented for the US ABX VAR models in this pre-crisis subperiod.

11.7.2   The Crisis Subperiod

This subperiod entails all data points in 2007 and is regarded as the crisis period during which the US subprime crisis unfolded. It is characterized by an increasing threat of subprime mortgage delinquencies and massive write downs of subprime portfolios in numerous financial institutions. The equity markets in our sample started to decline sharply at some point during this subperiod.

We find strong evidence of spillovers in both US equity and Treasury bond markets from the US subprime CDO market; that is, the F-statistics of most VAR models are highly significant. For the Treasury bond market, the F-statistics for the A, BBB and BBB- ABX indices VAR models are highly significant, with negative coefficient sums such that negative returns in the ABX indices lead to subsequent increases in Treasury bond market returns. This evidence suggests a possible flight-to-quality from equity to the safer Treasury bond

Table 11.4 Empirical findings of the ABX VAR models

y_t	ABX	2006 $\sum_{i=1}^4 \phi_i$	2006 R^2	2007 $\sum_{i=1}^4 \phi_i$	2007 R^2	2008 – Mar 2009 $\sum_{i=1}^4 \phi_i$	2008 – Mar 2009 R^2
Panel A: US							
US Gov Bond	AAA	-14.21	0.29	-0.51	0.40	-0.37**	0.55
	AA	-14.39	0.34	-0.31	0.38	-0.18**	0.54
Index	A	2.41	0.25	-0.13***	0.55	-0.09	0.49
	BBB	0.32	0.22	-0.09**	0.52	-0.09	0.47
	BBB-	-0.02	0.22	-0.12**	0.52	-0.10	0.48
S&P 500	AAA	23.18	0.49	2.05	0.38	-0.58	0.38
	AA	-11.45	0.45	1.04	0.39	-0.39	0.39
	A	-17.33	0.54	0.45**	0.51	-0.15	0.40
	BBB	0.81	0.51	0.26**	0.47	-0.08	0.37
	BBB-	0.52	0.44	0.35*	0.45	-0.13	0.36
US DS	AAA	35.91	0.47	2.13	0.49	-0.79	0.44
Financial	AA	-10.06	0.44	1.22*	0.53	-0.56	0.46
Index	A	-19.58	0.55	0.57***	0.60	-0.20	0.47
	BBB	-1.16	0.51	0.35**	0.59	0.00	0.46
	BBB-	-0.62	0.46	0.44***	0.57	0.00	0.45
PCA	AAA	16.61	0.46	0.35	0.37	0.05	0.44
Latent	AA	-0.10	0.37	0.33	0.37	-0.04	0.45
Factor	A	-13.50	0.45	0.16*	0.46	-0.01	0.48
	BBB	-0.10	0.44	0.08*	0.48	0.02	0.45
	BBB-	0.21	0.32	0.10	0.43	0.01	0.43
Panel C: France							
France	AAA	-44.76**	0.46	-0.88*	0.48	-0.01	0.29
Gov	AA	-16.26	0.41	-0.27	0.45	-0.01	0.37
Bond	A	0.78	0.28	-0.11***	0.56	-0.01	0.27
Index	BBB	-0.02	0.26	-0.08***	0.62	0.02	0.30
	BBB-	-0.08	0.25	-0.10***	0.60	0.00	0.31
France	AAA	97.82****	0.58	3.62**	0.48	-0.71	0.43
CAC 40	AA	10.40	0.35	1.27**	0.45	-0.36	0.47
	A	-23.62**	0.50	0.60***	0.51	-0.17	0.44
	BBB	-0.70	0.38	0.33**	0.47	-0.04	0.40
	BBB-	0.28	0.31	0.34*	0.42	-0.02	0.39

y_t	ABX	2006 $\sum_{i=1}^4 \phi_i$	2006 R^2	2007 $\sum_{i=1}^4 \phi_i$	2007 R^2	2008 – Mar 2009 $\sum_{i=1}^4 \phi_i$	2008 – Mar 2009 R^2
Panel B: UK							
UK Gov	AAA	-24.14	0.31	-0.37**	0.65	-0.11	0.37
Bond	AA	-10.63	0.32	-0.20	0.57	-0.09*	0.43
Index	A	3.03	0.34	-0.1	0.57	-0.04	0.37
	BBB	1.12	0.27	-0.06	0.56	-0.02	0.35
	BBB-	0.08	0.33	-0.06	0.54	-0.02	0.34
FTSE	AAA	20.80	0.46	1.83**	0.55	-0.29	0.36
100	AA	2.11	0.33	0.77**	0.54	-0.21	0.39
	A	-23.58	0.46	0.33***	0.60	-0.09	0.42
	BBB	-4.05	0.43	0.18***	0.58	-0.04	0.36
	BBB-	-1.47	0.37	0.21**	0.55	-0.09	0.38
UK DS	AAA	22.99	0.41	1.74*	0.57	-0.54	0.46
Financial	AA	-16.06	0.31	0.77	0.53	-0.35	0.47
Index	A	-34.96**	0.53	0.39*	0.58	-0.21	0.50
	BBB	-6.27	0.42	0.22*	0.58	-0.01	0.48
	BBB-	-3.08	0.37	0.27	0.54	-0.07	0.49
PCA	AAA	11.06	0.48	0.60**	0.50	-0.09	0.30
Latent	AA	3.65	0.37	0.29	0.45	-0.06	0.34
Factor	A	-13.87	0.45	0.16**	0.51	-0.03	0.36
	BBB	-2.21	0.46	0.10**	0.50	-0.02	0.32
	BBB-	-0.73	0.39	0.14*	0.48	-0.03	0.32
Panel D: Germany							
Germany	AAA	-18.19	0.45	-0.08	0.42	-0.08	0.45
Gov	AA	-6.97	0.49	-0.16	0.39	-0.02*	0.49
Bond	A	0.44	0.38	-0.06*	0.48	-0.01	0.41
Index	BBB	-0.23	0.39	-0.06*	0.49	0.00	0.45
	BBB-	-0.09	0.38	-0.08**	0.50	-0.01	0.45
Germany	AAA	-21.66	0.50	1.09	0.37	-0.17	0.33
DAX 30	AA	-41.54	0.50	0.80	0.40	-0.22	0.34
	A	-34.07***	0.63	0.34	0.42	-0.13	0.38
	BBB	-5.53	0.54	0.21	0.42	0.01	0.31
	BBB-	-3.51	0.45	0.27	0.40	-0.01	0.32

Table: France / Germany panels (top) — France columns on left, Germany columns on right.

France	AAA	125.26**	0.48	3.51	0.45	−1.37**	0.53	Germany	AAA	19.25	0.53	1.28	0.34	0.36	0.26
DS	AA	19.57	0.27	1.52	0.45	−0.41**	0.52	DS	AA	−29.07	0.44	1.10*	0.44	0.01	0.26
Financial	A	−29.77**	0.45	0.75**	0.52	−0.29*	0.51	Financial	A	−39.17**	0.60	0.44**	0.52	0.00**	0.38
Index	BBB	−1.35	0.29	0.40**	0.51	−0.10	0.49	Index	BBB	−4.30**	0.56	0.21**	0.46	0.06	0.26
	BBB-	0.42	0.23	0.44	0.46	−0.01	0.47		BBB-	−3.30	0.48	0.23	0.43	0.03	0.24
PCA	AAA	52.98**	0.48	1.63**	0.49	−0.18	0.44	PCA	AAA	3.98	0.44	1.01	0.42	−0.05	0.25
Latent	AA	14.62	0.24	0.62**	0.48	−0.11*	0.49	Latent	AA	−8.47	0.37	0.60**	0.49	−0.05	0.27
Factor	A	−10.54	0.33	0.29***	0.57	−0.06	0.45	Factor	A	−13.75***	0.54	0.26***	0.57	−0.03	0.31
	BBB	−0.53	0.29	0.16**	0.51	−0.03	0.41		BBB	−1.85	0.45	0.17**	0.51	0.00	0.23
	BBB-	0.32	0.21	0.17**	0.46	−0.04	0.41		BBB-	−0.98	0.35	0.19**	0.50	−0.01	0.23

Panel E: Japan

Japan	AAA	−11.35	0.40	−0.34	0.47	−0.09	0.33
DS Gov	AA	−8.27	0.43	−0.11	0.46	−0.05	0.37
Bond	A	7.09	0.40	−0.03*	0.56	−0.02	0.32
Index	BBB	0.91	0.35	−0.04	0.52	−0.02	0.32
	BBB-	0.24	0.33	−0.04	0.53	0.00	0.29
Japan	AAA	31.09	0.29	1.77*	0.57	0.32	0.34
Nikkei	AA	30.66	0.34	1.17**	0.60	0.02	0.36
225	A	−28.76	0.34	0.53***	0.75	−0.30	0.36
	BBB	−3.01	0.33	0.31***	0.64	0.03	0.38
	BBB-	−0.02	0.27	0.30**	0.61	−0.10	0.37
Japan DS	AAA	51.33	0.34	−0.57	0.61	1.13	0.49
Financial	AA	54.93	0.37	0.63	0.63	0.42	0.50
Index	A	−31.25	0.35	0.38***	0.75	−0.29	0.46
	BBB	0.61	0.32	0.21***	0.70	0.16	0.51
	BBB-	1.32	0.28	0.23*	0.66	0.01	0.50
PCA	AAA	−0.71	0.54	0.34	0.41	−0.03	0.37
Latent	AA	0.22	0.46	0.31	0.46	−0.02	0.40
Factor	A	−18.38***	0.67	0.13***	0.57	−0.04	0.40
	BBB	−1.89	0.53	0.08**	0.50	0.00	0.41
	BBB-	−0.40	0.46	0.08	0.46	−0.01	0.40

Notes: This table reports the results of the ABX VAR models for each G5 country. There are in total five ABX subindices included in our VAR estimations corresponding to credit ratings of AAA, AA, A, BBB and BBB- in the underlying CDO deals. Five VAR models are estimated for each subperiod and a total of 15 VAR models are estimated for each country. Each dependent variable is regressed against its own lags and the exogenous lagged returns of the ABX index and can be written as $y_t = \alpha_0 + \sum_{j=1}^{4} \beta_j y_{t-i} + \sum_{i=1}^{4} \phi_i x_{t-i} + \varepsilon_t$. For each equation within the VAR system, the (net) sum of the coefficients of the ABX lagged returns and the R^2 of the OLS equations are reported. Also reported are the significance level based on standard F-tests, which test the hypothesis: $\phi_1 = \phi_2 = \phi_3 = \phi_4 = 0$. Panel A, B, C, D, and E reports the findings of our US, UK, France, Germany and Japan VAR models. The ***, ** and * denote statistical significance at 1%, 5% and 10% level respectively.

273

markets during the crisis. For the Standard and Poor's (S&P) 500 composite index VAR models, the F-statistics of the three lower-rated ABX index models are highly significant, while for the financial equity sector, F-statistics for all ABX index models except the AAA index are very significant. As for the principal component VAR models, we find significant results for both the A and BBB ABX indices. Overall, we find that the ABX index lagged returns Granger-caused returns of the US domestic equity and Treasury bond market returns in this subperiod. Most of our significant VAR models refer to those ABX indices of lower credit ratings, that is, the A, BBB and BBB- ABX indices. This is consistent with our observation that the ABX indices with lower credit ratings experienced larger declines. Our results are qualitatively similar to Longstaff (2010), who finds significant contagion from the US subprime CDO market to other US domestic financial markets.

Next, we shall focus on our findings for the international markets. We find evidence of contagion in a number of markets, including the UK, French and Japanese equity markets. We also identified a possible flight-to-quality in the French and German markets as shown by the significant government bond market VAR models. In particular, for the UK, France and Japan, the F-statistics of all broader equity market VAR models are highly significant. The R^2 statistics of these VAR models except those in the French markets became higher compared to the pre-crisis subperiod, suggesting stronger explanatory power and improved specifications. For the financial equity models, we find significant F-statistics in the AAA, A and BBB ABX index models at the 10 per cent level for the UK and more significant F-statistics in the three lowest-rated ABX index models in Japan. The sums of ABX coefficients are in general positive for all these significant equity VAR models and suggest that the ABX shocks were translated into subsequent declines in these markets. On the other hand, we find possible contagion effects in the French and German government bond markets. All F-statistics except for the AA index of the French VAR models and those in the three lowest-rated ABX index models of Germany are highly significant with negative ABX coefficient sums. Our findings show that negative shocks to the US subprime CDO market led to subsequent increases in the government bond market returns in both France and Germany, consistent with a possible flight-to-quality phenomenon. However, the findings on the French and German financial equity VAR models are largely inconclusive due to the significant dependencies identified in the pre-crisis period. On the other hand, the PCA VAR models for all countries except Japan are largely significant, implying that the ABX indices have strong predictive power for the latent factors.

11.7.3   The Post-Crisis Subperiod

This subperiod includes data points from 2008 to March 2009, and consists of 62 observations. It covers the later stage of the subprime crisis, characterized by the global credit crunch and the six months of distress after the Lehman Brothers' collapse in September 2008. The equity markets largely continued their declines throughout the year 2008, tumbled shortly after the investment bank giant's collapse and then entered into a six-month period of distress. We test whether these further market failures were associated with any spillover effects from the US subprime CDO market.

Our findings in this subperiod were generally insignificant such that the predictive power of the ABX index returns almost completely disappeared except for a few markets. The two exceptions refer to the US Treasury bond market and the French financial equity sector. These aside, our findings suggest that the subsequent market declines in the later stage of the crisis and the six-month distress period were largely not spillovers of shocks from the US structured market.

11.7.4 Discussion

Overall, our analysis has shown empirically that there were substantial increases in market linkages between the US subprime CDO market and international financial markets during the subprime crisis. Strong predictive and explanatory power in the ABX lagged returns for weekly returns in a number of international financial markets have been identified. The predictive power largely ceased to exist in the last subperiod, suggesting that the further market declines were likely not attributed to spillovers.

Our analysis shows that international markets reacted differently to shocks from the US structured market during the crisis. Spillover effects are identified in almost every broader equity market and financial equity sector of our sample of countries. In other words, equity markets, and in particular the financial sectors, were vulnerable to shocks from the US subprime CDO market. One possible explanation relates to the significant increases in credit risks associated with the massive write-downs of subprime CDO portfolios in many financial institutions. Such heightened credit risk inherent in the financial sectors might have led to swift shrinkage of funding liquidity as evidenced by rising interbank lending rates and LIBOR–OIS (London Interbank Offered Rate–overnight indexed swap) spreads. This market information and downside investors' expectations then led to systematic changes in risk premia in a number of international markets. In addition, as pointed out by a number of researchers, investors might be obliged to liquidate cross-market investments in order to meet contingent liabilities resulting in a substantial amount of oversell and downside pressure in foreign asset markets. All these suggest spillover effects transmitted via funding liquidity and risk premia transmission channels.

On the other hand, we find evidence of a possible flight-to-quality in the US, French and German markets as shown by the negative sum of ABX coefficients in the significant government bond VAR models. During periods of extreme volatility, investors may be prone to switch from equities to government bonds, thereby increasing demand for government bonds and thus lowering bond yields. Flight-to-quality might be related to investors' risk tolerances and their need to adjust portfolio risk exposure after changes in risk premia. Flights could also be associated with market illiquidity such that investors prefer to hold more actively traded government bonds, which have higher liquidity, to fulfil their funding needs.

11.8   HOW DID CONTAGION TRANSMIT DURING THE SUBPRIME MORTGAGE CRISIS?

In the following sections, we investigate how shocks might have propagated from the US subprime CDO market to international markets during the crisis subperiod, and shed light on the dynamics of flights between domestic financial equity and government bond markets. Our findings provide implications for, in particular, the risk premia and funding liquidity transmission channels.

11.8.1   Methodologies

We adopt the same VAR(4) framework with the same sample subperiods to model the relationship between endogenous variables and the exogenous lagged returns of the ABX indices as a system of equations. However, instead of using weekly returns of financial markets, we introduce a few variables that track the weekly trading intensity in financial sectors, the level of credit risks and market illiquidity, and the level of market co-movement between returns of the financial equity sector and government bond markets.

11.8.2   Liquidity Ratios

Similar to Longstaff (2010), we compute the liquidity ratio by dividing the aggregate weekly trading volume in market value of the financial equity sector (using Datastream-calculated financial price indices) by the aggregate weekly trading volume in market value of the broader equity market for each country. The liquidity ratio for week t refers to the trading volume in market value in the week immediately before, including the Wednesday of week $t - 1$, and can be expressed as:

$$RATIO_{i,t} = \frac{\sum_{j=1}^{5} FinVol_{ij,t-1}}{\sum_{j=1}^{5} AlleqVol_{ij,t-1}}. \tag{11.2}$$

where $FinVol_{ij,t-1}$ refers to the daily trading volume in market value of the financial equity subindex in country i on trading day j of week $t - 1$, and $AlleqVol_{ij,t-1}$ refers to the daily trading volume in market value of the broader equity index in country i on trading day j of week $t - 1$.

Figure 11.2 plots the weekly liquidity ratios (financial trading volume ratios) of our five countries. We observe that the ratios for all countries were higher in 2007, suggesting increases in trading intensity of financial stocks. The numerous spikes in the ratios also suggest signs of clustering in the trades of financial stocks. Our analysis uses these liquidity ratio time series as endogenous variables in the VAR system and we test whether the trading intensity might be Granger-caused by the ABX lagged returns.

11.8.3   Interest Rate Swap Spreads

A large number of empirical studies have focused on investigating the determinant risk factors of IRSS and mostly follow two main research directions. One direction refers to an analysis of the liquidity convenience yield curve, while the other mainly discusses swap spreads in terms of credit and counterparty default risks (Brown et al., 1994; Grinblatt, 2001). A more recent paper by Liu et al. (2006) shows that the US interest rate swap spreads have both a default risk component and market illiquidity component for which strong time variation over the period 1988 to 2002 has been found. Moreover, Hui and Lam (2008) find that Hong Kong interest rate swap spreads were determined by credit risks during the period between July 2002 and September 2007 and by liquidity preference during the later period between September 2007 and April 2008.[7] These

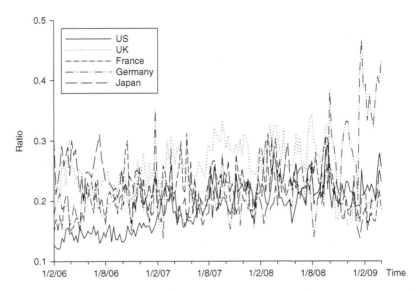

Note: This figure plots the liquidity ratios of the equity markets in the G5 countries. The ratios are computed by dividing the aggregate weekly trading volume in market value of the financial equity sector (using Datastream-calculated financial price indices) by the aggregate weekly trading volume in market value for the broader equity market for each country. It measures the trading intensity of the financial equity sector relative to the domestic broader equity market.

Source: Datastream; authors' calculations.

Figure 11.2 The liquidity ratios

studies suggest that interest rate swap spreads might contain a number of risk components that reflect levels of credit and market illiquidity risks in financial markets and provide implications for the contagion transmission mechanism.

We collect weekly quotes of ten-year interest rate swap middle rates for our sample of countries from Datastream, and then obtain the spreads by subtracting the corresponding ten-year government bond yields from them. Figure 11.3 plots the weekly interest rate swap spreads (IRSS) for each country. The spreads of all countries started to widen in the second half of 2007 reflecting possible heightened credit and market illiquidity risks. The spreads remained high throughout our entire sample period except those in the US, UK and Germany, which started to narrow from 2009 onwards. We examine the dependencies between the IRSS and ABX lagged returns to reveal any possible spillover effects via changes in credit or market illiquidity risks.

11.8.4 Implied Time-Varying Correlations

In earlier sections, we have found evidence of possible flights between equity and government bond markets during the crisis subperiod. Similar to a number of studies (e.g. De Goeij and Marquering, 2004; Li, 2003; Baur and Lucey, 2009), we examine the relationships between equity and government bond returns to identify any possible flight-to-quality phenomena, in particular, between financial equity sectors and government bond markets.

Note: This figure plots the interest rate swap spreads (IRSS) of the G5 countries. The spreads are computed by subtracting the ten-year government bond yields from the interest rate swap middle rates for each subject country.

Source: Datastream; authors' calculations.

Figure 11.3   The interest rate swap spreads

We employ an MGARCH diagonal VECH model to estimate the dynamics between the returns of domestic financial equity and government bond indices for each country and then obtain series of implied time-varying correlations for each pair of returns. We assume a VECH representation based on the conditional variances and conditional correlations that can be represented as follows:

$$\text{vech}(\mathbf{H}_t) = \mathbf{C} + \mathbf{A}\,\text{vech}(\Xi_{t-1}\Xi'_{t-1}) + \mathbf{B}\,\text{vech}(\mathbf{H}_{t-1})$$

$$\Xi_t | \mathcal{I}_{t-1} \sim N(0, \mathbf{H}_t). \qquad (11.3)$$

With the restricted form developed by Bollerslev et al. (1988), matrices $\mathbf{A}$ and $\mathbf{B}$ are assumed to be diagonal such that:

$$\mathbf{H}_t = \begin{bmatrix} h_{11t} & h_{12t} \\ h_{21t} & h_{22t} \end{bmatrix}, \ \Xi_t = \begin{bmatrix} u_{1t} \\ u_{2t} \end{bmatrix}, \ \mathbf{C} = \begin{bmatrix} c_{11} \\ c_{21} \\ c_{31} \end{bmatrix}, \ \mathbf{A} = \begin{bmatrix} \alpha_{11} & 0 & 0 \\ 0 & \alpha_{22} & 0 \\ 0 & 0 & \alpha_{33} \end{bmatrix}, \ \mathbf{B} = \begin{bmatrix} \beta_{11} & 0 & 0 \\ 0 & \beta_{22} & 0 \\ 0 & 0 & \beta_{33} \end{bmatrix}.$$

The conditional variances for our two asset returns in each country follow a GARCH(1,1) formulation characterized by:

$$h_{ij,t} = w_{ij} + \alpha_{ij} u_{i,t-1} u_{j,t-1} + \beta_{ij} h_{ij,t-1} \qquad \text{for } i,j = 1,2. \qquad (11.4)$$

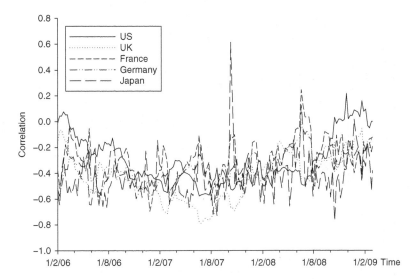

Note: This figure plots the implied correlations estimated using a MGARCH(1,1) model with a diagonal VECH specification between the weekly returns of Datastream-calculated financial price indices and the FTSE global government 10+ year bond clean price indices for each G5 country.

Source: Datastream; authors' calculations.

Figure 11.4   *The implied correlations between weekly returns of the financial indices and government bond indices*

where w_{ij}, α_{ij}, and β_{ij} are parameters to be estimated while $u_{i,t-1}$ and $u_{j,t-1}$ refer to the returns of assets i and j at time $t-1$ respectively.

Figure 11.4 plots the time-varying correlations between returns of the financial equity and government bond markets estimated using the MGARCH diagonal VECH specification described above. While most of the correlations remain negative throughout the entire sample period, these correlations appeared to be more negative during the 2007 crisis subperiod with the exception of the Japanese markets, which showed signs of an increase in the second half of 2007. These observations provide anecdotal evidence of a flight-to-quality between domestic financial equity and government bond markets.

In order to reveal the relationship between flights and ABX shocks, we use the time series of implied correlations as endogenous variables in our VAR models and examine the dependencies between the ABX lagged returns and the implied correlation series.

11.8.5   Empirical Findings: Liquidity Ratios, Interest Rate Swap Spreads and Implied Correlations

Table 11.5 presents the findings of our VAR models and reports the sum of the coefficients (multiplied by 100) for each exogenous ABX index lagged return, the R^2 statistic for each equation, and the 1 per cent, 5 per cent and 10 per cent significance levels of standard F-tests denoted by ***, ** and *, respectively. Similarly, the F-statistics associated with the null hypothesis of $\phi_1 = \phi_2 = \phi_3 = \phi_4 = 0$ are provided.

Table 11.5   Empirical results of the liquidity and credit risk VAR models

y_t	ABX	2006 $\sum_{i=1}^4 \phi_i$	2006 R^2	2007 $\sum_{i=1}^4 \phi_i$	2007 R^2	2008 – Mar 2009 $\sum_{i=1}^4 \phi_i$	2008 – Mar 2009 R^2
Panel A: US							
Liquidity	AAA	10.73	0.38	−0.46	0.74	−0.39	0.47
Ratio	AA	−4.02	0.37	−0.40**	0.78	−0.13	0.45
	A	−0.94	0.40	−0.20***	0.81	−0.09	0.43
	BBB	−1.19	0.36	−0.13**	0.78	−0.06	0.44
	BBB-	−0.35	0.37	−0.14	0.76	−0.06	0.43
IRSS	AAA	−147.81	0.77	−7.37	0.78	0.70	0.92
	AA	−2.65	0.72	−2.44	0.78	−0.03	0.92
	A	−10.97	0.72	−0.75***	0.84	−0.08*	0.93
	BBB	−5.01	0.73	−0.39***	0.81	0.16	0.93
	BBB-	−4.20	0.75	−0.50***	0.82	0.16	0.93
Implied	AAA	155.28	0.92	−2.44**	0.83	−0.59***	0.96
Corr.	AA	3.59	0.92	−1.14***	0.85	−0.13***	0.96
	A	1.46	0.92	−0.52*	0.82	−0.04**	0.96
	BBB	4.77	0.92	−0.30*	0.82	−0.03	0.95
	BBB-	2.51*	0.93	−0.25*	0.82	0.10	0.95
Panel C: France							
Liquidity	AAA	−20.62	0.44	−1.90	0.32	−0.14	0.58
Ratio	AA	−34.52	0.46	−0.92	0.34	−0.06	0.58
	A	−15.03	0.43	−0.36	0.38	−0.11	0.60
	BBB	−7.38	0.43	−0.22	0.33	−0.10	0.58
	BBB-	−4.34	0.45	−0.21	0.30	−0.14	0.61
IRSS	AAA	−84.95	0.48	−4.41***	0.83	0.12**	0.81
	AA	16.65	0.45	−0.91	0.78	−0.32***	0.83
	A	2.62	0.44	−0.41	0.77	−0.20	0.78
	BBB	−2.72	0.45	−0.26	0.79	−0.24	0.79
	BBB-	−1.28	0.46	−0.27	0.77	−0.34**	0.81

y_t	ABX	2006 $\sum_{i=1}^4 \phi_i$	2006 R^2	2007 $\sum_{i=1}^4 \phi_i$	2007 R^2	2008 – Mar 2009 $\sum_{i=1}^4 \phi_i$	2008 – Mar 2009 R^2
Panel B: UK							
Liquidity	AAA	−20.17	0.52	−1.26	0.70	−0.21	0.79
Ratio	AA	−44.09**	0.64	−0.12	0.69	−0.01	0.78
	A	−19.14*	0.61	−0.09	0.69	−0.07	0.80
	BBB	−6.93*	0.60	−0.13	0.70	−0.01	0.79
	BBB-	−3.38	0.58	−0.21	0.72	0.01	0.79
IRSS	AAA	76.02***	0.91	−3.26*	0.91	−0.02	0.89
	AA	34.47*	0.89	−1.80***	0.93	−0.07	0.89
	A	13.86*	0.89	−0.57***	0.92	−0.29	0.89
	BBB	0.25	0.87	−0.30*	0.90	−0.39	0.90
	BBB-	−0.12	0.87	−0.22	0.90	−0.48	0.90
Implied	AAA	118.13	0.84	−3.50**	0.85	0.17	0.74
Corr.	AA	89.46	0.84	−0.67***	0.86	0.06	0.75
	A	−31.75	0.84	−0.55***	0.87	0.22	0.74
	BBB	−1.41*	0.85	−0.44**	0.86	0.21	0.74
	BBB-	−3.71	0.83	−0.41	0.83	0.36	0.75
Panel D: Germany							
Liquidity	AAA	−11.54	0.17	5.10**	0.50	−0.47	0.61
Ratio	AA	−27.63	0.24	1.39***	0.53	−0.05	0.62
	A	7.60	0.22	0.61***	0.58	0.05	0.60
	BBB	−2.16	0.18	0.54**	0.51	−0.08	0.60
	BBB-	−4.53	0.21	0.26	0.37	−0.07	0.59
IRSS	AAA	−69.27	0.84	−3.03***	0.95	−0.89**	0.73
	AA	−17.27	0.81	−1.10**	0.95	−0.61**	0.73
	A	−10.33	0.82	−0.62***	0.95	−0.41	0.69
	BBB	−1.26	0.83	−0.43***	0.96	−0.40	0.68
	BBB-	−2.07	0.83	−0.42***	0.95	−0.48**	0.72

Implied Corr.	AAA	108.55	0.71	5.32	0.54	0.50	0.47	Implied Corr.	AAA	233.91	0.74	1.92*	0.65	0.76
	AA	37.56*	0.78	1.34	0.54	0.08	0.46		AA	83.12	0.75	0.78*	0.64	0.75
	A	33.08**	0.79	0.85	0.53	−0.43	0.49		A	−43.31*	0.78	0.42	0.61	0.74
	BBB	31.40**	0.81	0.76	0.54	−0.43	0.50		BBB	−4.51	0.75	0.33	0.62	0.74
	BBB-	13.16**	0.79	0.97	0.54	−0.44	0.51		BBB-	−3.34	0.75	0.40*	0.64	0.76

Panel E: Japan

Liquidity Ratio	AAA	12.67	0.56	−1.86	0.30	−0.05	0.59
	AA	−5.80	0.53	−0.43	0.24	−0.01	0.60
	A	−12.51	0.56	−0.17	0.27	0.00	0.59
	BBB	2.58	0.55	−0.25	0.34	0.07	0.59
	BBB-	0.12	0.50	−0.29*	0.37	0.04	0.58
IRSS	AAA	−42.77	0.76	−1.27**	0.57	0.37***	0.91
	AA	1.63	0.76	−0.32	0.51	0.09**	0.90
	A	−16.05**	0.81	−0.14	0.47	0.04**	0.90
	BBB	−0.31	0.79	−0.08	0.50	0.05	0.89
	BBB-	0.99	0.75	−0.08	0.50	0.01	0.88
Implied Corr.	AAA	35.11	0.39	−9.64	0.49	−1.36	0.35
	AA	135.77	0.39	−3.13	0.49	−0.97	0.38
	A	−29.97	0.45	−0.99	0.50	−0.84	0.41
	BBB	−14.95	0.46	−0.81	0.53	−0.95**	0.45
	BBB-	−3.25	0.46	−1.20	0.53	−1.13*	0.43

Notes: This table reports the sum of coefficients (multiplied by 100) of the ABX lagged returns in our liquidity and credit risk VAR models. With the same VAR framework, exogenous lagged returns of the ABX index and sample subperiods, we include different sets of endogenous variables in this analysis. The liquidity ratio is computed by dividing the weekly aggregate trading volume in market value of the Datastream calculated financial price index by the weekly aggregate trading volume in market value of the Datastream calculated market price index for each country. The IRSS refers to the interest rate differential between the interest rate swap middle rate and the corresponding 10 year government bond yield (or middle rate) quoted weekly. The implied corr. refers to the implied correlation variables, which are estimated using the MGARCH diagonal VECH model between the weekly returns of the Datastream calculated financial price index and the FTSE global government bond clean price index for each country. Panel A, B, C, D, and E reports the findings of our US, UK, France, Germany and Japan VAR models. The ***, ** and * denote statistical significance at 1%, 5% and 10% level respectively.

During the pre-crisis subperiod, we find little or no significant explanatory power in the ABX index returns for the liquidity ratios, IRSS and implied correlation variables except the UK liquidity ratio and IRSS VAR models and a few French implied correlation VAR models. Our findings show that the ABX lagged returns generally do not explain much of the variation in these series over this subperiod, consistent with our previous findings of low interdependence prior to the crisis.

Our findings become highly significant during the crisis subperiod, most remarkably for the US, UK and German models. In the US case, the F-statistics for the A, BBB and BBB- ABX IRSS VAR models and for the AA, A and BBB liquidity ratios VAR models become highly significant while all US implied correlation VAR models are highly significant. All ABX indices except the BBB- index in the UK implied correlation VAR models become highly significant. There are also slight increases in the predictive power of the ABX returns in the UK IRSS VAR models, in particular, referring to the AA and A ABX indices. Moreover, almost all German liquidity ratio and IRSS VAR models are significant. The AAA, AA and BBB- German implied correlation VAR models are also significant at the 10 per cent level. By contrast, our findings on the French and Japanese VAR models are largely insignificant, reflecting low degrees of dependence.

A number of points require highlighting. Firstly, the negative ABX coefficient sums in the significant US liquidity ratio models suggest that declines in the ABX index returns led to subsequent higher trading intensity in US financial stocks relative to the broader equity market during the crisis. By contrast, the German liquidity ratio VAR models were characterized by significant positive ABX coefficient sums. Secondly, for both US and German IRSS models, the negative ABX coefficient sums suggest that negative ABX shocks have strong predictive power for the subsequent widening of the US and German IRSS, consistent with spillover effects via changes in credit and illiquidity risk premia. Thirdly, and interestingly, we find negative ABX coefficient sums in the significant US and UK implied correlation VAR models, contrary to our expectations, and positive ABX coefficient sums in the German models. In other words, shocks to the US sub-prime CDO market translated into higher implied correlations between financial stocks and government bonds in the US and UK, with the opposite holding for the German markets. Our findings suggest that ABX shocks might have discouraged a flight-to-quality between financial stocks and government bonds in both the US and the UK while encouraging flights in Germany. This evidence contradicts our earlier findings of a possible flight-to-quality in the US market. Nonetheless, we believe that flights between these markets did indeed exist as evidenced by the negative time-varying implied correlations between financial stocks and government bonds throughout the crisis, as shown in Figure 11.4. One possible explanation is that there might be simultaneous flights from other assets (i.e. apart from financial equity) to the US government bond market that gave rise to the significant predictive power of the ABX returns as documented in our earlier analysis. However, further empirical work is required to verify such a claim.

11.9   CONCLUDING REMARKS

We demonstrate how to investigate contagion in financial markets. To do this, we extend Longstaff's (2010) work to investigate spillover effects from the US subprime

CDO markets to the G5 countries with an international market perspective. One major contribution to the body of knowledge is that we have shown empirically within a VAR framework that there were substantial increases in cross-market linkages between the US subprime structured market and a number of international equity and bond markets during the crisis period. Our findings also provide empirical support to the contagion transmission argument; in particular, via the changes in risk premia associated with heightened credit and market illiquidity risks during the crisis. Our study allows systematic comparisons of spillover effects across various developed financial markets and deepens our understanding of the mechanism of shock propagations during extreme market conditions. Moreover, we also provide evidence of a flight-to-quality between financial equity and government bond markets evinced by the negative time-varying implied correlations.

NOTES

1. Allen and Gale (2000) propose a model in which banking institutions might liquidate their cross-holdings of deposits across regions during crisis periods for funding liquidity requirements, while Kodres and Pritsker (2002) present a model within a hedging framework in which shocks might be propagated through investors' portfolio rebalancing for the purposes of adjusting exposure to macro-economic risks.
2. Interdependence refers to the level of cross-market linkages between two markets in all states of the world. Taking into account the level of interdependence, only in cases of significant increases in co-movement may contagion exist. The authors refer to their more restrictive definition of contagion as 'shift contagion', which is consistent with the crisis-contingent channels of contagion (Forbes and Rigobon, 2001; 2002, p. 2224).
3. Kaminsky et al. (2003, p. 55) define contagion as some immediate effects of some countries after experiencing a common shock, of which the consequences evolve over 'a matter of hours and minutes'. The authors also define the emergence of gradual or protracted consequences as 'spillovers'.
4. We do not define spillovers as the gradual effects of shock transmission as in Kaminsky et al. (2003), and we use the terms 'contagion' and 'spillover' interchangeably throughout the text.
5. By 2006, 75 per cent of the subprime loans and 91 per cent of the Alt-A loans were securitized. Besides, the proportion of non-agency issues of MBS had grown substantially with the largest growth in the Alt-A loans and subprime loans sectors.
6. The ABX PENAAA indices, which reference AAA-rated bonds that are second to last in principal distribution priority, were introduced in May 2008.
7. According to the authors, the liquidity preference refers more specifically to the strong demand for short-term exchange traded bills for liquidity purposes.

REFERENCES

Acharya, V.V. and L.H. Pedersen (2005), 'Asset pricing with liquidity risk', *Journal of Financial Economics*, **77** (2), 375–410.

Allen, F. and D. Gale (2000), 'Financial contagion', *Journal of Political Economy*, **108** (1), 1–33.

Amihud, Y. (2002), 'Illiquidity and stock returns: cross-section and time-series effects', *Journal of Financial Markets*, **5** (1), 31–56.

Baur, D.G. and B.M. Lucey (2009), 'Flights and contagion – an empirical analysis of stock-bond correlations', *Journal of Financial Stability*, **5** (4), 339–352.

Bollerslev, T., R.F. Engle and J.M. Wooldridge (1988), 'A capital-asset pricing model with time-varying covariances', *Journal of Political Economy*, **96** (1), 116–131.

Brown, K.C., W.V. Harlow and D.J. Smith (1994), 'An empirical analysis of interest rate swap spreads', *Journal of Fixed Income*, **3** (4), 61–78.

Brunnermeier, M.K. and L.H. Pedersen (2009), 'Market liquidity and funding liquidity', *Review of Financial Studies*, **22** (6), 2201–2238.

Calvo, G. (2000), 'Capital market contagion and recession: an explanation of the Russian virus', in E. Fernandes-Arias and R. Hausmann (eds), *Wanted: World Financial Security*, Washington, DC: IDB/ Johns Hopkins University Press, pp. 49–52.

Caruana, J. and L. Kodres (2008), 'Liquidity in global markets', *Financial Stability Review*, Special Issue on Liquidity, Banque de France, **11** (December), 65–74.

De Goeij, P. and W. Marquering (2004), 'Modeling the conditional covariance between stock and bond returns: a multivariate GARCH approach', *Journal of Financial Econometrics*, **2** (4), 531–564.

Dornbusch, R., Y.C. Park and S. Claessens (2000), 'Contagion: understanding how it spreads', *World Bank Research Observer*, **15** (2), 177–197.

Edwards, S. (1998), 'Interest rate volatility, capital controls, and contagion', National Bureau of Economic Research Working Paper Series, no. 6756, October.

Eichengreen, B., A. Mody, M. Nedeljkovic and L. Sarno (2009), 'How the subprime crisis went global: evidence from bank credit default swap spreads', National Bureau of Economic Research Working Paper Series, no. 14904, April.

Eichengreen, B., A.K. Rose and C. Wyplosz (1996), 'Contagious currency crises', National Bureau of Economic Research Working Paper Series, no. 5681, July.

Federal Housing Finance Agency – Office of Federal Housing Enterprise Oversight (2008), 'Widespread house price declines in fourth quarter [Press Release]', www.fhfa.gov/webfiles/1173/4q07hpi.pdf, accessed 26 February, 2008.

Fender, I. and P. Hördahl (2007), 'Overview: a cautious return of risk tolerance', *BIS Quarterly Review*, June, 1–16.

Fender, I. and M. Scheicher (2008), 'The ABX: how do the markets price subprime mortgage risk', *BIS Quarterly Review*, September, 67–81.

Forbes, K.J. and R. Rigobon (2001), 'Measuring contagion: conceptual and empirical issues', in S. Claessens and K.J. Forbes (eds), *International Financial Contagion*, Boston, MA: Kluwer Academic Publishers, pp. 43–66.

Forbes, K.J. and R. Rigobon (2002), 'No contagion, only interdependence: measuring stock market comovements', *Journal of Finance*, **57** (5), 2223–2261.

Grinblatt, M. (2001), 'An analytic solution for interest rate swap spreads', *International Review of Finance*, **2** (3), 113–149.

Kaminsky, G.L. and C.M. Reinhart (2000), 'On crises, contagion, and confusion', *Journal of International Economics*, **51** (1), 145–168.

Kaminsky, G.L., C.M. Reinhart and C.A. Vegh (2003), 'The unholy trinity of financial contagion', *Journal of Economic Perspectives*, **17** (4), 51–74.

King, M.A. and S. Wadhwani (1990), 'Transmission of volatility between stock markets', *Review of Financial Studies*, **3** (1), 5–33.

Kodres, L.E. and M. Pritsker (2002), 'A rational expectations model of financial contagion', *Journal of Finance*, **57** (2), 769–799.

Li, L. (2003), 'Macroeconomic factors and the correlation of stock and bond return', Yale School of Management Working Papers, November.

Lindsey, L.B. (2007), 'Fear and greed: why the American housing credit crisis is worse than you think', *International Economy*, **21** (2), 22–55.

Liu, J., F.A. Longstaff and R.E. Mandell (2006), 'The market price of risk in interest rate swaps: the roles of default and liquidity risks', *Journal of Business*, **79** (5), 2337–2359.

Longstaff, F.A. (2004), 'The flight-to-liquidity premium in US Treasury bond prices', *Journal of Business*, **77** (3), 511–526.

Longstaff, F.A. (2010), 'The subprime credit crisis and contagion in financial markets', *Journal of Financial Economics*, **97** (3), 436–450.

Park, Y.C. and C.-Y. Song (1999), 'The East Asian financial crisis: a year later', *IDS Bulletin*, **30** (1), 93–107.

Pericoli, M. and M. Sbracia (2003), 'A primer on financial contagion', *Journal of Economic Surveys*, **17** (4), 571–608.

Swan, P.L. (2009), 'The political economy of the subprime crisis: why subprime was so attractive to its creators', *European Journal of Political Economy*, **25** (1), 124–132.

Udell, G. (2009), 'Wall Street, Main Street, and a credit crunch: thoughts on the current financial crisis', *Business Horizons*, **52** (2), 117–125.

Vassalou, M. and Y. Xing (2004), 'Default risk in equity returns', *Journal of Finance*, **59** (2), 831–868.

Weaver, K. (2008), 'The sub-prime mortgage crisis: a synopsis', Global Securitisation and Structured Finance, Deutsche Bank Research, 22–31.

PART IV

CORPORATE FINANCE

12 Empirical mergers and acquisitions research: a review of methods, evidence and managerial implications

Andrey Golubov, Dimitris Petmezas and
Nickolaos G. Travlos

12.1 INTRODUCTION

Mergers and acquisitions (M&As) are among the most important corporate events in the finance and business world in terms of both size and impact. For instance, at the peak of the most recent merger wave in the year 2007, corporations spent more than US$4 trillion, or over 7.5 per cent of world gross domestic product (GDP) (in market exchange rates), on acquisitions worldwide.[1] Takeovers effect substantial reallocations of resources both within and across industries, and shape the corporate landscape.[2] A carefully designed and executed acquisition can create substantial value for the merging firms by improving operational efficiency and taking advantage of other synergistic gains from combining business activities. However, bad acquisition decisions can also destroy viable business entities and cost executives their jobs.

Academic research on the topic of corporate takeovers is abundant. This is not surprising given the above discussion. In addition, while M&As are of interest in themselves, they also serve as a testing ground for many economics and finance theories as these transactions are the largest and the most readily observable form of corporate investment; there are almost no data on the investment projects that firms routinely undertake during the course of their business.

In this chapter we review the relevant academic literature on M&A activity, motives and performance.[3] Such a review is timely given that empirical M&A research has exploded in the last two decades, mostly due to the availability of rich, machine-readable transaction data. Our discussion of relevant theory is fairly limited – in fact, a proper review of the theoretical M&A literature would require a whole separate survey.

Much of the evidence we review comes from studies based on United States (US) or United Kingdom (UK) data. The reason for this is twofold. Firstly, these are the largest and the most active takeover markets. Secondly, the availability of high-quality data on M&A deals is best. While some of the findings we review here may not be universal, many patterns are indeed found in other markets. We point out both cases in several instances. We also summarize the key managerial implications arising from the wealth of research on this topic. Overall, we intend this chapter to be a general introduction to M&A research covering major empirical methods and findings of this literature.[4]

The rest of this chapter is organized as follows. Section 12.2 reviews the history of M&A activity. Section 12.3 proceeds with a discussion of the key motives behind M&As. In section 12.4 we address the fundamental question of whether M&As create value, with a particular focus on the methodological aspects of this line of inquiry. Section 12.5 surveys the many factors that were found to affect acquisition performance. Some other notable M&A-related empirical research is briefly reviewed in section 12.6. We outline some of the managerial implications arising from the research findings in section 12.7, and close the chapter with some final remarks in section 12.8.

12.2   THE HISTORY OF M&A ACTIVITY

It is natural to start from a historical perspective and to review trends in M&As. Economic history has shown that there are distinct 'waves' in the frequency and volume of M&As over time. Often, the total of M&A deals at the peak of a cycle may be several times the amount taking place at the trough. Usually a cycle builds up, with more and more deals occurring, often at increasingly unrealistic prices, until some trigger almost grinds all the activity to a complete halt. Then, after some time, the entire process starts from the beginning and the next wave emerges.

Two major theories explain why mergers occur in waves. Firstly, the neoclassical theory posits that merger waves occur as firms in specific industries react to economic shocks (deregulation, emergence of new technologies or substitute products and services), which explains why merger activity clusters by industry. The empirical evidence in support of this theory is provided by Gort (1969) and more recently by Mitchell and Mulherin (1996) and Harford (2005). The size and length of each wave largely depends on the number of industries influenced. The emergence of the Internet for instance was more pervasive than the deregulation of utilities. The second theory suggests that market valuations cause merger waves. When firm valuations deviate from fundamentals, managers use the overvalued stock of their firms as currency to buy the assets of undervalued (or less overvalued) firms (Shleifer and Vishny, 2003; Rhodes-Kropf and Viswanathan, 2004), which explains the correlation of merger activity with stock market performance. Accordingly, the overvaluation theory posits that more acquisitions will happen in periods of bubbles. Rhodes-Kropf et al. (2005) provide empirical evidence consistent with the market valuations theory of merger waves.

The history of M&As has seen six merger waves so far:[5]

1. 1893–1904: the first merger wave was characterized by horizontal mergers which created mining, steel, oil, telephone and railroad giants, thus defining the basic manufacturing and transportation industries in the US. The adoption of antitrust laws in the early twentieth century and the First World War ended the wave.
2. 1919–1929: the second merger wave saw a continuation of the consolidation that started earlier with a very significant degree of vertical integration. The major car manufacturers, such as Ford, were created during this period. The stock market crash of 1929 and the Great Depression ended this wave.
3. 1955–1969: in the third merger wave, the conglomerate concept took hold of corporate America. Major conglomerates including LTV, Teledyne and Litton emerged. Their owners and managers were viewed as the heroes of the new organizational model. However, their stocks declined substantially in 1969–1970 as conglomerate companies never achieved the anticipated benefits.

4. 1980–1989: in the US, the merger wave of the 1980s was characterized by major hostile takeover battles, the invention of the 'poison pill', the rise of junk bond financing, and leveraged buyouts. In Europe, cross-border horizontal mergers took place as a preparatory step for the common market. Even the 1987 stock market crash was unable to bring this merger wave to an end, but it retreated with the demise of the junk bond market, the savings and loan bank crisis and the capital problems faced by commercial banks.
5. 1993–2000: the fifth merger wave was characterized by the globalization of competition and thriving stock prices putting pressure on managers to do deals. Deals of unthinkable proportions, such as the combinations of Exxon and Mobil, Citibank and Travelers, Chrysler and Daimler, AOL and Time Warner, were conducted. From over $300 billion in 1992 the volume of M&As worldwide increased by $3.3 trillion in 2000. The wave faded away as the tech bubble burst, but only to be reborn very soon.
6. 2003–2007: the sixth merger wave was characterized by consolidation in the metals, oil, gas and utilities, telecoms, banking and health care sectors. This wave was fuelled by increasing globalization and encouragement by the governments of certain countries (France, Italy and Russia being illustrative examples) to create strong national and global 'champions'. Private equity buyers played a significant role, accounting for a quarter of the overall takeover activity, stimulated by the availability of credit that markets were prepared to provide at low interest rates. Cash-financed deals were much more prevalent over this period (Alexandridis et al. 2012).

12.3 THE MAIN MOTIVES FOR M&AS

12.3.1 Synergy Motives

The common goal of all M&As is the pursuit of synergy gains. Synergy is achieved when the value of the combination of the two firms is greater than the sum of the two stand-alone values (Jensen and Ruback, 1983; Bradley et al., 1988). This effect is often described as '1 + 1 = 3'.

The synergy gains can be operational or financial. They may take the form of: cost reductions and improvements in operational efficiency; revenue enhancements due to optimization of the distribution network (e.g. cross-selling); an increase in market power (e.g. elimination of competition); or various financial advantages (such as tax efficiency and leverage) (see, e.g., Seth, 1990a, 1990b).

The most typical source of synergies – cost reductions – can be achieved from economies of scale and scope, opportunities for eliminating duplicate facilities and functions, and increased bargaining power against suppliers. Synergies may also stem from sharing managerial competences and practices between the two firms. In addition, certain strategic benefits can be achieved via acquisition of valuable technology, knowledge and skills that can be applied in the combined firm.

Revenue enhancement, another frequently cited source of synergy, occurs when the merged entity attains higher sales and growth than two stand-alone companies could enjoy on their own. This can arise due to more streamlined product offerings (e.g., complementary products) and an enhanced distribution network. In addition, revenue enhancement could be due to increased market power and the elimination of competitors.

Diversification is another often-cited source of synergies in mergers. For instance, diversified firms may create so-called internal capital markets, which allow the allocation of resources between divisions without the frictions and inefficiencies of external ones.[6] In addition, Doukas and Travlos (1988) suggest that the acquisitions of foreign firms serve as a diversification medium enabling the expansion of the boundary of the acquirer which allows the internalization of benefits that would be otherwise lost due to various market frictions.

Moreover, synergies may arise from improvements in corporate governance, as the effectiveness of governance mechanisms differs between firms. Wang and Xie (2009) show that 'corporate governance transfers' affect merger synergies which are then shared between the merging firms. This source becomes even more important in international acquisitions, as corporate governance standards vary significantly across different markets. Bris and Cabolis (2008) show how differences in corporate governance across countries can be a motive for cross-border mergers.

Firms can also be motivated to merge by financial synergies, such as tax considerations. For instance, savings could arise from fully utilizing tax shields by exploiting unused debt capacity or other tax shields of the target firm (such as loss carry-forwards or the ability to 'step up' the value of the target's assets for increased depreciation charges). Scholes and Wolfson (1990) demonstrate the effects of the US tax reforms of the 1980s on the M&A market. In addition, Hayn (1989) shows that merger gains are positively associated with the tax attributes of the target such as loss carry-forwards, tax credits, and the possibility of higher depreciation charges from asset value step ups. Finally, Manzon et al. (1994) provide evidence that differences in the tax regimes affect returns to cross-border acquisitions.

The empirical evidence is consistent with the existence of positive synergy gains in M&As. Using detailed cash flow projections, Devos et al. (2009) show that the synergy gains are, on average, 10 per cent of the combined firm value, with the majority of this value coming from operating synergies rather than tax savings. The operating synergies come mostly from reduced investment expenditure rather than improved operating profits, which is consistent with improved resource allocation and inconsistent with increased market power.[7] In addition, Houston et al. (2001), using data on bank mergers, provide evidence of positive synergy gains that are attributable mostly to cost savings and not revenue enhancement. Finally, Hoberg and Phillips (2010) show that firms using similar product descriptions language in their regulatory filings (i.e., firms with potential asset complementarities) are more likely to merge and that such mergers generate higher gains than those between dissimilar firms.

Measurement of synergy gains

More formally, the synergy gain is the difference between the value of the combined firm and the two stand-alone values of the merging firms (the bidder and the target). Empirically, researchers rely on stock market or accounting data to infer synergy gains. For instance, the synergy gain can be measured by the change in the market value of the firms involved at the acquisition announcement (net of the expected value change, or market-wide effects). Bradley et al. (1988) and Servaes (1991) define synergy gains as the cumulative abnormal return (CAR) of the combined firm, which is a weighted-average CAR of the bidding and target firms' stock surrounding the announcement of the deal. The weights are the market capitalizations of the respective firms measured several days prior to the announcement.[8]

Alternatively, one can look at accounting measures of efficiency improvements, such as the change in abnormal operating performance of the combined firm from the pre-merger abnormal operating performance of the bidder and the target (e.g. Wang and Xie, 2009). Typically, operating performance is defined as the return on (total) assets (ROA) or return on sales (ROS), where operating income before depreciation is divided by the book value of total assets or by sales.[9] Abnormal performance is usually measured against the industry median or against a control firm chosen on the basis of industry, size and the level of pre-event operating performance.[10] The average three-year post-acquisition abnormal operating performance is typically used and compared to the abnormal operating performance in the pre-acquisition (or the average of three pre-acquisition) year(s).[11]

12.3.2 Agency Motivations

Under the agency motive, managers may undertake acquisitions against the interests of shareholders. For instance, Amihud and Lev (1981) argue that managers engage in conglomerate mergers in order to diversify the activities of the firm and smooth out earnings, thereby securing their jobs; however, this is against shareholder interests as they can diversify on their own at a very low cost. Further, Jensen (1986), in his theory of free cash flow, posits that managers with access to surplus cash favor engaging in pet projects and unprofitable acquisitions instead of returning cash to shareholders. This is a manifestation of the agency conflicts between owners and managers. Firstly, executive compensation is often linked to firm size, so that managers have a preference for growing the firm ever larger. As paying out cash to shareholders reduces firm size and managerial discretion, managers tend to engage in negative net present value (NPV) investments (such as value-destroying acquisitions). Secondly, it is simply more prestigious to head a large organization. Empire-building chief executive officers (CEOs), in contrast to overconfident managers (see below) who truly believe in their abilities to create value, are seeking more power against shareholder interests. Thus, prospects of higher remuneration and the prestige of running a larger firm push managers into making acquisitions even if the deal is detrimental to firm value. In line with the hubris hypothesis, and in contrast to the synergy motive, the empirical evidence reviewed below suggests that agency costs destroy shareholder value.

Measuring agency costs
Measuring agency costs requires quantification of the degree of incentives misalignment and the readiness of managers to take advantage of it – quite an infeasible task. However, we know that agency costs can be mitigated by proper alignment of managerial interests with those of shareholders by means of compensation contracts or stock ownership, as well as by directly monitoring managers. Therefore, researchers can proxy for the severity of agency costs using various corporate governance structures.

On the incentives alignment front, several studies suggest that acquiring firm managers whose personal wealth is more closely linked to firm value make better acquisition decisions. For instance, Tehranian et al. (1987) show that acquirers with long-term compensation plans in place perform better than acquirers without such plans. Further, Datta et al. (2001) show that managers with more equity-based compensation (e.g., in the form of stock options) make better acquisitions.[12] In addition, Lewellen et al. (1985) show that acquirer returns are higher for firms with high managerial stock ownership. However, Hubbard and Palia (1995) show that this relationship between managerial stock ownership and acquirer returns is non-monotonic, as at the high levels of managerial ownership acquirer returns start to decline (due to entrenchment, as argued by the authors). Finally, Lin et al. (2011) show that acquirers whose officers and directors are insured against personal liability for the actions taken on behalf of the firm make worse acquisitions as they pay higher premiums and enter deals with smaller synergies; in fact, they demonstrate that bidder gains are decreasing in the amount of such insurance coverage.

Turning to monitoring, the evidence shows that more intensive supervision of managerial actions leads to better acquisition decisions. The board of directors is a typical monitoring device present in any listed firm. Here, increased board independence, coming from the presence of outside directors and from the separation of the roles of CEO and chairman of the board, is assumed to lead to more effective monitoring and lower agency costs as a result. A number of studies investigate the link between board structures and acquirer returns. Byrd and Hickman (1992) examine tender offers for public firms and show that acquirer returns increase with the proportion of outsiders on the board. However, Masulis et al. (2007) do not find such a relationship, while Bauguess and Stegemoller (2008) report a negative link for a sample of Standard & Poor's (S&P) 500 (large) acquirers.

Finally, the market for corporate control acts as a governance mechanism of last resort whereby agency-infected firms become targets of disciplining takeovers, and self-serving managers are replaced with more effective leaders.[13] However, firms can become insulated from this market force by adopting anti-takeover provisions (ATPs) in their charters and by-laws. Consistent with the effectiveness of takeover threats as a disciplining mechanism, Masulis et al. (2007) document that acquirers with fewer ATPs make better acquisitions.

As suggested by Jensen (1986), free cash flow (cash flow in excess of what can be profitably invested by the firm) exacerbates agency problems by increasing managerial discretion. Coupled with few profitable investment opportunities, free cash flow can lead to value-destroying acquisitions. Lang et al. (1991) show that this is indeed the case, as high free cash flow is associated with lower acquirer returns, particularly for firms with poor investment opportunities (proxied by Tobin's Q). In addition, Harford (1999) shows that cash-rich acquirers (those holding above-normal cash reserves) are more likely to attempt acquisitions, particularly diversifying deals, and on average tend to destroy shareholder value and suffer abnormal declines in operating performance.

12.3.3   Managerial Overconfidence (the Hubris Hypothesis)

Managerial overconfidence (also known as the hubris hypothesis), first introduced by Roll (1986), assumes market efficiency and suggests that CEOs engage in M&A deals due to excessive optimism regarding their ability to create value and the resultant overestimation of synergies. The empirical evidence suggests that managers affected by hubris are more likely to destroy shareholder value (Malmendier and Tate, 2008). Doukas and Petmezas (2007) and Billett and Qian (2008) posit that managers with overconfidence, sourced by self-attribution bias, tend to attribute their initial success from previous corporate decisions to their own ability and, as a consequence, conduct worse deals later on which significantly underperform acquisitions initiated by non-overconfident acquirers.

Measurement of managerial overconfidence
Overconfidence is a very ethereal concept and is difficult to operationalize. Researchers have to rely on imperfect proxies. One of the measures of managerial overconfidence is the takeover premium (defined as the difference between the offer price and the pre-offer value of the target firm divided by the latter). Managers that pay high premia are likely to be overconfident (Hayward and Hambrick, 1997). However, takeover premia are influenced by many factors and are thus a noisy proxy.

Malmendier and Tate (2008) propose an alternative measure of managerial overconfidence. They define as overconfident those managers who hold in-the-money stock options until the year before the expiration date. Arguably, the main reason for not exercising the options is the CEO's belief in their superior leadership and continually rising stock price.

Another measure, also suggested by Malmendier and Tate (2008), is media portrayal and is based on the way the press characterizes the CEOs of the bidding firms. The process to construct the business press proxy, which involves the calculation of two indices, is as follows. Firstly, articles characterizing the CEO with the words 'confident', 'confidence', 'optimistic', 'optimism', 'certain' and 'positive' are counted. Secondly, an index counting the number of articles referring to the manager by using the terms 'reliable', 'cautious', 'prudent', 'conservative', 'practical', 'sensible', 'frugal', 'careful' or 'steady' is created. This procedure is repeated for each manager by year and for all years. For each manager, the group of articles (i.e., overconfident versus non-overconfident) that outnumbers its counterpart is determined. Finally, the number of years when the overconfident articles index for a CEO is greater than the one characterizing them as non-overconfident and vice versa is also estimated.

As suggested by Doukas and Petmezas (2007) the decision of managers to engage in multiple acquisitions, that is, high acquisitiveness, is another proxy for overconfidence. Doukas and Petmezas (2007) classify as overconfident the managers of firms which make five or more acquisitions within a short period of time (three years). The intuition behind this measure is that managers making many acquisitions within a short period of time cannot carefully evaluate the potential synergies and negotiate efficiently, leading to shareholder value destruction.[14]

Finally, Kolasinski and Li (2013) suggest an insider trading-based measure of CEO overconfidence. They classify a firm-year as having an overconfident CEO if the latter, on average, loses money on their own company's open-market stock purchases in the next two years. A CEO purchasing the stock in the firm under their control and losing money on the trade reveals that they have overestimated the value of the firm, which is precisely the notion of managerial overconfidence. A virtue of this measure is that it is easily constructed from machine-readable data and is available for almost any listed firm.

12.3.4 Other M&A Motives

As stated earlier, industry shocks and market valuations drive takeover activity, forming merger waves. Industry shocks trigger merger activity as a prospect to capture synergies by increasing market share or eliminating excess capacity, improving operational efficiency and saving on costs (Gort, 1969; Jensen, 1993). Examples of industry shocks include changes in input prices and supply, innovations in technology, and currency movements (Mulherin and Boone, 2000; Andrade and Stafford, 2004).

Booming markets are another motivation for mergers. Stock market misvaluation creates opportunities for firms to buy relatively undervalued assets. Moreover, firms may use their overvalued stock to finance the deal, thereby locking in real assets. However, in contrast to the hubris theory, the overvaluation hypothesis assumes that acquirers are rational and undertake the opportunities offered by inefficient financial markets. Savor and Lu (2009) provide empirical evidence that overvalued acquirers can create value by using their overvalued stock as cheap currency to buy relatively less overvalued targets. Finally, influence from investment banks, that earn high fees from advising on M&A deals and therefore have an incentive to keep deals flowing, is also seen as a motive behind takeover transactions.

12.4 VALUE CREATION IN M&A

From the finance perspective, one of the most important questions regarding M&As is whether they benefit the shareholders of the firms involved. Generally, the empirical literature, mainly based on the US and UK takeover markets, documents that target firm shareholders enjoy significantly positive abnormal returns (in the order of 20–40 per cent on average) at acquisition announcements – quite an intuitive finding given the hefty premia offered by acquirers (e.g., Song and Walkling, 1993; Bauguess et al., 2009).

Unfortunately, things are less clear-cut for acquirers. Most studies agree that in acquisitions of listed targets, acquiring firms realize negative to zero abnormal returns at the acquisition announcement (Andrade et al. 2001). However, recent evidence from M&As around the world shows that acquiring firms do gain in acquisitions of public firms beyond the most competitive takeover markets (the US, UK and Canada) as they pay lower premia, while share-for-share offers are at least non-value-destroying for their shareholders (Alexandridis et al. 2010).[15] While the conclusions regarding acquisitions of public targets are not as unanimous as one would like them be, the evidence from private acquisitions is far clearer: acquiring firms gain, particularly when stock is used as a method of payment (Chang, 1998; Fuller et al., 2002).

The combined entity (target and acquirer) generally enjoys a positive abnormal return around the announcement date (Bradley et al., 1988; Mulherin and Boone, 2000; Bhagat et al., 2005). As noted above, the combined firm returns are used as a proxy for the overall synergy gains brought about by the deal.

Turning to studies of long-term performance, Malatesta (1983) and Asquith (1983), among others, report significant negative abnormal returns in the year following the outcome announcement. Further, Agrawal et al. (1992) observe that acquiring firm shareholders suffer a statistically significant loss of about 10 per cent over the five-year period after the merger. Loderer and Martin (1992) find evidence of underperformance over three, but not over five, years following an acquisition. Contrary to the above findings, Franks et al. (1991) do not find significant underperformance over three years after the acquisition. They conclude that previous findings of poor performance after takeovers are likely due to benchmark portfolio errors rather than mispricing at the time of the deal. In addition, Loughran and Vijh (1997) show that acquirers paying with cash outperform the relevant benchmark over five years following the deal, while the converse is true for acquirers paying with stock. Rau and Vermaelen (1998) show that the negative abnormal stock performance over the three years following the deal is mostly concentrated among high-valuation (low book-to-market) acquirers, so-called 'glamour' firms. Most recently, Bouwman et al. (2009) show that two-year post-acquisition returns for deals initiated during high stock market valuation periods underperform those initiated during low stock market valuation periods.

12.4.1   Measuring Value Creation

To measure value creation from M&As, one can examine the effect of these transactions on acquirer shareholder wealth, target shareholder wealth, the valuation of the combined entity, and the operating performance improvement. From the perspective of finance theory, managerial decisions should enhance shareholder wealth. Is the value of acquiring and target firms' shares increasing enough to compensate investors for the risk they bear around or following an acquisition? Is the return they earn higher than the cost of capital (assuming that the required rate of return equals the opportunity cost of investing elsewhere)? The most common approach to examine value creation is the use of event study methods.[16]

Short-run event studies
If stock markets operate efficiently, they should assess all the future benefits and costs associated with a deal and incorporate them into stock prices at the time of the announcement. In this case, a short event window surrounding the announcement captures the valuation effects from mergers. Hence, assuming efficient markets, acquisition announcements will be accompanied by abnormal increases in stock prices for value-creative deals, while value-destroying acquisitions will trigger an abnormal decline in stock prices. The most widely used event windows include 2 days $(-1, 0)$, 3 days $(-1, +1)$, 5 days $(-2, +2)$, and 11 days $(-5, +5)$, where 0 indicates the announcement day itself. Including the days just before the announcement allows for capturing potential information leakages, while a few extra trading days following the announcement account for any delays in the stock price reaction. Abnormal returns are computed using the expression below:

$$AR_{it} = R_{it} - E(R_{it})$$

where AR_{it} is the abnormal return for security i on day t; R_{it} is the actual, observed return for security i on day t, and $E(R_{it})$ is the expected return for security i on day t.

The expected return is typically estimated using two related approaches. The first is the market model, which involves estimation of the market model parameters by regressing security returns on a benchmark index (Brown and Warner, 1985). This approach is followed by, among others, Moeller et al. (2005) and Masulis et al. (2007). The market model parameters obtained in the estimation procedure are further applied to the return on a benchmark index for a day of interest to yield the expected return on a stock:

$$E(R_{i,t}) = \alpha_i + \beta_i R_{mt}$$

where α: is the regression intercept for security i, and β: is the slope coefficient for security i, and R_{mt} is either an equally weighted or a value-weighted market index return. The parameters for the market model are most often estimated over a given number of trading days period prior to the deal, such as $(-205, -6)$ or $(-210, -11)$.

The second approach, used by Fuller et al. (2002), Dong et al. (2006) and Faccio et al. (2006), among others, is a market-adjusted model:

$$AR_{it} = R_{it} - R_{mt}$$

This is a modified market model with $\alpha_i = 0$ and $\beta_i = 1$ as the market model parameters. This way of specifying the expected return may be particularly useful in samples containing frequent acquirers, which might render market model parameters to an extent biased given that the estimation period includes earlier deal announcements. Nevertheless, according to Brown and Warner (1980), the difference between the two approaches is minimal.

The abnormal returns for a given day and a given firm are then cumulated over the event window so as to arrive at a cumulative abnormal return (CAR):

$$CAR_i = \Sigma AR_{it}$$

The statistical significance of the resultant CARs is then tested using formal statistical procedures exploiting the time-series and cross-sectional variation in the returns. In addition, one can appreciate the economic significance of these estimates by translating the percentage value changes into dollar gains (losses) by multiplying the CARs by the market value of the firm measured immediately prior to the beginning of the event window.

A note of caution on interpreting announcement effects

An important caveat regarding the interpretation of M&A announcement wealth effects is in order. The existing literature tends to make conclusions regarding M&A value creation based on announcement-period abnormal stock returns as described in the previous subsection. However, for the announcement effects to accurately reflect the value creation from the deal, two important assumptions have to be maintained (apart from market efficiency, of course): (1) that the bid is not anticipated; and (2) that the bid announcement is uncontaminated with other information regarding the stand-alone values of the firms involved. There is growing evidence that neither of these assumptions is uncontested.

Regarding the anticipation effect, Cai et al. (2011) show that takeover bids are anticipated at the time of the first bid after a dormant period (at the industry level). As a result,
the announcement period returns for deals following the initial bid are underestimated.
When one takes into account the market reaction of future bidders to an industry's initial
bid, the returns to bidding firms are considerably higher.

Turning to the contamination issue, Bhagat et al. (2005) show that conventional
announcement period CARs are subject to revelation bias, that is, they reflect information about bidder stand-alone value in addition to the information regarding the bid
itself. Using intervening events, such as competing bids, they are able to disentangle
the two effects and show that conventional CARs are biased downward. In addition,
certain takeover bids, such as stock-financed public firm acquisitions, are essentially
joint announcements (a takeover and an equity issue). Issues of public equity are known
to be associated with negative abnormal stock returns; thus, one cannot attribute the
announcement period return purely to the takeover-related value changes. Golubov
et al. (2012a) address this issue and develop a method that allows for the estimation of
returns attributable to the implied equity issuance using a sample of seasoned equity
offerings (SEOs). Net of this effect, stock-financed acquisitions of public firms are found
to be non-value-destructive, and the method of payment does not explain the part of the
announcement return attributable to the acquisition decision. In general, one has to be
aware of potential confounding and anticipation effects in event studies and be careful
in drawing firm conclusions regarding the value implications of corporate actions based
on event study results.

Long-run event studies

While the stock market reacts to new information and does so fairly quickly, there
is some evidence of 'stickiness' in stock prices (i.e. the stock market reaction to corporate events may be delayed). Capital market participants may need the time to
revise their judgements based on new information about the acquisition integration
and the response of rivals. This implies that the wealth effects from acquisitions may
need to be assessed over long-run event windows. Most common windows used are
one, two, three and five years after the deal, and the most widely used methodologies
employed to calculate long-run abnormal returns are calendar time portfolio regressions (CTPRs), calendar time abnormal returns (CTARs), buy-and-hold abnormal
returns (BHARs) and cumulative abnormal returns (CARs).[17] However, there are two
main problems associated with long-run event studies: (1) difficulties with statistical
test procedures, which result in reduced reliability of results (Barber and Lyon, 1997;
Kothari and Warner, 1997; Lyon et al. 1999), and (2) other events or policy changes
occurring within the event window or expected beyond this window may impact upon
the value of the firm. As a matter of fact, it is not feasible to isolate the effect of a
takeover on long-term abnormal returns from other events affecting the firm during
the event window.

In general, given the 'bad model' problem (i.e., no model in finance can accurately
predict stock returns, and this problem is compounded with longer horizons), the
results of long-run studies may be biased and should therefore be interpreted with
caution.

Post-acquisition operating performance

If acquisitions create real economic efficiency improvements, they have to eventually show up in reported accounting numbers. Thus, an alternative approach to estimating merger gains utilizes changes in the (abnormal) operating performance of the merged firm.

The most common measure of the abnormal operating performance of the acquiring firm is the operating ROA or ROS (earnings before interest, taxes, depreciation and amortisation – EBITDA over total assets or sales, respectively) adjusted for industry median or operating performance of a control firm based on industry classification, size and pre-merger operating performance. If a control firm is used, the process can be described as follows.

In the year immediately prior to the acquisition announcement, the acquirer is matched to a control firm from the same industry based on Standard Industry Classification (SIC) codes or Fama–French classifications. The control firm is chosen such that its book value of total assets is within 90 per cent and 110 per cent of acquirer total assets and its ROA is closest to that of the acquirer. If there is no firm within the 90–110 per cent limit, it is expanded to 70–130 per cent and again the firm with the ROA closest to that of the acquirer is chosen. Finally, if the 70–130 per cent filter fails, the range is expanded to the entire industry and the firm with the ROA measure closest to that of the acquirer is picked. Each acquisition is typically followed for three years after its completion. If a matching firm does not have three years of data, the process is repeated to select another matching company to complete the three-year series. For each year, the ROA of the control firm is subtracted from the ROA of the merged firm, and the average for the three years is taken. This number can then be compared to the pre-acquisition abnormal operating performance. See Barber and Lyon (1996) for more details and an evaluation of different variations of abnormal operating performance methodology.

A number of studies examine the operating performance of the acquiring firms, reporting mixed results. Healy et al. (1992) observe increases in the post-merger cash flow operating performance of merged firms for a sample of 50 largest US mergers. Heron and Lie (2002) report evidence of operating performance improvements using a more comprehensive sample of US deals, while Powell and Stark (2005) show evidence of (modest) operating performance improvements following UK M&A deals. In contrast, however, no significant operating performance improvements are found by Ghosh (2001) for US acquirers or Sharma and Ho (2002) for Australian acquirers.

12.4.2   Bondholder Wealth Effects

Shareholder wealth effects are only a part of the overall change in the value of the firm. The value of the firms' debt may also change, for instance due to a co-insurance effect. The investigation of this phenomenon is complicated most notably by the following two issues: (1) few firms have publicly traded debt, and findings based on firms that do have bonds outstanding may not be generalizable to all acquirers; and (2) methodological issues, such as appropriate benchmarks, multiple bond issues and thin trading; the latter is especially serious as it may require researchers to use monthly bond returns, which lowers the power of the tests (Bessembinder et al. 2009).

Nevertheless, several studies examine bondholder wealth effects in M&As. Kim and McConnell (1977) and Asquith and Kim (1982) do not find any bondholder wealth changes surrounding M&A deals, while Dennis and McConnell (1986) find negative acquirer bondholder returns. Eger (1983) and Maquieira et al. (1998) focus on stock-for-stock mergers and find evidence of positive abnormal returns to acquiring-firm bondholders; however, Travlos (1987) reports the opposite, consistent with the release of negative information hypothesis. Billett et al. (2004) show that below investment grade target firm bonds earn significantly positive abnormal returns, while acquirer bondholders tend to experience negative abnormal returns, consistent with the existence of a co-insurance effect.

Bessembinder et al. (2009) address various methodological issues in measuring abnormal bond performance. They also show that when using daily data from the TRACE database, the power of the tests is significantly improved. They confirm that on average acquiring firm bondholders realize negative abnormal returns at acquisition announcements; however, this result is not detected when using monthly data. As the finer daily data have only recently become available to researchers, we expect more evidence on bondholder wealth effects in M&As to emerge; in fact, we see this as a fruitful area for further research.

12.5   DETERMINANTS OF ACQUISITION RETURNS

Apart from synergy, overconfidence and agency cost proxies described earlier, several firm and deal characteristics shape acquisition returns. Since the literature on M&A value creation is dominated by short-run event studies, we focus on the findings of this type of study.[18] Below, we present some of the most important characteristics noted in the literature, their association with bidder returns (and target returns where evidence exists), and the explanations put forward for these relationships.

12.5.1   Target Firm Listing Status

The organizational form of the target firm (whether the target is a public, private or subsidiary firm) is a very important determinant of takeover gains. Chang (1998) and Fuller et al. (2002) for the US, Faccio et al. (2006) for several Western European countries, and Draper and Paudyal (2006) for the UK, show that bids for listed (public) targets lead to zero-to-negative bidder returns, while acquisitions of non-listed (private or subsidiary) firms lead to positive returns for bidding firms. These findings are consistent with bidders acquiring privately held firms capturing an illiquidity discount.[19] In fact, Officer (2007a) shows that acquisitions of unlisted firms occur at 15–30 per cent lower multiples than otherwise comparable acquisitions of listed firms.

In addition, stock-financed acquisitions of private targets are associated with even larger positive bidder returns. This could be due to the following two effects. Firstly, acceptance of a stock offer by the shareholders of a private target, who are likely to have received private information from the bidder, conveys to the market that the bidder's shares are not overvalued (the information hypothesis). Secondly, given that the ownership in private targets is typically concentrated, a stock offer creates block holders. Since block holders have a significant stake in the combined firm, they have the incentives (and the ability) to monitor managers; thus, the market may be pricing the benefits of this expected monitoring at the time of the announcement (the monitoring hypothesis).

12.5.2   The Method of Payment

The method of payment is also among the most significant determinants of acquisition returns. Firstly, Travlos (1987) documents that bidders offering their own stock as the medium of exchange in public firm acquisitions experience lower (negative) returns than those offering cash payment (normal returns). This is consistent with the Myers and Majluf (1984) adverse selection framework whereby value-maximizing managers in possession of superior information regarding the value of the firm under their control decide to issue equity only when it is overvalued. Investors are aware of this behavior and adjust the stock price of equity issuers down accordingly.[20] Supporting this view, Chemmanur et al. (2009) show that acquirers whose stock prices are significantly higher than the intrinsic values estimated by accounting earnings-based models are more likely to use stock as means of payment, and that the degree of this overvaluation negatively affects bidder returns.

Secondly, Mitchell et al. (2004) show that almost half of the negative acquirer return at announcement of stock-financed public firm acquisitions can be attributed to price pressure effects rather than informed trading. Public firm takeover situations provide opportunities for merger arbitrage, whereby arbitrageurs assume the risk of deal completion by buying target firm stock at the post-announcement price hoping to receive the offer price at deal execution. However, when the offer consideration is stock, particularly in fixed exchange ratio stock offers, the value of the arbitrage position is uncertain and depends on the value of acquiring firm stock at deal completion. Arbitrageurs therefore short-sell acquirer shares to lock in the arbitrage spread existing at the announcement of stock-financed deals, thereby exerting negative price pressure on the acquirer stock. In this case, the negative announcement effect is not caused by trading on fundamentals as in the Myers and Majluf (1984) adverse selection framework.[21]

Target firms also gain less when the offer consideration is stock (Wansley et al., 1983; Huang and Walkling, 1987). Higher premia in cash offers can be explained by the fact that cash offers are usually taxable transactions, that is, selling shareholders become liable for tax on any capital gains on the shares sold; in contrast, there is no immediate tax liability in a stock swap deal (Brown and Ryngaert, 1991). Accordingly, stock offers can entail lower premia, other things being equal.[22]

Further, as noted above, the effects of the method of payment on bidder returns and target listing status are interrelated, as bidders paying with equity in acquisitions of non-listed firms (private and subsidiary) enjoy higher returns than those paying with cash (Chang, 1998; Fuller et al., 2002), which is the opposite to what is observed in listed-firm acquisitions.

Finally, recent evidence by Alexandridis et al. (2010) shows that acquirers do not experience negative returns even when using stock as a method of payment in acquisitions taking place in relatively less competitive takeover markets (outside the US, UK and Canada). The authors attribute this finding to the fact that the negative signalling effect of stock financing is subdued by the lower premium offered to target firms in less competitive takeover markets.

12.5.3 Industry Relatedness

The industry relatedness of the target firm also affects acquisition returns. Both Matsusaka (1993) and Hubbard and Palia (1999) show that during the conglomerate merger wave of the 1960s and early 1970s in the US, diversifying acquisitions were welcomed by the market with positive bidder returns. However, the former study reports that these gains are higher than those for related acquisitions, while the latter reports the opposite.

Focusing on a broader sample of M&A deals, Morck et al. (1990) provide evidence that diversifying acquisitions, defined as those where the acquirer and the target do not share the same primary four-digit SIC code, perform worse than focused deals.[23] Fan and Goyal (2006) find that mergers achieving vertical integration also generate higher acquirer returns than pure diversifying deals. Further, Hoberg and Phillips (2010) report that firms using similar product description language (a proxy for asset similarities and complementarities) generate higher acquisition gains. In bank mergers, DeLong (2001) documents that the most value-creating deals are those that are focused in terms of both activity and geography.

Finally, Moeller and Schlingemann (2005) show that deals diversifying the acquiring firm internationally exhibit lower returns than those decreasing international diversification (see also the section on cross-border acquisitions below).

12.5.4 Firm Size

The size of the bidding and target firms affects acquisitions returns. Bidder (target) size is typically defined as the bidding (target) firm market capitalization some time prior to the acquisition announcement, usually four weeks (see, e.g., Fuller et al., 2002).[24] Moeller et al. (2004) provide evidence that bidder announcement returns are negatively related to bidder size. Bidder size may proxy for the severity of agency costs, as the incentives of managers in small firms are better aligned with those of the shareholders. Managers in smaller firms should also be subject to closer monitoring due to higher ownership concentration as shown by Demsetz and Lehn (1985). In addition, managers of larger firms may be more prone to hubris given that these managers feel more important socially, have succeeded in growing the firm and face fewer obstacles in finding resources to finance the deal (Moeller et al., 2004). Schwert (2000) shows that larger targets also generate lower acquisition returns for target-firm shareholders given that larger targets receive lower percentage takeover premiums.

12.5.5 Firm Valuation and Investment Opportunities

The valuations of merging firms (which also proxy for growth opportunities) shape acquisition returns. Early studies adopt Tobin's Q as a measure of firm valuation. Tobin's Q is a ratio of the firm's market value of assets to their replacement cost. It is typically approximated as the book value of assets plus market value of common equity less the book value of common equity (and sometimes also less deferred taxes) divided by the book value of assets. Lang et al. (1989) and Servaes (1991) show that high Q bidders enjoy higher returns. Other studies employ a close counterpart of

Tobin's Q, the book-to-market ratio (B/M) as alternative proxy for firm valuation. B/M is usually defined as the book value of equity divided by the market value of equity. Dong et al. (2006) document that bidder and target short-run returns are positively associated with the B/M ratios of the respective firms, which comes in contrast to earlier evidence.

12.5.6   Pre-Announcement Stock Price Run-Up

The pre-announcement stock price behavior affects acquisition returns. The bidder (target) stock price run-up is most commonly calculated as the market-adjusted buy-and-hold stock return over a certain pre-announcement trading period, such as 200 trading days ending six days prior to the announcement date (Moeller et al., 2007). Rosen (2006) establishes a negative association between bidder returns and bidder stock price run-up, but Schwert (1996) does not find such a relationship between target returns and target stock price run-up.

12.5.7   Information Asymmetry

Information asymmetry regarding the value of merging firms affects acquisition returns. While information asymmetry is impossible to measure with precision, the most commonly used proxy is idiosyncratic stock return volatility introduced by Dierkens (1991). It is measured as the standard deviation of daily market-adjusted stock returns (or market model residuals) over a certain time period, such as starting 205 trading days and ending six days prior to the announcement of the deal (Moeller et al., 2007). The latter study provides evidence that high information asymmetry (high sigma) bidders generate lower announcement-period returns in stock-financed acquisitions. In addition, Officer et al. (2009) show that bidders gain more when stock is used for the acquisitions of high-sigma targets. Alternative proxies for information asymmetry include the number of analysts following the firm, the dispersion of analyst forecasts, mean analyst forecast error, firm age, bid–ask spread, the ratio of intangibles to total assets or the ratio of research and development (R&D) expenses to sales.

12.5.8   Cross-Border Acquisitions

The returns to merging firms also seem to be affected by the cross-border status of the deal. Holding the acquiring-firm nation fixed (the US), Doukas and Travlos (1988) show that multinational corporations expanding into new markets for the first time enjoy significantly positive returns. More recently, however, Moeller and Schlingemann (2005) show that cross-border acquisitions generate lower returns than domestic acquisitions for US acquirers; the same is true for UK acquirers (Conn et al., 2005). Holding the target-firm country fixed (Canada), Eckbo and Thorburn (2000) show that domestic acquirers perform better than foreign (US) acquirers.

Regarding cross-border deals, John et al. (2010) show that acquirer returns in cross-border public firm acquisitions are positive when the target-firm country has low shareholder protection, and negative when the target-firm country has high shareholder protection (but no such effect in private firm acquisitions). They also show that acquirer returns are increasing with the quality of accounting standards but decreasing with creditor protection in the target-firm nation.

On the target side, target-firm shareholders gain more when they are acquired by foreign firms (Harris and Ravenscraft, 1991; Shaked et al., 1991). However, Cebenoyan et al. (1992) argue that this is not always the case, and holds only when foreign competition is high. Servaes and Zenner (1994) show that returns to foreign acquisitions in the US vary with the tax regimes and reforms of the 1980s, suggesting that tax considerations are important in cross-border deals.

Bris and Cabolis (2008) document that cross-border acquisitions by firms located in high investor protection regimes acquiring firms from weaker investor protection regimes leads to higher target-firm returns. A similar relationship is observed for the differences in accounting standards of the merging firms. The authors argue that target gains (and thus premia) in cross-border acquisitions represent the value of shifts in investor protection.

12.5.9   The Acquisition Technique

The acquisition technique has also been found to affect acquisition returns. Jensen and Ruback (1983) document that tender offers are associated with higher bidder and target announcement period returns. Tender offers are, to a large extent, cash-financed deals, while mergers are more typically stock offers. As already described above, stock-financed deals are received by the market as signals of bidder overvaluation, leading to declines in bidder stock price. Thus, returns to bidders and targets in tender offers are, on average, higher than in mergers. In addition, Boone and Mulherin (2007, 2008) study whether the use of auctions versus negotiated deals affects the returns to the merging firms, but do not find such effects (this point is also related to takeover competition, see section 12.5.11).

12.5.10   Relative Size of the Deal

Relative size of the deal also affects merger gains. Relative size is usually defined as the deal value divided by bidder market value four weeks prior to the acquisition announcement. Target market values can be used instead of deal value in public firm acquisitions. Bidder returns have been shown to decrease with the relative size of the target in public firm acquisitions; however, bidders experience higher returns as the relative deal size increases in acquisitions of privately held firms (Fuller et al., 2002). Target-firm returns exhibit a negative relationship with the relative size of the deal (Officer, 2003).

12.5.11   Takeover Competition

Competition for the target is also important in explaining merger gains. Intuitively, competition for the target should decrease bidder returns and increase target returns as it raises the price that the successful acquirer must pay. Empirically, it is difficult to capture such competition. While the number of bidders in a given takeover contest is an obvious candidate, it does not capture competition that the acquirer may pre-empt by offering a sufficiently high premium. Michel and Shaked (1988) show that target returns in multiple bidder contests appear to be higher but this is only detectable after the arrival of the second bid, not at the announcement of the first bid.

In addition, while multiple bidder contests are rare, suggesting that most bidders are uncontested in their pursuit of a given target, there is significant pre-announcement competition for the target. However, it does not appear to affect the returns to the target (Boone and Mulherin, 2007) or bidding firms (Boone and Mulherin, 2008). James and Wier (1987) show that in bank mergers, where identification of potential competing bidders is relatively easy due to the nature of regulation, the returns to acquiring banks are negatively affected by potential takeover competition, while they are positively related to the availability of alternative target banks. Finally, Alexandridis et al. (2010) provide evidence that acquirers enjoy larger gains at the expense of target firms in countries with less competitive takeover markets, as proxied by the percentage of public firms taken over in a given country in a given year.

12.5.12 Hostility

The resistance of target-firm managers also affects acquisition returns. Hostile deals are acquisitions pursued without the acceptance of the target-firm's management. Servaes (1991) documents that hostile bids are associated with relatively lower bidder returns, while Schwert (2000) finds no significant effect for the bidder, but a positive effect for the target. Takeover premia tend to be higher in hostile deals in order to induce the selling shareholders to surrender to the predator.

12.5.13 Financial Advisor Reputation

Given that most acquisitions involve financial advisors responsible for carrying out the deal, several studies examine the effect of financial advisor (investment bank) reputation on acquisition returns. McLaughlin (1992) finds acquirers using lower-tier bankers as financial advisors enjoy higher returns. On the other hand, Servaes and Zenner (1996) find no such relationship. Rau (2000) finds that top-tier advisors do not deliver better returns apart from when tender offers are used, and that post-acquisition returns are more negative when a large part of advisory fees is contingent on deal completion. Kale et al. (2003) examine tender offers and show that only the relative reputation of the merging parties' advisors has a positive effect on bidder returns. Most recently, Golubov et al. (2012b) show that top-tier advisors are associated with higher bidder returns, but only in public firm acquisitions, arguing that the publicity of listed-firm takeover situations creates the exposure required for the reputation forces to come into effect.

12.5.14 Other Factors

As noted above, this is necessarily an incomplete list of determinants of takeover-related gains. We have only attempted to summarize the most prominent variables that are found to be important in many studies. Others have also established that factors influencing returns to merger announcements range from leverage (Maloney et al., 1993), accounting conservatism (Francis and Martin, 2010) and target-firm investor inertia (Baker et al., 2007) to stock market valuations (Bouwman et al. 2009), merger market sentiment (Rosen, 2006) and whether target-firm CEOs receive unscheduled stock option grants during merger negotiations (Fich et al., 2011). As the research goes forward, many new determinants of M&A-related gains will be uncovered.

12.6   OTHER M&A-RELATED EMPIRICAL RESEARCH

While the wealth effects of M&As and their determinants are the most popular lines of inquiry within empirical M&A research (hence our focus in this chapter), they are by no means the only ones. Other phenomena associated with M&A deals have also received considerable attention in the literature. Most notably they are (without going into the details of the findings): the choice of payment method (e.g., Martin, 1996; Ghosh and Ruland, 1988; Amihud et al., 1990; Faccio and Masulis, 2005; Chemmanur et al., 2009), the determinants of deal completion (e.g., Hoffmeister and Dyl, 1981; Walkling 1985; Samuelson and Rosenthal, 1986; Officer, 2003), questions pertaining to merger arbitrage (e.g., Brown and Raymond, 1986; Larcker and Lys, 1987; Baker and Savaşoglu, 2002; Mitchell and Pulvino, 2001; Jindra and Walkling, 2004; Hsieh and Walkling, 2005; Officer, 2007b), and the prediction of takeover targets (e.g., Palepu, 1986; Mitchell and Lehn, 1990; Ambrose and Megginson, 1992; Brar et al. 2009).

There also seem to be fruitful research avenues on the intersection of M&A and asset pricing. For instance, there is evidence that exposure to takeovers affects stock returns (Cremers et al., 2009), and that stock prices themselves affect takeover likelihoods (Edmans et al., 2012).

12.7   MANAGERIAL IMPLICATIONS

What can we as a society learn and gain from the wealth of studies on M&A transactions? What should managers keep in mind when carrying out their acquisition plans? What should board members remember when they approve deals? What should shareholders expect when they invest? Here we briefly outline some of the most prominent practical implications.

M&As are complex events, and so it is no wonder that many acquisitions fail to create value for acquirers, and some even destroy significant value. If one focuses on this general finding, one may question why managers are even allowed to pursue these deals at this scale. The 'M&A does not pay' conclusion is somewhat premature as it is based on the overall average. There is wide variation around this average. In fact, Moeller et al. (2005) show that while during the 1998–2001 period in the US acquisitions destroyed value on average, this overall loss is caused by a small number of large-loss deals. When one purges the sample of these unfortunate transactions, the overall bidding activity appears to be value-creating.[25] The truth is that there are firms that succeed in creating substantial wealth through acquisitions. How do they do this?

Perhaps the most important aspect is motivation. The right motive for acquisitions should be the pursuit of synergies, not personal gain for managers. The market appears to be able to see through agency-motivated managers and punishes them by depressing the firms' share prices. And even when the managers truly believe they are about to create value from another acquisition, they should bear in mind that they often tend to be overly optimistic and overestimate their abilities.[26] Again, the markets appear to sense these situations and respond accordingly. In light of this, it is reassuring that the synergy motive seems to be the driving force behind most deals; however, deals motivated by agency conflicts or hubris are also part of the M&A arena (see Berkovitch and Narayanan, 1993; Seth et al., 2000).

Another crucial issue is that acquirers often overpay for their targets, so that more than the created synergy is given away to the target-firm's shareholders, leaving the acquirer worse off even in well-motivated deals (Eccles et al., 1999). Other frequently cited reasons for M&A failure include poor business fit between the merging firms, undue influence from unscrupulous investment bankers or other advisors, and difficulties in post-merger integration arising from managerial power struggles and personnel tensions.

But of course, all of these issues should be considered once the firm has made a thorough review of its strategic alternatives in light of its industry's developments and a conclusion that M&A is the way forward has been reached. While M&A is a powerful tool for rapid growth and value creation (though not always), it is not the only one.

12.8   CONCLUSIONS

Empirical M&A research is vast and growing. We have attempted to summarize some of the most prominent results in this literature, relating them to the pertinent academic theory, and pointing out the possible managerial implications of these findings. As the empirical literature on M&A activity exploded during the last three decades, largely due to the availability of machine-readable transaction databases, academics have made considerable progress in their understanding of this complex activity. However, much is still to be discovered. For instance, the overwhelming majority of existing evidence pertains to the US takeover market, with some advances into Canadian and European (mostly UK) settings. As M&A activity becomes more global, many interesting tests exploiting the different institutional characteristics of various countries become amenable to researchers. And even for the well-researched markets, our understanding of M&As will improve as new and finer data become available. Meanwhile, M&As continue to be an integral part of the business world, a hotly debated issue for board members and policy makers, and a fruitful area for further research.

NOTES

1. Source: Thomson Financial SDC and International Monetary Fund.
2. The terms 'mergers', 'acquisitions' and 'takeovers' will be used interchangeably throughout this chapter. While there may be certain distinctions between these notions, the differences are of more interest to accountants and lawyers than to financial economists, managers and investors. The common theme is a combination of business activities and/or entities and the associated change in control over corporate assets.
3. The stream of empirical M&A research is vast and growing, making any survey inevitably selective; we make no claim of completeness.
4. As a next step, we recommend Betton et al. (2008) for a more quantitative treatment of research on

corporate takeovers. We also recommend Jensen and Ruback (1983) and Jarrell et al. (1988) for systematic reviews of the early M&A research, and Andrade et al. (2001) for a more recent overview.

5. This section draws on Lipton (2006).
6. There is a separate stream of research on corporate diversification and conglomeration. See Maksimovic and Phillips (2007).
7. Operating synergies were found to constitute the bulk of overall value gains in same-industry deals, while financial (tax) synergies were more important in diversifying mergers.
8. Effectively, this is a variant of event study methodology. See section 12.4.1 for more details.
9. On the one hand, a return measure based on operating profit before depreciation (and interest charges) is preferred as it allows for comparisons across firms with different depreciation policies and borrowing levels or costs. On the other hand, given that certain synergies are of a financial nature, such as tax efficiency due to increased depreciation or interest tax savings, a return measure based on operating profit would miss their effect.
10. The latter is done to account for mean-reversion. Barber and Lyon (1996) highlight the need for performance-matching, particularly in samples that are likely to exhibit pre-event abnormal performance.
11. See also section 12.4.1.
12. Minnick et al. (2011) also show that in bank mergers, managers with higher pay-for-performance sensitivity make fewer but better deals.
13. See Martin and McConnell (1991) for evidence of target firm top management turnover following takeovers, particularly in underperforming targets.
14. However, one has to be careful in dubbing managers engaging in multiple acquisitions as overconfident, given that the dynamics of certain industries (such as technology) may necessitate this strategy.
15. See section 12.5 for how the method of payment shapes the M&A-related shareholder wealth effects.
16. The reader can refer to Kothari and Warner (2007) for a chapter-length treatment of event study methods.
17. See Barber and Lyon (1997), Lyon et al. (1999) and Mitchell and Stafford (2000) for a discussion of these methodologies and issues arising in their implementation.
18. In fact, only a few variables are consistently found to be significant in explaining long-run acquirer returns, most notably the method of payment, stock market and acquirer valuation, and the type of the deal (tender offer versus merger). See section 12.4.1 on long-run event studies.
19. A related argument is as follows. If the market for corporate control is competitive, such as that for publicly traded firms, then any acquisition should represent a zero NPV investment. In the case of a privately held target, however, competition is likely limited, so that the likelihood of underpayment is high.
20. In fact, Houston and Ryngaert (1997), for a sample of bank mergers, and Officer (2004), for a larger sample of M&A deals, show that acquirer announcement returns are more negative when the value of consideration is more sensitive to the acquirer stock price (as is the case in fixed exchange ratio deals where the offer is fixed in the number of shares offered to the target but the value of the payment depends on the acquirer stock price at closing).
21. Note that the focus of this discussion is the method of payment (i.e., the medium of exchange). Several studies also examine the source of financing. Holding the method of payment fixed (e.g., cash deals), Schlingemann (2004) shows that acquisitions paid for with cash that is likely to have come from prior equity issues are associated with higher bidder returns (he argues that this is due to the resolution of uncertainty regarding the use of funds), while the amount of *ex ante* debt financing does not affect the returns. On the other hand, Bharadwaj and Shivdasani (2003) show that bank-debt-financed tender offers are associated with higher bidder returns due to the certification and monitoring effect of bank debt; Martynova and Renneboog (2009) report similar findings for European M&A deals.
22. Malmendier et al. (2011) provide an alternative explanation for why cash offers exhibit higher announcement returns for target firm shareholders. They argue that cash offers reveal positive information about the target firm's stand-alone value (while stock offers do not), so that part of the target firm's stock price increase at the announcement reflects this revaluation.
23. Another measure of industry relatedness proposed by the authors is the correlation between the monthly stock returns of the bidder and the target. Other studies have also used three-digit or two-digit SIC codes or Fama–French industry classifications.
24. Others also use the market or book value of assets.
25. In fact, Moeller et al. (2005) note that these large-loss deals were conducted by rather overvalued bidders, so that the wealth destruction they document could be attributed to a revaluation of bidder stand-alone values.
26. An example from the day-to-day world illustrates this point well: almost all people believe that their driving skills are above average, which is simply impossible.

REFERENCES

Agrawal, A., J.F. Jaffe and G.N. Mandelker (1992), 'The post-merger performance of acquiring firms: A re-examination of an anomaly', *Journal of Finance*, **47**, 1605–1622.

Alexandridis, G., C. Mavrovitis and N.G. Travlos (2012), 'How have M&As changed? Evidence from the sixth merger wave', *European Journal of Finance*, **18**, 663–688.

Alexandridis, G., D. Petmezas and N.G. Travlos (2010), 'Gains from M&As around the world: New evidence', *Financial Management*, **39**, 1671–1695.

Ambrose, B.W. and W.L. Megginson (1992), 'The role of asset structure, ownership structure, and takeover defenses in determining acquisition likelihood', *Journal of Financial and Quantitative Analysis*, **27**, 575–589.

Amihud, Y. and B. Lev (1981), 'Risk reduction as a managerial motive for conglomerate mergers', *Bell Journal of Economics*, **12**, 605–617.

Amihud, Y., B. Lev and N.G. Travlos (1990), 'Corporate control and the choice of investment financing: the case of corporate acquisitions', *Journal of Finance*, **45**, 603–616.

Andrade, G., M. Mitchell and E. Stafford (2001),'New evidence and perspectives on mergers', *Journal of Economic Perspectives*, **15**, 103–120.

Andrade, G. and E. Stafford (2004), 'Investigating the economic role of mergers', *Journal of Corporate Finance*, **10**, 1–36.

Asquith, P. (1983), 'Merger bids, uncertainty, and stockholder returns', *Journal of Financial Economics*, **11**, 51–83.

Asquith, P. and E.H. Kim (1982), 'The impact of merger bids on the participating firm's security holders', *Journal of Finance*, **37**, 1209–1228.

Baker, M., J. Coval and J.C. Stein (2007), 'Corporate financing decisions when investors take the path of least resistance', *Journal of Financial Economics*, **84**, 266–298.

Baker, M. and S. Savaşoglu (2002), 'Limited arbitrage in mergers and acquisitions', *Journal of Financial Economics*, **64**, 91–115.

Barber, B.M. and J.D. Lyon (1996), 'Detecting abnormal operating performance: the empirical power and specification of test statistics', *Journal of Financial Economics*, **41**, 359–399.

Barber, B.M. and J.D. Lyon (1997), 'Detecting long-run abnormal stock returns: the empirical power and specification of test statistics', *Journal of Financial Economics*, **43**, 341–372.

Bauguess, S.W., S.B. Moeller, F.P. Schlingemann and C.J. Zutter (2009), 'Ownership structure and target returns', *Journal of Corporate Finance*, **15**, 48–65.

Bauguess, S.W and M. Stegemoller (2008), 'Protective governance choices and the value of acquisition activity', *Journal of Corporate Finance*, **14**, 550–566.

Berkovitch, E. and M.P. Narayanan (1993), 'Motives for takeovers: an empirical investigation, *Journal of Financial and Quantitative Analysis*, **28**, 347–362.

Bessembinder, H., K.M. Kahle, W.F. Maxwell and D. Xu (2009), 'Measuring abnormal bond performance', *Review of Financial Studies*, **22**, 4219–4258.

Betton, Sandra, B.E. Eckbo and K.S. Thorburn (2008), 'Corporate takeovers', in B.E. Eckbo (ed.), *Handbook of Corporate Finance: Empirical Corporate Finance* (vol. 2), Amsterdam: Elsevier/North-Holland, pp. 291–429.

Bhagat, S., M. Dong, D. Hirshleifer and R. Noah (2005), 'Do tender offers create value? New methods and evidence', *Journal of Financial Economics*, **76**, 3–60.

Bharadwaj, A. and A. Shivdasani (2003), 'Valuation effects of bank financing in acquisitions', *Journal of Financial Economics*, **67**, 113–148.

Billett, M.T., T.-H.D. King and D.C. Mauer (2004), 'Bondholder wealth effects in mergers and acquisitions: New evidence from the 1980s and 1990s', *Journal of Finance*, **59**, 107–135.

Billett, M.T. and Y. Qian (2008), 'Are overconfident CEOs born or made? Evidence of self-attribution bias from frequent acquirers', *Management Science*, **54**, 1037–1051.

Boone, A.L. and J.H. Mulherin (2007),'How are firms sold?', *Journal of Finance*, **62**, 847–875.

Boone, A.L., and J.H Mulherin (2008), 'Do auctions induce a winner's curse? New evidence from the corporate takeover market', *Journal of Financial Economics*, **89**, 1–19.

Bouwman, C.H.S., K. Fuller and A.S. Nain (2009), 'Market valuation and acquisition quality: Empirical evidence', *Review of Financial Studies*, **22**, 633–679.

Bradley, M., A. Desai and E.H. Kim (1988), 'Synergistic gains from corporate acquisitions and their division between the stockholders of target and acquiring firms', *Journal of Financial Economics*, **21**, 3–40.

Brar, G., D. Giamouridis and M. Liodakis (2009), 'Predicting European takeover targets', *European Financial Management*, **15**, 430–450.

Bris, A. and C. Cabolis (2008), 'The value of investor protection: evidence from cross-border mergers', *Review of Financial Studies*, **21**, 2605–2648.

Brown, D.T. and M.D. Ryngaert (1991), 'The mode of acquisition in takeovers: taxes and asymmetric information', *Journal of Finance*, **46**, 653–669.

Brown, K.C. and M.V. Raymond (1986), 'Risk arbitrage and the prediction of successful corporate takeovers', *Financial Management*, **15**, 54–63.

Brown, S.J. and J.B. Warner (1980), 'Measuring security price performance', *Journal of Financial Economics*, **8**, 205–258.

Brown, S.J. and J.B. Warner (1985), 'Using daily stock returns: the case of event studies', *Journal of Financial Economics*, **14**, 3–31.

Byrd, J.W. and K.A. Hickman (1992), 'Do outside directors monitor managers?', *Journal of Financial Economics*, **32**, 195–221.

Cai, J., M.H. Song and R.A. Walkling (2011), 'Anticipation, acquisitions and bidder returns: industry shocks and the transfer of information across rivals', *Review of Financial Studies*, **24**, 1–44.

Cebenoyan, A.S, G.J. Papaioannou and N.G. Travlos (1992), 'Foreign takeover activity in the US and wealth effects for target firm shareholders', *Financial Management*, **21**, 58–68.

Chang, S. (1998), 'Takeovers of privately held targets, methods of payment, and bidder returns', *Journal of Finance*, **53**, 773–784.

Chemmanur, T.J., I. Paeglis and K. Simonyan (2009), 'The medium of exchange in acquisitions: does the private information of both acquirer and target matter?', *Journal of Corporate Finance*, **15**, 523–542.

Conn, R.L., A. Cosh, P.M. Guest and A. Hughes (2005), 'The impact on UK acquirers of domestic, cross-border, public and private acquisitions', *Journal of Business Finance and Accounting*, **32**, 815–870.

Cremers, M.K.J., V.B. Nair and K. John (2009), 'Takeovers and the cross-section of returns', *Review of Financial Studies*, **22**, 1409–1445.

Datta, S., M. Iskandar-Datta and K. Raman (2001), 'Executive compensation and corporate acquisition decisions', *Journal of Finance*, **56**, 2299–2336.

DeLong, G.L. (2001), 'Stockholder gains from focusing versus diversifying bank mergers', *Journal of Financial Economics*, **59**, 221–252.

Demsetz, H. and K. Lehn (1985), 'The structure of corporate ownership: causes and consequences', *Journal of Political Economy*, **93**, 1155–1177.

Dennis, D.K. and J.J. McConnell (1986), 'Corporate mergers and security returns', *Journal of Financial Economics*, **16**, 143–187.

Devos, E., P.-R. Kadapakkam and S. Krishnamurthy (2009), 'How do mergers create value? A comparison of taxes, market power, and efficiency improvements as explanations for synergies', *Review of Financial Studies*, **22**, 1179–1211.

Dierkens, N. (1991), 'Information asymmetry and equity issues', *Journal of Financial and Quantitative Analysis*, **26**, 181–199.

Dong, M.,D. Hirshleifer, S. Richardson and S.H. Teoh (2006), 'Does investor misvaluation drive the takeover market?', *Journal of Finance*, **61**, 725–762.

Doukas, J.A. and D. Petmezas (2007), 'Acquisitions, overconfident managers and self-attribution bias', *European Financial Management*, **13** (3), 531–577.

Doukas, J. and N.G. Travlos (1988), 'The effect of corporate multinationalism on shareholders' wealth: evidence from international acquisitions', *Journal of Finance*, **43** (5), 1161–1175.

Draper, P. and K. Paudyal (2006), 'Acquisitions: private versus public', *European Financial Management*, **12**, 57–80.

Eccles, R.G., K.L. Lanes and T.C. Wilson (1999), 'Are you paying too much for that acquisition?', *Harvard Business Review*, **77** (4), 136–146.

Eckbo, B.E. and K.S. Thorburn (2000), 'Gains to bidder firms revisited: domestic and foreign acquisitions in Canada', *Journal of Financial and Quantitative Analysis*, **35**, 1–25.

Edmans, A., I. Goldstein and W. Jiang (2012), 'The real effects of financial markets: the impact of prices on takeovers', *Journal of Finance*, **67**, 933–971.

Eger, C.E. (1983), 'An empirical test of the redistribution effect in pure exchange mergers', *Journal of Financial and Quantitative Analysis*, **18**, 547–572.

Faccio, M. and R.W. Masulis (2005), 'The choice of payment method in European mergers and acquisitions', *Journal of Finance*, **60**, 1345–1388.

Faccio, M., J.J. McConnell and D. Stolin (2006), 'Returns to acquirers of listed and unlisted targets', *Journal of Financial and Quantitative Analysis*, **41**, 197–220.

Fan, J.P.H. and V.K. Goyal (2006), 'On the patterns and wealth effects of vertical mergers', *Journal of Business*, **79**, 877–902.

Fich, E.M., J. Cai and A.L. Tran (2011), 'Stock option grants to target CEOs during private merger negotiations', *Journal of Financial Economics*, **101**, 413–430.

Francis, J.R. and X. Martin (2010), 'Acquisition profitability and timely loss recognition', *Journal of Accounting and Economics*, **49**, 161–178.

Franks, J.R., R.S. Harris and S. Titman (1991), 'The post-merger share-price performance of acquiring firms', *Journal of Financial Economics*, **29**, 81–96.

Fuller, K., J. Netter and M. Stegemoller (2002), 'What do returns to acquiring firms tell us? Evidence from firms that make many acquisitions', *Journal of Finance*, **57** (4), 1763–1793.

Ghosh, A. (2001), 'Does operating performance really improve following corporate acquisitions?', *Journal of Corporate Finance*, **7**, 151–178.

Ghosh, A. and W. Ruland (1998), 'Managerial ownership, the method of payment for acquisitions, and executive job retention', *Journal of Finance*, **53**, 785–798.

Golubov, A., D. Petmezas and N.G. Travlos (2012a), 'Do stock-financed M&As destroy value? New methods and evidence', Working Paper, Cass Business School, Surrey Business School and ALBA Graduate Business School.

Golubov, A., D. Petmezas and N.G. Travlos (2012b), 'When it pays to pay your investment banker: new evidence on the role of financial advisors in M&As', *Journal of Finance*, **67**, 271–312.

Gort, M. (1969), 'An economic disturbance theory of mergers', *Quarterly Journal of Economics*, **83**, 624–642.

Harford, J. (1999), 'Corporate cash reserves and acquisitions', *Journal of Finance*, **54**, 1969–1997.

Harford, J. (2005), 'What drives merger waves?', *Journal of Financial Economics*, **77**, 529–560.

Harris, R.S. and D. Ravenscraft (1991), 'The role of acquisitions in foreign direct investment: evidence from the US stock market', *Journal of Finance*, **46**, 825–844.

Hayn, C. (1989), 'Tax attributes as determinants of shareholder gains in corporate acquisitions', *Journal of Financial Economics*, **23**, 121–153.

Hayward M.L.A. and D.C. Hambrick (1997), 'Explaining the premiums paid in large acquisitions: evidence of CEO hubris', *Administrative Science Quarterly*, **42**, 103–127.

Healy, P., K. Palepu and R. Ruback (1992), 'Does corporate performance improve after mergers?', *Journal of Financial Economics*, **31**, 135–175.

Heron, R. and E. Lie (2002), 'Operating performance and the method of payment in takeovers', *Journal of Financial and Quantitative Analysis*, **37**, 137–155.

Hoberg, G. and G. Phillips (2010), 'Product market synergies and competition in mergers and acquisitions: a text-based analysis', *Review of Financial Studies*, **23**, 3773–3811.

Hoffmeister, J.R. and E.A. Dyl (1981), 'Predicting outcomes of cash tender offers', *Financial Management*, **10**, 50–58.

Houston, J.F., C.M. James and M.D. Ryngaert (2001), 'Where do merger gains come from? Bank mergers from the perspective of insiders and outsiders', *Journal of Financial Economics*, **60**, 285–331.

Houston, J.F. and M.D. Ryngaert (1997), 'Equity issuance and adverse selection: a direct test using conditional stock offers', *Journal of Finance*, **52**, 197–219.

Hsieh, J. and R.A. Walkling (2005), 'Determinants and implications of arbitrage holdings in acquisitions', *Journal of Financial Economics*, **77**, 605–648.

Huang, Y. and R.A. Walkling (1987), 'Target abnormal returns associated with acquisition announcements', *Journal of Financial Economics*, **19**, 329–349.

Hubbard, R.G. and D. Palia (1995), 'Benefits of control, managerial ownership, and the stock returns of acquiring firms', *RAND Journal of Economics*, **26**, 782–792.

Hubbard, R.G. and D. Palia (1999), 'A reexamination of the conglomerate merger wave in the 1960s: an internal capital markets view', *Journal of Finance*, **54**, 1131–1152.

James, C.M. and P. Wier (1987), 'Returns to acquirers and competition in the acquisition market: the case of banking', *Journal of Political Economy*, **95**, 355.

Jarrell, G.A., J.A.Brickley and J.M. Netter (1988), 'The market for corporate control: the empirical evidence since 1980', *Journal of Economic Perspectives*, **2**, 49–68.

Jensen, M.C. (1986), 'Agency costs of free cash flow, corporate finance and takeovers', *American Economic Review*, **76**, 357–398.

Jensen, M.C. (1993), 'The modern industrial revolution, exit, and the failure of internal control systems', *Journal of Finance*, **48**, 831–880.

Jensen, M.C. and R.S. Ruback (1983), 'The market for corporate control: the scientific evidence', *Journal of Financial Economics*, **11**, 5–50.

Jindra, J. and R.A. Walkling (2004), 'Speculation spreads and the market pricing of proposed acquisitions', *Journal of Corporate Finance*, **10**, 495–526.

John, K., S. Freund, D. Nguyen and G.K. Vasudevan (2010), 'Investor protection and cross-border acquisitions of private and public targets', *Journal of Corporate Finance*, **16**, 259–275.

Kale, J.R., O. Kini and H.E. Ryan (2003), 'Financial advisors and shareholder wealth gains in corporate takeovers', *Journal of Financial and Quantitative Analysis*, **38**, 475–501.

Kim, E.H and J.J. McConnell (1977), 'Corporate mergers and the co-insurance of corporate debt', *Journal of Finance*, **32**, 349–365.

Kolasinski A.C and X. Li (2013), 'Can strong boards and trading their own firm's stock help CEOs make better decisions? Evidence from acquisitions by overconfident CEOs', *Journal of Financial and Quantitative Analysis*, forthcoming.

Kothari, S.P. and J.B. Warner (1997), 'Measuring long-horizon security price performance', *Journal of Financial Economics*, **43**, 301–339.

Kothari, S.P. and Jerold B. Warner (2007), 'Econometrics of event studies', in B.E. Eckbo (ed.), *Handbook of Corporate Finance: Empirical Corporate Finance*, Amsterdam: Elsevier/North-Holland, pp. 3–36.

Lang, L.H.P, R.M. Stulz and R.A. Walkling (1989), 'Managerial performance, Tobin's q, and the gains from successful tender offers', *Journal of Financial Economics*, **24**, 137–154.

Lang, L.H.P., R.M. Stulz and R.A. Walkling (1991), 'A test of the free cash flow hypothesis: the case of bidder returns', *Journal of Financial Economics*, **29**, 315–336.

Larcker, D.F. and T. Lys (1987), 'An empirical analysis of the incentives to engage in costly information acquisition: the case of risk arbitrage', *Journal of Financial Economics*, **18**, 111–126.

Lewellen, W., C. Loderer and A. Rosenfeld (1985), 'Merger decisions and executive stock ownership in acquiring firms', *Journal of Accounting and Economics*, **7**, 209–231.

Lin, C., M.S. Officer and H. Zou (2011), 'Directors' and officers' liability insurance and acquisition outcomes', *Journal of Financial Economics*, **102**, 507–525.

Lipton, M. (2006), 'Merger waves in the 19th, 20th and 21st centuries', The Davies Lecture, Osgoode Hall Law School, York University.

Loderer, C. and K. Martin (1992), 'Post-acquisition performance of acquiring firms', *Financial Management*, **21**, 69–79.

Loughran, T. and A.M. Vijh (1997), 'Do long-term shareholders benefit from corporate acquisitions?', *Journal of Finance*, **52**, 1765–1790.

Lyon, J.D., B. Barber and C. Tsai (1999), 'Improved methods for tests of long-run abnormal stock returns', *Journal of Finance*, **54**, 165–201.

Maksimovic, Vojislav and Gordon Phillips (2007), 'Conglomerate firms and internal capital markets', in B.E. Eckbo (ed.), *Handbook of Corporate Finance: Empirical Corporate Finance*, Amsterdam: Elsevier/North-Holland, pp. 423–479.

Malatesta, P.H. (1983), 'The wealth effect of merger activity and the objective functions of merging firms', *Journal of Financial Economics*, **11**, 155–181.

Malmendier, U., M.M. Opp and F. Saidi (2011), 'Cash is king: revaluation and the medium of exchange in merger bids', Working Paper, U.C. Berkeley and New York University.

Malmendier, U. and G. Tate (2008), 'Who makes acquisitions? CEO overconfidence and the market's reaction', *Journal of Financial Economics*, **89**, 20–43.

Maloney, M.T., R.E. McCormick and M.L. Mitchell (1993), 'Managerial decision making and capital structure', *Journal of Business*, **66**, 189–217.

Manzon, Jr., G.B., D.J Sharp and N.G. Travlos (1994), 'An empirical study of the consequences of U.S. tax rules for international acquisitions by US firms', *Journal of Finance*, **49**, 1893–1904.

Maquieira, C.P., W.L. Megginson and L. Nail (1998), 'Wealth creation versus wealth redistributions in pure stock-for-stock mergers', *Journal of Financial Economics*, **48**, 3–33.

Martin, K.J. (1996), 'The method of payment in corporate acquisitions, investment opportunities, and management ownership', *Journal of Finance*, **51**, 1227–1246.

Martin, K.J. and J.J. McConnell (1991), 'Corporate performance, corporate takeovers, and management turnover', *Journal of Finance*, **46**, 671–687.

Martynova, M. and L. Renneboog (2009), 'What determines the financing decision in corporate takeovers: cost of capital, agency problems, or the means of payment?', *Journal of Corporate Finance*, **15**, 290–315.

Masulis, R.W., C. Wang and F. Xie (2007), 'Corporate governance and acquirer returns', *Journal of Finance*, **62**, 1851–1889.

Matsusaka, J.G. (1993), 'Takeover motives during the conglomerate merger wave', *RAND Journal of Economics*, **24**, 357–379.

McLaughlin, R.M. (1992), 'Does the form of compensation matter?', *Journal of Financial Economics*, **32**, 223–260.

Michel, A. and I. Shaked (1988), 'Corporate takeovers: excess returns and the multiple bidding phenomena', *Journal of Business Finance and Accounting*, **15**, 263–273.

Minnick, K., H. Unal and L. Yang (2011), 'Pay for performance? CEO compensation and acquirer returns in BHCs', *Review of Financial Studies*, **24**, 439–472.

Mitchell, M.L. and K. Lehn (1990), 'Do bad bidders become good targets?', *Journal of Political Economy*, **98**, 372–398.

Mitchell, M.L. and J.H. Mulherin (1996), 'The impact of industry shocks on takeover and restructuring activity', *Journal of Financial Economics*, **41**, 193–229.

Mitchell, M.L and T. Pulvino (2001), 'Characteristics of risk and return in risk arbitrage', *Journal of Finance*, **56**, 2135–2175.

Mitchell, M.L., T. Pulvino and E. Stafford (2004), 'Price pressure around mergers', *Journal of Finance*, **59**, 31–63.

Mitchell, M.L. and E. Stafford (2000), 'Managerial decisions and long-term stock price performance', *Journal of Business*, **73**, 287–329.

Moeller, S.B. and F.P. Schlingemann (2005), 'Global diversification and bidder gains: a comparison between cross-border and domestic acquisitions', *Journal of Banking and Finance*, **29**, 533–564.

Moeller, S.B., F.P. Schlingemann and R.M. Stulz (2004), 'Firm size and the gains from acquisitions', *Journal of Financial Economics*, **73**, 201–228.

Moeller, S.B., F.P. Schlingemann and R.M. Stulz (2005), 'Wealth destruction on a massive scale? A study of acquiring-firm returns in the recent merger wave', *Journal of Finance*, **60**, 757–782.

Moeller, S.B., F.P. Schlingemann and R.M. Stulz (2007), 'How do diversity of opinion and information asymmetry affect acquirer returns?', *Review of Financial Studies*, **20**, 2047–2078.

Morck, R., A. Shleifer and R. Vishny (1990), 'Do managerial objectives drive bad acquisitions?', *Journal of Finance*, **45**, 31–48.

Mulherin, J.H. and A.L. Boone (2000), 'Comparing acquisitions and divestitures', *Journal of Corporate Finance*, **6**, 117–139.

Myers, S.C. and N.S. Majluf (1984),'Corporate financing and investment decisions when firms have information the investors do not have', *Journal of Financial Economics*, **13**, 187–221.

Officer, M.S. (2003), 'Termination fees in mergers and acquisitions', *Journal of Financial Economics*, **69**, 431–467.

Officer, M.S. (2004), 'Collars and renegotiation in mergers and acquisitions', *Journal of Finance*, **59**, 2719–2743.

Officer, M.S. (2007a), 'The price of corporate liquidity: acquisition discounts for unlisted targets', *Journal of Financial Economics*, **83**, 571–598.

Officer, M.S. (2007b), 'Are performance based arbitrage effects detectable? Evidence from merger arbitrage', *Journal of Corporate Finance*, **13**, 793–812.

Officer, M.S., A. Poulsen and M. Stegemoller (2009), 'Target-firm information asymmetry and acquirer returns', *Review of Finance*, **13**, 467–493.

Palepu, K.G. (1986), 'Predicting takeover targets: a methodological and empirical analysis', *Journal of Accounting and Economics*, **8**, 3–35.

Powell, R.G. and A.W. Stark (2005), 'Does operating performance increase post-takeover for UK takeovers? A comparison of performance measures and benchmarks', *Journal of Corporate Finance*, **11**, 293–317.

Rau, R.P. (2000), 'Investment bank market share, contingent fee payments, and the performance of acquiring firms', *Journal of Financial Economics*, **56**, 293–324.

Rau, R.P. and T. Vermaelen (1998), 'Glamour, value and the post-acquisition performance of acquiring firms', *Journal of Financial Economics*, **49**, 223–253.

Rhodes-Kropf, M., D.T. Robinson and S. Viswanathan (2005), 'Valuation waves and merger activity: the empirical evidence', *Journal of Financial Economics*, **77**, 561–603.

Rhodes-Kropf, M. and S. Viswanathan (2004), 'Market valuation and merger waves', *Journal of Finance*, **59**, 2685–2718.

Roll, R. (1986), 'The hubris hypothesis of corporate takeovers', *Journal of Business*, **59**, 197–216.

Rosen, R.J. (2006), 'Merger momentum and investor sentiment: the stock market reaction to merger announcements', *Journal of Business*, **79**, 987–1017.

Samuelson, W. and L. Rosenthal (1986), 'Price movements as indicators of tender offer success', *Journal of Finance*, **41**, 481–499.

Savor, P.G. and Q. Lu (2009), 'Do stock mergers create value for acquirers?', *Journal of Finance*, **64**, 1061–1097.

Schlingemann, F.P. (2004), 'Financing decisions and bidder gains', *Journal of Corporate Finance*, **10**, 683–701.

Scholes, M.S. and M.A. Wolfson (1990), 'The effects of changes in tax laws on corporate reorganization activity', *Journal of Business*, **63**, S141–S164.

Schwert, G.W. (1996),'Markup pricing in mergers and acquisitions', *Journal of Financial Economics*, **41**, 153–192.

Schwert, G.W. (2000), 'Hostility in takeovers: in the eyes of the beholder?', *Journal of Finance*, **55**, 2599–2640.

Servaes, H. (1991), 'Tobin's Q and the gains from takeovers', *Journal of Finance*, **46**, 409–419.

Servaes, H. and M. Zenner (1994), 'Taxes and the returns to foreign acquisitions in the United States', *Financial Management*, **23**, 42–56.

Servaes, H. and M. Zenner (1996), 'The role of investment banks in acquisitions', *Review of Financial Studies*, **9**, 787–815.

Seth, A. (1990a), 'Sources of value creation in acquisitions: an empirical investigation', *Strategic Management Journal*, **11**, 431–446.

Seth, A. (1990b), 'Value creation in acquisitions: a reexamination of performance issues', *Strategic Management Journal*, **11**, 99–115.

Seth, A., K.P. Song and R. Pettit (2000), 'Synergy, managerialism or hubris? An empirical examination of motives for foreign acquisitions of US firms', *Journal of International Business Studies*, **31**, 387–405.

Shaked, I., A. Michel and D. McClain (1991), 'The foreign acquirer bonanza: myth or reality?', *Journal of Business Finance and Accounting*, **18**, 431–447.

Sharma, D.S and J. Ho (2002), 'The impact of acquisitions on operating performance: some Australian evidence', *Journal of Business Finance and Accounting*, **29**, 155–200.

Shleifer, A. and R.W. Vishny (2003),'Stock market driven acquisitions', *Journal of Financial Economics*, **70**, 295–311.

Song, M. and R. Walkling (1993), 'The impact of managerial ownership on acquisition attempts and target shareholder wealth', *Journal of Financial and Quantitative Analysis*, **28**, 439–457.

Tehranian, H., N.G. Travlos and J.F. Waegelein (1987), 'Management compensation contracts and merger–induced abnormal returns', *Journal of Accounting Research*, **25**, 51–76.

Travlos, N.G. (1987), 'Corporate takeover bids, method of payment, and bidding firm's stock returns', *Journal of Finance*, **52**, 943–963.

Walkling, R.A. (1985), 'Predicting tender offer success: a logistic analysis', *Journal of Financial and Quantitative Analysis*, **20**, 461–478.

Wang, C. and F. Xie (2009), 'Corporate governance transfer and synergistic gains from mergers and acquisitions', *Review of Financial Studies*, **22**, 829–858.

Wansley, J.W., W.R. Lane and H.C. Yang (1983), 'Abnormal returns to acquired firms by type of acquisition and method of payment', *Financial Management*, **12**, 16–22.

13 The construction and valuation effect of corporate governance indices[1]

Manuel Ammann, David Oesch and Markus Schmid

13.1 INTRODUCTION

There are two different channels through which corporate governance may help to overcome agency problems and thereby increase firm value. On the one hand, high corporate goverance standards may result in higher stock price multiples as investors anticipate that less cash flows will be diverted. Hence, a higher fraction of the firms' profits will come back to them as interest or dividend payments (Jensen and Meckling, 1976; La Porta et al., 2002). On the other hand, good corporate governance may reduce the expected return on equity as it reduces shareholders' monitoring and auditing costs resulting in lower costs of capital (Shleifer and Vishny, 1997). However, the implementation of a stronger corporate governance structure within firms is associated with costs and therefore it is not clear *ex ante* whether the benefits outweigh the costs of a strong firm-level corporate governance (e.g., Gillan et al., 2003; Chhaochharia and Grinstein, 2007; Bruno and Claessens, 2010).

The majority of prior research investigating the relationship between firm-level corporate governance and firm valuation finds better corporate governance to be associated with higher firm values (Yermack, 1996; Gompers et al., 2003; Cremers and Nair, 2005; Core et al., 2006; Bebchuck et al., 2009). While much of this literature deals with specific aspects of corporate governance, such as board structure or anti-takeover protection, some studies aggregate individual corporate governance attributes to corporate governance indices. Due to data availability and the relative size and importance of the capital market, the majority of research focuses on the United States (US). Using data on US companies, several studies demonstrate the value-relevance of such governance indices aggregating a number of individual governance attributes (Gompers et al., 2003; Bebchuck and Cohen, 2005; Bebchuck et al., 2009). Relatively few studies investigate the valuation effect of firm-level corporate governance in an international context. A few notable exceptions are La Porta et al. (2002), Klapper and Love (2004) and Durnev and Kim (2005). These studies use data compiled by La Porta et al. (1998) on minority shareholder rights protection and data from Credit Lyonnais Securities Asia (CLSA). The usefulness of both these data sources has been questioned, for example by Khanna et al. (2006). Other studies use governance attributes related to disclosure only as measured by the disclosure scores from the Center for International Financial Analysis and Research (CIFAR) database (e.g., Francis et al., 2005). To overcome the problem of data availability on non-US firm-level corporate governance, some studies use hand-collected and survey-based datasets regarding the firms' corporate governance structure, usually for one specific country. Examples are Drobetz et al. (2004), Beiner et al. (2006), Black et al. (2006) and Balasubramaniam et al. (2010) who document a positive relationship between corporate governance and firm valuation for German, Swiss, Korean and Indian listed companies, respectively.

With the recent availability of more detailed information on firm-level corporate governance for large international samples, a new stream of research has emerged. The prime provider of such data so far is RiskMetrics (which had acquired Institutional Shareholder Services, ISS, in 2007 before being acquired itself by MSCI in 2010). Aggarwal et al. (2009) use data from RiskMetrics and compare the corporate governance of non-US firms to the corporate governance of a matched set of US firms and find that the valuation of non-US firms falls as their governance index value decreases compared with the governance index of matched US firms. Bruno and Claessens (2010) also use RiskMetrics data and report a positive relationship between both firm value and firm-level corporate governance attributes, and between firm value and country-level shareholder protection laws. Moreover, they find these relationships to be more pronounced in companies that depend on external financing. Chhaochharia and Laeven (2009) also use data from RiskMetrics to distinguish between governance attributes that are legally required and attributes that are adopted voluntarily. Their results indicate that firms which voluntarily adopt a more rigorous corporate governance structure have high firm values.

In this chapter, we provide further evidence on the relationship between firm-level corporate governance and company valuation in an international setting and focus on the importance of corporate governance index construction. We use a largely unexplored dataset from Governance Metrics International (GMI) introduced by Ammann et al. (2011). Using such a new dataset is important as the quality of corporate governance data has been questioned (e.g., Khanna et al., 2006) and a check of prior results based on new datasets provides an important 'out-of-sample' test. The corporate governance data used in this chapter covers 22 developed countries (excluding the US) and spans five years from 2003 to 2007. The GMI dataset (Ammann et al., 2011) is much richer than those used in prior studies. It covers 64 corporate governance attributes which are classified by GMI into six categories: board accountability; financial disclosure and internal control; shareholder rights; remuneration; market for control; and corporate behaviour. One interesting aspect of the GMI data is that it includes attributes which document companies' social behaviour, also termed 'corporate social responsibility' (CSR). Moreover, the GMI data used in this chapter comprises the longest panel used in international studies on the valuation effect of firm-level corporate governance so far. The datasets in Aggarwal et al. (2009) and Bruno and Claessens (2010) cover only one cross-section and the dataset used in Chhaochharia and Laeven (2009) includes three years.

Even though there is an extensive literature investigating the relationship between corporate governance and firm value, there is little consensus so far on how to measure corporate governance (Larcker et al., 2007; Ertugrul and Hegde, 2009). In this chapter, we contribute to the literature by testing alternative approaches to constructing corporate governance indices. Prior literature almost exclusively uses additive indices giving mostly equal weights to each governance attribute considered. If data on certain attributes is missing, these attributes are usually dropped from the index construction to ensure a reasonably large sample size (Aggarwal et al., 2009). In this chapter, we use four alternative additive approaches to construct corporate governance indices. Moreover, in the construction of a fifth index, we rely on principal component analysis (PCA) to condense the information content of our 64 corporate governance attributes into one index. This approach is based on a recent study by Larcker et al. (2007).

The first additive index follows Aggarwal et al. (2009) and Chhaochharia and Laeven (2009). To construct this index, we first determine the number of governance attributes with data available for each firm-year observation and then define the governance index as the percentage of attributes a company has in place. Hence, attributes which are not reported are simply omitted from the index construction. To construct the second additive index, we use a similar procedure but treat governance attributes for which there is no information as if these attributes were not in place, instead of omitting such missing observations from the index construction. If firms are more likely to disclose information on governance attributes that are adopted, we would expect a stronger valuation effect of this second index compared to the first one. The third and fourth governance indices are similar to the first and second indices, respectively, with one important difference. We omit all governance attributes which every firm within the respective firm's country fulfils in a particular year. Hence, the third (fourth) index corresponds to the first (second) index but omits from the index calculation all attributes which every firm in a country fulfils in a particular year. The motivation for the construction of the third and fourth indices is that these indices allow us to focus on governance attributes which are truly firm-specific and not determined by country-specific differences in legal regimes (see Chhaochharia and Laeven, 2009). Hence, we expect these governance attributes to represent the firms' deliberate corporate governance choices. Finally, the fifth corporate governance index, which uses PCA and is based on Larcker et al. (2007), condenses the information contained in the individual corporate governance attributes into one corporate governance index by finding the linear combination of the original governance attributes that accounts for as much variation in the original dataset as possible (i.e., the first principal component). Hence, the weighting scheme in this fifth index is based on a statistical procedure instead of using equal or arbitrarily chosen weights.

Our results indicate a strong and positive relationship between all five of our firm-level corporate governance indices and firm value. This result is robust to the alternative calculation procedures for the corporate governance index, the omission of the largest sample countries from the analysis or a restriction to only the largest sample countries (with the exception of Japan), a breakdown of the sample by calendar year and also to the use of alternative estimation techniques. Besides investigating the statistical significance of the valuation effect of corporate governance, we also evaluate the economic importance of the valuation effect of the alternative corporate governance indices. Almost all previous studies focus on the statistical and not the economic significance of the results. Hence, there is little guidance from previous academic research on how large the potential valuation benefits associated with a good corporate governance are. When using the most standard approach to construct an additive corporate governance index, we find a similar valuation effect of corporate governance. Specifically, we find that a one standard deviation increase in the first additive governance index is associated with an increase in Tobin's Q of about 0.07 which corresponds to 3.85 per cent (4.80 per cent) of the mean (median) Q in our sample. However, further analyses show that the economic significance of the valuation effect strongly depends on the particular index construction. For example, when we penalize firms for not making information on certain attributes available by assuming that these attributes are not in place or when we focus on truly firm-specific governance attributes that are not influenced by country-specific differences in legal regimes, the economic importance of the valuation effect substantially increases and is estimated to be as high as a 0.16 increase in Tobin's Q for a one standard deviation increase in the index in some specifications. This represents an increase of 9.13 (11.37) per cent of mean (median) Q.

The remainder of the chapter is organized as follows. Section 13.2 describes the data, defines our variables and explains the construction of our corporate governance indices. Section 13.3 presents the main results on the valuation effect of corporate governance. Section 13.4 contains several robustness tests and section 13.5 concludes.

13.2   DATA AND VARIABLES

In this section of the chapter, we provide an overview of the sample data used in the empirical analyses. We also explain the construction of five alternative corporate governance indices based on 64 individual governance attributes. Finally, we outline the construction of financial control variables used in the multivariate analyses.

13.2.1   Data on Firm-Level Corporate Governance

We use firm-level corporate governance data from GMI. Starting in 2003, GMI provides information on firm-level corporate governance for over 4000 companies worldwide, covering important indices such as the MSCI World Index and the MSCI EAFE (Europe, Australasia and Far East) Index. GMI collects information on a large number of individual governance attributes and combines them to construct a governance rating for every firm in their universe. GMI constructs these ratings using a scoring algorithm that is proprietary. In this chapter, we do not use GMI's governance ratings but 64 individual corporate governance attributes collected by GMI. We use these 64 attributes to construct our own corporate governance indices. The dataset we obtain from GMI contains 7092 non-US firm-year observations on about 2300 firms for the time period from 2003 to 2007. This dataset is an unbalanced panel as the number of firms grows substantially over time (from 605 in 2003 to 2215 in 2007), reflecting the increase in companies covered by GMI. We exclude all observations from countries with fewer than ten firm-year observations in total. These countries are Argentina, Colombia, the Czech Republic, Egypt, Hungary, Iceland, Israel, Jordan, Morocco, Pakistan, Peru, the Philippines, Thailand and Venezuela. We also exclude developing and emerging countries (i.e., Brazil, Chile, China, India, Indonesia, Malaysia, Mexico, Russia, South Africa, South Korea, Taiwan and Turkey) because prior research suggests that the effect of firm-level corporate governance on firm valuation might substantially differ between developing and developed countries.[2] Applying these filters leaves us with a sample of 6663 firm-year observations covering 22 developed countries. The availability of financial variables for the multivariate analysis further reduces our sample size to 5511 firm-years. Table 13.1 reports the countrywise distribution of these 5511 firm-year

Table 13.1   Overview of sample countries

Country	Observations	% of sample
Australia	353	6.41
Austria	40	0.73
Belgium	68	1.23
Canada	223	4.05
Denmark	68	1.23
Finland	80	1.45
France	307	5.57
Germany	245	4.45
Greece	30	0.54
Hong Kong	185	3.36
Ireland	50	0.91
Italy	138	2.50
Japan	1651	29.96
Netherlands	108	1.96
New Zealand	43	0.78
Norway	49	0.89
Portugal	30	0.54
Singapore	189	3.43
Spain	134	2.43
Sweden	172	3.12
Switzerland	143	2.59
UK	1205	21.87
Total	5511	100

Notes: The table reports the number of observations (Observations) and the percentage each country accounts for in the full sample (% of sample) for each country covered in the study. The total sample consists of 5511 firm years. We drop countries for which we have less than ten firm-year observations (i.e., Argentina, Colombia, the Czech Republic, Egypt, Hungary, Iceland, Israel, Jordan, Morocco, Pakistan, Peru, the Philippines, Thailand and Venezuela) and emerging and developing countries (i.e., Brazil, Chile, China, India, Indonesia, Malaysia, Mexico, Russia, South Africa, South Korea, Taiwan and Turkey).

observations. Japan (1651), the UK (1205) and Australia (353) are the countries contributing the biggest number of firm-year observations to our sample. On the other hand, Austria (40), Portugal (30) and Greece (30) are the countries contributing the smallest number of firm-year observations.

The dataset we obtain from GMI contains 64 individual corporate governance attributes. GMI collects data on the implementation level for each of these attributes and then assesses whether a firm maintains a minimum level of implementation. GMI classifies the 64 attributes of our dataset into six categories. These six categories are board accountability, financial disclosure and internal control, shareholder rights, remuneration, market for control and corporate behaviour. In Table 13.2, we provide a survey of the 64 individual governance attributes used in our empirical analyses. Moreover, we show the percentage of firms meeting each governance criterion according to the thresholds set by GMI.

Two recent studies using firm-level corporate governance attributes for international

Table 13.2   List of corporate governance attributes and the percentage of firms meeting the requirement for these attributes

Individual governance attribute	% of firms meeting attribute
Board accountability	
1. Board members are subject to annual election by all shareholders	20.9
2. Non-executive board members have a formal session without executives once a year	51.0
3. Board performance is periodically evaluated	87.3
4. Company discloses a code of ethics for senior executives	42.1
5. Company discloses its corporate governance policies or guidelines	61.0
6. A board or committee is responsible for CEO succession planning	84.7
7. Company has not failed to adopt the recommendations of a shareholder proposal	99.8
8. All executive board members own shares after excluding options held	75.1
9. All non-executive board members own shares after excluding options held	35.5
10. Company has a separate chairman and CEO	85.8
11. All members attended at least 75% of the board meetings	81.5
12. Company has a designated 'lead' or senior non-executive board member	29.9
13. There have been no related-party transactions in the past three years	50.6
14. The governance/nomination committee is composed of independent board members	18.5
15. No former CEO of the company serves on the board	71.3
16. Nr. of shares held by officers and directors has not decreased by 10% or more	83.2
17. Nr. of shares held by officers and directors has increased by 10% or more	25.7
18. Governance/nomination committee has a written charter or terms of reference	48.9
19. Board size is greater than five but less than 16	81.2
20. Board is controlled by more than 50% of independent outside directors	36.9
Financial disclosure and internal control	
21. Company has not had a material earnings restatement in the past three years	98.5
22. Audit committee has a written charter or terms of reference	59.5
23. Company has not received a qualified audit opinion within the last two fiscal years	99.5
24. Company is not currently under investigation for accounting irregularities	98.9
25. Audit committee is wholly composed of independent board members	41.5
26. Someone other than senior management with sole authority to hire outside auditor	87.2
27. Audit committee with sole authority to approve non-audit services from outside auditor	36.9
28. Company did not pay its auditor less for audit related services than for other services	83.9
Shareholder rights	
29. Vote results for the last shareholder meeting are disclosed within 14 calendar days	80.4

Table 13.2 (continued)

Individual governance attribute	% of firms meeting attribute
Shareholder rights	
30. All common or ordinary equity shares have one-share, one-vote, with no restrictions	62.5
31. The company provides confidential voting with no or with reasonable exceptions	51.0
32. Shareholders have a right to convene an EGM with 10% or less of the shares requesting one	92.5
33. Shareowners have a right to act in concert through written communication	17.7
34. Voting rights are not capped at a certain percentage	96.0
Remuneration	
35. Non-executive board members paid in cash and some form of stock-linked compensation	16.2
36. Company discloses performance targets for the next fiscal year	33.0
37. Non-executive board members are paid entirely in some form of stock-linked compensation	0.3
38. CEO without an employment agreement that provides for guaranteed bonus payments	98.1
39. Goals used to determine incentive awards are aligned with the company's financial goals	38.2
40. CEO/Managing Director does not sit on the remuneration committee	94.5
41. Remuneration committee is wholly composed of independent board members	35.8
42. No repricing of outstanding executive stock options and no option exchange programme	98.8
43. Expensing of employee stock option grants	32.6
44. Remuneration committee has a written charter or terms of reference	55.4
45. Potential dilution from stock options outstanding is below 20%	66.4
46. Potential dilution from stock options outstanding and not yet granted is below 20%	52.0
Market for control	
47. Company has not adopted a shareholder rights plan ('poison pill')	97.0
48. Company does not have a staggered ('classified') board	50.2
49. Company cannot issue blank cheque preferred stock in the event of a hostile tender offer	90.9
50. Company's shareholder rights plan ('poison pill') has been ratified by a shareholder vote	2.3
51. Fair price provision in place or price protection under applicable law	73.0
52. Shareholder rights plan includes a TIDE provision or a three-year sunset provision	1.8
53. Company does not require a supermajority vote to approve a merger	43.9
54. No single shareholder or shareholder group with majority of voting power	82.3
55. Company allows cumulative voting in the election of directors	1.8

Table 13.2 (continued)

Individual governance attribute	% of firms meeting attribute
Corporate behaviour	
56. Company has a policy addressing workplace safety	89.4
57. Company does not have pending criminal litigation against it	96.6
58. No allegation that the company used sweat shops within the last three years	99.8
59. Company discloses its environmental performance	54.9
60. Company discloses its workplace safety record	36.8
61. No regulatory investigation for a material issue other than for accounting irregularities	92.2
62. Company discloses its policy regarding corporate level political donations	26.0
63. Company has not been charged with workplace safety violations within the last two years	98.0
64. It has not been alleged by a responsible party that the company used child labour	99.7

Notes: The table displays the 64 governance attributes of our sample grouped by the six sub-categories: Board Accountability, Financial Disclosure and Internal Control, Shareholder Rights, Remuneration, Market for Control and Corporate Behaviour. For each governance attribute we report the percentage of firms in our sample that meet the respective criteria associated with this attribute. The sample consists of 5511 firm-years.

samples are the papers by Chhaochharia and Laeven (2009) and Aggarwal et al. (2009). Both studies use data provided by RiskMetrics. The RiskMetrics data used in these two studies differ from our GMI data both in the number and contents of governance attributes. Chhaochharia and Laeven (2009) use 17 governance attributes and Aggarwal et al. (2009) use 44 governance attributes. One notable difference between the attributes provided by GMI and the attributes provided by RiskMetrics is that GMI's dataset contains information on nine attributes that pertain to a company's CSR. Additionally, the GMI dataset contains substantially more attributes in the category on financial disclosure and internal control. While our GMI sample includes eight attributes in this category, the datasets of Aggarwal et al. (2009) and Chhaochharia and Laeven (2009) include only two attributes and one attribute, respectively. In the remaining four categories, our dataset includes between three (shareholder rights and market for corporate control categories) and eight (remuneration category) attributes not included in Aggarwal et al. (2009). In fact, there is a substantial difference in the availability of governance attributes related to manager remuneration (and ownership) between the two databases.[3]

Table 13.2 shows that several of the 64 governance attributes in our dataset are met by a large fraction of sample firms. For example, nine of the 20 attributes from the category on board accountability are fulfilled by over 70 per cent of sample firms. Concerning the attributes on financial disclosure and internal control, five out of eight attributes are met by more than 70 per cent of sample firms. In the shareholder rights category, three out of six attributes are in place at more than 70 per cent of sample firms. More than 70 per cent of the firms in our sample meet three of the 12 governance criteria on remuneration. As for the attributes related to the market for corporate control, there are four attributes that more than 70 per cent of the companies in our sample fulfil. Finally, six of the attributes on corporate social responsibility are met by more than 70 per cent of sample firms. Comparing Table 13.2 with corresponding results from studies using the RiskMetrics database such as Aggarwal et al. (2009) reveals that the level of implementation is similar for the governance attributes that are provided by GMI and RiskMetrics.

13.2.2   Corporate Governance Index Construction

We use all 64 individual governance attributes provided by GMI to construct five alternative corporate governance indices. As all our governance attributes are binary, we first assign a value of one to each governance attribute that a firm has in place and a value of zero otherwise. As it is common in the literature (e.g., Aggarwal et al., 2009), our first governance index (CGI1) is simply calculated as the percentage of attributes a company has adopted (i.e., attributes which have been assigned a value of one). Attributes on which companies do not provide information are eliminated from the index construction. Hence, CGI1 reflects the percentage of attributes that are not missing and that a company satisfies. For example, if a company reports data on and satisfies all 64 attributes, CGI1 for this company will be equal to 100. If the company only reports data on 32 attributes and satisfies all of them, CGI1 for this company would again be equal to 100.

Our second governance index (CGI2) is constructed in a similar way as CGI1, with one exception: we do not exclude missing attributes from the index calculation but give each missing attribute a score of zero. Hence, we treat unreported attributes as if the company had not adopted the respective governance attribute. If the probability that a firm does not disclose information on a specific governance attribute is negatively correlated with the probability that an attribute is adopted, we would expect a stronger valuation effect of CGI2 as compared to CGI1.

The third and fourth governance indices are similar to CGI1 and CGI2, respectively, with one important difference: following Chhaochharia and Laeven (2009), we adjust the governance indices by omitting all governance attributes which every firm within the respective firm's country fulfils in the respective year. Hence, CGI3 corresponds to CGI1 but omitting all attributes which every firm within the firms' countries fulfils in the respective year from the index calculation. CGI4 corresponds to CGI2, again omitting all attributes which every firm within a country fulfils in the respective year from the index calculation. The motivation for the construction of CGI3 and CGI4 is that these indices allow us to focus on governance attributes which are truly firm-specific and not determined by country-specific differences in legal regimes. Hence, these governance attributes are likely to represent the firms' deliberate choices of corporate governance attributes.

The descriptive statistics of the four corporate governance indices are reported in Panel A of Table 13.3. The empirical distributions of all four indices are displayed in Figure 13.1. The means (medians) of CGI1 and CGI2 are 61.13 (60.38) and 52.97 (50.78), respectively. Both indices show a reasonably symmetric distribution. Moreover, approximately ten attributes are not reported for both the mean and median firm causing the difference between the mean and median values of CGI1 and CGI2. The mean and median values of CGI3 and CGI4 are somewhat lower. Subtracting attributes which

Table 13.3   Descriptive statistics

Panel A: Corporate governance indices

Variable	Obs.	Mean	25 percentile	Median	75 percentile	Std. Dev.
CGI1	5511	61.13	51.85	60.38	70.00	11.04
CGI2	5511	52.97	44.62	50.78	63.08	13.08
CGI3	5511	50.87	40.00	48.98	62.75	14.96
CGI4	5511	44.06	33.90	42.22	55.55	16.29
CGI5	5511	−0.12	−1.85	−0.20	1.40	1.68

Panel B: Financial data

Variable	Obs.	Mean	25 percentile	Median	75 percentile	Std. Dev.
Q	5511	1.72	1.13	1.38	1.88	1.13
LN(TOTAL ASSETS)	5511	8.56	7.55	8.41	9.49	1.43
PAST SALES GROWTH	5511	0.36	0.06	0.24	0.48	0.57
R&D/SALES	5511	0.02	0.00	0.00	0.02	0.06
CASH/ASSETS	5511	0.08	0.02	0.05	0.11	0.09
CAPEX/ASSETS	5511	0.05	0.02	0.04	0.07	0.06
PPE/SALES	5511	0.96	0.13	0.29	0.61	2.33
EBIT/SALES	5511	0.19	0.05	0.11	0.21	0.29
LEVERAGE	5511	0.57	0.42	0.58	0.71	0.20
ADR (Dummy)	5511	0.26	0.00	0.00	1.00	0.44
CLOSELY HELD	5511	0.30	0.13	0.25	0.45	0.22

Notes: The table provides summary statistics for the five corporate governance indices (Panel A) and the financial variables (Panel B). CGI1 denotes the governance index constructed in the same way as Aggarwal et al. (2009), i.e., by dividing the governance attributes a company fulfils by the number of governance attributes a company reports data for. CGI2 is constructed in the same way as CGI1 but with missing attributes treated as if these attributes were not fulfilled. CGI3 (CGI4) is an adjusted version of CGI1 (CGI2) where we omit the number of governance attributes that every firm in a given country fulfils in a given year. CGI5 denotes the governance index constructed by means of principal component analysis (PCA) as outlined in Table 13.4. Q denotes Tobin's Q and is computed as the sum of total assets less the book value of equity plus the market value of equity, divided by total assets, LN(TOTAL ASSETS) denotes the logarithm of total assets, PAST SALES GROWTH denotes the two-year growth of sales, R&D/SALES denotes the ratio of expenditures for research and development to sales, CASH/ASSETS denotes the ratio of cash to total assets, CAPEX/ASSETS denotes the ratio of capital expenditures to assets, PPE/SALES denotes the ratio of property, plant and equipment to sales, EBIT/SALES denotes the ratio of earnings before interest and taxes to sales, LEVERAGE denotes the ratio of total debt to total assets, ADR is a dummy variable which equals 1 if the firm has American Depository Receipts (ADR) and 0 otherwise and CLOSELY HELD is the percentage of closely held shares.

are fulfilled by all firms within a specific country and year naturally results in somewhat lower degrees of governance compliance. The mean (median) of CGI3 and CGI4 are 50.87 (48.98) and 44.06 (42.22). The 25 and 75 percentiles indicate that there is quite some variability in the cross-sectional distributions of all four indices. Figure 13.1 confirms that our four additive corporate governance indices are selected and constructed in a way that leads to sufficient variation across firms.

The first four corporate governance indices are all simple additive indices as commonly used in the literature (e.g., Gompers et al., 2003; Bebchuck and Cohen, 2005; Bebchuk

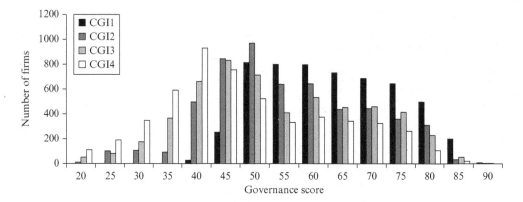

Notes: The figure shows the distribution of our four additively constructed corporate governance indices, CGI1, CGI2, CGI3 and CGI4. Black represents the scores according to CGI1, dark grey represents the scores according to CGI2, light grey represents the scores according to CGI3 and white represents the scores according to CGI4. CGI1 denotes the governance index constructed in the same way as Aggarwal et al. (2009), i.e., by dividing the governance attributes a company fulfils by the number of governance attributes a company reports data for. CGI2 is constructed in the same way as CGI1 but with missing attributes treated as if these attributes were not fulfilled. CGI3 (CGI4) is an adjusted version of CGI1 (CGI2) where we omit the number of governance attributes that every firm in a given country fulfils in a given year.

Figure 13.1   Empirical distribution of governance scores for CGI1, CGI2, CGI3 and CGI4

et al., 2009). In the construction of the fifth alternative governance index (CGI5), we follow Larcker et al. (2007) and apply principal component analysis (PCA) to condense the information contained in the large number of governance attributes provided by GMI. In fact, there is no well-developed conceptual basis for selecting relevant corporate governance variables to be included in an index and choosing their relative weights in the index. PCA is a simple mechanical tool which allows us to explore the unknown nature of the factor structure that is hidden behind our set of individual corporate governance attributes. We use PCA to condense the information contained in the individual corporate governance attributes into one corporate governance index by finding the linear combination of the original governance attributes which accounts for as much variation in the original dataset as possible. With respect to the index construction this means that the weighting scheme of our PCA-based index is based on a statistical procedure instead of using equal or arbitrarily chosen weights. These statistically determined weights ensure that as much of the underlying dimension or structure of the individual corporate governance attributes as possible is reflected in the index. Larcker et al. (2007) argue that such a governance index based on PCA has considerably less measurement error than any individual corporate governance variables or arbitrarily constructed indices.

Based on the analysis in Larcker et al. (2007), we use an oblique rotation that allows the principal components to be correlated and thereby enhances the interpretability of our PCA results. The PCA-based index that we use in the reported results only determines the weights based on PCA but not the choice of corporate governance factors. In unreported robustness tests, we also construct governance indices for which PCA not only determines the relative weights of the individual corporate governance attributes but also whether an attribute is included in the index in the first place. We do this by requiring a factor loading in excess of 0.40 in absolute value in the PCA (see Larcker et al., 2007). Instead of using the principal components directly as governance indices, we then construct governance indices by calculating equally weighted averages of standardized versions of these govern-ance attributes with factor loadings in excess of 0.40 in absolute value.

PCA requires the availability of all governance attributes for one specific firm-year observation for this observation not to be excluded from the analysis. As GMI does not provide the full set of governance attributes for many firm-years in our sample, we code all missing attributes to be zero (in the spirit of CGI2). Moreover, we restrict the number of governance attributes which are considered for the PCA-based index to the 17 presumably most important governance attributes reported in Panel A of Table 13.4. Including all 64 attributes in this analysis would make it harder for the PCA to extract a first principal component which reflects a meaningful proportion of the total variation in the original dataset.

For simplicity, in this chapter, we only use one PCA-based index which is precisely the first principal component and hence represents the linear combination of the 17 attributes that maximizes the variance explained in the dataset of 17 attributes. The choice of the 17 governance attributes for the PCA is based on prior empirical evidence. Many of the 17 variables have been analysed as individual corporate governance attributes in prior research. Examples are related-party transactions (e.g., Gordon et al., 2006), board size (e.g., Yermack, 1996), equity capital structure (e.g., Gompers et al., 2010) and board classification (e.g., Faleye, 2007). In addition, eight of these 17 attributes coincide with the attributes used in Chhaochharia and Laeven (2009) and 12 of them are included in Aggarwal et al. (2009).[4] Panel B of Table 13.4 shows that our CGI5 index, i.e., the first principal component of a PCA of the 17 governance attributes, explains 15.6 per cent of total variance in the 17 corporate governance attributes. Panel B of Table 13.4 also reports the expected sign of the correlation between the first five principal components and firm value. The expected sign is derived from the signs and magnitudes of the factor loadings of the individual governance attributes in each component. We sum all factor loadings over the 17 governance attributes and assign a positive expectation for the principal components with a value larger than one (the sums of factor loadings for the five components are 2.30, 0.55, 0.31, 1.79 and 2.07, respectively).[5] Panel A of Table 13.3 reports the descriptive statistics for CGI5. Of course, the scaling of CGI5 is completely different from that of the other, additive indices. However, the cross-sectional variability again seems reasonably large.

13.2.3   Financial Data

We collect the financial data for our sample firms from Thomson Financial's Worldscope database. Our measure of firm valuation is Tobin's Q. Following La Porta et al. (2000) and Doidge et al. (2004), we compute Tobin's Q as the sum of total assets minus the book value of equity plus the market value of equity, divided by total assets. In the multivari-ate analysis we use several control variables. The first control is firm size, calculated as the natural logarithm of total assets (LN(TOTAL ASSETS)). Following prior research investigating the relationship between corporate governance and firm value (e.g., Aggarwal et al., 2009), we control for: the past growth in sales over the last two years

Table 13.4   Corporate governance index based on principal component analysis

Panel A: Factor loadings for the first five principal components	PC1	PC2	PC3	PC4	PC5
Company has a designated 'lead' or senior non-executive board member	0.2599	-0.2257	0.1937	-0.0857	0.0474
No former CEO of the company serves on the board	0.1077	0.0117	-0.2898	**0.4990**	-0.0069
Board size is greater than five but less than 16	0.2027	0.0982	-0.0225	0.1701	0.0465
Company has not had a material earnings restatement in the past three years	-0.0995	-0.0682	-0.2107	0.3315	0.3572
Company has not received a qualified audit opinion within the last two fiscal years	0.0340	0.0893	-0.0464	0.0788	**0.6166**
Board members are subject to annual election by all shareholders	0.1170	**0.6069**	0.1686	0.0351	0.0784
No single shareholder or shareholder group with majority of voting power	-0.0198	-0.1126	0.2877	0.3995	-0.1337
All common or ordinary equity shares have one-share, one-vote, with no restrictions	0.3821	-0.1633	-0.1971	-0.1908	0.0945
Company discloses its corporate governance policies or guidelines	**0.4322**	-0.0739	-0.0690	-0.1139	0.0892
Voting rights are not capped at a certain percentage	-0.0344	-0.0296	0.1172	-0.1352	**0.6182**
Company allows cumulative voting in the election of directors	-0.0059	0.0156	-0.5452	0.0467	0.0665
Shareholders have a right to convene an EGM	0.0048	0.1159	0.5416	0.0536	0.1467
Company does not have a staggered ('classified') board	-0.0935	0.5208	-0.0450	-0.1002	0.0444
Company does not require a supermajority vote to approve a merger	0.0228	-0.4429	0.2241	0.0435	0.1521
Audit committee is wholly composed of independent board members	0.5117	0.0382	0.0874	0.0555	-0.0294
There have been no related-party transactions in the past three years	-0.0223	-0.0079	0.1113	0.5795	-0.0052
Board is controlled by more than 50% of independent outside directors	0.4989	0.1732	0.0076	0.1198	-0.1129

Panel B: Expected correlation with firm value and variance explained

Expected correlation with firm value (principal components)	+	?	?	+	+
Expected correlation with firm value (equally weighted averages of standardized governance attributes with factor loadings in excess of 0.40 in absolute value)	+	+	+	+	+
Variance explained by principal component	0.1561	0.1182	0.0837	0.0752	0.0703
Variance explained by principal component (cumulative)	0.1561	0.2743	0.3580	0.4332	0.5035

Notes: Panel A of the table reports the factor loadings of the 17 governance attributes included in the principal component analysis (PCA) for the first five principal components. The first principal component (PC1) corresponds to corporate governance index CGI5. The second to fourth principal components are used in unreported robustness tests as explained in section 13.2.2. Figures in bold print exhibit factor loadings in excess of 0.40 in absolute terms. In another robustness test, also outlined in section 13.2.2, we follow the approach proposed by Larcker et al. (2007) and calculate the equally weighted averages of standardized versions of the governance attributes with factor loadings in excess of 0.40 in absolute terms instead of using directly the first principal component. Panel B reports the expected sign of the correlation between the PCA-based governance indices and firm value. The expected sign is derived from the signs and magnitudes of the factor loadings of the individual governance attributes in each component. For the governance indices directly based on the principal components, we sum all factor loadings over the 17 governance attributes and attribute a positive expectation for the principal components with a value larger than one (the sums of factor loadings for the five components are 2.30, 0.55, 0.31, 1.79 and 2.07, respectively). For the governance indices based on the equally weighted averages of the standardized attributes, we derive the sign of the expected correlation from whether the sum of factor loadings in excess of 0.40 in absolute terms is larger than 0.5 (positive expectation), smaller than −0.5 (negative expectation), or between −0.5 and 0.5 (no expectation).

(PAST SALES GROWTH); the ratio of research and development expenditures to sales (R&D/SALES); the ratio of cash holdings to total assets (CASH/ASSETS); the ratio of capital expenditures to total assets (CAPEX/ASSETS); the ratio of property, plant and equipment to sales (PPE/SALES); the ratio of earnings before interest and taxes to sales (EBIT/SALES); leverage defined as the ratio of total debt to total assets (LEVERAGE); a dummy variable whether the firm has American Depository Receipts (ADR); and the percentage of shares held by blockholders with ownership stakes exceeding 5 per cent of the company's equity (CLOSELY HELD). All variables are measured in US dollars. To address the problem of outliers and influential observations, we winsorize the variables PAST SALES GROWTH, PPE/SALES and EBIT/SALES at the 1 and the 99 percentiles and restrict our sample to firm-years with a value of LEVERAGE which is less than or equal to one. The summary statistics for all financial variables are reported in Panel B of Table 13.3.[6]

13.3   THE VALUATION EFFECT OF MAIN CORPORATE GOVERNANCE INDICES

In this section, we investigate the valuation effect of the five alternative corporate governance indices in a multivariate framework. In addition to the statistical significance of the results, we also investigate the economic importance of the valuation effect of corporate governance. As the majority of previous research focuses on the statistical significance of the coefficients on the corporate governance variables only, it provides little insight into the economic significance of the effect of corporate governance on firm value. Hence, in a first step, we provide an overview of the economic effect of corporate governance on firm value as estimated in seven recent academic studies in the area. To be included in our survey, the studies have to use Tobin's Q as a measure of firm value, use a comprehensive corporate governance index and not individual corporate governance attributes, and include either the US or several non-US countries in the sample. Moreover, the paper has to provide an estimate of the standard deviation of the corporate governance index which allows the estimation of the economic effect. In the second step, we estimate panel regressions of Tobin's Q on our five alternative governance indices and various control variables.

The seven papers are surveyed in Table 13.5. Most importantly, the economic effect varies widely between the different studies and sometimes also within the studies. For example, in studies which attempt to control for endogeneity problems (e.g., Chhaochharia and Laeven, 2009) the economic magnitude may differ substantially across different analyses in the paper.[7] The smallest effect in any of the seven studies is reported in Cremers and Ferrell (2011), who find an increase in the G-index to be associated with a decrease in Q of approximately 0.033, or 2 per cent of mean Q in their US sample covering nearly 30 years. The largest effect of 0.421 (22 per cent of mean Q) is reported by Durnev and Kim (2005) when they account for endogeneity concerns by estimating a system of simultaneous equations with three-stage least squares. The average effect of OLS-based analyses in all seven surveyed papers is an increase in Q of 0.13 when the governance index increases (decreases in the case of the G-index) by one standard deviation (using the average of the minimum and maximum values in the study

Table 13.5   Survey of previous research investigating the valuation effect of corporate governance

Paper	Country/ countries	Sample period	Observations/ firms	Governance data source	# of governance attributes in index	Estimation approach(es)	Economic effect
Gompers et al. (2003)	USA	1990–99	NA/1500	IRRC (RiskMetrics)	24	OLS	An increase in the G-index by one standard deviation (2.8) leads to a decrease in Q by 0.120*
Klapper and Love (2004)	14 emerging markets	2000	374	Credit Lyonnais Securities Asia (CSLA)	57	OLS	An increase in the gov. index by one standard deviation (14.0) leads to an increase in Q by 0.322 (15% of mean, 23% of median Q)
Durnev and Kim (2005)	24 developed and emerging countries	2000	494	Credit Lyonnais Securities Asia (CSLA)	57	OLS/3SLS (system of two simultaneous equations)	An increase in the gov. index by one standard deviation (8.99) leads to an increase in Q by 0.175 (9% relative to mean Q); 3SLS increases the effect to 0.421 (22% of Q)
Aggarwal et al. (2009)	23 developed countries (incl. US)	2005	1527	Institutional Shareholder Services (ISS)	44	OLS/ Instrumental variable	Increasing the gov. index by the average gap to matched US firms increases Q by 0.094, an increase of 6.2% of median Q
Chhaochharia and Laeven (2009)	23 developed countries (incl. US)	2003–05	6134 firm-years/>2300 firms	Institutional Shareholder Services (ISS)	17	Panel regression with fixed effects (OLS); GMM (Arellano/ Bond)	A one standard deviation increase in the gov. index is associated with a 0.07 increase in Q, which is 4.4% (5.5%) of mean (median) Q; GMM leads to a substantially larger effect**

Table 13.5 (continued)

Paper	Country/ countries	Sample period	Observations/ firms	Governance data source	# of governance attributes in index	Estimation approach(es)	Economic effect
Ammann et al. (2011)	22 developed countries (excl. US)	2003–07	5511 firm-years/1638 firms	Governance Metrics International (GMI)	64	Panel regression with fixed effects (OLS)	An increase in the gov. index by one standard deviation leads to an increase in Q by between 0.06 (3.5% of mean, 4.2% of median Q) and 0.15 (9.4% of median Q) and 0.15 (9.4% of mean, 11.4% of median Q)
Cremers and Ferrell (2011)	USA	1978–2006	23 296 firm-years/approx. 1000 firms	IRRC (RiskMetrics), Hand-collected (10-K, 10-Q, proxy)	24	Panel regression with fixed effects (OLS)	An increase in the G-Index by one standard deviation (3) leads to a decrease in Q by about 0.033, a reduction of 2.1% of mean Q*

Notes: The table provides a survey of seven recent papers on the valuation effect of corporate governance with an emphasis on the economic magnitude. To be included in the survey, the studies have to use Tobin's Q as a measure of firm value, use a comprehensive corporate governance index and not individual corporate governance attributes and include either the US or several non-US countries in the sample. Moreover, the paper has to provide an estimate of the standard deviation of the corporate governance index in order to be able to estimate the economic effect. In general, a higher index value indicates better corporate governance. Papers in which a lower value of the corporate governance index (G-index) is associated with more shareholder rights and hence a better corporate governance are indicated by *. ** indicates that in this paper (Chhaochharia and Laeven, 2009), the economic effect cannot be inferred in the GMM regressions as the sample used is substantially larger than the one used in the other analyses of the paper and the corresponding descriptive statistics of the extended sample are not reported.

by Ammann et al., 2011). If we only consider the five studies focusing on developed countries, as we do in this chapter, the effect drops to 0.08. For developing and emerging countries, the economic effect is substantially larger and amounts to 0.25. This finding is not surprising given prior evidence of a stronger effect of corporate governance on firm value in less investor-friendly countries (e.g., Klapper and Love, 2004; Durnev and Kim, 2005).

To investigate both the statistical significance and the economic importance of the valuation effect of corporate governance, we estimate panel regressions of Tobin's Q on each of our five governance indices separately and a set of control variables. The choice of control variables is based on Aggarwal et al. (2009). As a measure of firm size, we include the natural logarithm of total assets (LN(TOTAL ASSETS)). We include the ratio of property, plant and equipment to sales (PPE/SALES) as companies operating with higher (lower) proportions of fixed (intangible) assets may consider it less optimal to adopt a strict corporate governance practice due to less scope to misuse assets. We control for several variables which have been shown to be significantly related to firm value: the two-year growth of sales (PAST SALES GROWTH); the ratio of capital expenditures to assets (CAPEX/ASSETS); the ratio of research and development expenditures to sales (R&D/SALES); the ratio of cash to total assets (CASH/ASSETS); the ratio of EBIT to sales (EBIT/SALES); leverage (LEVERAGE) and the percentage of closely held shares (CLOSELY HELD). Based on prior evidence showing that companies which are cross-listed on a US exchange have higher valuations (Doidge et al., 2004), we also include a dummy variable for whether the firm has American Depositary Receipts outstanding (ADR). To eliminate a potential omitted variables bias and control for the effect of unobserved variables that are constant over time, we include firm fixed effects. We use Driscoll and Kraay (1998) standard errors, which are heteroscedasticity-consistent and robust to general forms of cross-sectional and temporal dependence.[8]

The results are reported in the first five columns of Table 13.6. Most importantly, the coefficients on all five corporate governance indices are estimated to be positive and significant at the 5 per cent level or better. The coefficient estimate on CGI1 suggests that a one standard deviation (11.04) increase is associated with an increase in Tobin's Q of 0.07 which amounts to 3.85 (4.80) per cent of mean (median) Q in our sample. This valuation effect of corporate governance in our sample is comparable to those reported in Aggarwal et al. (2009) and Chhaochharia and Laeven (2009), which are the two studies most comparable to ours. As expected, the economic magnitude of the valuation effect of CGI2 is larger: a one standard deviation (13.08) increase is associated with an increase in Tobin's Q of 0.16, which amounts to 9.13 (11.37) per cent of mean (median) Q. Hence, accounting for the fact that companies are more likely to report information on corporate governance attributes they have adopted, leads to a substantial increase in the estimate of the valuation effect of corporate governance.

In the construction of CGI3 and CGI4, we follow Chhaochharia and Laeven (2009) and adjust CGI1 and CGI2 by omitting the governance attributes which all firms in the respective firm's country fulfil in a given year. This allows us to focus on governance attributes which are truly firm-specific and not influenced by country-specific differences in legal regimes. In fact, the economic magnitude of CGI3 is substantially larger than that of CGI1 and even larger than that of CGI2 and amounts to an increase in Tobin's Q of 0.16, or 9.57 (11.92) per cent of mean (median) Q, for a one standard deviation

Table 13.6   Fixed effects regressions of Tobin's Q on alternative governance indices and control variables

Dep. Variable: Tobin's Q	Firm fixed effects				
	(1)	(2)	(3)	(4)	(5)
Constant	3.134***	3.492***	3.153***	3.502***	3.477***
	(0.000)	(0.000)	(0.000)	(0.000)	(0.000)
CGI1	0.006**				
	(0.030)				
CGI2		0.012***			
		(0.000)			
CGI3			0.011***		
			(0.000)		
CGI4				0.010***	
				(0.000)	
CGI5					0.057***
					(0.000)
LN(TOTAL ASSETS)	−0.237***	−0.335***	−0.287***	−0.331***	−0.228***
	(0.000)	(0.000)	(0.000)	(0.000)	(0.000)
PAST SALES GROWTH	0.013	0.026	0.021	0.028	0.010
	(0.517)	(0.174)	(0.211)	(0.118)	(0.615)
R&D/SALES	0.041	−0.014	0.013	−0.008	0.042
	(0.863)	(0.951)	(0.957)	(0.973)	(0.862)
CASH/ASSETS	0.725***	0.715***	0.733***	0.725***	0.716***
	(0.000)	(0.000)	(0.000)	(0.000)	(0.000)
CAPEX/ ASSETS	0.702***	0.604***	0.674***	0.609***	0.700***
	(0.000)	(0.000)	(0.000)	(0.000)	(0.000)
PPE/SALES	−0.048***	−0.039***	−0.044***	−0.038***	−0.050***
	(0.000)	(0.000)	(0.000)	(0.000)	(0.000)
EBIT/SALES	0.242***	0.214***	0.224***	0.210***	0.238***
	(0.000)	(0.000)	(0.000)	(0.000)	(0.000)
LEVERAGE	−0.165*	0.024	−0.085	0.012	−0.172*
	(0.069)	(0.848)	(0.401)	(0.922)	(0.068)
ADR (Dummy)	1.159***	1.620***	1.423***	1.594***	1.138***
	(0.000)	(0.000)	(0.000)	(0.000)	(0.000)
CLOSELY HELD	−0.003***	−0.003***	−0.003***	−0.003***	−0.003***
	(0.001)	(0.002)	(0.002)	(0.002)	(0.001)
R-squared (within)	0.050	0.077	0.064	0.079	0.051
R-squared	–	–	–	–	–
Firms	1638	1638	1638	1638	1638
Observations	5511	5511	5511	5511	5511

Notes: The table reports estimates from fixed effects regressions of Tobin's Q on alternative corporate governance indices and control variables. CGI1 denotes the governance index constructed in the same way as Aggarwal et al. (2009), i.e., by dividing the governance attributes a company fulfils by the number of governance attributes a company reports data for. CGI2 is constructed in the same way as CGI1 but with missing attributes treated as if these attributes were not fulfilled. CGI3 (CGI4) is an adjusted version of CGI1 (CGI2) where we omit the number of governance attributes that every firm in a given country fulfils in a given year. CGI5 denotes the governance index constructed by means of principal component analysis (PCA) as outlined in Table 13.4. LN(TOTAL ASSETS) denotes the logarithm of total assets, PAST SALES GROWTH denotes the two-year growth of sales, R&D/SALES denotes the ratio of expenditures for research

	Country, industry and year fixed effects			
(6)	(7)	(8)	(9)	(10)
1.573***	1.363***	1.590***	1.472***	2.056***
(0.000)	(0.000)	(0.000)	(0.000)	(0.000)
0.008***				
(0.006)				
	0.013***			
	(0.000)			
		0.008***		
		(0.000)		
			0.010***	
			(0.000)	
				0.036***
				(0.004)
−0.216***	−0.226***	−0.219***	−0.225***	−0.210***
(0.000)	(0.000)	(0.000)	(0.000)	(0.000)
0.163***	0.165***	0.163***	0.165***	0.159***
(0.000)	(0.000)	(0.000)	(0.000)	(0.000)
1.169***	1.149***	1.159***	1.149***	1.185***
(0.000)	(0.000)	(0.000)	(0.000)	(0.000)
2.156***	2.145***	2.158***	2.149***	2.143***
(0.000)	(0.000)	(0.000)	(0.000)	(0.000)
1.108***	1.092***	1.107***	1.096***	1.129***
(0.002)	(0.002)	(0.002)	(0.002)	(0.002)
−0.086***	−0.085***	−0.086***	−0.085***	−0.085***
(0.000)	(0.000)	(0.000)	(0.000)	(0.000)
0.715***	0.723***	0.719***	0.721***	0.704***
(0.000)	(0.000)	(0.000)	(0.000)	(0.000)
0.201***	0.213***	0.201***	0.211***	0.223***
(0.000)	(0.000)	(0.000)	(0.000)	(0.000)
0.165***	0.152***	0.160***	0.151***	0.173***
(0.000)	(0.000)	(0.000)	(0.000)	(0.000)
0.004***	0.004***	0.004***	0.004***	0.003***
(0.000)	(0.000)	(0.000)	(0.000)	(0.000)
−	−	−	−	−
0.255	0.258	0.256	0.258	0.254
1638	1638	1638	1638	1638
5511	5511	5511	5511	5511

and development to sales, CASH/ASSETS denotes the ratio of cash to total assets, CAPEX/ASSETS denotes the ratio of capital expenditures to assets, PPE/SALES denotes the ratio of property, plant and equipment to sales, EBIT/SALES denotes the ratio of earnings before interest and taxes to sales, LEVERAGE denotes the ratio of total debt to total assets, ADR is a dummy variable which equals 1 if the firm has American Depository Receipts (ADR) and 0 otherwise and CLOSELY HELD is the percentage of closely held shares. The regressions reported in Columns 1 to 5 include firm fixed effects and the regressions in Columns 6 to 10 include industry, year and country fixed effects. The p-values (in parentheses) are based on Driscoll and Kraay (1998) standard errors which are heteroscedasticity-consistent and robust to general forms of cross-sectional and temporal dependence. ***, **, * denotes statistical significance at the 1%, 5%, 10% level.

increase in the index. Hence, increasing the volatility of the governance index by omitting variables without cross-sectional variation – at least at the country level – results in
a stronger economic effect of the governance index. The economic effect of CGI4, which
combines the adjustments of both CGI2 and CGI3, is very similar to that of CGI3.
Specifically, a one standard deviation (16.29) increase is associated with an increase in
Tobin's Q of 0.16, which amounts to 9.47 (11.80) per cent of mean (median) Q. Hence,
the focus on governance attributes that are likely to represent the firms' deliberate choice
of corporate governance mechanisms in place (CGI3) seems to have a stronger effect on
the economic magnitude of the valuation effect of corporate governance than the introduction of a penalty term for non-reported data (CGI2). Finally, the economic magnitude of the valuation effect of CGI5 is larger than that of CGI1 but smaller than that
of the other three indices: a one standard deviation (1.68) increase is associated with an
increase in Tobin's Q of 0.10 which amounts to 5.57 (6.93) per cent of mean (median) Q.

Regarding the control variables, our results largely correspond to those of Aggarwal
et al. (2009) with a few exceptions. Firstly, the coefficient on R&D/SALES is not significant in all five specifications. However, if we follow Aggarwal et al. (2009) and include
industry fixed effects (as we do in columns 6 to 10), the coefficient on R&D/SALES turns
positive and significant in all specifications. Secondly, and consistent with Aggarwal et
al. (2009), the coefficients on PPE/SALES are negative. However, in our regressions they
are all significant at the 1 per cent level while they are insignificant in Aggarwal et al.
(2009). Thirdly, the coefficient on LEVERAGE is negative and significant in two specifications of Table 13.6. In contrast, the leverage-coefficient is never significant in Aggarwal
et al. (2009). Finally, the coefficient on CLOSELY HELD is negative and significant in
all specifications. This finding contrasts with Aggarwal et al. (2009) and also other prior
research (e.g., La Porta et al., 1999; Stulz, 2005) and might be due to the relatively high
mean (30 per cent) and median (25 per cent) values of closely held shares in our sample.
Morck et al. (1988) report a negative relationship between share ownership of the board
of directors and firm value in the 5 to 25 per cent ownership range and attribute these
findings to a domination of the incentive alignment effect by the entrenchment effect. A
similar effect might be at work for block ownership more generally in our sample.

Cross-country variation in corporate governance practices have been shown to be
significant (e.g., Doidge et al., 2007). We aim to account for this fact controlling for
country-specific instead of firm-specific unobservable heteroscedasticity in our regressions. Specifically, we include country, industry and year fixed effects instead of firm
fixed effects in the subsequent regressions. The results are reported in columns 6 to 10
of Table 13.6. Most importantly, the coefficients on the governance indices all remain
positive and significant, now all at the 1 per cent level. With respect to the economic magnitude, the results are also largely consistent with those in columns 1 to 5. The smallest
economic effect is associated with CGI5 (0.06 increase in Q for a one standard deviation
increase in the index) followed by CGI1 (0.09 increase in Q for a one standard deviation
increase in the index). Omitting country-specific governance attributes (CGI3) strength-
ens the economic effect to an increase in Q of 0.12 for a one standard deviation increase
in the index. Penalizing firms for not making data on certain attributes available further
increases the economic magnitude to a 0.17 increase in Q for a one standard deviation increase in CGI2. Finally, a one standard deviation increase of CGI4 results in an
increase of Q of 0.16. Hence, as before, both a penalty term for non-reported attributes

and the omission of country-specific attributes are associated with a stronger economic effect of the corporate governance index. However, in contrast to the results in columns 1 to 5, this time the results suggest that the penalizing term for not reported attributes is somewhat more important than the omission of country-specific governance attributes from the index construction. The only notable changes in the control variables are that the coefficients on both R&D/SALES and LEVERAGE turn positive and significant when country dummy variables are included and, consistent with prior research, the coefficient on CLOSELY HELD also turns positive and significant.

Table 13.5 shows that alternative estimation techniques may strongly affect the estimate of the economic magnitude of the valuation effect of governance. In particular, methods that account for the endogeneity of corporate governance (and possibly other variables) seem to substantially increase the economic significance of the valuation effect (e.g., Durnev and Kim, 2005; Chhaochharia and Laeven, 2009). However, Beiner et al. (2006) and Black et al. (2006) show that instrumental variables approaches may lead to an overestimate of the valuation effect of corporate governance. Ammann et al. (2011) find little difference in the economic effect of corporate governance on Tobin's Q when comparing their ordinary least squares (OLS) results to those based on a dynamic panel GMM estimator.

13.4 ROBUSTNESS TESTS

The distribution of firm-year observations across countries, as reported in Table 13.1, shows that Japan and the UK combined make up more than 40 per cent of our sample. This gives rise to the concern that our results might be strongly driven by these two countries. To mitigate this concern, we re-estimate the firm-value regressions reported in columns 5 to 10 of Table 13.6 excluding all observations from these two countries. We present the results of this robustness test in Table 13.7. The results show that even after excluding all observations from Japan and the UK, all five corporate governance indices continue to have a significantly positive effect on firm value. Moreover, the sizes of the coefficients on the five governance indices are very similar to those reported for the full sample in Table 13.6. In further unreported robustness tests, we re-estimate the regressions in Table 13.6 for each individual year of our sample (2003, 2004, 2005, 2006, 2007) separately. We also re-estimate all regressions for the five largest sample countries (Japan, UK, Australia, France and Germany). We find the positive and significant coefficient on the five corporate governance indices to prevail for each sample year and for each of the five largest sample countries, with two exceptions. Firstly, possibly due to the relatively small sample size compared to the four subsequent years, in 2003 the coefficient on some corporate governance indices is insignificant. Secondly, the coefficient on all five corporate governance indices is insignificant for Japan. This latter finding is consistent with prior research documenting that the corporate governance of Japanese firms differs from that in other countries (e.g., Berglöf and Perotti, 1994; La Porta et al., 2000; Claessens et al., 2002). It is thus not surprising that we cannot find a significant relationship between our corporate governance indices and firm valuation for Japanese companies.[9]

When empirically investigating the relationship between corporate governance and

Table 13.7   Regressions of Tobin's Q on alternative governance indices and control variables: excluding Japan and the UK

Dependent variable: Tobin's Q	(1)	(2)	(3)	(4)	(5)
Constant	3.490***	3.443***	3.549***	3.496***	3.997***
	(0.000)	(0.000)	(0.000)	(0.000)	(0.000)
CGI1	0.009***				
	(0.000)				
CGI2		0.012***			
		(0.000)			
CGI3			0.007***		
			(0.000)		
CGI4				0.010***	
				(0.000)	
CGI5					0.043***
					(0.000)
LN(TOTAL ASSETS)	−0.261***	−0.267***	−0.262***	−0.267***	−0.254***
	(0.000)	(0.000)	(0.000)	(0.000)	(0.000)
PAST SALES GROWTH	0.127***	0.131***	0.128***	0.131***	0.126***
	(0.001)	(0.000)	(0.001)	(0.000)	(0.001)
R&D/SALES	1.967***	1.923***	1.947***	1.913***	1.976***
	(0.000)	(0.000)	(0.000)	(0.000)	(0.000)
CASH/ASSETS	2.256***	2.268***	2.275***	2.284***	2.222***
	(0.000)	(0.000)	(0.000)	(0.000)	(0.000)
CAPEX/ASSETS	0.724**	0.712**	0.733**	0.716**	0.748**
	(0.043)	(0.044)	(0.039)	(0.043)	(0.043)
PPE/SALES	−0.096***	−0.094***	−0.095***	−0.093***	−0.095***
	(0.000)	(0.000)	(0.000)	(0.000)	(0.000)
EBIT/SALES	0.613***	0.616***	0.612***	0.613***	0.598***
	(0.000)	(0.000)	(0.000)	(0.000)	(0.000)
LEVERAGE	−0.168**	−0.166**	−0.176**	−0.174**	−0.149*
	(0.034)	(0.035)	(0.033)	(0.033)	(0.062)
ADR (Dummy)	0.036	0.024	0.033	0.021	0.050
	(0.282)	(0.491)	(0.334)	(0.543)	(0.108)
CLOSELY HELD	0.004***	0.004***	0.004***	0.004***	0.003***
	(0.000)	(0.000)	(0.000)	(0.000)	(0.000)
R-squared	0.294	0.297	0.295	0.298	0.293
Firms	853	853	853	853	853
Observations	2655	2655	2655	2655	2655

Notes: The table reports estimates from fixed effects regressions of Tobin's Q on alternative corporate governance indices and control variables. CGI1 denotes the governance index constructed in the same way as Aggarwal et al. (2009), i.e., by dividing the governance attributes a company fulfils by the number of governance attributes a company reports data for. CGI2 is constructed in the same way as CGI1 but with missing attributes treated as if these attributes were not fulfilled. CGI3 (CGI4) is an adjusted version of CGI1 (CGI2) where we omit the number of governance attributes that every firm in a given country fulfils in a given year. CGI5 denotes the governance index constructed by means of principal component analysis (PCA) as outlined in Table 13.4. LN(TOTAL ASSETS) denotes the logarithm of total assets, PAST SALES GROWTH denotes the two-year growth of sales, R&D/SALES denotes the ratio of expenditures for research and development to sales, CASH/ASSETS denotes the ratio of cash to total assets, CAPEX/ASSETS denotes the ratio of capital expenditures to assets, PPE/SALES denotes the ratio of property, plant and equipment to

Table 13.7   (continued)

sales, EBIT/SALES denotes the ratio of earnings before interest and taxes to sales, LEVERAGE denotes the ratio of total debt to total assets, ADR is a dummy variable which equals 1 if the firm has American Depository Receipts (ADR) and 0 otherwise and CLOSELY HELD is the percentage of closely held shares. All regressions include industry, year and country fixed effects. The *p*-values (in parentheses) are based on Driscoll and Kraay (1998) standard errors which are heteroscedasticity-consistent and robust to general forms of cross-sectional and temporal dependence. ***, **, * denotes statistical significance at the 1%, 5%, 10% level.

firm value, endogeneity is an important issue. Recent academic literature suggests that such an endogenous relationship could be dynamic (e.g., Wintoki et al., 2012). Hermalin and Weisbach (2004) and Wintoki et al. (2012) argue that the current actions of a firm will affect both future corporate governance choices and performance, which will in turn affect the firm's future actions. We follow Wintoki et al. (2012) and employ the dynamic panel generalized method of moments (GMM) estimation procedure introduced by Arellano and Bover (1995) and Blundell and Bond (1998) to control for such dynamic endogeneity, unobservable heterogeneity and simultaneity. The estimation procedure consists of three steps. Firstly, we rewrite the regression equation as a dynamic model including lagged performance as an explanatory variable. Secondly, we compute the first differences of all variables to control for unobserved heterogeneity and to eliminate a potential omitted variables bias. Thirdly, we estimate the model by GMM and use lagged values of the governance indices and performance as instruments to control for potential simultaneity and reverse causality. This estimation procedure allows all the explanatory variables (i.e., the governance indices as well as all control variables) to be treated as endogenous. In unreported results, we find that the positive and significant relationship between our five alternative corporate governance indices and Tobin's Q prevails in such a dynamic panel GMM regression setup. The results of this analysis alleviate endogeneity concerns and may be regarded as evidence of a causal link between our corporate governance indices and firm value.

13.5   CONCLUSIONS

This chapter investigates the valuation effect of firm-level corporate governance using a new international corporate governance database provided by GMI. The dataset covers 64 individual corporate governance attributes on more than 2300 firms from 22 developed countries over a five-year period from 2003 to 2007. We aggregate the 64 corporate governance attributes to five alternative corporate governance indices using different additive and statistical techniques.

We find a strong and statistically significant and positive relationship between firm-level corporate governance and firm value. This result is robust to the different techniques used to construct the corporate governance indices, a breakdown of the sample by both calendar year and country, and to using a dynamic panel GMM estimator to account for endogeneity problems.

Moreover, the results in this chapter indicate that better corporate governance practices are reflected not only in statistically but also in economically significantly higher market values. Based on the most conservative estimate in our results, a one standard deviation increase in the (most simple additive) corporate governance index is associated with an increase in Tobin's Q of about 0.07, which corresponds to 3.85 per cent (4.80 per cent) of mean (median) Q in our sample. In other specifications, we use alternative governance indices that try to overcome two issues with the standard additive indices. Firstly, we account for the problem that the firm's decision to reveal information and the decision to comply are probably correlated. Secondly, we attempt to filter out governance standards at the country level. The results we obtain when we use these alternative indices indicate a much higher valuation impact and an increase in Q of up to 0.17 for a one standard deviation increase in the index or 9.88 per cent (12.32 per cent) of mean (median) Q. Hence, from the company's perspective, corporate governance should be understood as an opportunity to increase firm value and decrease the costs of capital rather than as an obligation and pure cost factor.

NOTES

1. The present chapter draws on findings presented in our recent paper: 'Corporate governance and firm value: international evidence', Ammann et al. (2011). We are grateful to Howard Sherman from Governance Metrics International (GMI) for providing us with the dataset used in this chapter.
2. The evidence presented by Klapper and Love (2004), for example, suggests that firm-level corporate governance is more important in countries with relatively weak legal environments. They argue that firms can partially compensate for ineffective laws and enforcement.
3. The 17 attributes used by Chhaochharia and Laeven (2009) are basically a subset of the 44 attributes used by Aggarwal et al. (2009) and 16 of them are included in the latter paper. In contrast to Aggarwal et al. (2009) and our analysis, Chhaochharia and Laeven (2009) do not include any attributes related to compensation and ownership and only a few attributes related to the board of directors.
4. In unreported robustness tests, we use an extended set of 21 governance attributes for the PCA-based index. The additional four attributes are: dummy variables whether the company has not adopted a shareholder rights plan ('poison pill'), whether the chief executive officer (CEO) or managing director does not sit on the remuneration committee, whether the remuneration committee is wholly composed of independent board members and whether the company has separated the chairman and CEO positions. The results remain virtually unchanged.
5. For the governance indices based on the equally weighted averages of the standardized attributes, which are used in unreported robustness tests, we derive the sign of the expected correlation from whether the sum of factor loadings in excess of 0.40 in absolute terms is larger than 0.5 (positive expectation), smaller than −0.5 (negative expectation), or between −0.5 and 0.5 (no expectation).
6. In unreported robustness tests, we find all our results to remain qualitatively unchanged when we omit the winsorization and sample restriction based on LEVERAGE.
7. For space reasons, we do not report all estimates reported in the seven studies and focus on those of the main regression specification of the paper. We report two values if there is a major change in the set-up within a paper (e.g., Chhaochharia and Laeven, 2009).
8. Driscoll and Kraay (1998) show that erroneously ignoring cross-sectional dependence in the estimation of linear panel models can lead to severely biased statistical inference. In the context of this chapter, cross-sectional correlation may arise when the decision to implement a specific corporate governance provision of one particular firm is related to or coincides with the decisions of other firms.
9. *Keiretsu* membership seems to be the most important corporate governance attribute in Japan, whereas others, such as ownership structure, appear to be less important. For example, Lins and Servaes (1999) find that a strong *keiretsu* membership is an indicator of potential governance problems while ownership structure is not. Claessens et al. (2002) do not include Japan in their analysis of ownership structure in East Asia because the *keiretsu* system affects corporate governance in ways not measurable by ownership variables.

REFERENCES

Aggarwal, R., I. Erel, R. Stulz and R. Williamson (2009), 'Differences in governance practice between U.S. and foreign firms: measurement, causes, and consequences', *Review of Financial Studies*, **22** (8), 3131–3169.

Ammann, M., D. Oesch and M. Schmid (2011), 'Corporate governance and firm value: international evidence', *Journal of Empirical Finance*, **18** (1), 36–55.

Arellano, M. and O. Bover (1995), 'Another look at the instrumental variable estimation of error-component models', *Journal of Econometrics*, **68** (1), 29–51.

Balasubramaniam, B.N., B.S. Black and V.S. Khanna (2010), 'The relation between firm-level corporate governance and market value: a case study of India', *Emerging Market Review*, **11** (4), 319–340.

Bebchuk, L. and A. Cohen (2005), 'The costs of entrenched boards', *Journal of Financial Economics*, **78** (2), 409–433.

Bebchuk, L., A. Cohen and A. Ferrell (2009), 'What matters in corporate governance?', *Review of Financial Studies*, **22** (2), 783–827.

Beiner, S., W. Drobetz, M. Schmid and H. Zimmermann (2006), 'An integrated framework of corporate governance and firm valuation', *European Financial Management*, **12** (2), 249–283.

Berglöf, E. and E. Perotti (1994), 'The governance structure of the Japanese financial keiretsu', *Journal of Financial Economics*, **36** (2), 259–284.

Black, B.S., W. Kim and H. Jang (2006), 'Does corporate governance affect firms' market values? Evidence from Korea', *Journal of Law, Economics and Organization*, **22** (2), 366–413.

Blundell, R. and S. Bond (1998), 'Initial conditions and moment restrictions in dynamic panel data models', *Journal of Econometrics*, **87** (1), 115–143.

Bruno, V. and S. Claessens (2010), 'Corporate governance and regulation: can there be too much of a good thing?', *Journal of Financial Intermediation*, **19** (4), 461–482.

Chhaochharia, V. and Y. Grinstein (2007), 'Corporate governance and firm value: the impact of the 2002 governance rules', *Journal of Finance*, **62** (4), 1789–1825.

Chhaochharia, V. and L. Laeven (2009), 'Corporate governance norms and practices', *Journal of Financial Intermediation*, **18** (3), 405–431.

Claessens, S., S. Djankov, J.P.H. Fan and L.H.P. Lang (2002), 'Disentangling the incentive and entrenchment effects of large shareholders', *Journal of Finance*, **57** (6), 2741–2771.

Core, J., W.R. Guay and T.O. Rusticus (2006), 'Does weak governance cause weak stock returns? An examination of firm operating performance and investors' expectations', *Journal of Finance*, **61** (2), 655–687.

Cremers, M. and A. Ferrell (2011), 'Thirty years of governance governance: firm valuation and stock returns', Working Paper, Yale School of Management.

Cremers, M. and V.B. Nair (2005), 'Governance mechanisms and equity prices', *Journal of Finance*, **60** (6), 2859–2894.

Doidge, C., G. Karolyi and R. Stulz (2004), 'Why foreign firms that list in the US are worth more?', *Journal of Financial Economics*, **71** (2), 205–238.

Doidge, C., G. Karolyi and R. Stulz (2007), 'Why do countries matter so much for corporate governance?', *Journal of Financial Economics*, **86** (1), 1–39.

Driscoll, J.C. and A.C. Kraay (1998), 'Consistent covariance matrix estimation with spatially dependent panel data', *Review of Economics and Statistics*, **80**(4), 549–560.

Drobetz, W., A. Schillhofer and H. Zimmermann (2004), 'Corporate governance and expected stock returns: evidence from Germany', *European Financial Management*, **10** (2), 267–293.

Durnev, A. and E.H. Kim (2005), 'To steal or not to steal: firm attributes, legal environment and valuation', *Journal of Finance*, **60** (3), 1461–1493.

Ertugrul, M. and S. Hegde (2009), 'Corporate governance ratings and firm performance', *Financial Management*, **38**(1), 139–160.

Faleye, O. (2007), 'Classified boards, firm value, and managerial entrenchment', *Journal of Financial Economics*, **83** (2), 501–529.

Francis, J., I. Khurana and R. Pereira (2005), 'Disclosure incentives and effects on cost of capital around the world', *Accounting Review*, **80** (4), 1125–1162.

Gillan, S., J. Hartzell and L. Starks (2003), 'Explaining corporate governance: boards, bylaws, and charter provisions', Working Paper, University of Texas at Austin.

Gompers, P.A., J. Ishii and A. Metrick (2003), 'Corporate governance and equity prices', *Quarterly Journal of Economics*, **118** (1), 107–155.

Gompers, P.A., J. Ishii and A. Metrick (2010), 'Extreme governance: an analysis of dual-class firms in the United States', *Review of Financial Studies*, **23** (3), 1051–1088.

Gordon, E.A., E. Henry and D. Palia (2006), 'Related party transactions: associations with corporate governance and firm value', working paper, Rutgers University.

Hermalin, B.E. and M.S. Weisbach (2004), 'Boards of directors as an endogenously determined institution: a survey of the economic literature', *Federal Reserve Bank of New York Economic Policy Review*, **9** (1), 7–26.

Jensen, M.C. and W.H. Meckling (1976), 'Theory of the firm: managerial behavior, agency costs and owner-ship structure', *Journal of Financial Economics*, **3** (4), 305–360.

Khanna, T., J. Kogan and K. Palepu (2006), 'Globalization and similarities in corporate governance: a cross country analysis', *Review of Economics and Statistics*, **88** (1), 69–90.

Klapper, L. and I. Love (2004), 'Corporate governance, investor protection and performance in emerging markets', *Journal of Corporate Finance*, **10** (5), 703–728.

La Porta, R., F. Lopez-De-Silanes and A. Shleifer (1999), 'Corporate ownership around the world', *Journal of Finance*, **54** (2), 471–517.

La Porta, R., F. Lopez-de-Silanes, A. Shleifer and R. Vishny (1998), 'Law and finance', *Journal of Political Economy*, **106** (6), 1113–1155.

La Porta, R., F. Lopez-de-Silanes, A. Shleifer and R.W. Vishny (2000), 'Investor protection and corporate governance', *Journal of Financial Economics*, **58** (1–2), 3–29.

La Porta, R., F. Lopez-de-Silanes, A. Shleifer and R.W. Vishny (2002), 'Investor protection and corporate valuation', *Journal of Finance*, **57** (3), 1147–1170.

Larcker, D., S. Richardson and I. Tuna (2007), 'Corporate governance, accounting outcomes and organiza-tional performance', *Accounting Review*, **82** (4), 963–1008.

Lins, K. and H. Servaes (1999), 'International evidence on the value of corporate diversification', *Journal of Finance*, **54** (6), 2215–2239.

Morck, R., A. Shleifer and R.W. Vishny (1988), 'Management ownership and market valuation: an empirical analysis', *Journal of Financial Economics*, **20** (1–2), 293–316.

Shleifer, A. and R.W. Vishny (1997), 'A survey of corporate governance', *Journal of Finance*, **52** (2), 737–783.

Stulz, R. (2005), 'The limits of financial globalization', *Journal of Finance*, **60** (4), 1595–1638.

Wintoki, M.B., J.S. Linck and J.M. Netter (2012), 'Endogeneity and the dynamics of corporate governance', *Journal of Financial Economics*, **103** (3), 581–606.

Yermack, D. (1996), 'Higher market valuation for firms with a small board of directors', *Journal of Financial Economics*, **40** (2), 185–211.

14 Does hedging reduce economic exposure? Hurricanes, jet fuel prices and airlines

David A. Carter, Daniel A. Rogers, Betty J. Simkins and *Stephen D. Treanor*

14.1 INTRODUCTION

Does hedging reduce corporate economic exposure to input cost risk factors? Surprisingly, this question has not been well addressed in prior literature. A recent survey article by Smithson and Simkins (2005) highlights that the population of published studies of the effect of hedging on firm risk factors is limited to those analyzing currency risk, financial institutions or commodity producers. Notably, none of the surveyed articles utilize a sample of firms for which an input cost factor poses significant risks to the financial health of the sample companies.

In this chapter, we demonstrate how the multivariate regression model (MVRM) can be used to analyze whether hedging affects economic exposures. We utilize information from extreme events to assess whether corporate hedging reduces an input cost risk exposure. In particular, we use the fact that two major hurricanes occurring in 2005 caused major spikes in jet fuel prices. We analyze whether jet fuel hedging by US airlines is able to reduce market value losses during unexpected increases in jet fuel prices. We argue that the standard methodology for measuring risk exposure is not well suited to improving our understanding of how hedging affects risk exposures across firms with differing risk management strategies. Because the cost of jet fuel is a significant operating expense for airlines, a sudden, unexpected increase in fuel costs could have a serious negative effect on their operating performance and stock price. In fact, we find that the stock price reactions of airlines to these extreme events is systematically greater than would be expected based on traditional jet fuel exposure coefficients. We find that airlines which hedge more are less affected by the price increases associated with the hurricanes. Our results highlight two important issues. Firstly, traditional measures of risk exposures might not adequately reflect how a firm's stock price reacts to an extreme event. Secondly, because traditional risk exposure measures might be systematically downward biased (in absolute value), the effect of hedging on risk exposure is better measured by analyzing how hedging affects value during extreme events.

The 2005 Atlantic hurricane season was extraordinary. With 27 named storms, 2005 was the most active Atlantic hurricane season on record. The year surpassed 1969 for the greatest number of hurricanes (14), tied with 1999 for the greatest number of Category 4 storms (5), and holds the record for the most Category 5 hurricanes (3).[1] In late August in the United States (US), Hurricane Katrina was responsible for killing almost 1400 people and causing $75 billion in damage as it devastated New Orleans and the Gulf Coast. Less than a month later, Hurricane Rita made landfall near the Texas–Louisiana border causing around $10 billion in damage. In both instances, oil production from

341

offshore oil rigs and refining capacity was affected by storm damage. The result was an increase in the already high prices of petroleum and petroleum products. Because jet fuel is a major operating expense for airlines, a sudden spike in fuel costs should be a major concern for airlines and their investors.

Several prior studies examine the relationship between stock returns and a variety of unexpected, catastrophic events, such as airline crashes (Barrett et al., 1987; Davidson et al., 1987), hurricanes (Lamb, 1995, 1998), and the September 11th terrorist attacks (Carter and Simkins, 2004). However, this investigation differs from these earlier studies because we account for the possibility that hedging could protect an airline from the sudden, unexpected increase in fuel costs resulting from the catastrophic hurricanes.

We use MVRM to investigate the market's reaction to the sudden increase in jet fuel prices caused by Hurricanes Katrina and Rita. The MVRM is an econometric technique to measure the effect of new information on asset prices that is superior to other techniques when certain econometric assumptions are violated. We find large, statistically significant, negative abnormal returns in response to actual or anticipated increases in jet fuel prices. The combined effects of the abnormal stock returns associated with the two hurricanes reduced the market value of the average US airline's stock by approximately 9.7 percent.

More importantly, we investigate cross-sectional differences in abnormal returns for our sample of US airlines. This analysis reveals a significant positive relationship between jet fuel hedging and the abnormal returns. In other words, airlines hedging a greater amount of their expected 2005 fuel needs had less negative abnormal returns. An airline with the average jet fuel hedged percentage (about 20 percent) generates approximately a 3.5 percent positive abnormal return relative to an unhedged airline during the two extreme dates.

The chapter proceeds as follows: section 14.2 discusses the literature related to risk exposure and hedging. Section 14.3 describes the data sources and the empirical methodology used in the investigation. Section 14.4 presents the results, and section 14.5 concludes.

14.2   EXPOSURE AND RISK MANAGEMENT

14.2.1   Traditional Measurement of Economic Exposures to Risk Factors

Measurement of economic exposures has spawned a considerable literature in which individual firms' stock returns are regressed on changes in interest rates, currency rates or commodity prices. Smithson and Simkins (2005) survey this literature and highlight 21 articles that, as a primary or sole aspect of their work, study the relationship between stock returns and either interest rate changes or currency rate changes. They conclude that financial institutions exhibit significant economic exposure to interest rate changes, but the evidence is mixed as to whether industrial companies are exposed to currency rate changes.

The basic models underlying the measurement of economic exposure rely on a regression of past stock returns on changes in the risk factor. For example, in the context of airline stock price exposure to jet fuel, the traditional approach to measuring risk exposure implies the following regression equation:

$$\tilde{R}_{i,t} = \alpha_i + \beta_{m,i}\tilde{R}_{m,t} + \gamma_{JF,i}\tilde{R}_{JF,t} + \varepsilon_{i,t}, \tag{14.1}$$

where:
$\tilde{R}_{i,t}$ is the stock return on airline i during time period t
$\tilde{R}_{m,t}$ is the return on a market index during time period t
$\tilde{R}_{JF,t}$ is the percentage change in jet fuel price during time period t
α_i, β_i are the standard market-model parameters for each airline i
$\gamma_{JF,i}$ is the jet fuel exposure coefficient for airline i
$\varepsilon_{i,t}$ is a random disturbance term.

Carter et al. (2006) use the above equation for an equally weighted portfolio of US airlines. They report a coefficient of −0.11, and note that a one standard deviation increase in monthly jet fuel prices would translate into a 2.75 percent decline in the return from a portfolio of US airline stocks. However, they do not analyze this exposure in any further detail, or at the individual company level.

The academic literature does not pay much attention to corporate exposure to input commodity price risks. Most articles studying commodity price exposure focus on the degree to which commodity producers are exposed to fluctuations in their asset markets. For example, Tufano (1998) and Petersen and Thiagarajan (2000) measure the gold price exposure of gold mining firms, while Jin and Jorion (2006) analyze the exposure of oil- and gas-producing firms. By focusing our analysis on commodity users rather than producers, we believe that our results are more generalizable to other industrial settings.

A potential weakness with the traditional methodology for measuring risk exposures is that, if the exposure coefficient is measured during 'normal' conditions for the risk factor, then the stock market reaction to 'abnormal' conditions for the risk factor might be significantly different than the expected reaction. In other words, the measured exposure may not work well in explaining the reaction to an extreme event.

In this chapter, we demonstrate how to use a modified event study methodology. We identify two extreme events, Hurricanes Katrina and Rita, to investigate three questions. Firstly, are individual airlines exposed to jet fuel prices according to the traditional exposure methodology? Secondly, do airline stock prices react to an extreme event as predicted by an *ex ante* exposure coefficient? Thirdly, does jet fuel hedging policy affect the exposure of airlines to extreme movements in jet fuel prices?

While this study is limited to airlines, we believe that the methodology is useful in other settings. For example, Smithson and Simkins (2005) state, 'The studies of FX risk in industrial companies reported that only a small percentage of individual firms exhibited (statistically) significant exposure.' However, if the firms in these studies are truly exposed to currency fluctuations, perhaps this fact can be better analyzed by studying the reactions of their stock prices to extreme events that affect the currency prices to which they are potentially exposed.

An additional difficulty associated with the traditional approach to measuring risk exposure occurs when trying to analyze whether hedging reduces the risk exposure. In a cross-sectional sample of firms, we might expect a hedger to exhibit a lower risk exposure coefficient than a non-hedger. However, this inference generally contains the implicit assumption that the two firms would have the same exposure in the absence of hedging. The appropriateness of such an assumption might be questionable in many empirical applications. By assessing the cross-sectional differences in abnormal stock returns occurring because of extreme events, we should be able to distinguish whether hedging is useful in mitigating the effects of a particular risk factor (in this case, jet fuel price risk).

14.2.2   The Multivariate Regression Model (MVRM)

As an alternative to the traditional approach to measuring exposure, we use the MVRM methodology, first suggested by Gibbons (1980), and further developed by Schipper and Thompson (1983), Binder (1985a, 1985b) and Malatesta (1986), to examine the stock price reaction to sudden, unanticipated increases in jet fuel prices. In these cases, stock return residuals will not be independently and identically distributed. For this reason, the MVRM approach is preferred to the standard event-study method first employed by Fama et al. (1969).[2] The Fama, Fisher, Jensen and Roll (FFJR) approach assumes that the residuals are independent and identically distributed. As Binder (1985a) states, there are three problems with this assumption: firstly, the abnormal returns are likely to differ across firms; secondly, the residual variance differs across firms; and thirdly, the residuals will not be independent if the events occur in the same time period for some firms (and these firms are in the same or similar industries). A key advantage of the MVRM is in the hypothesis testing since contemporaneous dependence of the disturbances and heteroscedasticity across equations are incorporated into the testing of hypotheses. Therefore, the MVRM is considered a leading technique to measure the effect of new information on asset prices and we demonstrate the use in a unique event study application: the impact of hurricanes on the stock prices of airlines.

To apply the MVRM technique, we estimate a system of equations in which the returns for each of our sample firms are represented as follows:

$$\tilde{R}_{i,t} = \alpha_i + \beta_i \tilde{R}_{m,t} + \gamma_{JF,t} \tilde{R}_{JF,t} + \sum_{j=1}^{n} \lambda_{i,j} D_j + \tilde{\varepsilon}_{i,t}, \tag{14.2}$$

where:
$\tilde{R}_{i,t}$ is the stock return on airline i on day t
$\tilde{R}_{m,t}$ is the return on the Standard & Poor's (S&P) 500 index on day t
$\tilde{R}_{JF,t}$ is the return on jet fuel prices on day t
α_i, β_i are the standard market-model parameters for each airline i
$\gamma_{JF,t}$ is the jet fuel exposure coefficient for airline i on day t
D_j is a dummy variable equal to 1 on event day j and 0 otherwise
$\lambda_{i,j}$ is the abnormal return for airline i on the event day j
$\tilde{\varepsilon}_{i,t}$ is a random disturbance term.

Equation (14.2) is estimated using daily returns beginning on January 3, 2005 and continuing through December 31, 2005. We include 18 dummy variables indicating trading days from August 23 to September 6, and September 19 to September 28, to capture any abnormal returns for the periods surrounding the landfalls of Hurricanes Katrina and Rita.

Within the MVRM framework, we first test the market's reaction to the hurricanes. This hypothesis is the standard event-study test to determine whether significant abnormal returns occurred in response to the extreme events. Rejection of the null hypothesis of no abnormal return suggests that the market viewed the hurricanes as having important implications for airlines and that the information was incorporated into share prices. Because we include the jet fuel return as an explanatory variable, negative abnormal returns on the event dates suggest that the traditional exposure coefficient provides an incomplete measure of exposure to extreme events. Prior research on large losses by firms finds an immediate negative market reaction (see Sprecher and Pertl, 1983; Barrett et al., 1987).

If significant abnormal returns are found, we hypothesize that cross-sectional differences in abnormal returns are due to the effectiveness of input commodity risk management (i.e., hedging). Specifically, we expect airlines that have hedged more of their remaining 2005 jet fuel requirements to experience less adverse stock price reactions on the event dates. To test this hypothesis, we run the following regression:

$$AR_{i,t} = \alpha_i + \beta*Size_i + \gamma*Lev_i + \delta*Perhedg_i + \tilde{\varepsilon}_{i,t}, \tag{14.3}$$

where:

$AR_{i,t}$	is the abnormal return on airline i on day t (September 1 or 21),
$Size_i$	is the natural log of assets for airline i,
Lev_i	is the ratio of long-term debt to total assets for airline i,
$Perhedg_i$	is the proportion of 2005 fuel requirements hedged by airline i

14.3 DATA

14.3.1 Chronology of Events

Hurricane Katrina initially formed as Tropical Depression 12 near the Bahamas on August 23, 2005. On this date, the spot price for Gulf Coast jet fuel (a primary benchmark for delivered airline jet fuel costs) was $1.872 per gallon. Katrina made landfall in southeastern Louisiana on Monday, August 29 as a strong Category 3 storm, devastating portion of southeastern Louisiana and coastal Mississippi. The spot price for Gulf Coast jet fuel on August 29 was $1.9723 (about 5.4 percent higher than the price when the hurricane initially formed). Because of the storm, the levees failed in New Orleans causing extensive flooding. Due to the resulting damage to oil production facilities and refineries, jet fuel prices increased drastically during the remainder of the week.[3] Closing Gulf Coast jet fuel prices were $2.295, $2.2884, $2.4225 and $2.205 on the following days.

Hurricane Rita initially formed on Saturday, September 17, 2005, and became a hurricane on September 20. The closing Gulf Coast jet fuel prices on Friday, September 16 and Tuesday, September 20 were $1.905 and $2.1529, respectively. Upon reaching warm

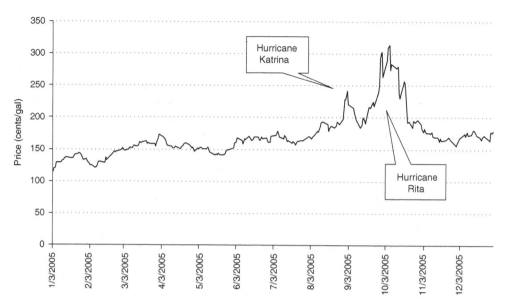

Source: Data obtained from the Energy Information Administration (www.eia.doe.gov).

Figure 14.1 Jet fuel prices (cents/gal) during 2005

Gulf of Mexico waters, Rita intensified dramatically. On September 21, Hurricane Rita was upgraded to a Category 5 storm with winds of 175 mph. Fortunately, Rita weakened significantly before making landfall on September 24. Nevertheless, due to the large amount of oil production and refining capacity in the Gulf region, Rita sparked a significant short-term spike in oil prices. Figure 14.1 presents the evolution of Gulf Coast jet fuel prices during 2005.

14.3.2 Sample Firms and Data

For this study, we use a sample of publicly traded US firms that operate in the commercial airline industry (SIC code of 4512). We obtain stock returns for each company from the Center for Research in Stock Prices (CRSP) at the University of Chicago. We eliminate firms with missing returns. Daily jet fuel prices are obtained from the Energy Information Administration website (www.eia.doe.gov). We obtain estimates of each firm's percentage of future jet fuel requirements hedged by reading the Management Disclosure and Analysis (MD&A) and financial statement footnote sections of 10-Q and 10-K filings with the Securities and Exchange Commission (SEC). Finally, we compute various financial metrics from accounting data on the Compustat Research Insight database. The resulting sample consists of 12 US airlines. Table 14.1 presents descriptive data for the firms in our sample, including the percentage of operating expenses made up by jet fuel costs and the percentage of 2005 expected fuel usage hedged, as of the end of 2004. Airline hedging policies varied considerably during this time frame. For example, Southwest Airlines hedged 85 percent of its anticipated 2005 fuel needs; three other airlines did not hedge at all.

Table 14.1   Selected financial data for sample passenger carriers (year-end 2004)

Airline	Total assets	Cash & short-term investments	Long-term debt	Return on assets (%)	Fuel costs as % of op. expenses	% of 2005 fuel needs hedged
Airtran Holdings	905.7	342.3	300.1	1.35	24.6	23.0
Alaska Air Group	3 335.0	873.9	989.6	−0.46	19.0	50.0
American Airlines	28 773.0	3 407.0	13 524.0	−2.64	21.1	4.0
Continental Airlines	10 511.0	1 669.0	5 167.0	−3.89	15.9	0.0
Delta Air Lines	21 801.0	2 147.0	13 005.0	−23.84	16.0	0.0
Frontier Airlines	792.0	204.7	282.8	−2.96	21.6	24.0
JetBlue Airways	2 798.6	449.2	1 395.9	1.70	22.1	22.0
Mesa Air Group	1 167.7	280.5	636.6	2.25	21.7	0.0
Midwest Express Holdings	360.7	110.6	64.6	−11.96	24.0	16.5
Northwest Airlines	14 042.0	2 611.0	8 023.0	−6.14	18.7	6.0
Southwest Airlines	11 337.0	1 305.0	1 700.0	2.76	16.7	85.0
United Airlines	20 705.0	2 178.0	301.0	−8.31	17.0	11.0
Mean	9 710.7	1 298.2	3 782.5	−4.35	19.9	20.1
Standard Deviation	9 391.3	1 051.2	4 812.3	7.30	2.9	24.0
Median	6 923.0	1 089.5	1 192.8	−2.80	20.1	13.8

Notes: This table presents selected financial data for sample airlines. Data for airlines are taken from SEC filings and are for the year ending 31 December 2004, except for Mesa Air Group (year ending 30 September 2004) and Frontier Airlines (year ending 31 March 2005).

14.4   EMPIRICAL RESULTS

To gain an initial assessment of airlines' sensitivities to jet fuel prices, we measure the jet fuel exposure coefficients of each company's stock using the traditional approach as shown in equation (14.1). We use daily returns for the period January–August 2005, prior to Hurricane Katrina. We report our estimates of jet fuel sensitivity in Table 14.2. All of the estimated jet fuel betas are negative. This result is consistent with the hypothesis that rising jet fuel prices are associated with decreasing stock returns for airline companies. Further, 10 of 12 jet fuel betas are statistically significant at the 10 percent level or better. The jet fuel sensitivities range between −0.0554 and −0.5254, and the average exposure coefficient is 0.26925. As a point of reference, the standard deviation of daily percentage changes in jet fuel prices from the beginning of 2005 through August 2005 is approximately 2.65 cents per gallon. Using a three standard deviation price change (to reflect an extreme move) and the average jet fuel exposure coefficient of −0.27, the average airline's expected stock market decline would be about 2.14 percent (beyond any market-related stock price changes). Thus, the jet fuel exposure coefficients do seem to reflect the fact that significant fuel price increases will reduce airline market values. However, a more important question is: 'Do the exposure coefficients do a reasonable job of explaining stock market changes when jet fuel prices are changing outside the realm of normality?'

Table 14.2   *Estimates of sensitivity to jet fuel prices for sample airlines (January–August 2005)*

Airline	Intercept	$\beta_{m,i}$	$\beta_{JF,i}$	R-squared	F-statistic
Airtran Holdings	0.0011	2.4060***	−0.2278***	0.3379	40.57***
	(0.0019)	(0.2928)	(0.0823)		
Alaska Air Group	0.0011	1.3410***	−0.2310***	0.3251	38.29***
	(0.0012)	(0.1900)	(0.0534)		
American Airlines	0.0032	1.6641***	−0.4494***	0.2785	30.68***
	(0.0020)	(0.3134)	(0.0880)		
Continental Airlines	0.0019	2.1836***	−0.3911***	0.2846	31.63***
	(0.0022)	(0.3444)	(0.0968)		
Delta Air Lines	−0.0085**	1.6965***	−0.2889*	0.0734	6.30***
	(0.0038)	(0.5905)	(0.1659)		
Frontier Airlines	0.0011	2.4155***	−0.2435***	0.3017	34.35***
	(0.0021)	(0.3222)	(0.0905)		
JetBlue Airways	−0.0001	1.7395***	−0.2483***	0.3091	35.56***
	(0.0016)	(0.2433)	(0.0684)		
Mesa Air Group	0.0007	2.1687***	−0.1104	0.2300	23.75***
	(0.0021)	(0.3270)	(0.0919)		
Midwest Express	0.0008	0.7078	−0.3232**	0.0470	3.92**
Holdings	(0.0033)	(0.5097)	(0.1432)		
Northwest Airlines	−0.0020	1.5444***	−0.5254***	0.1569	14.79***
	(0.0031)	(0.4738)	(0.1331)		
Southwest Airlines	−0.0006	1.2256***	−0.1366***	0.3994	52.86***
	(0.0009)	(0.1339)	(0.0376)		
United Airlines	0.0007	0.6952	−0.0554	0.0117	0.94
	(0.0036)	(0.5457)	(0.1533)		

Notes: This table presents jet fuel price sensitivities for sample airlines estimated using equation (14.3):

$$R_{i,t} = \alpha_i + \beta_{m,i} R_{m,t} + \gamma_{JF,i} R_{JF,t} + \varepsilon_{i,t}$$

Standard errors are reported in parentheses beneath the coefficient estimates. Statistical significance at the 10%, 5%, or 1% level is indicated by *, **, or ***, respectively.

For the next stage of our analysis, we use the MVRM methodology discussed in section 14.2.2. If traditional exposure coefficients measure airline jet fuel price risk fully, we expect to observe average abnormal returns of zero on event dates. If we observe negative abnormal returns in response to extreme events, then exposure coefficients are downward-biased (in absolute value) measures of true risk exposure.

We present the average abnormal returns for our sample airlines resulting from the estimation of equation (14.2) in Table 14.3. We note that two days (September 1 and September 21) exhibit statistically and economically significant average abnormal returns. On September 1, Gulf Coast jet fuel prices spiked to a new historical high of 242.25 cents per gallon (representing a 5.86 percent increase over the prior day) in response to damage to refineries caused by Katrina. The average abnormal return on September 1 was −5.71 percent.

Table 14.3   *Share-price response for airlines to jet fuel prices(23 August–28 September 2005)*

Variable	Coefficient estimate (standard error)
Intercept	0.0002
	(0.0012)
$R_{m,t}$	1.4144***
	(0.1918)
$R_{JF,t}$	−0.1251***
	(0.0376)
23 August	0.00336
	(0.0191)
24 August	−0.0053
	(0.0191)
25 August	0.0040
	(0.0190)
26 August	0.0052
	(0.0191)
29 August	−0.0154
	(0.0191)
30 August	−0.0014
	(0.0200)
31 August	−0.0119
	(0.0191)
1 September	−0.0571***
	(0.0192)
2 September	−0.0162
	(0.0194)
6 September	0.0095
	(0.0192)
19 September	−0.0061
	(0.0197)
20 September	−0.0063
	(0.0191)
21 September	−0.0400**
	(0.0191)
22 September	0.0110
	(0.0191)
23 September	0.0111
	(0.0191)
26 September	0.0120
	(0.0194)
27 September	0.0033
	(0.0191)
28 September	0.0176
	(0.0201)

Notes: This table presents average abnormal returns for sample airlines surrounding landfall of Hurricanes Katrina and Rita. Standard errors are reported in parentheses beneath the coefficient estimates. Statistical significance at the 10%, 5%, or 1% level is indicated by *, **, or ***, respectively.

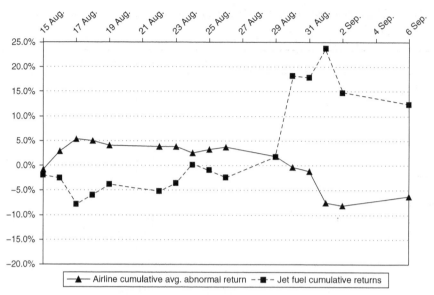

(a) Cumulative average abnormal returns for airlines and cumulative returns for jet fuel prices
surrounding Hurricane Katrina

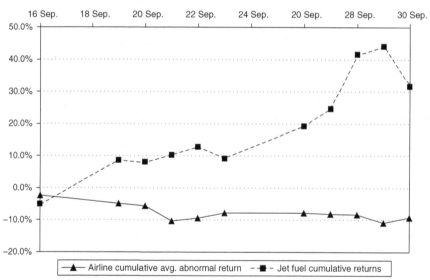

(b) Cumulative average abnormal returns for airlines and cumulative returns for jet fuel prices
surrounding Hurricane Rita

Figure 14.2   Cumulative average abnormal returns for airlines

Jet fuel prices increased approximately 2.1 percent on September 21, but average airline
stock prices declined significantly more than expected. The average abnormal return on
September 21 was −4 percent. Figures 14.2a and 14.2b graphically present cumulative
average abnormal returns for airlines and cumulative returns for jet fuel for the periods

surrounding hurricanes Katrina and Rita, respectively. Overall, the two days of significant abnormal returns associated with the two hurricanes caused a 9.71 percent market value loss for the average airline.

An interesting sidenote is that these abnormal returns occur on days after the most extreme jet fuel price changes. The largest jet fuel price change surrounding Katrina occurred on Tuesday, August 30 (16.4 percent increase), and Monday, September 19, saw a 13.6 percent increase. By comparison, the fuel price changes on September 1 and 21 were far less extreme (5.9 percent and 2.1 percent increases, respectively). Thus, the abnormal returns likely reflect the stock market's anticipation of damage to refining and production facilities (causing additional increases in fuel prices). We next turn to analyzing whether the extent to which airlines had managed jet fuel price risk was able to reduce the abnormal value loss associated with these two events.

We estimate cross-sectional regressions using the abnormal returns on September 1 and September 21 for each airline to determine whether hedging is effective in insulating the firms from sudden, unexpected spikes in commodity prices. We also include a measure of firm size (the natural logarithm of total assets) and leverage (long-term debt divided by total assets). The results of our cross-sectional regressions are reported in Table 14.4. We report results for estimates in which the dependent variable is the

Table 14.4 Cross-sectional regressions of abnormal returns on 1 September 2005 and 21 September 2005

	Constant	*LTASS*	*PERHEDG*	*LTDA*	R-squared	F-statistic
Panel A. Dependent variable is the abnormal return on 1 September 2005						
Model 1	−0.0599***		0.0538*		0.2874	4.03*
	(0.0084)		(0.0268)			
Model 2	−0.0852***		0.0758*	0.0554	0.4082	3.10*
	(0.0203)		(0.0304)	(0.0409)		
Model 3	−0.0467	−0.0016	0.0530*		0.2962	1.89
	(0.0405)	(0.0047)	(0.0281)			
Model 4	−0.0673	−0.0022	0.0756**	0.0578	0.4258	1.98
	(0.0418)	(0.0045)	(0.0318)	(0.0430)		
Panel B. Dependent variable is the abnormal return on 21 September 2005						
Model 5	−0.0575***		0.0764*		0.2441	3.23*
	(0.0133)		(0.0425)			
Model 6	−0.0888**		0.1037*	0.0687	0.3223	2.14
	(0.0335)		(0.0502)	(0.0675)		
Model 7	0.0331	−0.0107	0.0712*		0.4169	3.22
	(0.0568)	(0.0065)	(0.0395)			
Model 8	0.0042	−0.0116	0.1029**	0.0809	0.5240	2.94*
	(0.0586)	(0.0063)	(0.0446)	(0.0603)		

Notes: This table presents cross-sectional regressions for abnormal returns for airlines on 1 September 2005 and 21 September 2005. *LTASS* is the natural logarithm of total assets, *PERHEDG* is the percentage of estimated 2005 fuel needs hedged as of year-end 2004, and *LTDA* is the ratio long-term debt to total assets. Standard errors are reported in parentheses, beneath the parameter estimates. Statistical significance at the 10%, 5%, or 1% level is indicated by *, **, or ***, respectively.

September 1 abnormal return in Panel A, while the results for the abnormal returns of September 21 are reported in Panel B. We note that the percentage of 2005 expected fuel needs hedged is significant in all eight models. The coefficients are all positive and statistically significant at the 10 percent level or better. This result is consistent with the hypothesis that an effective risk management program can protect a firm against unexpected spikes in input commodity prices.

The economic significance of these results is worth noting. In Model 4 of Table 14.4, we illustrate a coefficient of 0.0756 on the percentage of jet fuel requirements hedged. The expected abnormal return for an airline with 85 percent of its future fuel requirements hedged is 6.4 percent higher than a similar company that is completely unhedged. This 'hedging premium' is even larger on September 21 (a coefficient of 0.1029 in Model 8). An airline with only about the average hedged exposure of 20 percent would expect to experience an abnormal return about 3.57 percent greater than an unhedged airline (i.e., 0.2 * (0.0756 + 0.1029)) on the two event dates. Evidently, investors took into account the fuel hedging positions of airlines during these two extreme events.

14.5   CONCLUSIONS

Extreme events may be associated with stock returns that are not adequately reflected by exposure coefficients measured using traditional methodologies. In this chapter, we illustrate how the MVRM econometric method can be used to analyze certain types of event studies. Using this technique, we show that Hurricanes Katrina and Rita are associated with greater negative stock returns than are implied by standard jet fuel exposure coefficients. For both hurricanes, the stock market seems to anticipate greater future fuel price shocks to occur because of the damage to production and refining facilities.

We find that the hedging of jet fuel price risk is able to reduce airline exposure to fuel price increases. While this result might not be terribly surprising, we find that jet fuel exposure coefficients are not significantly different for airlines that are heavier hedgers of jet fuel price risk. Thus, we are able to highlight the idea that traditionally defined exposure coefficients may be poor indicators of the relative risk exposure faced by a firm. If this is true in other settings, this finding might explain the low number of firms facing significant currency risk in studies of firms that would be expected to have significant exposure to currency fluctuations. We believe that the MVRM approach used in this chapter might be useful in other empirical studies to highlight the significance of corporate risk exposures.

NOTES

1. See Tanneeru, M., 'It's official: 2005 hurricanes blew records away,' CNN.com, December 30, 2005 (http:// www.cnn.com).
2. The MVRM method has been used by Smirlock and Kaufold (1987), Cornett and Tehranian (1989, 1990), Karafiath and Glascock (1989), Eyssell and Arshadi (1990), Madura et al. (1992), Cornett et al. (1996), Clark and Perfect (1996) and Sinkey and Carter (1999) to measure the stock price reaction to events which affect a number of firms in the same industry simultaneously.
3. See the Wikipedia entry 'Hurricane Katrina', http://en.wikipedia.org/wiki/hurricane_katrina.

REFERENCES

Barrett, B.W., A.J. Heuson, R.W. Kolb and G.H. Schropp (1987), 'The adjustment of stock prices to completely unanticipated events', *Financial Review*, **22**, 345–354.

Binder, J.J. (1985a), 'On the use of the multivariate regression model in event studies', *Journal of Accounting Research*, **23**, 370–383.

Binder, J.J. (1985b), 'Measuring the effects of regulation with stock price data', *Rand Journal of Economics*, **16**, 167–183.

Carter, D.A., D.A. Rogers and B.J. Simkins (2006), 'Does hedging affect firm value? Evidence from the US airline industry', *Financial Management*, **35**, 53–86.

Carter, D.A. and B.J. Simkins (2004), 'The market's reaction to unexpected, catastrophic events: the case of airline stock returns and the September 11th attacks', *Quarterly Review of Economics and Finance*, **44**, 539–558.

Clark, J.A. and S.B. Perfect (1996), 'The economic effects of client losses on OTC bank derivative dealers: evidence from the capital market', *Journal of Money, Credit, and Banking*, **28**, 527–545.

Cornett, M.M., W.N. Davidson III and N. Rangan (1996), 'Deregulation in investment banking: industry concentration following Rule 415', *Journal of Banking and Finance*, **20**, 85–113.

Cornett, M.M. and H. Tehranian (1989), 'Stock market reaction to the depository institutions deregulation and monetary control act of 1980', *Journal of Banking and Finance*, **13**, 81–100.

Cornett, M.M. and H. Tehranian (1990), 'An examination of the impact of the Garn–St Germain Depository Institutions Act of 1982 on commercial banks and savings and loans', *Journal of Finance*, **45**, 95–111.

Davidson, W.N. III, P.R. Chandy and M. Cross (1987), 'Large losses, risk management, and stock returns in the airline industry', *Journal of Risk and Insurance*, **54**, 162–172.

Eyssell, T.H. and N. Arshadi (1990), 'The wealth effects of risk-based capital requirement in banking', *Journal of Banking and Finance*, **14**, 179–197.

Fama, E.F., F. Fisher, M. Jensen and R. Roll (1969), 'The adjustment of stock prices to new information', *International Economic Review*, **10**, 1–21.

Gibbons, M.R. (1980), 'Econometric methods for testing a class of financial models – an application of the nonlinear multivariate regression model', PhD dissertation, University of Chicago, USA.

Jin, Y. and P. Jorion (2006), 'Firm value and hedging: evidence from US oil and gas producers', *Journal of Finance*, **61**, 893–919.

Karafiath, I. and J. Glascock (1989), 'Intra-industry effects of a regulatory shift: capital market evidence from Penn Square', *Financial Review*, **24**, 123–134.

Lamb, R.P. (1995), 'An exposure-based analysis of property-liability insurer stock values around Hurricane Andrew', *Journal of Risk and Insurance*, **62**, 111–123.

Lamb, R.P. (1998), 'An examination of market efficiency around hurricanes', *Financial Review*, **33**, 163–172.

Madura, J., A.J. Tucker and E. Zarrick (1992), 'Reaction of bank share prices to the third-world debt reduction plan', *Journal of Banking and Finance*, **16**, 853–868.

Malatesta, P. (1986), 'Measuring abnormal performance: the event parameter approach using joint generalized least squares', *Journal of Financial and Quantitative Analysis*, **21**, 465–477.

Petersen, M. and Thiagarajan, S. (2000), 'Risk management and hedging: with and without derivatives', *Financial Management*, **29**, 5–30.

Schipper, K. and R. Thompson (1983), 'The impact of merger-related regulations on the shareholders of acquiring firms', *Journal of Accounting Research*, **21**, 184–221.

Sinkey, J.F., Jr. and D.A. Carter (1999), 'The reaction of bank stock prices to news of derivatives losses by corporate clients', *Journal of Banking and Finance*, **23**, 1725–1743.

Smirlock, M. and H. Kaufold (1987), 'Bank foreign lending, mandatory disclosure rules, and the reaction of bank stock prices to the Mexican debt crisis', *Journal of Business*, **60**, 347–364.

Smithson, C.W. and B.J. Simkins (2005), 'Does risk management add value? A survey of the evidence', *Journal of Applied Corporate Finance*, **17** (3), 8–17.

Sprecher, C.R. and M.A. Pertl (1983), 'Large losses, risk management, and stock prices', *Journal of Risk and Insurance*, **50**, 107–117.

Tufano, P. (1998), 'The determinants of stock price exposure: financial engineering and the gold mining industry', *Journal of Finance*, **53**, 1015–1052.

PART V

RISK MODELLING

15 Quantifying the uncertainty in VaR and expected shortfall estimates

Silvia Stanescu and Radu Tunaru

15.1 INTRODUCTION

Since it was first proposed in 1996 by the RiskMetrics Group of J.P. Morgan, value-at-risk (VaR) has become the standard market risk metric. Assuming that the losses and profits given by a chosen portfolio are measured relative to a time horizon h, the $VaR_{\alpha,h}$ of that portfolio is the monetary amount such that a loss more severe than $VaR_{\alpha,h}$ can occur only with a probability smaller than α. In other words, the investor or risk manager is $100(1 - \alpha)\%$ confident that losses larger than $VaR_{\alpha,h}$ will not materialize at the horizon h. For example, if, for a portfolio, we consider $\alpha = 5\%$ and $h = 1$ year and $VaR_{5\%,1yr}$ is equal to £1 million, then there should be only a 5 per cent chance of losing £1 million or more over a one year period. An important point to make is that the definition of VaR is given under normal market conditions so that if extreme market conditions appear before the end of the horizon then large losses may materialize that could decimate the value of the portfolio. Hence, VaR is a measure of market risk but one should bear in mind that other types of risk, such as operational risk or credit risk, may impact negatively on the value of the portfolio. Calculating VaR is a forecasting exercise by nature and one may wonder what is the performance of this type of forecast. Over a long series of successive periods of the same length h, it is perfectly reasonable to have 'few' instances when losses are larger than the limits predicted by VaR. As long as the proportion of those instances is 'not too different' from α, the method used to construct the VaR measure is still reliable.

Furthermore, it is now known that VaR has some theoretical[1] and practical deficiencies. In particular, it does not tell us much about the magnitude of losses exceeding VaR. Hence, many financial practitioners augment their VaR assessments by an alternative measure of risk, such as expected tail loss (ETL), or expected shortfall (ES).

Given its wide applicability, the development of an effective model for estimating VaR has been the subject of many financial research papers and a plethora of VaR models have been put forward.[2] Different assumptions lead to different VaR models, and hence also to different VaR estimates. Furthermore, for each VaR model, the parameters need to be estimated based on financial data, and this further implies estimation error.[3] Therefore, no matter how complex the methodology used is, the VaR (or ETL) 'number' it produces remains an estimate, subject to estimation error. Thus, it is important to quantify the precision of risk measures if used in decision making.

In this chapter we review and provide examples for a number of alternative methods for building confidence intervals for VaR and ETL measures. We first provide formal definitions for VaR and its related risk measures ETL and ES in section 15.2. We next turn to the quantification of uncertainty in risk estimates: section 15.3 provides a brief overview of the approaches suggested in the finance literature for quantifying the uncertainty inherent in risk measures. A first method for assessing the precision of VaR estimation relies on asymptotic results: section 15.4 describes the standard error approach to construct confidence intervals for VaR estimates. Section 15.5 considers an alternative approach: confidence intervals for VaR are now based on theoretical results drawn from order statistics theory,[4] while section 15.6 deals with the case of quantifying the uncertainty in two or more VaR estimates – corresponding to different levels of significance – simultaneously.[5] Section 15.7 briefly discusses the uncertainty of ES estimates, while section 15.8 concludes.

15.2   CONCEPTUALIZATION OF RISK MEASURES

15.2.1   VaR

For a more formal definition, we denote by X the return of a portfolio with marked-to-market value Π, over the period h. If q_α is the left-tail α quantile of the probability distribution of X, that is $Pr[X \le q_\alpha] = \alpha$, then:

$$VaR_{\alpha,h} = -q_\alpha \times \Pi \qquad (15.1)$$

Without loss of generality we can assume that the current portfolio value is normalized to one unit of currency, that is $\Pi = 1$. More formally, the mathematical concept of VaR is defined as follows. Given a critical level α, for example $\alpha = 5\%$ or $\alpha = 1\%$, and for a probability distribution of returns characterized by the cumulative distribution function (cdf) F:

$$VaR_{F,\alpha} = -q^{F,\alpha} \qquad (15.2)$$

$$q^{F,\alpha} = \inf\{q : Pr(X \le q) > \alpha\} \equiv \sup\{q : Pr(X \le q) \le \alpha\} \qquad (15.3)$$

It is clear that from a statistical point of view the definition of VaR is intrinsically related to the concept of an α-quantile of X. However, as explained in Acerbi and Tasche (2002), the quantile used widely in defining VaR is the upper α-quantile of X as in (15.3). One can also use the lower α-quantile of X defined by:

$$q_{F,\alpha} = \inf\{q : Pr(X \le q) \ge \alpha\} \qquad (15.4)$$

The standard practice is to choose $\alpha = 1\%, 5\%$ or 10% but other values such as 2.5% have been used by banks. For h, the most widely employed values are one day, two weeks (ten trading days), one month (21 trading days), one quarter and one year (252 trading days). If the returns are independently and identically distributed (i.i.d.) and are calculated as logarithmic returns, the sum of n consecutive one-day log returns is the log return over the n-day horizon. Then, since the standard deviation of n-day returns is

$\sqrt{n} \times$ standard deviation of one-day returns, we could change the time scale of the VaR calculations as follows:

$$VaR_{\alpha,1-month} = VaR_{\alpha,1-day} \times \sqrt{21}$$

What horizon to take is not an easy question to answer. The Turner review (FSA, 2009) emphasized the sensitivity of the horizon chosen for VaR calculations in relation to bank capital. Lord Turner wrote:

> Measures of VaR were often estimated using relatively short periods of observation e.g., 12 months. As a result they introduced significant procyclicality, with periods of low observed risk driving down measures of future prospective risk, and thus influencing capital commitment decisions which were for a time self-fulfilling. At very least much longer time periods of observations need to be used.

Methods underpinned by the central limit theorem and requiring large samples of data may not comply with Lord Turner's request. In addition, the longer the horizon, the more difficult it is to accept that markets will not experience extreme movements due to external shocks. Since VaR calculations essentially cover a single period, we shall suppress the notation indicating the horizon h, for simplicity.

15.2.2 Expected Shortfall and Expected Tail Loss

Depending on the chosen quantile, lower or upper, and assuming that the returns X satisfy $\max(-X, 0) < \infty$, the ETL at critical level α is defined by:

$$ETL_{\alpha}(X) = -E[X|X \leq q_{F,\alpha}]$$

for the lower quantile, and:

$$ETL^{\alpha}(X) = -E[X|X \leq q^{F,\alpha}]$$

for the upper quantile. A careful analysis reveals that $ETL_{\alpha}(X) \geq ETL^{\alpha}(X)$. One major problem, though, with this risk measure is that it is not always sub-additive.

By definition the expected shortfall (ES) is the average of the worst losses greater than the corresponding VaR. Formally:

$$ES_{F,\alpha} = -\frac{1}{\alpha}\int_0^{\alpha} F^{-1}(u)\,du \tag{15.5}$$

Acerbi and Tasche (2002) proved that ES depends only on the distribution of X and the level α, but it is the same irrespective of the definition of the quantile chosen. Moreover, it was also proved that this measure is coherent. For practical purposes, it is good to remember that if X is a continuous random variable then $ETL = ES$ for any level α.

15.3   UNCERTAINTY IN RISK ESTIMATES: A SHORT OVERVIEW

One natural and easily interpretable approach for gauging the uncertainty in an estimate is through a confidence interval. Hence, for VaR the relevant confidence interval is that of a quantile of a distribution. Jorion (1996) determined a standard error formula for VaR under the assumption that losses are normally distributed. Soon after, Chappell and Dowd (1999) employed variance-ratio theory to provide exact confidence intervals for normal VaR when the mean is known. Other studies of VaR estimation uncertainty carried out under the normality assumption for the returns include Dowd (2000), who used Monte Carlo simulation to construct VaR distributions; and Dowd (2001, 2006), where the theory of order statistics was employed. More recently, Moraux (2011) accounted for the uncertainty around the mean parameter, deriving analytical results for VaR with the help of asymptotic theory and the delta expansion method.

Several generalizations away from normality have been proposed in the literature. Mausser (2001) suggested a new type of estimator for VaR, called the L-estimator, and he showed that the precision for this new VaR estimator is higher. Choosing a different methodology based on extrapolation, Inui and Kijima (2005) showed that the accuracy of VaR and ES estimators can be increased, exemplifying the case of the Student-t distribution. Dowd (2010) extended the order statistics approach to several risk measures and returns distributions.

In the search for analytical results, some authors successfully obtained asymptotic results. For stable Paretian distributions, Yamai and Yoshiba (2002) determined the asymptotic standard deviations of VaR and ES estimators, pointing out that ES becomes more uncertain than VaR for heavier tails. Similar results were obtained by Acerbi (2004) for log-normal and power-law distributions. Again, based on the asymptotic variances, estimators of VaR and ES perform roughly the same for moderately sized tails, but when the tails become heavier, ES is more uncertain than VaR. Hong et al. (2010) determined new asymptotic results for VaR that lead to confidence interval calculations. Their method requires the existence of the first four moments and requires large data samples.

In the non-analytic realm, Bams et al. (2005) rely on simulations to construct a confidence interval for VaR employing different generalized autoregressive conditional heteroscedastic (GARCH) models. Here the uncertainty about a particular VaR estimate stems only from uncertainty in the parameter estimates of the proposed return models. Therefore, this parameter uncertainty has to be taken into account in VaR calculations and they construct a region (confidence interval) for VaR using simulations. Contreras and Satchell (2003) and Christoffersen and Goncalves (2005) also express VaR uncertainty in the form of a confidence interval. Contreras and Satchell's approach is in effect Bayesian, since they use the posterior distributions of VaR model parameters to construct VaR confidence intervals, whereas Christoffersen and Goncalves (2005) suggest a bootstrap technique for this purpose, which can be used to approximate the distribution for the VaR metric. A bootstrap approach is also used in Hartz et al. (2006) to construct an empirical distribution for VaR.

15.4   ASYMPTOTIC STANDARD ERRORS FOR VAR

The definition of VaR is directly related to the definition of the quantile of the distribution of returns. Since the current practice is to report VaR as a positive number, by definition, VaR is the negative of the quantile. Thus, if all returns are non-negative (for example a long position in a call option), VaR would be negative, reflecting the fact that the holder of a call option has no downside risk. The second point is that VaR as outlined above is a concept defined at the 'population' level, to borrow a terminology from statistics. Moreover, for computational purposes, based on parametric models, VaR calculations depend on F. Nevertheless, in practice we do not know the population F and we have to work with an estimate $\hat{F}$ calibrated from a sample of data $X_1, \ldots, X_n$.

15.4.1   The Univariate Case

Stuart and Ord (1987) provide a formula for the asymptotic variance of a quantile. Adapting expression (10.29) from Stuart and Ord (1987) to our notation, we obtain an expression for the asymptotic variance of a VaR estimator:

$$var(VaR_{F,\alpha}) = var(q^{F,\alpha}) = \frac{\alpha(1-\alpha)}{nf(-VaR_{\hat{F},\alpha})^2} = \frac{\alpha(1-\alpha)}{nf(\hat{F}^{-1}(\alpha)^2)} \tag{15.6}$$

where n is the sample size and f is the density function of profit and loss (or returns). Therefore, asymptotically (when the sample size n is large enough), $VaR_{F,\alpha}$ follows a normal distribution with mean equal to $-\hat{F}^{-1}(\alpha)$, where F^{-1} is the generalized inverse of F and variance as given above in (15.6). Hence:

$$q^{F,\alpha} \sim_a N\left(\hat{F}^{-1}(\alpha), \frac{\alpha(1-\alpha)}{nf(\hat{F}^{-1}(\alpha))^2} \right) \tag{15.7}$$

$$VaR_{F,\alpha} \sim_a N\left(-\hat{F}^{-1}(\alpha), \frac{\alpha(1-\alpha)}{nf(\hat{F}^{-1}(\alpha))^2} \right) \tag{15.8}$$

from which asymptotic confidence intervals for VaR can be easily derived. If c is the chosen confidence level of the asymptotic confidence interval for the selected risk measure, Φ is the standard normal cumulative distribution function, and denoting by $\Psi = \sqrt{\frac{\alpha(1-\alpha)}{nf(\hat{F}^{-1}(\alpha))^2}}$ it follows that:

$$\Phi^{-1}\left(\frac{1-c}{2}\right)\Psi + \hat{F}^{-1}(\alpha) < q^{F,\alpha} < \Phi^{-1}\left(\frac{1+c}{2}\right)\Psi + \hat{F}^{-1}(\alpha) \tag{15.9}$$

$$\Phi^{-1}\left(\frac{1-c}{2}\right)\Psi - \hat{F}^{-1}(\alpha) < VaR_{F,\alpha} < \Phi^{-1}\left(\frac{1+c}{2}\right)\Psi - \hat{F}^{-1}(\alpha) \tag{15.10}$$

Note that this asymptotic result can also be applied to discrete distribution functions for which f is the mass density function.

In the numerical example below, we consider three such distributions employed in finance for VaR calculations, namely the normal, Student-t and Johnson SU distributions.[6]

15.5   EXACT CONFIDENCE INTERVALS FOR VAR

Although the asymptotic approach highlighted above is a quick starting point for producing confidence intervals for VaR estimates in closed form, it is only validly applied when the sample sizes are relatively large. Furthermore, the confidence intervals it produces may be large.

An alternative measure of accuracy for VaR can be obtained using the theory of order statistics.[7] Given an i.i.d. sample $X_1, X_2, \ldots, X_n$, we can order the observations from smallest to largest to obtain the ordered sample:

$$X_{(1)} \leq X_{(2)}. \ldots \leq X_{(n)}$$

$X_{(r)}$ is called the r-th order statistic, with $r = 1, 2, \ldots, n$. Thus $X_{(1)}$ is the sample minimum and $X_{(n)}$ is the sample maximum. If we set $r = [\alpha N]$, where $[a]$ is the largest integer smaller or equal to a, then $VaR_{F,\alpha}$ can be interpreted as the negative of r-th order statistic, with the underlying assumption that the observed sample is randomly drawn from a distribution with the cdf F. We can therefore employ a well-known result from the order statistics literature, namely the distribution function of an order statistic, to derive confidence intervals for *VaR*.

As David and Mishriky (1968) point out, the following results hold regardless of whether F is continuous or discrete:

$$P(j \text{ out of the } n \text{ observations do not exceed } x) = \binom{n}{j}[F(x)]^j[1 - F(x)]^{n-j} \quad (15.11)$$

and:

$$P(\text{at least } r \text{ out of the } n \text{ observations do not exceed } x) = P(X_{(r)} \leq x)$$

$$= F_{X_{(r)}}(x) = \sum_{j=r}^{n} \binom{n}{j}[F(x)]^j[1 - F(x)]^{n-j} \quad (15.12)$$

where $\binom{n}{j} = \frac{n(n-1)\ldots(n-j+1)}{j(j-1)\ldots1} = \frac{n!}{j!(n-j)!}$ is the binomial coefficient. The expression in (15.12) is the cdf of $X_{(r)}$. Confidence intervals can no longer be obtained in closed form (as in the asymptotic case above), but rather involve the following steps.

Step 1: decide what confidence interval and what VaR measure. Suppose we would like to obtain a 90 per cent confidence interval for $VaR_{1\%}$, based on an empirical sample of 1000 observations. We therefore have: $n = 1000$, $\alpha = 1\%$, which means that $r = [n\alpha] = 10$; hence we are interested in the distribution of the 10-th order statistic, and more specifically in finding its 5-th and 95-th percentiles, which will then be the lower and upper bounds of the 90 per cent confidence interval sought after.

Step 2: get the percentile points p_1 and p_2, such that:

$$F_{X_{(10)}}(x_1) = \sum_{j=10}^{1000} \binom{1000}{j} [p_1]^j [1 - p_1]^{1000-j} = 0.05$$

and:

$$F_{X_{(10)}}(x_2) = \sum_{j=10}^{1000} \binom{1000}{j} [p_2]^j [1 - p_2]^{1000-j} = 0.95$$

p_1 and p_2 would need to be determined via a numerical algorithm. For example, using the bisection algorithm suggested by Dowd (2010), we get that $p_1 = 0.0054$ and $p_2 = 0.0157$.

Step 3: the 90 per cent confidence interval for VaR is given by: $[\hat{F}^{-1}(p_1), \hat{F}^{-1}(p_2)]$. It is important to note that although the confidence interval for VaR depends on the choice of F, p_1 and p_2 do not depend on F; given a numerical algorithm for finding these probabilities, they depend solely on n and α.

15.5.1 Examples

Figure 15.1 plots 90 per cent confidence intervals for the 5 per cent VaR obtained using the standard normal distribution. The confidence intervals are computed using both the asymptotic approach (section 15.4) and the order statistics approach (earlier in this section), for different sample sizes. For both approaches, the confidence intervals become narrower as the sample size increases. Surprisingly, the asymptotic approach appears to be of comparable precision with the order statistics one.[8]

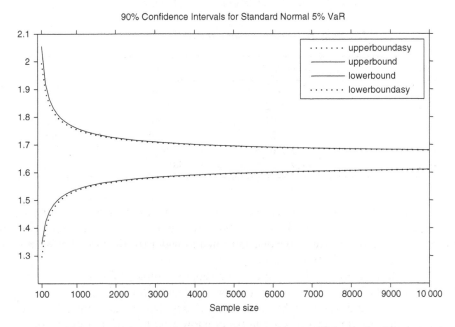

Note: 90% confidence intervals for the 5% standard normal VaR are constructed using the asymptotic (dotted lines) and order statistics (solid lines) approaches.

Figure 15.1   Confidence intervals for increasing sample size

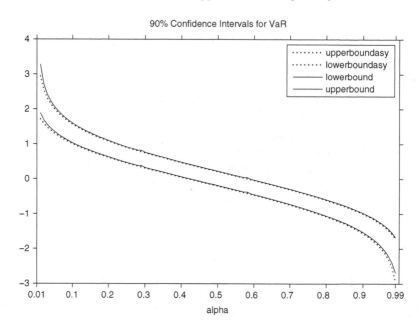

90% Confidence Intervals for VaR

Note: 90% confidence intervals for the alpha% standard normal VaR are constructed using the asymptotic (dotted lines) and order statistics (solid lines) approaches.

Figure 15.2   Confidence intervals for different confidence levels

Table 15.1   FTSE 100 daily returns: summary statistics

Sample period	2000–2011	2004–06	2008–10
Mean	−5.9E-05	0.0004	−0.0001
Standard deviation	0.0132	0.0067	0.0173
Volatility	0.2091	0.1061	0.2735
Skewness	−0.1127	−0.3798	−0.0275
Excess kurtosis	5.5960	1.6486	5.4092
Sample size (n)	3029	758	759

Figure 15.2 plots 90 per cent confidence intervals for standard normal VaR, for different levels of significance and a sample size of 100. Expectedly, the confidence intervals are narrowest towards the centre of the distribution and wider for the tails. The asymptotic and order statistics approaches yield similar results again.

For the results in Tables 15.1 and 15.2, we consider a sample of FTSE 100 daily returns (from 2000 to 2011) for which we compute the 1 per cent and 5 per cent VaR using the normal, Student-t and Johnson SU distributions detailed in the Appendix. We also report, for each estimate, the respective upper and lower bounds of 90 per cent confidence intervals computed using both the asymptotic and order statistics approaches. To capture any changes within the 11-year sample period, we repeat the analysis for two subperiods, namely 2004–2006, a low volatility subperiod, and 2008–2010, a high volatility subperiod.

Table 15.2 VaR estimates and 90% confidence interval bounds for FTSE 100 daily returns

Sample period	2000–2011		2004–06		2008–10	
VaR alpha	1%	5%	1%	5%	1%	5%
Normal						
VaR estimate	0.0308	0.0218	0.0152	0.0106	0.0404	0.0286
asy lower bound	0.0293	0.0210	0.0137	0.0098	0.0365	0.0264
asy upper bound	0.0323	0.0226	0.0167	0.0115	0.0442	0.0308
lower bound OS	0.0295	0.0210	0.0140	0.0099	0.0374	0.0267
upper bound OS	0.0325	0.0227	0.0172	0.0116	0.0455	0.0311
Student-t						
VaR estimate	0.0396	0.0206	0.0170	0.0103	0.0499	0.0259
asy lower bound	0.0342	0.0193	0.0143	0.0093	0.0372	0.0227
asy upper bound	0.0451	0.0219	0.0197	0.0114	0.0626	0.0291
lower bound OS	0.0322	0.0183	0.0149	0.0094	0.0394	0.0225
upper bound OS	0.0393	0.0206	0.0204	0.0115	0.0608	0.0284
Johnson SU						
VaR estimate	0.0364	0.0207	0.0180	0.0109	0.0471	0.0270
asy lower bound	0.0332	0.0196	0.0153	0.0098	0.0389	0.0241
asy upper bound	0.0396	0.0219	0.0206	0.0120	0.0552	0.0300
lower bound OS	0.0336	0.0197	0.0160	0.0099	0.0412	0.0246
upper bound OS	0.0401	0.0220	0.0217	0.0123	0.0591	0.0306

Table 15.1 summarizes the characteristics of the data. As expected, the mean return is very close to zero for the entire sample period considered (2000–2011), as well as the two subperiods, 2004–2006 and 2008–2010, respectively. The overall volatility is approximately 21 per cent.[9] The 2004–06 subperiod appears remarkably calm (volatility less than 11 per cent), while 2008–10 is, as expected, more turbulent, with a volatility higher than 27 per cent. All three time periods exhibit non-normal features (i.e. non-zero skewness and excess kurtosis); as expected for stock index returns, the skewness coefficient takes negative values, while the excess kurtosis is positive, for all three time periods considered.

Table 15.2 presents the VaR estimation results. For the entire sample period and the two subperiods mentioned above, we estimated VaR using three alternative distributional assumptions – namely, F is, in turn, the normal, Student-t, or Johnson SU cdf – and two significance levels: 1 per cent and 5 per cent. The degrees of freedom parameters of the Student-t distribution were determined using maximum likelihood for each of the samples, while the four parameters of the Johnson SU distribution (see the Appendix) were fitted using Tuenter's (2001) algorithm. Furthermore, we also obtained 90 per cent confidence intervals for each of these VaR estimates; the lower and upper bounds of the confidence intervals are given in Table 15.2, for both the asymptotic approach outlined in section 15.4, and the order statistics approach detailed earlier in this section. While for the normal and Johnson SU VaRs, the asymptotic and order statistics approaches produce confidence intervals of comparable width, the order statistics approach appears more accurate when used together with the Student-t distribution for VaR estimation.

15.6   VAR AT DIFFERENT SIGNIFICANCE LEVELS

Financial regulators usually require that banks measure their VaR for specific levels of significance: for example, Basel II regulations stipulate using 1 per cent as the level of significance for VaR calculations that subsequently form the basis for market risk capital requirements. However, for internal risk management purposes, banks may need to compute VaR for levels of confidence which are different from those imposed by the regulators. Hence, they may be interested in evaluating the precision of VaR measures at different levels of significance simultaneously. Established back-testing methodologies based on coverage tests – first proposed by Kupiec (1995) and later developed by Christoffersen (1998) – only consider the VaR estimates for one confidence level at a time. Thus, these back-testing approaches can deem one VaR method appropriate for one confidence level, but inappropriate for another confidence level. This section describes ways of assessing VaR estimates at different confidence levels jointly, via confidence intervals constructed based on either asymptotic (section 15.6.1) or exact (section 15.6.2) results on the distribution of quantiles.

15.6.1   Asymptotic Results

Section 15.4 showed how confidence intervals for VaR can be constructed based on asymptotic results for the distribution of quantiles. Asymptotic results are also available for the joint distribution of two or more quantiles; consequently, based on these multivariate distributions, we show below how multidimensional confidence domains can be constructed for VaR measures computed for different confidence levels.

The bivariate case

Following Stuart and Ord (1987), the asymptotic joint distribution for VaR_{F,α_1} and VaR_{F,α_2}, with $\alpha_1 < \alpha_2$, is given by the bivariate normal $N(\mu, \Sigma)$, where:

$$\mu = \begin{pmatrix} -\hat{F}^{-1}(\alpha_1) \\ -\hat{F}^{-1}(\alpha_2) \end{pmatrix} \tag{15.13}$$

$$\Sigma = \begin{pmatrix} \dfrac{\alpha_1(1-\alpha_1)}{nf(\hat{F}^{-1}(\alpha_1))^2} & \dfrac{\alpha_1(1-\alpha_2)}{nf(\hat{F}^{-1}(\alpha_1))f(\hat{F}^{-1}(\alpha_2))} \\ \dfrac{\alpha_1(1-\alpha_2)}{nf(\hat{F}^{-1}(\alpha_1))f(\hat{F}^{-1}(\alpha_2))} & \dfrac{\alpha_2(1-\alpha_2)}{nf(\hat{F}^{-1}(\alpha_2))^2} \end{pmatrix} \tag{15.14}$$

We note that the covariance between the two VaR measures is non-zero; thus, even if the assumed sample is i.i.d., the resulting quantiles are not i.i.d., which further motivates the need for analysing the precision of quantiles jointly rather than separately.

15.6.2   Exact Confidence Intervals

Section 15.5 elaborated on the application of established results from the order statistics literature to the computation of confidence intervals for VaR measures in a univariate framework. Similar results can also be derived for the joint distribution of two or more

VaR measures. As in section 15.5, we start from a random sample, $X_1, X_2, \ldots, X_n$; for $r < s$ and $x < y$, following David and Mishriky (1968), we can write:

$$F_{X_{(r)}, X_{(s)}}(x, y) = P(X_{(r)} \leq x, X_{(s)} \leq y)$$

$$= P\left(\begin{array}{l} \text{at least } r \text{ out of } n \text{ observations are not greater than } x \\ \text{and at least } s \text{ out of } n \text{ observations are not greater than } y \end{array}\right)$$

$$= \sum_{i=r}^{n} \sum_{j=max(0,s-i)}^{n-i} P\left(\begin{array}{l} i \text{ out of } n \text{ observations are not greater than } x \\ \text{and } j \text{ out of } n \text{ observations are not greater than } y, \\ \text{but greater than } x \end{array}\right)$$

$$= \sum_{i=r}^{n} \sum_{j=max(0,s-i)}^{n-i} \frac{n!}{i! j! (n - i - j)!} F(x)^i [F(y) - F(x)]^j [1 - F(y)]^{n-i-j} \quad (15.15)$$

15.6.3 Empirical Implementation

We are interested in constructing bidimensional confidence regions for VaR computed for two significance levels α_1 and α_2. For example, in order to construct a 90 per cent confidence region for the 1 per cent and 5 per cent VaRs, the 5-th and 95-th quantiles of the joint distribution of 1 per cent and 5 per cent VaRs are of interest: in the asymptotic case (section 15.6.1), this joint distribution is the bivariate normal, with mean vector and covariance matrix as given in (15.13) and (15.14); for the exact case (section 15.6.2), the joint cdf of the two quantiles is as given in formula (15.15). In either case, arriving at the confidence region is not a trivial exercise.

In the asymptotic case, using the notation from section 15.6.1, we are interested in the pairs (x_L, y_L) and (x_U, y_U) such that:

$$\Phi(x_L, y_L) = 0.05, \text{ and } \Phi(x_U, y_U) = 0.95$$

where Φ now stands for the bivariate normal distribution with mean μ and variance–covariance matrix Σ. This step would imply inverting a bivariate normal distribution, which is computationally cumbersome[10] and hence not developed further here.

In the exact case, using the notation from section 15.6.2 and with $r = n\alpha_1$, $s = n\alpha_2$, where $\alpha_1 = 1\%$ and $\alpha_2 = 5\%$ in our example, we would first need to find the pairs (p_{x_L}, p_{y_L}) and (p_{x_U}, p_{y_U}) such that:

$$F_{X_{(r)}, X_{(s)}}(x_L, y_L) = 0.05 \text{ and } F_{X_{(r)}, X_{(s)}}(x_U, y_U) = 0.95$$

where $x_L = \hat{F}^{-1}(p_{x_L})$; $y_L = \hat{F}^{-1}(p_{y_L})$; $x_U = \hat{F}^{-1}(p_{x_U})$; $y_U = \hat{F}^{-1}(p_{y_U})$. Again, the step of finding the pairs, (p_{x_L}, p_{y_L}) and (p_{x_U}, p_{y_U}), is non-trivial. As in the univariate case, these probabilities can be recovered via a numerical technique, but this time we would operate in a bivariate rather than univariate framework and the solutions may not be unique. Assuming that we can solve this numerical step and find the two pairs of probabilities, (p_{x_L}, p_{y_L}) and (p_{x_U}, p_{y_U}), the limits of the confidence region will be given by the pairs (x_L, y_L) and (x_U, y_U).

15.7   EXTREME LOSS ESTIMATION AND UNCERTAINTY

One major criticism of VaR is that it does not reflect the size of extreme losses that a portfolio may experience. ETL and ES are risk measures that are used in practice precisely to circumvent this drawback. While there are differences between the two from a theoretical point of view, the two measures coincide when the cdf F is a continuous function. Hence, when parametric models are used and X is a continuous random variable with cdf F, then:

$$VaR_{F,\alpha} = -q^{F,\alpha} = -q_{F,\alpha} \tag{15.16}$$

and:

$$ETL_\alpha(X) = ETL^\alpha(X) = ES_{F,\alpha} = E[X|X \le -VaR_{F,\alpha}] \tag{15.17}$$

One source of uncertainty in estimating the risk measures of extreme losses is due to parameter estimation for F. Thus, if ϑ is the vector of parameters describing F, that is $F \equiv F(\cdot\,;\vartheta)$, then one has to work with $\hat{F} = F(\cdot\,;\hat{\vartheta})$. Clearly, changing the method of parameter estimation may result in different values for $\hat{\vartheta}$ which will lead to different values for $VaR_{\hat{F},\alpha}$ and this in turn may give different estimates for ES.

Despite its desirable theoretical properties, ES as a measure of risk has been less covered in the literature. Regarding its estimation, order statistics can be used to construct a point estimator of ES from a historical data sample. Acerbi and Tasche (2002) proved that:

$$ES_\alpha = \lim_{n \to \infty} -\frac{1}{[n\alpha]}\sum_{i=1}^{[n\alpha]} X_{(i)}. \tag{15.18}$$

Therefore, an easy to implement estimator of ES is given by $-\frac{1}{[n\alpha]}\sum_{i=1}^{[n\alpha]} X_{(i)}$. Note that this estimator is model free, which is a great advantage.

Furthermore, Inui and Kijima (2005) showed that, denoting $k = [n\alpha]$ and $m = n\alpha - k$, then:

$$\widehat{ES}_\alpha = \begin{cases} -\overline{X}_{(k)}, & \text{if } n\alpha \text{ is a positive integer;} \\ -(1-m)\overline{X}_{(k)} - m\overline{X}_{(k+1)}, & \text{otherwise} \end{cases} \tag{15.19}$$

where $\overline{X}_{(k)} = \frac{X_{(1)} + \ldots X_{(k)}}{k}$.

Dowd (2010) presents an easily implementable approach for quantifying the uncertainty in ES estimators, namely he suggests a modification of the univariate order statistics approach (detailed in section 15.5) for the case of the expected shortfall risk measure, and obtains the upper and lower bounds of confidence intervals for ES_α by simply averaging the respective upper and lower bounds of the corresponding VaR_a estimates, where $0 < a \le \alpha$.

Nevertheless, it is difficult to derive the exact distribution of ES suggested in (15.18) and in (15.19) and subsequently a confidence interval. Given that these two estimators are linear combinations of order statistics, and that the joint distribution of these order statistics is known, one may envisage a way of calculating a confidence internal with simulation methods. However, due to the large values of the multinomial combinatorial coefficient, this is known to be a difficult problem computationally, but we hope to report on some results in this area in the near future.

15.8 CONCLUSIONS

There are many methods to estimate VaR and to a lesser extent ES. However, research on the uncertainty (and on the construction of confidence intervals in particular) associated with the VaR and ES risk measures is relatively sparse. The problem of estimation uncertainty and more specifically of uncertainty of risk measures should preoccupy not only the regulators of financial markets and central banks but market participants as well.

A single number calculated with the most complex procedure is still a single number and it cannot convey a detailed picture of the exposure to risk. Confidence intervals can be used to give a measure of the uncertainty surrounding point estimates of risk measures. They can be constructed from asymptotic results and using exact probability distributional formulae.

One easy way to estimate VaR and ES is by using order statistics. When using this approach, VaR estimators at different levels of confidence are correlated and any back-testing routine should take that into consideration.

NOTES

1. For example, it is not a coherent risk measure in the sense of Artzner et al. (1999).
2. Recent reviews of VaR methodologies are given in Angelidis and Degiannakis (2009) and Alexander (2008). ETL is comparatively less covered in this literature, Alexander and Sheedy (2008) being a notable exception. For other related issues, we also refer to Brooks and Persand (2000) who examine the pitfalls of established VaR methodologies in times of crisis and ways to correct the inherent biases.
3. This point was made early on by Jorion (1996) and Pritsker (1997), and it has been revisited in Chistoffersen and Goncalves (2005).
4. See David (1981) and Stuart and Ord (1987).
5. As explained below, regulators require back-testing and VaR computed for specific parameters, while for internal risk management, banks may need to compute VaR for different confidence levels. As it will be shown below, VaR estimates computed for the same VaR model but for different significance levels are not independent, and hence their precision ought to be investigated jointly.
6. The leptokurtic SU distribution was proposed by Johnson (1949); see also Bowman and Shenton (1983). The density functions as well as the formulae used to calculate VaR for each of these distributions are given in the Appendix to this chapter.
7. See David (1981) and Stuart and Ord (1987).
8. Similar results (available from the authors upon request) are also obtained for the Student-t distribution.
9. We used 252 risk days per year to annualize the standard deviation into volatility.
10. For example, the (x,y) pairs are not necessarily unique.

REFERENCES

Acerbi, C. (2004), 'Coherent representations of subjective risk-aversion', in Giorgio Szego (ed.), *Risk Measures for the 21st Century*, New York: Wiley, pp. 147–207.

Acerbi, C. and D. Tasche (2002), 'On the coherence of expected shortfall', *Journal of Banking and Finance*, **26**, 1487–1503.

Alexander, C. (2008), *Market Risk Analysis, Volume IV: Value at Risk Models*, Chichester: Wiley.

Alexander, C. and E. Sheedy (2008), 'Developing a stress testing framework based on market risk models', *Journal of Banking and Finance*, **31**, 2220–2236.

Angelidis, T. and S. Degiannakis (2009), 'Econometric modelling of value-at-risk', in W.N. Toggins (ed.), *New Econometric Modelling Research*, New York: Nova, pp. 9–60.

Artzner, P., F. Delbaen, J.-M. Eber and D. Heath (1999), 'Coherent measures of risk', *Mathematical Finance*, **9** (3), 203–228.

Bams, D., T. Lehnert and C.C.P. Wolff (2005), 'An evaluation framework for alternative VaR-Models', *Journal of International Money and Finance*, **24**, 944–958.

Bowman, K.O. and L.R. Shenton (1983), 'Johnson's system of distributions', in S. Kotz, N.L. Johnson and C.B. Read (eds) *Encyclopedia of Statistical Sciences*, Vol. 4. New York: Wiley, pp. 303–314.

Brooks, C. and G. Persand (2000), 'Value at risk and market crashes', *Journal of Risk*, **2** (4), 5–26.

Chappell, D. and K. Dowd (1999), 'Confidence intervals for VaR', *Financial Engineering News*, March, 1–2.

Christoffersen, P.F. (1998), 'Evaluating interval forecasts', *International Economic Review*, **39**, 841–862.

Christoffersen, P.F. (2003), *Elements of Financial Risk Management*, San Diego, CA: Academic Press.

Christoffersen, P.F. and S. Goncalves (2005), 'Estimation risk in financial risk management', *Journal of Risk*, **7** (3), 1–28.

Contreras, P. and S. Satchell (2003), 'A Bayesian confidence interval for VaR', Cambridge Working Papers in Economics no. 0348.

David, H.A. (1981), *Order Statistics*, 2nd edn, New York: Wiley.

David, H.A. and R.S. Mishriky (1968), 'Order statistics for discrete populations and for grouped samples', *Journal of the American Statistical Association*, **63** (324), 1390–1398.

Dowd, K. (2000), 'Assessing VaR accuracy', *Derivatives Quarterly*, **6** (3), 61–63.

Dowd, K. (2001), 'Estimating VaR with order statistics', *Journal of Derivatives*, **8** (3), 23–30.

Dowd, K. (2006), 'Using order statistics to estimate confidence intervals for probabilistic risk measures', *Journal of Derivatives*, Fall, 1–5.

Dowd, K. (2010), 'Using order statistics to estimate confidence intervals for quantile-based risk measures', *Journal of Derivatives*, Fall, 9–14.

FSA (2009), 'The Turner review, a regulatory response to the global banking crisis', www.fsa.gov.uk/pubs/other.

Hartz, C., S. Mittnik and M.S. Paolella (2006), 'Accurate value-at-risk forecasting based on the (good old) normal-GARCH model', National Centre of Competence in Research Financial Valuation and Risk Management Working Paper no. 333.

Hong, J., J. Knight, S. Satchell and B. Scherer (2010), 'Using approximate results for validating value-at-risk', *Journal of Risk Model Validation*, **4** (3), 69–81.

Inui, K. and M. Kijima (2005), 'On the significance of expected shortfall as a coherent risk measure', *Journal of Banking and Finance*, **29**, 853–864.

Johnson, N.L. (1949), 'Systems of frequency curves generated by methods of translation', *Biometrica*, **36**, 149–176.

Jorion, P. (1996), 'Risk2: measuring the risk in value at risk', *Financial Analysts Journal*, **52** (6), 47–56.

Kupiec, H. (1995), 'Techniques for verifying the accuracy of risk management models', *Journal of Derivatives*, **3**, 73–84.

Mausser, H. (2001), 'Calculating quantile-based risk analytics with L-estimators', *ALGO Research Quarterly*, **4** (4), 33–47.

Moraux, F. (2011), 'Large sample confidence intervals for normal VaR', *Journal of Risk Management in Financial Institutions*, **4** (2), 189–200.

Pritsker, M. (1997), 'Evaluating value at risk methodologies: accuracy versus computational time', *Journal of Financial Services Research*, **12**, 201–242.

Stuart, A. and K. Ord (1987), *Kendall's Advanced Theory of Statistics, Vol. 1. Distribution Theory*, 5th edn, London: Arnold.

Tuenter, H.J.H. (2001), 'An algorithm to determine the parameters of SU-curves in the Johnson system of probability distributions by moment matching', *Journal of Statistical Computation and Simulation*, **70**, 325–347.

Yamai, Y. and T. Yoshiba (2002), 'Comparative analyses of expected shortfall and Value-at-Risk: their estimation error, decomposition, and optimization', *Monetary and Economic Studies*, **20** (1), 87–121.

APPENDIX: CONTINUOUS DISTRIBUTIONS USED FOR VAR CALCULATIONS

Normal Distribution

If F is the normal distribution $N(\mu, \sigma^2)$, then VaR is given by:

$$VaR_{N,\alpha} = -\Phi^{-1}(\alpha)\sigma - \mu$$

where Φ^{-1} is the inverse distribution function (quantile function) of the standard normal distribution. The corresponding density function is the well-known:

$$\phi(x) = \frac{1}{\sqrt{2\pi}\sigma} \exp\left[-\frac{1}{2}\left(\frac{x - \mu}{\sigma}\right)^2 \right]$$

Student-T Distribution

If we denote the profit and loss (or returns) by X, such that $X = \mu + \sigma T$, where T has a standardized Student-t distribution, the expression for VaR now becomes:

$$VaR_{T,\alpha} = -\sqrt{\frac{\upsilon - 2}{\upsilon}} t_\upsilon^{-1}(\alpha)\sigma - \mu,$$

where t_υ^{-1} is the inverse cdf of a Student-t distribution with υ degrees of freedom, which has density function:

$$f_\upsilon(x) = \frac{1}{\sqrt{\upsilon\pi}} \frac{\Gamma(\frac{\upsilon + 1}{2})}{\Gamma(\frac{\upsilon}{2})} \left(1 + \frac{x^2}{\upsilon}\right)^{-\frac{\upsilon+1}{2}}$$

The degrees of freedom parameter υ, if not pre-specified, is usually determined via maximum likelihood.[1]

Johnson SU Distribution

The Johnson SU VaR is given by:

$$VaR_{J,\alpha} = -\lambda\sinh\left(\frac{\Phi^{-1}(\alpha) - \gamma}{\delta}\right) - \xi$$

and the corresponding density function now becomes:

$$f_{JSU}(z) = \frac{\delta}{\lambda\sqrt{2\pi}\sqrt{z^2 + 1}} \exp\left[-\frac{1}{2}(\gamma + \delta\sinh^{-1}(z)) \right]$$

where $z = \frac{x - \xi}{\lambda}$. The four parameters of the Johnson SU distribution δ, γ, λ, ξ can be calibrated using Tuenter's (2001) very fast moment matching algorithm.

Note

1. A full explanation as well as Excel implementation of the maximum likelihood procedure is given in Christoffersen (2003) and Alexander (2008); both authors also suggest a quick approximation for υ using moment matching.

16 Econometric modeling of exchange rate volatility and jumps

Deniz Erdemlioglu, Sébastien Laurent and Christopher J. Neely

16.1 INTRODUCTION

Volatility measures the dispersion of asset price returns. Recognizing the importance of foreign exchange volatility for risk management and policy evaluation, academics, policymakers, regulators and market practitioners have long studied and estimated models of foreign exchange volatility and jumps. Financial economists have sought to understand and characterize foreign exchange volatility, because the volatility process tells us about how news affects asset prices, what information is important and how markets process that information. Policymakers are interested in measuring asset price volatility to learn about market expectations and uncertainty about policy. For example, one might think that a clear understanding of policy objectives and tools would tend to reduce market volatility, other things being equal.

More practically, understanding and estimating asset price volatility is important for asset pricing, portfolio allocation and risk management. Traders and regulators must consider not only the expected return from their trading activity but also the trading strategy's exposure to risk during periods of high volatility. Traders' risk-adjusted performance depends upon the accuracy of their volatility predictions. Therefore, both traders and regulators use volatility predictions as inputs to models of risk management, such as value-at-risk (VaR).

The goal for volatility modelers has been to simultaneously account for the most prominent features of foreign exchange volatility: (1) it tends to be autocorrelated; (2) it is periodic, displaying intraday and intraweek patterns; and (3) it includes discontinuities (jumps).

To account for these characteristics, researchers started modeling weekly and daily volatility with parametric autoregressive conditional heteroskedastic (ARCH) generalized ARCH (GARCH) models in the 1980s. Practitioners often use the RiskMetrics statistical model, which is a member of the large ARCH/GARCH family. These models effectively described the autocorrelation in daily and weekly volatility. At intraday horizons, however, institutional features – that is, market openings/closings and news announcements – create strong intraday patterns, including discontinuities in prices. Much research on intraday data sorted out the factors behind these periodic patterns and discontinuities. The use of intraday data enabled the next big advance in volatility modeling: 'realized volatility', which is the use of very high-frequency returns to calculate volatility at every instant. A few years later, researchers began to develop increasingly sophisticated models that estimate jumps and that combine autoregressive volatility and jumps.

In short, academic researchers have improved volatility estimation remarkably quickly in the last 30 years, and policymakers, traders and regulators have benefitted from these advances. This chapter reviews those advances and provides some suggestions for further research.

16.1.1   Exchange Rate Data

We start our review of the foreign exchange volatility literature by illustrating some stylized facts of currency markets with intradaily data for the EUR/USD and USD/JPY exchange rates over a period from January 3, 1995 to December 30, 2009.[1] Olsen & Associates provides the last mid-quotes (average of the logarithms of bid and ask quotes) of five-minute intervals throughout the global 24-hour trading day. Following Andersen and Bollerslev (1998a), one trading day extends from 21:00 GMT on day $t - 1$ to 21:00 GMT on day t. Let us denote the i-th price of day t by $P_{t,i}$. The i-th return (in percent) of day t, denoted $(y_{t,i})$, is computed as $100(p_{t,i} - p_{t,i-1})$ where $p_{t,i} = \log P_{t,i}$ and by convention $p_{t,i} = P_{t-1,M}$.

We omit trading days that display either too many missing values or low trading activity because they will provide poor estimates of volatility. Similarly, we delete weekends plus certain fixed and irregular holidays, trading days for which there are more than 57 missing values at the five-minute frequency (corresponding to more than 20 percent of the data), and trading days with too many empty intervals and consecutive prices.[2] These criteria leave 3716 and 3720 days, respectively, for the EUR/USD and the USD/JPY exchange rates. We obtain return series of lower frequencies by summing 5-minute returns at 30-minute, one-hour, daily, weekly and monthly horizons.

16.1.2   Stylized Facts

The top-left panels of Figures 16.1 and 16.2 show that nominal exchange rates have stochastic trends, that is, they are nonstationary. The top-right panels of Figures 16.1 and 16.2 plot daily returns in percentages. Those returns clearly exhibit volatility clustering; that is, periods of low volatility mingle with periods of high volatility. The bottom-left panels of Figures 16.1 and 16.2 illustrate another stylized fact of daily exchange rate return series that returns are not normally distributed. The empirical distribution is more peaked than the normal density and it has fatter tails or excess kurtosis.[3]

The bottom-right panels of the figures plot the correlogram (with 100 lags) of the squared returns and the upper bound of the 95 percent Bartlett's confidence interval for the null hypothesis of no autocorrelation. These graphs illustrate that exchange rates exhibit volatility clustering (that is, volatility shows positive autocorrelation) and the shocks to volatility take several months to die out. In addition, both exchange rates exhibit autocorrelation at much longer horizons than one would expect.

16.1.3   Statistical Properties of Exchange Rates

Tables 16.1 and 16.2 confirm that exchange rate returns are not normally distributed (the last column of Table 16.1 and *JB* test in Table 16.2), and exhibit autocorrelation in squared returns or 'ARCH effects' (see the *LM*-test and the *Q*-test on the squared returns in Table 16.2). The last column of Table 16.2 suggests that the exchange rate returns do not have a unit root at any sampling frequency.

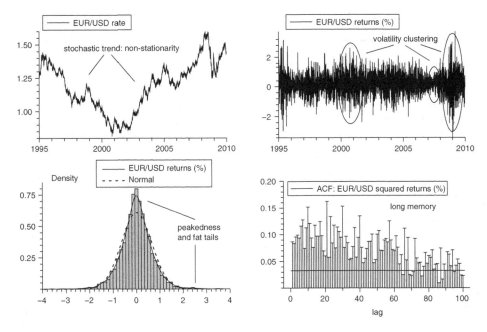

Figure 16.1   Stylized facts of the daily EUR/USD exchange rate

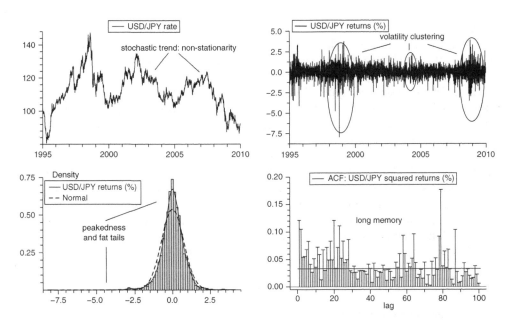

Figure 16.2   Stylized facts of the daily USD/JPY exchange rate

Table 16.1   Summary statistics for exchange rate returns

	#Obs	Mean	Min	Max	Std	Skew	Kurt
5-min returns							
EUR/USD	1 070 208	0.00	−1.43	2.79	0.04	0.49	59.85
USD/JPY	1 071 360	0.00	−2.89	1.98	0.05	−0.49	65.59
30-min returns							
EUR/USD	178 368	0.00	−2.28	2.64	0.10	0.16	23.95
USD/JPY	178 560	0.00	−3.39	3.54	0.11	−0.19	41.34
1-hour returns							
EUR/USD	89 184	0.00	−2.36	2.19	0.14	0.08	17.00
USD/JPY	89 280	0.00	−3.36	4.05	0.16	−0.30	30.64
Daily returns							
EUR/USD	3716	0.00	−3.59	3.53	0.66	0.03	4.89
USD/JPY	3720	0.00	−7.91	3.90	0.74	−0.62	9.36
Weekly returns							
EUR/USD	743	0.02	−6.72	8.60	1.47	0.14	5.54
USD/JPY	744	−0.01	−12.72	5.65	1.58	−0.99	9.25
Monthly returns							
EUR/USD	185	0.09	−10.71	10.63	3.06	0.08	4.06
USD/JPY	186	−0.04	−12.67	9.97	3.21	−0.42	4.06

Note: The sample covers the period from 3 January 1995 to 30 December 2009.

We calculate Ljung–Box test statistics with 20 lags, denoted $LB(20)$, to diagnose serial correlation in the returns.[4] While the $LB(20)$ statistic fails to reject the null hypothesis of no serial correlation for daily and lower frequencies, the robust test does reject that hypothesis for intradaily frequencies except for the 1-hour EUR/USD returns.

These characteristics in Figures 16.1 and 16.2 and Tables 16.1 and 16.2 suggest that a good model for exchange rate series should capture serial correlation, time-varying variance, long-memory, peakedness and fat tails. The next section presents that attempt to capture those features with parametric models.

The remainder of the chapter is organized as follows. Section 16.2 begins with parametric methods before section 16.3 describes non-parametric models. Section 16.4 describes how researchers have modeled intraday periodicity. Section 16.5 introduces the subject of testing for jumps or discontinuities in foreign exchange data. Section 16.6 evaluates the important literature on how news, including central bank intervention, affects volatility and jumps in foreign exchange rates. Section 16.7 concludes.

16.2   PARAMETRIC VOLATILITY MODELS

16.2.1   The Conditional Mean

To correctly model the conditional variance of exchange rates, one must model the conditional mean. If Ω_{t-1} is the information set at time $t-1$, the exchange rate return, y_t, is usually modeled as follows:

Table 16.2   Time series properties and preliminary tests for exchange rate returns

	#Obs	JB	Q(20)	LB(20)	Q²(20)	LM(5)	ADF(2)
5-min returns							
EUR/USD	1 070 208	1.4×10^{8}**	4311.82**	816.12**	24883.30**	2329.20**	-625.59**
USD/JPY	1 071 360	7×10^{8}**	5236.13**	627.58**	66991.10**	6405.30**	-627.85**
30-min returns							
EUR/USD	178 368	3.3×10^{6}**	127.32**	58.14**	6566.12**	692.48**	-243.64**
USD/JPY	178 560	1.1×10^{7}**	285.11**	45.28**	30157.90**	2173.5**	-245.09**
1-hour returns							
EUR/USD	89 184	7.3×10^{5}**	44.27**	25.76	4082.98**	354.94**	-173.06**
USD/JPY	89 280	2.8×10^{6}**	156.52**	42.39**	20007.80**	1846.90**	-176.52**
Daily returns							
EUR/USD	3716	554.67**	23.65	16.50	778.59**	24.14**	-35.93**
USD/JPY	3720	6517.3**	43.64**	28.73	356.83**	21.41**	-35.63**
Weekly returns							
EUR/USD	743	202.55**	22.98	17.39	165.81**	6.68**	-14.85**
USD/JPY	74	1329.80**	23.67	16.99	43.37**	3.51**	-14.94**
Monthly returns							
EUR/USD	185	8.93*	9.25	15.02	39.21**	4.84**	-7.32**
USD/JPY	186	13.99**	21.67	14.96	21.91	3.32**	-7.55**

Note: The sample covers the period from 3 January 1995 to 30 December 2009. *#Obs* corresponds to the total number of observations. *JB* is the statistic of the Jarque–Bera normality test. *Q*(20) and *Q*²(20) correspond respectively to the Box–Pierce test of serial correlation in the raw and squared returns with 20 lags. *LB*(20) is the robust Ljung–Box statistic on raw returns with 20 lags and *LM*(5) is the statistic of the ARCH–LM test for 5 lags. *ADF*(2) denotes the Augmented Dickey–Fuller unit root test statistics with two lags, without intercept and time trend. Davidson and MacKinnon (1993) provide asymptotic critical values for the ADF tests. ** Indicates significance at the 1% level.

$$y_t = E(y_t|\Omega_{t-1}) + \varepsilon_t, \tag{16.1}$$

where $E(.|.)$ denotes the conditional expectation operator and ε_t is the disturbance term, with $E(\varepsilon_t) = 0$ and $E(\varepsilon_t\varepsilon_s) = 0, \forall t \neq s.$[5]

Researchers have often modeled the conditional mean $E(y_t|\Omega_{t-1})$ with autoregressive (AR) and moving average (MA) terms, as well as explanatory variables, $x_{i,t}$. Using such a specification, we obtain the ARMAX(n, s) process:

$$\Psi(L)(y_t - \mu_t) = \Theta(L)\varepsilon_t$$

$$\mu_t = \mu + \sum_{i=1}^{n_1}\delta_i x_{i,t}, \tag{16.2}$$

where L is the lag (or backshift) operator, that is $L^k y_t = y_{t-k}$, $\Psi(L) = 1 - \sum_{i=1}^{n}\psi_i L^i$ and $\Theta(L) = 1 + \sum_{j=1}^{s}\theta_j L^j$.

16.2.2   The ARCH Model

In order to model the volatility clustering in economic variables, Engle (1982) developed the autoregressive conditional heteroskedastic (ARCH) model. An ARCH process of order q can be written as follows:

$$\varepsilon_t = z_t \sigma_t$$

$$\sigma_t^2 = \omega + \sum_{i=1}^{q} \alpha_i \varepsilon_{t-i}^2, \tag{16.3}$$

where z_t is an independently and identically distributed (i.i.d.) process with $E(z_t) = 0$ and $Var(z_t) = 1$. The model assumes that ε_t is serially uncorrelated, and mean zero, with time-varying conditional variance, σ_t^2. To ensure that σ_t^2 is positive for all t, it is sufficient to impose $\omega > 0$ and $\alpha_i \geq 0$.[6]

The ARCH model can describe volatility clustering because the conditional variance of ε_t is an increasing function of ε_{t-1}^2. Consequently, if ε_{t-1} was large in absolute value, σ_t^2 and thus ε_t is expected to be large (in absolute value) as well. The unconditional variance of ε_t exists if $\omega > 0$ and $\sum_{i=1}^{q} \alpha_i < 1$, and is given by:

$$\sigma^2 \equiv E[E(\varepsilon_t^2 | \Omega_{t-1})] = \frac{\omega}{1 - \sum_{i=1}^{q} \alpha_i}. \tag{16.4}$$

Explanatory variables (for example macro-news announcements, central bank interventions, and so on) can be introduced in the conditional variance equation.

16.2.3   The GARCH Model

Bollerslev (1986) usefully generalized the simple ARCH model with the parsimonious and frequently used generalized ARCH (GARCH) model, which models current conditional variance with geometrically declining weights on lagged squared residuals. The GARCH (p, q) model can be expressed as:

$$\sigma_t^2 = \omega + \sum_{i=1}^{q} \alpha_i \varepsilon_{t-i}^2 + \sum_{j=1}^{p} \beta_j \sigma_{t-j}^2. \tag{16.5}$$

Using the lag operator L, the GARCH (p, q) model becomes:

$$\sigma_t^2 = \omega + \alpha(L)\varepsilon_t^2 + \beta(L)\sigma_t^2,$$

with $\alpha(L) = \alpha_1 L + \alpha_2 L^2 + \ldots + \alpha_q L^q$ and $\beta(L) = \beta_1 L + \beta_2 L^2 + \ldots + \beta_p L^p$. As in the ARCH case, some restrictions are needed to ensure σ_t^2 to be positive for all t. For example, one can impose $\omega > 0$, $\alpha_i \geq 0$ and $\beta_j \geq 0$ as proposed by Bollerslev (1986).

16.2.4 The Leverage Effect

Stocks exhibit a 'leverage effect' in which large negative returns are more likely to predict high volatility than large positive returns. To account for the leverage effect, Glosten et al. (1993) have proposed a simple asymmetric model, the eponymous GJR model, which can be expressed as:

$$\sigma_t^2 = \omega + \sum_{i=1}^{q} (\alpha_i \varepsilon_{t-i}^2 + \gamma_i S_{t-i}^- \varepsilon_{t-i}^2) + \sum_{j=1}^{p} \beta_j \sigma_{t-j}^2, \tag{16.6}$$

where $S_t^- = 1$ when $\varepsilon_t < 0$ and 0 otherwise.[7]

In contrast to the results for equity markets, foreign exchange returns usually exhibit symmetric volatility; that is, past positive and negative shocks have similar effects on future volatility (Diebold and Nerlove, 1989; Andersen et al., 2001; Hansen and Lunde, 2005a; Laurent et al., 2012). For instance, Bollerslev et al. (1992) argue that 'whereas stock returns have been found to exhibit some degree of asymmetry in their conditional variances, the two-sided nature of foreign exchange markets makes such asymmetries less likely'.[8]

16.2.5 FIGARCH

Section 16.1 illustrated the long-range dependence in squared foreign exchange returns. That is, the effects of a volatility shock can take a considerable time to fully decay. Ding et al. (1993) find that the squared Standard & Poor's (S&P) 500 daily returns series has positive autocorrelations over more than 2500 lags (or more than ten years). Therefore, neither an I(0) process with an exponential decay in autocorrelations nor an I(1) volatility process with no decay in autocorrelations can easily explain this phenomenon.[9]

To mimic the behavior of the correlogram of the observed volatility, Baillie et al. (1996a) (hereafter BBM) introduce the fractionally integrated GARCH (FIGARCH) model. The conditional variance of the FIGARCH (p, d, q) is given by:

$$\sigma_t^2 = \underbrace{\omega[1-\beta(L)]^{-1}}_{\omega^*} + \underbrace{\{1-[1-\beta(L)]^{-1}\phi(L)(1-L)^d\}}_{\lambda(L)} \varepsilon_t^2, \tag{16.7}$$

or $\sigma_t^2 = \omega^* + \sum_{i=1}^{\infty} \lambda_i L^i \varepsilon_t^2 = \omega^* + \lambda(L)\varepsilon_t^2$ with $0 \le d \le 1$ and $\phi(L)$ is a polynomial of order q. It is fairly easy to show that $\omega > 0, \beta_1 - d \le \phi_1 \le \frac{2-d}{3}$ and $d(\phi_1 - \frac{1-d}{2}) \le \beta_1(\phi_1 - \beta_1 + d)$ are sufficient to ensure that the conditional variance of the FIGARCH $(1, d, 1)$ is positive almost surely for all t.[10] Setting $\phi_1 = 0$ gives the condition for the FIGARCH $(1, d, 0)$.

16.2.6 Estimation

Researchers commonly estimate ARCH-type models by maximum likelihood (ML), which requires that they specify the distribution of the innovation process z_t. Weiss (1986) and Bollerslev and Wooldridge (1992) show that under the normality assumption, the quasi-maximum likelihood (QML) estimator is consistent if the conditional mean and the conditional variance are correctly specified. The log-likelihood function of the standard normal distribution is given by:

$$L_{Gauss} = -\frac{1}{2} \sum_{t=1}^{T} [\log(2\pi) + \log(\sigma_t^2) + z_t^2], \tag{16.8}$$

where T is the number of observations, $z_t = \varepsilon_t/\sigma_t$ and $\varepsilon_t = y_t - E(y_t|\Omega_{t-1})$.

The normal distribution cannot account for the pronounced 'fat tails' of exchange rate returns, however – see Figure 16.1 and Table 16.1. To account for this characteristic, researchers widely use fat-tailed distributions, such as the Student-t distribution and the generalized error distribution (GED) (see Palm, 1996; Pagan, 1996; Bollerslev et al., 1992). The log-likelihood for a Student-t distribution is:

$$L_{Stud} = T \left\{ \log \Gamma\left(\frac{\upsilon + 1}{2}\right) - \log \Gamma\left(\frac{\upsilon}{2}\right) - \frac{1}{2} \log[\pi(\upsilon - 2)] \right\}$$

$$- \frac{1}{2} \sum_{t=1}^{T} \left[\log(\sigma_t^2) + (1 + \upsilon) \log\left(1 + \frac{z_t^2}{\upsilon - 2}\right) \right], \tag{16.9}$$

where υ is the degrees of freedom, $2 < \upsilon \leq \infty$ and $\Gamma(.)$ is the gamma function. The GED log-likelihood function is given by:

$$L_{GED} = \sum_{t=1}^{T} \left[\log\left(\frac{\upsilon}{\lambda_\upsilon}\right) - 0.5 \left|\frac{z_t}{\lambda_\upsilon}\right|^\upsilon - (1 + \upsilon^{-1})\log(2) - \log \Gamma\left(\frac{1}{\upsilon}\right) - 0.5 \log(\sigma_t^2) \right], \tag{16.10}$$

where $0 < \upsilon < \infty$ and:

$$\lambda_\upsilon \equiv \sqrt{\frac{\Gamma(1/\upsilon)2^{(-2/\upsilon)}}{\Gamma(3/\upsilon)}}.$$

These densities account for fat tails but not asymmetry. However, both skewness and kurtosis are important in financial applications, such as in asset pricing models, portfolio selection, option pricing theory and value-at-risk. To properly model skewness, Lambert and Laurent (2000, 2001) and Bauwens and Laurent (2005) apply and extend the skewed-Student density proposed by Fernández and Steel (1998) to the GARCH framework. The log-likelihood of the standardized (zero mean and unit variance) skewed-Student is:

$$L_{SkSt} = T \left\{ \log \Gamma\left(\frac{\upsilon + 1}{2}\right) - \log \Gamma\left(\frac{\upsilon}{2}\right) - 0.5 \log[\pi(\upsilon - 2)] + \log\left(\frac{2}{\xi + \frac{1}{\xi}}\right) + \log(s) \right\}$$

$$- 0.5 \sum_{t=1}^{T} \left\{ \log\sigma_t^2 + (1 + \upsilon)\log\left[1 + \frac{(sz_t + m)^2}{\upsilon - 2}\xi^{-2I_t}\right] \right\}, \tag{16.11}$$

where:

$$I_t = \begin{cases} 1 & \text{if } z_t \geq -\frac{m}{s} \\ -1 & \text{if } z_t < -\frac{m}{s}, \end{cases}$$

ξ is the asymmetry parameter, υ is the degree of freedom of the distribution:

$$m = \frac{\Gamma(\frac{\upsilon + 1}{2})\sqrt{\upsilon - 2}}{\sqrt{\pi}\,\Gamma(\frac{\upsilon}{2})}\left(\xi - \frac{1}{\xi}\right),$$

and:

$$s = \sqrt{\left(\xi^2 + \frac{1}{\xi^2} - 1\right) - m^2}.$$

There are other definitions of skewed-Student distribution (see for example Hansen, 1994; Mittnik and Paolella, 2000; Aas and Haff, 2006; Dark, 2010; Deschamps, 2011). For instance, Aas and Haff (2006) extend the skewed-Student distribution to the generalized hyperbolic skewed-Student distribution (GHSST), while Deschamps (2012) proposes a Bayesian estimation of GARCH models with GHSST errors. Forsberg and Bollerslev (2002) use a GARCH model with normal inverse Gaussion (NIG) error distributions on exchange rate data.

16.2.7 An Application

How do the models described above compare? Tables 16.3 and 16.4 report model estimates for the EUR/USD and USD/JPY return series, respectively.[11]

The first columns of those tables report the quasi-maximum likelihood estimation of an ARCH (1) model. The Box–Pierce statistics on squared standardized returns are far too high, suggesting that the model is misspecified for both series. The GARCH (1, 1) clearly improves upon the ARCH (1) model because it has a much higher log likelihood and no serial correlation.

We then ask whether the EUR/USD and USD/JPY return series display asymmetric volatility or leverage effects. The GJR model (column 3) does not significantly improve on the fit of the GARCH (1, 1) model and so provides no evidence of a leverage effect for either exchange rate. This result implies that the news impact curve is likely to be symmetric; that is, past positive shocks have the same effect on today's volatility as past negative shocks.

To account for the potential presence of long-memory in volatility (as suggested by Figures 16.1 and 16.2), we also estimate a FIGARCH (1, d, 1) model. The data do not reject the additional flexibility of the FIGARCH model. This might be due to breaks in the volatility process, however, rather than genuine long-memory. Furthermore, the last three columns of Tables 16.3 and 16.4 report parameter estimates of the FIGARCH model with Student, skewed-Student and GED distributions, respectively. As expected, the normal distribution is rejected. For the EUR/USD data, the estimated log(ξ) parameter is not statistically different from 0, which allows us to conclude that the conditional

Table 16.3   Estimation results of parametric volatility models for daily EUR/USD returns

	ARCH	GARCH	GJR	FIGARCH	FIGARCH-t	FIGARCH-St	FIGARCH-GED
μ	0.002	0.009	0.009	0.008	0.006	0.008	0.005
	(0.010)	(0.010)	(0.010)	(0.010)	(0.009)	(0.010)	(0.009)
ω	0.392	0.002	0.002	0.001	0.001	0.001	0.001
	(0.015)	(0.001)	(0.001)	(0.001)	(0.001)	(0.001)	(0.001)
α_1	0.087	0.030	0.030	–	–	–	–
	(0.026)	(0.004)	(0.006)	–	–	–	–
β_1	–	0.966	0.966	0.944	0.943	0.943	0.944
	–	(0.004)	(0.004)	(0.016)	(0.013)	(0.013)	(0.014)
γ_1	–	–	−0.001	–	–	–	–
	–	–	(0.008)	–	–	–	–
d	–	–	–	0.883	0.902	0.905	0.896
	–	–	–	(0.056	(0.044	(0.044)	(0.048)
ϕ_1	–	–	–	0.074	0.042	0.040	0.055
	–	–	–	(0.048)	(0.037)	(0.037)	(0.041)
υ	–	–	–	–	8.406	8.412	1.464
	–	–	–	–	(1.132)	(1.133)	(0.053)
$log(\xi)$	–	–	–	–	–	0.018	–
	–	–	–	–	–	(0.021)	–
$log\text{-}l$	−3684.11	−3488.06	−3488.05	−3485.57	−3444.75	−3444.42	−3441.84
$Q(20)$	22.64	20.24	20.20	20.03	19.99	19.98	20.03
$Q^2(20)$	524.15**	20.03	20.14	14.47	15.39	15.44	14.71

Note: Parameter estimation of ARCH(1), GARCH(1,1), GJR(1,1) and FIGARCH(1,d,1) models. Robust standard errors are reported in parenthesis. The first four models are estimated by quasi-maximum likelihood. Student-t, skewed Student-t and GED distributions are chosen respectively for the last three models. $Q(20)$ and $Q2(20)$ correspond respectively to the Box–Pierce statistics on standardized and squared standardized residuals with 20 lags. ** Indicates significance at the 1% level.

distribution of the daily returns is likely to be well described as symmetric but has fatter tails than the normal.[12]

To investigate the stability of the parameters, we split the EUR/USD sample into two subperiods, that is, before and during the subprime mortgage crisis. The results suggest that the d parameter of the FIGARCH model was smaller than 0.5 during the pre-crisis period and about 0.9 during the crisis and thus volatility shocks display much higher persistence during the turbulent periods than in normal times.[13]

In summary, our empirical results show that FIGARCH models with fat-tailed distributions are capable of capturing serial correlation, time-varying variance, long-memory and peakedness as well as fat tails. In line with the literature, we find no evidence of a leverage effect for the EUR/USD and USD/JPY exchange rates.

Table 16.4   Estimation results of parametric volatility models for daily USD/JPY returns

	ARCH	GARCH	GJR	FIGARCH	FIGARCH-t	FIGARCH-St	FIGARCH-GED
μ	0.009	0.006	0.002	0.009	0.019	0.009	0.016
	(0.012)	(0.011)	(0.011)	(0.011)	(0.010)	(0.011)	(0.010)
ω	0.442	0.005	0.006	0.021	0.030	0.029	0.026
	(0.021)	(0.002)	(0.003)	(0.010)	(0.012)	(0.012)	(0.011)
σ_1	0.197	0.042	0.031	–	–	–	–
	(0.046)	(0.011)	(0.010)	–	–	–	–
β^1	–	0.950	0.948	0.686	0.583	0.591	0.608
	–	(0.013)	(0.016)	(0.098)	(0.092)	(0.087)	(0.094)
γ_1	–	–	0.019	–	–	–	–
	–	–	(0.013)	–	–	–	–
d	–	–	–	0.342	0.337	0.333	0.328
	–	–	–	(0.067)	(0.066)	(0.064)	(0.060)
ϕ_1	–	–	–	0.453	0.301	0.313	0.355
	–	–	–	(0.104)	(0.068)	(0.066)	(0.085)
υ	–	–	–	–	5.654	5.823	1.315
	–	–	–	–	(0.494)	(0.516)	(0.044)
$log(\xi)$	–	–	–	–	–	-0.062	–
	–	–	–	–	–	(0.023)	–
log-l	−4072.13	−3905.84	−3902.60	−3903.72	−3787.18	−3783.56	−3802.27
$Q(20)$	33.99	27.46	27.38	25.88	26.29	26.50	25.92
$Q^2(20)$	282.10**	12.61	12.53	11.43	13.16	13.05	11.37

Note: Parameter estimation of ARCH(1), GARCH(1,1), GJR(1,1) and FIGARCH(1,d,1) models. Robust standard errors are reported in parenthesis. The first four models are estimated by quasi-maximum likelihood. Student-t, skewed Student-t and GED distributions are chosen respectively for the last three models. $Q(20)$ and $Q^2(20)$ correspond respectively to the Box–Pierce statistics on standardized and squared standardized residuals with 20 lags. **: Indicates significance at the 1% level.

16.3   NON-PARAMETRIC VOLATILITY ESTIMATORS

16.3.1   Realized Volatility

The models described in the previous section are parametric and usually designed to estimate the daily, weekly or monthly volatility using data sampled at the same frequency. The recent widespread availability of intradaily asset prices have permitted econometricians to use high-frequency data to compute *ex post* measures of volatility at a lower frequency (see French et al., 1987). This method is known as the 'realized volatility' approach. The popular continuous-time diffusion provides the most commonly used framework to model realized volatility:

$$dp(t) = \mu(t)dt + \sigma(t)dW(t), t \geq 0, \tag{16.12}$$

where $dp(t)$ denotes the logarithmic price increment, $\mu(t)$ is a continuous locally bounded variation process, $\sigma(t)$ is a strictly positive and *càdlàg* (right-continuous with left limits) stochastic volatility process and $W(t)$ is a standard Brownian motion. Security prices evolve in a nearly continuous fashion throughout the trading day and so it is natural to think of the price and return series of financial assets as arising through discrete observations from an underlying continuous-time process.

Assuming that the time length of one day is one, what does equation (16.12) imply for the one-period daily return? It follows immediately that:

$$r_t \equiv p(t) - p(t-1) = \int_{t-1}^{t} \mu(s)\,ds + \int_{t-1}^{t} \sigma(s)\,dW(s). \tag{16.13}$$

The volatility for the continuous-time process over $[t-1, t]$ is therefore linked to the evolution of the spot volatility $\sigma(t)$. Furthermore, returns are normally distributed, conditional on the sample path of the drift and the spot volatility processes:

$$r_t \sim N\!\left(\int_{t-1}^{t} \mu(s)\,ds, IV_t\right), \tag{16.14}$$

where IV_t denotes the so-called integrated variance (which converges also to the quadratic variation in this case), and is defined as follows:

$$IV_t \equiv \int_{t-1}^{t} \sigma^2(s)\,ds. \tag{16.15}$$

IV_t is latent because $\sigma^2(s)$ is not directly observable. The daily squared return y_t^2 provides a simple unbiased non-parametric estimate of IV_t in this framework.

Andersen and Bollerslev (1998a) were the first to point out that a much more precise *ex post* estimator than y_t^2 can be obtained by simply summing intraday squared returns. They called this estimator realized volatility.[14] This estimator is defined as follows:

$$RV_t = \sum_{i=1}^{M} y_{t,i}^2. \tag{16.16}$$

The sum of the high-frequency squared returns is an 'error free/model free' measure of the daily volatility that is relatively insensitive to sampling frequency. The literature finds that under model (16.12) and some suitable conditions (like the absence of serial correlation in the intraday returns) RV_t consistently estimates the integrated volatility in the sense that when $\Delta \to 0$, it measures the latent integrated volatility IV_t perfectly. However, in practice, at very high frequencies, returns are polluted by microstructure noise (bid-ask bounce, unevenly spaced observations, discreteness). This 'errors-in-variables' problem produces autocorrelation in the high-frequency returns (see Table 16.2). Researchers have proposed several solutions, such as sparse sampling (e.g., Bandi and Russell, 2008, 2005), subsampling and two time-scale estimators (e.g., Zhang et al., 2005), and kernel-based estimators (e.g., Hansen and Lunde, 2004, 2005b, 2006; Barndorff-Nielsen et al., 2008), to tackle these microstructure problems, McAleer and Medeiros (2008) compare these methods and provide a practical guide to estimate integrated variance under micro-

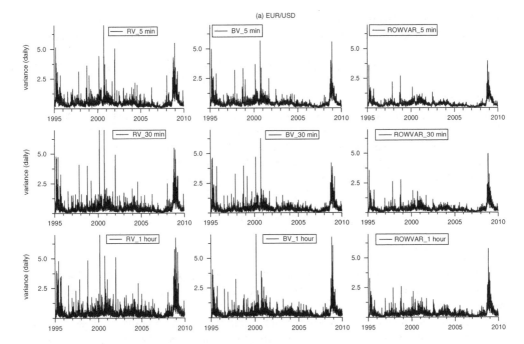

Figure 16.3 RV$_t$, BV$_t$ *and* ROWVar$_t$ *constructed from 5-min., 30-min. and 1-hour intraday returns for the EUR/USD series*

structure noise. The left-block graphs of Figure 16.3 illustrate the similarity of realized volatility (RV) measures using five-minute, 30-minute and one-hour EUR/USD returns.

16.3.2   Bi-Power Variation

Empirical studies have shown that a continuous diffusion model as in equation (16.12) fails to explain some characteristics of asset returns such as sudden spikes or jumps. The inadequacy of the standard stochastic diffusion model has led to developments of continuous time jump-diffusion and stochastic volatility models.

One class of these models is known as the 'Brownian semi-martingale with finite activity jumps' (hereafter denoted BSMFAJ) model. This model has two main components: (1) a diffusion component to capture the smooth variation of the price process; and (2) a jump component to account for the discontinuities in the observed prices. Intuitively, a jump process is defined to be of finite activity if the number of jumps in any interval of time is finite.[15] Andersen et al. (2007b) cite several authors who found that this is a realistic model for the price series of many financial assets. A BSMFAJ log-price model admits the representation:

$$dp(t) = \mu(t)dt + \sigma(t)dW(t) + \kappa(t)dq(t), t \geq 0, \qquad (16.17)$$

where $q(t)$ is a counting process with $dq(t) = 1$ corresponding to a jump at time t and $dq(t) = 0$ otherwise. The (possibly time-varying) jump intensity is $l(t)$ and $\kappa(t)$ is the size of the corresponding jump. Model (16.17) implies that realized volatility converges in probability to the sum of integrated diffusion variance and the sum of squared jumps:

$$RV_t \rightarrow \int_{t-1}^{t} \sigma^2(s)\,ds + \sum_{t-1<s\leq t} \kappa^2(s), \tag{16.18}$$

when $\Delta \rightarrow 0$.

In other words, in the absence of jumps, the realized volatility consistently estimates the integrated volatility, but does not do so in the presence of jumps. Barndorff-Nielsen and Shephard (2004) showed that under model (16.17), the normalized sum of products of the absolute value of contiguous returns (that is bi-power variation) is a consistent estimator for IV_t (see equation 16.15). The bi-power variation is defined as:

$$BV_t \equiv \mu_1^{-2} \frac{M}{M-1} \sum_{i=2}^{M} |y_{t,i}||y_{t,i-1}|, \tag{16.19}$$

where $\mu_1 \equiv \sqrt{2/\pi} \simeq 0.79788$.

Unlike RV_t, BV_t is designed to be robust to jumps because its building block is the product between two consecutive returns instead of the squared return. If one of the returns corresponds to a jump and the next one follows the BSM diffusion process, then the product has a small impact on BV_t, being the sum of many of these building blocks. If the jump process has finite activity then 'almost surely' jumps cannot affect two contiguous returns for $\Delta \rightarrow 0$ (or equivalently $M \rightarrow \infty$) and the jump process has a negligible impact on the probability limit of BV_t, which coincides with the IVar. Under the BSMFAJ model, bi-power variation converges in probability to diffusion variance as the sampling frequency increases to infinity:

$$p\lim_{\Delta\rightarrow 0} BV_t = \int_{t-1}^{t} \sigma^2(s)\,ds. \tag{16.20}$$

The middle graphs of Figure 16.3 show that there are fewer spikes in BV_t than in RV_t, suggesting that BV_t is indeed more robust to jumps.

16.3.3 Realized Outlyingness Weighted Variance

One of the disadvantages of the BV_t is that it is downward biased in the presence of 'zero' measured returns in the sample. Moreover, jumps might significantly affect BV_t when returns are computed over longer time intervals such as five or 30 minutes. For these reasons, Boudt et al. (2011a) have proposed a robust-to-jumps alternative to BV_t. The realized outlyingness weighted variance ($ROWVar_t$) is defined as:

$$ROWVar_t = c_w \frac{\sum_{i=1}^{M} w(d_{t,i})\,y_{t,i}^2}{\frac{1}{M}\sum_{i=1}^{M} w(d_{t,i})}, \tag{16.21}$$

where $w(.)$ is the weight function, $d_{t,i}$ is an outlyingness, and the c_w is a correction factor to ensure that the $ROWVar_t$ is consistent for the IV_t under the BSM and BSMFAJ models.[16] To compute $ROWVar_t$, one should measure the outlyingness $d_{t,i}$ of return $y_{t,i}$ as the square of the robustly standardized return. That is:

$$d_{t,i} = \left(\frac{y_{t,i}}{\hat{\sigma}_{t,i}}\right)^2, \tag{16.22}$$

where $\hat{\sigma}_{t,i}$ is a robust estimate of the instantaneous volatility computed from all the returns belonging to the same local window as $y_{t,i}$.[17] Because of the presence of intra-day periodicity in volatility, Boudt et al. (2011a) propose to compute $d_{t,i}$ on returns that have their intraday periodicity filtered out instead of raw returns.[18] Further, Boudt et al. (2011b) chose a weight function that maintains a compromise between robustness and efficiency. They recommend using the soft-rejection (SR) weight function with 95 percent quantile of the χ_1^2 distribution function. The SR weight function is defined as:

$$w_{SR(z)} = \min\{1, k/z\}, \tag{16.23}$$

where k is a tuning parameter to be selected. The right-hand graphs of Figure 16.3 show that the $ROWVar_t$ is less affected by jumps than RV_t or BV_t.

16.3.4   MinRV and MedRV

Andersen et al. (2008) propose two estimators of IV_t, $MinRV_t$ and $MedRV_t$, that are consistent in the presence of jumps and are less sensitive to zero returns than BV_t. These estimators are defined as follows:

$$MinRV_t \equiv M\frac{M}{M-1}\mu_2\sum_{i=2}^{M}\min(|y_{t,i}|,|y_{t,i-1}|)^2 \tag{16.24}$$

$$MedRV_t \equiv M\frac{M}{M-2}\mu_3\sum_{i=3}^{M}med(|y_{t,i}|,|y_{t,i-1}|,|y_{t,i-2}|)^2, \tag{16.25}$$

where $\mu_2 \equiv \pi/(\pi - 2)$ and $\mu_3 \equiv 3\pi/(6 - 4\sqrt{3} + \pi)$, *Min* stands for minimum and *Med* for median.

   Figure 16.4 plots $MinRV_t$ and $MedRV_t$ for the three sampling frequencies. It is hard to conclude which measure is superior at the sampling frequencies considered.

16.3.5   Truncated Power Variation

We have reviewed several robust-to-jumps estimators – that is, BV_t, $ROWVar_t$, $MinRV_t$ and $MedRV_t$ – of integrated volatility, which have been proved robust for BSMFAJ models. Indeed, Aït-Sahalia (2004), Barndorff-Nielsen et al. (2006), and Lee and Hannig (2010) show the presence of other types of jumps in the evolution of prices. These type of jumps are called infinite activity Lévy-type jumps. That is, if the jumps are a type of infi-nite activity, then the number of jumps (the intensity) in any interval of time is infinite.

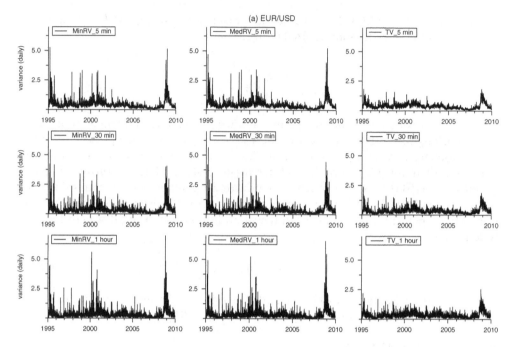

Note: We set $g = 0.3 \times 9$ and $\tilde{\omega} = 0.47$ as thresholds for TV_t.

Figure 16.4   MinRV$_t$, MedRV$_t$ and TV$_t$ constructed from 5-min., 30-min. and 1-hour
                intraday returns for the EUR/USD series

In this regard, several estimations of IV_t have been also designed to be immune to jumps
with infinite activity (hereafter denoted IA).

We now consider log-price processes that belong to the Brownian semi-martingale
with infinite activity jumps (BSMIAJ) family of models. In a BSMIAJ model, the diffusion component captures the smooth variation of the price process as before, while the
jump component accounts for both rare, large discontinuities and frequent, small jumps
in the prices. A BSMIAJ log-price diffusion admits the representation:

$$dp(t) = \mu(t)dt + \sigma(t)dW(t) + \kappa(t)dq(t) + h(t)dL(t), t \geq 0, \qquad (16.26)$$

$$\underbrace{\qquad\qquad}_{\text{finite activity}} \underbrace{\qquad\qquad}_{\text{infinite activity}}$$

where $q(t)$ is a counting process (possibly a Poisson process) as in model (16.17), and
$L(t)$ represents either an α-stable process or a Cauchy process as in Lee and Hannig
(2010). $\kappa(t)$ and $h(t)$ further denote the jump sizes of the corresponding jump processes,
respectively. The jump component of model (16.26) captures both finite and infinite
activity price jumps as in the studies of Aït-Sahalia and Jacod (2009a, 2009b, 2010, 2012),
Todorov and Tauchen (2006) and Carr and Wu (2003), among others.

Under the BSMIAJ, Mancini (2009) and Bollerslev and Todorov (2011) suggest using

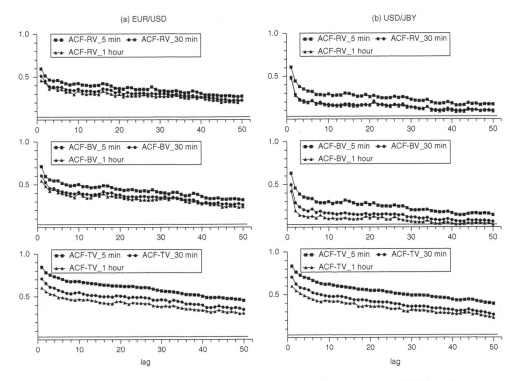

Figure 16.5 *ACFs of the realized volatility (RV$_t$), bipower variation (BV$_t$) and truncated power variation (TV$_t$) constructed from 5-min., 30-min. and 1-hour intraday returns*

the truncated power variation TV_t to consistently estimate IV_t. The truncated power variation TV_t is defined as:

$$TV_t(\Delta) \equiv \sum_{i=1}^{M} (y_{t,i})^2 1_{|y_{t,i}| \le g(\Delta)^{\tilde{\omega}}} \xrightarrow{\mathbb{P}} \int_{t-1}^{t} \sigma^2(s)\,ds, \qquad (16.27)$$

where $g > 0$, and $\tilde{\omega} \in (0, 1/2)$ are the thresholds to truncate the returns. TV_t eliminates the large returns and retains the ones that are lower than the specified thresholds. To estimate TV_t, we use the parameter values of $g = 0.3 \times 9$, and $\tilde{\omega} = 0.47$, following Aït-Sahalia and Jacod (2009b).

The block-graphs on the right of Figure 16.4 plot the truncated power variation for the EUR/USD, constructed from the five-minute, 30-minute and one-hour intraday returns. The graphs show that the TV_t is highly robust to jumps in that it exhibits fewer spikes than $MinRV_t$ and $MedRV_t$.

As an alternative comparison, Figure 16.5 plots the first 50 lags of the autocorrelation function of RV_t, BV_t and TV_t constructed from five-minute, 30-minute and one-hour returns. This figure clearly suggests the presence of long-memory in volatility. The estimated long-memory parameters given by the log-periodogram regression method of Geweke and Porter-Hudak (1983) are about 0.30, 0.35 and 0.45 for RV_t, BV_t and TV_t,

Table 16.5   Distributions of the non-parametric volatility measures for exchange rates

	mean	min.	max.	std	skew	kurt	Q(20)	d
EUR/USD								
$RV_{(5min)}$	0.52	0.05	10.95	0.49	5.82	75.69	13946.60**	0.34**
$RV_{(30min)}$	0.45	0.04	9.18	0.49	5.79	62.98	9999.38**	0.31**
$RV_{(1hour)}$	0.44	0.03	8.42	0.52	5.34	48.96	8393.41**	0.29**
$BV_{(5min)}$	0.46	0.04	5.65	0.41	4.37	34.81	19510.50**	0.41**
$BV_{(30min)}$	0.39	0.03	6.25	0.41	4.79	40.12	13446.60**	0.35**
$BV_{(1hour)}$	0.38	0.02	7.59	0.44	5.79	61.00	11624.10**	0.33**
$TV_{(5min)}$	0.41	0.05	1.85	0.24	1.83	8.22	35104.10**	0.54**
$TV_{(30min)}$	0.36	0.04	2.38	0.25	2.11	9.87	22706.70**	0.42**
$TV_{(1hour)}$	0.35	0.02	2.54	0.26	2.11	10.24	16969.00**	0.34**
USD/JPY								
$RV_{(5min)}$	0.70	0.03	32.90	0.96	13.73	371.52	6859.34**	0.42**
$RV_{(30min)}$	0.59	0.02	49.42	1.13	24.29	959.81	2617.29**	0.34**
$RV_{(1hour)}$	0.58	0.02	48.57	1.17	21.90	796.02	2381.10**	0.34**
$BV_{(5min)}$	0.62	0.03	27.06	0.82	12.85	327.95	8542.60**	0.45**
$BV_{(30min)}$	0.52	0.02	41.00	0.94	24.25	953.58	3262.92**	0.35**
$BV_{(1hour)}$	0.51	0.02	58.08	1.21	31.27	1388.60	1696.90**	0.30**
$TV_{(5min)}$	0.50	0.03	2.09	0.29	1.57	6.13	30602.20**	0.57**
$TV_{(30min)}$	0.43	0.02	2.24	0.30	1.83	7.44	9417.80**	0.45**
$TV_{(1hour)}$	0.42	0.02	2.42	0.32	1.93	8.00	14471.00**	0.37**

Note: Descriptive statistics on the non-parametric volatility measures of the EUR/USD and USD/JPY exchange rates. The sample is from 3 January 1995 to 30 December 2009. Realized volatilities, bipower variations and truncated power variations are constructed from 5-min, 30-min and 1-hour returns. $Q(20)$ corresponds to the Box–Pierce statistic for serial correlation with 20 lags. The last column reports the log-periodogram regression estimates of the long-memory parameter, based on the method of Geweke and Porter-Hudak (1983). ** Indicates significance at the 1% level.

respectively (see the last column in Table 16.5). These coefficient estimates suggest that the more robust-to-jumps estimators also imply more evidence of long-memory persistence in volatility.[19]

16.4   INTRADAY PERIODICITY

A time series is periodic if it shows a regular, time-dependent structure. Foreign exchange volatility shows strong intraday periodic effects caused by regular trading patterns, such as the openings and closings of the three major markets – Asia, Europe and North America – as well as effects from regularly scheduled macroeconomic announcement effects.

Andersen and Bollerslev (1997) show that failure to account for this intradaily periodicity is likely to result in misleading statistical analyses because intraday returns do not conform at all to the theoretical aggregation results for the GARCH models. This section documents the intraday periodicity found in foreign exchange volatility and discusses methods of modeling it.

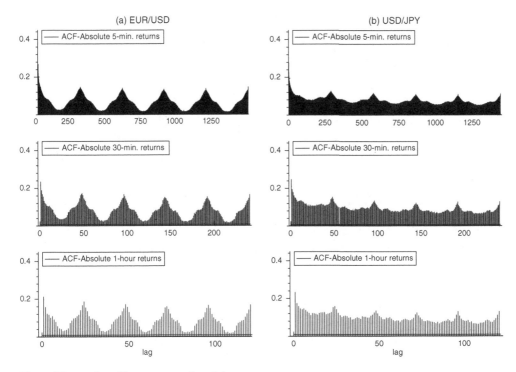

Note: The number of lags corresponds to 5 days.

Figure 16.6   ACF of the absolute EUR/USD and USD/JPY returns at 5-min., 30-min. and 1-hour sampling frequencies

Figure 16.6 displays distinct U-shaped patterns in the ACF for the five-minute, 30-minute and one-hour absolute returns $|y_{t,i}|$. Standard ARCH models imply a geometric decay in the absolute return autocorrelation structure and simply cannot accommodate strong regular cyclical patterns of the sort displayed in Figure 16.6.

Figure 16.7 depicts the mean absolute EUR/USD returns over the (288) five-minute intervals. This intraday pattern is quite similar across all days of the week with discrete changes in quoting activity marking the opening and closing of business hours in the three major regional centres, all of which have their own activity pattern.

In illustrating the properties of intraday foreign exchange volatility, we use the following hours of active trading: the Far East is open from 16:00 EST (21:00 GMT) to 1:00 EST (6:00 GMT); Europe trades between 2:00 EST (7:00 GMT) and 11:00 EST (16:00 GMT); and trading in North America occurs from 7:00 EST (12:00 GMT) to 16:00 EST (21:00 GMT). Using the discussion of market opening and closures presented above, we explain the intraday periodic volatility as follows. At 19:00 EST, the Far Eastern market has already been trading for around three hours and market activity is high. From 19:00 EST until about 22:00 EST, activity levels and volatility remain high. The lunchtime in Tokyo (22:00 EST – 23:45 EST) is the point of the day corresponding to the most prominent feature of the series. Volatility drops sharply and

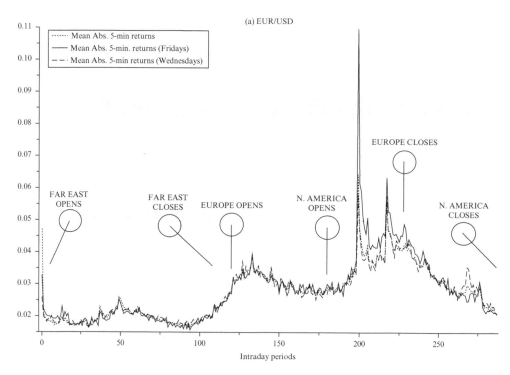

Figure 16.7 *Mean absolute 5-min. EUR/USD returns on whole sample, Wednesdays, and Fridays*

regains its former value at about 0:00 EST. Generally, there is a small peak in volatility as Europe begins to contribute to activity at around 2:00 EST and the Far Eastern market activity begins to wane. During European lunch hours (starting around 6:30 EST), both activity and volatility show a slight lull. The most active period of the day is clearly when both the European and North American markets are open (between 7:00 EST and 11:00 EST). Volatility starts to decline as first the European and then US markets wind down. At around 16:00 EST, the Asian market begins to trade again and the daily cycle is repeated after midnight. This intraday pattern is consistent with previous evidence reported in the literature; see Andersen and Bollerslev (1998b) among others.

16.4.1 Classical and Robust Estimation of Intraday Periodicity

Recall that we use T days of $\lfloor 1/\Delta \rfloor \equiv M$ equally spaced and continuously compounded intraday returns and that $y_{t,i}$ is the i-th return of day t. Assume first that the log-price follows a Brownian semi-martingale (BSM) diffusion as in equation (16.12). If Δ is sufficiently small, returns are conditionally normally distributed with mean zero and variance $\sigma_{t,i}^2 = \int_{t+(i-1)\Delta}^{t+i\Delta} \sigma^2(s)\,ds$, that is $y_{t,i} \approx \sigma_{t,i} z_{t,i}$, where $z_{t,i} \sim N(0,1)$. Due to the daily/

weekly cycle of opening and closing times of the financial centers around the world, the high-frequency return variance $\sigma_{t,i}^2$ has a periodic component $f_{t,i}^2$.

At daily frequencies, the intraday periodic component accounts for almost all variation in variance. Andersen and Bollerslev (1997, 1998b), Andersen et al. (2007b) and Lee and Mykland (2008) use local windows of one day. It is therefore realistic to set $\sigma_{t,i}^2 = s_{t,i} f_{t,i}$, where $s_{t,i}$ is the stochastic part of the intradaily volatility that is assumed to be constant over the day but varies from one day to another.

Andersen and Bollerslev (1997, 1998b) suggest estimating $s_{t,i}$ by $\hat{s}_t = \sqrt{\frac{1}{M} h_t}, \forall i = 1,\ldots,M$, where h_t is the conditional variance of day t obtained by estimating a GARCH model on daily returns. Under the BSM model, a more efficient estimator for $s_{t,i}$ is $\hat{s}_t = \sqrt{\frac{1}{M} RV_t}$.

As explained above, under the BSMFAJ model, the daily integrated volatility is better estimated using Barndorff-Nielsen and Shephard's (2004) realized bi-power variation, that is, $\hat{s}_{t,i} = \sqrt{\frac{1}{M-1} BV_t}$, where BV_t is the bi-power variation computed on all the intraday returns of day t (see equation 16.19). In the presence of infinite activity Lévy jumps – model (16.26) – the truncated power variation TV_t – equation (16.27) – would be a better choice for estimating daily integrated volatility. In this case, $\hat{s}_{t,i} = \sqrt{\frac{1}{M-1} TV_t}$, where TV_t is the truncated power variation computed on all the intraday returns of day t.[20]

Under this model, the standardized high-frequency return $\bar{y}_{t,i} = y_{t,i}/\hat{s}_{t,i} \sim N(0, f_{t,i}^2)$ as $\Delta \to 0$. This result suggests estimating the periodicity factor using either a non-parametric or parametric estimator of the scale of the standardized returns.

16.4.2 Non-Parametric Estimation of Periodicity

The non-parametric estimates of intraday volatility patterns are all based on average variation in volatility across different periods of the week. In other words, the non-parametric estimates for the volatility periodicity factor on Wednesdays at 10:00 AM are some sort of weighted average of the magnitude of the returns on all Wednesdays at 10:00 AM. The non-parametric estimators differ in whether or how they compensate for the presence of jumps, which should be excluded from the estimation of the periodic diffusion volatility factor.

The classical periodicity estimator is based on the standard deviation:

$$\hat{f}_{t,i}^{SD} = \frac{SD_{t,i}}{\sqrt{\frac{1}{M} \sum_{j=1}^{M} SD_{t,j}^2}}, \tag{16.28}$$

where $SD_{t,i} = \sqrt{\frac{1}{n_{t,i}} \sum_{j=1}^{n_{t,i}} \bar{y}_{j,t,i}^2}$. This estimator is similar to Taylor and Xu (1997)'s periodicity estimate based on averages of squared returns. In the absence of jumps, $\hat{f}_{t,i}^{SD}$ efficiently estimates $f_{t,i}^{SD}$ if the standardized returns are normally distributed. In the presence of jumps, this estimator is useless, since it suffices that one observation in the sample is affected by a jump to make the periodicity estimate arbitrarily large.

Because $\hat{f}_{t,i}^{SD}$ does not robustly estimate its population counterpart in the presence of jumps, Boudt et al. (2011b) propose replacing the standard deviation in (16.28) by a robust non-parametric estimator. One candidate is the median absolute deviation (MAD), which is proportional to the size of the median deviation from the median of a series. The MAD of a sequence of observations $y_1,\ldots,y_n$ is defined as:

$$1.486 \cdot \text{median}_i |y_i - \text{median}_j y_j|, \tag{16.29}$$

where 1.486 is a correction factor to guarantee that the MAD is a consistent scale estimator at the normal distribution. The MAD estimator for the periodicity factor of $y_{t,i}$ equals:

$$\hat{f}_{t,i}^{MAD} = \frac{MAD_{t,i}}{\sqrt{\frac{1}{M} \sum_{j=1}^{M} MAD_{t,j}^2}}. \tag{16.30}$$

Among the large number of robust-scale estimators available in the literature (see Maronna et al., 2006, for an overview), Boudt et al. (2011b) also recommend the use of the shortest half scale estimator proposed by Rousseeuw and Leroy (1988) because it remains consistent in the presence of infinitesimal contaminations by jumps in the data. Importantly, the shortest half scale estimator has the smallest jump-induced bias among a wide class of estimators. Under normality the shortest half scale estimator is as efficient as the MAD and the interquartile range. It is also computationally convenient and does not need any location estimation.

To define the shortest half scale estimator, we denote the corresponding order statistics $\bar{y}_{(1);t,i}, \ldots, \bar{y}_{(n_{t,i});t,i}$ such that $\bar{y}_{(1);t,i} \leq \bar{y}_{(2);t,i} \leq \ldots \leq \bar{y}_{(n_{t,i});t,i}$. The shortest half scale is the smallest length of all 'halves' consisting of $h_{t,i} = \lfloor n_{t,i}/2 \rfloor + 1$ contiguous order observations. These halves equal $\{\bar{y}_{(1);t,i}, \ldots, \bar{y}_{(h_{t,i});t,i}\}, \ldots, \{\bar{y}_{(n_{t,i}-h_{t,i}+1);t,i}, \ldots, \bar{y}_{(n_{t,i});t,i}\}$, and their lengths are $\bar{y}_{(h_{t,i});t,i} - \bar{y}_{(1);t,i}, \ldots, \bar{y}_{(n_{t,i});t,i} - \bar{y}_{(h_{t,i});t,i}$ respectively. The corresponding scale estimator (corrected for consistency under normality) equals the minimum of these lengths:

$$\text{Short H}_{t,i} = 0.741 \cdot \min\{\bar{y}_{(h_{t,i});t,i} - \bar{y}_{(1);t,i}, \ldots, \bar{y}_{(n_{t,i});t,i} - \bar{y}_{(n_{t,i}-h_{t,i}+1);t,i}\}. \tag{16.31}$$

The shortest half estimator for the periodicity factor of $y_{t,i}$ equals:

$$\hat{f}_{t,i}^{\text{ShortH}} = \frac{\text{Short H}_{t,i}}{\sqrt{\frac{1}{M} \sum_{j=1}^{M} \text{Short H}_{t,j}^2}}. \tag{16.32}$$

The shortest half dispersion is highly robust to jumps, but it has only a 37 per cent relative efficiency under normality of the $\bar{y}_{t,i}$'s. Boudt et al. (2011b) show that the standard deviation applied to the returns weighted by their outlyingness under the ShortH estimate offers a better trade-off between the efficiency of the standard deviation under normality and robustness to jumps, that is:

$$\hat{f}_{t,i}^{WSD} = \frac{WSD_{t,i}}{\sqrt{\frac{1}{M} \sum_{j=1}^{M} WSD_{t,j}^2}}, \tag{16.33}$$

where:

$$WSD_{t,j} = \sqrt{1.081 \cdot \frac{\sum_{l=1}^{n_{t,j}} w[(\bar{y}_{l;t,j}/\hat{f}_{t,j}^{\text{Short H}})^2] \bar{y}_{l;t,j}^2}{\sum_{l=1}^{n_{t,j}} w[(\bar{y}_{l;t,j}/\hat{f}_{t,j}^{\text{ShortH}})^2]}}.$$

Because the weighting is applied to the squared standardized returns, which are extremely large in the presence of jumps, Boudt et al. (2011b) recommend the use of the hard rejection with threshold equal to the 99 percent quantile of the χ^2 distribution with one degree of freedom, that is:

$$w(z) = \begin{cases} 1 & \text{if } z \leq 6.635 \\ 0 & \text{else.} \end{cases} \tag{16.34}$$

The factor 1.081 ensures the consistency of the estimator under normality. The weighted standard deviation (WSD) in (16.33) has a 69 percent efficiency under normality of the $\bar{y}_{t,i}$'s.

16.4.3 Parametric Estimation of Periodicity

The non-parametric periodicity estimators use the standardized returns that have the same periodicity factor. This means that if we are interested in the impact of calendar effects, the non-parametric estimators take the returns that are observed at the same time of the day and on the same day of the week. Alternatively, Andersen and Bollerslev (1997) show that one can efficiently estimate the periodicity process with trigonometric functions of time. These trigonometric functions implicitly constrain the periodicity to be 'smooth' over time in ways that the non-parametric techniques, which estimate the periodicity factor independently during each time period, do not. Under the assumption that returns are not affected by jumps, Andersen and Bollerslev (1997) show that $\log(\frac{|y_{t,i}|}{s_{t,i}}) \approx \log f_{t,i} + \log|z_{t,i}|$, which isolates $f_{t,i}$ as follows:

$$\log(|y_{t,i}/s_{t,i}|) - c = \log f_{t,i} + u_{t,i}, \tag{16.35}$$

where the error term $u_{t,i}$ is i.i.d. distributed with mean zero and has the density function of the centered absolute value of the log of a standard normal random variable, that is:

$$g(z) = \sqrt{2/\pi} \exp[z + c - 0.5 \exp(2(z + c))]. \tag{16.36}$$

The parameter $c = -0.63518$ equals the mean of the log of the absolute value of a standard normal random variable. Andersen and Bollerslev (1997) then propose modeling $\log f_{t,i}$ as a function h of a vector of variables x (such as sinusoid and polynomial transformations of the time of the day) that is linear in the parameter vector θ:

$$\log f_{t,i} = h(x_{t,i}; \theta) = x'_{t,i}\theta. \tag{16.37}$$

Combining (16.35) with (16.37), we obtain the following regression equation:

$$\log(|\bar{y}_{t,i}|) - c = x'_{t,i}\theta + u_{t,i}. \tag{16.38}$$

Researchers commonly estimate the parameter θ in (16.38) by ordinary least squares (OLS). This approach is neither efficient nor robust because the error terms are not normally distributed. Denote the loss functions of the OLS and ML estimators by $\rho^{OLS}(z) = z^2$ and by:

$$\rho^{ML}(z) = -0.5 \log(2/\pi) - z - c + 0.5 \exp(2(z + c)),$$

respectively The OLS and ML estimates equal:

$$\hat{\theta}^{OLS} = \arg\min \frac{1}{MT} \sum_{t=1}^{T} \sum_{i=1}^{M} \rho^{OLS}(u_{t,i}) \text{ and } \hat{\theta}^{ML} = \arg\min \frac{1}{MT} \sum_{t=1}^{T} \sum_{i=1}^{M} \rho^{ML}(u_{t,i}), \quad (16.39)$$

where $u_{t,i}$ is a function of θ.

As an alternative to the OLS and ML estimators, Boudt et al. (2011b) propose using the truncated maximum likelihood (TML) estimator introduced by Marazzi and Yohai (2004). This estimator assigns a zero weight to outliers, as defined by the value of the ML loss function evaluated at the corresponding residual computed under the robust non-parametric estimator $\hat{f}^{WSD}$ in (16.33). Let:

$$u_{t,i}^{WSD} = \log \bar{y}_{t,i} - c - \log \hat{f}_{t,i}^{WSD}. \quad (16.40)$$

Observations for which $\rho^{ML}(u_{t,i}^{WSD})$ is large have a low likelihood and are therefore likely to be outliers (Marazzi and Yohai, 2004). Denote by q an extreme upper quantile of the distribution of $u_{t,i}$. The TML estimator is defined as:

$$\hat{\theta}^{TML} = \frac{1}{\sum_{t=1}^{T} \sum_{i=1}^{M} w_{t,i}} \sum_{t=1}^{T} \sum_{i=1}^{M} w_{t,i} \rho(u_{t,i}), \quad (16.41)$$

with:

$$w_{t,i} = \begin{cases} 1 & \text{if } \rho^{ML}(u_{t,i}^{WSD}) \le \rho^{ML}(q) \\ 0 & \text{else.} \end{cases}$$

The parametric estimate for the periodicity factor equals:

$$\hat{f}_{t,i}^{TML} = \frac{\exp x_{t,i}' \hat{\theta}^{TML}}{\sqrt{\frac{1}{M} \sum_{j=1}^{M} (\exp x_{t,j}' \hat{\theta}^{TML})^2}}, \quad (16.42)$$

and similarly for $\hat{f}_{t,i}^{OLS}$ and $\hat{f}_{t,i}^{ML}$. Boudt et al. (2011b) show that parametric methods are generally much more efficient than non-parametric ones. They also show that in the presence of jumps, the TML estimator is the most robust method. However, the main weakness of this approach is that little is known about the asymptotic distribution of the TML estimates in the presence of jumps, which makes the statistical inference based on this method challenging.

Figures 16.8 and 16.9 depict the non-parametric and parametric periodicity estimates of the EUR/USD and USD/JPY series. In Figure 16.8, we see that the SD method (that is, the Taylor and Xu, 1997 filter) is indeed more sensitive to jumps than the other non-parametric estimators. Among the parametric candidates given in Figure 16.9, TML periodicity estimates seem to be smoother than the OLS and ML estimates.

Are the periodic volatility patterns common to several time series? To investigate this issue, Hecq et al. (2012) propose a reduced rank method to examine the presence of such commonalities in the intraday cyclical movements. This approach, along with a

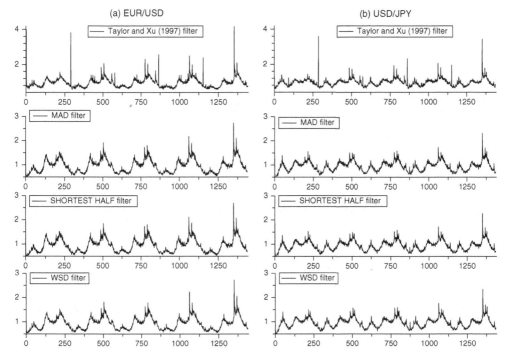

Figure 16.8   Estimates of the non-parametric periodicity filters for the 5-min. EUR/USD and USD/JPY exchange rates

multivariate information criteria, further allows the determination of the variables that explain the common periodic features. In an application to 30 US stocks, their empirical results suggest using three common sources to describe the periodic patterns, whereas they find no evidence of common factors in the intradaily periodic volatility of the major exchange rates.

16.5   JUMPS

Researchers have noted jumps (that is, discontinuities) in asset prices for some time. The efficient markets hypothesis easily explains many jumps because it predicts very rapid systematic price reactions to news surprises to prevent risk-adjusted profit opportunities. Decomposing volatility into jumps and time-varying diffusion volatility is important because these two components have different implications for modeling, forecasting and hedging. For example, persistent time-varying diffusion volatility would help forecast future volatility, while jumps might contain no predictive information or even distort volatility forecasts (Neely, 1999; Andersen et al., 2007a). Therefore, it makes sense to detect jumps and either model them separately or clean them from the data. This section describes recent tests for jumps in foreign exchange rates.

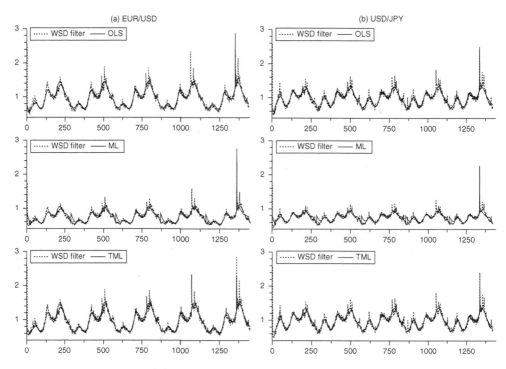

Figure 16.9   *Estimates of the parametric periodicity filters for the 5-min. EUR/USD and*
USD/JPY exchange rates

16.5.1   Daily Non-Parametric Tests for Large Jumps

The difference between RV_t and any robust-to-jumps estimator of IV_t, denoted $\hat{IV}_t$,
estimates the jump contribution or realized jumps under the BSMFAJ model. That is,
the realized jump measure equals a realized volatility measure less a robust-to-jumps
measure of diffusion volatility:

$$RJ_t \equiv RV_t - \hat{IV}_t \rightarrow \sum_{t-1 < s \leq t} \kappa^2(s),\qquad(16.43)$$

where $\hat{IV}_t$ is, for instance, BV_t or $ROWVar_t$. We will review several statistics that estimate
jumps using the difference between RV and robust-to-jumps estimates of IV.

Based on the theoretical results of Barndorff-Nielsen and Shephard (2006) that:

$$\sqrt{\Delta}\left(\frac{RV_t - IV_t}{\hat{IV}_t - IV_t}\right) \xrightarrow{d} MN\left(0, \begin{pmatrix} 2 & 2 \\ 2 & \theta \end{pmatrix} IQ_t\right) \text{ if } \Delta \to 0,\qquad(16.44)$$

where $IQ_t \equiv \int_{t-1}^{t} \sigma^4(s)\,ds$ is the integrated quarticity. Andersen et al. (2007a) have developed a formal test for (daily) jumps, that is:

$$Z_t \equiv \frac{RV_t - \hat{IV}_t}{\sqrt{(\theta - 2)\frac{1}{M}\hat{IQ}_t}},$$ (16.45)

where $\hat{IQ}_t$ is a robust-to-jumps estimate of the integrated quarticity, IQ_t. Andersen et al. (2007a) estimate integrated variance with bi-power variation and use the tri-power quarticity TQ_t to estimate IQ_t, where:

$$TQ_t \equiv M\frac{M}{M-2}\mu_{4/3}^{-3}\sum_{i=3}^{M}|y_{t,i}|^{4/3}|y_{t,i-1}|^{4/3}|y_{t,i-2}|^{4/3},$$ (16.46)

with $\mu_{4/3} \equiv 2^{2/3}\Gamma(7/6)\Gamma(1/2)^{-1}$.

Another popular estimator for IQ_t, in the spirit of the bi-power (or multi-power) variation, is the Quad-power quarticity QQ_t, that is:

$$QQ_t \equiv M\frac{M}{M-3}\mu_1^{-4}\sum_{i=4}^{M}|y_{t,i}||y_{t,i-1}||y_{t,i-2}||y_{t,i-3}|$$ (16.47)

when $\hat{IV}_t = BV_t$, $\theta = \mu_1^{-4} + 2\mu_1^{-2} - 3 \approx 2.609$. The main drawback of TQ_t and QQ_t is that, like BV_t, they are downwardly biased in the presence of zero returns. To overcome this problem, Boudt et al. (2011a) have proposed replacing $\hat{IV}_t$ in equation (16.45) by $ROWVar_t$ and $\hat{IQ}_t$ by the realized outlyingness weighted quarticity:

$$ROWQuarticity_t = d_w\frac{\sum_{i=1}^{M}w(d_{t,i})y_{t,i}^4}{\sum_{i=1}^{M}w(d_{t,i})},$$ (16.48)

where $w(.)$ is the hard rejection weight function. Table 16.6 reports the correction factor d_w and the asymptotic variance of the $ROWVar_t$ θ for several choices of the critical level β (used to get the outlyingness threshold k).

In the spirit of their MinRV and MedRV estimators, Andersen et al. (2008) propose two alternative robust estimators of the integrated quarticity, namely the MinRQ and MedRQ. The formulas are:

$$MinRQ_t \equiv M\frac{M}{M-1}\mu_4\sum_{i=2}^{M}\min(|y_{t,i}|,|y_{t,i-1}|)^4$$ (16.49)

Table 16.6   The correction factor d_w *and the asymptotic variance of the ROWVar* θ

β	1	0.99	0.975	0.95	0.925	0.90	0.85	0.80
c_w HR	1	1.081	1.175	1.318	1.459	1.605	1.921	2.285
c_w SR	1	1.017	1.041	1.081	1.122	1.165	1.257	1.358
θ HR	2	2.897	3.707	4.674	5.406	5.998	6.917	7.592
θ SR	2	2.072	2.184	2.367	2.539	2.699	2.989	3.245
d_w HR	0.333	0.440	0.554	0.741	0.945	1.177	1.760	2.566

Note: c_w, θ and d_w for different critical levels β (such that the threshold $k = \chi_1^2(\beta)$, with $\chi_1^2(\beta)$ the β quantile of the χ_1^2).

$$MedRQ_t \equiv M\frac{M}{M-2}\mu_5 \sum_{i=3}^{M} med(|y_{t,i}|,|y_{t,i-1}|,|y_{t,i-2}|)^4, \tag{16.50}$$

where $\mu_4 \equiv \pi/(3\pi - 8)$ and $\mu_5 = 3\pi/(9\pi + 72 - 52\sqrt{3})$. Note also that Andersen et al. (2008) show that both the MinRV and MedRV satisfy (16.44), where θ equals 3.81 for the former and 2.96 for the latter (the MedRV being asymptotically more efficient than the MinRV in absence of jumps).

Barndorff-Nielsen and Shephard (2006) advocated the use of a log version of the z_t statistics. According to them, the statistic:

$$log Z_t \equiv \frac{log(RV_t) - log(\hat{IV}_t)}{\sqrt{(\theta - 2)\frac{1}{M}\hat{IQ}_t\hat{IV}_t^{-2}}}, \tag{16.51}$$

has better finite sample properties.

They also proposed another version of this statistic, denoted *maxlog* Z_t:

$$maxlog\ Z_t \equiv \frac{log(RV_t) - log(\hat{IV}_t)}{\sqrt{(\theta - 2)\frac{1}{M}\max\{1,\hat{IQ}_t\hat{IV}_t^{-2}\}}}. \tag{16.52}$$

Under the null of no jump on day t, Z_t, $logZ_t$ and *maxlog* Z_t are asymptotically (as $\Delta \to 0$) standard normal. The sequences $\{Z_t\}_{t=1}^{T}$, $\{log\ Z_t\}_{t=1}^{T}$ and $\{maxlogZ_t\}_{t=1}^{T}$ provide estimates of the daily occurrence of jumps in the price process.

16.5.2   Intradaily Non-Parametric Tests for Large Jumps

The tests presented in the previous section rely on intraday returns to test for jumps at a lower frequency, for example, over one day. This section describes the tests that examine whether any given intraday return $y_{t,i}$ is from a purely continuous diffusion or is due to a jump in the price process. Lee and Mykland (2008) propose detecting intraday jumps by comparing returns to a local volatility measure. However, what constitutes an abnormally big return depends on the prevailing level of volatility. That is, in times of high volatility, an abnormal return is expected to be bigger than an abnormal return in times of low volatility. Hence, Lee and Mykland (2008) study the properties of the ratio of the tested return over a measure of local volatility. They propose a powerful and parsimonious methodology that allows us to test whether any return contains a jump component.

Their jump statistic, denoted $J_{t,i}$, is defined as the absolute return divided by an estimate of the local standard deviation $\hat{\sigma}_{t,i}$, that is:

$$J_{t,i} = \frac{|y_{t,i}|}{\hat{\sigma}_{t,i}}. \tag{16.53}$$

Under the null of no jump in the ith return, that the process belongs to the family of BSMFAJ models described in equation (16.17), and a suitable choice of the window size for local volatility, $\frac{y_{t,i}}{\hat{\sigma}_{t,i}}$ asymptotically follows a standard normal distribution.

Lee and Mykland (2008) recommend replacing $\hat{\sigma}_{t,i}$ by $\hat{s}_t = \sqrt{\frac{1}{M-1}BV_t}$, where BV_t is the bi-power variation computed on all the intraday returns of day t. Boudt et al. (2011b) propose to account for the strong periodicity in volatility and show that replacing $\hat{\sigma}_{t,i}$ by either $\hat{f}_{t,i}^{\text{WSD}}\hat{s}_t$ or $\hat{f}_{t,i}^{\text{TML}}\hat{s}_t$ is more appropriate. They show that ignoring periodic volatility patterns leads to spurious jump identification. Indeed, the original Lee–Mykland statistic, which neglects the periodicity, tends to overdetect (underdetect) jumps in periods of high (low) intraday periodic volatility.

Under the null of no jump and a consistent estimate $\hat{\sigma}_{t,i}$, $J_{t,i}$ follows the same distribution as the absolute value of a standard normal variable. Brownlees and Gallo (2006) propose comparing $J_{t,i}$ with the $1 - \alpha/2$ quantile of the standard normal distribution. This rule might spuriously detect many jumps, however. Andersen et al. (2007b) use a Bonferroni correction to minimize spurious jump detection. To minimize the risk of falsely finding jumps, Lee and Mykland (2008) propose inferring jumps from a conservative critical value which they obtain from the distribution of the statistic's maximum over the sample size. If the statistic exceeds a plausible maximum, one rejects the null of no jump. Under the stated assumptions and no jump in the interval $i - 1, i$ of day t, then when $\Delta \to 0$, the sample maximum of the absolute value of a standard normal variable (that is, the jump statistic $J_{t,i}$) follows a Gumbel distribution. We reject the null of no jump if:

$$J_{t,i} > G^{-1}(1 - \alpha)S_n + C_n, \tag{16.54}$$

where $G^{-1}(1 - \alpha)$ is the $1 - \alpha$ quantile function of the standard Gumbel distribution, $C_n = (2\log n)^{0.5} - \frac{\log(\pi) + \log(\log n)}{2(2\log n)^{0.5}}$ and $S_n = \frac{1}{(2\log n)^{0.5}}$. When $n = 1$ the test is similar to the one of the Brownlees and Gallo (2006) in the sense that the expected number of spuriously detected jumps (under the null) can be extremely large, that is, αMT. When $n = M$ (the number of observations per day) and $n = MT$ (the total number of observations), this number equals respectively αT and α (that is ≈ 0). So if we choose a significance level of $\alpha = 0.0001$, then we reject the null of no jump at testing time if $J_{t,i} > S_n\beta^* + C_n$ with β^* such that $P(\psi \leq \beta^*) = \exp(-e^{-\beta^*}) = 0.9999$, that is $\beta^* = -\log(-\log(0.9999)) = 9.21$.

Lee and Hannig (2010) propose a method to decompose jump risk into big jump risk and small jump risk. To identify big jump arrivals, they propose using the statistic:

$$J_{t,i}^{LH} = \frac{|y_{t,i}|}{\hat{\sigma}_{t,i}}, \tag{16.55}$$

where $\hat{\sigma}_{t,i}$ is now replaced by $\hat{s}_t = \sqrt{\frac{1}{M-1}TV_t}$, where TV_t is the truncated power variation given in equation (16.27), and computed on all the intraday returns of day t. The test detects the arrival times of the big jumps when the data follow a BSMIAJ model as in equation (16.26).[21] The detection method for the big jumps is the same as the Lee and Mykland test, and is thus given by the rule in (16.54).

Like the Lee–Mykland statistic, $J_{t,i}^{LH}$ neglects periodic volatility. To account for such cyclical patterns in volatility, one can replace $\hat{\sigma}_{t,i}$ by $\hat{f}_{t,i}\hat{s}_t$, which is a periodicity-robust volatility measure. Indeed, the left-block graphs of Figure 16.10 show that ignoring periodicity leads to spurious jump identification.[22] Like the Lee–Mykland test, the original Lee–Hannig test (without periodicity filtration) tends to overdetect (underdetect) jumps

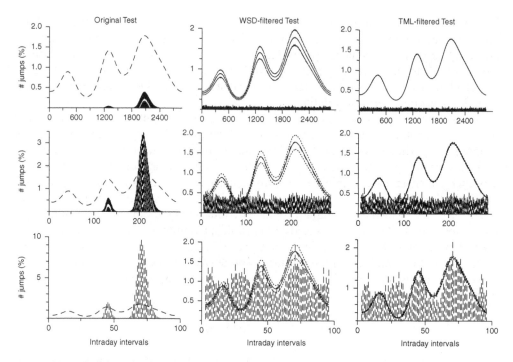

Note: The periodicity estimators are WSD and TML. DGP: Continuous-time GARCH diffusion model. Number of days: 250. Number of replications: 1000. Sampling frequencies: 30-seconds (top-row panels), 5-minutes (middle-row panels), 15-minutes (bottom-row panels). n = M and α = 0.1. Rejection thresholds: 4.74 (for 30-seconds) , 4.30 (for 5-minutes), and 4.10 (for 15-minutes).

Figure 16.10   *Proportion of intraday returns affected by spurious jumps according to the original and the filtered Lee–Hannig tests*

in periods of high (low) intraday periodic volatility. The figure also suggests that the filtered Lee–Hannig test (by either $\hat{f}_{t,i}^{\text{WSD}}\hat{s}_t$ or $\hat{f}_{t,i}^{\text{TML}}\hat{s}_t$) leads to a more uniform distribution of the number of spurious jumps over a day (see middle and right-block graphs in Figure 16.10).

16.5.3   An Application

This section applies the daily and intradaily jump tests described in the previous sections to five-minute returns.

Table 16.7 reports the number of detected daily jumps and their proportions to all sample days. The table clearly shows the presence of jumps in the exchange rates. The tests using BV_t, $MinRV_t$ and $MedRV_t$ as integrated volatility measures detect about 300–400 daily jumps. Furthermore, Figure 16.11 illustrates the time series of these detected jumps. Jumps occur more frequently during the financial crisis period, 2007–09, particularly for the USD/JPY exchange rate.

We now turn our attention to intraday jumps. Table 16.8 reports the results of the Lee–Mykland-test and the Lee–Hannig-test, as well as their periodicity-free versions.

Table 16.7 Daily jump tests

Statistic	BV_t	$MinRV_t$	$MedRV_t$
EUR/USD			
Z_t	475 [0.13]	373 [0.10]	516 [0.14]
$logZ_t$	366 [0.10]	243 [0.07]	374 [0.10]
$maxlogZ_t$	364 [0.10]	243 [0.07]	374 [0.10]
USD/JPY			
Z_t	441 [0.12]	360 [0.10]	500 [0.13]
$logZ_t$	366 [0.10]	224 [0.06]	381 [0.10]
$maxlogZ_t$	365 [0.10]	224 [0.06]	381 [0.10]

Note: Results of the daily jump tests. The sample covers the period from 3 January 1995 to 30 December 2009. The table reports the number of daily jumps detected and the jump proportion in brackets (p(jumps) $=100\times$#jumps/#days). The significance level of the tests is 0.0001. IV_t is computed by BV_t, $MinRV_t$, and $MedRV_t$.

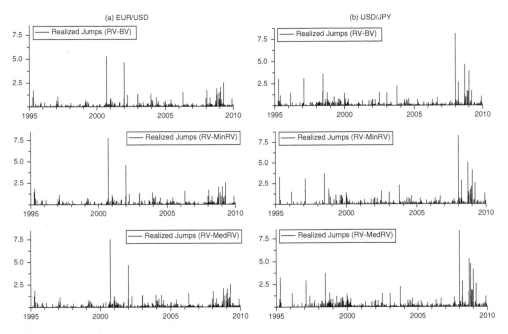

Note: The test statistics are based on $maxlogZ_t$. The significance level of the tests is 0.0001.

Figure 16.11 EUR/USD and USD/JPY daily realized jumps

The table indicates that there are about 2000 intraday jumps detected in both exchange rates. Nevertheless, the intraday jumps do not occur very often. For instance, the likelihood of observing an intraday return as a jump (that is $p(jumps)$ in the second column) is less than 1 percent in general.

How does periodicity in volatility affect intraday jump identification? Figure 16.12

Table 16.8　Intraday jump tests: LM-test and LH-test

Statistic	#jump	p(jumps)(%)	#jumpdays	p(jumpdays)(%)
EUR/USD				
Lee/Mykland	2105	0.20	1580	42.52
Lee/Hannig	2589	0.24	1619	43.57
Lee/Mykland(filt)	1863	0.17	1345	36.19
Lee/Hannig(filt)	2254	0.21	1411	37.97
USD/JPY				
Lee/Mykland	1866	0.17	1456	39.14
Lee/Hannig	2738	0.26	1576	42.37
Lee/Mykland(filt)	1838	0.17	1341	36.04
Lee/Hannig(filt)	2640	0.25	1480	39.78

Note: Results of the intraday jump tests. The sample covers the period from 3 January 1995 to 30 December 2009. Equation (16.53) and equation (16.55) give the jump detection statistics of the tests. '(filt)' implies that the corresponding test accounts for the periodicity based on the estimator WSD. *#jumps* is the number of intradaily jumps detected, *p(jumps)* is the jump proportion (that is *p(jumps)*=100×*#jumps*/*#obs*), *#jumpdays* is the number of days with at least one intraday jump and *p(jumpdays)* denotes the jump-day proportion (that is *p(jumpdays)* =100×*#jumpdays*/*#days*). The significance level of the tests is 0.1.

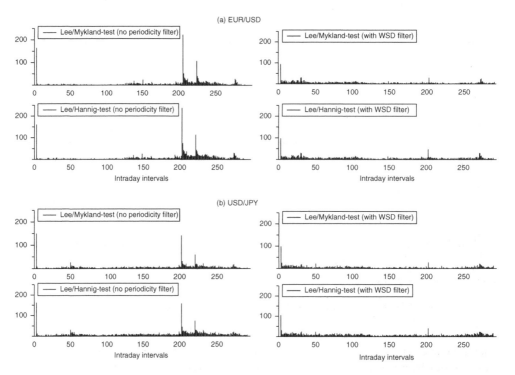

Figure 16.12　Number of EUR/USD and USD/JPY jumps per intraday period of time

plots the number of jumps per intraday interval. The fact that the filtered and unfiltered tests detect different returns as jumps (see the right and left-block graphs in Figure 16.12) suggests that one should account for intraday periodicity in jumps. The unfiltered tests tend to underdetect jumps at times of low periodicity and overdetect jumps at high periodicity times, in line with our simulation results. Accounting for periodicity leads to a more uniform distribution for intraday jump occurrences (see the right-block graphs in Figure 16.12).

16.6   MACRO NEWS AND CENTRAL BANK INTERVENTIONS

Because asset prices react to news about discount rates or future earnings, researchers have long recognized that announcements affect foreign exchange volatility. Scheduled announcements can help explain two important properties of foreign exchange volatility: periodicities and discontinuities in prices.

The study of announcement effects on volatility grew out of an earlier literature on autocorrelation, intraday and intraweek patterns in volatility. Researchers sought to distinguish patterns caused by market opening/closing from those caused by regular macro announcements. Links between announcements and volatility have implications for policy: a strong relationship between volatility and news argues against taxing foreign exchange transactions to reduce allegedly meaningless churning that creates 'excess' volatility (Melvin and Yin, 2000). Recent research has clearly linked macro announcements to price discontinuities (jumps), which have implications for volatility forecasting (Neely, 1999; Andersen et al., 2007a). Finally, microstructure theory has motivated studies showing that the prolonged impact of news announcements on volatility occurs through the persistent release of private information through order flow.

16.6.1   Research Methods

The literature has devoted disproportionate attention to US announcements because they are scheduled and expectations of those announcements and accompanying exchange rate data have been widely available for a long time.[23] Tables 16.9 and 16.10 show commonly used US announcements, their source and the delay in their release.

Researchers have commonly used three measures of volatility to study announcement effects: implied volatility, realized volatility and variants of GARCH models (Engle, 1982; Bollerslev, 1986).[24] Implied volatility is strongly forward looking and often insensitive to short-lived volatility effects from macro announcements. GARCH models fitted to daily data predict daily volatility through essentially autoregressive processes, but such models cannot estimate intraday effects. In contrast, high-frequency data – which can be used with parametric models such as GARCH – are well suited to measuring short-lived, intraday effects.

Researchers also study the extent to which a scheduled announcement itself – rather than the surprise component – could be expected to change volatility. To separate the effects of the announcement itself from the effects of the surprise component, researchers generally estimate the expectation of the announcement with the median response from

Table 16.9 US macroeconomic announcements

Name of announcement	Units of announcement	Frequency	Release lag	Source	Release time
Average Hourly Earnings	$ per hour	Monthly	Almost none	BLS	8:30 AM
Beige Book		8 times per year		FRB	2:15 PM
Business Inventories		Monthly	~6 weeks	CB	10:00 AM
Capacity Utilization Rate	Index (2002 = 100), % m-m	Monthly	~2 weeks	FRB	9:15 AM
Construction Spending	% m-m	Monthly	~5 weeks	CB	10:00 AM
Consumer Confidence Index	Index (1985 = 100)	Monthly	None	Conf. Board	10:00 AM
Consumer Credit Report	% m-m	Monthly	~5 weeks	FRB	3:00 PM
Consumer Installment Credit	% m-m, % q-q, No.	Monthly	~5 weeks	FRB	3:00 PM
Consumer Price Index	% m-m	Monthly	~2 weeks	BLS	8:30 AM
	(1982 = 100)				
Domestic Vehicle Sales	Millions of vehicles	Monthly	Almost none	BEA	3:00 PM
Durable Goods Orders	% m-m	Monthly	~3–4 weeks	CB	8:30 AM
Employment Cost Index	% q-q	Quarterly	~2–3 weeks	BLS	8:30 AM
	(2005 = 100)				
Existing Home Sales	No. of sales	Monthly	~4 weeks	NAR	10:00 AM
Factory Inventories	$ billion change	Monthly	~4 weeks	CB	10:00 AM
Factory Orders	$ billion change	Monthly	~4 weeks	CB	10:00 AM
Federal Budget/Deficit	$ Trillions	Monthly	–	CBO	2:00 PM
FOMC Minutes		8 times per year	~2–3 weeks	FRB	2:00 PM
GDP	% q/q	Quarterly		BEA	8:30 AM
GDP-Advance	% q/q	Quarterly	1 month lag	BEA	8:30 AM
GDP-Deflator	% q/q	Quarterly		BEA	8:30 AM
GDP-Final	% q/q	Quarterly	3 month lag	BEA	8:30 AM
GDP-Preliminary	% q/q	Quarterly	2 month lag	BEA	8:30 AM
Housing Starts	No. of units,	Monthly	~ 3 weeks	CB	8:30 AM
	% m-m				
Humphrey–Hawkins Testimony		Semiannual		FRB Chairman	10:00 AM
Index of Coincident Indicators	m-m	Monthly	~3 weeks	Conf. Board	10:00 AM
Industrial Production	Index (2002 = 100),% m-m	Monthly	~2 weeks	FRB	9:15 AM
Initial Unemployment Claims	No. of claims	Weekly	~5 days	ETA	8:30 AM
International Trade in Goods and Services	$ Billions	Monthly	~6 weeks	Commerce	8:30 AM
Inventories and Sales Ratio		Monthly	~6 weeks	CB	10:00 AM

Note: See Table 16.10. The release lag for FOMC minutes was about 6 weeks from February 1993 to 2005.

Table 16.10   US macroeconomic announcements (continued)

Name of announcement	Units of announcement	Frequency	Release lag	Source	Release time
ISM Index (formerly the NAPM Survey)	Index	Monthly	Almost none	ISM	10:00 AM
Lagging Indicators	m-m	Monthly	~3 weeks	Conf. Boar	10:00 AM
Leading Indicators	m-m	Monthly	~3 weeks	Conf. Board	10:00 AM
M1	Change in $ billions	Weekly		FRB	4:30 PM
M2	Change in $ billions	Weekly		FRB	4:30 PM
Merchandise Trade Balance				CB	8:30 AM
New Home Sales	Thousands	Monthly	~3–4 weeks	CB	10:00 AM
Nonfarm Payrolls	Thousands	Monthly	A few days	BLS	8:30 AM
Personal Consumption Expenditure Index (PCE)	% m-m	Monthly	~4 weeks	BEA	8:30 AM
Personal Income	% m-m	Monthly	~4 weeks	BEA	8:30 AM
Personal Spending	% m-m	Monthly	~4 weeks	BEA	8:30 AM
Producer Price Index	% m-m	Monthly	~2 weeks	BLS	8:30 AM
Productivity Costs	Index (1982 = 100) Index of output/ index of hours worked	Quarterly	Several months	BLS	8:30 AM
Retail Sales (Advance)	% m-m	Monthly	~2 weeks	CB	8:30 AM
Retail Trade	$ Millions	Monthly	~6 weeks	CB	8:45 (Sales) 10:15 (Inventories)
Target Federal Funds Rate	%	8 times a year		FRB	2:15 PM
Trade Balance	$ Billions	Monthly	~6–7 weeks	BEA	8:30 AM
Treasury Auction Results		Weekly		Treasury	11:00 AM
Unemployment rate	% of labor force	Monthly	A few days	BLS	8:30 AM
US Exports	% m-m (2000 = 100)	Monthly	~5–6 weeks	CB	8:30 AM
US Imports	% m-m (2000 = 100)	Monthly	~5–6 weeks	CB	8:30 AM
Value of New Constr. put in place	$ Millions % m-m	Monthly	~5 weeks	CB	10:00 AM

Note: CPI, consumer price index; GDP, gross domestic product; M1, M2, NAPM, National Association of Purchasing Managers; NFP, nonfarm payroll; PCE, personal consumption expenditures; PMI, Purchasing Managers' Index; PPI, producer price index. The following abbreviations are used for announcements: BEA, Bureau of Economic Analysis; BLS, Bureau of Labor Statistics; CB, US Census Bureau; Conf. Board, Conference Board; CBO, Congressional Budget Office; Commerce, US Department of Commerce; ETA, Department of Labor's Employment and Training Administration; FRB, Federal Reserve Board; ISM, Institute for Supply Management; NAR, National Association of Realtors; Treasury, US Department of the Treasury. % m-m, percent change from month to month; % q/q, percent change quarter over quarter; % q-q, percent change quarter to quarter. Descriptions of the announcements are available upon request.

the Money Market Services (MMS) Friday survey of 40 money managers on their expectations of coming economic releases.[25] Grossman (1981), Engel and Frankel (1984), Pearce and Roley (1985) and McQueen and Roley (1993) show that the MMS survey data provide approximately unbiased and informationally efficient estimates of news announcements that outperform time series models.[26]

To compare coefficients on announcement surprise series with different magnitudes, researchers have typically followed Balduzzi et al. (2001) in standardizing surprises by subtracting the MMS expectation from the release and dividing those differences by the SD of the series of differences. For example, the standardized surprise for announcement j is as follows:

$$S_t^j = \frac{R_t^j - E_t^j}{\hat{\sigma}_j},$$

(16.56)

where R_t^j is the realization of announcement j at day t, E_t^j is the MMS market expectation, and $\hat{\sigma}_j$ is the estimated standard deviation (SD) of the series of the differences. Thus, announcement surprises are close to mean zero and have a unit SD.

16.6.2   Early Studies of Volatility Patterns

Early studies of volatility patterns by Engle et al. (1990) and Harvey and Huang (1991) motivated specific investigation of announcement effects on volatility, despite the fact that the latter paper did not explicitly incorporate macro announcements.

Harvey and Huang (1991) discover an intraday U-shaped volatility pattern in hourly foreign exchange returns as well as intraweek effects. The authors speculate that important news announcements at the end of the week raise volatility on Thursday and Friday. Volatility is highest during the traded currency's own domestic business hours, particularly so for non-USD (US dollar) cross rates. Engle et al. (1990) extend this research in intraday volatility patterns by introducing the concepts of 'heat waves' and 'meteor showers' in the foreign exchange market. 'Heat waves' refer to the idea that volatility is geographically determined: that is, a heat wave might raise volatility in New York on Monday and Tuesday but not in London on Tuesday morning. Heat waves might occur if most or all important news that affects volatility occurs during a particular country's business day and there is little price discovery when that country's markets are closed. In contrast, 'meteor showers' refer to the tendency of volatility to spill over from market to market, from Asian to European to North American markets, for example. Therefore, meteor showers imply volatility clusters in time, not by geography. Using a GARCH model with intraday data, Engle et al. (1990) find that the meteor shower hypothesis better characterizes foreign exchange volatility engendered by balance of trade announcements. Baillie and Bollerslev (1991) confirm the meteor shower effect but also find some evidence of heat wave behavior. In retrospect, it seems unsurprising that meteor showers should predominate over heat waves in a world of global trading and a high degree of autocorrelated common shocks across countries: News tends to cluster in time and will surely affect volatility across the globe.

16.6.3   Decomposing Announcements and Periodic Volatility Patterns

Ederington and Lee (1993, 1994, 1995) argued that announcements explain most of the daily and intraweek volatility patterns, leaving little residual explained by a periodic pattern. Because announcements and periodicity are correlated, however, one must jointly model them to consistently estimate and compare their impact (Payne, 1996; Andersen and Bollerslev, 1998b). In doing so, Andersen and Bollerslev (1998b) affirm the importance of macro releases as addressed by Ederington and Lee (1993), but argue that these are secondary to the intraday pattern; periodic patterns and autoregressive volatility forecasts explain more of intraday and daily volatility than do announcements. The debate on the relative importance of announcement versus periodic effects continued in Han et al. (1999) and Ederington and Lee (2001).

Announcements and intraday patterns are not the whole story, however: Andersen and Bollerslev (1998b) find that – after accounting for the intraday volatility pattern – including ARCH terms still significantly improves forecasting power, even in a high-frequency volatility process.

To illustrate the issues involved in disentangling announcements, other periodic effects and autocorrelation, one can regress absolute hourly foreign exchange returns – 24 hours a day, five days a week – on announcement variables and periodic components. The following equation describes such a regression for hourly returns:

$$\log(|y_{t,i}|/\hat{s}_{t,i}) - c = \alpha_0 + \beta_0^{(US)}D_{t,i}^{(US)} + \beta_1^{(For)}D_{t,i}^{(For)} + \sum_{j=1}^{N}\beta_{2,j}|Surprise_{t,i}^{(j)}| + \sum_{q=1}^{4}\beta_{3,q}\cos\left(\frac{i2\pi q}{24}\right)$$

$$+ \sum_{q=1}^{4}\beta_{4,(4+q)}\sin\left(\frac{i2\pi q}{24}\right) + \sum_{l=1}^{5}\beta_{5,l}|y_{t,i-1}| + \sum_{h=19}^{23}\beta_{6,h}D_{t,i}^{(Friday_h)} + \varepsilon_{t,i}, \qquad (16.57)$$

where $\log(|y_{t,i}|/\hat{s}_{t,i})$ is the standardized log return (annualized) from period i to $i + 1$; c is as defined in section 16.4; $D_{t,i}^{(US)}$ and $D_{t,i}^{(For)}$ are dummy variables that take the value 1 if there is any US or foreign announcement, respectively during i to $i + 1$, and 0 otherwise; $Surprise_{t,i}^{(j)}$ is the standardized surprise of announcement j at period i on day t; $\cos(\frac{i2\pi q}{24})$ and $\sin(\frac{i2\pi q}{24})$ are trigonometric functions that allow parsimonious estimation of an intra-day periodic component.[27] Finally, $D_{t,i}^{(Friday_h)}$ takes the value 1 if the observation i coincides with hour h of a Friday, and 0 otherwise.

We estimate equation (16.57) by OLS on one-hour log changes in the EUR/USD exchange rate over the period November 5, 2001 to March 12, 2010, after first removing weekends and the following holidays from the sample: New Year's Day (December 31–January 2), Good Friday, Easter Monday, Memorial Day, Fourth of July (July 3 or 5 when the Fourth falls on a Saturday or Sunday), Labor Day, Thanksgiving (and the Friday after), and Christmas (December 24–26). We use daily annualized GARCH (1,1) volatility (that is, σ_t), and also RV_t to estimate $s_{t,i}$ for equation (16.57).

Table 16.11 shows the relative explanatory power of the various components of equation (16.57) for absolute returns. When we use RV_t to compute an endogenous variable (that is SYSTEM-II), the full regression has a substantial R^2 of 0.1828, with the greatest explanatory power coming from lagged absolute returns, with a partial R^2 of 0.0644, and 0.0457 for the intraday periodicity. The announcement dummies provide a very low

Table 16.11 R^2 and partial R^2s

Independent variable(s)	SYSTEM-I log($|yt, i|/\sigma_{t,i}$)	SYSTEM-II log($|y_{t,i}|/RV_{t,i}$)
Full regression (adjusted)	0.1175	0.1828
Announcement dummies	0.0009	0.0002
Absolute announcement surprises	0.0035	0.0044
Seasonal effect	0.0659	0.0457
Lags of absolute returns	0.0134	0.0644
Friday night dummies	0.1036	0.0008

Note: The table displays the R^2 and partial R^2s from regression (16.57) and various combinations of its regressors: the announcement dummies, $\beta_0^{(US)}D_{t,i}^{(US)}$ and $\beta_1^{(For)}D_{t,i}^{(For)}$; the absolute announcement surprises, $\sum_{j=1}^N \beta_{2,j}|Surprise_{t,i}^{(j)}|$; the periodic component, $\sum_{q=1}^4 \beta_{3,q}\cos(\frac{i2\pi q}{24})$ and $\sum_{q=1}^4 \beta_{4,(4+q)}\sin(\frac{i2\pi q}{24})$; five lags of absolute returns, $\sum_{i=1}^5 \beta_{5,i}|yt, i-1|$; and the Friday night indicators, $\sum_{h=19}^{23}\beta_{6,h}D_{t,i}^{(Friday_h)}$. Endogenous variables are log($|y_{t,i}|/\sigma_{t,i}$) in SYSTEM-I, and log($|y_{t,i}|/RV_{t,i}$) in SYSTEM-II.

partial R^2 of 0.0002 and the absolute announcement surprises provide a statistic of only 0.0044. Thus, the announcement surprises are fairly important but not as important as some other features of the data, confirming the views of Andersen and Bollerslev (1998b).

Tables 16.12 and 16.13 show the estimated regression coefficients and the robust *t*-statistics from equation (16.57). Most (but not all) of the news surprise coefficients are positive, indicating that larger surprises increase volatility. Some of the news surprise coefficients are perverse (negative), which often results from their correlation with the periodic components and/or the announcement indicators. Of all the German/euro announcements, German real GDP growth, euro area producer price index, and euro area industrial production indicators are significant and positive (see the columns of SYSTEM-II). The German preliminary cost of living indicator is slightly significant and negative. The US announcement indicator is significant, whereas the German/euro indicator is essentially zero – that is, US announcements raise volatility but German announcements do not. The significance of the US announcement indicator confirms the results of Andersen et al. (2003), who use high-frequency (five-minute) data from 1992 through 1998 to study the effects of a large set of US and German announcements on the conditional mean and the conditional volatility of DEM/USD, USD/GBP (British pound sterling), JPY/USD, CHF (Swiss franc)/USD, and USD/EUR (euro) exchange rates. The authors find that both the magnitude of the surprise and the pure announcement effect are significant.

In summary, the results in Table 16.11 indicate that Andersen and Bollerslev (1998b) were correct to argue that announcements are important explanatory variables for volatility, though not as important as intraday periodicity. Likewise, Tables 16.12 and 16.13 confirm the findings of Ederington and Lee (1993) that US non-farm payroll and US trade balance surprises are among the most important for volatility.

16.6.4   Volatility and News Arrival

Although the first studies of news volatility effects used US news reports and USD exchange rates, later studies branched out to study the effect of foreign news and broader definitions of news. Most such work has found that US news has stronger effects on

Table 16.12 *Regression coefficients*

Independent variable	SYSTEM-I			SYSTEM-II		
	Coefficient	t-HACSE	Impact	Coefficient	t-HACSE	Impact
Constant	-0.777	-85.100	(-)	-5.149	-287.000	(-)
US Announcement Dummy	0.240	6.360	(+)	0.114	2.560	(+)
German/Euro Announcement Dummy	-0.054	-1.380	.	-0.065	-1.290	.
US: Real GDP: Advance	0.417	2.890	(+)	0.478	2.020	(+)
US: Real GDP: Preliminary	-0.138	-0.779	.	-0.238	-1.090	.
US: Real GDP: Final	0.158	1.810	(+)	0.135	1.320	.
US: Business Inventories	-0.041	-0.396	.	-0.062	-0.399	.
US: Capacity Utilization Rate: Total Industry	-0.409	-2.840	(-)	-0.439	-2.480	(-)
US: Consumer Confidence	0.222	2.050	(+)	0.355	3.000	(+)
US: Construction Spending	0.265	2.670	(+)	0.434	4.390	(+)
US: Consumer Price Index	0.040	0.386	.	0.154	1.160	.
US: Consumer Credit	-0.287	-2.930	(-)	-0.068	-0.568	.
US: New Orders: Advance Durable Goods	0.128	1.320	.	0.211	1.890	.
US: New Orders	-0.284	-2.430	(-)	-0.306	-1.970	(-)
US: Housing Starts	-0.019	-0.223	.	0.035	0.316	.
US: Industrial Production	0.307	2.110	(+)	0.544	3.860	(+)
US: Composite Index of Leading Indicators	-0.107	-1.050	.	-0.016	-0.137	.
US: ISM: Mfg Composite Index	0.345	3.080	(+)	0.519	4.310	(+)
US: Employees on Non-farm Payrolls	0.842	5.490	(+)	1.688	7.030	(+)
US: New Home Sales	0.061	0.585	.	0.070	0.630	.

Table 16.12 (continued)

Independent variable	SYSTEM-I			SYSTEM-II		
	Coefficient	t-HACSE	Impact	Coefficient	t-HACSE	Impact
US: PCE	-0.041	-0.461	.	-0.013	-0.106	.
US: Personal Income	-0.181	-1.490	.	-0.115	-0.511	.
US: Producer Price Index	-0.034	-0.344	.	-0.010	-0.084	.
US: Retail Sales	0.170	1.300	.	0.151	1.330	.
US: Retail Sales ex Motor Vehicles	0.127	0.922	.	0.193	1.290	.
US: Trade Balance: Goods & Services [BOP]	0.350	3.720	(+)	0.49	4.540	(+)
US: Government Surplus/Deficit	-0.049	-0.588	.	0.038	0.443	.
US: Initial Claims	-0.004	-0.075	.	0.072	1.260	.
Euro area: CPI Flash Estimate Y/Y %Chg	0.121	1.630	.	0.277	1.060	.
Euro area: Industrial Production Y/Y %Chg WDA	0.236	2.750	(+)	0.298	2.370	(+)
Euro area: Money Supply M3 Y/Y %Chg	-0.051	-0.574	.	-0.010	-0.082	.
Euro area: Harmonised CPI Y/Y %Chg	-0.019	-0.175	.	-0.046	-0.337	.
Euro area: Unemployment Rate	0.109	1.310	.	0.110	1.070	.
Euro area: Producer Price Index Y/Y %Chg	0.130	1.670	.	0.196	2.210	(+)
Euro area: Retail Sales WDA Y/Y %Chg	-0.183	-1.650	.	-0.171	-1.340	.
Euro area: Trade Balance Eurostat	0.005	0.047	.	-0.061	-0.380	.
Euro area: Preliminary Real GDP Y/Y %Chg	-0.287	-1.420	.	-0.012	-0.044	.
Euro area: Final Real GDP Y/Y %Chg	0.039	0.303	.	-0.215	-0.649	.

Note: See Table 16.13.

Table 16.13 Regression coefficients (continued)

Independent variable	SYSTEM-I			SYSTEM-II		
	Coefficient	t-HACSE	Impact	Coefficient	t-HACSE	Impact
Germany: Current Account Balance	−0.089	−0.660	.	−0.016	−0.083	.
Germany: Final Cost of Living	0.066	0.466	.	−0.033	−0.232	.
Germany: Prelim Cost of Living	−0.137	−1.720	(−)	−0.310	−1.870	(−)
Germany: IP: Total Industry M/M %Chg	−0.028	−0.279	.	0.067	0.565	.
Germany: Producer Price Index: Mfg Y/Y %Chg	−0.001	−0.014	.	0.053	0.374	.
Germany: Real Retail Sales Y/Y %Chg	0.075	0.627	.	0.151	1.030	.
Germany: Current Account: Trade Balance	0.138	1.180	.	0.058	0.322	.
Germany: Real GDP Q/Q %Chg	0.447	4.570	(+)	0.445	2.970	(+)
Cos_q1	−0.136	−19.200	(−)	0.013	1.250	.
Cos_q2	0.021	3.400	(+)	0.012	1.620	.
Cos_q3	−0.157	−24.200	(−)	−0.171	−21.800	(−)
Cos_q4	−0.120	−18.400	(−)	−0.140	−18.300	(−)
Sin_q1	0.248	39.700	(+)	0.249	28.400	(+)
Sin_q2	−0.021	−3.210	(−)	−0.015	−1.840	(−)
Sin_q3	0.027	4.060	(+)	0.058	6.920	(+)
Sin_q4	−0.074	−11.600	(−)	−0.072	−9.540	(−)
Abs Return Lag1	1.124	17.300	(+)	2.465	30.900	(+)
Abs Return Lag2	0.714	10.700	(+)	1.811	21.100	(+)
Abs Return Lag3	0.566	8.280	(+)	1.765	18.600	(+)
Abs Return Lag4	0.582	8.790	(+)	1.764	19.600	(+)
Abs Return Lag5	0.450	6.940	(+)	1.642	18.900	(+)
Friday_1900	−0.494	−3.510	(−)	−1.050	−5.310	(−)
Friday_2000	−0.269	−1.520	.	−0.624	−1.620	.
Friday_2100	−0.056	−0.178	.	0.041	0.500	.
Friday_2200	−0.375	−1.760	(−)			.
Friday_2300	−1.039	−72.000	(−)			.

Note: The table shows the regression coefficients from estimating equation (16.57) on $\log(|yt,i|/\hat{s}_i)$, over the sample period November 5, 2001, to March 12, 2010. Endogenous variables are $\log(|yt,i|/\sigma_{t,i})$ in SYSTEM-I, and $\log(|y_{t,i}|/RV_{i,t})$ in SYSTEM-II. BOP, balance of payments; CPI, consumer price index; GDP, gross domestic product; IP, industrial production; ISM, Institute for Supply Management; PCE, personal consumption expenditures; PPI, producer price index; WDA, work days adjusted. *t*-HACSE: Heteroskedasticity and autocorrelation corrected robust *t*-statistics. (+): Indicates statistically significant positive coefficient. (−): Indicates statistically significant negative coefficient.

foreign exchange volatility than does foreign news (Cai et al., 2009; Evans and Speight, 2010; Harada and Watanabe, 2009).

Not all news consists of macro announcements. Information about the international economy and politics arrives continuously in financial markets via newswire reports. Although most papers documenting the impact of information arrival measure that variable by the frequency of headlines from wire service news agencies, DeGennaro and Shrieves (1997) use unexpected quote arrivals instead. The most common theme in this literature is that information arrival typically increases volatility (DeGennaro and Shrieves, 1997; Eddelbüttel and McCurdy, 1998; Joines et al., 1998; Melvin and Yin, 2000; Chang and Taylor, 2003). Melvin and Yin (2000) interpret this result as casting doubt on proposals to apply 'sand-in-the-wheels' transaction taxes that would reduce allegedly self-generated foreign exchange volatility.

Although news arrival usually boosts volatility, DeGennaro and Shrieves (1997) find that unscheduled announcements actually reduce volatility for 20 minutes, perhaps inducing traders to pause to consider unexpected information.

Eddelbüttel and McCurdy (1998) confirm that use of the Reuters news headlines as a proxy for news arrival renders the GARCH-implied variance process much less persistent. This fact appears to confirm the intuitively attractive proposition that persistence in news arrival drives part of the volatility persistence captured by GARCH models. The literature also shows, however, that public information arrival cannot explain the entire increase in volatility.

Joines et al. (1998) and Chang and Taylor (2003) argue that trading must also release private information that hikes volatility. Researchers working with order flow data would further explore this point.

16.6.5   Announcements and Jumps

Goodhart et al. (1993) first suggested the importance of accounting for news-induced discontinuities in exchange rates. The authors claim that including news indicators in the conditional mean and variance equations of a GARCH-in-mean (GARCH-M) model renders both of these processes stationary (Perron, 1990). The short (three-month) span of their data would seem to preclude useful inference about the degree of persistence in the processes.

To link daily jumps in the JPY, GBP and DEM exchange rates to four announcements from US, British, German and Japanese sources, Johnson and Schneeweis (1994) introduce an announcement effect parameter to Jorion's (1988) jump-diffusion model, permitting the conditional variance to depend on an announcement indicator. Real announcements – US trade balance and industrial production news – cause larger volatility movements than do money supply and inflation news and US news influences currency market variance more than does foreign news. Using data from 1982 to 2000, Fair (2003) relates the largest changes in US foreign exchange (and stock and bond) futures tick prices to changes in monetary, price level, employment and trade balance news.

Advances in econometric jump modeling enabled later researchers to better examine the relationship between announcements and jumps. Barndorff-Nielsen and Shephard (2004) used their method of bi-power variation to pinpoint jump dates and to observe that they often correspond to days of macroeconomic releases, which is consistent with

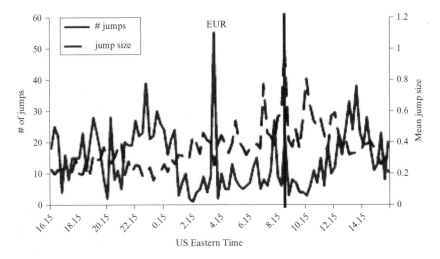

Note: The X-axis represents intraday time (US ET). The left Y-axis displays the number of significant jumps ($\alpha = 0.1$), while the right Y-axis shows the mean of absolute values of significant jumps. Solid lines denote the number of jumps and dashed lines denote mean jump size. The vertical lines denote the interval containing 8:30 a.m., the time of most news arrivals. The sample period is 1987–2004.

Source: From Figure 2 in Lahaye et al. (2011).

Figure 16.13   Number and sizes of jumps at different times of the day

Andersen et al. (2003) and Andersen et al. (2007c) (see for example equations (16.51) and (16.52)).[28]

The Barndorff-Nielsen and Shephard (2004) bi-power procedure estimates the sum of jumps during a period, usually a day, but does not pin down the precise times of those jumps, which precludes linking jumps to specific news releases. Lahaye et al. (2011) use the Lee and Mykland (2008) technique – which more precisely identifies jump times and sizes – to determine that US macro announcements explain jumps and cojumps – simultaneous jumps in multiple markets – across equity, bond, and foreign exchange markets. Non-farm payroll and federal funds target announcements are the most important news across asset classes, while trade balance shocks are also important for foreign exchange jumps (see equation (16.53)).

Figure 16.13 illustrates the intraday frequency and size of jumps in the USD/EUR market (Lahaye et al. 2011). Exchange rate jumps are more frequent around the times of major US macro news announcements, at 8:30 a.m., and during periods of low liquidity, that is, the gap between the US and the Asian business day, 4 p.m. to 8 p.m., and the Tokyo lunch, 10 p.m. to 2 a.m. US ET.

Lahaye et al. (2011) use tobit-GARCH and probit models to formally confirm the relationship between US news and a variety of asset price jumps and cojumps, respectively. Table 16.14 shows the tobit-GARCH results: from non-farm payroll (NFP), federal funds target announcements, trade balance reports, preliminary gross domestic product (GDP), government fiscal announcements, and consumer confidence surprises, to foreign exchange jumps. Table 16.15 likewise shows that a probit model consistently

Table 16.14 Tobit-GARCH models for jumps

	S&P futures Coef.	S&P futures P>|t|	Nasdaq futures Coef.	Nasdaq futures P>|t|	Dow Jones futures Coef.	Dow Jones futures P>|t|	US bond futures Coef.	US bond futures P>|t|	USD/EUR Coef.	USD/EUR P>|t|	JPY/USD Coef.	JPY/USD P>|t|	USD/GBP Coef.	USD/GBP P>|t|	CHF/USD Coef.	CHF/USD P>|t|
CONSCONF	–	–	–	–	0.71	0.88	0.96	0.01	–	–	0.74	0.00	0.38	0.08	0.43	0.02
CONSCONF (−1)	–	–	–	–	–	–	–	–	–	–	–	–	–	–	–	–
CONSCRED	–	–	–	–	0.98	0.10	–	–	–	–	–	–	0.06	0.99	−0.13	0.99
CPI	2.13	0.00	1.90	0.59	0.81	0.68	1.20	0.00	–	–	–	–	–	–	−0.06	0.99
FFRTARGET	1.06	0.49	1.39	0.63	1.65	0.00	0.74	0.05	0.01	1.00	0.09	0.99	0.66	0.00	0.57	0.00
FFRTARGET (−1)	–	–	–	–	–	–	0.66	0.02	0.88	0.00	0.72	0.00	–	–	–	–
GDPADV	2.19	0.01	3.47	0.01	2.09	0.00	–	–	–	–	–	–	0.40	0.83	0.48	0.81
GDPPRE	–	–	–	–	1.17	0.51	–	–	0.81	0.00	0.84	0.01	–	–	0.58	0.04
GVFISCDEF	0.97	0.69	–	–	–	–	0.30	0.88	−0.55	0.17	−0.72	0.08	−0.32	0.66	−0.62	0.08
MFGIND	–	–	–	–	2.61	0.00	1.69	0.74	0.24	0.81	−0.21	1.00	−0.04	1.00	0.54	0.12
NFPAYROL	2.28	0.00	4.75	0.00	1.78	0.00	1.52	0.00	0.98	0.00	0.35	0.25	0.16	0.94	0.43	0.00
PPI	1.05	0.14	−0.12	0.96	0.49	0.70	0.55	0.10	−0.70	0.99	−0.82	0.99	−0.15	0.58	−1.02	0.67
RETSALES	0.78	0.04	1.37	0.05	0.59	0.27	0.41	0.27	−0.21	0.99	–	–	–	–	−1.18	0.99
TRADEBAL	−10.09	0.79	–	–	0.10	0.92	−3.99	0.81	0.43	0.05	0.02	1.00	0.17	0.89	0.47	0.02
ω	1.65	0.03	11.58	0.00	0.90	0.10	0.69	0.06	0.30	0.00	0.26	0.00	0.25	0.00	0.52	0.00
α_1	0.27	0.02	0.34	0.00	0.11	0.01	0.19	0.02	0.19	0.00	0.18	0.00	0.28	0.00	0.26	0.00
α_2	–	–	–	–	–	–	–	–	–	–	–	–	–	–	0.09	0.00
β_1	0.46	0.01	–	–	0.72	0.00	0.46	0.04	0.49	0.00	0.60	0.00	0.28	0.00	–	–
Function value	−877.44	0.00	−1204.57	0.00	−924.59	0.00	−917.35	0.00	−7090.68		−7542.77		−7727.96		−7331.87	
# obs	49135.00	0.00	49662.00	0.00	53909.00	0.00	40559.00	0.00	352127.00	0.00	351359.00	0.00	352799.00	0.00	352319.00	

Note: The latent Tobit jump variable is given by $Jump^*_{t,i} = \mu + \eta_{t,i} + \mu_{t,i} + \xi_{5,i} + \varepsilon_{t,i}$, where $|Jump_{t,i}| = Jump^*_{t,i}$ if $Jump^*_{t,i} > 0$ and $|Jump_{t,i}| = 0$ if $Jump^*_{t,i} \leq 0$, $\varepsilon_{t,i}|\mathcal{I}_{t,i-1}$ is $N(0, \sigma_i^2)$. The variance σ_i^2 is assumed to follow an ARCH or GARCH process. $|Jump_{t,i}|$ represents significant jumps ($\alpha = 0.1$) as defined in the theoretical part. $\eta_{t,i}$ controls for day of the week effects (not reported) and $\mu_{t,i}$ includes surprises concerning macro announcements. For each series, we regress jumps in absolute value on surprises in absolute value. $\xi_{5,i}$ controls for intradaily periodicity (not reported). Estimates and robust p-values ($2 \times (1 - Prob(X < |stat|))$. X being a t-distributed random variable with $N - K$ (# obs. - #parameters) degrees of freedom, and tstat being the estimated coefficient over its std. error) are reported for surprise coefficient (if it is significant at 10% in at least one series), as well as the ARCH and GARCH coefficients. Regressors with no contemporaneous match with significant jumps are excluded from the model. See Lahaye et al. (2011) for the sample periods.

Table 16.15 Probit models for cojumps

	USD/EUR – USD/GBP		USD/EUR – JPY/USD		USD/EUR – CHF/USD		USD/GBP – JPY/USD		USD/GBP – CHF/USD		JPY/USD – CHF/USD	
	Coef.	$P > |t|$	Coef.	$P > |t|$	Coef.	$P > |t|$	Coef.	$P > |t|$	Coef.	$P > |t|$	Coef.	$P > |t|$
CNSTRSPEND	–	–	–	–	–7.41	0.00	–	–	–	–	0.73	0.00
CONSCONF	–	–	–	–	–	–	–	–	–	–	0.74	0.01
FFRTARGET	1.08	0.00	0.86	0.00	0.83	0.00	0.90	0.00	0.89	0.00	0.83	0.00
GDPPRE	–	–	0.87	0.00	0.60	0.02	–	–	–	–	0.25	0.05
GVFISCDEF	–	–	0.23	0.07	0.17	0.18	–	–	–	–	–	–
MFGIND	–	–	–	–	1.50	0.00	–	–	–	–	–	–
NFPAYROL	–	–	0.65	0.00	0.79	0.00	–	–	–	–	0.61	0.00
TRADEBAL	–	–	–	–	0.76	0.02	–	–	–	–	–	–
Function value	–1842.90		–1181.87		–3130.59		–742.60		–1610.76		–933.24	
Pseudo R^2	0.04		0.04		0.03		0.05		0.04		0.05	
# obs	349355		348967		349557		348593		349542		348619	

Note: The latent probit cojump variable is given by $CO\,Jump^*_{t,i} = \mu + \eta_{t,i} + \mu_{\nu,i} + \xi_{t,i} + \varepsilon_{t,i}$, where $CO\,Jump_{t,i} = 1$ if $CO\,Jump^*_{t,i} > 0$ and $CO\,Jump_{t,i} = 0$ if $CO\,Jump^*_{t,i} \leq 0$. $\varepsilon_{t,i}$ is $NID(0,1)$. $CO\,Jump_{t,i}$ is the cojump indicator. $\eta_{t,i}$ controls for day of the week effects (not reported) and $\mu_{\nu,i}$ includes surprises concerning macro announcements. For each series, we regress cojumps on surprises in absolute value. $\xi_{t,i}$ controls for intradaily seasonality (not reported). Estimates and robust p-values $(2 \times (1 - Prob(X < |tstat|))$, X being a t-distributed random variable with $N - K$ (# obs. – #parameters) degrees of freedom, and $tstat$ being the estimated coefficient over its std. error are reported for each surprise coefficient. Regressors with no contemporaneous match with significant cojumps are excluded from the model. We further report the maximized log-likelihood function value, and the McFadden R^2 (defined as $1 - \frac{LogLik_1}{LogLik_0}$, i.e. 1 minus the ratio of the log likelihood function value of the full model to the constant only model one). See Lahaye et al. (2011) for the sample periods.

and strongly links cojumps to macro surprises, such as those to the federal funds rate target, NFP and preliminary GDP. Federal funds target surprises significantly explain cojumps in every currency pair.

16.6.6   Order Flows and Foreign Exchange Volatility

News might create order flows – signed transaction flows – that transmit private information to the foreign exchange market. Private agents combine public news releases with their own private information, and their publicly observable decisions may convey that private information. For example, a business might revise its estimates of future demand from a positive industrial production surprise and decide to build a new plant – but only if the firm's privately known cost structures would make it expect to profit from that decision. The release of private information creates a channel by which news can affect volatility over a prolonged period.

Obtaining order flow data is difficult and/or expensive, prompting some researchers to use proxies for order flow, while others have used relative short spans from electronic brokers such as Reuters D2000-1, Electronic Brokerage Services or proprietary datasets from commercial banks. The limited length and market coverage of order flow data has hindered clear inference about the effect of specific announcements on order flow.

The main finding from the literature on order flow and announcements is that news releases public information, which immediately affects prices and volatility and – after a delay – volume through release of private information through order flow (Evans and Lyons, 2005). The delayed effects of order flow can contribute to volatility for hours after announcements, particularly if the announcement is important and unscheduled, as in Carlson and Lo (2006).

Berger et al. (2009) conclude that both persistence in order flow and persistence in sensitivity to that order flow contribute to the persistence of volatility. In other words, the type of order flow matters for volatility transmission: financial customers are thought to be 'informed traders', to have better information on asset prices than commercial firms, which trade currency to import/export. Frömmel et al. (2008) find that only order flow from banks and financial customers (that is, informed order flow) is linked to higher foreign exchange volatility.[29] Savaser (2011) finds that informed traders substantially increase their use of limit orders prior to news releases and that accounting for this surge substantially improves the ability to explain exchange rate jumps that follow news.

16.6.7   Summary

The research on announcements and volatility highlights the role of announcements in contributing to two of the main characteristics of volatility: periodicity and jumps. Trading and volatility typically increase for about an hour after certain announcements: non-farm payrolls, trade balance, advance GDP and interest rate changes (Ederington and Lee, 1993).

Early researchers disentangled the contributions of macroeconomic news from those of other periodic market effects – such as market openings and closings, showing that both had significant effects on volatility (Payne, 1996; Andersen and Bollerslev, 1998b).

Further studies showed that news flow (that is, headline counts) influence volume and volatility (Ederington and Lee, 2001; Melvin and Yin, 2000; Chang and Taylor, 2003). More generally, researchers have established that news has a prolonged effect on order flow, which channels private information to market prices and produces sustained increases in volatility (Cai et al., 2001; Evans, 2002; Evans and Lyons, 2005; Frömmel et al., 2008).

The development of better tests for price discontinuities has aided more recent studies to connect jumps to macro announcements and other news (Goodhart et al., 1993; Fair, 2003; Andersen et al., 2003; Lahaye et al., 2011). Removing such jumps from the volatility process improves autoregressive volatility forecasts (Neely, 1999; Andersen et al., 2007a).

16.6.8 Central Bank Intervention, Foreign Exchange Volatility and Jumps

Foreign exchange intervention is the practice by monetary authorities or finance ministries of buying or selling foreign currency to influence exchange rates. From 1985 through 2004, the US, Japanese and German (European) central banks intervened more than 600 times – about three times per month, on average – in either the DEM-dollar (DEM/USD or EUR/USD after the introduction of the euro) or the yen–dollar (JPY/USD) market.[30]

The importance of foreign exchange markets for international trade and finance makes it unsurprising that central banks should frequently intervene in markets that are of crucial importance for international trade and finance. Specifically, central banks often motivate intervention with a desire to respond to 'disorderly markets', an ill-defined term that could include excess volatility. The International Monetary Fund's (IMF) document: 'Surveillance over exchange rate policies', for example, states that: 'A member should intervene in the exchange market if necessary to counter disorderly conditions, which may be characterized inter alia by disruptive short-term movements in the exchange value of its currency.'[31] In practice, authorities have often referred to market volatility in justifying intervention: On March 17, 2011, for example, the G-7 announced a coordinated intervention to sell the yen in response to unwanted appreciation after the Japanese earthquake of the previous week. The G-7 press release contained the following text:

> [A]t the request of the Japanese authorities, the authorities of the United States, the United Kingdom, Canada, and the European Central Bank will join with Japan, on 18 March 2011, in concerted intervention in exchange markets. As we have long stated, excess volatility and disorderly movements in exchange rates have adverse implications for economic and financial stability. (G-7, 2011)

Foreign exchange intervention is a type of unscheduled news; market participants generally quickly find out about such transactions. Many researchers have studied the relationship between intervention and foreign exchange volatility and, more recently, with jumps.

Although intervention is often motivated by a desire to counter volatility, research has usually found that interventions generally increase foreign exchange volatility. This result is robust to the use of any of the three main measures of asset price volatility:

univariate GARCH models (Baillie and Osterberg, 1997; Dominguez, 1998; Beine et al., 2002a); implied volatilities extracted from option prices (Bonser-Neal and Tanner, 1996; Dominguez, 1998; Galati and Melick, 1999) and realized volatility (Beine et al., 2009; Dominguez, 2006). Hung (1997) says that results could be sample dependent: intervention reduced both JPY/USD and DEM/USD volatilities during 1985–86, but increased them during 1987–89. Fratzscher (2008) finds that oral – not actual – interventions tend to reduce exchange rate volatility. Using bi-power variation to determine the days of jumps, Beine et al. (2007) likewise find that although jumps are not more likely to occur on days of intervention, the jumps that do occur are larger than average. Their analysis strongly suggests that intervention normally generates the jumps, rather than reacting to them. The only period in which intervention appears to respond to jumps is that of the 'Louvre Accords', when central banks were very keen to dampen volatility by leaning against the wind. In addition, coordinated operations statistically explain an increase in the persistent (continuous) part of exchange rate volatility. This correlation is even stronger on days with jumps.

While most studies find that intervention raises uncertainty, the literature is not unanimous on this point. Failure to correctly resolve the difficult issues of simultaneity and identification of the cross-effects of volatility and intervention might explain the finding that intervention raises volatility. That is, intervention responds to volatility, so these variables will be positively correlated. Volatility does tend to decline in the hours and days following intervention, but it is difficult to ascertain whether the decline is the result of intervention or simply the natural tendency of very volatile markets to return to normal volatility levels over time. That is, Figure 16.14, excerpted from Neely (2011), shows that both realized and implied volatility drop remarkably after the March 18, 2011 G-7 intervention. After the intervention, short-horizon implied volatility dropped much more than long-horizon volatility, which suggests that the unexpected intervention did calm markets.

Although high-frequency data or more sophisticated econometric techniques might account for simultaneity, another method would be to ask market participants – who observe very high-frequency data – about the effect of intervention on volatility. Cheung and Clement (2000) report that traders believe that intervention increases volatility, though they also believe that it helps restore equilibrium. Neely (2008) reports that central bankers who are directly involved with intervention generally do not believe that it raises volatility.

In summary, intervention and volatility are clearly correlated. The effect of intervention on volatility likely depends on the intervention reaction function and market conditions at the time of intervention.

16.7   CONCLUSION

This chapter has reviewed the recent developments in modeling exchange rate volatility and jumps. Volatility models of foreign exchange inform a variety of agents, including academic researchers, policymakers, regulators, and traders. A good volatility model fits the three characteristics of volatility: intraday periodicity, autocorrelation and allowance for discontinuities in prices.

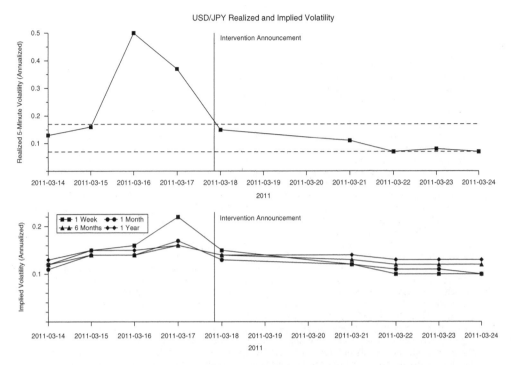

Note: Top panel shows the annualized realized volatility, computed from 5-minute squared returns, for the JPY/USD market from March 14 to March 24, 2011. The horizontal lines show the 10th and 90th percentiles of volatility for the USD/JPY over the March 26, 1998–March 31, 2011, period. Bottom panel shows option-implied volatility over four horizons for the same market during the same period in March 2011.

Figure 16.14 Realized and implied volatilities around an intervention announcement

Early research focused on ARCH/GARCH modeling of the autocorrelation in daily and weekly squared residuals. We show that a FIGARCH model with a fat-tailed distribution describes daily exchange rate volatility dynamics quite well. Researchers soon discovered the value of high-frequency data for better volatility and jump estimation, however. Using high-frequency exchange rate data, we presented several methods to estimate the quadratic variation, integrated volatility, jumps and intraday periodicity in a continuous-time framework. In doing so, we illustrate the prevalence of jumps in the data and show that one must account for intraday periodicity in detecting jumps. We concluded our chapter by discussing the effects of macro news announcements and central bank interventions on exchange rate volatility and jump dynamics. Macro news affects volatility but not as much as periodicity caused by market openings and closings. The effect of interventions on volatility depends on market conditions.

More recently, researchers have investigated the impact of central bank communication on exchange rates. Does communication calm foreign exchange markets? How and when do markets process communication news? Future research may shed more light on these issues.

NOTES

1. We splice DEM/USD returns with EUR/USD returns on January 1, 1999, and call the resulting series EUR/USD for simplicity.
2. These holidays include New Year (December 31 – January 2), Martin Luther King Day, Washington's Birthday or Presidents' Day, Good Friday, Easter Monday, Memorial Day, Independence Day, Labor Day, Thanksgiving Day and Christmas (December 24–26).
3. See also Table 16.1.
4. The weakness of the Ljung–Box test is that its asymptotic distribution is known under the very restrictive assumption that errors are i.i.d. Francq et al. (2005) propose a robust version of that test whose distribution is derived under the weaker assumption of a martingale difference sequence. This test is therefore robust to ARCH effects. See also Francq and Zakoïan (2009).
5. For the sake of simplicity, we present the parametric volatility models for the daily frequency only.
6. However, these conditions are not necessary as shown by Nelson and Cao (1992).
7. Researchers have proposed other specifications accounting for this leverage effect. See the EGARCH of Nelson (1991), the TARCH of Zakoïan (1994) and the APARCH of Ding et al. (1993), among others.
8. Nevertheless, some empirical studies do find evidence of asymmetry for some exchange rates (Oh and Lee, 2004; McKenzie and Mitchell, 2002).
9. Granger (1980) and Granger and Joyeux (1980) initially developed the ARFIMA process to model long memory in time series processes. An ARFIMA specification fills the gap between short and complete persistence, so that the ARMA parameters capture the short-run behavior of the time-series and the fractional differencing parameter models the long-run dependence. Baillie (1996) surveys this topic. ARFIMA models have been combined with an ARCH-type specification by Baillie et al. (1996b), Tschernig (1995), Teyssière (1997), Lecourt (2000) and Beine et al. (2002b). However, among these studies, Tschernig (1995) and Beine et al. (2002b) find evidence of only weak long-memory in the conditional mean of some exchange rate returns. To check this result using our dataset, we estimated an ARFIMA(1, d, 1) model for the EUR/USD exchange rate. We found that the long-memory parameter d in the conditional mean equation is not statistically different from zero, which is consistent with the main body of the literature. For brevity, we do not report these results but they are available upon request.
10. Conrad and Haag (2006) further derive necessary and sufficient positivity constraints for FIGARCH models.
11. We first estimated an ARFIMA-GARCH model to test for the long-memory in the conditional mean. We did not find any evidence of long-range dependence and therefore only reported short-memory models for the conditional mean.
12. The Student-t and GED distribution are not nested and hence one cannot rely on a standard likelihood ratio test to discriminate between the two distributions.
13. For brevity, these results are not reported yet they are available upon request. Note that the pre-crisis sample covers the periods 2004-01-05 to 2006-12-29, and the crisis sample spans 2007-01-03 to 2009-12-30.
14. The origin of realized volatility is not as recent as it would seem at first sight. Merton (1980) already mentioned that, provided data sampled at a high frequency are available, the sum of squared realizations can be used to estimate the variance of an i.i.d. random variable.
15. In other words, a counting process (such as the Poisson process) is defined to be of finite activity if the change in the counting process over any time interval is finite with probability one.
16. Even in the absence of jumps, some squared returns are down-weighted and therefore $c_w > 1$ is intended to compensate for this, to make the weighted sum of squared returns consistently estimate IV_t.
17. The length of the local window is usually set to one day.
18. We discuss the periodicity estimation methods in section 16.4.
19. One can also compare the non-parametric volatility estimators based on their volatility forecasting performance. One candidate model is an ARFIMA. As an alternative to ARFIMA models, Corsi (2009) proposed a simple AR-type model that considers volatilities realized over different horizons (typically three, that is daily, weekly and monthly). This model is called a heterogeneous auto-regressive (HAR) model.
20. Note that it is standard practice to normalize the integral of the periodicity factor (or its square) to equal one over the day.
21. Lee and Hannig (2010) also propose a detection rule to identify small jumps in the data. In our study, we only focus on the big jump detection test.
22. Unreported simulation results. The underlying DGP is a continuous-time GARCH model. There are no jumps in the process. These results are available upon request.
23. Money Market Services (MMS) expectations have been available for other countries for some time.
24. Neely (2005) discusses the measurement and uses of implied volatility estimated from options prices.

Engle (1982) developed the autoregressive conditionally heteroskedastic (ARCH) model that Bollerslev (1986) extended to the GARCH formulation. GARCH models usefully account for the time-varying volatility and fat-tailed distributions of daily and intraday financial returns.

25. The number of survey participants and the dates of the survey have changed over time. Hakkio and Pearce (1985) report that MMS surveyed about 60 money market participants during the early 1980s. MMS conducted the surveys on both Tuesdays and Thursdays before February 8, 1980 and on Tuesdays after that date.

26. Rigobon and Sack (2008) discuss two methods to compensate for the error inherent in estimating market expectations with survey data. Bartolini et al. (2008) apply this methodology.

27. Equation (16.57) could be altered to take into account a host of effects, including asymmetry or business cycle dependence, for example.

28. Beine et al. (2007) use macro announcements as control variables in a study of the effects of US, German, and Japanese foreign exchange intervention on the continuous and discontinuous components of DEM-EUR/USD and JPY/USD exchange rate volatility. They estimate exchange rate jumps with bi-power variation.

29. Informed order flow would be order flow that is generated by private information and speculates on a change in asset prices. In contrast, uninformed order flow would be generated by demands for commercial or hedging purposes and would not be predicated on private information that informs expectations of changes in asset prices.

30. The central banks of major economies have tended to intervene far less frequently since 1995. See Savaser (2011).

31. See http://www.imf.org/external/pubs/ft/sd/2011/123110.pdf.

REFERENCES

Aas, K. and I.H. Haff (2006), 'The generalized hyperbolic skew Student's t-distribution', *Journal of Financial Econometrics*, **4**, 275–309.

Aït-Sahalia, Y. (2004), 'Disentangling diffusion from jumps', *Journal of Financial Economics*, **74**, 487–528.

Aït-Sahalia, Y. and J. Jacod (2009a), 'Estimating the degree of activity of jumps in high-frequency data', *Annals of Statistics*, **37**, 2202–2244.

Aït-Sahalia, Y. and J. Jacod (2009b), 'Testing for jumps in a discretely observed process', *Annals of Statistics*, **37**, 184–222.

Aït-Sahalia, Y. and J. Jacod (2010), 'Is Brownian motion necessary to model high-frequency data?', *Annals of Statistics*, **38**, 3093–3128.

Aït-Sahalia, Y. and J. Jacod (2012), 'Analyzing the spectrum of asset returns: jump and volatility components in high frequency data', *Journal of Economic Literature*, **50**, 1007–1050.

Andersen, T.G. and T. Bollerslev (1997), 'Intraday periodicity and volatility persistence in financial markets', *Journal of Empirical Finance*, **4**, 115–158.

Andersen, T.G. and T. Bollerslev (1998a), 'Answering the skeptics: yes, standard volatility models do provide accurate forecasts', *International Economic Review*, **39**, 885–905.

Andersen, T.G. and T. Bollerslev (1998b), 'DM–dollar volatility: intraday activity patterns, macroeconomic announcements and longer run dependencies', *Journal of Finance*, **53**, 219–265.

Andersen, T., T. Bollerslev and F. Diebold (2007a), 'Roughing it up: including jump components in the measurement, modelling and forecasting of return volatility', *Review of Economics and Statistics*, **89** (4), 701–720.

Andersen, T., T. Bollerslev and D. Dobrev (2007b), 'No-arbitrage semi-martingale restrictions for continous-time volatility models subject to leverage effects, jumps and i.i.d. noise: theory and testable distributional implications', *Journal of Econometrics*, **138**, 125–180.

Andersen, T.G., T. Bollerslev, F.X. Diebold and P. Labys (2001), 'The distribution of exchange rate volatility', *Journal of the American Statistical Association*, **96**, 42–55.

Andersen, T.G., T. Bollerslev, F.X. Diebold and C. Vega (2003), 'Micro effects of macro announcements: real-time price discovery in foreign exchange', *American Economic Review*, **93**, 38–62.

Andersen, T.G., T. Bollerslev, F.X. Diebold and C. Vega (2007c), 'Real-time price discovery in stock, bond and foreign exchange markets', *Journal of International Economics*, **73**, 251–77.

Andersen, T.G., D. Dobrev and E. Schaumburg (2008), 'Jump-robust volatility estimation using nearest neighbor truncation', Working Paper, Kellogg School of Management, Northwestern University, USA.

Baillie, R.T. (1996), 'Long memory processes and fractional integration in econometrics', *Journal of Econometrics*, **73**, 5–59.

Baillie, R.T. and T. Bollerslev (1991), 'Intra-day and inter-market volatility in foreign exchange rates', *Review of Economic Studies*, **58**, 565–585.

Baillie, R.T., T. Bollerslev and H.O. Mikkelsen (1996a), 'Fractionally integrated generalized autoregressive conditional heteroskedasticity', *Journal of Econometrics*, **74**, 3–30.

Baillie, R.T. C.F. Chung and M.A. Tieslau (1996b), 'Analyzing inflation by the fractionally integrated ARFIMA-GARCH model', *Journal of Applied Econometrics*, **11**, 23–40.

Baillie, R.T. and W.P. Osterberg (1997), 'Why do central banks intervene?', *Journal of International Money and Finance*, **16**, 909–919.

Balduzzi, P., E.J. Elton and T.C. Green (2001), 'Economic news and bond prices: evidence from the US Treasury market', *Journal of Financial and Quantitative Analysis*, **36**, 523–543.

Bandi, F.M. and J.R. Russell (2005), 'Realized covariation, realized beta and microstructure noise', Working Paper, Graduate School of Business, University of Chicago, USA.

Bandi, F.M. and J.R. Russell (2008), 'Microstructure noise, realized volatility, and optimal sampling', *The Review of Economic Studies*, **75**, 339–369.

Barndorff-Nielsen, O.E., P.H. Hansen, A. Lunde and N. Shephard (2008), 'Designing realised kernels to measure the ex-post variation of equity prices in the presence of noise', *Econometrica*, **76**, 1481–1536.

Barndorff-Nielsen, O.E. and N. Shephard (2004), 'Power and bipower variation with stochastic volatility and jumps (with discussion)', *Journal of Financial Econometrics*, **2**, 1–48.

Barndorff-Nielsen, O.E. and N. Shephard (2006), 'Econometrics of testing for jumps in financial economics using bipower variation', *Journal of Financial Econometrics*, **4**, 1–30.

Barndorff-Nielsen, O.E., N. Shephard and M. Winkel (2006), 'Limit theorems for multipower variation in the presence of jumps', *Stochastic Processes and Their Applications*, **116**, 796–806.

Bartolini, L., L. Goldberg and A. Sacarny (2008), 'How economic news moves markets', *Federal Reserve Bank of New York Current Issues in Economics and Finance*, **14**, 1–7.

Bauwens, L. and S. Laurent (2005), 'A new class of multivariate skew densities, with application to GARCH models', *Journal of Business and Economic Statistics*, **23**, 346–354.

Beine, M., A. Bènassy-Quèrè and C. Lecourt (2002a), 'Central bank intervention and foreign exchange rates: new evidence from FIGARCH estimations', *Journal of International Money and Finance*, **21**, 115–144.

Beine, M., J. Lahaye, S. Laurent, C.J. Neely and F.C. Palm (2007), 'Central bank intervention and exchange rate volatility, its continuous and jump components', *International Journal of Finance and Economics*, **12**, 201–223.

Beine, M., S. Laurent and C. Lecourt (2002b), 'Accounting for conditional leptokurtosis and closing days effects in FIGARCH models of daily exchange rates', *Applied Financial Economics*, **12**, 589–600.

Beine, M., S. Laurent and F. Palm (2009), 'Central bank forex interventions assessed using realized moments', *Journal of International Financial Markets, Institutions and Money*, **19**, 112–127.

Berger, D., A. Chaboud and E. Hjalmarsson (2009), 'What drives volatility persistence in the foreign exchange market?', *Journal of Financial Economics*, **94**, 192–213.

Bollerslev, T. (1986), 'Generalized autoregressive conditional heteroskedasticity', *Journal of Econometrics*, **31**, 307–327.

Bollerslev, T., R.Y. Chou and K.F. Kroner (1992), 'ARCH modeling in finance: a review of the theory and empirical evidence', *Journal of Econometrics*, **52**, 5–59.

Bollerslev, T. and V. Todorov (2011), 'Estimation of jump tails', *Econometrica*, **79**, 1727–1783.

Bollerslev, T. and J.M. Wooldridge (1992), 'Quasi-maximum likelihood estimation and inference in dynamic models with time-varying covariances', *Econometric Reviews*, **11**, 143–172.

Bonser-Neal, C. and G. Tanner (1996), 'Central bank intervention and the volatility of foreign exchange rates: evidence from the options market', *Journal of International Money and Finance*, **15**, 853–878.

Boudt, K., C. Croux and S. Laurent (2011a), 'Outlyingness weighted quadratic covariation', *Journal of Financial Econometrics*, **9**, 657–684.

Boudt, K., C. Croux and S. Laurent (2011b), 'Robust estimation of intraweek periodicity in volatility and jump detection', *Journal of Empirical Finance*, **18**, 353–367.

Brownlees, C. and G. Gallo (2006), 'Financial econometric analysis at ultra-high frequency: data handling concerns', *Computational Statistics and Data Analysis*, **51**, 2232–2245.

Cai, F., H. Joo and Z. Zhang (2009), 'The impact of macroeconomic announcements on real time foreign exchange rate in emerging markets', International Finance Discussion Paper No. 973, Board of Governors of the Federal Reserve System.

Cai, J., Y.-L. Cheung, R.S.K. Lee and M. Melvin (2001), '"Once-in-a-generation" yen volatility in 1998: fundamentals, intervention, and order flow', *Journal of International Money and Finance*, **20**, 327–347.

Carlson, J.A. and M. Lo (2006), 'One minute in the life of the DM/US$: public news in an electronic market', *Journal of International Money and Finance*, **25**, 1090–1102.

Carr, P. and L. Wu (2003), 'What type of process underlies options? A simple robust test', *Journal of Finance*, **58**, 2581–2610.

Chang, Y. and S.J. Taylor (2003), 'Information arrivals and intraday exchange rate volatility', *Journal of International Financial Markets, Institutions and Money*, **13**, 85–112.

Cheung, Y.-W. and Y.-P.W. Clement (2000), 'A survey of market practitioners' views on exchange rate dynamics', *Journal of International Economics*, **51**, 401–419.

Conrad, C. and B.R. Haag (2006), 'Inequality constraints in the fractionally integrated GARCH model', *Journal of Financial Econometrics*, **4**, 413–449.

Corsi, F. (2009), 'A simple approximate long-memory model of realized volatility', *Journal of Financial Econometrics*, **7**, 174–196.

Dark, J.G. (2010), 'Estimation of time varying skewness and kurtosis with and application to value-at-risk', *Studies in Nonlinear Dynamics and Econometrics*, **14**, article 3.

Davidson, R. and J. MacKinnon (1993), 'Estimation and inference in econometrics', New York: Oxford University Press.

DeGennaro, R.P. and R.E. Shrieves (1997), 'Public information releases, private information arrival, and volatility in the foreign exchange market', *Journal of Empirical Finance*, **4**, 295–315.

Deschamps, P. (2012), 'Bayesian estimation of generalized hyperbolic skewed student GARCH models', *Computational Statistics and Data Analysis*, **56** (11), 3035–3054.

Diebold, F.X. and M. Nerlove (1989), 'The dynamics of exchange rate volatility: a multi-variate latent factor ARCH model', *Journal of Applied Econometrics*, **4**, 1–21.

Ding, Z., C.W.J. Granger and R.F. Engle (1993), 'A long memory property of stock market returns and a new model', *Journal of Empirical Finance*, **1**, 83–106.

Dominguez, K.M. (1998), 'Central bank intervention and exchange rate volatility', *Journal of International Money and Finance*, **17**, 161–190.

Dominguez, K.M. (2006), 'When do central bank interventions influence intra-daily and longer-term exchange rate movements', *Journal of International Money and Finance*, **25**, 1051–1071.

Eddelbüttel, D. and T.H. McCurdy (1998), 'The impact of news on foreign exchange rates: evidence from high frequency data', unpublished manuscript, Rotman School of Management.

Ederington, L.H. and J.H. Lee (1993), 'How markets process information: news releases and volatility', *Journal of Finance*, **48**, 1161–1191.

Ederington, L.H. and J.H. Lee (1994), 'The response of the dollar/yen exchange rate to economic announcements', *Asia-Pacific Financial Markets*, **1**, 111–128.

Ederington, L.H. and J.H. Lee (1995), 'The short-run dynamics of the price adjustment to new information', *Journal of Financial and Quantitative Analysis*, **30**, 117–134.

Ederington, L.H. and J.H. Lee (2001), 'Intraday volatility in interest-rate and foreign-exchange markets: ARCH, announcement, and seasonality effects', *Journal of Futures Markets*, **21**, 517–552.

Engel, C.M. and J.A. Frankel (1984), 'Why interest rates react to money announcements an explanation from the foreign exchange market', *Journal of Monetary Economics*, **13**, 31–39.

Engle, R.F. (1982), 'Autoregressive conditional heteroscedasticity with estimates of the variance of United Kingdom inflation', *Econometrica*, **50**, 987–1007.

Engle, R.F., T. Ito and W.-L. Lin (1990), 'Meteor showers or heat waves? Heteroskedastic intra-daily volatility in the foreign exchange market', *Econometrica*, **58**, 525–542.

Evans, K. and A. Speight (2010), 'International macroeconomic announcements and intraday euro exchange rate volatility', *Journal of the Japanese and International Economies*, **24**, 552–568.

Evans, M.D.D. (2002), 'FX trading and exchange rate dynamics', *Journal of Finance*, **57**, 2405–2447.

Evans, M.D. and R.K. Lyons (2005), 'Do currency markets absorb news quickly?', *Journal of International Money and Finance*, **24**, 197–217.

Fair, R.C. (2003), 'Shock effects on stocks, bonds, and exchange rates', *Journal of International Money and Finance*, **22**, 307–341.

Fernández, C. and M.F.J. Steel (1998), 'On Bayesian modelling of fat tails and skewness', *Journal of the American Statistical Association*, **93**, 359–371.

Forsberg, L. and T. Bollerslev (2002), 'Bridging the gap between the distribution of realized (ECU) volatility and ARCH modeling (of the euro): the GARCH-NIG model', *Journal of Applied Econometrics*, **17**, 535–548.

Francq, C., R. Roy and J.-M. Zakoïan (2005), 'Diagnostic checking in ARMA models with uncorrelated errors', *Journal of the American Statistical Association*, **100**, 532–544.

Francq, C. and J.-M. Zakoïan (2009), 'Bartlett's formula for a general class of non linear processes', *Journal of Time Series Analysis*, **30**, 449–465.

Fratzscher, M. (2008), 'Communication and exchange rate policy', *Journal of Macroeconomics*, **30**, 1651–1672.

French, K.R., G.W. Schwert and R.F. Stambaugh (1987), 'Expected stock returns and volatility', *Journal of Financial Economics*, **19**, 3–29.

Frömmel, M., A. Mende and L. Menkhoff (2008), 'Order flows, news, and exchange rate volatility', *Journal of International Money and Finance*, **27**, 994–1012.

Galati, G. and W. Melick (1999), 'Perceived central bank intervention and market expectations: an empirical study of the yen/dollar exchange rate, 1993–96', BIS Working Papers, No. 77.

Geweke, J. and S. Porter-Hudak (1983), 'The estimation and application of long memory time series models', *Journal of Time Series Analysis*, **4**, 221–238.

Glosten, L.R., R. Jagannathan and D.E. Runkle (1993), 'On the relation between expected value and the volatility of the nominal excess return on stocks', *Journal of Finance*, **48**, 1779–1801.

Goodhart, C.A.E., S.G. Hall, S.G.B. Henry and B. Pesaran (1993), 'News effects in a high-frequency model of the sterling–dollar exchange rate', *Journal of Applied Econometrics*, **8**, 1–13.

Granger, C.W.J. (1980), 'Long memory relationships and the aggregation of dynamic models', *Journal of Econometrics*, **14**, 227–238.

Granger, C.W.J. and R. Joyeux (1980), 'An introduction to long-memory time series models and fractional differencing', *Journal of Time Series Analysis*, **1**, 15–29.

Grossman, J. (1981), 'The "rationality" of money supply expectations and the short-run response of interest rates to monetary surprises', *Journal of Money, Credit, and Banking*, **13**, 409–424.

Hakkio, C.S. and D.K. Pearce (1985), 'The reaction of exchange rates to economic news', *Economic Inquiry*, **23**, 621–636.

Han, L.-M., J.L. Kling and C.W. Sell (1999), 'Foreign exchange futures volatility: day-of-the-week, intraday, and maturity patterns in the presence of macroeconomic announcements', *Journal of Futures Markets*, **19**, 665–693.

Hansen, B. (1994), 'Autoregressive conditional density estimation', *International Economic Review*, **35**, 705–730.

Hansen, P.R. and A. Lunde (2004), 'An unbiased measure of realized variance', unpublished manuscript.

Hansen, P.R. and A. Lunde (2005a), 'A forecast comparison of volatility models: does anything beat a GARCH(1,1)', *Journal of Applied Econometrics*, **20**, 873–889.

Hansen, P.R. and A. Lunde (2005b), 'A realized variance for the whole day based on intermittent high-frequency data', *Journal of Financial Econometrics*, **3**, 525–554.

Hansen, P.R. and B. Lunde (2006), 'Realized variance and market microstructure noise (with discussion)', *Journal of Business and Economic Statistics*, **24**, 127–218.

Harada, K. and T. Watanabe (2009), 'News effects on high frequency yen/dollar exchange rate and its volatility behavior', Working Paper.

Harvey, C.R. and R.D. Huang (1991), 'Volatility in the foreign currency futures market', *Review of Financial Studies*, **4**, 543–569.

Hecq, A., S. Laurent and F. Palm (2012), 'Common intraday periodicity', *Journal of Financial Econometrics*, **10** (2), 325–353.

Hung, J.H. (1997), 'Intervention strategies and exchange rate volatility: a noise trading perspective', *Journal of International Money and Finance*, **16**, 779–793.

Johnson, G. and T. Schneeweis (1994), 'Jump-diffusion processes in the foreign exchange markets and the release of macroeconomic news', *Computational Economics*, **7**, 309–329.

Joines, D.H., C.S. Kendall and P.E. Kretzmer (1998), 'Excess volatility and the arrival of public information: evidence from currency futures markets', unpublished manuscript.

Jorion, P. (1988), 'On jump processes in the foreign exchange and stock markets', *Review of Financial Studies*, **1**, 427–445.

Lahaye, J., S. Laurent and C.J. Neely (2011), 'Jumps, cojumps and macro announcements', *Journal of Applied Econometrics*, **26**, 893–921.

Lambert, P. and S. Laurent (2000), 'Modelling skewness dynamics in series of financial data', Discussion Paper, Institut de Statistique, Louvain-la-Neuve.

Lambert, P. and S. Laurent (2001), 'Modelling financial time series using {GARCH}-type models and a skewed student density', mimeo, Université de Liège.

Laurent, S., J. Rombouts and F. Violante (2012), 'On the forecasting accuracy of multivariate GARCH models', *Journal of Applied Econometrics*, **27** (6), 1099–1255.

Lecourt, C. (2000), 'Dépendance de court et long terme des rendements de taux de change', *Economie et Prévision*, **5**, 127–137.

Lee, S.S. and J. Hannig (2010), 'Detecting jumps from Lévy jump-diffusion processes', *Journal of Financial Economics*, **96**, 271–290.

Lee, S.S. and P.A. Mykland (2008), 'Jumps in financial markets: a new nonparametric test and jump dynamics', *Review of Financial Studies*, **21**, 2535–2563.

Mancini, C. (2009), 'Non-parametric threshold estimation for models with stochastic diffusion coefficient and jumps', *Scandinavian Journal of Statistics*, **36**, 270–296.

Marazzi, A. and V.J. Yohai (2004), 'Adaptively truncated maximum likelihood regression with asymmetric errors', *Journal of Statistical Planning and Inference*, **122**, 271–291.

Maronna, R.A., D.R. Martin and V.J. Yohai (2006), *Robust Statistics: Theory and Methods*, NewYork: Wiley.

McAleer, M. and M.C. Medeiros (2008), 'Realized volatility: a review', *Econometric Reviews*, **27**, 10–45.

McKenzie, M. and H. Mitchell (2002), 'Generalized asymmetric power ARCH modeling of exchange rate volatility', *Applied Financial Economics*, **12** (3), 555–564.

McQueen,G. and V.V. Roley (1993), 'Stock-prices, news, and business conditions', *Review of Financial Studies*, **6**, 683–707.

Melvin, M. and X. Yin (2000), 'Public information arrival, exchange rate volatility, and quote frequency', *Economic Journal*, **110**, 644–661.

Merton, R.C. (1980), 'On estimating the expected return on the market: an exploratory investigation', *Journal of Financial Economics*, **8**, 323–361.

Mittnik, S. and M.S. Paolella (2000), 'Conditional density and value-at-risk prediction of Asian currency exchange rates', *Journal of Forecasting*, **19**, 313–333.

Neely, C.J. (1999), 'Target zones and conditional volatility: the role of realignments', *Journal of Empirical Finance*, **6**, 177–192.

Neely, C.J. (2005), 'Using implied volatility to measure uncertainty about interest rates', *Federal Reserve Bank of St. Louis Review*, **87**, 407–425.

Neely, C.J. (2008), 'Central bank authorities' beliefs about foreign exchange intervention', *Journal of International Money and Finance*, **27**, 1–25.

Neely, C.J. (2011), 'A foreign exchange intervention in an era of restraint', *Federal Reserve Bank of St. Louis Review*, **93**, 303–324.

Nelson, D.B. (1991), 'Conditional heteroskedasticity in asset returns: a new approach', *Econometrica*, **59**, 349–370.

Nelson, D.B. and C.Q. Cao (1992), 'Inequality constraints in the univariate GARCH model', *Journal of Business and Economic Statistics*, **10**, 229–235.

Oh, S. and H. Lee (2004), 'Foreign exchange exposures and asymmetries of exchange rates: Korean economy is highly vulnerable to exchange rate variations', *Journal of International Financial Management*, **17** (1), 8–21.

Pagan, A. (1996), 'The econometrics of financial markets', *Journal of Empirical Finance*, **3**, 15–102.

Palm, F.C. (1996), 'GARCH models of volatility', in G. Maddala and C. Rao (eds), *Handbook of Statistics*, Amsterdam: Elsevier Science, pp. 209–240.

Payne, R. (1996), 'Announcement effects and seasonality in the intra-day foreign exchange market', FMG Discussion Paper No. DP238, Financial Markets Group.

Pearce, D.K. and V.V. Roley (1985), 'Stock prices and economic news', *Journal of Business*, **58**, 49–67.

Perron, P. (1990), 'Testing for a unit root in a time series with a changing mean', *Journal of Business and Economic Statistics*, **8**, 153–162.

Rigobon, R. and B. Sack (2008), 'Noisy macroeconomic announcements, monetary policy, and asset prices', in J. Campbell (ed.), *Asset Prices and Monetary Policy*, Chicago, IL: University of Chicago Press, pp. 335–370.

Rousseeuw, P. and A. Leroy (1988), 'A robust scale estimator based on the shortest half', *Statistica Neerlandica*, **42**, 103–116.

Savaser, T. (2011), 'Exchange rate response to macro news: through the lens of microstructure', *Journal of International Financial Markets, Institutions and Money*, **21**, 107–126.

Taylor, S.J. and X. Xu (1997), 'The incremental volatility information in one million foreign exchange quotations', *Journal of Empirical Finance*, **4**, 317–340.

Teyssière, G. (1997), 'Double long-memory financial time series', paper presented at the ESEM, Toulouse.

Todorov, V. and G. Tauchen (2006), 'Simulation methods for Lévy-driven CARMA stochastic volatility models', *Journal of Business and Economic Statistics*, **24**, 455–469.

Tschernig, R. (1995), 'Long memory in foreign exchange rates revisited', *Journal of International Financial Markets, Institutions and Money*, **5**, 53–78.

Weiss, A.A. (1986), 'Asymptotic theory for ARCH models: estimation and testing', *Econometric Theory*, **2**, 107–131.

Zakoïan, J.-M. (1994), 'Threshold heteroskedasticity models', *Journal of Economic Dynamics and Control*, **15**, 931–955.

Zhang, L., P.A. Mykland and Y. Aït-Sahalia (2005), 'A tale of two time scales: determining integrated volatility with noisy high frequency data', *Journal of the American Statistical Association*, **100**, 1394–1411.

17 Predicting financial distress of companies: revisiting the Z-Score and ZETA® models[1]

Edward I. Altman

17.1 BACKGROUND

This chapter discusses two of the venerable models for assessing the distress of industrial corporations. These are the so-called Z-Score model (1968) and the ZETA® (1977) credit risk model. Both models are still being used by practitioners throughout the world. The latter is a proprietary model for subscribers to ZETA Services, Inc. (Hoboken, NJ, USA).

The purposes of this summary are twofold. Firstly, those unique characteristics of business failures are examined in order to specify and quantify the variables which are effective indicators and predictors of corporate distress. By doing so, I hope to highlight the analytic as well as the practical value inherent in the use of financial ratios. Specifically, a set of financial and economic ratios will be analyzed in a corporate distress prediction context using a multiple discriminant statistical methodology. Through this exercise, I will explore not only the quantifiable characteristics of potential bankrupts but also the utility of a much-maligned technique of financial analysis: ratio analysis. Although the models that I will discuss were developed in the late 1960s and mid-1970s, I will extend the tests and findings to include applications to firms not traded publicly, to non-manufacturing entities, and also refer to a new bond-rating equivalent model for emerging markets corporate bonds. The latter utilizes a version of the Z-Score model called Z″. This chapter also updates the predictive tests on defaults and bankruptcies through to 1999.

As I first wrote in 1968, and it seems even truer today, academicians seem to be moving toward the elimination of ratio analysis as an analytical technique in assessing the performance of the business enterprise. Theorists downgrade arbitrary rules of thumb (such as company ratio comparisons) widely used by practitioners. Since attacks on the relevance of ratio analysis emanate from many esteemed members of the scholarly world, does this mean that ratio analysis is limited to the world of 'nuts and bolts'? Or has the significance of such an approach been unattractively garbed and therefore unfairly handicapped? Can we bridge the gap, rather than sever the link, between traditional ratio analysis and the more rigorous statistical techniques which have become popular among academicians in recent years? Along with my primary interest, corporate bankruptcy, I am also concerned with an assessment of ratio analysis as an analytical technique.

It should be pointed out that the basic research for much of the material in this paper was performed in 1967 and that several subsequent studies have commented upon the Z-Score model and its effectiveness, including an adaptation in 1995 for credit analysis of emerging market corporates. And this author has co-developed a 'second generation' model (ZETA) which was developed in 1976.

17.2 TRADITIONAL RATIO ANALYSIS

The detection of company operating and financial difficulties is a subject which has been particularly amenable to analysis with financial ratios. Prior to the development of quantitative measures of company performance, agencies were established to supply a qualitative assessment of the credit-worthiness of particular merchants. For instance, the forerunner of the well-known Dun & Bradstreet, Inc. was organized in 1849 in Cincinnati, OH, USA in order to provide independent credit investigation. Formal aggregate studies concerned with portents of business failure were evident in the 1930s.

One of the classic works in the area of ratio analysis and bankruptcy classification was performed by Beaver (1966). In a real sense, his univariate analysis of a number of bankruptcy predictors set the stage for the multivariate attempts, by this author and others, which followed. Beaver found that a number of indicators could discriminate between matched samples of failed and non-failed firms for as long as five years prior to failure. He questioned the use of multivariate analysis, although a discussant recommended attempting this procedure. The Z-Score model did just that. A subsequent study by Deakin (1972) utilized the same 14 variables that Beaver analyzed, but he applied them within a series of multivariate discriminant models.

The aforementioned studies imply a definite potential of ratios as predictors of bankruptcy. In general, ratios measuring profitability, liquidity and solvency prevailed as the most significant indicators. The order of their importance is not clear since almost every study cited a different ratio as being the most effective indication of impending problems.

Although these works established certain important generalizations regarding the performance and trends of particular measurements, the adaptation of the results for assessing the bankruptcy potential of firms, both theoretically and practically, is questionable. In almost every case, the methodology was essentially univariate in nature and emphasis was placed on individual signals of impending problems. Ratio analysis presented in this fashion is susceptible to faulty interpretation and is potentially confusing. For instance, a firm with a poor profitability and/or solvency record may be regarded as a potential bankrupt. However, because of its above-average liquidity, the situation may not be considered serious. The potential ambiguity as to the relative performance of several firms is clearly evident. The crux of the shortcomings inherent in any univariate analysis lies therein. An appropriate extension of the previously cited studies, therefore, is to build upon their findings and to combine several measures into a meaningful predictive model. In so doing, the highlights of ratio analysis as an analytical technique will be emphasized rather than downgraded. The questions are: (1) Which ratios are most important in detecting bankruptcy potential? (2) What weights should be attached to those selected ratios? and (3) How should the weights be objectively established?

17.3 DISCRIMINANT ANALYSIS

After careful consideration of the nature of the problem and of the purpose of this analysis, I chose multiple discriminant analysis (MDA) as the appropriate statistical technique. Although not as popular as regression analysis, MDA has been utilized in a variety of disciplines since its first application in the 1930s. During those earlier years, MDA was used mainly in the biological and behavioral sciences. In recent years, this technique has become increasingly popular in the practical business world as well as in academia. Altman et al. (1981) discusses discriminant analysis in-depth and reviews several financial application areas.

MDA is a statistical technique used to classify an observation into one of several a priori groupings dependent upon the observation's individual characteristics. It is used primarily to classify and/or make predictions in problems where the dependent variable appears in qualitative form; for example, male or female, bankrupt or non-bankrupt. Therefore, the first step is to establish explicit group classifications. The number of original groups can be two or more. Some analysts refer to discriminant analysis as 'multiple' only when the number of groups exceeds two. I prefer that the multiple concepts refer to the multivariate nature of the analysis. After the groups are established, data are collected for the objects in the groups; MDA in its most simple form attempts to derive a linear combination of these characteristics which 'best' discriminates between the groups. If a particular object, for instance, a corporation, has characteristics (financial ratios) which can be quantified for all of the companies in the analysis, the MDA determines a set of discriminant coefficients. When these coefficients are applied to the actual ratios, a basis for classification into one of the mutually exclusive groupings exists. The MDA technique has the advantage of considering an entire profile of characteristics common to the relevant firms, as well as the interaction of these properties. A univariate study, on the other hand, can only consider the measurements used for group assignments one at a time.

Another advantage of MDA is the reduction of the analyst's space dimensionally, that is, from the number of different independent variables to G-1 dimension(s), where G equals the number of original a priori groups. This analysis is concerned with two groups, consisting of bankrupt and non-bankrupt firms. Therefore, the analysis is transformed into its simplest form: one dimension. The discriminant function, of the form $Z = V_1 X_1 + V_2 X_2 + \ldots + V_n X_n$ transforms the individual variable values to a single discriminant score, or Z value, which is then used to classify the object where V_1, $V_2, \ldots V_n$ = discriminant coefficients, and $X_1, X_2, \ldots X_n$ = independent variables.

The MDA computes the discriminant coefficient, V_i, while the independent variables X_i are the actual values. When utilizing a comprehensive list of financial ratios in assessing a firm's bankruptcy potential, there is reason to believe that some of the measurements will have a high degree of correlation or collinearity with each other. While this aspect is not serious in discriminant analysis, it usually motivates careful selection of the predictive variables (ratios). It also has the advantage of potentially yielding a model with a relatively small number of selected measurements which convey a great deal of information. This information might very well indicate differences among groups, but whether or not these differences are significant and meaningful is a more important aspect of the analysis.

Perhaps the primary advantage of MDA in dealing with classification problems is the potential of analyzing the entire variable profile of the object simultaneously rather than sequentially examining its individual characteristics. Just as linear and integer programming have improved upon traditional techniques in capital budgeting, the MDA approach to traditional ratio analysis has the potential to reformulate the problem correctly. Specifically, combinations of ratios can be analyzed together in order to remove possible ambiguities and misclassifications observed in earlier traditional ratio studies.

As we will see, the Z-Score model is a linear analysis in that five measures are objectively weighted and summed up to arrive at an overall score that then becomes the basis for classification of firms into one of the *a priori* groupings (distressed and non-distressed).

17.4   DEVELOPMENT OF THE Z-SCORE MODEL

17.4.1   Sample Selection

The initial sample is composed of 66 corporations with 33 firms in each of the two groups. The bankrupt (distressed) group (Group 1) are manufacturers that filed a bankruptcy petition under Chapter X of the United States (US) National Bankruptcy Act from 1946 through 1965. A 20-year period is not the best choice since average ratios do shift over time. Ideally, I would prefer to examine a list of ratios in time period t in order to make predictions about other firms in the following period (t + 1). Unfortunately, it was not possible to do this because of data limitations. Recognizing that this group is not completely homogeneous (due to industry and size differences), I attempted to make a careful selection of non-bankrupt (non-distressed) firms. Group 2 consists of a paired sample of manufacturing firms chosen on a stratified random basis. The firms are stratified by industry and by size, with the asset size range restricted to between $1 and $25 million. The mean asset size of the firms in Group 2 ($9.6 million) was slightly greater than that of Group 1, but matching the exact asset size of the two groups seemed unnecessary. Firms in Group 2 were still in existence at the time of the analysis. Also, the data collected are from the same years as those compiled for the bankrupt firms. For the initial sample test, the data are derived from financial statements dated one annual reporting period prior to bankruptcy. The data were derived from Moody's Industrial Manuals and also from selected annual reports. The average lead time of the financial statements was approximately seven and one-half months.

An important issue is to determine the asset-size group to be sampled. The decision to eliminate both the small firms (under $1 million in total assets) and the very large companies from the initial sample essentially is due to the asset range of the firms in Group 1. In addition, the incidence of bankruptcy in the large-asset-size firm was quite rare prior to 1966. This changed starting in 1970 with the appearance of several very large bankruptcies, for example PennCentral R.R. Large industrial bankruptcies also increased in appearance since 1978. In all, there have been at least 100 Chapter 11 bankruptcies with over $1 billion in assets since 1978 (the year of the existing Bankruptcy Code's enactment).

A frequent argument is that financial ratios, by their very nature, have the effect of deflating statistics by size, and that therefore a good deal of the size effect is eliminated. The Z-Score model, discussed below, appears to be sufficiently robust to accommodate large firms. The ZETA model did include larger-sized distressed firms and is unquestionably relevant to both small and large firms.

17.4.2 Variable Selection

After the initial groups are defined and firms selected, balance sheet and income state-ment data are collected. Because of the large number of variables found to be significant indicators of corporate problems in past studies, a list of 22 potentially helpful variables (ratios) was complied for evaluation. The variables are classified into five standard ratio categories, including liquidity, profitability, leverage, solvency and activity. The ratios are chosen on the basis of their popularity in the literature and their potential relevance to the study, and there are a few 'new' ratios in this analysis. The Beaver (1966) study concluded that the cash flow to debt ratio was the best single ratio predictor. This ratio was not considered in my 1968 study because of the lack of consistent and precise depre-ciation and cash flow data. The results obtained, however, were still superior to the results Beaver attained with his single best ratio. Cash flow measures were included in the ZETA model tests (see later discussion).

From the original list of 22 variables, five are selected as doing the best overall job together in the prediction of corporate bankruptcy. This profile did not contain all of the most significant variables measured independently. This would not necessarily improve upon the univariate, traditional analysis described earlier. The contribution of the entire profile is evaluated and, since this process is essentially iterative, there is no claim regard-ing the optimality of the resulting discriminant function. The function does however do the best job among the alternatives which include numerous computer runs analyzing different ratio profiles.

In order to arrive at a final profile of variables, the following procedures are utilized: (1) observation of the statistical significance of various alternative functions, including determination of the relative contributions of each independent variable; (2) evaluation of inter-correlations among the relevant variables; (3) observation of the predictive accu-racy of the various profiles; and (4) judgment of the analyst.

The final discriminant function is:

$$Z = 0.012X_1 + 0.014X_2 + 0.033X_3 + 0.006X_4 + 0.999X_5$$

where X_1 = working capital/total assets, X_2 = retained earnings/total assets, X_3 = earn-ings before interest and taxes/total assets, X_4 = market value equity/book value of total liabilities, X_5 = sales/total assets, and Z = overall index.

Note that the model does not contain a constant (Y-intercept) term. This is due to the particular software utilized and, as a result, the relevant cut-off score between the two groups is not zero. Other software programs, such as SAS and SPSS, have a constant term, which standardizes the cut-off score at zero if the sample sizes of the two groups are equal.

X_1, working capital/total assets (WC/TA)

The working capital/total assets ratio, frequently found in studies of corporate prob-lems, is a measure of the net liquid assets of the firm relative to the total capitalization. Working capital is defined as the difference between current assets and current liabilities. Liquidity and size characteristics are explicitly considered. Ordinarily, a firm experi-encing consistent operating losses will have shrinking current assets in relation to total assets. Of the three liquidity ratios evaluated, this one proved to be the most valuable. Two other liquidity ratios tested were the current ratio and the quick ratio. These were found to be less helpful and subject to perverse trends for some failing firms.

X_2, retained earnings/total assets (RE/TA)

Retained earnings is the account which reports the total amount of reinvested earnings and/or losses of a firm over its entire life. The account is also referred to as earned surplus. It should be noted that the retained earnings account is subject to 'manipulation' via corporate quasi-reorganizations and stock dividend declarations. While these occurrences are not evident in this study, it is conceivable that a bias would be created by a substantial reorganization or stock dividend and appropriate readjustments should be made to the accounts.

This measure of cumulative profitability over time is what I referred to earlier as a 'new' ratio. The age of a firm is implicitly considered in this ratio. For example, a relatively young firm will probably show a low RE/TA ratio because it has not had time to build up its cumulative profits. Therefore, it may be argued that the young firm is somewhat discriminated against in this analysis, and its chance of being classified as bankrupt is relatively higher than that of another older firm, *ceteris paribus*. But, this is precisely the situation in the real world. The incidence of failure is much higher in a firm's earlier years. In 1993, approximately 50 percent of all firms that failed did so in the first five years of their existence (Dun & Bradstreet, 1994).

In addition, the RE/TA ratio measures the leverage of a firm. Those firms with high RE, relative to TA, have financed their assets through retention of profits and have not utilized as much debt.

X_3, earnings before interest and taxes/total assets (EBIT/TA)

This ratio is a measure of the true productivity of the firm's assets, independent of any tax or leverage factors. Since a firm's ultimate existence is based on the earning power of its assets, this ratio appears to be particularly appropriate for studies dealing with corporate failure. Furthermore, insolvency in a bankrupt sense occurs when the total liabilities exceed a fair valuation of the firm's assets with value determined by the earning power of the assets. As I will show, this ratio continually outperforms other profitability measures, including cash flow.

X_4, market value of equity/book value of total liabilities (MVE/TL)

Equity is measured by the combined market value of all shares of stock, preferred and common, while liabilities include both current and long term. The measure shows how much the firm's assets can decline in value (measured by market value of equity plus debt) before the liabilities exceed the assets and the firm becomes insolvent. For example, a company with a market value of its equity of $1000 and debt of $500 could experience a two-thirds drop in asset value before insolvency. However, the same firm with $250 equity will be insolvent if assets drop only one-third in value. This ratio adds a market value dimension which most other failure studies did not consider. The reciprocal of X_4 is a slightly modified version of one of the variables used effectively by Fisher (1959) in a study of corporate bond yield-spread differentials. It also appears to be a more effective predictor of bankruptcy than a similar, more commonly used ratio; net worth/total debt (book values). At a later point, I will substitute the book value of net worth for the market value in order to derive a discriminant function for privately held firms (Z') and for non-manufacturers (Z").

More recent models, such as the KMV approach, are essentially based on the market value of equity and its volatility. The equity market value serves as a proxy for the firm's asset values.

X_5, sales/total assets (S/TA)

The capital–turnover ratio is a standard financial ratio illustrating the sales generating ability of the firm's assets. It is one measure of management's capacity to deal with competitive conditions. This final ratio is quite important because it is the least significant ratio on an individual basis. In fact, based on the univariate statistical significance test, it would not have appeared at all. However, because of its unique relationship to other variables in the model, the sales/total assets ratio ranks second in its contribution to the overall discriminating ability of the model. Still, there is a wide variation among industries in asset turnover, and I will specify an alternative model (Z"), without X_5 at a later point.

17.4.3   A Clarification

The reader is cautioned to utilize the model in the appropriate manner. Due to the original computer format arrangement, variables X_1 through X_4 must be calculated as absolute percentage values. For instance, the firm whose net working capital to total assets (X_1) is 10 percent should be included as 10.0 percent and not 0.10. Only variable X_5 (sales to total assets) should be expressed in a different manner: that is, a S/TA ratio of 200 percent should be included as 2.0. The practical analyst may have been concerned by the extremely high relative discriminant coefficient of X_5. This seeming irregularity is due to the format of the different variables. Table 17.1 illustrates the proper specification and form for each of the five independent variables.

Over the years many individuals have found that a more convenient specification of the model is of the form: $Z = 1.2X_1 + 1.4X_2 + 3.3X_3 + 0.6X_4 + 1.0X_5$. Using this formula, one inserts the more commonly written proportion, for example, 0.10 for 10 percent, for the first four variables (X_1-X_4) and rounds the last coefficient off to equal 1.0 (from 0.99). The last variable continues to be written in terms of the number of times.

Table 17.1   Variable means and test significance

Variable	Bankrupt group mean[n](%)	Non-bankrupt group mean[n](%)	F ratio[n]
X_1	−6.1	41.4	32.50*
X_2	−62.6	35.5	58.86*
X_3	−31.8	15.4	26.56*
X_4	40.1	247.7	33.26*
X_5	1.5X	1.9X	2.84

Notes: $N = 33$, $F_{1.60}(0.001) = 12.00$; $F_{1.60}(0.01) = 7.00$; $F_{1.60}(0.05) = 4.00$.* Significant at the 0.001 level.

The scores for individual firms and related group classification and cut-off scores remain identical. We merely point this out and note that we have utilized this format in some practical applications, for example, Altman and LaFleur (1981).

17.4.4   Variable Tests

A test to determine the overall discriminating power of the model is the F-value which is the ratio of the sums-of-squares between-groups to the within-groups sums-of-squares. When this ratio is maximized, it has the effect of spreading the means (centroids) of the groups apart and, simultaneously, reducing dispersion of the individual points (firm Z-values) about their respective group means. Logically, this test is appropriate because the objective of the MDA is to identify and utilize those variables which best discriminate between groups and which are most similar within groups.

The group means of the original two-group sample are:

$$\text{Group 1} = -0.29 \qquad F = 20.7$$
$$\text{Group 2} = +5.02 \qquad F_{4n}(0.01) = 3.84$$

The significance test therefore rejects the null hypothesis that the observations come from the same population.

Variable means measured at one financial statement prior to bankruptcy and the resulting F-statistics were shown in Table 17.1. Variables X_1 through X_4 are all significant at the 0.001 level, indicating extremely significant differences in these variables among groups. Variable X_5 does not show a significant difference among groups and the reason for its inclusion in the variable profile is not apparent as yet. On a strictly univariate basis, all of the ratios indicate higher values for the non-bankrupt firms. Also, all of the discriminant coefficients display positive signs, which is what one would expect. Therefore, the greater a firm's distress potential, the lower its discriminant score. It is clear that four of the five variables display significant differences between groups, but the importance of MDA is its ability to separate groups using multivariate measures.

Once the values of the discriminant coefficients are estimated, it is possible to calculate discriminant scores for each observation in the samples, or any firm, and to assign the observations to one of the groups based on this score. The essence of the procedure is to compare the profile of an individual firm with that of the alternative groupings. The comparisons are measured by a chi-square value and assignments are made based upon the relative proximity of the firms' score to the various group centroids.

17.4.5   Initial Sample (Group 1)

The initial sample of 33 firms in each of the two groups is examined using data compiled one financial statement prior to distress. Since the discriminant coefficients and the group distributions are derived from this sample, a high degree of successful classification is expected. This should occur because the firms are classified using a discriminant function which, in fact, is based upon the individual measurements of these same firms. The classification matrix for the original sample is shown in Table 17.2.

The model is extremely accurate in classifying 95 percent of the total sample correctly.

Table 17.2   Classification results, original sample

	Number correct	% correct	% error	n	Actual	Predicted	
						Group 1	Group 2
					Group 1	31	2
					Group 2	1	32
Type I	31	94	6	33			
Type II	32	97	3	33			
Total	63	95	5	66			

Table 17.3   Classification results, two statements prior to bankruptcy

	Number correct	% correct	% error	n	Actual	Predicted	
						Group 1 (Bankrupt)	Group 2 (Non-bankrupt)
					Group 1	23	9
					Group 2	2	31
Type I	23	72	28	32			
Type II	31	94	6	33			
Total	54	83	17	65			

The Type I error proved to be only 6 percent while the Type II error was even lower at 3 percent. The results, therefore, are encouraging, but the obvious upward bias should be kept in mind, and further validation techniques are appropriate.

17.4.6   Results Two Statements Prior to Bankruptcy

The second test observes the discriminating ability of the model for firms using data compiled two statements prior to distress. The two-year period is an exaggeration since the average lead time for the correctly classified firms is approximately 20 months, with two firms having a 13-month lead. The results are shown in Table 17.3. The reduction in accuracy is understandable because impending bankruptcy is more remote and the indications are less clear. Nevertheless, 72 percent correct assignment is evidence that bankruptcy can be predicted two years prior to the event. The Type II error is slightly larger (6 percent versus 3 percent) in this test, but still it is extremely accurate. Further tests will be applied below to determine the accuracy of predicting bankruptcy as much as five years prior to the actual event.

17.4.7   Potential Bias and Validation Techniques

When the firms used to determine the discriminant coefficients are reclassified, the resulting accuracy is biased upward by: (1) sampling errors in the original sample; and

(2) search bias. The latter bias is inherent in the process of reducing the original set of variables (22) to the best variable profile (five). The possibility of bias due to intensive searching is inherent in any empirical study. While a subset of variables is effective for the initial sample, there is no guarantee that it will be effective for the population in general.

The importance of secondary sample testing cannot be overemphasized. One type of secondary sample testing is to estimate parameters for the model using only a subset of the original sample, and then to classify the remainder of the sample based on the parameters established. A simple t-test is then applied to test the significance of the results. Five different replications of the suggested method of choosing subsets (16 firms) of the original sample are tested.

The test results reject the hypothesis that there is no difference between the groups and substantiate that the model does, in fact, possess discriminating power for observations other than those used to establish the parameters of the model. Therefore, any search bias does not appear significant.

17.4.8   Secondary Sample of Bankrupt Firms

In order to test the model rigorously for both bankrupt and non-bankrupt firms, two new samples are introduced. The first contains a new sample of 25 bankrupt firms whose asset size range is similar to that of the initial bankrupt group. On the basis of the parameters established in the discriminant model to classify firms in this secondary sample, the predictive accuracy for this sample for one statement prior to bankruptcy is described in Table 17.4.

The results here are surprising in that one would not usually expect a secondary sample's results to be superior to the initial discriminant sample (96 percent versus 94 percent). Two possible reasons are that the upward bias normally present in the initial sample tests is not manifested in this investigation and/or that the model, as stated before, is not optimal.

17.4.9   Testing the Model on Subsequent Distressed Firm Samples

In three subsequent tests, I examined 86 distressed companies from 1969–75, 110 bankrupts from 1976–95, and 120 from 1997–99. I found that the Z-Score model, using a cut-off score of 2.675, was between 82 percent and 94 percent accurate. For an in-depth discussion of these studies, see below. In repeated tests up to 1999, the accuracy of the Z-Score model on samples of distressed firms has been in the vicinity of 80–90 percent, based on data from one financial reporting period prior to bankruptcy.

Table 17.4   Classification results, secondary sample of bankrupt firms

	Bankrupt Group (Actual)			Predicted	
	Number correct	% correct	% error	Bankrupt	Non-bankrupt
				24	1
Type I (Total)	24	96	4	n = 25	

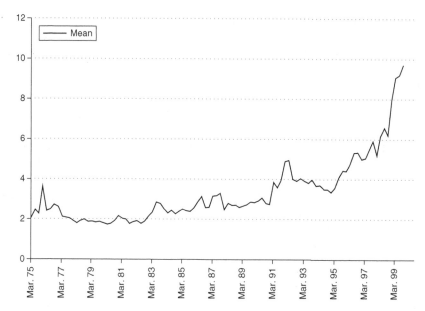

Source: Osler and Hong (2000).

Figure 17.1   Average Z-Scores: US industrial firms 1975–1999

The Type II error (classifying the firm as distressed when it does not go bankrupt), however, has increased substantially with as much as 15–20 percent of all firms and 10 percent of the largest firms having Z-Scores below 1.81. Recent tests, however, show the average Z-Score increasing significantly with the average rising from the 4–5 level in the 1970–95 period to almost 10 in 1999 (see Osler and Hong, 2000 for these results, shown in Figure 17.1). But the median level has not increased much. The majority of increase in average Z-Scores was due to the dramatic climb in stock prices and its impact on X_4.

I advocate using the lower bound of the zone of ignorance (1.81) as a more realistic cut-off Z-Score than the score 2.675. The latter resulted in the lowest overall error in the original tests. In 1999, the proportion of US industrial firms, listed on the Compustat data tapes that had Z-Scores below 1.81, was over 20 percent.

17.4.10   Secondary Sample of Non-Bankrupt Firms

Up to this point, the sample companies were chosen either by their bankruptcy status (Group 1) or by their similarity to Group 1 in all aspects except their economic well-being. But what of the many firms that suffer temporary profitability difficulties yet do not actually become bankrupt? A bankruptcy classification of a firm from this group is an example of a Type II error. An exceptionally rigorous test of the discriminant model's effectiveness would be to search out a large sample of firms that have encountered earnings problems and then to observe the Z-Score's classification results.

In order to perform the above test, a sample of 66 firms is selected on the basis of net income (deficit) reports in the years 1958 and 1961, with 33 from each year. Over 65 percent of these firms had suffered two or three years of negative profits in the previous three years. The firms are selected regardless of their asset size, with the only two criteria being that they were manufacturing firms which suffered losses in the year 1958 or 1961. The companies are then evaluated by the discriminant model to determine their bankruptcy potential.

The results show that 14 of the 66 firms are classified as bankrupt, with the remaining 52 correctly classified. Therefore, the discriminant model correctly classified 79 percent of the sample firms. This percentage is all the more impressive when one considers that these firms constitute a secondary sample of admittedly below-average performance. The t-test for the significance of the result is significant at the 0.001 level. Another interesting facet of this test is the relationship of these 'temporarily' sick firms' Z-Scores with the 'zone of ignorance'. The zone of ignorance is that range of Z-Scores where misclassification can be observed.

Of the 14 misclassified firms in this secondary sample, ten have Z-Scores between 1.81 and 2.67, which indicates that although they are classified as bankrupt, the prediction of their bankruptcy is not as definite as it is for the vast majority in the initial sample of bankrupt firms. In fact, just under one-third of the 66 firms in this last sample have Z-Scores within the entire overlap area, which emphasizes that the selection process is successful in choosing firms which showed signs (profitability) of deterioration. Although these tests are based on data from over 40 years ago, they do indicate the robustness of the model which is still in use today.

17.4.11   Long-Range Accuracy

The previous results give important evidence of the reliability of the conclusions derived from the initial and holdout samples of firms. An appropriate extension would be to examine the overall effectiveness of the discriminant model for a longer period of time prior to bankruptcy.

To answer this question, data are gathered for the 33 original firms from the third, fourth and fifth years prior to bankruptcy. One would expect on an *a priori* basis that, as the lead time increases, the relative predictive ability of any model would decrease. This was true in the univariate studies cited earlier, and it is also quite true for the multiple discriminant model. We will shortly see, however, that the more recent model (e.g., ZETA®) has demonstrated higher accuracy over a longer period of time.

Based on the above results, it is suggested that the Z-Score model is an accurate forecaster of failure up to two years prior to distress, and that accuracy diminishes substantially as the lead time increases. I also performed a trend analysis on the individual ratios in the model. The two most important conclusions of this trend analysis are: (1) that all of the observed ratios show a deteriorating trend as bankruptcy approaches; and (2) that the most serious change in the majority of these ratios occurred between the third and the second years prior to bankruptcy. The degree of seriousness is measured by the yearly change in the ratio values. The latter observation is extremely significant as it provides evidence consistent with conclusions derived from the discriminant model. Therefore, the important information inherent in the individual ratio measurement trends takes on deserved significance only when integrated with the more analytical discriminant analysis findings.

Table 17.5   *Classification and prediction accuracy Z-Score (1968) failure model**

Year prior to failure	Original sample (33) (%)	Holdout sample (25) (%)	1969–75 Predictive sample (86) (%)	1976–95 Predictive sample (110) (%)	1997–99 Predictive sample (120) (%)
1	94 (88)	96 (92)	82 (75)	85 (78)	94 (84)
2	72	80	68	75	74
3	48	–	–	–	–
4	29	–	–	–	–
5	36	–	–	–	–

Note: * Using 2.67 as cut-off score (1.81 cut-off accuracy in parenthesis).

17.4.12   Average Z-Scores over Time

As Table 17.5 shows, I have tested the Z-Score model for various sample periods over the last 30 years. In each test, the Type I accuracy using a cut-off score of 2.67 ranged from 82–94 percent, based on data from one financial statement prior to bankruptcy or default on outstanding bonds. Indeed, in the most recent test, based on 120 firms which defaulted on their publicly held debt during 1997–99, the default prediction accuracy rate was 94 percent (113 out of 120). Using the more conservative 1.81 cut-off, the accuracy rate was still an impressive 84 percent. The 94 percent, 2.67 cut-off accuracy is comparable to the original sample's accuracy which was based on data used to construct the model itself.

We can, therefore, conclude that the Z-Score model has retained its reported high accuracy and is still robust despite its development over 30 years ago. In the last decade, however, the Type II accuracy has increased to about 15–20 percent of those manufacturing firms listed on Compustat.

17.4.13   Adaptation for Private Firms' Application

Perhaps the most frequent inquiry that I have received from those interested in using the Z-Score model is, 'What should we do to apply the model to firms in the private sector?' Credit analysts, private placement dealers, accounting auditors and firms themselves are concerned that the original model is only applicable to publicly traded entities (since X_1 requires stock price data). And, to be perfectly correct, the Z-Score model is a publicly traded firm model and ad hoc adjustments are not scientifically valid. For example, the most obvious modification is to substitute the book value of equity for the market value and then recalculate V_4X_4. Prior to this chapter, analysts had little choice but to follow this procedure since valid alternatives were not available.

17.4.14   A Revised Z-Score Model

Rather than simply insert a proxy variable into an existing model to calculate Z-Scores, I advocate a complete re-estimation of the model, substituting the book value of equity for the market value in X_4. One expects that all of the coefficients will change (not only the

Table 17.6 Revised Z'-Score model: classification results, group means and cut-off boundaries

Actual	Classified		Total
	Bankrupt	Non-bankrupt	
Bankrupt	30	3	33
	(90.9%)	(9.1%)	
Non-bankrupt	1	32	33
	(3.0%)	(97.0%)	

Notes:
Bankrupt group mean = 0.15; non-bankrupt group mean = 4.14.
Z'<1.21 = Zone I (no errors in bankruptcy classification); Z'>2.90 = Zone II (no errors in non-bankruptcy classification); grey area = 1.23 to 2.90.

new variable's parameter) and that the classification criterion and related cut-off scores would also change. That is exactly what happens.

The results of our revised Z-Score model with a new X_4 variable are:

$$Z' = 0.717(X_1) + 0.847(X_2) + 3.107(X_3) + 0.420(X_4) + 0.998(X_5)$$

The equation now looks different than the earlier model; note, for instance, the coefficient for X_1 went from 1.2 to 0.7. But the model looks quite similar to the one using market values. The actual variable that was modified, X_4, showed a coefficient change to 0.42 from 0.6001; that is, it now has less of an impact on the Z-Score. X_3 and X_5 are virtually unchanged. The univariate F-test for the book value of X_4 (25.8) is lower than the 33.3 level for the market value but the scaled vector results show that the revised book value measure is still the third most important contributor.

Table 17.6 lists the classification accuracy, group means, and revised cut-off scores for the Z'-Score model. The Type I accuracy is only slightly less impressive than the model utilizing the market value of equity (91 percent versus 94 percent) but the Type II accuracy is identical (97 percent). The non-bankrupt group's mean Z'-Score is lower than that of the original model (4.14 versus 5.02). Therefore, the distribution of scores is now tighter with larger group overlap. The grey area (or ignorance zone) is wider, however, since the lower boundary is now 1.23 as opposed to 1.81 for the original Z'-Score model. All of this indicates that the revised model is probably somewhat less reliable than the original, but only slightly less. Due to the lack of a private firm database, I have not tested this model extensively on a secondary sample of distressed and non-distressed entities. However, a model from Moody's et al. (2000), utilizing data on middle-market firms and over 1600 defaults, concentrates on private firms.

17.4.15 A Further Revision: Adapting the Model for Non-Manufacturers

The next modification of the Z-Score model analyzed the characteristics and accuracy of a model without X_1, sales/total assets. I do this in order to minimize the potential industry effect which is more likely to take place when such an industry-sensitive variable as asset turnover is included. In addition, I have used this model to assess the financial health of non-US corporates. In particular, Altman et al. (1995) have applied this enhanced Z"-Score model to emerging markets corporates, specifically Mexican firms that had issued Eurobonds denominated in US dollars. The book value of equity was used for X_4 in this case.

The classification results are identical to the revised five-variable model (Z"-Score). The new Z"-Score model is:

$$Z" = 6.56 (X_1) + 3.26 (X_2) + 6.72 (X_3) + 1.05 (X_4).$$

All of the coefficients for variables X_1 to X_4 are changed, as are the group means and cut-off scores. This particular model is also useful within an industry where the type of financing of assets differs greatly among firms and important adjustments, like lease capitalization, are not made. In the emerging market model, we added a constant term of $+3.25$ so as to standardize the scores with a score of zero (0) equated to a D (default) rated bond.

17.4.16   Emerging Market Scoring Model and Process

Emerging markets' credits may initially be analyzed in a manner similar to that used for traditional analysis of US corporates. Once a quantitative risk assessment has emerged, an analyst can then use a qualitative assessment to modify it for such factors as currency and industry risk, industry characteristics, and the firm's competitive position in that industry. It is not often possible to build a model specific to an emerging market country based on a sample from that country because of the lack of credit experience there. To deal with this problem, Altman et al. (1995) have modified the original Altman Z-Score model to create the emerging market scoring (EMS) model.

The process of deriving the rating for a Mexican corporate credit is as follows:

1. The EMS score is calculated, and equivalent rating is obtained based on the calibration of the EMS scores with US bond-rating equivalents (see Table 17.7).
2. The company's bond is then analyzed for the issuing firm's vulnerability concerning the servicing of its foreign currency-denominated debt. This vulnerability is based on the relationship between the non-local currency revenues minus costs, compared with non-local currency expense. Then the level of non-local currency cash flow is compared with the debt coming due in the next year. The analyst adjusts the rating downward depending on the degree of vulnerability seen.
3. The rating is further adjusted downward (or upward) if the company is in an industry considered to be relatively riskier (or less risky) than the bond-rating equivalent from the first EMS result.
4. The rating is further adjusted up or down depending on the dominance of the firm's position in its industry.
5. If the debt has special features, such as collateral or a bona fide guarantor, the rating is adjusted accordingly.
6. Finally, the market value of equity is substituted for the book value in variable X_4, and the resulting bond-rating equivalents are compared. If there are significant differences in the bond-rating equivalents, the final rating is modified, up or down.

Table 17.7   US bond-rating equivalent based on EM score

US equivalent rating	Average EM score
AAA	8.15
AA+	7.60
AA	7.30
AA−	7.00
A+	6.85
A	6.65
A−	6.40
BBB+	6.25
BBB	5.85
BBB−	5.65
BB+	5.25
BB	4.95
BB−	4.75
B+	4.50
B	4.15
B−	3.75
CCC+	3.20
CCC	2.50
CCC−	1.75
D	0

Source: In-depth Data Corp. Average based on over 750 US Corporates with rated debt outstanding: 1994 data.

For relative value analysis, the corresponding US corporates' credit spread is added to the sovereign bond's option-adjusted spread. Only a handful of the Mexican companies were rated by the rating agencies. Thus, risk assessments such as those provided by EMS are often the only reliable indicators of credit risk to overseas investors in Mexico. Altman et al. (1995) report that the modified ratings have proven accurate in anticipating both downgrades and defaults (Grupo Synkro, Situr, GMD, Tribasa, etc.) and upgrades (Aeromexico in July 1995).

17.5   THE ZETA® CREDIT RISK MODEL

Altman et al. (1977) constructed a second generation model with several enhancements to the original Z-Score approach. The purpose of this study was to construct, analyze and test a new bankruptcy classification model which considers explicitly recent develop-ments with respect to business failures. The new study also incorporated refinements in the utilization of discriminant statistical techniques. Several reasons for building a new model, despite the availability of several fairly impressive 'old' models, are presented below and the empirical results seem to substantiate the effort. The new model, which is called ZETA®, was effective in classifying bankrupt companies up to five years prior to failure on a sample of corporations consisting of manufacturers and retailers. Since the ZETA® model is a proprietary effort, I cannot fully disclose the parameters of the market.

17.5.1 Reasons for Attempting to Construct a New Model

There are at least five valid reasons why a revised Z-Score bankruptcy classification model can improve and extend upon those statistical models which had been published in the literature in the prior decade. These include:

1. The change in the size, and perhaps the financial profile, of business failures. The average size of bankrupt firms had increased dramatically with the consequent greater visibility and concern from financial institutions, regulatory agencies and the public at large. Most of the past studies had used relatively small firms in their samples with the exception of Altman's (1973) railroad study and the commercial bank studies. Any new model should be as relevant as possible to the population to which it will eventually be applied. This present study utilizes a bankrupt firm sample where the average asset size two annual reporting periods prior to failure was approximately $100 million. No firm had less than $20 million in assets.
2. Following (1) above, a new model should be as current as possible with respect to the temporal nature of the data.
3. Past failure models concentrated either on the broad classification of manufacturers or on specific industries. I feel that with the appropriate analytical adjustments, retailing companies, a particularly vulnerable group, could be analyzed on an equal basis with manufacturers.
4. An important feature of this study is that the data and footnotes to financial statements have been scrupulously analyzed to include the most recent changes in financial reporting standards and accepted accounting practices. Indeed, in at least one instance, a change which was scheduled to be implemented in a very short time was applied. The purpose of these modifications was to make the model not only relevant to past failures, but to the data that will appear in the future. The predictive as well as the classification accuracy of the ZETA® model is implicit.
5. To test and assess several of the then recent advances and still controversial aspects of discriminant analysis.

17.5.2 Principal Findings

In Altman et al. (1977) we concluded that the new ZETA® model for bankruptcy classification appeared to be quite accurate for up to five years prior to failure with successful classification of well over 90 percent of the sample one year prior and 70 percent accuracy up to five years. We also observed that the inclusion of retailing firms in the same model as manufacturers does not seem to affect the results negatively. This is probably true due to the adjustments to the data based on recent and anticipated financial reporting changes – primarily the capitalization of leases.

We also find that the ZETA® model outperformed alternative bankruptcy classification strategies in terms of expected cost criteria utilizing prior probabilities and explicit cost of error estimates. In the investigation, we were surprised to observe that, despite the statistical properties of the data which indicate that a quadratic structure is appropriate, the linear structure of the same model outperformed the quadratic in tests of model validity. This was especially evident regarding the long-term accuracy of the model and in holdout sample testing.

17.5.3 Sample and Data Characteristics and Statistical Methodology Sample Characteristics

Our two samples of firms consist of 53 bankrupt firms and a matched sample of 58 non-bankrupt entities. The latter are matched to the failed group by industry and year of data. Our sample is almost equally divided into manufacturers and retailer groups and 94 percent of the firms failed during the period 1969–75. The average asset size of the failed group is almost $100 million, indicative of the increasing size of failures. The bankrupt firms represent all publicly held industrial failures which had at least $20 million in assets, with no known fraud involved and where sufficient data was available. Five non-bankruptcy petition companies were included due to either: (1) substantial government support; (2) a forced merger; or (3) where the banks took over the business or accepted a distressed restructuring rather than forcing the Chapter 11 petition.

17.5.4 Variables Analyzed

A number of financial ratios and other measures have been found in other studies to be helpful in providing statistical evidence of impending failures. We have assembled data to calculate these variables and in addition have included several 'new' measures that were thought to be potentially helpful as well. The 28 variables are listed in the Appendix, along with certain relevant statistics which will be discussed shortly. Note that in a few cases – such as nos 7 and 8, tangible assets and interest coverage – the variables are expressed in logarithmic form in order to reduce outlier possibilities and to adhere to statistical assumptions. The variables can be classified as profitability (1–6), coverage and other earnings relative to leverage measures (8–14), liquidity (15–18), capitalization ratios (19–23), earnings variability (24–26) and a few miscellaneous measures (7 and 27).

17.5.5 Reporting Adjustments

As noted earlier, we adjusted the basic data of our sample to consider explicitly several of the most recent and, in our opinion, the most important accounting modifications. These adjustments include the following:

1. Capitalization of leases. Without doubt, the most important and pervasive adjustment made was to capitalize all non-cancelable operating and finance leases. The resulting capitalized lease amount was added to the firms' assets and liabilities and also we have imputed an interest cost to the 'new' liability. The procedure involved preparation of schedules of current and expected lease payment obligations from information found in footnotes to the financial statements. The discount rate used to capitalize leases was the average interest rate for new-issue, high-grade corporate

bonds in the year being analyzed plus a risk premium of 10 percent of the interest rate. An amount equal to the interest rate used in the capitalization process times the capitalized lease amount is added to interest costs. Subsequent to our analysis, FASB 13 (1980) stipulated that the appropriate discount rate to use is the lessee's cost of debt capital (before taxes) or the internal rate of return on the lease to the lessor, whichever is lower.

2.   Reserves. If the firms' reserves were of a contingency nature, they were included in equity and income was adjusted for the net change in the reserve for the year. If the reserve was related to the valuation of certain assets, it was netted against those assets. If the reserve is for contingent liabilities, for example lawsuits, then it is added to the liabilities. This was the case for Johns Manville (1982) and A.H. Robins (1985) and several other healthcare lawsuits.

3.   Minority interests and other liabilities on the balance sheet. These items were netted against other assets. This allows for a truer comparison of earnings with the assets generating the earnings.

4.   Captive finance companies and other non-consolidated subsidiaries. These were consolidated with the parent company accounts as well as the information would allow. The pooling of interest method was used. This was made mandatory by the Financial Accounting Standards Foundation (FASF) in 1987.

5.   Goodwill and intangibles. Deducted from assets and equity because of the difficulty in assigning economic value to them.

6.   Capitalized research and development costs, capitalized interest and certain other deferred charges. These costs were expensed rather than capitalized. This was done to improve comparability and to give a better picture of actual funds flows.

17.5.6   Statistical Methodology

Distress classification was again attempted via the use of a multivariate statistical technique known as discriminant analysis. In this study, the results using both linear and quadratic structure are analyzed. The test for assessing whether a linear or quadratic structure is appropriate – sometimes referred to as the H_1 test – provides the proper guidance when analyzing a particular sample's classification characteristics. Essentially, if it is assessed that the variance–covariance matrices of the G groups are statistically identical, then the linear format which pools all observations is appropriate. If, however, the dispersion matrices are not identical, then the quadratic structure will provide the more efficient model since each group's characteristics can be assessed independently as well as between groups. Efficiency will result in more significant multivariate measures of group differences and greater classification accuracy of that particular sample. What has not been assessed up to this point is the relative efficiency of the linear versus quadratic structures when the sample data are not the same as those used to construct the model, that is, holdout or secondary samples. I will analyze this point in the next section.

17.6   EMPIRICAL RESULTS

17.6.1   The Seven-Variable Model

After an iterative process of reducing the number of variables, we selected a seven-variable model which not only classified our test sample well, but also proved the most reliable in various validation procedures. That is, we could not significantly improve upon the results by adding more variables, and no model with fewer variables performed as well:

- X_1 Return on assets, measured by the earnings before interest and taxes/total assets. This variable has proven to be extremely helpful in assessing firm performance in several past multivariate studies.
- X_2 Stability of earnings, measured by a normalized measure of the standard error of estimate around a five- to ten-year trend in X_1. Business risk is often expressed in terms of earnings fluctuations and this measure proved to be particularly effective. We did assess the information content of several similar variables which attempted to measure the potential susceptibility of a firm's earnings level to decline which could jeopardize its ability to meet its financial commitments. These variables were quite significant on a univariate basis but did not enter into our final multivariate model.
- X_3 Debt service, measured by the familiar interest coverage ratio, that is, earnings before interest and taxes/total interest payments (including that amount imputed from the capitalized lease liability). We have transposed this measure by taking the log 10 in order to improve the normality and homoskedasticity of this measure.
- X_4 Cumulative profitability, measured by the firm's retained earnings (balance sheet)/total assets. This ratio, which imputes such factors as the age of the firm, debt and dividend policy as well as its profitability record over time, was found to be quite helpful in the Z-Score model, discussed earlier. As the results will show, this cumulative profitability measure is unquestionably the most important variable measured univariately and multivariately.
- X_5 Liquidity, measured by the familiar current ratio. Despite previous findings that the current ratio was not as effective in identifying failures as some other liquidity measures, we now find it slightly more informative than others, such as the working capital/total assets ratio.
- X_6 Capitalization, measured by common equity/total capital. In both the numerator and the denominator, the common equity is measured by a five-year average of the total market value, rather than book value. The denominator also includes preferred stock at liquidating value, long-term debt and capitalized leases. We utilized a five-year average to smooth out possible severe, temporary market fluctuations and to add a trend component (along with X_2 above) to the study.
- X_7 Size, measured by the firms' total assets. This variable, as is the case with the others, was adjusted for financial reporting changes. No doubt, the capitalization of leasehold rights has added to the average asset size of both the bankrupt and non-bankrupt groups. We also transformed the size variable to help normalize

the distribution of the variable due to outlier observations. Again, a logarithmic transformation was applied.

17.6.2   Relative Importance of Discriminant Variables

The procedure of reducing a variable set to an acceptable number is closely related to an attempt to determine the relative importance within a given variable set. Several of the prescribed procedures for attaining the 'best' set of variables, for example stepwise analysis, can also be used as a criterion for ranking importance. Unfortunately, there is no one best method for establishing a relative ranking of variable importance. Hence, we assessed this characteristic by analyzing the ranks suggested by five different tests. These tests are (1) forward stepwise; (2) backward stepwise; (3) scaled vector (multiplication of the discriminant coefficient by the appropriate variance–covariance matrix item); (4) separation of means test; (5) the conditional deletion test, which measures the additional contribution of the variable to the multivariate F-test given that the other variables have already been included. In several studies that we have observed, the rankings across these tests are not very consistent and the researcher is left with a somewhat ambiguous answer. This was definitely not the case in our study.

Regardless of which test statistic is observed, the most important variable is the cumulative profitability ratio, X_4. In fact, our scaled vector analysis indicates that this single ratio contributes 25 percent of the total discrimination. Second in importance is the stability of earnings ratio (X_2) and, except for the univariate test of significance, it too has a consistency across tests.

17.6.3   Linear versus Quadratic Analysis

The H_1 test of the original sample characteristics clearly rejects the hypothesis that the group dispersion matrices are equal. Therefore, the linear structure classification rule (excluding error costs), is not appropriate and the quadratic structure appears to be the more efficient one.

As can be observed in Table 17.8, the quadratic and linear models yield essentially equal total sample accuracy results for the original sample classifications, but the holdout sample test indicates a clear superiority for the linear framework. This creates

Table 17.8   Overall classification accuracy (%)

Years prior to bankruptcy	Bankrupt firms		Non-bankrupt firms		Total	
	Linear	Quadratic	Linear	Quadratic	Linear	Quadratic
1 Original sample	96.2	94.3	89.7	91.4	92.8	92.8
2 (Lachenbruch validation test)	(92.5)	(85.0)	(89.7)	(87.9)	(91.0)	(86.5)
3 Holdout	84.9	77.4	93.1	91.9	89.0	84.7
4 Holdout	74.5	62.7	91.4	92.1	83.5	78.9
5 Holdout	68.1	57.4	89.5	87.8	79.8	74.0
6 Holdout	69.8	46.5	82.1	87.5	76.8	69.7

a dilemma and we have chosen to concentrate on the linear test due to: (1) the possible high sensitivity to individual sample observations of the quadratic parameters (that is, we observe 35 different parameters in the quadratic model compared with only seven in the linear case, not including the intercept); and (2) the fact that all of the relative tests of importance are based on the linear model.

17.6.4   Classification Accuracy: Original and Holdout Samples

Table 17.8 presents classification and holdout sample accuracy of the original sample based on data from one year prior to bankruptcy. Lachenbruch (1967) suggests an almost unbiased validation test of original sample results by means of a type of jack-knife, or one isolated observation at a time approach. The individual observations' classification accuracy is then cumulated over the entire sample. Years 2–5 'holdout' sample results are also presented. These results are listed for both the linear and quadratic structures of the seven variable model.

The linear model's accuracy, based on one year prior data, is 96.2 percent for the bankrupt group and 89.7 percent for the non-bankrupt. The upward bias in these results appears to be slight since the Lachenbruch results are only 3 percent less for the failed group and identical for the non-failed group. As expected, the failed group's classification accuracy is lower as the data become more remote from bankruptcy, but still quite high. In fact, we observe 70 percent accuracy as far back as five years prior to failure. This compares very favorably to the results recorded by the Z-Score model, where the accuracy dropped precipitously after two years prior.

An interesting result was observed by comparing the quadratic structure's results for that of the linear model (Table 17.8). As noted earlier, the total samples' classification accuracy is identical for the two structures in period 1, with the linear showing a slight edge in the bankrupt group and the quadratic in the non-bankrupt group. The most obvious and important differences, however, are in the validation and 'holdout' tests of the bankrupt group. Here, the linear model is clearly superior, with the quadratic misclassifying over 50 percent of the future bankrupts five years prior. The Lachenbruch validation test also shows a large bankrupt classification accuracy difference (over 7 percent favoring the linear model). Subsequent analysis will report only the linear results.

17.6.5   Comparison with the Z-Score Model

Table 17.9 compares the original sample classification accuracy and also the accuracy for up to five years prior to financial distress of the Z-Score and ZETA® models. Note that the one-year prior classification accuracy of bankrupt firms is quite similar for both models (96.2 percent for ZETA® and 93.9 percent for Z-Score), but that the accuracy is consistently higher for the ZETA® model in years 2–5 prior to the distress date. Indeed, by the fifth year, the ZETA® model is still about 70 percent accurate but the Z-Score's accuracy falls to 36 percent. Note also that the Z-Score's accuracy on the ZETA® sample (columns 6 and 7) is actually considerably higher in years 2–5 than on the original sample. Finally, when we recalibrate the Z-Score model's coefficients based on the ZETA® sample, the classification results (column 8) are much better than the originals (column 4) in all but the first year prior.

Table 17.9   Classification accuracy between the ZETA model and various forms of the Z-Score model (%)

Year prior to bankruptcy (1)	ZETA model		Altman's 1968 model		1968 model, ZETA sample		1968 variables, ZETA parameters	
	Bankrupt (2)	Non-bankrupt (3)	Bankrupt (4)	Non-bankrupt (5)	Bankrupt (6)	Non-bankrupt (7)	Bankrupt (8)	Non-bankrupt (9)
1	96.2	89.7	93.9	97.0	86.8	82.4	92.5	84.5
2	84.9	93.1	71.9	93.9	1	89.3	83.0	86.2
3	74.5	91.4	48.3	n.a.	2	91.4	72.7	89.7
4	68.1	89.5	28.6	n.a.	3	86.0	57.5	83.0
5	69.8	82.1	36.0	n.a.	4	86.2	44.2	82.1

450

17.6.6 Group Prior Probabilities, Error Costs and Model Efficiency

Earlier, we showed the classification rules for both linear and quadratic analyses. If one assumes equal prior probabilities of group membership, the linear model will result in a cut-off or critical score of zero. This is due to the constant term in the ZETA® model. All firms scoring above zero are classified as having characteristics similar to the non-bankrupt group and those with negative scores similar to bankrupts. The same zero cut-off score will result if one desired to minimize the total cost of misclassification. That is, assuming multi-normal populations and a common covariance matrix, the optimal cut-off score ZETA®, is equal to:

$$ZETA_c = \ln\left(\frac{q_1 C_1}{q_2 C_{11}}\right)$$

where q_1, q_2 = prior probability of bankrupt (q_1) or non-bankrupt (q_2), and C_1, C_{11} = costs of type I and type II errors, respectively.

Further, if one wanted to compare the efficiency of the ZETA® bankruptcy classification model with alternative strategies, the following cost function is appropriate for the expected cost of ZETA (EC_{ZETA}).

$$EC_{ZETA} = q_1 (M_{12} / N_1)C_1 + q_2 (M_{21} / N_2)C_{11},$$

where M_{12}, M_{21} = observed type I and type II errors (misses) respectively, and N_1, N_2 = number of observations in the bankrupt (N_1) and non-bankrupt (N_2) groups.

In our tests, we have implicitly assumed equal prior probabilities and equal costs of errors, resulting in a zero cut-off score. We are actually aware, however, of the potential bias involved in doing so. Instead of attempting earlier to integrate probability priors and error costs, we have assumed equal estimates for each parameter, because to a great extent the two parameters neutralize each other, and it was much easier than attempting to state them precisely. The following is our reasoning.

The 'correct' estimate of q_1 is probably in the 0.01–0.05 range. That is, the prior probability that a firm will go bankrupt within one or two years in the future is probably in this 0.01–0.05 range. Although the ZETA® model's parameters are based on data from one year prior to bankruptcy, it is not specifically a one-year prediction model. The procedure in this sense is atemporal. It is, in our opinion, incorrect to base one's prior probability estimates on a single year's reported statistics. In addition, there are many definitions of financial distress which economically approximate bankruptcy. These include non-judicial arrangements, extreme liquidity problems which require the firm's creditors or other external forces to take over the business or agree to a distressed restructuring (composition or extension of claims), bond default, and so on. In the final analysis, we simply do not know the precise estimate of bankruptcy priors, but at the same time assert that one must assume the estimate to be greater than a single year's reported data. Hence, we believe the prior probability estimate is in the 1–5 percent range and in the subsequent analysis we utilize the 2 percent fiture.

17.6.7 Cost of Classification Errors

Another input that is imperative to the specification of an alternative to the zero cut-off score is the cost of error in classification. No study prior to the ZETA® analysis (Altman et al. 1977) had explicitly included this element. In an attempt to incorporate the cost component into an analysis of model efficiency, it is necessary to specify the decision-maker's role. In this study we utilize the commercial bank loan function as the framework of analysis. The type I bankruptcy classification is analogous to that of an accepted loan that defaulted and the type II error to a rejected loan that would have resulted in a successful payoff. Many of the commercial factors involved in assessing these error costs were first noted in an excellent discussion (following Beaver's 1966 paper) by Neter.

An empirical study was performed to assess the costs of these lending errors with the following specification for the equivalent type I (C_1) and type II (C_{11}) error costs:

$$C_1 = 1 - \frac{LLR}{GLL}, C_{11} = r - i,$$

where:

LLR	=	amount of loan losses, recovered
GLL	=	gross loan losses (charged-off)
r	=	effective interest rate on the loan
i	=	effective opportunity cost for the bank

The commercial bank takes the risk of losing all or a portion of the loan should the applicant eventually default. The exact amount is a function of the success the bank has in recovering the loan principal. We are quite aware that there are additional costs involved in the recovery process, including legal, transaction and loan charge-off officer opportunity costs. These costs are not reported but obviously increase the type I error cost. In addition, if the type II error (C_{11}) is positive, i.e., $r > 1$, then there will be an added cost element in C_1. This added element involves the lost interest on that remaining part of the loan which is not recovered (GLL-LLR) for the duration of the defaulted loan. We will examine C_{11} below, but will not include this added element in our calculation of C_1. Again, however, it is clear that we are underestimating C_1 somewhat.

17.6.8 Recoveries in the Public Bond Market

While there have been almost no rigorous studies published which quantify the effective costs of lending errors for loans and other private placements, a number of recent studies have documented losses in the public bond markets, for example Altman and Eberhart (1994), Moody's (1995) and Standard & Poor's (1995). The former documents recoveries at default and also upon emergence from Chapter 11 bankruptcy. These public bond market studies observe recoveries stratified by bond seniority. For commercial loans, the most likely equivalents to the public bond market are the straight (non-convertible) senior secured and senior unsecured classes. Table 17.10 lists these recoveries at the time of default and upon emergence from Chapter 11.

Table 17.10   *Bond recoveries (% of par value), by seniority, at default and upon emergence from Chapter 11*

Bond priority	N	Recovery at default	Recovery upon emergence
Senior secured	24	60.51	100.91
Senior unsecured	71	52.28	81.05
Senior subordinated	35	30.70	23.38
Subordinated	54	27.96	32.41

Sources: Altman and Eberhart (1994) and Altman (1993).

We have measured C_1 based on annual report data from 26 of the largest US commercial banks and questionnaire returns from a sample of smaller, regional banks in the Southeast US. A questionnaire was sent to approximately 100 Southeast banks with 33 usable responses. The range of commercial bank asset sizes in this small-bank sample was between $12 million and $3 billion, with the average equal to $311 million and the median equal to $110 million. The large-bank sample's asset size averaged $13.4 billion with a $10 billion median.

Both the data sources encompass a five-year period, 1971–75 inclusive, and we measure the average loan loss recovery statistics for senior unsecured loans on a contemporary and a one-year lag (recoveries lagging charge-offs) basis. The results of this investigation show that the average C_1 on a contemporary basis is in the 76.7–83.0 percent range; when measured on a one-year lag basis, the averages are lower (68.6–72.2 percent). The year 1975 was an abnormally high loan charge-off year in the US banking system and since these data are included in the contemporary statistics but not in the one-year lag data, we believe the more representative result for C_1 is in the vicinity of 70 percent. We use this statistic for C_1.

The simple formula for C_{11} specifies that the decision not to lend to an account that would have repaid successfully forgoes the return on that loan, but the loss is mitigated by the alternative use of loanable funds. In its strictest sense, the bank's opportunity cost implies another loan at the same risk which is assumed to pay off. In this case, C_{11} is probably zero or extremely small. Conservatively speaking, however, an account that is rejected due to its high risk characteristics and alternative uses will probably carry lower risk attributes. Hence, r-i will be positive but still quite low. Carried to the other extreme, the alternative use would be an investment in a riskless asset, that is, government securities of the same maturity as the loan, and r-i will be somewhat higher – perhaps 2–4 percent. The relationship between r-i will vary over time and is particularly sensitive to the demand and supply equilibrium relationship for loanable funds. As an approximation, we specify $C_{11} = 2\%$, hence C_1/C_{11} is equal to 35 times (0.70/0.02).

17.6.9 Revised Cut-Off Score and Model Efficiency Tests

With respect to the calculation of the critical or cut-off score ZETA®, we have:

$$ZETA_c = \ln\left(\frac{q_1 C_1}{q_2 C_{11}}\right) = \frac{0.02 \times 0.70}{0.98 \times 0.02} = \ln 0.714,$$

$$ZETA_c = -0.338.$$

Before comparing the efficiency of the various alternative bankruptcy classification strategies, it should be noted that the observed classification accuracy of a model such as ZETA® will change with the new cut-off score. For example, with the cut-off score of −0.337, the number of type I errors increases from two (3.8 percent) to four (7.6 percent), while the number of type II errors decreases from six (10.3 percent) to four (7.0 percent).

17.6.10 Adjustments to the Cut-Off Score and Practical Applications

In addition to the utilization of prior probabilities of group membership and cost estimates of classification errors for comparative model efficiency assessment, these inputs could prove valuable for practical application purposes. For instance, the bank lending-officer or loan review analyst may wish to be able to logically adjust the critical cut-off score to consider their own estimates of group priors and error costs and/or to reflect current economic conditions in the analysis. One could imagine the cut-off score falling (thereby lowering the acceptance criterion) as business conditions improve and the banker's prior probability of bankruptcy estimate falls from say 0.02 to 0.015. Or, a rise in cut-off scores could result from a change (rise) in the estimate of the type I error cost vis-à-vis the type II error cost. The latter condition will possibly occur for different decision-makers. For instance, the cost to a portfolio manager of not selling a security destined for failure is likely to be extremely high relative to their cost of not investing in a stock (which does not fail) due to its relatively low ZETA®. The portfolio manager may indeed want to raise the cut-off or threshold level to reduce the possibility of intangible (lawsuit) as well as tangible (lower prices) costs involved with holding a failed company's stock.

Another example of a practical application of cut-off score adjustment is the case of an accounting auditor. They might wish to use the model to decide whether a 'going concern' qualified opinion should be applied. Their expected cost for doing so is likely to be quite high (loss of client) relative to the expected cost of a stockholder law suit. This might lead to a fairly low cut-off score. On the other hand, the environment may be such that the lawsuit expected cost is prohibitive.

17.7 CONCLUSIONS

The ZETA® model for assessing the bankruptcy risk of corporations demonstrates improved accuracy over an existing failure classification model (the Z-Score) and, perhaps more importantly, is based on data more relevant to current conditions and to a larger number of industrial firms. Recall, however, our use of the Z" model for non-manufacturers. We are concerned with refining existing distress classification techniques by the use of the most relevant data combined with developments in the application of discriminant analysis to finance. The ZETA® model's bankruptcy classification accuracy ranges from over 96 percent (93 percent holdout) one period prior to bankruptcy, to 70 percent five annual reporting periods prior. We have assessed the effect of several elements involved with the application of discriminant analysis to financial problems. These include linear versus quadratic analysis for the original and holdout samples, introduction of prior probabilities of group membership and costs of error estimates into the classification rule, and comparison of the model's results with naive bankruptcy classification strategies.

The potential applications of the ZETA® bankruptcy identification model are in the same spirit as previously developed models. These include creditworthiness analysis of firms for financial and non-financial institutions, identification of undesirable investment risk for portfolio managers and individual investors, and to aid in more effective internal and external audits of firms with respect to going-concern considerations, among others.

NOTE

1. This chapter is adapted and updated from Altman (1968) and Altman et al. (1977).

REFERENCES

Altman, E. (1968), 'Financial ratios, discriminant analysis and the prediction of corporate bankruptcy', *Journal of Finance*, **23**, 589–609.

Altman, E. (1973), 'Predicting railroad bankruptcies in America', *Bell Journal of Economics and Management Service*, **4**, 184–211.

Altman, E. (1993), *Corporate Financial Distress and Bankruptcy*, 2nd edn, New York: John Wiley & Sons.

Altman, E.I., R.A. Avery, A.A. Eisenbeis and J.F. Sinkey (1981), *Application of Classification Techniques in Business, Banking and Finance*, Greenwich: Jai Press.

Altman, E. and A.C. Eberhart (1994), 'Do seniority provisions protect bondholders' investments?', *Journal of Portfolio Management*, **20**, 67–75.

Altman, E., R. Haldeman and P. Narayanan (1977), 'ZETA analysis: a new model to identify bankruptcy risk of corporations', *Journal of Banking and Finance*, **1**, 29–54.

Altman, E., J. Hartzell and M. Peck (1995), 'Emerging markets corporate bonds: a scoring system', New York: Salomon Brothers.

Altman, E. and J.K. LaFleur (1981), 'Managing a return to financial health', *Journal of Business Strategy*, **2**(1), 31–38.

Beaver, W. (1966), 'Financial ratios as predictors of failures', *Journal of Accounting Research*, **4** (Supplement), 71–111.

Deakin, E.B. (1972), 'A discriminant analysis of predictors of business failure', *Journal of Accounting Research*, **10**, 167–179.

Dun & Bradstreet (1994), *The Failure Record*.

Fisher, L. (1959), 'Determinants of risk premiums on corporate bonds', *Journal of Political Economy*, **67**, 217–237.

Lachenbruch, P.A. (1967), 'An almost unbiased method of obtaining confidence intervals for the probability of misclassification in discriminant analysis', *Biometrics*, **23**, 639–645.

Moody's (1995), 'Corporate bond defaults and default rates', L. Carty, D. Lieberman and J. Fons, January.

Moody's, E. Falkensten, A. Boral and L. Carty (2000), 'RiskCalc™ private model: Moody's default model for private firms', Global Credit Research, May.

Osler, C. and G. Hong (2000), *Rapidly Rising Corporate Debt: Are Firms Now Vulnerable to an Economic Slowdown?*, Current Issues in Economics & Finance, Federal Reserve Bank of New York, June.

Standard & Poor's (1995), 'Corporate defaults level off in 1994', L. Brand, T.K. Ho and R. Bahar, CreditWeek, May 1.

APPENDIX

Table 17A.1   Listing of all variables, group mean, and F-tests based on one period prior to bankruptcy data (ZETA model sample)

No.	Name	Population means Failed	Population means Non-failed	Univariate F-test
1	EBIT/TA	−0.0055	0.1117	54.3
2	NATC/TC	−0.0297	0.0742	36.6
3	Sales/TA	1.3120	1.6200	3.3
4	Sales/TC	2.1070	2.1600	0.0
5	EBIT/Sales	0.0020	0.0070	30.2
6	NATC/Sales	−0.0153	0.0400	33.1
7	Log tang. assets	1.9854	2.2220	5.5
8	Interest coverage	−0.5995	5.3410	26.1
9	Log no. (8)	0.9625	1.1620	26.1
10	Fixed charge coverage	0.2992	2.1839	15.7
11	Earnings/debt	−0.0792	0.1806	32.8
12	Earnings 5 yr. maturities	−0.1491	0.6976	8.8
13	Cash flow/fixed charges	0.1513	2.9512	20.9
14	Cash flow/TD	−0.0173	0.3136	31.4
15	WC/LTD	0.3532	2.4433	6.0
16	Current ratio	1.5757	2.6040	38.2
17	WC/total assets	0.1498	0.3086	40.6
18	WC/cash expenses	0.1640	0.2467	5.2
19	Ret.earn/total assets	−0.0006	0.2935	114.6
20	Book equity/TC	0.2020	0.5260	64.5
21	MV equity/TC	0.3423	0.6022	32.1
22	5yr.MV equity/TC	0.4063	0.6210	31.0
23	MV equity/total liabilities	0.6113	1.8449	11.6
24	Standard error of estimate of EBIT/TA (norm)	1.6870	5.784	33.8
25	EBIT drop	−3.2272	3.179	9.9
26	Margin drop	−0.2173	0.179	15.6
27	Capital lease/assets	0.2514	0.178	4.2
28	Sales/fixed assets	3.1723	4.179	3.5

Notes: EBIT = earnings before interest and taxes; NATC = net available for total capital; TA = total tangible assets; LTD = long term debt; MV = market value of equity; TC = total capital; TD = total debt; WC = working capital; CF = cash flow (before interest #13, after interest #14).

18 Quantifying time variation and asymmetry in measures of covariance risk: a simulation approach

Ólan T. Henry, Nilss Olekalns and Kalvinder K. Shields

18.1   INTRODUCTION

It is well known that equity returns display volatility clustering (Mandelbrot, 1962). This implies that in periods of relatively high risk, the rational risk-averse investor will demand a relatively high expected return and be willing to pay more to hedge exposure to volatility. Similarly, there is evidence that equity volatility responds asymetrically to news; for example, Engle and Ng (1993) argue that bear markets are more volatile than bull markets, all else being equal. If this is the case, then the price of risk should display asymmetry. Braun et al. (1995), Engle and Cho (1999) and Brooks and Henry (2000) detect evidence of such asymmetric responses in various equity markets.

In this chapter we present new methods based upon the variance impulse response function methodology of Shields et al. (2005) to detect and quantify the dynamic response to news of measures of undiversifiable risk and benefits to diversification. We demonstrate how these dynamic responses can be used to construct time profiles measuring the effects of news on the future behaviour of unobserved variables such as rates of expected return, conditional correlations, and measures of systematic risk and benefits to diversification. We develop metrics based upon these time profiles to investigate whether these unobserved variables respond asymmetrically in a statistically significant and economically important fashion to news.[1] We illustrate the usefulness of this approach with a simple example, namely the international capital asset pricing model (ICAPM).

This chapter has six further sections. Section 18.2 outlines the CAPM in an international setting. The methods used to capture time variation and asymmetry in measures of country risk are discussed in the section 18.3. An empirical application is presented in sections 18.4 to 18.6. The final section presents a summary and some concluding comments.

18.2   THE ICAPM

Our approach is simulation based and can be adapted to complex multifactor asset pricing models. To illustrate our methodology, we follow Harvey's (1991) description of the conditional CAPM in an international setting.

Harvey (1991) assumes that the entire world operates under the same risk structure. If the markets are integrated, the model implies that the expected return in country i conditional on the information set used by investors to determine prices, Ω_{t-1}, is given by:

$$E[R_{i,t}|\Omega_{t-1}] = r_{f,t} + \frac{COV[R_{i,t},R_{M,t}|\Omega_{t-1}]}{VAR[R_{M,t}|\Omega_{t-1}]}E[R_{M,t} - r_{f,t}|\Omega_{t-1}], \qquad (18.1)$$

where $E[R_{M,t} - r_{f,t}|\Omega_{t-1}]$ is the expected excess return to the world portfolio and $r_{f,t}$ is the rate of return on the risk-free asset.[2] The measure of undiversifiable risk for country i is:

$$\beta_{i,t} = \frac{COV[R_{i,t},R_{M,t}|\Omega_{t-1}]}{VAR[R_{M,t}|\Omega_{t-1}]}.$$

Defining the time-varying price per unit risk, λ_t, as:

$$\lambda_t = \frac{E[R_{M,t} - r_{f,t}|\Omega_{t-1}]}{VAR[R_{M,t}|\Omega_{t-1}]}, \qquad (18.2)$$

we can write (18.1) as:

$$E[R_{i,t}|\Omega_{t-1}] = r_{f,t} + \lambda_t COV[R_{i,t},R_{M,t}|\Omega_{t-1}]. \qquad (18.3)$$

As equation (18.3) makes clear, the model predicts that risk depends solely on the conditional sensitivity or covariance of the return to investing in a particular country with the world stock return. In this context the expected return to the world portfolio would be:

$$E[R_{M,t}|\Omega_{t-1}] = r_{f,t} + \lambda_t COV[R_{M,t},R_{M,t}|\Omega_{t-1}] = r_{f,t} + \lambda_t VAR[R_{M,t}|\Omega_{t-1}] \qquad (18.4)$$

In the international setting the CAPM implies that the risk measure at the highest level of aggregation is the own variance of the world portfolio. Similar models are used by Giovannini and Jorion (1989), Chan et al. (1992) and De Santis and Gerard (1997).

18.2.1   Benefits to Diversification

In the case where national financial markets are affected by country-specific factors, correlations across markets are likely to be lower than correlations within markets. In this situation, international diversification can be a practical strategy to improve portfolio performance. There are some caveats associated with taking a position that is exposed to international risks. Firstly, markets have become more integrated in recent years, increasing correlations across countries. Secondly, recent studies suggest that bear markets spill over at an international level; see Lin et al. (1994), De Santis and Gerard (1997) and Brooks and Henry (2000) inter alia. In this case, the benefits to diversification disappear just as they become most valuable to the investor.

The CAPM framework can be used to assess the potential benefits from international diversification. Consider an internationally diversified portfolio, D, paying a return $R_{D,t}$ with the same level of conditional volatility as a domestic portfolio paying return $R_{i,t}$. The expected benefit to diversification, $E(BD_{i,t}|\Omega_{t-1})$, can be defined as:

$$E(BD_{i,t}|\Omega_{t-1}) = E[R_{D,t} - R_{i,t}|\Omega_{t-1}] \tag{18.5}$$

where $R_{D,t} = \Psi_t R_{M,t} + (1 - \Psi_t)r_{f,t}$. Here $\Psi_t > 0$ is the optimal weight that satisfies $\Psi_t^2 = VAR[R_{i,t}|\Omega_{t-1}]/VAR[R_{M,t}|\Omega_{t-1}]$.[3] The CAPM predicts that the expected return to country i should satisfy (18.1) and that the expected return to D should satisfy:

$$E[R_{D,t}|\Omega_{t-1}] = r_{f,t} + \lambda_t COV[\Psi_t R_{M,t}, R_{M,t}|\Omega_{t-1}] = r_{f,t} + \lambda_t \Psi_t VAR[R_{M,t}|\Omega_{t-1}] \tag{18.6}$$

Combining (18.1) and (18.6), the benefit to diversification implied by the CAPM is:

$$E[BD_{i,t}|\Omega_{t-1}] = \lambda_t[\Psi_t VAR[R_{M,t}|\Omega_{t-1}] - COV[R_{i,t}, R_{M,t}|\Omega_{t-1}]]. \tag{18.7}$$

In order to highlight the main influences underlying the conditional benefit to diversification, we consider the special case where the portfolio D is 100 per cent invested in $R_{M,t}$, which is equivalent to setting $\Psi_t = 1$. This allows us to rewrite (18.7) as:

$$E[BD_{i,t}|\Omega_{t-1}] = \lambda_t[VAR[R_{i,t}|\Omega_{t-1}] - COV[R_{i,t}, R_{M,t}|\Omega_{t-1}]]. \tag{18.8}$$

The term inside the brackets in (18.8) can be interpreted as a measure of the time-varying non-systematic risk of country i, for which investors are not compensated. It is clear from (18.8) that the benefits to diversification are increasing in the exposure to country risk.

The conditional correlation between market i and the world portfolio M, $\rho_{iM,t}$, can be defined as:

$$\rho_{iM,t} = \frac{COV(R_{i,t}, R_{M,t}|\Omega_{t-1})}{\sqrt{VAR(R_{i,t}|\Omega_{t-1})VAR(R_{M,t}|\Omega_{t-1})}}. \tag{18.9}$$

Using (18.9) and again setting $\Psi_t = 1$ for illustrative purposes, we can rewrite (18.7) as:

$$E[BD_{i,t}|\Omega_{t-1}] = \lambda_t(1 - \rho_{iM,t})VAR(R_{i,t}|\Omega_{t-1}). \tag{18.10}$$

Equation (18.10) shows that diversification benefits are decreasing in the level of correlation with the world as, *ceteris paribus*, $\rho_{iM,t} \to 1$, implies that $E[BD_{i,t}|\Omega_{t-1}] \to 0$; there is no benefit to diversification if country i is perfectly correlated with the world. Furthermore, the benefit to hedging is increasing in λ_t, the price per unit risk, and in $VAR(R_{i,t}|\Omega_{t-1})$, the simple risk of the country.

Note that setting $\Psi_t = 1$ is a special case used for illustration only. In the empirical work that follows below, the portfolio D is diversified optimally.

18.3 THE EMPIRICAL FRAMEWORK

Let $\tilde{R}_{k,t} = R_{k,t} - r_{f,t}$ represent the excess return to the kth asset or market. Consider the k dimensional vector of excess returns $\tilde{R}_t$:

$$\tilde{R}_t = (\tilde{R}_{M,t}, \tilde{R}_{1,t}, \ldots \tilde{R}_{k-1,t})'. \tag{18.11}$$

We can write the conditional mean of our model as:

$$\tilde{R}_t = \mu_t(\phi) + \varepsilon_t, \tag{18.12}$$

where $\mu_t(\phi)$ is the conditional mean vector and $\varepsilon_t = (\varepsilon_{M,t}, \varepsilon_{1,t}, \ldots, \varepsilon_{k-1,t})'$, is the innovation vector. Here $\varepsilon_t = H_t^{1/2}(\phi) z_t$, and $H_t^{1/2}(\phi)$ is a $k \times k$ positive definite matrix where H_t is the conditional variance matrix of $\tilde{R}_t$ and z_t is the $k \times 1$ vector of standardized innovations $z_t = (z_{M,t}, z_{1,t}, \ldots, z_{k-1,t})'$. Note that H_t is:

$$H_t = \begin{bmatrix} h_{M,t} & h_{M,1,t} & \cdots & h_{M,k-1,t} \\ h_{M,1,t} & h_{1,t} & \cdots & h_{1,k-1,t} \\ \vdots & \vdots & \ddots & \vdots \\ h_{M,k-1,t} & h_{1,k-1,t} & \cdots & h_{k-1,t} \end{bmatrix} \tag{18.13}$$

Consider $\tilde{R}_{k,t}$ the kth element of $\tilde{R}_t$. Holding $|\varepsilon_t| = \varepsilon^*$, a variable is said to display own variance asymmetry if:

$$VAR[\tilde{R}_{k,t+1}|\Omega_t]|_{\varepsilon_{k,t}<0} - \sigma_{k,t}^2 > VAR[\tilde{R}_{k,t+1}|\Omega_t]|_{\varepsilon_{k,t}>0} - \sigma_{k,t}^2. \tag{18.14}$$

for all values of ε^*. Here, a negative excess return innovation for market k leads to an upward revision of the expected conditional variance of $\tilde{R}_{k,t+1}$. This increase in the expected conditional variance exceeds that for a shock of equal magnitude but opposite sign. Similarly, if a negative excess return innovation for market j leads to an upward revision of the expected conditional variance of $\tilde{R}_{k,t+1}$, then $\tilde{R}_{k,t+1}$ is said to display cross-variance asymmetry:

$$VAR[\tilde{R}_{k,t+1}|\Omega_t]|_{\varepsilon_{j,t}<0} - \sigma_{k,t}^2 > VAR[\tilde{R}_{k,t+1}|\Omega_t]|_{\varepsilon_{k,t}>0} - \sigma_{k,t}^2. \tag{18.15}$$

Covariance asymmetry occurs if:

$$COV[\tilde{R}_{k,t+1}, \tilde{R}_{j,t+1}|\Omega_t]|_{\varepsilon_{j,t}<0} - \sigma_{jk,t}^2 \neq COV[\tilde{R}_{k,t+1}, \tilde{R}_{j,t+1}|\Omega_t]|_{\varepsilon_{k,t}>0} - \sigma_{jk,t}^2 \tag{18.16}$$

or:

$$COV[\tilde{R}_{k,t+1}, \tilde{R}_{j,t+1}|\Omega_t, \varepsilon_{j,t} < 0]|_{\varepsilon_{j,t}<0} - \sigma_{jk,t}^2 \neq COV[\tilde{R}_{k,t+1}, \tilde{R}_{j,t+1}|\Omega_t, \varepsilon_{j,t} > 0]|_{\varepsilon_{j,t}>0} - \sigma_{jk,t}^2. \tag{18.17}$$

Given the definition of $\beta_{i,t}$, from the CAPM we may write:

$$\beta_{i,t} = \frac{COV(\tilde{R}_{M,t}, \tilde{R}_{i,t}|\Omega_{t-1})}{VAR(\tilde{R}_{M,t}|\Omega_{t-1})} \tag{18.18}$$

for $i = 1,\ldots k - 1$. If the data display own variance, cross-variance or covariance asymmetry, it follows that $\beta_{i,t}$ may respond asymmetrically to positive and negative return innovations. Holding $|\varepsilon_t| = \varepsilon^*$, we define beta asymmetry as:

$$E[\beta_{i,t+1}|\Omega_t]|_{\varepsilon_{j,t}<0} - E[\beta_{i,t+1}|\Omega_t]|_{\varepsilon_{j,t}>0} \neq 0, \qquad (18.19)$$

for all values of ε^*. Here the impacts of positive and negative shocks of equal magnitude to the kth market may lead to differing revisions to the conditional measure of risk.

Asymmetry in one or all of the elements of H_t has potentially important implications for measures of exposure. If the return to the world portfolio displays own or cross-variance asymmetry, and/or if covariance asymmetry exists between the returns to country i and the world portfolio, then $\beta_{i,t}$ will display asymmetry.

Similarly, own or cross-variance asymmetry to the returns of market i and the world portfolio and/or covariance asymmetry will give rise to asymmetry in the measure of benefits to diversification. Diversification asymmetry may be defined as:

$$E[BD_{i,t+1}|\Omega_t]|_{\varepsilon_{j,t}<0} - E[BD_{i,t+1}|\Omega_t]|_{\varepsilon_{j,t}>0} \neq 0 \qquad (18.20)$$

A method of modelling the responses of the joint distribution of world and country returns and detecting asymmetric responses to positive and negative shocks is central to this study and has potentially important implications for risk estimation and portfolio allocation. This chapter presents a unified framework for this task.

18.3.1 Generalized Impulse Responses

Define the vector $\Lambda_t = vech(H_t)$, where $vech$ is the column stacking operator of a lower triangular matrix; Λ_t is of dimension $k(k + 1)/2$. Stacking $\beta_{i,t}$, $\rho_{i,t}$ and $BD_{i,t}$ into the vector Ξ_t, we can now define the $4k + k(k + 1)/2 - 2$ dimensional vector Q_t as:

$$Q_t = (\tilde{R}_t, \Lambda_t, \Xi_t). \qquad (18.21)$$

The generalized impulse function, *GIRF*, for a specific shock v_t and history ω_{t-1} can then be given as:

$$GIRF_Q(n, v_t, \omega_{t-1}) = E[Q_{t+n}|v_t, \omega_{t-1}] - E[Q_{t+n}|\omega_{t-1}] \qquad (18.22)$$

for $n = 0,1,2,\ldots$. Hence the *GIRF* is conditional on v_t and ω_{t-1} and constructs the response by averaging out future shocks given the past and present. A natural reference point for the impulse response function is the conditional expectation of Q_{t+n} given only the history ω_{t-1}. In this benchmark case the current shock is also averaged out. Assuming that v_t and ω_{t-1} are realizations of the random variables V_t and Ω_{t-1} that generate realizations of $\{Q_t\}$ then (following the ideas proposed in Koop et al., 1996) the *GIRF* defined in (18.22) can be considered to be the realization of a random variable given by:

$$GIRF_Q(n, V_t, \Omega_{t-1}) = E[Q_{t+n}|V_t, \Omega_{t-1}] - E[Q_{t+n}|\Omega_{t-1}]. \qquad (18.23)$$

Note that the first k elements of $GIRF_Q(n,V_t,\Omega_{t-1})$ contain the impulse responses for the excess returns, the next remaining $k(k+1)/2$ elements contain the variance impulse responses, $VIRF_\Lambda(n,V_t,\Omega_{t-1})$,[4] while the remaining $3k-2$ elements are the impulse responses for the elements of Ξ_t, $IRF_\beta(n,v_t,\omega_{t-1})$, $IRF_\rho(n,v_t,\omega_{t-1})$, and $IRF_{BD}(n,v_t,\omega_{t-1})$, respectively.

A number of alternative conditional versions of $GIRF_Q(n,V_t,\Omega_{t-1})$ can be defined.[5] In this study we are particularly interested in evaluating the significance of the asymmetric effects of positive and negative world and country shocks on the elements of Q_t. For instance, the response functions can be used to measure the extent to which negative shocks may (or may not) be more persistent than positive shocks. It is also possible to assess the potential diversity in the dynamic effects of positive and negative shocks on the conditional volatilities and on the conditional covariances.

Van Dijk et al. (2000) present a measure of asymmetry in the response of the conditional mean to positive and negative innovations. Let $GIRF_Q(n,V_t^+,\Omega_{t-1})$ denote the impulse response function from conditioning on the set of all possible positive shocks, where $V_t^+ = \{v_t|v_t > 0\}$ and $GIRF_Q(n,-V_t^+,\Omega_{t-1})$ denote the response from conditioning on the set of all possible negative shocks. The random asymmetry measure:

$$ASY_{\tilde{R}}(n,V_t,\Omega_{t-1}) = GIRF_{\tilde{R}}(n,V_t^+,\Omega_{t-1}) + GIRF_{\tilde{R}}(n,-V_t^+,\Omega_{t-1}), \qquad (18.24)$$

will be centred on zero if positive and negative shocks have exactly the same effect on the conditional mean vector, $\tilde{R}_t$. Grier et al. (2004) describe the application of (18.23) and (18.24) for multivariate asymmetric GARCH in mean models.

Shields et al. (2005) present a measure of asymmetry in the response of the conditional variance–covariance matrix to shocks. Let $VIRF_\Lambda(n,V_t^+,\Omega_{t-1})$ denote the variance impulse response function from conditioning on the set of all possible positive shocks, where $V_t^+ = \{v_t|v_t > 0\}$ and $VIRF_\Lambda(n,-V_t^+,\Omega_{t-1})$ denote the response from conditioning on the set of all possible negative shocks. The random asymmetry measure:

$$ASY_\Lambda(n,V_t,\Omega_{t-1}) = VIRF_\Lambda(n,V_t^+,\Omega_{t-1}) - VIRF_\Lambda(n,-V_t^+,\Omega_{t-1}), \qquad (18.25)$$

will be insignificantly different from zero if positive and negative shocks have exactly the same effect on the conditional variance. The distribution of (18.25) can provide an indication of the asymmetric effects of positive and negative shocks.

The asymmetry measure ASY_Λ is analogous to the measure proposed in van Dijk et al. (2000) for the case of $GIRF$s. However, a notable distinction is that the measure in (18.25) is comprised of the difference between the variance response functions, $VIRF_\Lambda(n,V_t^+,\Omega_{t-1})$ and $VIRF_\Lambda(n,-V_t^+,\Omega_{t-1})$, in contrast to the summation of the corresponding generalized impulse response versions in (18.24). This distinction arises because $VIRF$s are made up of the squares of the innovations (and will therefore be of the same sign), in contrast to the case of $GIRF$s, where positive and negative shocks cause the response functions to take opposite signs.

The random asymmetry measure:

$$ASY_\beta(n,V_t,\Omega_{t-1}) = IRF_\beta(n,V_t^+,\Omega_{t-1}) - IRF_\beta(n,-V_t^+,\Omega_{t-1}), \qquad (18.26)$$

will be insignificantly different from zero if positive and negative shocks have the same effect. The distribution of (18.26) can provide an indication of the asymmetric effects of positive and negative shocks to $\beta_{i,t}$. Similarly, the asymmetry measure

$$ASY\rho_{jk}(n,V_t,\Omega_{t-1}) = IRF\rho_{jk}(n,V_t^+,\Omega_{t-1}) - IRF\rho_{jk}(n,-V_t^+,\Omega_{t-1}), \qquad (18.27)$$

can be used to evaluate the asymmetric effects of positive and negative return realizations to markets j and k on ρ_{jk}. Note that (18.26) and (18.27) are composed of the elements of Λ_t and therefore the asymmetry measures, analogous to the *VIRF*s, will be made up of the difference between the respective impulse responses for positive and negative shocks. Finally, the asymmetry measure:

$$ASY_{BD_i}(n,V_t,\Omega_{t-1}) = IRF_{BD_i}(n,V_t^+,\Omega_{t-1}) + IRF_{BD_i}(n,-V_t^+,\Omega_{t-1}), \qquad (18.28)$$

can be used to evaluate the asymmetry effects of positive and negative return realizations to markets i and M on the benefit to diversification. In other words, we may evaluate the extent to which the one period benefit to hedging displays asymmetry.

18.4   DATA DESCRIPTION

To illustrate the techniques described in the previous sections we use weekly price index data, P_t, denominated in USD for Hong Kong (*HK*), Singapore (*SP*) and the World (*M*), downloaded from Datastream.[6] The sample runs from 1 January 1973 to 28 July 2003, a total of 1597 observations.[7] The continuously compounded returns to each index, adjusted for dividends, were calculated using:

$$R_{k,t} = 100 \times \log\left(\frac{P_{k,t}}{P_{k,t-1}}\right) \qquad (18.29)$$

for $k = M,HK,SP$.

The continuously compounded risk-free return, $r_{f,t}$ was calculated from secondary market yields on three-month US Treasury Bills obtained from the FRED II database at the Federal Reserve Bank of Saint Louis.[8] Our analysis is performed on the returns in excess of the riskless rate for each index, $\tilde{R}_{k,t} = R_{k,t} - r_{f,t}$. The price and excess return data are plotted in Figure 18.1. In particular, the excess return data appear to display the volatility clustering usually associated with such data. Large (small) shocks of either sign tend to follow large (small) shocks.

Table 18.1 presents summary statistics for the excess returns. The data are non-normal with clear evidence of negative skewness and excess kurtosis. The Bera–Jarque (1982) test rejects the null of normality at all usual levels of significance. There is strong evidence of conditional heteroscedasticity in the data with Engle's (1982) Lagrange multiplier (LM) test for up to fifth-order ARCH rejecting the null of no ARCH at all usual levels of significance.

There is also evidence of asymmetry in volatility for each of the series. Engle and Ng (1993) present tests of the null hypothesis of own variance asymmetry; however,

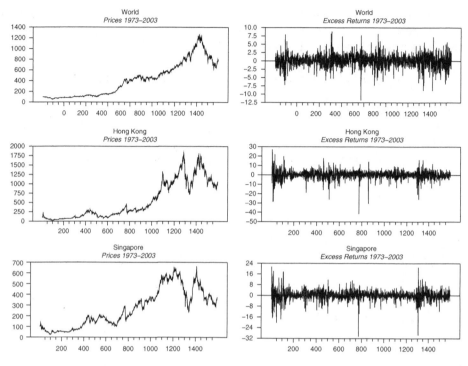

Figure 18.1   The data

Table 18.1   Data description

	World	Hong Kong	Singapore
Mean	0.1299	0.1470	0.0822
	[0.0110]	[0.2322]	[0.4058]
Variance	4.1572	24.1506	15.5973
SK	−0.3635	−1.0331	−0.6126
	[0.0000]	[0.0000]	[0.0000]]
EK	2.7221	8.3991	7.5541
	[0.0000]	[0.0000]	[0.0000]
JB	527.5898	497.9738	3892.1574
	[0.0000]	[0.0000]	[0.0000]
ARCH(5)	384.5812	239.6484	314.0226
	[0.0000]	[0.0000]	[0.0000]
Sign Bias	0.7288	−2.3748	−2.4684
	[0.4662]	[0.0177]	[0.0137]
Negative Size Bias	−1.2710	0.3309	0.3595
	[0.2039]	[0.7407]	[0.7193]
Positive Size Bias	0.0058	1.5663	1.8013
	[0.9953]	[0.1175]	[0.0718]
Joint Test	8.2601	8.1399	8.1316
	[0.0409]	[0.0432]	[0.0434]

this test cannot detect cross-variance or covariance asymmetry. For Hong Kong and Singapore the negative sign bias test of Engle and Ng (1993) suggests that negative innovations will lead to higher levels of conditional volatility than positive innovations of equal magnitude. This implies that a symmetric model would tend to systematically under forecast volatility when prices are trending downwards and over forecast volatility in an environment where prices are appreciating. Furthermore, time variation and asymmetry in $VAR[R_{M,t}|\Omega_{t-1}]$ implies that λ_t, the price per unit risk, $\beta_{i,t}$, the measure of risk for country i, and $BD_{i,t}$, the benefit to diversifying out of country i, are likely to display time variation and asymmetry unless $E[R_{M,t} - r_{f,t}|\Omega_{t-1}]$, $E[R_{i,t} - r_{f,t}|\Omega_{t-1}]$ and $COV[R_{i,t},R_{M,t}|\Omega_{t-1}]$ display sufficient offsetting asymmetry and time variation. Our empirical model described below is a trivariate model, and allows for all three types of asymmetry.

18.5   THE STATISTICAL MODEL

We illustrate our methodology using a multivariate asymmetric GARCH model. However, the approach is sufficiently general to apply to a far wider class of multivariate non-linear models.

Consider the 3×1 excess return vector $\tilde{R}_t = (\tilde{R}_{M,t},\tilde{R}_{HK,t},\tilde{R}_{SP,t})'$. The conditional mean of our model is written as:

$$\tilde{R}_t = \mu_t(\phi) + \varepsilon_t, \tag{18.30}$$

where $\mu_t(\phi)$ is the conditional mean vector and $\varepsilon_t = (\varepsilon_{M,t},\varepsilon_{HK,t},\varepsilon_{SP,t})'$ is the innovation vector where:

$$\varepsilon_t = H_t^{1/2}(\phi)z_t, \tag{18.31}$$

and $H_t^{1/2}(\phi)$ is a 3×3 positive definite matrix with H_t being the conditional variance matrix of $\tilde{R}_t$ and z_t is the 3×1 vector of standardized residuals, $z_t = (z_{M,t},z_{HK,t},z_{SP,t})'$. Here H_t is:

$$H_t = \begin{bmatrix} h_{M,t} & h_{M,HK,t} & h_{M,SP,t} \\ h_{M,HK,t} & h_{HK,t} & h_{SP,HK,t} \\ h_{M,SP,t} & h_{SP,HK,t} & h_{SP,t} \end{bmatrix}. \tag{18.32}$$

For simplicity, we assume that the excess return to the market portfolio follows a GARCH-M process written as:

$$\tilde{R}_{M,t} = \phi_0 + \phi_1 h_{M,t} + \varepsilon_{M,t}. \tag{18.33}$$

The country returns, given by the CAPM, are written as:

$$\tilde{R}_{i,t} = \beta_{i,t}\tilde{R}_{M,t} + \varepsilon_{i,t}, \tag{18.34}$$

for $i = HK,SP$. We condition on the sigma field generated by all the information available until week $t - 1$, contained in the information set Ω_{t-1}.

It is possible to assume that $\{z_t\}$ is i.i.d. with $E(z_t) = 0$ and $Var(z_t) = I_3$ where I_3 is a 3×3 identity matrix. Maximum likelihood estimation is then possible under the assumption of the conditional normality of z_t. However, such an assumption must be considered tenuous given the extreme levels of non-normality present in the data as reported in Table 18.1. Our approach is to assume that the data follow a conditional Student-t density with unknown degrees of freedom η. As η tends to infinity the Student-t density converges to the normal distribution. We further assume that $\eta > 2$ to ensure the existence of the first and second order moments and to retain the interpretation of H_t as a conditional variance–covariance matrix. The Student-t density for our case is:

$$g(z_t|\phi,\Omega_{t-1},\eta) = \frac{\Gamma(\frac{\eta+3}{2})}{\Gamma(\frac{\eta}{2})\,[\pi\,(\eta-2)\,]^{3/2}}\left[1 + \frac{z_t'z_t}{\eta-2}\right]^{-\frac{3+\eta}{2}}. \tag{18.35}$$

The conditional variance matrix H_t is parameterized as:

$$H_t = C_0^{*\prime}\,C_0^* + A_{11}^{*\prime}\,\varepsilon_{t-1}\varepsilon_{t-1}'A_{11}^* + B_{11}^{*\prime}H_{t-1}B_{11}^* + D_{11}^{*\prime}\xi_{t-1}\xi_{t-1}'D_{11}^*, \tag{18.36}$$

where C_0^* is a 3×3 upper triangular parameter matrix to ensure that the model is identified, and A_{11}^*, B_{11}^* and D_{11}^* are 3×3 parameter matrices with elements a_{jk}, b_{jk}, and d_{jk}, respectively for all combinations of $j,k = 1.2.3$. Defining $\xi_{i,t} = \min\{0,\varepsilon_{i,t}\}$, and $\xi_t = (\xi_{M,t},\xi_{HK,t},\xi_{SP,t})'$, our model captures the negative size bias evident in Table 18.1 through the main diagonal elements of the D_{11}^* matrix. Significance of the off-diagonal elements of D_{11}^* indicates the presence of cross-variance asymmetry and/or covariance asymmetry.

To close the model we require a definition of $\beta_{i,t}$ the time-varying measure of undiversifiable risk for each country. Given the definition of $\beta_{i,t}$ from the CAPM we write:

$$\beta_{i,t} = \frac{COV(\tilde{R}_{M,t},\tilde{R}_{i,t}|\Omega_{t-1})}{VAR(\tilde{R}_{M,t}|\Omega_{t-1})} = \frac{h_{M,i,t}}{h_{M,t}} \tag{18.37}$$

for $i = HK,SP$.

The conditional variance–covariance structure allows for asymmetry to enter through the elements of the outer product matrix $\xi_{t-1}\xi_{t-1}'$ in (18.36). Hence, if the matrix of coefficients, D_{11}^*, defined in (18.36) are statistically insignificantly different from zero, then the *VIRF* will not distinguish between a positive or negative shock. If, on the other hand, the elements of D_{11}^* are significant, then the possibility of asymmetric responses to positive and negative shocks arises.

Table 18.2 presents parameter estimates of the full model. Consistent with the results displayed in Table 18.1 there is strong evidence of GARCH in the data. The estimates of the main diagonal elements of the $\hat{B}_{11}^*$ coefficient matrix are all strongly significant. Conversely, the off-diagonal elements are insignificant. This suggests that persistence in variance is largely due to own market effects. All the elements of the first row of the $\hat{A}_{11}^*$ matrix are significant, indicating the presence of possible spillover effects between

Table 18.2   Maximum likelihood estimates of the model

$$\tilde{R}_{M,t} = 0.1185 + 0.0209\,h_{M,t} + \varepsilon_{M,t}$$
$$\qquad\quad \{0.1603\}\;\{0.0874\}$$

$$\tilde{R}_{i,t} = \beta_{i,t}\tilde{R}_{M,t} + \varepsilon_{i,t}$$

$$\varepsilon_t = \begin{bmatrix} \varepsilon_{M,t} \\ \varepsilon_{HK,t} \\ \varepsilon_{SP,t} \end{bmatrix}; z_t \sim ST(0,H_t,\eta) \quad \hat{\eta} = 8.4884$$
$$\qquad\qquad\qquad\qquad\qquad\qquad\quad \{0.6934\}$$

$$H_t = C_0^{*\prime}C_0^* + A_{11}^{*\prime}\varepsilon_{t-1}\varepsilon_{t-1}^{\prime}A_{11}^* + B_{11}^{*\prime}H_{t-1}B_{11}^* + D_{11}^{*\prime}\xi_{t-1}\xi_{t-1}^{\prime}D_{11}^*$$

$$\xi_t = \begin{bmatrix} \xi_{M,t} \\ \xi_{HK,t} \\ \xi_{SP,t} \end{bmatrix}; \xi_{K,t} = \min\{0,\varepsilon_t\}$$

$\hat{C}_0^* =$	$\begin{array}{ccc} 0.3150 & 0.1116 & 0.0863 \\ \{0.0596\} & \{0.0538\} & \{0.0533\} \\ 0 & 0.6461 & 0.1708 \\ & \{0.0517\} & \{0.0540\} \\ 0 & 0 & 0.4149 \\ & & \{0.0323\} \end{array}$	$\hat{A}_{11}^* =$	$\begin{array}{ccc} 0.0510 & -0.1251 & -0.0611 \\ \{0.0199\} & \{0.0371\} & \{0.0322\} \\ 0.0014 & 0.3444 & 0.0012 \\ \{0.0034\} & \{0.0132\} & \{0.0076\} \\ 0.0140 & -0.0072 & 0.2740 \\ \{0.0069\} & \{0.0254\} & \{0.0134\} \end{array}$
$\hat{B}_{11}^* =$	$\begin{array}{ccc} 0.9618 & 0.0088 & -0.0112 \\ \{0.0092\} & \{0.0095\} & \{0.0088\} \\ 0.0004 & 0.9235 & 0.0023 \\ \{0.0015\} & \{0.0045\} & \{0.0033\} \\ -0.0026 & 0.0041 & 0.9474 \\ \{0.0026\} & \{0.0057\} & \{0.0020\} \end{array}$	$\hat{D}_{11}^* =$	$\begin{array}{ccc} 0.2990 & 0.1346 & 0.2264 \\ \{0.0296\} & \{0.0348\} & \{0.0334\} \\ 0.0384 & 0.0028 & -0.0179 \\ \{0.0117\} & \{0.0268\} & \{0.0178\} \\ -0.0707 & 0.0840 & -0.0859 \\ \{0.0204\} & \{0.0395\} & \{0.0439\} \end{array}$

the World index and the Hong Kong and Singapore indices. Additionally, $\hat{d}_{11}$ and $\hat{d}_{33}$ are significant, indicating own variance and cross-variance asymmetry in the World and Singapore returns. The significance of the off-diagonal elements of $\hat{D}_{11}^*$ is consistent with the presence of cross-variance and covariance asymmetry.

The model appears well specified. Table 18.3 presents specification test results for the model based on orthogonality conditions suggested by Nelson (1991). The standardized residuals from the model, z_{it}, display dramatically reduced levels of skewness and kurtosis and are largely free from serial correlation and conditional heteroscedasticity.

In addition the moment conditions $E(\hat{\varepsilon}_{j,t}\hat{\varepsilon}_{k,t}) = \hat{h}_{jk,t}$ were satisfied for all combinations of j and k. To conserve space these results are not reported but are available upon request.

Finally, Figure 18.2 displays the estimated benefits to diversification for Hong Kong and Singapore. Here, Ψ_t, the weight attached to portfolio M in the diversified portfolio paying return $R_{D,t} = \Psi_t R_{M,t} + (1-\Psi_t)R_{f,t}$, is set optimally, satisfying $\Psi_t^2 = VAR[R_{i,t}|\Omega_{t-1}]/VAR[R_{M,t}|\Omega_{t-1}]$. Clearly $BD_{i,t}$ displays time variation and sometimes sharp reactions to shocks. It is interesting to note that $BD_{i,t}$ is uniformly positive for both countries suggesting that a diversified strategy should be the norm for investors in these countries.

Table 18.3   Specification test results

Orthogonality Condition	World	Hong Kong	Singapore
$E[\hat{z}_{k,t}] = 0$	−0.0145	0.0464	0.0179
	[0.5614]	[0.0698]	[0.4798]
$E[\hat{z}^2_{k,t} - 1] = 0$	−0.0114	0.0440	0.0196
	[0.8241]	[0.4439]	[0.7272]
$E[\hat{z}^3_{k,t}] = 0$	−0.5299	−0.5442	−0.3480
	[0.0315]	[0.0383]	[0.1776]
$E[\hat{z}^4_{k,t} - 3] = 0$	2.1501	3.3389	3.0893
	[0.01373]	[0.0132]	[0.0277]
$E[(\hat{z}^2_{k,t} - 1)(\hat{z}^2_{k,t-1} - 1)] = 0$	0.3204	0.4395	0.3901
	[0.3146]	[0.2030]	[0.0769]
$E[(\hat{z}^2_{k,t} - 1)(\hat{z}^2_{k,t-2} - 1)] = 0$	0.1133	0.7237	0.0064
	[0.1612]	[0.2148]	[0.9518]
$E[(\hat{z}^2_{k,t} - 1)(\hat{z}^2_{k,t-3} - 1)] = 0$	0.0907	−0.0834	0.1091
	[0.3401]	[0.2251]	[0.2517]
$E[(\hat{z}^2_{k,t} - 1)(\hat{z}^2_{k,t-4} - 1)] = 0$	−0.0803	0.0466	0.3314
	[0.2171]	[0.5883]	[0.3412]
$E[(\hat{z}^2_{k,t} - 1)(\hat{z}^2_{k,t-5} - 1)] = 0$	0.0366	−0.1332	0.0212
	[0.6431]	[0.0586]	[0.8099]
$E[\hat{z}_{k,t}\hat{z}_{k,t-1}] = 0$	0.0001	0.0739	0.0457
	[0.9986]	[0.0995]	[0.1271]
$E[\hat{z}_{k,t}\hat{z}_{k,t-2}] = 0$	0.0455	0.0360	0.0741
	[0.0823]	[0.1520]	[0.0038]
$E[\hat{z}_{k,t}\hat{z}_{k,t-3}] = 0$	0.0343	0.0017	0.0252
	[0.1862]	[0.9485]	[0.3498]
$E[\hat{z}_{k,t}\hat{z}_{k,t-4}] = 0$	0.0004	−0.0248	0.0437
	[0.9850]	[0.3083]	[0.1367]
$E[\hat{z}_{k,t}\hat{z}_{k,t-5}] = 0$	0.0077	0.6727	0.0054
	[0.7606]	[0.4121]	[0.8232]

18.6   THE IMPULSE RESPONSE ANALYSIS

It is impossible to construct analytical expressions for the conditional expectations for the non-linear structure proposed in this chapter. Therefore, Monte Carlo methods of stochastic simulation need to be used. Following the algorithm described in Koop et al. (1996), impulse responses are computed for all 1597 histories in the sample for horizons $n = 0,1,...N$, with $N = 50$. At each history, 500 draws are made from the joint distribution of the innovations and $R = 100$ replications are used to average out the effects of the shocks.

Following Hafner and Herwartz (2001) and Shields et al. (2005), one can define news in terms of the i.i.d. innovation z_t and use a decomposition strategy to overcome the general problem that the error vector shows contemporaneous correlation. The Jordan decomposition of H_t can be used to obtain the symmetric matrix:

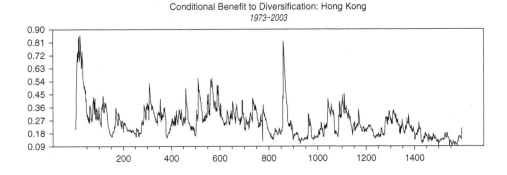

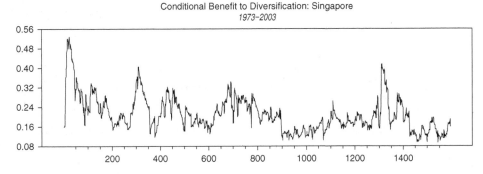

Figure 18.2   Time series plots for $\hat{BD}_{i,t}$

$$H_t^{1/2} = \Upsilon_t \Psi_t^{1/2} \Upsilon_t'$$

with $\Upsilon_t = (\upsilon_{t1}, \ldots \upsilon_{tN})$ and $\Psi_t^{1/2} = diag(\psi_{t1}, \ldots, \psi_{tN})$, where $\upsilon_{ti}, i = 1, \ldots, N$ denote the eigenvalues of H_t with corresponding eigenvectors ψ_{t1}. Using $z_t = H_t^{-1/2}\varepsilon_t$ to identify the independent news requires no zero restrictions and is independent of the ordering of the variables in the state vector. In the case where ε_t is Gaussian, z_t is not unique. However if z_t is a vector of independent standardized variates, the only occasion where non-identifiability occurs is where z_t is normally distributed. News can be considered to be identified if the innovation vector is not normally distributed.

Generalized impulse responses and associated asymmetry measures were calculated for the elements of Q_t. To conserve space, we report a selection of the results.

18.6.1   Generalized Impulse Responses

Figures 18.3, 18.4 and 18.5 display the cumulative dynamic response of $\beta_{i,t}$, $\rho_{i,k,t}$ and $BD_{i,t}$, respectively, for $i = HK$ and SP and for $k = M, HK$ and SP, to orthogonal shocks to each market. The responses are scaled to have unit impact on each of the respective measures. The figures are drawn for $N = 8$ horizons which is sufficient for the long-run response to the shock to be achieved in each case.

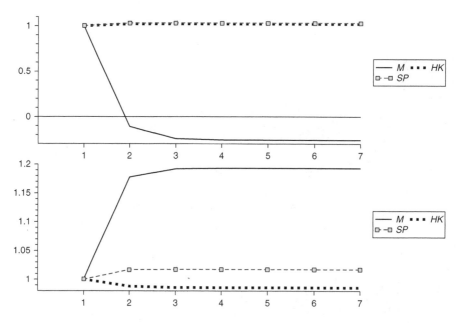

Figure 18.3   *Cumulative generalized impulse responses:* $\beta_{HK,t}$ *upper panel;* $\beta_{SP,t}$ *lower panel*

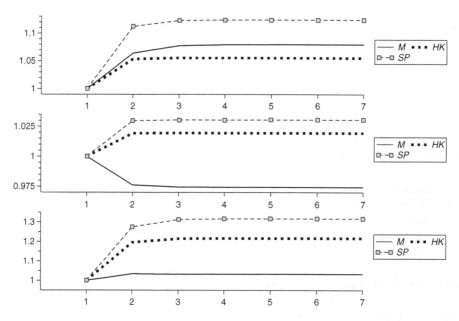

Figure 18.4   *Cumulative generalized impulse responses:* $\rho_{HK,M}$ *upper panel;* $\rho_{SP,M}$ *middle panel* $\hat{B}D_{i,t}$; $\rho_{HK,SP}$ *lower panel*

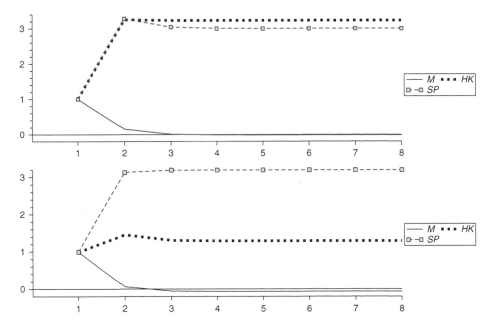

Figure 18.5   *Cumulative generalized impulse responses:* $BD_{HK,t}$ *upper panel;* $BD_{SP,t}$ *lower panel* $\hat{BD}_{i,t}$

Cumulative GIRFs for $\beta_{HK,t}$ and $\beta_{SP,t}$ are displayed in the upper and lower panels of Figure 18.3, respectively. The long-run impact of an orthogonalized shock to the market portfolio that causes $\beta_{HK,t}$ to rise by one unit on impact is essentially zero. Moreover, news about the world dissipates within two periods. In contrast, a world shock that causes $\beta_{SP,t}$ (in the lower panel) to rise by 1 per cent on impact leads to a greater than 1 per cent long-run effect. This result is driven by the higher persistence of the covariance of Singapore returns with the world, $h_{M,SP,t}$, compared with $h_{M,HK,t}$, in response to an orthogonal shock to the world portfolio.

News about Singapore or Hong Kong that causes $\beta_{HK,t}$ or $\beta_{SP,t}$ to rise by one unit on impact have approximately one unit of impact in the long run. This implies that country-specific news leads to a persistent increase in the measure of risk for country i. Here, diversification of this country-specific risk is desirable.

Figure 18.4 displays GIRFs for $\rho_{iM,t}$. In all but one case a shock to the system that causes the correlation to rise by one unit on impact results in a greater than one unit long-run increase in the level of correlation across the individual countries and with the world index. News about Singapore which causes the correlation between $R_{SP,t}$ and $R_{M,t}$ to rise by one unit on impact leads to a 0.95 unit long-run increase in the correlation. Recall that if $\Psi_t = 1$, and we invest 100 per cent of our wealth in the diversified portfolio in M, we can rewrite (18.7) as $E[BD_{i,t}|\Omega_{t-1}] = \lambda_t(1 - \rho_{iM,t})VAR(R_{i,t}|\Omega_{t-1})$. Our results imply that, *ceteris paribus*, any news will increase correlation leading to a reduction in the benefit to diversification across markets.

The upper panel of Figure 18.5 implies that the long-run impact of an orthogonal shock to $R_{M,t}$ that causes $BD_{HK,t}$ to rise by one unit on impact is zero. Furthermore, the impulse dissipates after three periods. On the other hand the long-run response to an orthogonal shock to $R_{HK,t}$, or $R_{SP,t}$ that causes $BD_{HK,t}$ to rise by one unit on impact is almost three units. The system achieves this long-run level after three periods. A similar pattern is evident in the lower panel of Figure 18.5. Shocks to $R_{M,t}$ have zero long-run impact on $BD_{SP,t}$ while shocks to Hong Kong and in particular Singapore have lasting impact on the benefit to diversification. International diversification reduces exposure to country-specific shocks for any one market and these benefits to diversification appear to be lasting.

Unlike for GIRFs, the property of linearity in the impulse no longer holds for VIRFs and correspondingly for the impulse responses for $\beta_{i,t}$, $\rho_{iM,t}$, and $BD_{i,t}$. Therefore, an innovation of ρv_t, where ρ is a scalar, will not have ρ times the effect of v_t, if we consider conditional volatility responses. Given the quadratic nature of the VIRFs, the magnitude of the response will be in terms of the square of ρ, implying that the larger is the shock, the greater will be the correlation between the variables and so the smaller will be the benefit to diversification. For large shocks to Hong Kong and Singapore there will be an increasingly larger benefit to holding a diversified portfolio.

18.6.2   Measuring Asymmetry in the Response to News

Tables 18.4–18.7 display asymmetry measures for $\tilde{R}_{k,t}$, $\beta_{i,t}$, $\rho_{i,k,t}$ and $BD_{i,t}$, respectively, for $i = HK$ and SP and for $k = M, HK$ and SP. These measures are designed to highlight differences in average responses to positive and negative orthogonal shocks to each market. These random asymmetry measures will be zero in expectation if positive and negative shocks have equal effect.

Table 18.4   Measures of asymmetry in return

	$ASY_{\tilde{R}_M}$	$ASY_{\tilde{R}_{HK}}$	$ASY_{\tilde{R}_{SP}}$
M	−0.0011	−0.1167	−0.1146
	(−0.0828)	(−22.7761)	(−16.3076)
HK	0.0244	0.0221	−0.0178
	(3.3600)	(2.8325)	(−2.2751)
SP	0.0181	−0.1350	−0.0903
	(2.0001)	(−19.0217)	(−12.9588)

Table 18.5   Measures of asymmetry in $\beta_{i,t}$

	$ASY_{\beta_{HK,t}}$	$ASY_{\beta_{SP,t}}$
M	−0.0292	−0.0264
	(−13.8511)	(9.5003)
HK	0.0595	0.00119
	(24.7067)	(12.1141)

Table 18.6   Measures of asymmetry in $\rho_{i,k,t}$

	$ASY_{\rho_{M,HK,t}}$	$ASY_{\rho_{M,SP,t}}$	$ASY_{\rho_{HK,SP,t}}$
M	−0.0031	0.0063	−0.0025
	(−4.3452)	(12.4159)	(−10.0956)
HK	0.0133	0.0085	−0.0111
	(22.6024)	(18.5639)	(21.9407)
SP	0.0013	0.0004	0.0001
	(4.0402)	(1.2603)	(0.5321)

Table 18.7   Measures of asymmetry in $BD_{i,t}$

	$ASY_{BD_{HK,t}}$	$ASY_{BD_{SP,t}}$
M	0.0361	0.0132
	(8.0606)	(2.9235)
HK	0.0789	0.1149
	(27.3461)	(4.6970)
SP	0.0333	−0.1031
	(9.2520)	(−27.6489)

There is no evidence that the return to the world portfolio responds asymmetrically to positive and negative orthogonal shocks to $R_{M,t}$ of equal magnitude. Conversely both $R_{HK,t}$ and $R_{SP,t}$ respond asymmetrically to news about the world portfolio, with bad news about $R_{M,t}$ having greater impact than good news. There is some statistical evidence that good news about $R_{HK,t}$ has greater long-run impact than bad news, but the magnitude of the effect, at approximately two basis points, is unlikely to be significant economically.

In Table 18.5 there is evidence of asymmetric response in $\beta_{i,t}$ to news. The total impact of a negative shock to $R_{M,t}$ on $\beta_{HK,t}$ and $\beta_{SP,t}$ will be greater than the total impact of a positive shock of similar magnitude. Positive shocks to $R_{HK,t}$ and $R_{SP,t}$ have a greater long-run impact on $\beta_{HK,t}$ and $\beta_{SP,t}$ although the asymmetric response of $\beta_{SP,t}$ to news about Singapore is not statistically significant.

The results in Table 18.6 suggest that positive shocks to Hong Kong lead to a greater long-run response in $\rho_{HK,M,t}$, $\rho_{SP,M,t}$ and $\rho_{HK,SP,t}$ than negative shocks of equal magnitude. However only $\rho_{HK,M,t}$ responds in a statistically significant fashion to news about Singapore. Bad news about the world portfolio has a greater long-run impact on $\rho_{HK,M,t}$ and $\rho_{HK,SP,t}$ than good news of equal magnitude. The effect of a positive shock to $R_{M,t}$ on $\rho_{M,SP,t}$ in the long run exceeds the impact of a negative shock of equal magnitude.

Finally, Table 18.7 presents asymmetry measures for $BD_{i,t}$. With the exception of the response of $BD_{SP,t}$ to news about Singapore, the evidence suggests that positive shocks have a greater long-run impact on the benefit to diversification than negative shocks of similar magnitude. This suggests that as markets trend downwards, the benefit to international diversification is eroded.

18.7   SUMMARY AND CONCLUSIONS

We illustrate how stochastic simulation techniques may be used to obtain impulse responses for important, unobserved risk management measures. Using the CAPM as an illustrative framework, we develop impulse response functions for the first and second moments of the joint distribution of country and world returns, the conditional beta, the conditional correlation and the conditional benefit to diversification. This allows an examination of the dynamic response of these measures to shocks. Using these dynamic responses, we develop a metric for measuring the degree of asymmetry in the reaction of the measures to positive and negative shocks.

Using weekly total returns data for three markets, the World, Hong Kong and Singapore, we illustrate our methodology using a multivariate asymmetric GARCH model. We provide strong evidence that these markets respond asymmetrically to shocks, and importantly that news raises the conditional sensitivity of each country's return with the world return, raising the price of risk and reducing the conditional benefit to diversification. We further provide strong evidence of asymmetry in the response; the market distinguishes between good and bad news. The implication is that when these markets are trending downwards sharply, the degree of correlation between the country and world return increases. This implies that the price of risk and the benefits from diversification may differ in a statistically and economically meaningful fashion to good and bad news.

Our approach is sufficiently general to apply to a wide class of asset pricing models and to a range of multivariate non-linear models including GARCH and non-parametric models. These extensions are the subject of ongoing research.

NOTES

1. Previous studies simply report statistically significant asymmetry in equity market volatility (see Campbell and Hentschel, 1992; Bekaert and Harvey, 1997; Brooks and Henry, 2000; Bekaert et al., 2002, inter alia) or the usual measures of risk in an international context (Harvey, 1991; De Santis and Gerard, 1997, inter alia).
2. The world portfolio aggregates across countries such that all assets are held in terms of their value weights.
3. The weight Ψ_t is given by $VAR(R_{i,t}|\Omega_{t-1}) = VAR(R_{D,t}|\Omega_{t-1})$ and $VAR(R_{D,t}|\Omega_{t-1}) = \Psi_t^2 VAR(R_{M,t}|\Omega_{t-1})$. Rearranging yields $\Psi_t^2 = VAR[R_{i,t}|\Omega_{t-1}]/VAR[R_{M,t}|\Omega_{t-1}]$.
4. Hafner and Herwartz (2001) also consider such an extension and derive analytical expressions for the VIRFs for the case of symmetric multivariate generalized autoregressive conditional heteroscedastic (GARCH) models.
5. For instance, it is possible to condition on a particular shock and treat the variables generating the history as random, or condition on a particular history and allow the shocks to be the random variables. Alternatively, particular subsets of shocks/histories could be conditioned on; see Koop et al. (1996) for further details.
6. In this study, the returns in equations (18.1) and (18.4) are expressed in units of a common currency, the US dollar. This is a trivial assumption in the case of Hong Kong which has a fixed exchange rate with the US dollar. In markets with floating exchange rates, this approach assumes that investors do not hedge against currency fluctuations. Hence this approach can be viewed as a restricted version of an ICAPM where the price of exchange rate exposure is zero.
7. The datastream codes are TOTMHK$, TOTMSG$ and TOTMKWD for the Hong Kong, Singapore and World indices, respectively.
8. http://research.stlouisfed.org/fred2/. The secondary market yields are contained in the file WTB3MS.

REFERENCES

Bekaert, G., R.H. Campbell and N. Angela (2002), 'Market integration and contagion', working paper, Hong Kong University of Science and Technology.

Bekaert, G. and C.R. Harvey (1997), 'Emerging equity market volatility', *Journal of Financial Economics*, **43**, 29–77.

Braun, P.A., D.B. Nelson and A.M Sunier (1995), 'Good news, bad news, volatility and betas', *Journal of Finance*, **50**, 1575–1603.

Brooks, C. and Ó.T. Henry (2000), 'Linear and non-linear transmission of equity return volatility: evidence from the US, Japan and Australia', *Economic Modelling*, **17**, 497–513.

Campbell, J.Y. and L. Hentschel (1992), 'No news is good news: an asymmetric model of changing volatility in stock returns', *Journal of Financial Economics*, **31**, 281–318.

Chan, K.C., G.A. Karolyi and R.M. Stulz (1992), 'Global financial markets and the risk premium on US equity', *Journal of Financial Economics*, **32**, 137–168.

De Santis, G. and B. Gerard (1997), 'International asset pricing and portfolio diversification with time varying risk', *Journal of Finance*, **52**, 1881–1912.

Engle, R.F. and Y-H. Cho (1999), 'Time varying betas and asymmetric effects of news: empirical analysis of blue chip stocks', NBER Working Paper No 7330.

Engle, R.F. and V.K. Ng (1993), 'Measuring and testing the impact of news on volatility', *Journal of Finance*, **48**, 1749–1778.

Giovannini, A. and P. Jorion (1989), 'The time variation of risk and return in the foreign exchange and stock markets', *Journal of Finance*, **44**, 307–325.

Grier, K., Ó.T. Henry, N. Olekalns and K.K. Shields (2004), 'The asymmetric effects of uncertainty on inflation and output growth', *Journal of Applied Econometrics*, **19** (5), 551–565.

Hafner, C.M. and H. Herwartz (2001), 'Volatility impulse response functions for multivariate GARCH models', CORE Discussion Paper.

Harvey, C.R. (1991), 'The world price of covariance risk', *Journal of Finance*, **46**, 111–157.

Koop, G., M.H. Pesaran and S.M. Potter (1996), 'Impulse response analysis in non-linear multivariate models', *Journal of Econometrics*, **74**, 119–147.

Lin, W.-L., R.F. Engle and T. Ito (1994), 'Do bulls and bears move across borders? International transmissions of stock returns and volatility', *Review of Financial Studies*, **7**, 507–538.

Mandelbrot, B.B (1962), 'The variation of certain speculative prices', IBM External Research Report NC-87.

Nelson, D. (1991), 'Conditional heteroscedasticity in asset returns: a new approach', *Econometrica*, **59**, 347–370.

Shields, K., N. Olekalns, Ó.T. Henry, and C. Brooks (2005), 'Measuring the response of macroeconomic uncertainty to shocks', *Review of Economics and Statistics*, **87** (2), 362–370.

van Dijk, D., P.H. Franses and H.P. Boswijk (2000), 'Asymmetric and common absorption of shocks in non-linear autoregressive models', Econometric Institute Research Report 2000-01/A.

Index